Feuerbach

Dedicated to the memory of
my father and my son
Isaac Leon Wartofsky (1893–1944)
Ira Leon Wartofsky (1952–1958)

Feuerbach

MARX W. WARTOFSKY

PROFESSOR OF PHILOSOPHY
BOSTON UNIVERSITY

Cambridge University Press

CAMBRIDGE

LONDON   NEW YORK   MELBOURNE

Published by the Syndics of the Cambridge University Press
The Pitt Building, Trumpington Street, Cambridge CB2 1RP
Bentley House, 200 Euston Road, London NW1 2DB
32 East 57th Street, New York, NY 10022, USA
296 Beaconsfield Parade, Middle Park, Melbourne 3206, Australia

First published 1977

Printed in the United States of America
by Heritage Printers, Inc., Charlotte, NC 28202, USA

Library of Congress Cataloging in Publication Data
Wartofsky, Marx W.
Feuerbach.
Bibliography: p.
Includes index.
1. Feuerbach, Ludwig Andreas, 1804–1872.
B2973.W37   193   76–9180
ISBN 0 521 21257 X

Contents

❁

113174

Preface

✿

Prefaces are misplaced epilogues. Only at the end of my study and reconstruction of Feuerbach's philosophical development did it occur to me clearly that Feuerbach's thought exemplifies the very dialectic of consciousness that he so powerfully describes. And only at the end of this work did I come to recognize that I had participated in it in my own thinking. The core of the Feuerbachian dialectic is Socratic: The analysis and critique of concepts and theories is a process of self-discovery, and of self-transformation. The idea is certainly not new. Hegel's systematic elaboration of dialectic as a process of self-objectification and self-alienation provided his student, Feuerbach, with both a theory of dialectic and a host of applications (for example, phenomenology, history of philosophy, social theory, philosophy of religion, natural philosophy, among others). Feuerbach rejected Hegel's theory of dialectic. In his critique of his master, Feuerbach discovered what he saw as the basic confusion in Hegel's application of it. But Feuerbach did not reject the practice of dialectic. In fact, one may say that Feuerbach's own course of development provides us not only with his own account of the dialectic of consciousness, but with an account of the dialectic of his own consciousness, which is equally striking. For Feuerbach's development proceeds as a series of self-rejections and reconstructions. It does so, however, not as internal monologue, but as dialogue. Feuerbach discovers himself in the course of his critique of religion and philosophy. And that is how we discover him as well, in the detail and struggle of his emerging thought.

This work therefore proposes to set forth the development of Feuerbach's thought as a dialectic. It focuses, therefore, on the transformation of Feuerbach's early Hegelianism into that empirical realism and materialist humanism that Feuerbach himself saw as the negation of speculative German idealism, and indeed, as the end of philosophy in the old sense. What I hope to present here is the process and the stages of critical self-transformation in the case of a philosopher who not only reconstructs this process itself in the objective form of his critique of the history of philosophy, but engages subjectively in this process in his own work, in the form of self-criticism. Feuerbach's greatness, it seems to me, lies not so much in the truth of what he says, but rather in the way in which his own thought becomes subject to the very mode of criticism that he levels at the thought of others.

In the first chapter, by way of introduction, I will set out the intent and scope of this study of Feuerbach, by asking and answering three questions: First, *Why may Feuerbach be taken seriously?* Second, *What is dialectic? And why may Feuerbach be taken as a dialectical philosopher?* Third, *What is materialism? In what sense may Feuerbach be said to be a materialist, and what are the limits of his materialism?*

These three questions are answered in the study itself only implicitly, in the concrete details and analysis of Feuerbach's philosophic development. Yet this work may be understood as a case study of the philosophic dialectic that attempts to answer these questions. Feuerbach engages in this dialectic; and in this study, so do I; and if it is read in this spirit, so will the reader. As such, the study of Feuerbach has become as much a matter of my own critical self-reflection on these issues as it is a reconstruction of Feuerbach's own *Gedankengang.* My own present views on these questions, arrived at in this way, are not what they were when I started, and this is both disturbing and revealing. As I hope to explain, this process of active self-reflection in the other is the very method of dialectic itself, as a self-transformative critical activity. Thus it is only at the end of this study and reconstruction of Feuerbach's own development that such prefatory reflections could have come to be articulated.

Let me say why I think these reflections are important. First, they give the reader a clue to my own understanding of Feuerbach, and of the importance and thrust of his work. My study may then be read and understood neither simply as an exposition nor as an interpretation (though it is both of these), but as the implicit elaboration of a thesis—my own—about the nature of the history of philosophy and of the relation of this history to contemporary philosophic problems and their resolution. I discovered this only in the process of the work itself, and it seems to me now to appear there only in its latent form. Thus, the work was not written in order to elaborate a thesis; rather, it has come to reveal one to me. Second, these reflections bear on what I take to be crucial contemporary questions in philosophy. The first question, as to why Feuerbach may be taken seriously, bears on more than a historical acknowledgment of Feuerbach's importance. Rather, it is a question about how one is to understand philosophy itself, after Feuerbach's fundamental critique of it.

Feuerbach may be taken seriously because his critique of philosophy forces a reassessment of what the enterprise is. The critique makes philosophy self-conscious in a way that reveals its human foundations and its social and epistemological uses in a new way. By means of this critique, by putting philosophy itself fundamentally in question, Feuerbach enabled Marx to transform the method of theoretical critique and self-reflection into a method of practical critique, or critical reflection on society. But more than this: Feuerbach reveals the extent to which both religion and philosophy are masked and esoteric forms of practical, human thought; how they serve, and distort, human needs and purposes; and most important, what is the mechanism of the distortion, what is the method behind the mystification. In short, Feuerbach provides the basis for a fuller epistemological critique of the nature and function of ideology. In this sense, Feuerbach's analysis provides a crucial epistemological context for the contemporary discussion of ideology, of the nature of social belief and of concept formation.

The questions concerning dialectic and materialism are equally central in contemporary philosophy. Having gone through the rigors and revisions of a half century of logical positivism, logical empiricism, and linguistic analysis, we cannot reconsider the more traditional formulations of dialectic, or of materialism simply by recapitulating them in the old way. That such questions reemerge with the force that they do—after the methodological injunctions as to their "meaninglessness" as metaphysical, or as to their vacuousness, as uninterpretable in testable or empirically or cognitively significant form—is itself an important fact about contemporary philosophy. The emergence of a wide interest in Hegel and in Marx and Marxism speaks to a felt lack of a crucial dimension in philosophy, namely, its social and its historical contexts, and its relevance to practical social life and to human concerns. Though the existential and phenomenological movements in philosophy attempted to respond to this felt need, they, like analytic and empiricist philosophies, remained ahistorical and asocial—or social in only inadequate ways, focusing on a subject which remained radically individual.[1] What remains at issue is the historicity and sociality of philosophy, and moreover, the historicity and sociality of knowledge itself.

In this context the question "What is dialectic?" cannot remain a formal question. It is not simply a matter of method, and not, in the narrower sense, a matter of logic. Rather, it is a question concerning the role and nature of criticism, and the possibility of self-criticism as a means of transcending the present. The present will be transcended by the inexorability of time. But the question is not a metaphysical one in that sense; rather, it concerns the rational, cognitive, and deliberate transcendence of the human present, by the agency of conscious human action or praxis. The question "What is dialectic?" then becomes transformed into the question "What is history?" or "How is one to understand the process of self-transformation and self-transcendence by conscious human agency as history?" Insofar as this conscious agency involves reflective consciousness, or philosophical thought, Feuerbach provides both a theory and a model of this dialectic and thus a model of historical development, at least in thought. But his theory is implicit and his model is given by way of exemplification, rather than construction. I therefore pose the same question in two ways: *What is dialectic? And why may Feuerbach be taken as a dialectical philosopher?* In the first chapter, by way of an introduction, I try to answer both questions.

What remains problematic for me there, and unresolved, is the question of whether dialectic is to be taken as a theory of historical development in the contexts of human action and human consciousness alone—that is, as a social dialectic—or whether it can be also reasonably interpreted beyond that as an "objective" dialectic, that is, a dialectic of nature or of matter. In a much earlier study,[2] it all seemed much clearer to me. There I saw Diderot and Feuerbach as precursors of a viable conception of the dialectic as a universal theory of development, from matter to mind, so to speak. An emergentist materialist monism, such as dialectical materialism represented, in its formulations by, for example, Engels, Plekhanov, and Lenin, seemed to satisfy the demands for a holistic, unified, and scientifically viable metaphysics. Feuerbach seems to be heading in that direction, and his early Hegelianism becomes transformed into an empirical realism and what I characterize as a humanistic or anthropological materialism. But he balks, stumbles, and runs into problems he cannot resolve here. And so do I. The simple-minded version of the problem resolves it too easily and one-sidedly: If dialectic is a logic, and negation and contradiction are taken as logical terms, then the imputation of dialectics to nature or to matter is the simple confusion of ontologizing a logic beyond its proper domain—that is, the domain of human discourse, or language. This is the force of the standard critique of Engels (e.g., by Zhitlowski, by Masaryk, by Hook and Popper, and by all those who want to separate humanistic, social Marx from objectivistic, scientistic Engels). As forceful as this critique of dialectic as logic is, it is not satisfying. It rests on a simple bifurcation of discourse or thought from nature or the material world. This critique therefore does not resolve the question, but rather sharpens it. Whether negation and contradiction are mistaken imputations from the realm of logic to the realm of being, or whether negation and contradiction are the mediated discursive forms that reflect the deeper truths of our practice and knowledge of the world–this remains for me an open question, not resolvable by neat cuts. My approach to this question, by means of the "purgatory of the fiery brook," emerges as what I believe is Feuerbachian in method: How do such questions come to be posed in the way that they are in different historical periods? My name for this approach is historical epistemology, and Feuerbach and Marx lead me to the brink, but not further; nor does the easy resolution of the issue of materialism and dialectics by way of the neat separation of nature from society, of matter from mind, of bodily motions from actions, of being from thought.

Marx resolved the question of dialectic by reconstructing not thought, but historical social practice itself as a dialectic. He, like Feuerbach, placed thought into its practical social context, but he did so historically, and by way of a fundamental reinterpretation of human praxis as labor. The ontological domain of the dialectic thus becomes social-historical praxis itself–the history of social development. Thus, historical materialism embodies and exhibits the dialectic in *this* "material" form. Here the "logic" of negation and contradiction is translated into the domain of social strife, of opposition and polarity of interests, purposes, needs. These are matters of human action and of the forms of life that are permeated by our consciousness and intentionality, and also by our discourse. Therefore, the extension of the logical sense of negation and contradiction to what concerns conscious agency may be problematic, but it is not obviously false. What seems obviously false is the imputation of logical structure, and of discursive contexts to matter, or to nature itself. The seventeenth century achieved its scientific and philosophical revolution by imputing mathematical structure to nature. The nineteenth seems to have extended this by imputing logical structure to both nature and society. So why the fuss? Obviously because *dialectic* as a "logic" seems to accept what is logically unacceptable: that contradictions *exist*, and not that what is contradictory *cannot* exist, or is *impossible* (the older form of logicism ontologized). How can matter itself be "logical" in its structure if this simply embodies what logic rejects, namely, contradiction? Further, what sense does it make in the first place to impute a logical or discursive, or even narrowly sentential function to matter itself?

Therefore, though one may make some sense of a social dialectic, because opposition and polarity in human life may be expressible in the very discourse that both is shaped by and shapes that life, how can one make any sense of a dialectic of nature or of matter, where agency is not at work (unless one is ready to concede objective mind, or panpsychism or some other form of natural theology; and one is not).

It is easy, therefore, to split the social from the natural, and Marx from Engels, on this score. Especially where the ghost of Stalinism hovers over the grave of "objectivism," to scare off the superstitious and the easily frightened, and to warn others of where this objectivism may lead. Thus, the question of a materialist interpretation of dialectics in this form leads to resolutions of two sorts: Dialectics is *not* "logic," but rather a vacuous theory of development, which says no more than that things change and that there is strife and opposition, in some sense, in nature, in society, and in thought (e.g., Popper); or that dialectics is an appropriate logic of social reality, but not of nature. This latter move regarding materialism and dialectic has become fashionable and has come to express itself in the wider domain of the contemporary issue concerning the "essential" difference between the social sciences and the natural sciences. One should remember that Feuerbach looms in the immediate background of the nineteenth-century movement of *Geisteswissenschaft*, of Dilthey et al., which formulated this difference in a sharp, methodological way. The relevance of Feuerbach's thought to this question is therefore both historical and substantive. However, his thought has been most clearly and popularly represented not in these contexts, but in the form of a crude philosophical materialism: "Man is what he eats," which says little and resolves nothing. It certainly is not what Feuerbach's anthropological materialism comes to, and has served to characterize not only Feuerbach, but Marx as well, as reductive economic, if not gastronomic, materialists.

What is of greater issue in the question "What is materialism" goes beyond either such simpleminded formulations or such simpleminded resolutions. To talk of "material human existence" is to talk of neither atoms and molecules nor blood, cells, and organs (including the brain); rather, it is to talk of social and historical human existence. But in what sense is this "material"? Is the metaphysical extension from physical "matter" inevitably reductive? Does emergentism provide anything but the pious accommodation of a programmatic materialism, and cover up rather than reveal the problems raised by the claim for continuity and unity between the natural, the social, and the mental? There is a further question, namely, "What epistemological, metaphilosophical, and methodological issues are raised by the theoretical claim to the common (or uncommon) materiality of nature and the human?" The movement for the unity of science tried to resolve this question as a methodological one, with minimal ontology, or even with a claim to the elimination of ontology. It failed. Dialectical materialism raises this question to the level of *identifying* methodology with ontology. It fails as well. But failure is instructive. It forces us to consider what combination of heuristic force and ideological need makes failed programs important. In short, it forces us to that critique of philosophy and method that, in our own day, parallels Feuerbach's.

The introductory chapter deals with these questions, therefore, by way of setting Feuerbach's own philosophical development in this perspective. The succeeding chapters do not, or do so only implicitly and occasionally. They go into the details of the development itself, for that is where the claim that Feuerbach's development is dialectical stands or falls. And that is where the implicit definition of dialectic as self-transformative critical activity is concretely given.

I confess that I am puzzled now about the larger questions. I hope to address myself to them systematically, in my current work. This book, therefore, has become my own prolegomenon, and a test of whether I can participate in the dialectic, as Feuerbach did.

In my reflections and revisions of the text, my discussions with many colleagues and students were helpful. I want to thank Professor Joseph Agassi of Boston University especially for the terrible time he gave me on these questions. I cannot agree with him on very much, but our disagreements have been fruitful and interesting, and our friendship has survived them. Agassi, in a more mundane way, also tried to curb my stylistic excesses and barbarisms and helped to cut a monstrous manuscript to more manageable size. For this, I am mundanely grateful. In a historical sense (reducing history to biography for the moment), my debt to Professor John Herman Randall, Jr., of Columbia University, who introduced me to a lifelong passion for the history of philosophy during my student days, is great. His virtues, as my major professor more than twenty-five years ago, was his nonintrusiveness. He left me alone. And I learned from his work and his teaching. So, too, I wish to acknowledge the discussion over the years with my close associate, Professor Robert S. Cohen; with our mutual friend, Professor Herbert Marcuse; and with that fine group of Feuerbach scholars who gathered at the first international symposium on Feuerbach at Bielefeld, in 1973. For their critical response and discussion of my own paper there,[3] and for what I learned from their papers, I am indeed grateful; and especially so to the organizers of the symposium, Professor Dr. Hans-Martin Sass, of Bochum University; Professor Dr. Herman Lübbe, University of Bielefeld; and Professor Dr. Werner Schuffenhauer, of the German Academy of Sciences in Berlin, G.D.R. From the many whose critical discussion helped me there, I want to thank particularly Professor Claudio Cesa of the University of Siena; Professor Dr. Alfred Schmidt and Professor Dr. Irving Fetscher, both of Frankfurt University; Professor Henri Arvon, of the University of Paris, Nanterre; Professor Dr. Friedrich Richter of Berlin, G.D.R.; and Professor Eugene Kamenka, of the Australian National University, Canberra. Among older friends and cohorts, in matters Feuerbachian and Marxian, I wish especially to thank Professor John Glasse, of Vassar College, Professor Manfred Vogel, of Northwestern University, and Professor Shlomo Avineri, of the University of Jerusalem, for our discussion and correspondence over the years. Most recently, at the end of my labors, I have profited from the discussion and criticism of Dr. Fred Gordon, whose penetrating study of Feuerbach and Stirner raised sharp questions of interpretation for me.

This work has stretched over many years, and my gratitude extends backward through this period: to my friends, colleagues and students at Boston University and elsewhere who provided the ambiance for my study and teaching; to the Boston University Graduate School, for its occasional research support for the project; and to Maureen Hill, Judith Bleiwas Wilkis, Marian Cox, and Elizabeth Clark, who typed and retyped and retyped various versions of the manuscript. I also wish to thank the late Dr. Karl Marx, of Berlin, Paris, and London, for the theoretical and practical stimulation of his thought and his example.

M. W. W.

Boston, Massachusetts

Author's Note

※

This work is the first major full-length study of the philosophy of Ludwig Feuerbach in English. Let me explain, but not qualify, this apparently immodest claim. There are indeed two other books, several dissertations, and many brief treatments and allusions to Feuerbach in English.* The early and still cogent discussion by Sidney Hook occurs in his work *From Hegel to Marx* (1936). The first full-length book on Feuerbach is the oddly titled *Heaven Wasn't His Destination*, by William Chamberlain (1941). Most recently, Eugene Kamenka's book, *The Philosophy of Ludwig Feuerbach*, provides a comprehensive and engaging, if brief and breezy, treatment of major themes. So mine is not the first book in English, nor the first full-length study. Yet it is the first *major* study, not, I hope, simply as the *longest*, but rather in its scope and detail, and in the account it gives of the dialectic of the development of Feuerbach's thought. The term "major" here bears the weight of my intentions. The reader must judge whether this weight is borne well or ill.

That the book is in English is hardly important. However, it does suggest that the author's conceptual framework as well as his native language may cast Feuerbach's work into a different light from that in

* There is one study, which is just about to appear, that was not available when I was writing this book but deserves mention here. It is Frederick Gregory's *Scientific Materialism in Nineteenth Century Germany* (Dordrecht and Boston: D. Reidel, 1977). Gregory's work deals with Vogt, Moleschott, Buchner, and Czolbe and treats Feuerbach's major influence on these "scientific materialists." I should also note Frederick M. Gordon's doctoral dissertation, "The Development of Marx's Conception of Human Nature" (San Diego: University of California, 1975), which is especially important with respect to the relations among Stirner, Feuerbach, and Marx on the concept of "species being."

which it had been seen by the continental scholars–primarily German –who have interpreted Feuerbach. The fundamental work of scholarship on Ludwig Feuerbach remains that of the late Professor Simon Rawido-wicz, published in 1931. I have also benefited from the extraordinary range of scholarship, older and recent, which has revealed the many-sidedness as well as the problems of Feuerbach's work. My debt to the community of scholars shows itself, I hope, in this work.

ABOUT THE CITATIONS

The references to Feuerbach throughout the text are, with few excep-tions, to two standard editions of the collected works. The first is the older Bolin-Jodl edition, published between 1903 and 1910, in ten volumes, by Frommann Verlag, Stuttgart. This edition was reissued in a facsimile reprint, under the editorship of Hans-Martin Sass, and was enlarged by an eleventh volume of the early writings, containing the full Latin text of Feuerbach's inaugural dissertation of 1828 and a facsimile reprint of the original 1830 edition of the *Thoughts on Death and Immortality*; and by a double volume (XII–XIII) that reprints the two-volume *Selected Correspondence from and to Ludwig Feuerbach*, originally issued by Wilhelm Bolin in 1904. Sass also adds twenty-one previously unpublished letters (351–72). All *initial* page references in the text are to this edition and are given by volume in roman numerals and page in arabic numerals (e.g., II, 223). An occasional reference to the original 1846 edition of the collected works, which Feuerbach edited, is given as S.W.$_1$, with volume and page numbers following.

The second edition is the recent and newly edited critical edition that is now appearing (1967–) and will, when completed, comprise sixteen volumes. This edition, edited by Werner Schuffenhauer and issued by Akademie-Verlag in Berlin, is occasionally referred to in the second-place page references, preceded by G. W. (*Gesammelte Werke*). Because none of the volumes were yet available when I commenced my research, and only some were available during it, I have not been able to give full parallel references to this fine recent edition.

References to *The Essence of Christianity* are, first, to the Bolin-Jodl edition (*S.W.*) and second, to the critical two-volume reedition of the work edited by Werner Schuffenhauer and issued by Akademie-Verlag in Berlin in 1956. The second-place references are marked S (Schuffen-hauer). Because Schuffenhauer's critical edition gives the text variations of all three editions of Feuerbach's *Essence of Christianity*, and the Bolin-Jodl edition reprints the third edition, of 1849, where the quotation is from the first edition only, the reference gives only S.

Feuerbach's Life: A Brief Sketch

✿

Ludwig Andreas Feuerbach was born July 28, 1804, in Landshut, Bavaria, into the large family of a noted jurist, Paul Johann Anselm von Feuerbach. His father, born in Frankfurt-am-Main, and himself the son of a lawyer, studied at Jena and Kiel, and held a post at the University of Landshut at this time, but left shortly thereafter for Munich, where, in the Bavarian state service, he worked on reform of criminal law. He later became presiding judge of the Appelate Court in Ansbach. In the context of the clerical politics of the time, Anselm von Feuerbach represented a libertarian tradition, and the family environment was an enlightened one. Of Feuerbach's four brothers, each achieved a certain distinction. The oldest, Joseph, was an archaeologist, whose son Anselm (Feuerbach's nephew) became a distinguished painter. The next oldest, Karl Wilhelm, who died tragically at the age of thirty-four after political imprisonment and persecution, was a first-rate mathematician. Eduard August, born one year before Ludwig, became a jurist like his father. Ludwig's younger brother, Friedrich, was a philologist and a devoted adherent of his older brother's philosophy.

Feuerbach came to philosophy by way of theology. He began his studies in theology at Heidelberg, in 1823, where he attended the lectures of H.E.G. Paulus and Karl Daub. Paulus' lectures on church history and exegesis attempted a "rationalized" theology, but Feuerbach was soon put off by what he later characterized as a "web of sophisms," and stopped attending the lectures. Karl Daub, who lectured on Dogmatics, represented the newer "speculative theology," strongly influenced by Hegel and by the Berlin theologians Schleiermacher and Marheineke. The appeal of Berlin grew strong, and after a confrontation with his father over his new choice, and after difficulties caused by police surveillance (in the atmosphere of antistudent reaction following the Karlsbad Decrees of 1819), Feuerbach went to Berlin to attend Hegel's lectures, as well as those of the theologians Schleiermacher and Marheineke, and matriculated in the faculty of philosophy there in the following year (1825). A year later, Feuerbach left Berlin to complete his study requirements at the University of Erlangen because of financial problems. The government stipend he had been receiving, as son of a civil servant, was cut off upon the death of King Max Joseph of Bavaria, and expenses were lower in Erlangen than in Berlin. At Erlangen, he planned to study the natural sciences and attended lectures in physiology and anatomy (under Koch and Fleischmann). But penury made continued study impossible. In 1828, he earned his doctoral degree with a dissertation on *Reason: Its Unity, Universality, and Infinity*, a work whose rationalist-Hegelian analysis goes beyond classical objective idealism and points in the humanist direction already adumbrated in Hegel's *Phenomenology of Mind*. From 1829 to 1835, as docent at the University of Erlangen, Feuerbach lectured on the history of modern philosophy. There were intermittent trips during this time, and unsuccessful attempts to get a university post. These attempts were doomed forever after the appearance of Feuerbach's first postdoctoral published work, which appeared anonymously in 1830 under the title *Thoughts on Death and Immortality*. The work is an irreverent and incisive treatment of themes that continue to intrigue Feuerbach thereafter. Moreover, it is an open attack on theology in the service of the police state, and was taken, in the context of the clerical reaction of the time, as a dangerous and revolutionary document. Its authorship was soon recognized, however, and it was enough to bar Feuerbach from university posts. It also put the seal on Feuerbach's hopes for a literary career, and he turned thereafter to philosophical work.

In 1833, the first of three volumes on the history of modern philosophy appeared: *The History of Modern Philosophy, from Bacon to Spinoza*. This was followed in 1836 by a second volume: *Exposition, Development and Critique of Leibnizian Philosophy*; and in 1838, by a third: *Pierre Bayle: A Contribution to the History of Philosophy and Humanity*. During these difficult years, Feuerbach met and married Berta Löw, and moved to Bruckberg, where she was part owner of a family porcelain factory. He lived there in rustic isolation, and in comfortable means for many years. He did most of his important work in this retreat, having separated himself once and for all from the prospects of a professorial life, and also from its demands. In 1839, there appeared his *Critique of Hegelian Philosophy*, marking the open break with Hegelian idealism. In 1841, his fundamental work, *The Essence of Christianity*, was published. His friends, Christian Kapp and Arnold Ruge, tried in vain to lure him to Heidelberg, and to Halle, respectively, and away from his rural isolation. Ruge, as editor of the *Hallische Jährbucher*, encouraged Feuerbach's publication in its pages, after the *Berliner Jährbucher*, official organ of the Hegelian school, began to demand revisions and changes in his writings that Feuerbach would not countenance. In 1842 and 1843, the explicitly empiricist-materialist works *Preliminary Theses for the Reform of Philosophy* and *Foundations of the Philosophy of the Future* appeared, and in 1845 and 1846, there followed *The Essence of Religion* and *The Question of Immortality from the Standpoint of Anthropology*. In 1846, too, Feuerbach began the publication of the ten-volume *Collected Works*.

It is during this period, of the early 1840s, that Feuerbach became the theoretical leader of the left-Hegelian school and had such an important influence on Marx and Engels. It is of this period that Engels writes, "We were all Feuerbachians." In 1845, Marx sketched his *Theses on Feuerbach*, marking his critique of the limits of Feuerbach's materialism and anthropologism, and his break with Feuerbachian modes of thought.

Feuerbach took a curiously passive and skeptical attitude toward the revolution of 1848, though he was lionized by the students and radical intellectuals of the time. At the invitation of the revolutionary student body, Feuerbach gave public lectures from December 1, 1848, to March 2, 1849, at the City Hall in Heidelberg. These *Lectures on the Essence of Religion* were published in 1851, as Volume 8 of Feuerbach's *Collected Works*.

After the 1849 reaction, Feuerbach was in despair over the state of political and intellectual freedom in Germany and thought seriously of migrating to the United States, where he had friends (notably Friedrich Kapp) and a circle of readers and admirers in St. Louis and in New York City. His next published work was the large and complex *Theogonie*, in which he carried further the program of *The Essence of Christianity* with respect to other religions, and to Greek and Roman mythology. It was published in 1857 as Volume 9 of his *Collected Works*.

In 1860, Feuerbach's life was seriously uprooted. His wife's factory in Bruckberg went bankrupt and he found himself, at the age of fifty-six, once again penurious and without a source of income. He moved to Rechenberg, near Nurenberg, where he lived until his death. The final publication during his lifetime was the work "Spiritualism and Materialism," which together with his "On Ethics: Eudaimonism" and other shorter works of the 1850s and 1860s appeared as Volume 10 of his collected works in 1866. In 1868, he read, with enthusiasm, Marx's *Capital* (published a year before), and in 1870, he joined the German Social Democratic Party. Two years later, on September 13, 1872, Feuerbach died and was buried at the Johannisfriedhof in Nürenberg.

CHAPTER I

Prefatory Reflections
by Way of an Introduction

✵

WHY MAY FEUERBACH BE TAKEN SERIOUSLY?

I take Feuerbach seriously. This is not always easy to do. There are too many echoes of a derived Hegelianism. There is too much truth to Marx's and Engel's critique of Feuerbach's limitations. There is too much in Feuerbach that is simplistic, sentimental, prolix. As to Feuerbach's finest insights, they have been absorbed and transformed in the works of Marx, Freud, Dewey, and Lukács. So it seems we shall lose nothing if we touch on him lightly. True, there are others who have taken him seriously. Feuerbach's radical critique of religion has been adopted with almost indecent fervor by radical theology itself, as a way of saving God for mankind and of rescuing religion from total irrelevance to this world. Sartre, Marcel, and Buber have taken over Feuerbach's *I-Thou* as the touchstone of the relation of self to other. The existential psychology and psychiatry of Rogers, Laing, and others has repeated and elaborated the theory and the implicit therapy of Feuerbachian psychology. Though I have little sympathy with these views, I too take Feuerbach seriously. But for different reasons. He has too long been treated either as a transitional figure (between Hegel and Marx), as a purveyor of aphorisms ("Man is what he eats," a pun in German that is not even Feuerbach's own), or as a crude and simple materialist.

I take Feuerbach seriously as a philosopher, for the depth and clarity of his insights and for the subtle analysis and argument by which he works them out and defends them. What is more—and this, I think, is missed by almost all Feuerbach commentators and critics—he is an epochal figure in the history of philosophy, for the originality and fundamental character of his critique of philosophy itself.

Feuerbach is the first and the greatest of the modern critics of philosophy outside the positivistic tradition. His is a devastating critique of professional and professorial philosophy. Moreover, it is a systematic and thorough one, and not merely rhetorical or aphoristic, like that of Schopenhauer or Nietzsche. Though Feuerbach is easily quoted in his aphoristic asides (e.g., "My religion is no religion; my philosophy is no philosophy"), what is more striking and more substantive is the detail and the character of his critique of philosophy. It is a historical critique, which gives it range and an extraordinarily rich content.

Feuerbach acquired his historical method from Hegel, of course. What takes him beyond Hegel, however, is Feuerbach's distinctive characterization of philosophy as a human activity–specifically, as a highly evolved mode of the human effort at self-understanding. But Feuerbach sees philosophy, in its traditional forms, as a hidden and self-deceiving mode of human self-understanding. The fundamental human content of philosophy is masked behind its metaphysical façade. Where speculative philosophy lays claim to the Absolute, to Truth, to a realm of essences as its proper subject matter, Feuerbach sees in this "nothing but" the abstruse form of self-conceptions of human nature and of human consciousness itself. Philosophy is thus interpreted as an abstract and esoteric form of anthropology and psychology.

In Feuerbach's "reduction" of philosophy to anthropology, he is not alone, nor entirely original. One may say that the "reduction" of philosophy to psychology–in the analytic and empiricist tradition of Hobbes, Locke, and Hume–is an earlier parallel move. Insofar as epistemology becomes "naturalized," in Quine's sense, we have echoes of this reduction in contemporary philosophy as well. In the empiricist tradition, philosophical thought itself is seen to emerge from the operation of a combinatory or associative reflex in the human mind. Such abstract ideas as Substance, Cause, Space, and Time are seen to be rooted in the ordinary modes of human sense experience and are thus "reduced" (or reducible) to the merely human. That is, for empiricism, the essences, substances, and universals of the rationalist-speculative tradition are reductively analyzed in terms of facts about the conditions and modes of human knowledge itself, rather than in terms of facts about the world, or about *Being*. And we know how Kant proceeds from Hume, in this "Copernican revolution." But Feuerbach's approach goes beyond the analytic and psychological critique and reduction of philosophy in the empiricist tradition, and also beyond Kant's reconstruction of the transcendental conditions of any possible empirical knowledge. Rather, Feuerbach's "reduction" proceeds from the basis of an anthropological and cultural critique of philosophy. The contexts of his "reduction" are not those of empiricism (i.e., the sense impressions or ideas that are given to an undifferentiated, merely receptive, or merely associative sensory apparatus), nor are they the Kantian contexts of the a priori forms of perception or of the understanding. Rather, Feuerbach's are the Hegelian contexts of the forms of life, the modes of need and dependency, the fuller contexts of human social existence–and more. It is this social or species nature that becomes for Feuerbach the very condition and ground of philosophy. He finds the primary mode of expression of this species nature not in an undifferentiated sense perception, but in religious consciousness. Yet, in his later work, Feuerbach's insistence on *Sinnlichkeit* (sensibility) as the primary mode of conscious existence, and the origin and test of all our ideas, is certainly not Hegelian, and indeed sounds like nothing else so much as good old British or French seventeenth- and eighteenth-century sensationalism. It is this tension between a reductive psychologism and a fuller anthropologism or social empiricism that creates major difficulties in Feuerbach's later philosophy, as we shall see.

Yet Feuerbach's forceful characterization of philosophy as "nothing but" the process of human self-understanding, as the attempt at human self-knowledge, carries him beyond either the transcendental precincts of speculative idealism, whether of Kant or of Hegel, or the reductive precincts of traditional empiricism, whether British or French. The process of human self-consciousness he describes is one that is directly expressive of human feelings, human needs, human actions. Once philosophy is understood in this way, says Feuerbach (i.e., as the esoteric and abstract reflection by an active consciousness of ordinary life conditions and life activities) philosophy is demystified and is recognized, in its "positive" content, for what it is–namely, anthropology. Traditional philosophy dissolves, then, into the deliberate and secular scientific study of human nature and the reflective elaboration in thought of the very conditions of human life itself. These range from the biological needs of individual and species survival–food, water, air, sex– to the human needs for love, for social existence, for creative activity, for law, and for hope.

In Feuerbach's view, these ordinary and daily human needs are concretely expressed in religion, in forms generated by the sensuous imagination. Theology, by contrast, imposes an abstruse and esoteric form of expression on these needs, making them otherworldly in their import and their fulfillment. Philosophy then proceeds to give a fully abstract representation of these same needs, casting them in the forms of metaphysical discourse. Thus, Feuerbach says, "the secret of philosophy is theology" (i.e., philosophy is abstract theology). And in turn, "the

3

secret of theology is anthropology" (i.e., theology is an esoteric and mythical account of the human). By derivation, then, philosophy itself is abstract, demythologized anthropology. Once the secret is out, the human intent and content of abstract metaphysical thought are revealed. Thus, Feuerbach's critique of philosophy is carried out by way of his critique of religion, or of religious consciousness. On his view, religion and philosophy are not separate but are rather stages of the same process, namely, the process by which human beings come to understand and to recognize their own human nature. But this self-understanding and self-recognition become possible only after they have been projected into or objectified as something other than human, whether as "God," or "Nature," or "Being." Philosophy, as "speculative philosophy" or metaphysics, is the continuation of theology by other means. It is the study of God's nature transformed into the study of the Nature of Being. It is "abstract" or "esoteric" theology, and thereby it is doubly abstract and esoteric. From the theological abstraction of the human, as a superhuman essence, philosophy effects the further abstraction from the Godlike to the metaphysical, from divinity to *Being* itself. In its rigorous abstraction, philosophy strips away the still personal, still sensuously conceived aspects of the divine image of man until only the most severe logical and metaphysical attributes remain, and are reconceived as attributes of a hypostatized abstract *Being*. Thus, philosophy simply continues that mystification and conceptual inversion that theology began. Namely, where theology takes the human and hypostatizes it as divine, philosophy doubly hypostatizes this divinity as metaphysical, or as Essential Being.

This process of the double alienation of human self-consciousness, first in theology and then in metaphysics becomes more than a programmatic sketch in Feuerbach's treatment. Indeed, the force of his critique is precisely in the details of his illustration of this process. He shows, in the most interesting and often exciting and original ways, just *how* philosophy and theology effect this inversion. He offers the translation, point for point, of the proffered truths of theology and philosophy into human truths, or truths about human nature. In this sense, he has been identified with the antimetaphysical positivist tradition, or that part of it that argues for a reductive naturalism. And, indeed his work has striking similarities to that of his contemporary, Auguste Comte. It is not surprising that the young and brilliant philosophical radicals of the Vienna Circle counted Feuerbach as among their spiritual predecessors (together with Hume, Kant, Mach, and the French philosophers of the eighteenth-century Enlightenment).[1] Nor is it wrong to see Feuerbach as a foundation stone of modern atheism. Still, both of these

4

characterizations of Feuerbach, as antimetaphysical positivist or as atheist, are misleading and need to be severely qualified. Certainly, Feuerbach proposes a "naturalistic" or "anthropological" *reduction* of theology and of metaphysics. Moreover, his problematic empiricist realism or sensationism would make him appear as a direct heir of Locke and Condillac, and a forebear of Mach and the sense-datum theorists. But Feuerbach's reduction is neither physicalist nor sensationist (and certainly not phenomenalist, in this latter tradition). True, the *God* of the theologians, or the *Being* or *Substance* of the metaphysicians, is, in Feuerbach's view, "nothing but" human consciousness of its own nature, or human self-consciousness formulated in an alienated and hypostatized way. But this reduces neither the human being to a conglomerate of physical atoms nor his or her consciousness to a bundle of sense impressions. Rather, the human is raised up from the status of a mere reflection or image of the divine, or from a mere mode of Universal Being, to the status of a conscious and sensate individual who constitutes this universality by his activity. *God* and *Being* are, for Feuerbach, the images of the universality of human species consciousness and species sensibility (*Sinnlichkeit*). The individual human being is the ontological ground of the universality of the human species. This universality is not only a characteristic of the "infinity" of reason, for Feuerbach. Indeed, the human senses themselves, and human feelings as well, tend toward universality. It is the universal and infinite capacities of human thinking, sensing, and feeling that find their echo and their embodiment in the conceptions of an infinite and universal God, or in an infinite and universal Nature. Spinoza's *Deus sive Natura* is seen as the projection of the infinity, universality, and unity of human nature itself.

The secret of this universalizing tendency of human nature is that it is essentially a species nature, a social nature. That is, the human being *is* what he takes God to be, insofar as man conceives of himself as a *species being*, and most simply within the limits of his natural and finite individuality. Feuerbach argues that it is the very *human* capacities for sensibility, feeling, thought, action (or praxis) that raise human beings beyond their animal finitude, and make possible for them the appropriation of the universe and of their fellow creatures as the objects of their knowledge and of their action. On Feuerbach's view, then, the human is not "reduced" to a physical or natural being. But *because* human beings are natural beings of a certain kind; because their sensation and perception are already involved with consciousness and with the possibility of language, thought, reflection, science; because their life of feeling, of sensibility, of animal need is already a matter of *fellow* feeling, or sympathy, of compassion, of mutual needs, human life transcends animal life. Culture and thought themselves derive from the practical human needs, sensibilities, conscious dependencies of human beings, as these express themselves in their conscious praxis. In this sense, Feuerbach is neither a positivist nor an atheist, in the ordinary (and narrower) senses, but rather an emergentist, for whom religion is a serious (and dialectically necessary) expression of a certain stage of human self-understanding.

That Feuerbach was able to take religious consciousness seriously, that he did not simply denigrate its insights or ignore its formulations made him the most powerful critic of the psychology of religion and of the function of religious consciousness. Unlike the atheist critics of the eighteenth century (and closely akin to Hume of the *Dialogues* and of the *Natural History of Religion*), Feuerbach sought to make the phenomenon of religion an object of deliberate rational and scientific study. He sought, in a way to be emulated by the best of our contemporary anthropologists and sociologists of religion, to understand the phenomenon theoretically, to give it its full due as a social phenomenon. Feuerbach understood religion as a stage of the growth of human self-consciousness, to be investigated in its own forms of expression—from the "inside," so to speak. His early training in theology, indeed his Hegelian training, equipped him superbly for such an internal critique. He was a master of the theological literature, and together with Strauss, Bauer, and the other Young Hegelians, he helped to lay the foundations for the so-called Higher Criticism, that is, the scientific, textual, sociological, and historical analysis of the Gospels, and of the history of Christian dogmas, as expressions of human imagination and of a mystified and esoteric human rationality. Rather than simply to reject the Gospels as dogmas, as blind superstition, or as folk mythology, he tried to find a philosophical, indeed, an epistemological explanation of their form and a humanistic interpretation of their content. This was his "anthropological reduction." The humanistic "decoding" of the Christian tradition then served as the basis of his critique of philosophy itself. Philosophy, too, is revealed as a "mystified" and inverted form of human self-consciousness, or self-knowledge.

But if philosophy is a human construction, and beyond this, also an expression of human need—of the human need to know, to relate to one's fellow beings, and to one's world *theoretically*—whence does such a need to theorize arise? How is it related to the basic human needs, to human existence itself? Why does it arise and develop in the peculiar form of a self-deception? Feuerbach adopts the logic of this dialectic, as a process of self-revelation through self-deception, from Hegel's analysis in the *Phenomenology of Mind*, the seminal work that is all-important in understanding not only Feuerbach's thought but that of Marx as well. But if this were all there is to Feuerbach's (or Marx's) work, if the contribution of Feuerbach (and of the young Marx) were no more than a fleshing out, or an elaboration or a humanistic or socio-historical interpretation of Hegel's *Phenomenology*, then I should have to characterize Feuerbach (and Marx) not as epochal figures but as epigones. And I think this is false.

However tempting it is (and for the historical scholar, the temptation is almost irrepressible!) to read back into Hegel all that Feuerbach, and after him, Marx, went on to say, it is wrong to do so (just as it is wrong to dissolve Marx's unique contribution into its "Feuerbachian" components). The game of "adumbritis" or "precursoritis" is easy to play, but it is, in the end, a trivial game and is, at its worst, a misleading one. At most, it shows the continuity of human thought, whether in the history of philosophy or of the arts and sciences generally. But it does not serve to show the identity of one man's thought or discovery with another's (except in those rare instances of parallel discovery, or in the degenerate case of outright plagiarism). Thus, if we are so inclined, we can map Hegel's *Phenomenology* onto Feuerbach, onto Marx, certainly onto whole portions of Freud, Sartre, or who not?

Feuerbach himself gives the lie to such a simplistic approach. He does a devastating critique of Hegel's *Phenomenology* that at once reveals what he sees as its principal philosophical error–that it is an idealism that reduces existence to thought–and at the same time retains Hegel's brilliant analysis of the dialectic of consciousness. Feuerbach's critique of Hegel stands, I think, as a fundamental critique in the history of philosophy. It does so not simply because in it Feuerbach arrives at the "right" conclusions. I happen to think he did, but that is not what is important. Rather, the philosophical profundity of the critique is in its methodology, in the way in which Feuerbach uses the dialectic itself to reveal the flaws in the dialectic of Hegel. His early critique of Hegel is, in a sense, the critical *Vorschule* for his critique of religion, but then, his critique of religion, in turn, becomes the (methodological, as well as substantive) basis for his critique of philosophy itself. And the methodological import of Feuerbach's critique is that it is dialectical.

What Is Dialectic? And Why May Feuerbach Be Taken as a Dialectical Philosopher?

This brings me to the methodological question par excellence: namely, what is dialectic? And how does the Feuerbachian dialectic compare with those of Hegel, Marx, or Engels? In the broader context of the varieties of the dialectic, how does it compare with Socratic dialectic, or with the more recent interpretation of the dialectic by Popper? In the scholarly literature, there is debate over whether Feuerbach, in breaking with Hegelianism, also gave up the Hegelian dialectic. For my part, I am clearly on the side of those who say he never gave it up.[2] Furthermore, there is a debate over whether there is a "Socratic" dialectic by contrast to its "perversion" and "betrayal," in the Hegelian dialectic. Here I think Popper's "What is Dialectic?"[3] is simply in error, that he either misreads or misunderstands Hegel. But Feuerbach *is* anti-Hegel, and Marx is anti-Feuerbach, and I am claiming that the dialectic is somehow retained through all these *bouleversements*. This had better be made clear, and now.

There are, it seems to me, two ways of approaching the question "What is dialectic?" The first may be characterized as a reflective or external approach; the second may be thought of as immanent or internal. The first, and more obvious approach proceeds by setting out some *theory* of dialectic that may be said to have two components: (1) a specification of the domain of the dialectic, that is, what the dialectic is a dialectic *of* or the context in which it is concretely exhibited, and (2) a theoretical reconstruction of the form of the dialectic in this context. Here there are a number of alternative and even conflicting views. Thus, the dialectic may be taken as a *method* of critical refutation in the domain of discourse or of argument. The Socratic dialectic serves as the classic example here. Or, in a Hegelian interpretation, the dialectic may be taken to be the actual *process* of the self-differentiation and development of the Idea or as a dialectic of consciousness or thought. Or again, in Marx's version, the dialectic may be understood as the social process of human action in which human beings create and change their own nature in their *praxis*, that is, in their social interaction and in the activity of transforming nature. On another reading the dialectic may be seen as an "objective" process of history or of social change. It may also be taken to be an "objective" dialectic of nature, that is, of the processes of evolution and transformation of forms in nature. It may be considered a "logic" of the processes of change in the material world (as in Engels). In Popper's view, by contrast, it may be taken to be a method of trial and error common to both animal and human learning. Or, more specifically, it may be considered a method of self-correction through criticism.

In all of these variations, the *theory* of dialectic answers the question "What is dialectic?" by a reflective reconstruction of the method or the form that is taken to be exhibited in some concrete process, whether of discourse, thought, social life, nature, practical activity, and so forth. Such an approach is external in that it takes the embodied dialectic, "out there," so to speak, as the object of a theoretical reflection. The theory, then, is *about* the dialectic, but it is not yet conceived of as participating *in*, or being itself a constituent *of*, the dialectic.

The second way of answering the question I would characterize, by contrast, as *internal*. It consists in exhibiting the method in actual practice—not simply by exemplifying it, however, as the manifest expression of some a priori form or logic of development or change, but rather, by *engaging* in it. In this sense, this second way of answering the question "What is dialectic?" may also be characterized as *participative* or *immanent*. Plato presents us with examples of this approach in the so-called Socratic dialogues and in the Socratic discussions in later dialogues, in which Socrates engages, with others, in a critical dialectical discourse, by way of questions and answers. Similarly, though Hegel is preeminently a theorist of the dialectic, he is also a practitioner. But it is hard to say whether his practice is participatory or merely exemplificative. That is, though Hegel presents us with the "embodied" dialectic, in his works, it is not clear to me that Hegel subjects *himself* to an engagement *in* the dialectic, in his own thought. For Hegel, the dialectic is *objectified*, and taken, either in its exemplification or in its theory, as something to be written about, described, or reflectively reconstructed. Because, for Hegel, "philosophy is its own time, apprehended in thought," and appears as reflection *after* the fact, it plays no active role *in* the fact. Thus, though Hegel's philosophy is preeminently dialectical in *form*, yet, by his own strictures, it does not engage *in* the very dialectic that it reflects. The owl of Minerva takes wing only at dusk, in Hegel's own metaphor.

A participative approach to dialectic, by contrast, is one in which a self-transformation occurs as a result of the process. Feuerbach's work is a striking example of such participative or immanent dialectic. One may reconstruct Feuerbach's development as a process of self-transformation, in which Feuerbach himself, his thought, his beliefs, indeed his philosophical practice, are always engaged as an active element *in* the very dialectic he presents. The method of Feuerbach's engagement is precisely the same as that which he *represents* in his account of the development of human self-consciousness. It is a method in which the I or the self comes to know itself first, by way of its objectification in alienated form, in an other. The "other" for Feuerbach is, in the first instance, the history of philosophy; in the second instance, Hegel's philosophy; and in the third, the forms and modes of human belief. Feuerbach mirrors himself in all these contexts, but he does so actively.

9

That is to say, the reflection is already a transformation, for it takes on the forms and changes introduced by critique. In short, one may say that Feuerbach transforms both his object–philosophy, religion, belief–and himself, as thinker, in his engagement with and critique of this "object."

The development of Feuerbach's thought is therefore an immanent dialectic, presented in the form of his critique of religion and philosophy. Its presentation requires a reconstruction of this series of engagements, in their concrete contexts. Feuerbach *becomes* Feuerbach, comes to know himself, in this very dialectic. What he "negates" or "overcomes" at each stage is no less Feuerbach than what he achieves or posits by way of replacement. In short, I see the process of Feuerbach's own development as an exemplary case of what, in Hegelian theoretical terms, is called "determinate negation," that process in which what is negated, refuted, critically rejected is not simply eliminated, but transformed and incorporated at the next level or stage of development.

Concretely, Feuerbach's early Hegelianism, his idealist epistemology and his recapitulation of Hegel's phenomenology, as an *I-Thou* relation in thought, is first critically transformed in his coming to terms with the history of modern philosophy. Here Feuerbach uses the Hegelian dialectic *externally*, as a device for reconstructing this history. But at the same time, in this very use, it is clear that he reads himself into that history, and only slowly comes to articulate his own *Problematik*, by means of his critique of other philosophers. When he writes his work on Leibniz, he is already struggling with an empiricism and nominalism at odds with his prior Hegelianism. But he is still hiding it from himself, and he presents it only in the outward form of a dialogue, in which the two conflicting views confront each other. In the subsequent book on Pierre Bayle, the "confessional" nature of the work (noted, for example, by Rawidowicz) is clear. It is Feuerbach contra Feuerbach, thinly veiled. There follow a series of highly polemical shorter works, in which Feuerbach in effect defends *himself* against the questions and criticisms that others have raised, ostensibly against Hegel and the young Hegelians. Feuerbach defends himself against the provocative expressions of outright empiricism and materialism in the interpretation of the nature of thinking, and against the charges of atheism leveled at Hegel's and the young Hegelians' interpretations of religion and theology. But, as it turns out, Feuerbach is defending himself against himself. In this very polemic, he comes to grapple with views that are only nascent or half-formed in his own thought and that he as yet rejects. Only by a massive effort at reinterpretation does Feuerbach come to preserve the content of traditional religion, theology, and philosophy in a form acceptable to him. This reinterpretation of the manifest content and claims of religion, theology, and philosophy entails a rejection of the present form of this content and a reconstitution of it in what appears to be a radically altered form. "My philosophy is–no philosophy; my religion is–no religion," he exclaims, in an aphoristic expression of his rejection. But, indeed, *both* philosophy and religion, translated as expressions of human self-understanding, demythologized, demystified, "naturalized," are preserved in terms of what Feuerbach now comes to understand as their latent, or hidden, content. Finally, as the theoretical basis for this reinterpretation, Feuerbach is forced to formulate an empirical-realist and ostensibly materialist-humanist epistemology, a theory of concept formation that finds its genesis in human need, human sensibility, and human dependence on nature and other human beings.

This brief account of Feuerbach's odyssey is not intended as summary, but rather as an indication of the way in which Feuerbach discovers himself, so to speak, by the way of his critical argument with his own beliefs and theories, in their objectified form as they are presented by others. Feuerbach, in reading himself into these others, reconstructs their own views, therefore, from the point of view of his own ongoing *Problematik*. We, in reading Feuerbach's critique, may therefore come to understand his own course of development immanently from the reconstruction of the historical development of this critique. Feuerbach's own methodological statement–*"Die wahre Kritik liegt in der Entwicklung selbst"* ("The true critique lies in the development itself," i.e., in the critical reconstruction of the history of theory, or of dogma, or of belief)–may be taken reflexively, about Feuerbach. He exemplifies his coming to know himself; he articulates himself in the very process of his critique. And we come to know him through it as well. This is why this study is devoted to the struggling, emerging, Feuerbach–not to the mature, complete one.

One may say, therefore, that Feuerbach shows himself in what he says about others. It is noteworthy that, upon the first publication of his collected works, beginning in 1846, Feuerbach reflected upon his earlier views in a variety of contexts and commented on them retrospectively. He reveals there a certain self-consciousness about his own development. But this self-conscious self-reflection *after* the fact is not more valid than the self-revelation that takes place *in* the fact, in the moment of the ongoing work itself.

Feuerbach's method is as much a method of self-revelation and self-articulation as a method of revealing how self-revelation and self-articulation take place in the general development of human consciousness. In this sense, Feuerbach is himself a concrete exemplification of his own analysis. And to take him thus is to take his analysis most seriously, as reflexively valid. That is to say, his method is one that may be used in understanding his own work, and as a basis for a critique of his own work. It is therefore a self-critical method.

Now what I want to say in all this is that the essence of dialectic is self-criticism, but that self-criticism requires objectification, that is, the positing of one's own thought or action as an object. Another way of saying this, less bound to the Hegelian terminology, is that self-criticism requires engagement in the very practice that is to be the subject of that criticism, for only in this practice can one's thoughts, beliefs, or actions; one's commitments; or one's proffered truths be tested. It is therefore not sufficient to characterize dialectic as "criticism" *tout court*, or as criticism of someone *else's* thoughts, beliefs, or actions. (The *reductio ad absurdum* of this version of "criticism and self-criticism" is expressed well in an old left joke: "Comrades! I believe in self-criticism; and I would like to begin by self-criticizing *you*.") Yet the critique of received wisdom, of established beliefs, or of established institutions is the *beginning* of self-criticism, for the self is discovered not as *tabula rasa*, not as innocent and uncontaminated by its history, but as the heir and embodiment of its history. This is why the negative or destructive moment of Socratic dialectic, the casting in doubt of one's presuppositions and present beliefs, is so crucial to the dialectic.

Feuerbach's recognition of his philosophical "self" is not simply the discovery of his "own" personal history as thinker, or as philosopher, but the recognition of himself as species being, that is, as heir to and product of the whole history of philosophy. Feuerbach's "Thou" is Plato, is Descartes, is Leibniz, is Spinoza, is Hegel. Yet the *uncritical* self-recognition in the other, the mere identification of self and other is loss of self. In effect, such sheer self-mirroring identity is *undialectical*, because uncritical. Such a "self" is in effect epiphenomenal, as only a reflex or image of the other. This, curiously enough, is just Feuerbach's own critique of unselfconscious religious consciousness that takes its "God" as real and itself as God's image. Feuerbach's transcendence of this self-deception, the liberation from the idolatry that takes the image as real, is to recognize that "God" is in fact one's own species nature, or rather, the specific form of the understanding that one has attained of one's own species nature. And because the species constitutes itself in the very activity of self-understanding, by means of this alienated mode of self-projection, it transforms itself both in changing its own self-understanding—that is, in the history of religious or philosophical thought and belief—and by coming to recognize itself as the subject or ground of this projection.

The overcoming of the sheer identity with the image is the work of critique. This critique raised to the level of self-recognition *in* the image is *self*-criticism. Self-transformation requires both self-objectification and the critique of this objectification. Dialectic is nothing less than this process of self-transformative praxis, therefore.

This is, I believe, the common core of the dialectical tradition. The variations are important because they map this common core onto different contexts, with very different outcomes. The classic variations are those of Socrates, Plato, Hegel, Marx, and Engels. One needs to add here the contemporary reintroduction by Popper of the Socratic dialectic in the form of a theory of the growth of knowledge by the method of conjectures and refutations. Let me sketch some of the classic variations here, in order to place Feuerbach's dialectical model in the tradition and also to see its distinctiveness.

That the Socratic dialectic is a critical method, that it is a negative or destructive method, is quite clear. What it effects, in its brilliant exemplifications in Plato's Socratic dialogues is the destruction of an argument, or better yet, the destruction of a universal proposition *by* an argument—by the discovery of a contradiction in the views of those who propound it. If, in a valid chain of inference from admitted premises, uncompromised by equivocation or ambiguity, one can show that a contradiction ensues, then one has shown that the premises in question are false, in the sense that they contain at least one falsehood. Thus, the Socratic dialectic does not tell us what is true, or even where the falsehood lies, but only that some premise is false (except in the irrelevant mathematical case of the *reductio ad absurdum* proof, in which the premise is utterly refuted and hence its negation established). Furthermore, one can characterize Socratic dialectic as a *probative* logic, that is, a logic of testing tentative propositions, where the test is that of criticism, and where criticism, as a method, is the search for contradictory consequences of a universal proposition. As such, this is a rational test, rather than an empirical test (though it has an empirical component). The searched-for refutation takes the form of an analytically false proposition—a contradiction—rather than a synthetically false proposition—one that is shown false by empirical test. For, ultimately, all contradiction is logical, because the universal proposition that is shown to be false by empirical test together with the outcome of the test generate the formal contradiction p and not-p. (It remains a matter of fact—i.e., of empirical discovery—as to whether a case exists to instantiate not-p, the so-called basic or falsifying statement.)

Now what is destructive about the Socratic dialectic is that it proposes no universal statements (beyond the undisputed ones that belong to the logic of discourse itself–notably, the principle of noncontradiction). Rather, it eliminates proffered truths by critical examination and test. Yet there is a constructive consequence of this destruction: One may then ask, "What, hypothetically, would have to be posited in order to overcome the critical refutation?" How, in other words, would the premises have to be reformulated so as to evade the admitted criticism? In fact, the dialectical *process* (as distinct from the dialectical *method*, if we take the *method* to be this search for the negative instance of a given premise) is the process of reconstructing alternatives to the failed premises. Such a reconstruction may indeed be in the mode of "conjecture," as Popper proposes–or more deliberately, as a salvage operation, as a reconstruction of refuted premises (by elimination of what is refuted and by addition of new elements to the premises, or new premises).

The constructive consequence of the negative dialectic is thus the generation of new premises, or of hypotheses, as claims to truth, instigated by the failure of previous claims. This is, in effect, the *process* of the dialectic, and what makes it a process rather than a series of disconnected and sporadic episodes is that the same question is being asked, the same "problem situation" is being addressed, and therefore there is a continuity in the scope of the inquiry, which also makes for a continuity in the content or the "history" of the inquiry. (Thus, for example, Socrates endlessly repeats the *same* question, at different stages of a dialogue.) Moreover, continuity may be preserved even when a question is shifted, in accord with the logic of the situation. In this sense, one refutation leads to another proposal (or "conjecture"), designed to meet the desiderata both of the original (failed) proposal *and* of its refutation or negation. That which continues through this series of Socratic debates therefore, *transcends* the refutation and is carried into the reconstruction. Where this fails, of course, the inquiry is at an impasse, it has degenerated in a cul de sac (e.g., in the *Euthyphro*), and a new start, departing imaginatively from the original, is required.

These are features of the Socratic dialectic. But Plato goes beyond this in providing an explicit theory of those conditions (or necessary presuppositions) that would have to hold if the dialectic itself is to proceed as more than idle discourse, that is, if it is to proceed as an inquiry into truth. I find that the Socratic dialectic is embodied in its fullest clarity in such a dialogue as the *Euthyphro*, which is, to all appearances, without issue (unless one derives from it a skeptical conclusion). Yet, as against this skeptical conclusion, Plato theorizes in his later writings. Plato's question, recast in perhaps too Kantian a mold, might be phrased, "How is the finding of truth possible?" That is, what would have to be the case if our (dialectical) inquiry is to be more than an exercise in skepticism, more than an endless series of discursive exclusions?

Here Plato and Hegel (and the long tradition of dialectic that binds them) are at one, and here too is the continuity of Hegel with the Socratic dialectic. Hegel's ontology–his idealism, if you like–is dialectical in precisely this way: What must *Being* be, such that an inquiry into it is conceivably also a way of knowing it, of "arriving" at the truth if only in the limit? To put it differently, what ontology is requisite for intelligibility? Quite clearly, Hegel answers, the *real* would have to be such that the very nature of intelligibility is in accord with it. *Being* is rational–or better, "rationable," available to reason and therefore, in this sense, *one* or identical in both substance and form with reason. Insofar as Hegel's dialectic, like Socrates', sees in the progress of reason the constant negation of partiality, the growing self-awareness that results from the elimination of error, or of contradiction, it can be seen both as a radically destructive or negative method of criticism and as a constructive generation of alternative or reconstructed hypotheses.

One may question, however, the constructive thrust of the Socratic dialectic and ascribe to Plato, rather than to Socrates, this ontological or theoretical dimension. In short, one may see Plato as the betrayer rather than the successor of Socratic skepticism. Socrates' claim to knowledge, after all, was that he knew that he did not know, knew his ignorance, and thereby earned the Delphic oracle's characterization of his wisdom.

For Plato, by contrast, these skeptical limits of the Socratic dialectic are superseded. If knowledge of the truth is to be possible at all, then the prerequisites for rational discourse itself as the mode of truth acquisition have to be ontologically grounded.

I would suggest that for Plato this requirement of an ontological ground for the possibility of truth or for certain knowledge of the truth has two sources: mathematics and politics. In both domains, Plato sees the need to establish the independent reality that would assure the objectivity of mathematical truth on the one hand and of law on the other. In the first case, the truth of mathematics undergirds the possibility of our rational understanding of the natural world; in the second, the objective necessity of law, the ontological status of the Good, undergirds the possibility of rational political rule and of justice. Thus, Plato proposes a ground for mathematical truth–that is, that its objects be real and that its true statements refer to them. Second, he proposes a ground for the political rule of law–that is, that it be based on the ontic nature of human beings and preeminently on their essential rationality. In both mathematics and politics this transcendental ground is taken to be the principle of rationality itself– that is, noncontradiction–which is therefore hypostatized as the very nature of Being itself. This move, in effect, embodies in the object of knowledge or of rational discourse the very conditions of such knowledge or discourse in order to guarantee the very possibility of objectivity. On such a reading, Plato's ontology is the consequence of a transcendental deduction to the very condition of the possibility of truth. The object of knowledge, if truth is possible, is, in effect, knowledge's own "other," the hypostatized image of its own preconditions. The nature and forms of *Being* are thus hardened hypostatizations of the very categories and prerequisites of rational discourse itself.

Such a reconstruction sees the dialectic as two sided: radically negative in its method of criticism, which discovers contradictory consequences of proffered truth claims, and conservatively constructive, in that it reifies the universals that are taken to be the conditions of rational discourse.

But such a reading separates, within the dialectical method, the very polarity that is the condition of dialectic. For without the constructed (or reconstructed) premise, or hypothesis, or categorical assertion, or conjecture, no critique is possible. The very condition of critique is this "other," its *object*, so to speak. Criticism, like consciousness, is a two-termed relation. Its "subjective" side, the dissolution and refutation of a claim to truth, requires its "objective" side, the claim itself. Hegel raises this condition to the very condition of consciousness itself: without this "other" as "object," consciousness is inconceivable; in other words, pure subjectivity is impossible. Moreover, what consciousness, as subject, comes to know, it comes to know on the joint condition that its object is *both unlike itself* (as *object*, or *other*, and therefore *"for* consciousness") *and like* itself (capable of being appropriated *by* consciousness [i.e., its "otherness" overcome]: its *ansichsein*, or being in itself, transformed into its *fureinandersein*, or being for another [i.e., its phenomenality]; and finally, as it is reappropriated by the subject, or as it becomes, *for me*, an object of knowledge). The subject-object identity, the "unity in difference" of the synthetic moment of consciousness, is the recognition by consciousness of the "other" as consciousness' *own* other, or as its *own* othersidedness. Knowledge is possible, truth is possible, only if the object of knowledge is knowable, that is, only if what is to be known is of the nature of consciousness itself. If we translate this back into the Socratic context, it becomes: "Knowledge is possible only if what is criticized is criticizable," namely, only if claims to truth are subject to the norm of noncontradiction. For otherwise all criticism that leads to the demonstration of a contradiction is vain. This methodological requirement of the dialectic, which ensures its legitimacy as *negative* critique, short of sheer skepticism or agnosticism, becomes both for Plato, as for Hegel, a systematic and theoretical requirement of the object of knowledge itself.

On the Hegelian model of the dialectic, this overcoming of contradiction is a limit. It is "achieved" only in the complete and absolute Identity of the subject and object. Therefore, at the limit, one comes to the "end" of the dialectic, in the sense that the dialectic simply ends, and in the sense that further criticism is impossible. Truth has been "achieved." Thus, this notion of limit also has the sense of what is the *telos* or goal of the dialectic: It aims at truth. The problem of this "end" of the dialectic is itself a dialectical problem. For if we are talking here of a dialectic of *concepts*, or of *theories*, then we are talking of the limit as the end of conceptual or theoretical evolution, or of the grasping, in immediacy (i.e., *un*dialectically) of a final truth. Whatever dogmatism is engendered by Hegelianism is derived from the *un*dialectical assertion of this claim to finality. For with it inquiry ends, and indeed, *consciousness* ends, if we are to take Hegel himself seriously about the conditions of consciousness itself. For then, in the identity of subject and object in the limit, the very condition of consciousness, its requirement of an object, is overcome. What remains is the infinite self-enjoyment of God, in that static and eternal "fullness of Being" with which rationalistic theology filled the heavenly void. At best, we have that realm of being that "surpasseth all understanding"—we have mystery, the *via negativa*, and the absolute breach of reason. In short, we have faith.

Enter Feuerbach. If anything, his successive removals from the Hegelian mode, from speculative philosophy, and from the stylish jargon of the Hegelian school—his opting for an enlightened empiricism, for a ramified sensationalism, for a nominalistic ontology of individuals, for a humanistic anthropologism, or naturalism, or materialism (the exact characterization is at issue, and is a subject for this study)—all of these would suggest his progressive detachment from the dialectical method itself. But this is belied both by the method and the content of his work. Methodologically, Feuerbach's critical *and* constructive work is thoroughly imbued with both the Socratic element of negative critique and the reconstructive element of theory formation.

His method is not to destroy religion, or philosophy, but to translate and interpret them *dialectically*, that is, as the alienated forms of an essentially human activity. He sees in them the reflective and constructive activity of consciousness, the conscious representation of practical life. Feuerbach's whole "demystification" of religion and philosophy, his "nothing but," is not reductionist but is rather a dialectical negation and transformation of religion and philosophy: the *aufhebung*, the "raising up" of a confused and inverted consciousness, to enlightenment and self-knowledge. The model for this dialectic is clearly Hegel's *Phenomenology of Mind*. But the radical departure from Hegel is in the use of this very dialectic to criticize the very foundation of Hegel's idealism, and of Hegel's claim as to what philosophy itself is.

WHAT IS MATERIALISM? IN WHAT SENSE MAY FEUERBACH BE SAID TO BE A MATERIALIST? AND WHAT ARE THE LIMITS OF HIS MATERIALISM?

The source of Feuerbach's profound influence on Marx is often said to be Feuerbach's materialism. But it is not enough to say that Feuerbach provided the young Marx with "materialism," as the textbooks tell us. It is the content and thrust of this materialism, as a *critical* materialism, whose objects of criticism are "here below," whose attack is on the mystification and alienation of everyday life, in the human, political, economic realm of ordinary existence (captured best by that much-inflated yet workaday German expression, *Dasein*). This materialism, therefore, transfers, in Marx's own phrase, the critique of the Holy Family to the critique of the earthly family, turns attention from heaven to earth, from theology to this-worldly salvation, from philosophy of the state to politics. Therefore, Feuerbach's impact on the young Feuerbachians, Marx and Engels, was profound. It made it possible to conceive of the relation of philosophical theory to human practice, to human weal and woe, to human history, society, political economy, culture itself; and thereby to turn philosophy first into a critique of philosophy itself, insofar as such a "speculative philosophy" conceived of its object as other than human, or transcendental; and thereby, into a critique of culture, of society, of the "forms of life" that speculative philosophy expresses in its abstract, "rational," and esoteric form.

Thus, the Feuerbachian dialectic, in its application, is not simply a formal *theory* of dialectic that Feuerbach interprets in the domain of the psychology of concept formation in religious or philosophical thought that is then "transferred" by Marx and Engels to the domain of social critique. One may say, then, that dialectics is not a formal theory, but a methodology or a practice of criticism. Yet this practice does have its explicit formal theory, or theories. Hegel, after all, gives us not only the exemplified dialectic of his *Phenomenology of Mind*, or of his *History of Philosophy*, or of the *Philosophy of Right*, or of his *Philosophy of Nature*, or of *Art*. He also gives us the theoretical and abstracted form of the dialectic as a logic, in his *Science of Logic* and in the *Shorter Logic*. In Engels too we have an explicit *theory* of dialectic as objective negation, that is, as an interpretation of "criticism" in terms of ontological negation. Engels is more explicit than Marx and more "objective" than Hegel in his interpretation of the dialectic as a natural process. That is, the "objective" dialectic is taken neither as the internal dialectic of the *Idea* "objectified" in nature merely as the *Idea's* other—for this remains an idealist dialectic—nor only as a social dialectic albeit of material social life, that is, the activity of the social production of the means of human existence and the reproduction of species life. Rather, in the full-blown version of a materialist dialectic, the "laws" of the dialectic—negation of the negation, transformation of quantitative into qualitative change, and interpenetration of opposites—are seen as laws of *Being*, or in physicalist-materialist terms, as laws of the self-transformation of matter, of physical nature itself. Thus, Engels clearly states that the materialist dialectic is Hegel's idealist dialectic stood back on its (physical) feet, not simply in terms of the relation of social being to social consciousness, but in terms of the internal and self-differentiating dialectical process of matter itself, as a self-transformative process. In the *Dialectics of Nature*, Engels sketchily develops this view of dialectic as an elaboration and extension of that dialectic whose domain remains that of human society, human history, and human praxis.

Popper appears to eschew such a formal theory of dialectic. Yet he proposes a method of dialectical criticism whose logic he does attempt to elaborate in great detail. Popper's account of theoretical refutation or falsification is taken by him to be the elaboration, into the domain of theory, and therefore of a discourse whose norms are those of valid inference or logic, of the common pretheoretical practice of trial and error, whose roots are in animal behavior. Thus, for Popper, dialectic is simply the highest evolved form of a fundamental life activity. It becomes dialectic at the level of critical or self-critical (i.e., argumentative) discourse, which is the evolved instrumentality for the growth of knowledge and the hallmark of scientific knowledge. Popper's formal theory of dialectic is therefore the logical theory of falsificationism, together with his demarcation of the logic of inquiry from the nonlogical and therefore nonrational domains of thinking. Popper openly rejects any attempt to ground knowledge either on positive evidence or on what comes to the same thing, so-called inductive inference. His anti-justificationism, so called, recapitulates the negative content of the Socratic dialectic.

In all these versions, however, self-transformation through self-criticism or self-negation emerges as the invariant core of the dialectic. This self-criticism remains a function of a discourse bounded by the norm of noncontradiction, in the Socratic and Popperian versions. Although the discourse is not a disembodied one and concerns the practice of social and moral life in Socrates and the practice of scientific inquiry, or the acquisition or growth of knowledge, in Popper, the dialectic proper is assigned to the domain of discourse itself. In Plato, Hegel and Engels, it is ontologized: The conditions of discourse, or of reason, or of consciousness itself are the conditions of Being. The transcendental grounds of reason are the transcendental grounds of reality itself. Moreover, the practical world of our feelings, beliefs, actions, and sense experience achieves its small measure of reality only derivatively, as the partial and incomplete exemplification of the forms of Being or of Reason themselves.

Feuerbach's radical move is to see the dialectic as a dialectic of consciousness rooted in the very condition of material human existence: in needs, interests, wants; in the human being's dependency on other human beings, and on nature. Thus, because the primary reality for human beings is their sensible existence, the dialectic is a dialectic of this sensibility, of *Sinnlichkeit*.

Feuerbach's materialism in this context consists of his interpretation of the dialectic of consciousness as a dialectic of conscious needs and dependencies where these needs and dependencies are given by human sensibility (*Sinnlichkeit*). This sensibility, in turn, is rooted in or is an expression of the material conditions of human existence. "Material conditions" connote, for Feuerbach, both the physical requirements for human life–that is, food, air, water–and the social requirements, that is, other human beings. Feuerbach thus means by "material" something as vague as "real" or "existing" as opposed to "imaginary" or "in consciousness alone." But that doesn't take us very far. He certainly does *not* mean by "material" anything as specific, as "physical," as atoms in motion or chemical elements. And it is only in his later works that his conception of "sensibility" (*Sinnlichkeit*) takes a physiological turn. "Matter" then becomes not simply the object of sensation, but rather of digestion! It is literally what becomes incorporated, the external world transformed into living substance or into consciousness by metabolic activity. But what gives this "matter" its character is that it is needed, acted upon, transformed by human activity as a means of satisfying life needs, both natural and social.

In the dialogue *D'Alembert's Dream*, Diderot had proposed that marble could become living flesh (by grinding it, ingesting it, and incorporating it in living tissue). This eighteenth-century parable about how the inorganic can be transformed into the organic is echoed by the later Feuerbach in the 1850s in his enthusiasm over Moleschott's physiological materialism. But the crucial form of Feuerbach's materialism remains his theory of sensibility; and here, the central features are the conscious neediness or dependency of the sentient human being that is the source and motive of human agency and also the content that human consciousness discovers in its reflection upon itself. Thus, the dialectic is not taken to be a dialogue of consciousness with itself but rather a dialogue of consciousness with its "other" as the object or material of sensibility. This object is given, so to speak, in sensation and in feeling, and our human awareness of this object is suffused with our awareness of our neediness and dependency upon it. The practical form of this neediness, however, is not action but belief. The object remains an object of our practical activity only within the category of belief.

Marx's critique of Feuerbach is not, therefore, that Feuerbach's intentions are wrong, or that the dialectic is wrongly grounded. Rather, it is that the sensibility, which Feuerbach takes as the domain of the dialectic, remains an abstract sensibility: It remains, for all Feuerbach's protestations, a reflected-upon praxis, or a praxis within reflection, a praxis of belief and of thought. It remains *philosophy*. It needs to become, says Marx, a social and political praxis and preeminently a historical one. Insofar as it does, the dialectic is embodied not in consciousness, as such, nor in sensibility as such, but in revolutionary praxis, in world-changing praxis. Thus, in Marx's view, Feuerbach fails to fulfill his very intentions, by conceiving of this concrete praxis as an abstract one, in the sense that it is ahistorical, and remains concerned with belief, feeling, and awareness of needs as human. But this awareness remains only abstract insofar as it is not yet historically determinate and historically differentiated and insofar as it remains a reflective awareness and is not yet embodied in action.

Both Feuerbach and Marx, therefore, see the fundamental character of dialectic as an embodied practice–whether of belief or of labor and of social and political action. Both are theorizers. Yet neither has an explicit or formal theory of dialectic. Both are practitioners of the theoretical reconstruction of this embodied dialectic, but neither gives us the theory of this reconstruction, except in occasional and scattered remarks. Both in fact are wary of formal or methodological explication, like artists wary of aestheticians or practicing scientists wary of philosophers of science. And with good reason. Yet both give the richest materials for such a *theoretical* reconstruction, not simply in what they present, but in the practical method of their critiques.

Of the theoretical reconstructions of the dialectic, Hegel's is by far the richest. Plato presents it to us, in the form of Socratic dialogue, and achieves a remarkable range of theoretical discussions in the development of his theory of forms. But the theoretical emphasis is on the ontology, not on the methodology, which is given only implicitly, by exemplification. Engels, in his attempt at an explicit theory, remains sketchy, and elementary, and fills in with examples from the natural sciences. The fuller theoretical reconstruction of the dialectic method, and of the intimate relations between its form and its content, remains to be achieved, I believe. The study of two of its most eminent modern practitioners, Feuerbach and Marx, provides the most articulate models of its practice and evidence of its forcefulness and effectiveness as a critical method.

In this framework, the present study of Feuerbach's development, though it does not attempt an explicit theoretical formulation of the dialectic, does attempt to show it in its operation. The crucial element in the presentation, then, is the attempt to show how criticism and self-criticism are interrelated, how, in effect, the praxis of criticism becomes a self-transformative praxis in Feuerbach's own case. Thus, what the dialectic is, in Feuerbach, we can best learn from reading and analyzing his own applied analysis and critique of religion and philosophy and his own construction of the dialectical continuity of sensing, perceiving, imagining, and thinking, his "dialectic of sensibility."

I hope to show this in the present work, and merely make a claim for it here. But, then, what is *my* methodology? It is, I hope, dialectical as well, and in its substantive import, a critical method. That is to say, I purport to set forth, in detail, the actual development of Feuerbach's thought, in its own terms; to give a substantive exposition not simply of his conclusions and tenets, but of the *process* of his thought and the character of his distinctive *Problematik*; and therefore, *also, to show the dialectical process of negation by which Feuerbach refutes Feuerbach; and further, to show where Feuerbach fails to refute Feuerbach.* In short, this account of Feuerbach's philosophy is not an exposition or a summary. I hope to enter into the very grain of Feuerbach's mode of thought and to show how the dialectical transformation of the young Hegelian took place. I have found the tracking of this spoor an intellectual adventure. But because the process, in a sense, is central, the details are important, and patience for them is the price of the intellectual reward.

For this purpose, my focus is on the period of transformation—from the earliest writings to the principal work of Feuerbach's "middle period," *The Essence of Christianity*—and only secondarily on his later works (which are, in fact, philosophically weaker and less interesting for my purposes). I include enough on them to show where Feuerbach's own constructive philosophy tended. But if anything in Feuerbach is second rate, this is. It is interesting, but not innovative; thorough, but not exciting. His philosophical humanism, like most philosophical humanism, tends to be bland, uncritical, and too often sentimental.

It is also clear that Marx's critique of Feuerbach is well founded. It is precisely at the point of drawing the fullest consequences of his own critique that Feuerbach fails. He remains too "philosophical," even "abstract" in his conception of human nature, as a fixed "species nature." But the import of these terms—"philosophical," "abstract," "species nature"—as *critical* terms derives from Feuerbach's own analysis. Moreover, he touches more fully and more explicitly on the psychology of belief, on the epistemological problem of the relation of our consciousness to our everyday life, on the mind-body problem, and on the mechanism of human self-knowledge and self-deception than does Marx. That is not to say that we have here a Marxist epistemology or psychology, in germ. Assuredly not, for as Marx pointed out, Feuerbach lacked *that* sense of historical concreteness, of the world of human praxis itself (rather than its reflected image in our conscious reconstruction of it) to fulfill his *humanist* materialism as a *historical* materialism. But the subtlety and richness of Feuerbach's insights into the modes of human consciousness and self-consciousness provide a needed corrective for the tendencies of some Marxists to dogmatize on what Marx said, instead of being creatively philosophical and critical with respect to what Marx did not say, or failed to say.

Now in claiming that my approach and method are critical, I should also point to a shortcoming in my own work. Were this study to be a sustained piece of analysis both of the intellectual-philosophical dialectic of Feuerbach's thought *and* of its concrete historical matrix, then I should have to show, in detail, the relation of Feuerbach's philosophy to its social roots and examine its social and political role. This I have failed to do. It would require historical scholarship beyond my present grasp to reconstruct and interpret the details of German and European political and socioeconomic history, in this context. But had I undertaken this, one warning would have been in order: The simplistic reconstruction of Feuerbach's philosophy as, somehow, the reflection of the class struggle in Germany in his time would be far from enough, or even distorting. At best, were it done well, this would provide only the necessary (or *a* necessary) but not a sufficient condition for such a critical historical-materialist reconstruction. The intricacy and subtlety of the interplay between the sociohistorical factors, the relatively autonomous philosophical dialectic, the cultural and conceptual matrix of German intellectual life, and the personal biography of Feuerbach demand a masterful synthesis. Such a work, a truly historical study in all this depth, remains to be written. Indeed, there are few philosophers who have been dealt with in this way, let alone adequately. But such a biographical-historical-intellectual study demands more than vulgar sociology, or what Marx would have called "mechanical materialism," and certainly more than a "vulgar Marxism" (i.e., a mechanistic and flat-footed economic determinism). In short, this is a genre of philosophical history as yet underdeveloped, and I regret not having attained it in this work.[4]

For all this, my own stance in this work remains, philosophically, that of a critical materialist. By this I mean that my sympathies and commitments lie with Feuerbach's humanism and naturalism–with his attempt to explain the ideal, the transcendental, the metaphysical in terms of the natural and this-worldly activities and capacities of mankind; to see consciousness as a "form of life" (to borrow Wittgenstein's phrase in what I take to be its deepest significance). This is not yet materialist, but only naturalist–only "shamefaced materialism." Yet what is "materialist" is precisely what is at issue here. The reductive materialism of a blood-and-guts physicalism–"All is atoms in motion and the void"–is as inappropriate to the categories of "species-being" and to the social, cultural, and historical realities of human action as the more contemporary "analytical materialism" (my name for the current preoccupation with mind-brain identity theories, based on linguistic and explanatory reduction). My materialism is, I would hope, akin to Marx's–fluent and nondogmatic, emergentist, and sensitive to the requirements for an explanation and understanding of human praxis and of human history. Therefore, it is nonreductionist, and, indeed, antireductionist. But here is where both my sympathy for and my criticism of Feuerbach's materialism lie. As concrete and "natural" as Feuerbach's conception of man is, it lacks, as Marx saw, the historical, social, and developmental categories that would concretize the notion of "species being." Feuerbach provides a phylogeny and ontogeny for the human species concept. But he fails to provide a *history*, and thereby ends with a historically abstract "species being," the Human as such. Yet the richness of his phylogeny, in terms of abiding and universal species-characteristics, especially in terms of the psychological processes of self-knowledge, is unsurpassed. Here he is, at least programmatically, historical as well as systematic. He traces this history in the history of religions and of philosophic consciousness–but not yet in the relation of this reflected-upon consciousness to historical, political, and social praxis. There are suggestions of this relation here and there in Feuerbach, but no more.

If I am critical of Feuerbach, then, it is at those points where he himself *fails* to break with the very philosophical inversion he attacked in Hegel and in speculative philosophy generally–the failure to see the abstractly human or abstractly material as themselves derived, by the philosophical consciousness (in this case, Feuerbach's own), from the more concrete circumstances of historical human activity, in concrete social, political, and economic contexts. However, I do not fault Feuerbach with having failed to write an *Eighteenth Brumaire* or a *Civil War in France* or a *Critique of Political Economy*. That is not the point. Moreover, Feuerbach himself is sometimes clearly aware, and explicit, about the limits of his own enterprise. In answer to the early critics of his *Essence of Christianity* (e.g., Julius Müller, who accused him of a benighted anthropomorphism and who declared that for Feuerbach it would appear that nature itself had no independent status, except as a reflection of man's own self-image) Feuerbach replied that his specific and delimited subject matter was indeed *only* that process of self-projection, only the phenomenon of human self-consciousness, in which "nature" serves as a clue to self-conception. But ultimately, Feuerbach's defense fails, not because what he says in his defense is not so, but because he fails finally to establish a *more* than anthropomorphic or phenomenological account of "nature," or of the objectivity of the natural world. He *asserts* it certainly, but his philosophy does not systematically sustain that assertion. And here, I think, his materialism fails. Nature remains what it is capable of becoming *for* man; it remains the *object* of human consciousness, the reflected-upon and transformed construction of human needs, desires, wishes–and, at the materialist limits, of human sensation. Feuerbach's sensationalistic empiricism is as close as he comes to materialism, and it remains a sensationalistic materialism, though it promises and suggests more. His theory of sensation is an enlightened and advanced theory, far beyond that of eighteenth-century empiricism, and more directly akin to the subtle and advanced views of Diderot.[5] In this sense, it is a viable corrective and guide to the simplistic empiricist sensationalism of much of contemporary psychology, and is related to such contextualist and organicist views as that of J. J. Gibson and to the still rich suggestions of Dewey. But insofar as Feuerbach's sensationist materialism fails to be adequate to concrete historical contexts, it falls short of being an adequate materialist epistemology. And insofar as his anthropologism—his insistence on the human origin and derivation of all religious and philosophical categories—fails to see *these* categories in their concrete historical evolution, it too falls short of being an adequate materialist anthropology.

But what is an "adequate materialism"? If my own materialist view is "critical," it is so in the sense that I think an "adequate materialism" is a goal, not an achievement. The goal functions heuristically here. It is a set of desiderata that a materialist philosophy will have to meet, but not yet the actual meeting of these desiderata. They will be met differently as human knowledge increases, and so "adequacy" is bound to cases, to specific answers to specific questions, and is not a metaphysical *terminus ad quem*. Therefore, an "adequate materialism" is a touchstone for criticism rather than a theory *as such*. It is, I would hope, a dialectical concept, whose content and whose embodiment are realized in the actual practice of philosophical criticism. The minimal desiderata for such criticism are analogous to those of the Socratic dialectic: there the desideratum is a discursive or logical one—noncontradiction; here the desiderata are ontological and methodological: that the explanation and understanding of human beings, as of nature, take fully into account the material conditions and genesis of man and of nature, where "material" connotes what we can come to know objectively by means of our theoretical and empirical practice. This is, obviously, bald and bare—but a heuristic will be bald and bare; it is not an algorithm, nor a security blanket, nor a dogma.

"Empirical practice" itself is an open concept, but it includes, at least, the activity of bold theorizing as well as the activity of rigorous criticism and practical test of the consequences of our theories. Its epistemological prejudice is realist: What we know exists independently of our knowing it. But it is also relativist or interactionist: Our knowing transforms the *object*, makes it an object for us. I gladly acknowledge the traditional and contemporary difficulties of this viewpoint, even as barely as it is stated here. Indeed, it is Feuerbach's coping with just such questions that gives him the philosophical cutting edge that he has.

To acknowledge the difficulties is not to allay them, but rather to promise that the work itself will cope with them in situ, and concretely, where they arise. The *profession de foi* here is simply to disabuse the reader of any expectations of philosophical neutrality, rather than to enlighten him on the tough and analytical questions to which such a formulation gives rise–and also it is to give some sense that materialism is not a philosophical dogma, but a critical standpoint, which must also take *itself* as an object of criticism.

CHAPTER II

Early Hegelian Epistemology: The Dissertation

Feuerbach's *Dissertation*,[1] though it is a thoroughly Hegelian exercise, is significant in the suggestions it already bears of themes he is to develop later. Two readings of the *Dissertation* are possible: first, one may read it as a continuation of Hegel's dialectical phenomenology, as it is fully developed in the *Phenomenology of Mind*. In this case, one reads the *Dissertation* historically from *its* present, relating it to what preceded it in Hegel's work. Second, one may read it retrospectively, from its future or *from our* present, so to speak. Such a reading is historically informed by a knowledge of what Feuerbach's subsequent philosophical development was. In this case, one discovers in it sources and suggestions of Feuerbach's later thought. On these two readings, two different judgments are possible: first, that Feuerbach is simply a good Hegelian, in his mastery of the mode of dialectical analysis of the subject-object relation, of the relation of self and other in consciousness, and of the rationalist-idealist commitment to Reason as the universal ground for the identity of knowing and being. On this first reading, what is distinctively Feuerbachian is perhaps the humanist interpretation of Hegel's *Phenomenology of Mind* that Feuerbach suggests: that is, that Reason—"One, universal and infinite"—is the essence of man, that it is a species essence; and that its embodiment is in human consciousness, as a species consciousness and not as an individual consciousness. I say that this is "perhaps" what is distinctively Feuerbachian, because at least one tradition of Hegel scholarship—that represented in the French School, principally by Kojève[2]—reads Hegel's *Phenomenology of Mind* itself in this spirit. At the very least, then, Feuerbach's *Dissertation* provides the first model for such a reading of Hegel.

On the second, retrospective reading, from *our* present, an alternative judgment is suggested: that the *Dissertation* contains, in germ, major themes that Feuerbach is to develop later. Thus, in the *Dissertation* there is already a discussion of the species concept (*Gattungsbegriff*) of man and of his essence as species being (*Gattungswesen*). Thus, too, there is a discussion of the relation of the individual to the species, in the context of an *I-Thou* relationship, though this is understood there only in its idealist-rationalist form, as a relation *in* thought activity alone.

These two alternative readings of the *Dissertation* are not mutually exclusive, of course. They vary in standpoint. For our purposes, we may adopt either standpoint, flexibly, when it is useful to an understanding of the text. But because the main object of this study is Feuerbach's philosophical development, the dominant organizing principle of the discussion will be the retrospective standpoint, from our present. It is thus not an object of this study to show all the connections with Hegel's thought. It *is* a major object of this exposition, analysis, and critique of Feuerbach's early work to understand the content and character of Feuerbach's break with Hegel, and with speculative idealist philosophy in general; and this demands a full treatment of Feuerbach's understanding of Hegelianism. For this purpose, the *Dissertation* is, though a work of Feuerbach's discipleship and youth, a crucial work. In this context, it has not been seriously treated by Feuerbach scholars.[3]

The *Dissertation* is an explicitly rationalist-idealist work. In the Platonic-Hegelian tradition, Reason is the Idea, the Form, the ultimate ground from which all individual existences derive. Only reason can know universals, because only it is universal: Thus, only in Reason is there the identity of knowing and being; only in Reason does the individual overcome his finitude and become one with the species. The senses can know only particulars. Insofar as it is *only* the individual who thinks and insofar as the individual knows only individuals in his thinking, human reason remains finite. It is not yet *species* consciousness, not yet universal reason, that transcends human finitude. Yet, in Feuerbach's explicit formulation of this idealist rationalism, there already appear the grounds, and the modes of analysis, in terms of which Feuerbach is to do his about-face, in his critique of Hegel and of idealism in general. What he begins here, realistically (in terms of the ontological ultimacy of universals), he is to conclude nominalistically (in terms of the ontological ultimacy of individuals). In his later work, he will derive Reason, its infinity, universality, and unity, *from* the very individuals and particulars of sensibility that here he derives instead *from* Reason. In its inverted form, the *Dissertation* establishes the language and context of the later critique. But the critique is not to be achieved until

Feuerbach's thought goes through the purgatory of its Hegelian exposition. And Feuerbach's "positive" formulation of a sensuous materialism is not to be achieved until the Hegelian formulation is transformed by Feuerbach's "anthropological" or humanist critique of theology and speculative philosophy.

THINKING, KNOWING, AND SENSING

The program of the *Dissertation* is clearly set forth: "We wish to consider, first, pure thought; then that thought which thinks itself; finally, the unity of thinking and knowing, in order to show that there is but one universal and infinite reason. That this reason is not finite and not individual, the examination of thought itself will show" (IV, 301). Despite this, Feuerbach begins the *Dissertation* with an assertion of the finitude of human reason. The recognition of the finitude of human reason is the threshold of all philosophy, he says. But, he adds, this is not skepticism, is not Pyrrhonistic as regards the limits of human knowledge. The mistake of Pyrrhonistic skepticism is that it confuses the limits of the individual knower with the rational capacities of the human spirit in general. The mistake, says Feuerbach, is to regard reason as a property of individuals. In this sense, it is taken merely as an individual function, as an *instrument* of the individual understanding. Thus, it is comprehended as an instrument in the same sense that the foot is an instrument for walking, the ear for hearing, the eye for seeing. The "new philosophy," on the contrary, understands reason properly as "the unified and general *ground* of all individuals," says Feuerbach. In effect, reason is not an activity *of* individuals, *as* individuals; rather, individuals are only finite modes of the universal activity of reason. In thinking and knowing, individuals become rational by transcending their individuality, by "abolishing" or overcoming their finitude.

To discover *what* it is that thinks and knows, therefore, says Feuerbach, we do not start with the individual. The ontological status of the thinker and knower, of the Being who thinks and knows, is to be derived instead from an analysis of what thinking and knowing are. The character of the activity defines the agent. Moreover, for the young Hegelian, the essence of Being *is* thought itself. This he characterizes (in his *History of Modern Philosophy*, to be treated later) as the foundation stone of modern philosophy, and the "great thought" of Descartes and Leibniz, the innovation of the "new philosophy." It is not simply that *man's* being is his thinking activity; this would relegate this activity to one among many, as man is one among many beings. Rather, Feuerbach continues, because it is in thought that universals come to be known and because Being is ultimately *universal, one* and *infinite,* thought, in coming to know Being, must be of the same nature. The relation of the thinking subject to its proper object is possible only if the subject and the object are of the same nature. Thus, the Hegelian identity philosophy establishes the subject-object relation as reflexive, that is, ultimately, as a relation in which Reason stands to itself. Whatever is, is *what* it is by virtue of this relation of Reason, or of the Idea, to itself. Reason and Being are ultimately identical, therefore.

"Ultimately" means, in the Hegelian dialectic, at the point at which the subject-object identity is fully realized or achieved. In this self-relation of Reason, however, there is a dialectical *process* of self-identification. The identity is not simply given, but achieved. In this process, the universal relation of identity appears (in its "moments" or stages of the process) in different modes of self-relation. The *kinds* of being that there are, are ultimately to be defined and determined by the analysis of these kinds or modes of Reason's self-relation. All of them, to be sure, are modes of one and the same relation of Reason to itself; however, this relation appears, in the process, in finite and determinate modes. The *being* of anything is therefore nothing but what it exemplifies as *a* mode of this self-relation. The thinking, knowing, and sensing being is defined and determined therefore by these activities, as modes of the self-relation of Reason. It is on the basis of this abstract, formal Hegelian structure of the subject-object relation that Feuerbach distinguishes between thinking, knowing, and sense perception.

In the *Dissertation*, Feuerbach asserts the privacy of sense perception, its incommunicable immediacy. The essence of sense perception, in distinction from thought, is that it cannot be shared through discourse. The unique "ownness" of one's perceptions is contrasted with the communal nature of discourse; and thinking is defined as such a discursive function. He writes,

The inner senses, such as, for example, the perception of pleasure and pain, are true senses, and cannot be separated from the subject, whereas the object which is the stimulus of my sensation can be shared in common with all others. In describing the object, I am able to publicize my sensation, and another can understand my condition. The grounds of such understanding do not lie in sensibility itself, however, but in thought. Sense-perception in and for itself remains forever mine alone, and is locked within the boundaries of the *I*. The word is always the expression for a universal; sensibility gives only the particular. To be sure, I can say to another, "my head hurts," "this thing smells sweet," etc.; but this pain, this odor itself cannot be shared; otherwise, the other person would have to have the same pain or odor perceptions simultaneously with my expression of them in words. (IV, 302)

This privacy of sense experience, then, makes it impossible to explain human communication in empiricist terms. For sense experience itself is the mark of individuality, whereas communication, even of this sense experience itself, requires community. The exclusiveness of individuals, in sensing, vanishes in that community that characterizes thought. "Insofar as I think," writes Feuerbach, "I cease to be an individual; and thought, therefore, is nothing but the being of universality" (IV, 302). In effect, says Feuerbach, the "problem" of communication is a pseudo-problem. There is no problem, because, in fact, men do communicate. But the attempt to explain this communication in empirical terms, in the terms of sense experiences that are ultimately private, exclusively "my own," leads to insurmountable problems. "Were man, insofar as he thinks, as differentiated from all others as he is when he lives, feels and senses, then all sharing and communication of thoughts would be entirely impossible" (IV, 304).

However exclusive and incommunicable my sense experiences are, however "my own" they are in this sense, my thoughts are no less my own; but my own in a different way, which characterizes my very being as ultimately *not* individual, but communal; not particular, but of a "species nature." Thus, my senses do not mark my essence, but are "mediated" by the objects that stimulate them. What is my "own," as individual, is not determined by anything outside or beyond my individuality itself. It is in this sense "immediate." Insofar as sense perception introduces an external stimulus object, my perception is thereby a "mediated" mode of consciousness, determined by something whose nature is *not*-myself. However, my thinking *is* my nature in itself, though not as individual. "For [my thoughts] are my self, my real, inner nature. At the same time, my thoughts can be communicated to another, so that this other may recognize them as his own" (IV, 303). This double ownership, this shared thought is no less my own for being shared. In sense perception, the *other* or object of my perception is other than myself; however, in thought, the *other* with whom the thought is shared is myself *as* other, the *I* that transcends its privacy, and becomes its *own* object. Thus, Feuerbach distinguishes between sense perception and thought:

On these grounds, since sense experience separates me from the other, since in perception I am only myself and the other is an other-for-me, no other can in any real sense participate in my sense experience. Insofar as I think, however, I can at the same time be another, and in fact I *am* another; my essence is also his. What I have in my inmost being can be, and shall be also a part of his self. Nothing is so entirely my own as my thinking; and no element of my person, of what I own, can be so fully alienated and at the same time incorporated in another, as my thinking. ... To put it another way: to think is to differentiate one's self-unity, to be dual, within the context of the highest unity, and vice versa. (IV, 304)

This dialectic of the self-differentiation of the *I*, in the activity of thinking, serves Feuerbach, as it served Hegel, to establish the subject-object identity. It is not simply that in thinking, some *part* of me becomes shared with another, or becomes at the same time a *part* of another (though the text falls into this usage). Rather, in thinking, the *I is* its thinking activity, and nothing else. Its identity is its thought. It is what it does, so to speak. The ontological identity of the subject is not given, or presupposed, apart from this activity, which defines it. Thus, man thinking is not, a priori, an individual who thinks (i.e., an individual, *one* of whose properties is thought), but rather a thinking being, a being whose essence is thinking. In the act of thought, therefore, what may be particular and individual in other respects—that is, in terms of sensation, or feeling, and therefore, as the marks of an empirical individual—is no longer particular and individual, or distinct from other individuals. Thus, in thought, individuality is negated, transcended. The identity of the self, in thinking, is not the same, therefore, as the identity of particular individuals. In recognizing myself in the other, in another self, or in a *Thou*, I recognize not my particular individual self-identity, but rather my *species* identity. The *I* is a *species-I*, and it is this distinctive identity that marks it off from merely *natural beings,* and distinguishes it as *human being*. Self-recognition, therefore, is not *simple* self-identity, which is the condition of the individuality of *natural beings.* The unique *individuality* of man is the recognition of himself as species-being. Feuerbach dsitinguishes between *mere* individuality (of natural being) and human individuality on these grounds.

Man as an individual is man in general; i.e., every individual recognizes in himself other men, or *all* other men, simply in knowing himself as man. For in my awareness of myself as man, I know myself both as *this* individual, and as man in general. Insofar, then, as I know myself, and posit myself, I know and posit the other, or mankind in general, as well. And thereby I cease to be merely an individual. This mere individuality is the necessary condition of every other natural being which has no self-knowledge. Were my self-awareness not also at the same time a comprehension of other men, then I would not be a man, but a plant, and would have only a vegetative soul.... But this self-awareness which we ascribe here to plants cannot be, nor can it be called, self-knowledge. It is only life, growth.... (IV, 308)[4]

What is suggested here is that continuum of "grades" or "levels" of self-relation, characteristic of the stages of the Hegelian dialectic. The notion that "self-awareness" is one form of self-relation that characterizes lower levels of "life"—that is, vegetative or animal life—has its antecedents in the neo-Platonic tradition of grades of nature. It finds its modern expression and systematic presentation in Leibniz's *Monadology*, and later, in Schelling's notion of "grades of potentiation of Spirit," in his philosophy of nature; and obviously, in Hegel's philosophy of nature, in which the dialectic of self-differentiation and self-relation is embodied in a systematic view of grades of nature. In Feuerbach's *Dissertation*, it forms the basis for the distinction between such "natural being" and "human being." In natural beings, the mode of self-relation is one that is mediated by an external object; for sensate beings, by an object of sensory awareness, or an object of perception. In such a relation, the other is not yet a *Thou*, but merely another individual thing. In the human case, however, Feuerbach holds this to be a distinctive relation of *I*-and-*Thou*, which he first introduces in the *Dissertation* and which is to shape (if not to haunt) all his subsequent work.

I-THOU: THE INDIVIDUAL AND THE SPECIES

In the relation of an *I* to a *Thou*, which is the characteristic relation of human, thinking consciousness, the *I* recognizes its own *species* nature in the *Thou*. The *Thou* is therefore not merely another individual, but that distinctive "individual" that is recognized as a universal, namely, as man's own essence. This mode of self-relation is achieved uniquely through the recognition of universality. But this recognition is both consummated in and constituted by the act of thought. It is in thinking, says Feuerbach, that man expresses and realizes his species nature. In this thinking activity, the thinking individual, the *I*, is in unity with the "other," the object of this thought, which is a *Thou*. This "unity" is that of the thinking essence or of thought activity with *itself*, because the "other" is of the same essence as this thought activity, or is, in effect, the other-sidedness of this thought activity itself. The peculiarity of attributing universality to this activity of thought is the peculiarity of rationalism. But the peculiarity of seeing this self-relation as an *internal* relation is a peculiarity of dialectical rationalism, in particular, and this is the model Feuerbach adopts. It is the old model of contemplative activity, inherited from the Greeks: Aristotle's "mind thinking itself" or the neo-Platonic, self-contemplation of God in which the universal knows itself *as* universal, in the immediacy and unity of God's self-knowledge. The dialectical character of this internal relation is in the unity of the subject and the object. The "other" is only *apparently* "other." Its externality, its "otherness," is a false appearance. This unity is realized in the recognition of the self in the other. The essential unity of the subject and the object is achieved, therefore, despite, and also by means of, the differentiation of the subject from itself as its own object. The *Thou*, as the self's other, is therefore *not* a particular individual; insofar as it is merely individual, its individuality is indifferent. Thus, any *Thou* and all *Thous* are *one*, in that they are indifferently the same in the act of conscious thought. Moreover, the self, in being internally related to this universal *Thou*, is in unity with it, and is, therefore, likewise, universal, or becomes *universalized*, in thinking. Thus, Feuerbach says, "It makes no difference whether I say 'Insofar as I think, I am *Thou*' or 'Insofar as I think, I am all men.' For the concept of universality requires only the *one* and the *other* in its unity; for every community is a unity" (IV, 306).

In sense perception or in feeling, on the other hand, there is never a unity with the other, never an internal relation, but only an external relation, says Feuerbach. Shared feelings, for example, still presuppose two distinct individuals, who remain mutually exclusive.

Where there is present a community of sense-perception, or of any feelings, we talk of *mitgefühl, mitleid* (sympathy, compassion). But it would be patently ridiculous to talk of *mitdenken* or *mitgedanken* (co-thinking or co-thoughts). This follows from the nature of thought.... What I think is, of course, my thought. But it can be separated from me in such a way as to become the entire individual property of another, because if it is taken up by another, it must still be newly brought forth by him.... All sharing of sensibility never leads to anything more than sympathy or compassion. Zeno's statement that a friend is another self is valid in this sense. And thus, in general, in every relation of man to man, the other may be called another self. However, in thinking, the other is *in* myself. I am at the same time *I* and *Thou*–not any determinate particular *Thou*, however, but *Thou* in general, as a species (*Gattung*). (IV, 305)

There are difficulties and muddles in Feuerbach's notion of *individual* here. He is to carry them along into his transformed version of the *I-Thou* relation, in his later work, in which it is not *thinking*, but rather *sensibility* and *feeling* that constitute the unity of *I* and *Thou*. The difficulty in Feuerbach's account is in the notion of the individual's transcendence or overcoming of his own individuality–here, in the act of thought, and in the later works, in the act of sensibility or feeling. In Feuerbach's view of this transcendence, or negation of individuality, the uniqueness of the species is expressed *in* the individual. The individual *loses* his determinateness as a *particular* individual; nevertheless, he becomes a *species* individual, namely, that *kind* of individual capable of transcending itself, or of being one with the species. The retention of the term "individual" in this case requires a sharp distinction from the notion of individual as natural individual and also requires some dialectical formulation of how the relation *I-Thou remains* a relation between an *I* and a *Thou*, if the two are, so to speak, one in essence. It requires one to talk of an individual whose determinateness or essence is not its particularity, but its universality. But because the ontology is derived from an analysis of the mode of activity—in this case, of the mode of self-relation of thinking activity—we cannot come to the question with ontological presuppositions about individuality. In Feuerbach's formulation, the *Thou* is not *this* or *that Thou*; the *otherness* of the *Thou* is as much my own otherness as it is that of any other self. It is the principle of *otherness*, the general form of *otherness*—in short, the principle of self-differentiation of the *species-I*, not of the particular *I*. The relation of the individual to the species, therefore, is a relation of self-transcendence, a transformation of natural being into human being, in the distinctive act of thinking consciousness. The individual does not become a *member* of the species, as one individual in an aggregate. Rather, the individual becomes a species being, in this negation of determinate or finite individuality. In this dialectical transformation, Feuerbach argues, the individual rises beyond sensibility and feeling, beyond sense perception, and thus beyond the external relations he has to others as objects of these activities. "In one and the same act of thought," Feuerbach writes, "all men are equal, no matter how different they are in other respects. As a thinker, I am connected with all others; moreover, I am unified with them. One can say, in fact, that 'as thinking being, I am all people'" (IV, 306). Further, he says, "Through consciousness, therefore, I am able to comprehend all other men in myself, though as a sensate individual, I am external to them all" (IV, 308).

It is no longer a matter of a common rationality shared in by all men; rather, it is the essence of man, his species nature, that determines his being *as* man. Whether this goes beyond the classical definition of man as a rational animal (his specific essence being his rationality) depends on how much of the Hegelian dialectic of self-transcendence one is willing to accept. For Feuerbach, as Hegelian rationalist here, the crucial thing is precisely this emphasis on the transcendence of individuality, or of *separate* individuality, in the *I-Thou* relation. Through the relation to the *Thou*, I universalize myself. The *Thou* is the principle or form in relation to which I *become* a species being. It is not the flesh and blood person to whom I relate in feeling, in recognition, in sympathy and compassion; rather, it is the bloodless *Thou* of discourse, it is Reason itself, in its role as the necessary and sufficient condition of dialogue. Thus, what constitutes the *I*, in thinking activity, is this discursive universality. We have an "individual" who is not an individual, or, in Feuerbach's own phrase, whose individuality is constituted by its universality and infinity, and therefore by its transcendence of particularity and finitude.

The Modes of Relation of Consciousness

THE DISTINCTION BETWEEN THINKING AND KNOWING

To establish the infinity and universality of thought, Feuerbach must, within the context of his scheme, differentiate between those modes of relation in which thought remains finite and determinate and those in which it is infinite and universal. As a good Idealist, here, Feuerbach must also show that all modes of thought are ultimately modes of self-relation, that the ultimate ground and object of Reason (i.e., that to which it is related in its activity) is Reason itself.

He makes a series of distinctions for this purpose. First, he distinguishes between consciousness and self-consciousness. Consciousness, as *form*, is empty of any content and is formally undetermined by its content. Its scope is the capacity for any content whatever, but this content leaves the *form* of consciousness unmodified. For the *form* of consciousness is determined by nothing but its relationship to itself *as* consciousness. So, Feuerbach continues, consciousness is thinking, but as unmediated self-related, self-conscious *thought* it is to be distinguished from *knowing*, which is consciousness that is mediated by an other; that is, related to itself only *through* its relation to other things. He asks, "Were this relation of consciousness to things not also at the same time a relation to itself, how would it know anything about things?" (IV, 322). Insofar as consciousness has itself as unmediated object, it is, by virtue of this lack of self-limitation, undifferentiated, infinite, one and universal. But as such, it is merely formal, or abstract, empty consciousness, albeit the "empty" form of all modes of self-relation. The Hegelian sense of this "merely formal" or "empty" or "abstract" character of undifferentiated consciousness, is that it is lacking in concrete–that is, specific and determinate–*content*. Consciousness *without* such content is an abstraction. It becomes "concrete" when it is content-full consciousness. This concrete mode of consciousness is *knowing*, which, says Feuerbach, is "characterized by its relation to specific, individual things, which constitute its proper domain, and which are apprehended under specific forms of thought. It is no more than a particular mode of the original and constant relation of consciousness to itself" (IV, 322).

What is the relation of these finite modes of the self-relation of consciousness to its infinite form? In short, how are the *many* related to the *one*? If concrete relations are only those exhibited in the various instances of knowing, then is the self-relation of consciousness, in its "pure" form, no more than an abstraction? Feuerbach, like Hegel, proposes a conceptualist, even Aristotelian approach to this question. The universal form, or the species consciousness, exists only in and through its concrete instances. It may be abstracted, however, as an object of thought, or as a merely conceptual entity:

> The species is . . . (in nature) . . . an abstract concept. Concrete Being, the material of species is, however, constituted by individual beings, and only in their coming-to-be and passing away does the species exist. The species as such is manifested in the death of individuals, for the universal perdures and remains, whereas the individual vanishes. But even the individual vanishes only in form, not in reality, and not completely. Death is the common destiny of all individuals. . . . But if the innumerable individuals of a species which come to be and exist at a given time . . . pass away and vanish, all together and each separately, so the new individuals grow to replace them. Thus is the particular individual overcome by nature, and thus is it destroyed; but not so individual Being as such, Individuality itself. Thus material being as such can never become universal. In the same sense, consciousness is the species, and knowing is its subtype, for knowing is nothing but a relation of consciousness which expresses its simple and self-identical relation to itself in terms of various objects which consciousness presents to an extent in a fragmented way. (IV, 323)

If indeed consciousness is constituted only by the totality of its finite modes of self-relation, then it is constituted only as *potentially*, but not *actually* infinite. The universal may exist only in and through its concrete instances, its finite modes of self-relation, but is not identical with the aggregate or sum of these modes; it is not merely the sum of individuals. Such an aggregate is a "potential infinity" or a "bad or spurious infinity" in Hegel's terms. That is, it is an infinity that simply incorporates every "next" individual, in a sequence of coming to be and passing away. But then, there is no transcendence of the individuals, no ideal totality, as in a "good infinity," but only a collection or aggregate of finite entities. Feuerbach therefore needs to find a ground for the type of infinity that transcends this merely constitutive or aggregative "identity" of individuals. Yet consciousness abstracted from these concrete individuals is an empty form, and as such, non-Being:

> Consciousness which is not determined by any content, can be considered as not-Being, and . . . in the same way, knowing can be considered as Being i.e. as the actual existence of consciousness. And so, just as the species in nature is constituted by the coming-to-be and passing away of individuals, so self-consciousness has its present existence (*Dasein*) only in the finite and individual "knowings" which constitute its knowing activity. On the other hand, however, it is the grave, so to speak, of all its "knowings," their fate, in that it dissolves all that is individual and determinate equally into nothing. (IV, 324)

The notion of consciousness as constituted by its activity, its "knowings," leaves no substantive "consciousness" as such, but only the process of its instances of self-relation. Its "activity" is its "form," in the Hegelian-Feuerbachian sense (and in the Aristotelian sense of ἐνέργεια)· Yet the "Form" of individuality is the activity of determination, definition, the active *principium individuationis* of consciousness. Consciousness becomes "concrete," has Being, in its activity of knowing. Its universality, however, is directly opposite to this individuation, is the negation of this individuation, so to speak. This negation of individuality is the negation of individuals; that is, their ultimate finitude, their "death." The principle or "form" of individuality is this very finitude itself. Thus, "individuality as such" is concomitant with concrete existence as such—that is, with actuality—which for Feuerbach, as for Hegel, derives from the relations of consciousness with its finite "other," the realm of objects, which are known only mediately.

SELF-CONSCIOUSNESS AND THE INFINITY OF CONSCIOUSNESS

Only when consciousness is its *own* object, when the mode of self-relation is reflexive and immediate (i.e., in self-consciousness) is individuality overcome. Thus, Feuerbach says,

> One can say, therefore, that self-consciousness, or more correctly, the self-conscious individual ... knows only itself as infinite, and places itself outside of, and beyond that reason which is nothing but determinative and knowing thought. And this is the proof that the individual is independent with respect to the form of thought, but not with respect to its content; or is independent only insofar as he thinks, but not insofar as he knows. (IV, 324)

Thus, on Feuerbach's view, *knowing* is consciousness of an other, as a determinate content. The self, in knowing, is mediated by an other, *not* itself. Self-consciousness, on the other hand, has as its *unmediated* object the *form of consciousness* itself. Insofar as it is not mediated by an object outside itself, it has, in effect, no determinate content. But then it is not a case of *knowing*, strictly speaking, because there is nothing that is known in this case. Thought "thinks" its own "pure" or "empty" form. Such self-consciousness has as its object a purely formal, "transparent" self. Further, in having nothing outside itself as object, in being unmediated, in this sense, it is not limited by an other. In this sense, it is independent, and, in effect, infinite. "Infinity" here is that traditional, scholastic notion of a being that is not determined from without (i.e., that is unlimited). Thus, such an infinite or unlimited consciousness cannot be anything but pure form, or the pure form of the activity of consciousness, transcending the individual and determinate occasions of knowing. It cannot, therefore, be constituted by the sum or aggregate of such individual occasions, which at best constitute a "spurious infinity." In other terms, one may characterize such a summation as a finite totality, whereas the form of the activity, by contrast, may be characterized as a function of infinitely summing, constituting an ideal, but not an actual totality. The first Feuerbach characterizes as the *material* of species; the second, as the *form*. In self-consciousness, therefore, the form of consciousness alone is an object of thought, and it is completely devoid of content, or constitutes *its own* (purely formal) content. In this (peculiar) sense, Feuerbach describes it as a unity of form and content.

Because knowing, by contrast, is mediated by the objects of knowledge, and because these are objects of sense perception, such perceptual knowledge is always limited by the particularity and partiality of its sensory content. Here Feuerbach argues that each particular sense modality gives only that sense content appropriate to its nature. Each of these, in turn, is "partial," unique to that modality. The eye, the ear, and so on, do not "impose" on each other; the sense contents that they present as the objects of mediated, empirical thought, are discrete. But thereby, says Feuerbach, *within* each sense modality, in any act of sensing, there is no intrusion from without that modality. Thus, he says, in sensing, we feel no limitation. In itself, sensing is fully self-sufficient. There is no more to an instance of visual perception than what is contained in sight; there is nothing missing, and to that extent every act of sense is infinite (i.e., nonlimited) *in its kind*. However,

Thought is not so confined as the individual senses; it is also not a determinate and separate form, as each sense is, (which therefore delimits the latter to a determinate and limited content). *Thinking is simply form itself* [my italics, M. W.]; as such, it is universal and unlimited, and relates to the universal nature of things, to unity, wholeness, entirety, universality and infinity, with the same necessity that the eye relates to light and color, the ear to tone, each sense to its specific content. (IV, 326–7)

Pressing this analogy, Feuerbach goes on to distinguish the unmediated self-relation of consciousness as characteristic of "Spirit," whereas nature is precisely that content that is only mediately a self-relation of consciousness.

Whereas in nature that which sees and that which is seen are two, the Spirit is at the same time eye, light and object; it sees itself, and does so through no other medium than itself alone. In this way, thought, as infinite form, is capable of knowledge of the infinite, because it is already in itself, the unity of form and content. (IV, 327)

The individual consciousness, insofar as it *is* consciousness, strives for this unity out of "natural necessity"; that is, the *Being* of Consciousness is itself the *activity* of thus unifying, or universalizing, a determinate content, and the object of self-consciousness is this process of universalizing, which is infinite. As the individual thus strives to realize his "species existence" as conscious individual, the bifurcation between infinite form and finite content, between thinking and knowing, is transcended (*aufgehoben*). The object of infinite knowledge is an infinite "content," that is, knowledge *of* the infinite. This is no longer knowledge of individuals known by consciousness, but "knowledge" (now an analogous usage) of the infinity of consciousness itself. Anything less than this is *content* knowledge, not yet knowledge or *form itself*. But knowledge of the form of consciousness itself (i.e., of its activity) cannot be achieved apart from the process of knowing its content. Thus, it is not the *objects of thought* (i.e., determinate sense contents) that are the objects of self-consciousness, but the activity of thinking itself, and this activity not as a finite set of instances of thought, but as a universal form. Thus, in self-consciousness, thought takes its own essence as its object; it "thinks itself" in its universal and infinite form. ("Infinite" because the object of thought is not limited by anything other than itself, or its own nature; it is, in Kant's term, autonomous Reason, free in the sense that it is not other-determined, or heteronomous.) Feuerbach foreshadows his later formulation here but as yet in an unselfconscious way. Later (in a typically reflexive Hegelian locution), he is to define the consciousness of infinity (e.g., in religious or metaphysical thought) as "nothing but the consciousness of the infinity of consciousness." But the sense of this "infinity of consciousness" is the one given here in the *Dissertation*.

Infinite Reason as Human Essence

Only in his critique of Hegelian philosophy (some eleven years later) is Feuerbach to grasp the utter abstract formalism of this dialectic. There, he will characterize Hegel's (and his own present) approach as mistaking a phenomenological *logic* for a phenomenology of consciousness itself, that is, mistaking the abstract form of consciousness for the essence of consciousness itself. Yet even in the *Dissertation*, Feuerbach attempts to understand Reason as the form of *human* consciousness, as man's species being. He tries to relate the thought activity of individual human beings to thinking as such, that is, to Reason as "one, infinite and universal."

Feuerbach's orientation here is already incipiently "anthropological," in the sense that he was later to develop as the cornerstone of his philosophic view. What, after all, is this infinite consciousness? How is it related to human consciousness, to human thought?

The relation of the many to the one becomes the specific relation of the thought activity of individual human beings to thinking as such, in Feuerbach's treatment. The one, infinite, and universal reason becomes

113/74

that toward which human rationality strives "out of natural necessity." The natural necessity is the *form*, or the *activity* of human reason itself, its *entelechy* in the Aristotelian sense. This striving, this "desire for knowledge" that is the natural condition of human reason, never actually attains to unity. But its *form* is *the process of attaining to unity*. This form transcends the sum of individual strivings. Thus, Feuerbach writes, "Reason is neither finite nor merely human. For by 'human' we mean the sum of individual human beings, and the adjective 'human' expresses the properties and capacities which all of these innumerable individuals possess. But I believe I have adequately shown that Reason is not individual, but is universal or general . . . and . . . that there is only one Reason" (IV, 335).

If Reason is *one*, and "not merely human," in the sense Feuerbach gives it here, it is confusing to assert that it is *man's* essence. For then it would appear to be some superhuman essence, in which men "participate" (*pace* all the notorious difficulties of the "participation" model), but not insofar as they are "merely" human. We have either a simple confusion, in Feuerbach's use of "human" here, or a real disaster: that is, a flat contradiction at the heart of the theory. The "confusion" can be fixed up, by adducing two senses of "human," as we have two senses of "individual"–one, the more or less common sense class concept (all those beings are human who are members of the class "human"); the other, a dialectical concept (all those beings are human not as *members* of a class, but as a unity transcending their individuality). They do not *have* a common essence, as a property of each individual; they *are* that essence. Therefore, "they" are not many, but one. The individuality that constitutes an aggregate, a "they," is negated, transcended, *aufgehoben*, in the unity or oneness of this essence. This is no longer "human," but rather Humanity, in a fully hypostatized form. But then, man's species being, his essence, stands beyond his existence. It is, so to speak, his perfection. The flat contradiction, disastrous to the theory, lies just a hair's breadth beyond this, however. If man's species being is "more than human," if, in fact, it has all the earmarks of divine being, it is no longer man's essence at all, but God's. Yet Feuerbach speaks of it as the universal essence of mankind, distinguishing it from the individual existence of men:

The essence of individuals is . . . something other than the particular individuals themselves, insofar as they are distinct and differentiated from each other. Were not the essence of individuals something which transcended the individuals as units; were it, in other words, contained separately in each individual there would be as many individual essences as there were individuals: each unit would be its own substance and essence. (IV, 341)

Such a plurality of essence violates the concept of essence, however. So Feuerbach says, "Insofar as essence is actually essence, it must be simple, homogeneous, undifferentiated in itself, unified: not manifold, and self-differentiated as individuals are . . . the essence of men is identical with their absolute unity. This essence is thinking. Therefore, in thought I attain to absolute unity with all mankind" (IV, 342).

Though Feuerbach talks about "absolute unity with all mankind," this "essence of men" is described in all the ways traditionally associated with God's essence: "simple, homogeneous, undifferentiated in itself," and so on. That it is *Reason*, or *thinking*, that has all these traditionally divine properties–one, universal, infinite–is precisely what makes it transcend the "merely human," in Feuerbach's terms. Yet he persists in defining it as the species essence of *man*. He writes, "Man is man only insofar as he is Spirit (*Geist*); and Spirit is Spirit only insofar as it thinks. Its ground and activity are one . . ." (IV, 339). And further, "Thought is therefore the absolute essence of man as species" (IV, 341). The "absolute essence of man" turns out to be "Spirit," whose "ground and activity are one," that which alone is its own ground, whose essence and existence are one. But this is nothing else than the God of the theologians and of the metaphysicians, in the classical and scholastic traditions. Knowing where Feuerbach is to take this thought later, it is hard *not* to read the resolution of the contradiction between human and divine essence into the *Dissertation*: Man's essence is divine; Man, as species being, *is* God. Man is species being insofar as he thinks, or is a rational being. Perfect rationality is perfect humanity; but perfect humanity is identical, therefore, with God. This divine perfection is the essence of man as species being, but not of man as individual. Because it is thought that raises man beyond individuality and makes him *all men*, or species being, it is thought that makes man God.

Feuerbach does not draw these conclusions in the *Dissertation*. When he does draw them, most fully in *The Essence of Christianity*, in 1841, it comes to him almost as a revelation that all of rationalist theology and metaphysics is simply an esoteric recognition by man of his *own* species nature, and not God's; but of his own species nature only as a thinking being, and therefore of only one aspect of his total nature.

In the *Dissertation*, however, Feuerbach says that man attains to his species nature *only* in thought. Feuerbach's conceptualism saves him from the hypostatization of this Thought, or Reason, as a substantive essence in itself, apart from its realization *in* humanity. But it does not save him from hypostatizing human essence, from going beyond that which is "merely human," in the sense of a constitutive or aggregative humanity (i.e., the class of all humans), to "Humanity" as such, the

43

essence of which is thought. The "unity with all mankind" is a unity *in thought*, of the concept of thinking with the concept of humanity, or man as such. The tension here between the dynamic notion of mankind as a constitutive community and the static notion of a metaphysical "essence" of man is the characteristic tension within Hegelianism itself, between absolute Idea and the dialectic process itself. "Reason," as one, infinite, and universal, as "empty" form finds its actualization in a "living community." The Being of Reason is humanity, as being human is the activity of thinking itself. As thought is the transcendence of individuality and the achievement of universality, so the "living community" is the condition for this universality. As *nature* is the principle of individuation, the differentiation of one individual from another, so *spirit* is the activity of overcoming this differentiation. Specifically, Feuerbach claims for man an "insatiable desire to unite with others from whom he is divided by nature." This *eros* is the process of humanization itself. "It is only by means of the interrelationship between man and man, that the individual becomes a human being" (IV, 342).

In a striking passage, Feuerbach adds,

In this sense, one can say that the human being is not born, but is developed. For in nature, he is not a thinking being, but a reason-less being who is completely separate from others. Reason is not inborn, or implanted, as magnetic force is in a magnet. Nor does it grow in man as fruit does on a tree. As a single individual man has no part of Reason at all. For Reason is community, universality; but man as a single individual is completely divided and separated from every other. ... As reason is a communal thing, not an inborn property of single individuals, so man, unless he lives in a community, cannot attain to Reason. He comes to Reason not by himself, but through the actual presence of Reason in the form of a living community. ... From the very beginnings of the race, we find man in living communities. Animals are animals as single individual beings; men are men only as one man, as the human race, as a whole, as a community. The origins of Reason, insofar as they are present in single human beings, can only be understood in terms of the totality of mankind ... it follows that the individual, in the strict sense of the word, is only a fiction; and whoever wants to look for a human being *in himself*, i.e. one who is still untouched and untainted by society, must look for one who was neither born, nor raised, but must have been created from nothing. For the poor human being is already tainted by his fellow men, even in his mother's womb. (IV, 342, n.)

This "taint" of humanity, this condition of being human is not its limitation, however, but its transcendence of limitation. It is not the finitude of the human condition that marks its essence, but its *infinity*. The human condition is not the existential uniqueness or singleness of individuality, but the essential species nature of humanity, its infinity *in* community, its total self-relatedness; and because it is only in thought that such a transcendence is possible, says Feuerbach, the essence of man is his thinking activity, that activity in which any one man *is* all men. Insofar as man is a sensing or feeling being, his limitations are the limitations of this sensing activity. Insofar as man is a rational being, he is fully universalized (i.e., his limitations are the limitations of this thinking activity); and because thinking as self-activity is *not* limited by anything but its *own* nature, because it has, in this ultimate simplicity and immediacy of self-relation, no relation to an *other*, but is immediately self-identical, it is *one, infinite,* and *universal.*

The guidelines of the dissertation are clear. It is a restatement of classical rationalism, that same rationalism that, from the Greeks on through Descartes, Spinoza, Kant, and Hegel, had, in one or another form, discovered reason to be the essence of man, the ground of his common *humanitas,* the achievement in activity of his oneness, and the source of his moral obligation to fulfill his species nature as rational being. From Stoic sources, from Kant's notion of a "cosmopolitical" destiny, in which history fulfilled the conditions of this unity, and from Hegel's vast architectural drama of the Spirit's Odyssey, Feuerbach draws the "social" conclusion: Man becomes man only in a society of men. But this society is more than the conglomerate of individuals, whose essence as *individuals* is their externality to each other. It is the "living community" in which every relation is a mode of the relation of reason to itself. But as reason is the essence of man, every relation in the living community is a relation of man to his essence; and the classical dialectical problem of the relation of the many to the one is resolved in a classical way:

All the interconnections of man to man such as love and friendship are limited, particular, finite, in nature. . . . There must therefore be some way in the depths of man in which the yearning for the Thou can be fulfilled: where the *I* and the *Thou* are no longer counterposed, where this unity is not only a virtual one, not only a mere connection, but is absolute, unconditional, fully realized. And such a unity exists only in thought. (IV, 344)

On Feuerbach's view, therefore, to ask whether this unity actually *exists* or whether it is rather an ideal that is the object of "natural striving" can be seen to be a confused way of stating the question. The relation of the process to its end, its *entelechy,* is a relation of immanence. The unity of thought is not a substantive unity, not the oneness of a "thing," not singularity, nor individuality. Rather, it is the formal unity that characterizes the process of thinking itself. Its *being one* is identical with its *becoming one.* Thus, Feuerbach evades the hypostatization of thought as some substantive Reason, or Idea. "The existence of reason signifies nothing but reason in action" (IV, 345). One might paraphrase this, in characterizing the unity of reason or thought as its activity of *unifying*, its *universality* in its *universalizing*, and its *infinity* in the *infinity of the process of Thought*. If anything is hypostatized, it is that human essence that is seen as identical with Reason.

In retrospect, this identity already suggests the consequences that Feuerbach was to draw later. If we have transformed all the characteristic attributes of the theologian's God into the attributes of Reason, then we have done no more than what classical metaphysics has done, as Feuerbach was later to recognize. But to the extent that we identify these attributes with those of human essence, we are led to the next identification: of human essence as divine, or as that which heretofore was taken to be divine, in the sense of *non*human, or superhuman. Classical rationalistic theology saw in human reason the element of divinity. Man is like God, or imitates God in his rational activity. By virtue of this likeness, man can know God by reason. The accord of man's reason, with the archetypal ideas in God's mind, the "consent of Being to Being" is possible because of this likeness. Thus far go the classical participation and imitation models, adapted from Greek thought. But if the divine essence is, in fact, "nothing but" (to use Feuerbach's favorite reductive locution) the unity, infinity, and universality of Reason, and if it is precisely this that constitutes *human* essence, as the "living community," then human essence and the "living community" are divine. And then, once this formulation is broken free from its ordinary position and "turned upside down," the transformation becomes the foundation stone of Feuerbach's "anthropological critique": Divine essence is nothing but the externalized and alienated form of human essence; man has made God in his own image.

This conclusion goes far beyond the *Dissertation* itself. It is not at all clear that Feuerbach had anything like this in mind in 1828. In fact, despite what one may read back into the dissertation, on the basis of a knowledge of Feuerbach's later development of its theme, in 1828 Feuerbach considered himself, in the most ardent terms, a disciple of Hegel and saw the *Dissertation* as a student's tribute to his teacher. In November, 1828, Feuerbach, having submitted the work to Hegel, wrote to him:

I am taking the liberty of sending you . . . my dissertation, not because I place any special value on it, or because I imagine that it commands any great interest in itself. . . . Rather, I send it to you only because I, the author, am a most devoted student of yours, who attended your lectures in Berlin for two years, and I wish to express to you in this way, the high regard and esteem which I owe you as a student, and which it is my pleasure to acknowledge as a duty. (IV, 357)

In this discipleship, Feuerbach would not have been ready to interpret the Hegelian dialectic as "merely" a human dialectic, even in the exalted form of the dialectic of human reason. It is possible to read Hegel this way, if one takes the young Hegel at all seriously. Lukács, Löwith, Rawidowicz, and Arvon, among others, have noted the similarities between the young Hegel and the older Feuerbach. But the young Feuerbach did not know the young Hegel (of the early theological writings, or of the Jena period). He therefore conceived of his dissertation as a development of the consequences of Hegel's philosophy in its mature form, that of the Berlin lectures of 1826–8.

Feuerbach's disciple Wilhelm Bolin[5] holds that in the dissertation, Feuerbach already showed his independence from Hegel. The deepest modern student of Feuerbach, S. Rawidowicz, takes issue with Bolin on this and purports to show that both in substance and in form (in the triadic division of the work), as well as in the characteristics of the terminology and the form of argument, the *Dissertation*, as well as many later writings, are the works of a devoted Hegelian.

Whatever reading one wishes to give Feuerbach here, on the basis of his subsequent development, it is quite clear that Feuerbach thought of himself as a full-fledged Hegelian at the time. It is also clear that twelve years later, in 1840, when Feuerbach reconsidered his dissertation, he wrote that the solution that he there proposed for the problem of the unity of the universal and the particular, "from the standpoint of Hegelian philosophy," was "one-sided and abstract." Its one-sidedness and abstractness lay not in its assertion of a human essence, but in the characterization of this essence as Thought or Reason. The limitation of this view, says Feuerbach, in retrospect, is that it founds the unity and community of man on his reason alone. But if this is to be the unity and continuity of a *living* community, then reason is not enough. For the living man does not live by reason alone, but by sensation and feeling as well. Contrary to the thesis of the *Dissertation*, that the senses give only individuals and that therefore sensate man is only an individual (i.e., not yet *species* man), in 1840 Feuerbach was to assert that the unity and essentiality of man, his reason itself, is founded upon sensation.

What is missing [in my dissertation] and what is characteristically missing in the whole approach of Absolute philosophy is that this continuity, this unbroken unity holds not only for thought, but also for sensation, for life in general. The point is missed that the other *thinks* in my stead only because he also *senses* in my stead. For just as there is no sensation for man without thought, without consciousness, the converse is also true: There is no consciousness without sensation. For what else is consciousness but the conscious, or sensed sensation? (IV, 421)

In this radical revision of his epistemological standpoint, Feuerbach went from a classic and dialectical rationalism to empiricism. In its emphasis on the *activity* of sensation, Feuerbach's empiricism went beyond British seventeenth- and eighteenth-century empiricism and even beyond its French inheritors, Helvétius and D'Holbach—and beyond the sensationalism of Condillac. This revision was achieved in the decade in which Feuerbach broke with Hegelian idealism. The break was itself a long process, which tells much about its end product. Without an understanding of the stages of Feuerbach's emancipation from Hegel, the interpretation of his later philosophy—his psychological and anthropological critique of religious belief and of theology, and his development of a humanistic materialism—becomes superficial and one-sided. The early epistemology of the *Dissertation* sets the context for this revision. This is what Feuerbach changed *from*. What he changed *to* is unfortunately most widely known in superficial and vulgarized "popular" presentations of Feuerbach's philosophy, or in terms of the rather simplistic and aphoristic conclusions with which he advertised his own thought. However, the path of Feuerbach's philosophical development is often more interesting and significant than the sometimes simple conclusions to which it led. Nor can even these be properly assessed, in terms of their forcefulness and effectiveness in their own time, without an understanding of their genesis and their intent. Feuerbach's revision of his earlier thought, his attack on Hegelian idealism, which became the starting point of Marx's and Engels' materialism, was concerned mainly with epistemological questions, before it became a full-fledged philosophical anthropology. These epistemological questions were worked out most fully by Feuerbach in the three volumes he wrote on the history of philosophy; in the critical and polemical writings and reviews of the late 1830s; and in his defense, and then critique, of Hegel. Throughout, the themes and even the language of the *Dissertation* appear and reappear, in their transformations, and this earliest work therefore gives us an important key to the mode of Feuerbach's thought, and to the *Problematik* in terms of which it developed.

CHAPTER III

History of Philosophy: Genetic Analysis
as the Critique of Concepts

Feuerbach's first major publication, after the 1828 *Dissertation*, and the traumatic incident of the anonymous publication of his *Todesgedanken* in 1830, was a work entitled *History of Modern Philosophy from Bacon to Spinoza*, published in 1833. This work is usually acknowledged in passing, by Feuerbach scholars, as a journeyman's piece, but it has been little studied in its own right. Nor has its significance in Feuerbach's philosophical development been assessed seriously. I want to argue that it is a crucial work in understanding Feuerbach's development. In it, Feuerbach comes to discover his own views in the course of his critique of major philosophical figures. Moreover, in an as yet unselfconscious way, Feuerbach already initiates the method of analysis that eventuates in his systematic critique of religion and of philosophy in the later works. There are several elements that reveal themselves in this *History* in an especially important way: (1) Feuerbach's mastery of the Hegelian dialectic as a dialectic of concepts–that is, as a dialectic unfolding of an Idea by means of critical refutation or negation, or by means of revealing the contradictions contained in one conceptual system, as the full consequences of its premises are articulated; and the subsequent replacement of this system by another, in which these contradictions are resolved but in which new contradictions emerge. Thus, Feuerbach develops the Hegelian logic of replacement, in the concrete context of the history of philosophy. He develops it, therefore, not as a *formal*, but as an *applied* logic of conceptual or theoretical change. (2) This logic of replacement– of the replacement of one conceptual framework or system, or of one world view by another–is seen as a historical logic. That is, it is seen as a logic of the history of philosophy, which is therefore reconstructed

49

not simply as a chronicle or a mere sequence, but as a development. The internal motive force of this development comes to define the very nature of philosophy itself, for Feuerbach, as criticism, or as the critique of concepts, whose outcome or product is a *history* (albeit an "internal" conceptual history). (3) In the *History*, Feuerbach begins to formulate the criteria for an adequate empiricism and materialism in his critique of the one-sidedness or abstractness of previous empiricism and atomism, and of the previous concepts of matter (e.g., in Bacon, Hobbes, Descartes, Gassendi, Spinoza). He also begins to formulate a critique of the one-sidedness of idealism, in its reduction of the empirical, the material, and of sensibility and feeling, to thought.

Thus, three elements of Feuerbach's philosophy—his use of dialectical method and a dialectical construction; his historical interpretation of this dialectic; and his attempt to construct an adequate empiricism—emerge as implicit themes in the *History of Modern Philosophy*.

There is still a more important aspect to the reading of the work, that is, the question of *how* to read it. An external reading reveals it as a highly competent, if somewhat tendentiously structured history of philosophical ideas. It remains informative at this level as one among the better critical histories of modern philosophy. Beyond this, however, there is another way to read this work (and also the subsequent works of Feuerbach's transition, the historical studies of Leibniz and of Bayle). That is to see it as an exemplification of Feuerbach's own thesis, derived from Hegel's phenomenology, about how consciousness comes to know itself through the recognition of itself in another. In brief, Feuerbach's own philosophic consciousness comes to articulate itself first by recognizing its own content, its own themes, its own theses in the mirror of the history of philosophy. What Feuerbach reads back from the critique of this history can be understood, in retrospect, as the process of the formulation of his own distinctive ideas. Feuerbach re-creates the history of philosophy in his own image. But this image is not already formed. Rather, it takes shape in this very process of re-creation, of historical reconstruction. We may characterize Feuerbach's enterprise not simply as historical reconstruction, but as *projective* history, that is, as a history in which Feuerbach comes to form and to recognize his own distinctive theses, his own "image." The methodology of this self-reflection in another is explicitly recognized by Feuerbach as a feature of the historical process of philosophy itself. For example, as we shall see, he gives an explicit account of it in his characterization of Protestantism and of the Italian Renaissance, and in his analysis of Bacon's achievements and shortcomings. He does not yet realize how accurate a *self*-characterization he achieves here. Nor could he. Only in retrospect can we see (as Feuerbach also does, in later discussion of his earlier works) that Feuerbach's own philosophical development, his own self-articulation and self-recognition takes place in and through the concrete details of his critique of the philosophical ideas of others.

For this reason, this chapter follows Feuerbach's critique and appreciation of the philosophers—Bacon, Hobbes, Descartes, Gassendi, Malebranche, Spinoza, and others—in some detail, not as exposition, but as an implicit process of unselfconscious self-revelation, on Feuerbach's part. For the dialectic of his own development yields to no abstract schema, but only to a concrete analysis of the details of his critique. It is this second reading of the *History* that is intended here.

THE ROLE OF "HISTORY OF PHILOSOPHY" IN FEUERBACH'S DEVELOPMENT

In 1835, Feuerbach wrote an appreciative review[1] of the first two volumes of Hegel's *History of Philosophy*, first published two years earlier. He marks Hegel's work as the first *philosophical* history of philosophy, as something more than mere wooden exposition and chronicle. His characterization of Hegel's intimacy with his subject matter precedes a methodological statement on the nature of the study of the history of philosophy. Feuerbach writes,

> No other historian of ancient philosophy has ever treated his subject with such intimacy as has Hegel. These are not strangers whom Hegel engages in stiff formal conversation; these are his forebears, his intimates, with whom he carries on a confident discussion on the most important issues of philosophy. He is at home in the foreign land; as much at home with Parmenides and Heracleitus, with Plato and Aristotle, as he is with himself. In his lectures, we breathe the authentic air of the Greek homeland, of the Greek sky, which vitalizes and stirs us. Hegel's history is therefore unquestionably the first to give us a real knowledge of the history of philosophy, and to afford us the revelation of the authentic sense of the various systems and concepts of Greek thought. (II, 4)

What we need, says Feuerbach, is just such a history that reveals the inner sense not simply of this or that philosopher, but of philosophy itself. This demands a point of view.

> Whoever would approach the history of philosophy must have some definite ... conception of what philosophy is. Were one to begin with no such concept, the object would never once be granted him; he wouldn't be able to guarantee whether he were delivering to us a history of philosophy, or in its place, a history of wigs, or of beards, or of any other subject far removed from philosophy. Every study is necessarily subjective, and in this sense, *a priori*. The only

difference is whether one starts with inflexible, wooden, one-sided concepts, which stultify and limit thought, and restrict the study of a subject, or from concepts which themselves are of the spirit and life of the subject-matter, concepts of an omnipresent, all-encompassing and all-comprehending nature. (II, 4–5)

Hegel, writes Feuerbach, leads us through the temple of Greek philosophy not like a porter, or a janitor, but as one who understands its art and architecture. Here, as in other places, Feuerbach counterposes the philologist to the philosopher. In the philosophical fragments, Feuerbach has noted (with respect to his own lectures on logic and metaphysics when he was *privatdocent* at Erlangen, in 1829–32) that his own exposition of Hegel's logic was to be carried forth "not in Hegel's words, but in his spirit, not philologically, but philosophically" (II, 366). The analysis of a historical figure in philosophy is, therefore, not a textual exposition, but an attempt to elucidate the essential spirit of his thought. In such an elucidation, the basis for a *philosophical* history of philosophy becomes clear. What is philosophically *essential*, what is continuous throughout the whole of such a history is the Idea of Truth. Thus, Feuerbach writes,

> The history of philosophy is not a history of accidental, subjective thoughts, i.e., of *opinions*. Considered superficially, it would appear so, in that such a history seems to offer us nothing so much as a constant alternation of different systems, whereas Truth is changeless and one. But Truth is not one in the sense of abstract unity; i.e., it is not a simple Thought to which differentiation stands opposed. Rather it is Spirit, Life, a self-determining and self-differentiating unity, i.e., Concrete Idea. The difference among systems has its basis in the Idea of Truth itself. The history of philosophy is nothing but the temporal exposition of the different determinations, which together constitute the content of Truth. The valid, objective category in which this content must be exhibited is the Idea of Development. This latter is a necessary and rational process, in itself, an unbroken, progressive and active process of knowledge of Truth. (II, 6)

The dialectic unfolding of the Idea, in the history of philosophy, thus forms *that* subjective a priori concept that most adequately conforms to the criterion of an all-encompassing scheme for the study of this complex subject; one that is, in effect, appropriately contemporaneous with its subject matter and is, therefore, always relevant to it, and understands it "from the inside." The unifying thread of this history is the concrete Idea of Truth—concrete in that Truth here is not merely a formal, or abstract, norm with respect to which philosophical systems or concepts are judged "true" or "false," but concrete in that it is expressible concretely only *in* the history of philosophy itself. The expression of this truth is not accidental, or random, but rather is a development, whose temporal dimension is the history of philosophy itself and whose normative dimension is the critical *progress* of philosophy.

In 1835, then, Feuerbach is an *echt-Hegelianer,* dialectic included, at least insofar as the study of the history of philosophy is concerned. This history is not the subject of an antiquarian interest. It is a living history in the sense that the present stage in philosophy can only be grasped as the latest moment of the process itself. It has no isolated significance, in itself. Thus, Feuerbach writes,

> The history of philosophy is therefore concerned not with the past, but with the present, with what is still living. It is not the principle of a philosophy which perishes, but only the claim that such a principle is the absolute and total determination of the Absolute. The later and richer philosophy always retains the essential elements of the principles of the earlier system. *The study of the history of philosophy is thus the study of philosophy itself.* [My stress, M. W.] (II, 6–7)

To what extent is this early, distinctly Hegelian view of the history of philosophy exhibited in Feuerbach's own three major works in this area? The simplest answer is "less and less." After Michelet's publication of Hegel's *History of Philosophy* in 1832 (two years after Hegel's death), the great German school of historical scholarship in this field was launched. In 1834, Johann Eduard Erdmann published his epochal *Versuch einer wissenschaftlichen Darstellung der Geschichte der neueren Philosophie.* A year earlier, Feuerbach had won the admiration of the Hegelians with his *Geschichte der neuren Philosophie von Bacon von Verulam bis Benedict Spinoza* (to be referred to hereafter as "the *History*"). In 1836, he published his *Darstellung, Entwicklung und Kritik der Leibniz'schen Philosophie* (to be referred to hereafter as "the *Leibniz*"). And in 1838, the last of the historical works was published: the large and significant *Pierre Bayle–Ein Beitrag zur Geschichte der Philosophie und Menschheit* (to be referred to hereafter as "the *Bayle*"), the work Rawidowicz astutely calls Feuerbach's "Confessional of 1838" (Rawidowicz, *L.F.,* p. 63). The book on Bayle was no longer the work of a dedicated Hegelian. One year after its publication, Feuerbach published his open attack on German Idealism, his *Zur Kritik der Hegelschen Philosophie.* The transformation of the ardent student apprentice into the sharply critical journeyman took a full decade.

An understanding of this process of transformation, from the *Dissertation* to the *Kritik* is crucial to an understanding of Feuerbach, and also to a deeper appreciation of the force of Feuerbachian thought among the young Hegelians, and the left Hegelians, whose master he was. In the course of this "radicalization" of his thought, Feuerbach's Germany approached the momentous decade of the 1840s, whose culmination in the revolution of 1848 was to no small extent reflected in the apex of Feuerbach's intellectual influence on the political and philosophical thinkers at the forefront of the revolution.[2]

What led the young "Hegeling"[3] to become the philosophical Nestor to Marx and Engels, however, was not his politics, but his philosophy, not his philosophy of history, but his epistemology, not his economic theory (which was crudely naive and hardly to be called a theory), but his analysis of the nature of human belief. It is in the gestation period of the 1830s that Feuerbach developed his distinctive methodology, his humanistic ontology, his genetic-analytic method, and his rejection of rationalist idealism for a materialist empiricism.

His work in the history of philosophy, valuable for its contribution to the critical study of this history, has a special value as the record of Feuerbach's own philosophical development. It has been too little studied in this regard.

THE HISTORY OF MODERN PHILOSOPHY

THE GENESIS OF MODERN PHILOSOPHY

Because for Feuerbach the history of philosophy is not mere chronicle, but rather the very process of the unfolding of the truth itself, the context for the study and characterization of "modern philosophy" is the analysis of its genetic development out of what preceded it. Here Feuerbach, in the sway of the grand schematism of his master, prepares the way in a broad characterization of the *stages*, the large, dialectically unfolding epochs of philosophy. Dialectic continuity demands not only a "beginning" in philosophy, but an account of this beginning as itself a "next stage" of what preceded it. Thus, characteristically, it is not the pre-Socratics who are the first subject of interest in this preliminary sketch, but the more broadly conceived "essence of the pagan world view." Feuerbach's use of "pagan" here is in the tradition of Hegel's *Weltgeschichte*, and marks clearly the sense in which Christianity is taken as a fundamental divide not only in the history of religion, but in the history of philosophy as well. In fact, on Feuerbach's view, it is the interweaving of the elements of "pagan" and "Christian" world views that constitutes the fabric of classical philosophical thought itself. The other common division that Feuerbach also makes, between secular and theological, or this-worldly and otherworldly, is not a synonymous one, but rather interpenetrates with the first. Feuerbach's later attack on speculative philosophy as the last stage of theology has its roots in the analysis, in this still idealist *History*, of the intimate interplay between the theological and the secular throughout the whole history of philosophy. Here too lies the significance of his dating of "modern philosophy" from Bacon, rather than more traditionally from Descartes: Bacon is the first philosopher to establish philosophy as distinct from and as essentially opposed to theology.

Feuerbach begins his *History of Modern Philosophy*, then, with a broad and schematic characterization of the "pagan world view" in terms of its fundamental antithesis. The essence of this world view is the "unity of religion and politics, spirit and nature, God and man." Still, the very terms of this unity are not "universal" in scope, as they are intended, but are instead "fatally limited," according to Feuerbach. Thus, in this world view,

man was not man as such, but the nationally defined man: the Greek, the Roman, the Egyptian, the Jew. Consequently, his god was also a nationally defined God; specifically, a god or being set over against the gods of other peoples; a being therefore, in contradiction to the spirit of humanity, which is the essence of humanity, and as its essence, is that of all peoples, of all men. (III, 1)

Thus, the pagan world view reveals its essential limitations. On the one hand, it claims universality over the domain of man, and a unity of God and man; on the other, it negates this very claim in the limited "rational" form in which man and God are conceived. The sources of this limitation are in the religiomythical *form* in which the unity of spirit and nature, God and man, religion and politics is conceived. Feuerbach intimates that precisely because of its imagistic nature, that is, its pictorial or dramatic form, bound as it is to representation in terms of sensory imagery, the form of this world view is limited, local, national, anthropomorphic. It is either Greek or Roman or Egyptian or Jewish in essence, and thus not universal. In its development, however, pagan *philosophy* transcends this limitation of pagan myth and religion by rejecting this imagistic form, which Feuerbach characterizes here as "superstition." The "resolution of this contradiction, within paganism itself, is pagan philosophy" (III, 1).

The Hegelian dialectical form of Feuerbach's reconstruction is clear: first, the assertion, in paganism, of the unity of man and nature, state and religion; second, the contradiction within this ostensible unity and universality because of its ethnic and local limitedness; third, the overcoming of the contradiction in the universalism of Greek rational-scientific thought (as nonethnic and nonlocal in its claims). This last stage, then, is pagan *philosophy*, as against pagan religion. Pagan philosophy, as the negation of the negation–the negation, that is, of the ethnic limitedness of the claim to universality–is the synthesis achieved

55

in paganism, on the grounds of the pagan world view itself. Pagan philosophy "tore man from his national exclusiveness and self-sufficiency, raised him beyond the limitations of folk-darkness and folk-belief, and set him on a cosmopolitical standpoint" (III, 1).

But if pagan philosophy is the resolution of this contradiction within the context of paganism itself, it is not yet the resolution of the contradiction within the pagan world view, that is, not yet its dissolution and its replacement by a higher synthesis. Feuerbach holds that pagan philosophy was the "fate" of antiquity, the *spiritual* ground of the downfall of the pagan world view. Nevertheless, pagan philosophy resolved the contradiction "only in thought, only abstractly"; that is, it was the *form* of the resolution of this contradiction, but not its content. "The actual resolution of this contradiction came about only in Christianity," that is to say, only when paganism was overcome and replaced (III, 2).

The Hegelian schematism shows itself here. Only that which is nonpagan "really" resolves the contradictions within paganism—only Christianity, by definition, is nonpagan in the exclusive disjunction that divides up the universe as either pagan or Christian. But Feuerbach intends more than would appear on this merely formal construal. He distinguishes the *mere* Christian consciousness, the "idea" of Christianity, from the actual event, that is, the embodiment or actualization of this idea in a historical, and therefore not merely formal or abstract, "resolution" of the contradiction. The "unconditional event" of Christianity, the person of Christ and the crucifixion itself, becomes, in this context, a concrete "stage" in the dialectic, prepared for dialectically by the *abstract* universality of pagan philosophy.

What is important here beyond the dialectical form of Feuerbach's account is that this early formulation is a model for his own later critique of Hegelian philosophy, and for his insistence upon the "unconditional event" of human existence. At this point, however, Feuerbach speaks of the existential event only in terms of the consciousness that "expresses itself," "actualizes itself" in it.

Christ is nothing but man's consciousness of his Being-with divine being—a consciousness which, when the time came for it to become a world-historical consciousness, to express itself as an unconditional event, to manifest itself as a single person, to actualize itself as an individual, then had to set itself against the darkness of the age-old contradiction of the world view of ethnic particularity, as the creator of a new world age. (III, 2)

The dialectic of this development, Christianity's very assertion of universality, leads Christianity, in course, to become a "world-denying religion." Ethnic particularity is overcome in the personality of the

Christ, who in his very individuality as universal savior transcends all particularity. However, this very negation of ethnic particularity itself develops its antithetical character in a one-sided way, as Feuerbach continues his dialectical account. "In Christianity, God therefore becomes an object to man as Spirit. God is Spirit, insofar as he is conceived in Christianity, as universal essence cleansed of all national and other difference and separateness" (III, 2).

The concrete personality of Christ is lost in the conception of universality as *spiritual*. The grasp of this spirituality asserts itself as a denial of the flesh.

The difference between flesh and spirit, between the sensible and supersensible ... develops to the point of an opposition, a bifurcation of spirit and matter, of God and the world, ... as the moments of the development of Christianity in history become determinate. And in this development of the supersensible as what is alone essential, & of the sensible as non-essential, Christianity, in its historical development, becomes a ... world-denying religion. (III, 2–3)

This development of the one-sidedness of spirituality, the "negative religious spirit" as Feuerbach calls it, is what is fundamentally responsible for the destruction of the art and science of antiquity. Not wars, but this negative religious spirit is what causes Nature itself to "sink into this night of oblivion and ignorance," because Nature, in this "negative spirit," is the opposition to real Being, that is, Spirit; it has no Being in itself.

How can the Spirit concentrate on, or take as an object of serious concern that which has significance only as finite, vain and empty? What sort of interest can the Spirit have in the temporal creature, in the knowledge of the miserable product of creation, when it knows the Creator? How can one who lives in trusting intercourse with the Lord of Creation so demean himself as to enter into the same relation with the handservant. Indeed, what other aspect and significance does nature have, from this standpoint of negative religiosity, than that of God's handservant? The theological-teleological conception of nature is the only one which is suited to this point of view. But this is not an objective, physical conception of nature, or one which allows for the deep investigation of nature. (III, 4–5)

The limitedness of "negative religiosity" is not its ethnic or its local character, but rather its claims to transcend *all* this-worldly particularity. Its limitation *is* its peculiarly abstract universality. Universality is denied to nature, and only the supersensible, that is, nonnature, is the realm of the universal. Thus, the study of nature is admitted only under the ruling idea of a theological-teleological world view. Whatever natural studies take place (e.g., in the monasteries) are conceived in this way, and are submitted to the absolute legislation and executive power of the church. Though theology tends, even here, to pass over into philosophy,

57

that is, into the form of nonimagistic and abstract thought, still it is constrained by the absolute power of the church. The Greek philosophical tradition, the "autonomy of reason," the "free productive activity" of the Greek tradition must degenerate in this atmosphere, and the free development of logic and metaphysics is stifled.

Feuerbach thus characterizes the fundamental contradiction of this world-negating "stage" as the conflict between body and soul, between the flesh and the spirit. Yet here too the negation of this Christian world view develops within the context of the world view itself. Just as pagan philosophy was, in its development, the negation and resolution of the contradiction in the pagan world views, so too Christian philosophy itself leads to the dissolution of the Christian world view. Feuerbach interprets scholastic philosophy as this very resolution within the limits of the "negative religious spirit." In a boldly appreciative passage, Feuerbach characterizes scholastic philosophy as the *science* of the Middle Ages, thus:

> Even though scholastic philosophy stood in the service of the church, insofar as it recognized, demonstrated and defended the positions of the church, still it derived from a scientific interest, and awakened and engendered the free spirit of inquiry. It made the object of belief an object of thought, raised man from the sphere of unconditional belief to the sphere of doubt, of inquiry and of knowledge. Insofar as scholasticism sought to *demonstrate* what was otherwise only an authoritative belief, and sought grounds for this belief, it thereby established—in most cases without willful intent or knowledge of what it was doing—the authority of reason; and thus brought a different principle into the world than that of the Church. It brought the principle of the thinking spirit, the self-consciousness of reason—or at least it prepared the ground for it.[4] Even the monstrosities and obscurities of scholasticism, the many absurd *Quaestiones* ..., even its thousandfold unnecessary and arbitrary distinctions, its curiosities and subtleties, must be understood in terms of a rational principle, in terms of a thirst for enlightenment and a spirit of inquiry which could express itself only in this way, under the oppressive domination of the old Church spirit in those times. (III, 8)

In Feuerbach's historicist view, the "dead hand of scholasticism" makes itself felt only when its original impetus is spent, and its categories and techniques become fossilized strictures on further development. In "its time," Feuerbach sees it as a progressive attempt to break through the walls of Church authority. "It is only when scholasticism was a dead historical reliquary that it stood in contradiction to its original significance ... and became the worst enemy of an awakened spirit" (III, 9).

The "awakened spirit" is, in Feuerbach's view, "the essence of Protestantism," that is, its spirit of freedom from external authority. But this development encompasses both the reconstruction of the ideal of classical antiquity, in humanism, and Luther's appeal to *belief* as an ontological and ontologizing activity. It is in introducing this central topic, which dominates so much of his later thought, that Feuerbach describes the advent of a new idea:

> Whatever comes forth into the world as a new principle must at the same time express itself as a religious principle. Only thus does it strike the world as a shattering and fearsome thunderbolt. Only thus does it become common property, a world-fact dominating the passions. Only the individual through whom the spirit sets to work, who recognizes this spirit as God, who sees his deed, his apostacy from the previous principle–(which also expressed itself as a religion)–who sees this as a divine necessity, as a religious act–only such an individual acquires the irresistible energy before which all external force is powerless. (III, 13)

Feuerbach's emphasis shifts here from the reconstruction of a rational dialectic to the role which belief, faith, commitment play in this dialectic. The genesis of a "new principle" requires conviction, the motive force of belief in "divine necessity," the instrumentality for "dominating the passions," without which the principle remains abstract, contemplative, and, in this sense, unactualized. Here, in an early form, are Feuerbach's intimations of the *diesseitigkeit*, of the subjective practical activity that makes the history of philosophy more than a history of ideas. Rather, it is also a history of beliefs and ultimately, therefore, a history of *action*, of "concrete activity." It is in Luther that Feuerbach finds the concretization of belief into action; and in Protestantism the "new principle" that expresses itself religiously. Like all "new" principles, it must already have been present in the bosom of the old. Thus, he sees the new principle as already at work in scholasticism itself, "insofar as (scholasticism) was an instrument of liberation from external authority."

The three strands of this "liberation" are (1) the humanist reconstruction of a classical ideal of rationality, (2) the recognition of the authority of the *activity* of belief, and (3) the recognition of the authority of sense experience.

The Humanist Reconstruction
of Classical Rationality

The return to classical learning becomes, in Feuerbach's scheme, a consolidation of an earlier achievement, and an objectification of it, necessary for the development of self-conscious reason. Feuerbach writes,

Before the newly awakened, thinking, self-conscious Spirit could achieve the strength and the capacity to create itself out of itself, to create new matter and content from its own essence, it had to acknowledge itself, and to transform, into a vitalized, developing and creative matter that essence which was already present in this Spirit. This already present essence had initially been encountered only in the form of its own striving and desire, i.e. as actuality, as an acknowledged, already completed and realized world. (III, 17)

This acknowledged form of the striving of the "thinking, self-conscious," that is, rational, spirit, is Greek philosophy. The rationalism of Protestant humanism and of the Italian Renaissance could develop only by acknowledging itself first in this external or projected form. It found the means for its own self-realization in the fact of an already realized, objectively complete rationalism. Thus, says Feuerbach, the Greek model becomes the "other," as object, in which the subject mirrors and recognizes its own striving. The analogy to the development of human self-consciousness, which is to become Feuerbach's central theme, is pursued in a Fichtean-Hegelian interpretation:

Just as the first notion which man has of himself is as an other; i.e. it is at first only as another person, who is an object for him, that man perceives and recognizes himself in his essence; just as it is only in an other who is like him and continues his own essence, that man arrives at self-consciousness, so too does the human spirit attain to self-consciousness, (and thereby to productivity) by means of representing itself as an *object*. This representation takes place in the study and assimilation of classical antiquity. . . . (III, 17)

The Renaissance enthusiasm for Aristotle and Plato is evidence of the degree of recognition of one's *own* rationality in their works. "One sees in them the product of one's own thinking spirit, as free, universal," under the limiting condition of a rational spirit that has not yet the power to speak for itself. Feuerbach interprets the Renaissance-humanist appreciation of Greek rationality as the latent, unselfconscious form of the appreciation of its own rational spirit, and thus as a necessary stage on the way to its self-recognition as rational spirit.

The Authority of Belief

Though Protestantism could express its rational spirit only indirectly, in the image of classic rationalism, Feuerbach argues it expressed itself most directly and clearly in its "essentially" religious spirit. Here, not thinking but rather feeling and belief are its essence, and Luther is its clearest spokesman.

Where Descartes says *I think, I am*, i.e. my thinking is my being, Luther says, in this respect, *my belief is my being*. Just as Descartes recognizes the unity of thinking and being as the principle of philosophy, and recognizes the Spirit as this unity, whose being is only in thinking, so Luther professes the unity of Being and Believing, and expresses this unity as Religion. (III, 15)

In the *History*, Feuerbach was not yet ready to come to grips with the issue of the relation between Protestantism and philosophy, between faith and reason. His critical treatment was to come in his later work, on *Pierre Bayle*, which completed the historical trilogy and marked Feuerbach's struggle and transition to a materialist-empiricist viewpoint. Still, Feuerbach's characterization of *belief* as an *activity*, as itself productive in the ontological sense, that is, as itself the *creation* of a world of belief in which man lives and has his being, is already clear here. Thus, human reality or human ontology is concerned not only with the being of a thinking being but with the being of a believing being. The comparison of Descartes and Luther is instructive here. For in both cases, ontology is interpreted functionally. A thing *is* what it *does*, its essence is its activity; thus, Being is not given, but produced.

The Authority of Experience

Yet Feuerbach sees that, historically, in the Renaissance, what is produced by Spirit is its this-worldly existence, its concretization in Nature. Nature becomes the object with which the Spirit comes to identify itself. This third strain in Feuerbach's characterization of the "Essence of Protestantism" is the new scientific interest in nature, particularly during the Italian Renaissance, which eventuates in the "authority of experience" finally expressed in the first "modern" philosophers, Bacon and Descartes.

In Renaissance philosophy, Feuerbach sees the progress of the spirit, of human consciousness from the "religious-imagistic" phase to the "philosophical-theoretical," by way of "poetical or anthropological Idealism." Knowledge of nature is achieved in anthropomorphic form. The duality, nature—man, flesh—spirit, is overcome in the identification of man and nature, in the naturalistic pantheism and pananthropism of Renaissance natural philosophy. Man no longer denies nature, but makes it like himself, anthropomorphizes it. Feuerbach sees "the first real beginnings of modern philosophy . . . in the nature-philosophies of the Italians, Cardano, Bernardino Telesio, Francesco Patrizzi, Giordano Bruno, who expressed the view of Nature in her godly fullness and infinity, and in the most striking and clear way" (III, 19).

The fault in this development, says Feuerbach, is that in overcoming the total alienation of man from nature, expressed in the dualism of body and soul, or in the medieval negation of nature, which placed human essence totally outside it, Renaissance humanism also negates nature by finding *only* man there. Thus, the joyful Renaissance sense of the immediacy and patent clarity of our experience of nature, the Neo-platonic

61

intuition of the fullness and adequacy of natural being requires the mediation of a critical empiricism, a concept of experience that is scientific and not poetic. Despite his characterization of the Renaissance philosophy as "the first real beginning," Feuerbach sees its limitations: He insists on the critical appreciation of sense experience as the starting point for modern philosophy, and this he finds only in Bacon and Descartes, the "founders of modern philosophy."

Experience—in the sense of scientific experience not in the sense of that experience which is one with life, with living—is not that unmediated, self-evident and simply understood sort of thing it was formerly represented to be. It isn't a childish, or native and original affair.... The standpoint of experience, as is self-evident, exhibits the drive to know and to explain nature; a drive which is the result of the consciousness of the difference between appearance and reality, a consequence of the doubt as to whether the essence of nature is so simply available to our understanding, without further ado. Thus, this point of view of experience is characterized by criticism, skepticism. Therefore, the founders of modern philosophy, Bacon and Descartes, began expressly with this point of view; the former, in that he made the rejection of all prejudgments and previously held opinions the precondition for the knowledge of nature; the latter, in his demand that, to begin with, we should doubt everything. (III, 20)

Francis Bacon, says Feuerbach, is then seen as the "immediate or sense-oriented father of modern natural science" in that he was the first "to express the principle of experience as the *method* of science, with unreserved vigor." And with this introduction of the experimental and empirical study of nature as his starting point, Feuerbach is ready to begin the series of studies that constitute the bulk of his *History of Modern Philosophy*. He is content that the genetic background for his "beginning" is reasonably clear: the transition from an ethnic to a pagan-universal standpoint; from pagan "universalism" in form to the world-denying "universalism" of Christianity; from the medieval dualism of body and soul to the reidentification of the two in the "poetic idealism" of the Renaissance; from the negation of the autonomy of reason and its subordination to authority, to its piecemeal reconstruction in scholasticism and in humanism. At the culmination of this historical development, Feuerbach sees the development of Protestantism in religion, and a critical skepticism and empiricism in philosophy. Both of these he regards as "beginnings," in themselves merely setting the task of modern philosophy and establishing its background. The *History* provides the main stages of the philosophic critique of empiricism, and it culminates in the subsequent volume on Leibniz. The heart of the critique of the religious standpoint, in both Catholicism and Protestantism, is in the volume on *Pierre Bayle*. But the Feuerbach who writes the *Bayle* no longer is the Feuerbach of the *History*. His own odyssey, which hugs the Hegelian coastline closely at the outset, then takes off for the open sea. The later critique of religion ends in a humanist atheism in which the "essence of religion," man's self-knowledge, is fulfilled. The critique of empiricism ends in a completely explicit sensationalism, in which the truth of the senses is enthroned.

However contrary and perverse these conclusions seem, given the Hegelian starting point, it can be shown that the germs of this outcome are in Hegel himself (particularly the young Hegel), and (with respect to this study) in the very method and analysis Feuerbach presents in the early historical works. We now turn to these studies of Bacon, Hobbes, Gassendi, Böhme, Descartes, Spinoza, Leibniz, and Bayle.

In the introduction to the 1846 edition of the *Collected Works*, Feuerbach writes of himself: "Take a look then, at the content of your work, particularly the historical writings, in which you expressed your own thoughts under the name of others" (SW$_1$, I, ix–x). To the extent that Feuerbach did this, it helps to explain what, in effect, is an increasingly *ad hominem* kind of analysis in the historical works and in the critique of Hegel. Rawidowicz aptly characterized the work on Bayle as "Feuerbach's Confessional (*Bekentnissbuch*) of 1838."[5] "Every study," he had written, "is necessarily subjective, and in this sense a *priori*" (see p. 51). Still, the canons of objectivity in historical study are maintained if this "subjectivity" is flexible and comprehensive, shares in the spirit and life of the subject matter, and is open to criticism. This is the method of the historical studies, and also their significance for a study of Feuerbach's philosophy.

BACON

It is in this context that Feuerbach is concerned in each of the studies to give a sketch of the philosopher's life. The "Reflections on Bacon's Life and Character" precede the estimate of Bacon's philosophical significance, in a way that suggests the two are intimately connected, without thereby making the fatal error of judging one in terms of the other. It is interesting that Feuerbach concludes that Bacon was not *enough* of a philosopher; that his basic flaw was his lack of singlemindedness about philosophy and scholarship. In splitting himself between the world of learning and the world of politics, Bacon "destroyed the unity of his spirit." Feuerbach also finds Bacon's desire for the life of singleminded and undistracted scholarship in his description of Galileo (*Acta Philosopharum*, vol. III, 15, and in the *Philosophical Letters*) and Bacon's estimate of the virtues of a rural retreat. When Galileo wanted to write his great dialogue, he went to the country, far from Florence ("because," writes Bacon, "it appeared to him that the city of Florence was like a prison for the speculative disposition, whereas the free rural life was a book of Nature wherein everything is open to one's eyes, if one only chooses to read and study with the eye of the understanding").

Feuerbach is inclined to a German-romantic reading of Bacon. The sense in which "nature" means the countryside, "observation of nature" means rural inspection, and the "city" is the death of the speculative— that is, the "scientific"—spirit, is the classically romantic sense of the "back to nature" idyll, which dogged Feuerbach through his life and fatally delimited his understanding of science. Had he studied Galileo more carefully and seen the close relation the foundations of mechanics and the analysis of motion bear to the technology of the "city," his views might have been modified.

Then too this praise of rural life is significant in the personal sense for Feuerbach, who spent most of his years in what was effectively the rural exile of Bruckberg. The detachment of science from politics, which he would have urged on Bacon, is the same detachment Feuerbach himself practiced during the 1848 revolution, though his reasons for doing so were complex.

The demand for a "unity of the spirit," an undivided pursuit of "theory" is also an aspect of that German romantic intellectualism that found its metaphysical arguments not only in the idealism of Hegel, but in Spinoza and Leibniz as well. Feuerbach quotes both in his criticism of Bacon as a thinker: Spinoza's "We are active only insofar as we know" and Leibniz's "We were created to think. It is not necessary that we live; but it is necessary that we think"—both express, for Feuerbach, the ideal of a rationalist pursuit of truth as man's end. He writes, "The true thinker, the true intellectual serves mankind in that he serves truth. He regards knowledge as the greatest good, as the truly useful; its demands are his practical life goal. Every hour which is not dedicated to knowledge is regarded by him as a loss in his life" (III, 28).

Feuerbach sees such a loss in Bacon's life. However great a statesman Bacon was, this was not his *essence*; thus, in the sphere of statesmanship, Bacon had no firm character, "for in that which is not essential to one, he has no center of gravity, and therefore wavers from one position to another" (III, 28). In the light of the general task of a universal science that Bacon set for himself, Bacon "committed a sin against the Holy Ghost" in failing to commit himself fully to the life of the mind, thereby limiting his contribution to science.

Here the ardent young Hegelian intellectual speaks: The service of the Spirit makes total demands; one is free only in recognizing its necessity. All else is bondage to accident, to passion, in effect, to irrationality, which is (in the metaphor that so suits the transcendental absolutism of the system) "sinful."

> If Bacon had not so fragmented his life, if he had dedicated his whole life to the service of science, after the example of other great scholars, he would not have remained merely at the grandiose imperative, at superficial proposals concerning the great structure of science, without having worked out some of the details. Instead, he would have steeped himself in the depths of different subject matters, and with the use of his exceptional mental gifts, would have arrived at certain conclusive results out of the mass of facts, inquiries and observations which were available to him. He would have discovered particular laws of nature, as did Galileo and Descartes. Thus, instead of merely proposing plans, he would have exhibited the universality of his spirit in the penetration and mastery of the particular, in the raising up of the particular to the general. . . . He wouldn't have skimmed so lightly over so many different subjects. In short, he would have accomplished infinitely more than in fact he did. (III, 30–1)

Whatever interest Feuerbach's estimate of Bacon may have, for our purposes this passage is intriguing with respect to Feuerbach himself. It is in effect Feuerbach's self-administered call to intellectual arms, his resolution with respect to the concentrated self-discipline that eschews programs and requires the "real work" of concrete and detailed accomplishment and discovery. There was, as Feuerbach early recognized, the great temptation of dilettante eclecticism, the urge to aphorismic summation, to the flash of a *bon mot*, and the attraction of the joys of sheer writing and of poetry.

The picture is characteristic, and may be said to describe the youthful enthusiasms and poetic intentions of, for example, Plato, Hegel, and the untold thousands of students for whom the "free life of the spirit" is constituted by giving free rein to the "imagination." Art and poetry struggle with the more "mature" commitment to science, philosophy, disciplined theory. Feuerbach was to be torn between "programs and proposals" and "conclusive results" all his life. And it was to science as he understood it that he made a pathetically unfulfilled vow of allegiance later on. But this remained at the level of amateur and enthusiastic study of geology, in which he constantly recognized his lack of professional training. The early critique of Bacon as an incomplete thinker reveals how soon the parallel problem presented itself to Feuerbach in his own search for a vocation.

Yet, in 1847, when the second edition of the *History* appeared, Feuerbach reflected a different view of his own development in his notes to the new edition. The critique of Hegel was behind him; his *Foundations for the Philosophy of the Future* and the *Preliminary Theses Toward the Reform of Philosophy* had appeared. *The Essence of Christianity* had established his leadership of the radical left among the young Hegelians. He was now ready to approve the programmatic nature of Bacon's work in a considered way. The note is in effect a self-justification.

> Bacon accomplished what he set out to accomplish, and he accomplished enough. He wanted only to establish the foundations of the house. The construction itself he left to others. He knew that what he wanted he could not accomplish by himself, nor would it be accomplished in his time. Its accomplishment would be the work of innumerable men, and of centuries to come. He appeals, therefore, to the future. (III, 31)

Bacon's significance in the history of philosophy is most positively assessed, from the start; the limitations of Bacon the man, the "dualism in his spirit, or in his metaphysical spiritual principle" as Feuerbach writes, are not seen to compromise his philosophical significance, only to delimit its fullest realization. Generally, Feuerbach holds that Bacon made natural knowledge the principle of all knowledge, and based natural knowledge on experience. The achievement was not merely in emphasizing the empirical foundations of knowledge, however, but in raising experience from an "accidental object," as it was previously conceived, to a "philosophical object," an object of science.

> The essence of Bacon's contribution is that he gave us a method, an organon, a logic of experience, a clear guide to sure and successful experience. He raised blind experience, feeling-around-in-the-dark in the realm of particulars, to an experimental technique based on logical laws and rules, and tried to give to a mankind till then awkward, unpractised and unused to experience, the instruments for its comprehension. (III, 34)

Bacon's contribution lies in the method, the technique, the means of considering and dealing with experience. Though Bacon is an empiricist par excellence, still Feuerbach exempts him from the general critique of empiricism on the grounds of his Platonic commitment to formal essences. Thus, writes Feuerbach, though Bacon was an empiricist in the "ordinary sense,"

> Yet for him experience was only a means, not a goal, only the beginning, not the result, which only philosophy, or philosophical knowledge itself could be. Thus, he defines the goal and object of natural science to be the knowledge of "the eternal and unchangeable form of things"...as immanent in nature (as *fons emanationes*, as *natura naturans*). (III, 35)

Bacon is characterized as a "positive" rather than a "negative" empiricist in that his emphasis on *form* is physical rather than mathematical. The forms are primary physical *qualities*, and Quality is "his ruling and determining concept." The reduction of experience to physical

66

qualities makes quality the primary object of the experience of nature, and this experience is the immediacy of sensation, sense perception. Experience becomes an object for thought only mediately, and only in this mediation is it mathematizable. Thus, mathematics has a subordinate role to physics "insofar as it is physics, and not merely applied mathematics." The ultimate reality for experience is physical quality, and not the *mediated* mathematical quantity.

> In this regard, Bacon stands alone. The ruling concept for Hobbes and Descartes and of other investigators of nature, in his time and later, is that of Quantity; nature is an object for them only from the point of view of its mathematical determinability. Bacon, however, makes Quality the primary form of Nature. Nature is an object for him only under this form. Therefore he says that primary matter must be thought of in connection with motion and quality. (III, 38)[6]

Unclear as Feuerbach is here, it is interesting to note how he is caught up by the "concreteness" of Bacon's physical orientation. He opposes this qualitative empiricism to the abstractness of a mathematical construction of nature, which nowhere enters into the direct experience of the senses. This emphasis on the physics of qualities as the "real stuff" of experience already foreshadows the kind of empiricism that Feuerbach himself developed later. That the "truth" of nature is given to us directly in sense experience; that the senses serve not merely as sources of inference, but as bearers of the existence of things beyond them—this direct empirical realism is not formulated here. But Feuerbach makes an exception of Bacon in his general critique of empiricism in the *History*. The exception is informative, for it already appears that within the context of the rationalist-idealist approach, Feuerbach distinguishes between two sorts of empiricism, "positive" and "negative," or "narrow," empiricism. The sources of his later affirmation of empiricism are here. The *History* provides Feuerbach with the opportunity to examine these distinctions, albeit not yet in a fully deliberate way, and still within the framework of Hegel's historical criticisms of empiricism, which he largely adopts as his own.[7] Bacon's approach to all previous philosophy, his outright rejection of the authority of the schools, and with them, of Plato and Aristotle, is critically assessed by Feuerbach. "The French proverb '*Il veut appendre à sa mère à faire des enfants*' (He would teach his mother how to have children) suits Bacon well, in his reasoning . . . concerning Greek science" (III, 40). As to Bacon's own Christianity, in the light of his naturalism, Feuerbach sees him as straddling a contradiction: He is both Christian and un-Christian. For Christianity, the ultimate reality of the world is nothing. In Feuerbach's analysis, the very concept of creation *from nothing* expresses this ultimacy in Christian belief. For science, however, nature gives truth, in sense experience. Thus, insofar as he is a natural philosopher, Bacon's approach leads to materialism, and atheism, if it is consistently pursued. It is therefore fundamentally un-Christian. Apart from that, says Feuerbach, Bacon is a Christian *comme il faut* (III, 76). Though the theme of the basic irreconcilability of the scientific and the theological world views is merely asserted here, it is to be the subject of his later studies. Still, this theme runs through the *History*, in his characterization of Descartes, Leibniz, and others, and culminates in the open attack on theology in the *Bayle*.

Feuerbach compares Bacon's place in the historical development of modern philosophy, by analogy, to that of a student leaving school. In school, he is separated from life. Upon leaving, in the full feeling of his new independence, he throws himself at life. Thus, with Bacon, the human spirit leaves the *Gymnasium* of scholasticism and medieval authoritarianism, in which all one's concerns were with the realm of the "higher," the supersensible. Now it "empties itself of its own content" (III, 77). Empiricism is seen here as a purgative process; the accretion of theology and metaphysics is "emptied," and in this emptiness, the human spirit confronts itself in its empirical and materialist aspect. The transition from Bacon to Hobbes is this "emptying." Hobbes represents this empirical materialism in its clearest form. But what Hobbes sought to accomplish is impossible, says Feuerbach, namely, "to make empiricism express itself as philosophy, and to make it do" (III, 77–8).

HOBBES

Feuerbach's fundamental critique of "negative" or "empty" empiricism is clearest in his evaluation of Hobbesian materialism. What empiricism and materialism (here identified) lack is the ground for a *system*, which alone would qualify them as philosophical. And Hobbes' system is no system, but a "thinking machine."

> His thought is pure mechanism, as external in nature, as loosely held together as a machine is, whose parts, despite their interconnections, remain unliving, without unity, external to each other. For Hobbes, thought is as tedious, monotonous and as dull as a mechanical operation; as indifferent and as blind as accident, or as external, mechanical necessity, in that it indifferently levels all the various specific content of things, without distinction. Or worse yet, by negating the difference between particular laws or categories, each of which hold only for limited, subordinate sets of determinate objects, it seeks to extend the laws of finite, or of external mechanism to all objects. (III, 78)

Feuerbach's critique of philosophical mechanism does not deny its adequacy as a theory of abstract quality, whose domain is that "subordi-

nate set of determinate objects," that is, bodies in motion, treated mathematically. But he argues that such a view is fatally inadequate as a theory
of "physical" nature, in that it leaves out the "specific contents," the
range of qualitative differences in nature. The "emptiness" of such an
empiricism as Hobbes' is its reduction of qualities to the one aspect,
motion, and the reduction of this motion itself to quantitative change.
But *quantity* as a category, is already mediated, by thought; it is an abstraction from sense experience, in which qualities are directly apprehended. In this sense, "Hobbes' philosophy is not a natural philosophy,
but a theory of bodies in motion" (III, 89), an *abstract* philosophy as
distinct from the concreteness of a natural philosophy concerned with
"actual" experience. A theory of bodies in motion is already fatally abstract if it is essentially a mathematical theory. "For Hobbes, mathematics has a primary productive significance, unlike Bacon, for whom
it is secondary. Hobbes derives nature from mathematics, so to speak.
For him, body as body, conceived only in terms of quantity or magnitude, is the only thing which is substantive or actual in nature" (III, 89).

As *body* is conceived abstractly by Hobbes, so too is *motion*. Because
every motion is mechanically caused by another motion, motion itself has
no ground in nature; every motion is conditional, "merely relative," and
is itself an abstraction "introduced into nature only by the thinking
subject, which comes upon it as an activity in experience. In Hobbes,
then, motion is not immanent in nature. So, too, *qualities* become 'ac-
cidents,' *phantasmata*, appearances, images, representations of sensing
subjects" (III, 89–90).[8]

Again, it is not motion itself that is rejected by Feuerbach as the
ground of a natural philosophy, but mechanical motion, that abstraction
of motion whose domain of validity, as a model, is limited to mechanical
rather than "natural" objects. Feuerbach writes,

It is a profound and true notion that motion is the principle of nature. . . .
The error of Hobbes and Descartes was not in making motion the principle
of the determination and differentiation of things (and thereby the principle
of Nature in general); it was rather that they were limited to the concept of
motion as a mechanical, mathematically definable motion, and it was this that
they raised to a general principle. As long as mathematical ideas had exclusive
dominion, there could be no true idea of life or of the nature of quality, which
in fact have a physical origin. The mathematician must make mechanical motion his leading principle; he must conceive of nature as a machine, because
he cannot construe it other than mathematically. Quality, which ensouls nature,
and physical nature, in which the fire of life breathes, is merely a hypostatization, in the quantitative view of nature; it is merely an accident, an unreality.
And life itself is conceived only as a machine, in this view. It may be conceived
only on a hydraulic model or on some other mechanical model. (III, 90)

The concepts "motion," "principle of nature," and "life" are clearly understood in the Hegelian tradition here. Moreover, they are conceived in an older Greek sense by Feuerbach. "Motion" is activity, that is, "real" activity, the principle of change itself. It is process, development, unfolding, and in this sense, it is the principle of that physical nature "in which breathes the fire of life." Feuerbach here speaks of "quality which ensouls nature" in precisely the Aristotelian sense of Ψυχήν, that principle "in" or "of" anything by virtue of which it moves, where "motion" is taken to mean its characteristic activity or "principle of life" (though Aristotle saw this only as the principle of living organisms, rather than of nature as a whole).

Feuerbach's critique of Hobbes' "bodies in motion," then, is that both "body" and "motion" are abstract constructions of *thought*, and not the physical nature that is given in experience. Hobbes is being criticized for not being *enough* of an empiricist! And insofar as "materialism" is understood by Feuerbach to mean the materialism of quantitatively described bodies in motion, it stands opposed to an empirical realism of *qualities*, and is instead a representational or phenomenalistic empiricism, the *shadow* of "real" experience. The limitation, interestingly enough, is suggested as a limitation by choice of language framework. In the framework of mathematical description, *only* abstract bodies and abstract motion can be conceived. The conception itself is a function of the descriptive predicates. Thus, the "model" is limited to what can be conceived under and described by such predicates.

The clearest exception that Feuerbach takes to Hobbes, on idealist grounds, is that thought cannot be seen to have any "self-origin" in this system, because thought, for Hobbes, depends on motion in the parts of an organic body. Thus, for Hobbes, thought has no beginning in itself, and vanishes in the infinite regress of mechanical causes, says Feuerbach. It is precisely this idealism, of thought as somehow original, "self-originative," that Feuerbach is later to criticize in Hegel, and to reject. It is this concept, too, that he will seek to explain, genetically, in terms of its psychological origins and its uses. For Feuerbach, the term "materialism" often connotes the Hobbesian reduction, which he never adopts. Yet when he proclaims himself a materialist, a confusion ensues concerning the two (at least two) senses of "materialism" that he uses (which parallel the two senses of "empiricism"), the "abstract" and merely quantitative, on the one hand, and the "concrete," "qualitative," on the other.[9] For all this, Feuerbach, in the spirit of "genetic" history of philosophy, finds a historical role which Hobbes fulfills:

it is precisely in this emptying and alienation of the Spirit, in this *excentric* materiality of thought that Hobbes' system is interesting and historically significant. This is its connection with the history of modern philosophy, and is also its justification and its value. For it was entirely appropriate, in its transition from the narrow and stifling cloister of the middle ages, from the limited circle of its previous withdrawal and separation from life, and from the world, to the free university of the new age, that the Spirit should go to the opposite extreme, and reject as worthless all that is Ideal, supersensible and metaphysical. (III, 79)

The *historical* partiality of Hobbes' "empty" and "abstract" empiricism is, in the history of the spirit, inevitable, in this Hegelian scheme. The claim appears to be wider in the *History*: that *any* empiricism is thus fatally limited, "has no beginning, no middle and no end" and thus cannot be a system, that is, cannot be "philosophical" in this sense. There is nothing but a hint at some wider empiricism that might approach "living reality," but in the *History* this is still vague and unclear. In the 1847 edition, however, Feuerbach sees fit to note his later appreciation of empiricism, in this qualification of his earlier view:

To be sure, it is a contradiction to try to make empiricism express itself as a philosophy–at least in the case of a raw, unqualified, incomplete empiricism. One might still ask "Even if empiricism were completed, wouldn't it get lost in the infinite?" [i.e., in the infinite regress of conditional connections–my note, M. W.] My answer to this would be: Is philosophy itself ever completed? In his own view, every philosopher sees his philosophy as complete; his conclusions appear to him as absolute, adequate, final, plainly necessary and universal. But is this so for those others who came after him? By no means. The "Absolute Knowledge" of every philosophy is shown in time to be only finite knowledge, its "universal truths" only particular truths, its "absolute necessity" as no more than a temporal, historical necessity. And philosophy will run on into infinity, i.e. as long as time follows upon time, and man follows upon man. The objections which speculative philosophy raises against empiricism return upon speculative philosophy itself. Besides, Hobbesian empiricism, or modern empiricism in general, is in no way the absolute empiricism, but only a finite limited empiricism. It hypostatizes determinate phenomena, makes absolute Beings of them. So, Hobbes, for example, makes of arithmetic computation the essence of thought, and makes of the phenomenon of man in civil strife the fundamental nature of man. (III, 78)

Thus, twelve years after the first publication of the *History*, Feuerbach assesses the limitations of empiricism as intrinsic not to empiricism as such, but to philosophy in general. In effect, he rejects the claim that philosophy, in order to be philosophy, needs an overarching "substantive concept." The history of philosophy needs such substantive concepts if it is to progress and if the dialectic of criticism is to be pursued. Yet the only thing truly substantive or universal about such concepts is their historical role in this dialectic.

Later, Feuerbach will say: Once this requirement is *seen* as historically relative, traditional philosophy (i.e., classical metaphysics) is at an end; its essence has been revealed, and no further "philosophical" claims to universality and necessity can be made for *any* system.

GASSENDI

Feuerbach's critique of the Hobbesian concept of "body" as abstract leads him directly to the fuller consideration of atomism in general. This he does in his analysis of Gassendi. The criticism of Gassendi is a criticism of the formal inadequacies of atomism, rather than a critique of empiricism. In fact, insofar as sense and feeling are unrelated to the atoms, Feuerbach finds that atomism, as an intellectual construct, leaves the empirical rationally unaccounted for, and thus consigns it to the realm of belief and feeling, to the "utility-bag of the heart." The "atomic principle" lacks any "internal" ground or necessity,

for the atoms combine with each other, in one or another way, to form any particular aggregate; and all there is is an external and fortuitous connection. The world is only an aggregate, not a system. It has no unity, no necessity; it is a *thing*, a work of accident. External necessity can be reconciled with the atomic principle, but this is not distinguished from chance. To make the atom the principle of things is to make chance the world principle. (III, 123)

In this criticism, the equation of mechanical, "external" necessity or of mechanistic determinism with chance is not a mere contradiction. The atoms themselves, as individuals, "follow no rule." In Feuerbach's metaphor, they are "absolute atheists, or at least free thinkers, which have as little relation to God, as Epicurus' God had to the world and the atoms. These atoms are autocrats, monarchs–they abide no co-regents, they are a world unto themselves" (III, 121). The "autocracy" of the atoms is their ruleless behavior–that is, they have no internal rule, but behave completely arbitrarily in this respect. Their arbitrariness, or randomness, is delimited only by the external "subjection" of their motion to impact, to the action, equally ruleless, of the other atoms. In this respect they are "externally" constrained by a necessity that has no ground in their own nature, but is itself merely the expression of their "inner" fortuitousness. Feuerbach had no clear notion of laws of chance nor of statistical laws. In any event, such "laws" or "rules" are not *systematic* in the sense of speculative philosophy; they are not principles, but the work of chance. Thus mechanical and atomistic determinism has chance as its "ground" with respect to individual atoms. The lawfulness in the aggregate is merely the *appearance* of lawfulness since no law is being "obeyed." The animistic overtones of this analysis hide the more profound problems of the relation of cause and chance. Feuerbach's critique of atomism is that it cannot, by itself, suffice for the construction of a metaphysical system. In general, this becomes a criticism of induction: "To derive the truly general representation from the particular is as if one were to derive light from the combination of different colors" (III, 116), says Feuerbach. From the aggregate of constituents, no true class representation can be achieved. And it is only such a class representation (i.e., of the universal) that is a "true, conscious, rational representation." If there is none, then there is no object of thought, and if no thought, no mind or reason. "And a mind or reason which has no thoughts is therefore no mind or reason at all, just as a light which doesn't illuminate is no light at all. For what else is reason, in this regard, but thinking-activity?" (III, 117).

A rationalistic idealism demands universals as its objects; without them, there is no rational idea. In this conceptual form, there are no abstract universal ideas without objects, for the very being of Idea is its activity, and its activity is a thought with content. On such a priori grounds, then, Feuerbach rejects atomism in that it provides no object, that is, no class concept, that rises beyond enumerative induction.

What is equally, or perhaps more, important to Feuerbach is the impossibility or rational belief under these conditions. He is flirting with the classical problem of induction, but he does not recognize it as such. The "belief" or "degree of rationality of belief" in a disjunctive world of atoms is thus impossible to attain on any rational, or "necessary," grounds. The pity of it, says Feuerbach, is that "belief" is then consigned to the "hothouse atmosphere" of feelings, sans reason. This dichotomy of the realms of thought and feeling has its source in the inadequacies of the atomic model. Thus, Feuerbach notes that Gassendi, like Bacon and Hobbes, is a split personality: He thinks differently from the way he feels or believes; his rational principle contradicts his religious principle. The identification here of the "religious principle" with belief and feeling is a central thought in Feuerbach, the source of his later analysis. For as long as feeling and belief are not accounted for in the rational principle, that is, as long as the rational principle remains delimited in this regard, as it does in atomism, religion becomes what Spinoza viewed as the *asylum ignorantiae* for the feeling-believing activity of man. Anticipating the positivism of Comte and of Spencer, in this respect, Feuerbach sees religion as the residual domain of ignorance, the realm of the abdication of reason. Insofar as atomism is "atheist" in its delimited domain, it leads to theism. In his 1847 note to the discussion of Gassendi, Feuerbach adds, "Bacon says that atomism leads necessarily to theism. And he is right. Every delimited natural principle demands, for its full realization, some supernatural cause" (III, 121).

This split into two worlds, of "Godless" rationalism and irrational religious belief, is exhibited in Gassendi, for example, in his belief in the immortality of the soul–unaccountable on the "rational," but inadequately rational grounds, of atomism. Feuerbach's picturesque description of the "contradiction" is worth citing:

> It is the same contradiction [in Bacon, Hobbes, Gassendi] which expresses itself in recent and in contemporary philosophy in the most varied, and in the crassest ways. It goes so far that . . . nothing but the empty shell of Reason, the flayed skin of things, remains. The *content* however is stuffed into the utility-bag of the heart. When God is driven from the Temple of Reason, from the open, free, clear and distinct world of thought into the secret recesses, the Old Ladies' Home, the *Asylum Ignorantiae* of the heart; when everything that pertains to God is consigned to the comfortable room-temperature of intricate and sophistical feelings, like a hot-house plant which cannot stand the fresh air –then, one becomes an intellectual atheist, in the open market-place of the understanding; but in the private backrooms of reason, one remains the most superstitious Christian, the most religious man in the world. In this way, however, God is honored only as a household idol. (III, 124)

God as rational or philosophical world principle, God out in the "market-place of the understanding"–this is ostensibly the aim here. And Feuerbach is to see this later, in effect, as the principle of rational idealism, of Hegelianism, of speculative philosophy in general–as the "last stage of theology." Here, however, it is the charge of repressing God, of instituting a dichotomy of thought and feeling, that Feuerbach brings against atomism. It is hardly the charge that atomism is too empirical, but that it is not empirical enough, and not consistently empirical. Gassendi's value in the history of philosophy is that his consistency in the atomistic model *underlines* the contradictions in atomism, showing most clearly what its intrinsic limits are.

BÖHME

What "principle" *is* to suffice then as the *ground* for a world view? The most striking anticipation of Feuerbach's later views is found in his treatment of Jakob Böhme, the great German mystic. Böhme represents, for Feuerbach, the antithesis to Hobbes, Descartes, Spinoza, Leibniz–to every "separation" of the rational principle from feeling and belief (III, 178, "Note of 1847"). Wherein do the two poles meet? In man, of course. And for Böhme's theosophy, the key to God is man. The vague, metaphorical pantheism of Böhme's speculation is seen by Feuerbach as "esoteric psychology." The explanation of reason and feeling is the revelation of their human content. Feuerbach quotes Böhme:

> The book in which all secrets lie hidden is man himself: he himself is the Book of the Essence of all Essences. Because he is like unto God, he contains

the great Arcanum. . . . Why do you seek God in the depths or beyond the stars? You shall not find him there. Seek Him in your heart, in the center of your life's origin. There shall you find Him.[10] (III, 173)

This theological commonplace is interpreted by Feuerbach as the profound clue to Böhme's (and, ultimately, to religion's) significance. In a fantastic form, Böhme unites the "one" and its "other." The duality of thought and feeling, of "being one" and "knowing an other" is overcome in the "Book of the Essence of all Essences," man. This reading of the "inner" as the revelation of the "outer"; this interpretation of the "outer" as itself a mode of the self-knowledge of the "one"; the various elements of the typical dialectic of "internal differentiation," of "internal opposition"–all this is already contained in Böhme. Feuerbach chooses Böhme as the *only* German philosopher to deal with in the *History*, and it is quite clear that he sees Böhme as archetypal in this regard. Speculative philosophy is an elucidation, or an explication of the *Urprinzipen* already adumbrated in Böhme. But Feuerbach seems even more interested in the "anthropological" interpretation of Böhme, focusing on the latent content *not* in its speculative-dialectical aspect, but in its anthropological-psychological aspect. And it is this that marks the special significance of Feuerbach's analysis here. It is one of the earliest models of that sort of reduction to anthropological-psychological terms that characterizes Feuerbach' later full-scale attack on speculative metaphysics and theology, his attempt to get at its positive content, in human-pragmatic terms. Feuerbach's formulation of this approach is given here:

Böhme is the most profound unconscious and unlettered psychologist . . . because he feels what he thinks and says, because he creates the stuff of his explanations and his examples from the source of all suffering and joy, from his own feelings and sensations. J. Böhme is the most instructive and also the most interesting proof that the mysteries of theology and metaphysics find their explanation in psychology, that metaphysics is nothing but "esoteric psychology"–for all his metaphysical and theosophical conclusions and expressions have a pathological [in the sense of "feelings," M. W.] and a psychological sense and origin. (III, 177)

This psychological "reduction" of theology and metaphysics, the foundation of Feuerbach's critique of traditional philosophy, is facilitated by the view that states, though in a "fantastic" form, that the essence of the nature of thought and of belief is to be found inwardly, in man's *own* nature. Feuerbach sees a relation between Böhme and Descartes in this regard. Thus, in both Descartes and Böhme, says Feuerbach, "the consciousness of nature is inseparable from self-consciousness" (III, 179). The *cogito* is compared to Böhme's "I am my own book," whose paraphrase Feuerbach points to in Montaigne's *"je suis moi-même le sujet de*

75

mon livre." This stands in apparent contradiction to Böhme's "I have but one teacher—the whole of nature," but this "naturalism" is a pananthropic naturalism, one that sees an identity of nature and man, asserts it *as* a unity in duality, and "reads nature" while it "feels itself." Our knowledge of an "other" is ultimately a mode of self-knowledge. And the profound and *immediate* way in which we "know" ourselves is in the activity of feeling, or of belief. But there is something in Böhme's appeal to the *directness* of self-knowledge in *feeling*, in "the source of all suffering and joy," that attracts Feuerbach strongly and that he later translates into a kind of empiricism that is the source of the pragmatic and existentialist readings of Feuerbach's own philosophy.

DESCARTES

Feuerbach's treatment of Descartes and the Cartesians (Geulincx, Malebranche) and of Spinoza completes the first volume of the *History*. In the preceding studies of Bacon, Hobbes, and Gassendi, he suggests that the origins of modern philosophy lie in empiricism, materialism, or naturalism, and atomism, in the negation of the authoritarian spirit of medieval philosophy, of its otherworldliness and its foundation in the supersensible. The emphasis on *body*, on *motion*, in the mechanistic sense, on the *experience* of nature as the ground of natural philosophy in the initial studies is Feuerbach's foil for the introduction of idealism, however. The negation of the supersensible world by this empiricism and naturalism is, however, also a negation of *thought*, of the philosophical conception of thinking activity. Neither the empiricism, nor the naturalism, nor the atomism of the founders of modern philosophy is adequate for the systematic relation of thinking and being. The empiricism itself is inadequate to account for the experience of feeling, sensation, belief; and it is crucially inadequate to account for the experience of thinking.

In eschewing the essential difference between body and spirit, between matter in motion and the distinctive activity of consciousness, the "systems" of Bacon, Hobbes, and Gassendi are unable to account for thought, experience, feeling. They fail, therefore, as adequate, rational "philosophical" systems, that is, as systems based on "substantive concepts" that are "philosophical" in the sense of inherently necessary, universal, fully coherent.

Whereas Cartesian doubt, as the beginning of philosophy, has the same apparent content, in its rejection of external authority, as has the antiauthoritarianism of Bacon, its *methodological* character is supplemented by its distinctive content. It is a rejection of the "authority" of the senses, as well as of the authority of faith without the assent of and derivation from rational intuition. The ultimate distinction between spirit and body is the very activity of doubting itself, the activity of a being that can doubt. Descartes' rejection of external authority is thus not merely an "external" rejection, an unselfconscious turning to a different authority, *again* characterized as "external" (e.g., nature, body, sense experience as the image or phantasm of bodily activity). Rather, says Feuerbach, the thrust of Descartes' philosophy of the spirit, is to establish the difference of body and spirit in a *positive* characterization of the essence of spiritual activity, that is, thinking. So Feuerbach assesses Descartes' view:

> Descartes differentiates spirit from body and says that it is entirely and essentially different. What however is the difference? *Thinking itself,* which alone constitutes the essence of spirit. What else is thinking, however . . . but doubting? And what is doubting except separation, differentiation, abstraction from the body, and from the sensible? "By thought, I mean nothing but consciousness" says Descartes. But is consciousness itself, in Descartes' sense, anything other than self-consciousness? And is self-consciousness itself anything but the self-differentiation from body and from the sensible in general? And this differentiation, which establishes the self with certainty as the absolutely and unmediatedly real—isn't this what spirit is; a doubting of the reality of the sensible, or a negation thereof? Isn't doubt then the same as consciousness? Spirit is therefore differentiated from body, and it is thinking which constitutes the difference. But thinking is the same as doubting, and doubting the same as differentiating. It is differentiated from body by its self-differentiation. It is Spirit in that it thinks, and is differentiated from body in that it differentiates itself from body. Doubt . . . is therefore the essence of spirit, and spirit is essentially that which doubts the reality of sensible things. . . . (III, 204–5)

Feuerbach thus identifies Cartesian doubt with the *Cogito.* Descartes' thinking substance is understood in an Aristotelian, functional sense as constituted by its essential activity: There is no entity, Thought, apart from the activity of thinking, and, as Feuerbach repetitively asserts, the essence of thinking activity is doubting, where doubt itself is defined as self-differentiation, separation from body. It follows as an analytic conclusion, therefore, that thought is not corporeal.

On Gassendi's classical criticism of the *Cogito* as a syllogistic deduction, with the suppressed premise "whatever thinks, is," Feuerbach sides with Descartes, taking an essentialist view. The immediacy of the *intuition* of the *Cogito* is upheld on the grounds that for Descartes thinking is not *an* activity of the spirit, but *the* activity of the spirit. Its thinking is essentially identical with its being; there is no need for a third, mediating term. Still, Feuerbach sees the criticism of Gassendi in another light. Where Gassendi proposes, "Whatever acts, is," Descartes replies, "I walk, therefore I am—but only if I am aware of my walking." This *awareness* of an activity yields, however, only *phenomenal* self-existence, a self-existence that is "merely" empirical, or sensory, in its dependence on *awareness* (i.e., an experience) of a "real activity." Thus, this kind of awareness cannot yield "real self-existence," as can the essential activity of doubting, which takes self-existence itself as its object.

If Descartes had only asserted that Spirit is *not* body, then the philosophical significance of this assertion would have been small indeed.

Descartes' contribution is in the fact that he made this distinction not merely in the sense of the indefinite idea, (expressed as "Spirit is different from Body") which remains merely a negative, empty definition, in terms of *Im*materiality, *In*corporeality, *In*divisibility – all of which give no warrant at all for positive knowledge. His contribution is rather that he defined this distinction, this Immateriality and Simplicity, positively, as the living self-differentiation of Spirit – i.e. placed it in the activity of thinking, of consciousness, and made the actual, living, self-determining and self-conscious spirit, or the spirit as self, the very principle of philosophy. (III, 206)

Given Feuerbach's interpretation of the *Cogito* as the very act of self-differentiation from body, the immateriality of the Spirit follows analytically from the essence of this spirit as self-differentiating.

the sense of "I think, therefore, I am" is none other than "I differentiate myself from body, from the material, and therefore, and therein am I differentiated from it: My differentiating myself is my difference. . . . *Were I not different, I couldn't differentiate myself. Thus the proof of my difference is that I differentiate myself.* This differentiation of myself *is* my consciousness, the knowledge of myself, of my *Ego*, and as the unmediated affirmation of my self, it is the unmediated negation of all corporeality and materiality, it is the unmediated certainty that I am a self, and not an other, not a body. (III, 207)

Descartes does not mean, says Feuerbach, that it is an immaterial substance that thinks, "as if immateriality were a predicate in itself, or the universal predicate." Rather, spirit is immaterial *in that it thinks.* Its immateriality and its incorporeality are one and the same as its thinking. Therefore, the question as to whether spirit is or is not corporeal is "inadmissible, invalid"; the demand for a proof of the incorporeality of the spirit is "an improper demand, based on misunderstanding."

There is a basic defect in Descartes' philosophy of the Spirit, in his very separation of spirit from body, in the very sharpness of the distinction itself, according to Feuerbach. Though his exposition of Descartes' own concept of thinking is sympathetic, and though his insight into the relation between Cartesian doubt and the *Cogito* is an enlightened one, Feuerbach is critical of the sort of thinking entity or thinking activity that results. It is no longer the "living spirit," but an empty, abstract, and metaphysical essence, whose attribute, thinking, stands to it in the same relation as extension does to extended substance. Feuerbach's criticism here seems unclear and confused. For if, as he himself alleges, thinking is not the attribute of a logically or metaphysically prior substance, but is *itself*, as an activity, *what* that substance is, and also determines *that* such a substance is, then the charge that the substance-attribute relation is abstract and metaphysical seems unwarranted. He has answered his own charge (and a traditional charge) against Descartes as a "substance" philosopher (in the "entity" or "thing" sense of substance). However Feuerbach means that the abstractness and emptiness of "thinking substance" is its absolute separateness from body; in characterizing "Spirit" as thought alone, Descartes "conceived of spirit only in relation to itself (in subjectivity) and took this self-relation as its entire essence." The mistake here is one-sidedness, which "remains at the opposition between spirit and body." That is, Spirit has no *essential* relation to body, and from this, says Feuerbach, stem the other defects in Descartes' natural philosophy and view of the mind-body relation. The illicit transformation from self-certainty to certainty with regard to objective reality is achieved by Descartes in a "highly unphilosophical, popular, theological" way; in the "comfortable" way of going from self-consciousness, to consciousness of God and of God's existence, to innate ideas.

In effect, the methodological achievement of Descartes is the doubt-*Cogito* formulation, which establishes the distinctiveness of thought as the very activity of self-differentiation. The error or defect in Descartes lies in his use of the ontological argument to make up for the subjectivity, the one-sidedness, of thinking activity as *mere* self-relation. For the young Hegelian, Spirit had to have more than consciousness, that is, self-consciousness, as its essence. It had to encompass all; it had to have body itself as essential to it. Spirit's "otherness" had to be as systematically identical with Spirit, as its "this-sidedness," in self, or ego. Clearly, then, Spinoza is Descartes' fate, in this historical unfolding of the Spirit, as we shall see.

Feuerbach goes on to show how the one-sidedness of Descartes' characterization of thinking issues in an analogous one-sidedness in his natural philosophy, and in his account of the mind-body relation. In Feuerbach's critique of the natural philosophy, it is the concept of motion that is seen to reveal the defects of Cartesian dualism.

It is motion alone which transcends the mere extensionality, and external relations of the parts of matter, which shakes the parts out of their dead indifference, thoroughly interactivates them and . . . to this extent . . . "spiritualizes" matter. Motion is therefore the first abstract form of life, or the first abstract principle of all quality, of all life. The fact that Descartes cannot have motion

originate in matter itself, that he doesn't recognize motion as intrinsically inherent in matter, but rather has recourse to God's power as the source of motion, and thus drags it into nature in such an external way, is a major defect in
[Descartes'] natural philosophy. (III, 230)

Feuerbach's criticism of the natural philosophy is analogous in form
to his criticism of the one-sidedness and insufficiency of Descartes' spiritual principle. Extended substance, or matter, is inadequate in itself as
the basis for a world construction. This both Hobbes and Descartes
realized, says Feuerbach. But the introduction of motion as merely "external" to matter makes the material principle no more sufficient, in that
motion is conceived only as a "subjective necessity" of matter, and not as
an objective one, that is, *a necessity of matter itself*. Feuerbach identifies
motion with life, with animateness, with self-activity, and thus ultimately
with spirit itself, in the Greek and Hegelian traditions; thus, no external
"dragging in" of motion from some other source will give us that unitary
principle of spirit-matter that will suffice for a comprehensive world system. Unless matter is already potentially spiritual, in its "objective essence," the concept of matter itself remains abstract and one-sided.
Unless motion is an "objective necessity of matter itself" (III, 230) matter
suffers the same deficiency as does Descartes' "Spirit"–it is *mere* extension, as Spirit is *mere* thought. Descartes' solution is "unphilosophical,
popular and theological" here too. The mind-body dualism in Descartes
is the result of a joint deficiency in Descartes' concept of mind and in his
concept of body.

Feuerbach's pejorative use of "metaphysical essence," in this criticism
is noteworthy. "Metaphysical" or "merely metaphysical" connotes an
abstract essence, which exists merely in *thought*; further, because it is
merely in *thought*, it is subjective, lacks objectivity, concreteness, and
moreover, lacks "life" (that much-used Hegelianism that connotes process, change, development on the basis of some intrinsic and "real" self-
differentiation–in short, *dialectical* process). It is this that "metaphysical" is basically opposed to, not merely in the formal mode of "static"
versus "dynamic" categories, but in the material mode of "abstract"
versus "concrete" essence or being. This usage, part of the common language of the young Hegelians, passes into the works of Marx and Engels
in an important way. The rejection of "metaphysics" here is not, therefore, to be simply identified with the characteristic later *positivist* rejection of metaphysics as "meaningless." It is the *special* rejection of
metaphysics in that sense of a priori, *speculative* construction on the
basis of pure thought alone that Hegel and the Hegelians in common
eschewed. Much Anglo-American contemporary philosophy is at fault
in missing this distinction, particularly in Hegelianism. The oversight

has left a whole generation of Hegel criticism superficial, and has resulted in a marvelous confusion in the philosophical discussion of Marx. In Feuerbach's critique of Descartes, what is rejected is sometimes referred to as the "older metaphysics," that is, scholasticism, which delimits the framework of Cartesian philosophy (e.g., III, 236). The explicit charge, however, is that Descartes "transformed the living spirit into an empty, abstract essence, . . . into a *metaphysical* essence" [stress mine, M. W.] (III, 208).

Feuerbach's use of "materialism" is also noteworthy here. Feuerbach calls Descartes a "pure materialist" (III, 237) in respect to his view of the automatism of bodies (e.g., Descartes' treatment of *flinching*, in *Of the Passions*, art. 13, as, in effect, an unconditioned reflex). It is clear, both in his treatment of Hobbes and of Descartes, that "materialism" means "mechanical" or "abstract materialism," the system of merely external relation of bodies, which themselves are moved, but are not the source of motion, and are merely the translators of motion. Feuerbach rejected such a materialism through his whole career, even when he called himself a materialist. It was precisely this deficiency in mechanistic materialism that he sought to make up. Still, his later usage is confusing, because his characteristic use of "materialism" as Hobbesian-Cartesian mechanism persists, usually without qualifications or distinctions, and superficially Feuerbach often appears to be contradicting himself. There is more than an ambiguity of usage involved, however, in his later work. The concept of materialism he attempts to develop remains itself ambiguous, often unclear, and reflects Feuerbach's own struggle to achieve a satisfactory alternative to the *rejected* form of materialism.

It is clear also that despite the sharp differences in the conceptual framework between the atomism of Hobbes and Gassendi and the anti-atomism of Descartes, between the alternatives of a discontinuous and a continuous model of world structure, Feuerbach identifies both alternatives as "mechanist." An essential feature of mechanism is the externality of the relations between (or among) ultimate constituents. In the atomist case, there is radical spatiotemporal discontinuity among the atoms, and the external relation is action by contact among bodies. In the Cartesian case, it is the more fundamental metaphysical discontinuity, and the consequent problem of relation between two substances. The latter in itself is not necessarily mechanistic, and apart from the confused and unclear suggestion about the pineal gland and the passage of "animal spirits," Descartes' solution is not mechanistic, but theological. Still, by his insistence on the priority and independence of thought, Descartes makes the conditions for the *conception* (though not for the *existence*) of matter or extended substance mechanistic, in raising the category of *Quantity* to the supreme position in this conception. As Feuerbach points out, this is exhibited in Descartes' deduction of the concept of matter *from* the mathematical concepts of magnitude, divisibility, and so on. That is, the concept of extended substance is not derived from sense impressions or from the imagination (though it is related to them). Rather, it is derived from reason. As *rational object* (i.e., in *conception*), matter is thinkable in terms of the language of mathematics; or rather, it is *essentially* thinkable in this way, apart from the accidental properties that *may* be thought with it. But this is precisely the abstractness or one-sidedness that Feuerbach charges against mechanism, whether in its atomistic or nonatomistic (Cartesian) form: that it is not empirical enough; that the mechanist concept of matter is only matter as it is *for thought*, and not, as Bacon suggests, matter as it is for the direct, qualitative intuitions of sense. Thus, alleges Feuerbach, in the idea of extension as the very essence of matter lies the one-sidedness and the intellectual abstractness of Cartesian mechanism. The *general* similarity of both atomistic and Cartesian mechanism is not in the special concept of extension. Feuerbach sums this up thus:

> Natural science, especially physics, remains Cartesian in its viewpoint, to the present day, in its essential and general aspects, i.e. in its metaphysics and its philosophy of nature, even though most physicists are not Cartesians, but are, on the contrary, atomists in their orientation. But this atomism is not essentially different from Descartes' philosophy of nature, for both rest on a bare mechanism and materialism. (III, 232)

Despite these shortcomings, Feuerbach credits Descartes with having made a new start here also, as well as in his special scientific findings. Feuerbach says that the highest praise is due Descartes for having established that experience itself requires a spiritual principle as its ground, though Descartes expressed this only in an abstract and limited form.

MALEBRANCHE

For Feuerbach, the development and fulfillment of Descartes' philosophy is in the work of Malebranche and Spinoza. He deals briefly with the Cartesian school in a chapter on Geulincx. In a lengthier chapter on Malebranche, he characterizes the distinctiveness of this follower of Descartes as lying in his views on the dependency and finitude of the spirit.

Because, according to Malebranche, the soul is a particular, finite, and imperfect being, it cannot itself be the ground of the objectivity and universality of knowledge. Rather, only in its dependence on God, as universal and perfect Being, does the soul attain to such objectivity. In

Feuerbach's view, this is a more consistent account of the ground of certainty than that which Descartes gives in the *Cogito*. This latter has its "certainty" and "objectivity" only in the form of subjective activity, or the subjective validity of thinking itself; but since, in the *Cogito* argument, neither thought nor matter are given independent existence–are not, in the classical scholastic sense, *causa sui*–there is no ground of objective validity beyond the subject's own activity. Now it is true that Descartes goes beyond this, in his dependence on a form of the ontological argument and on the "necessity" of a nondeceiving God. But this is not of a piece with the *Cogito* argument. In this sense, Malebranche is more consistent than Descartes, in that he ascribes independent being to God alone.

With respect to God, as infinite being, the mutually exclusive and mutually finite "opposites" spirit and matter have no real being, but only apparent being. The source of all existence, as of all knowledge, is in God; thus also, both matter and spirit are "created beings," and not, in either case, *causa sui*. Any instance of knowing, then, is God's knowing *in us*. Feuerbach writes, "The true sense of Malebranche's main idea is this: God is the reason or the Spirit in us, or the reason, the Spirit in us is God" (III, 288).

Though Malebranche makes the transition from theology to philosophy, says Feuerbach, he does not free himself from theology. He retains a fundamental dualism in a way different from Descartes, but still in the Platonic-Augustinean tradition.

The chief defect [in Malebranche] that derives from the fusion of theological concepts and philosophical thought is this: God is conceived as the universal Being; all other being, including material being, is contained and subsumed in God. In this sense, then, matter should not be an insurmountable reality for God, should not be in opposition to His nature, and thus spirit should be able to perceive and to know material things in God, since matter is ideally posited in Him, and the opposition of matter and spirit is transcended. For all this, however, the division, or rather the absolute bifurcation between the spiritual, intelligible world and the material, sensual world remains in effect. Matter is not subsumed in God in any truly positive way, i.e. it is not conceived in its necessity. For God, as universal, infinite and absolutely real being, is here conceived as the most spiritual, immaterial being, i.e. as that which is completely divorced from all matter, and His essential nature is seen to lie in this immateriality. Thus, matter, and with it, nature is posited as un-Godly, as nothing, as unreal. . . . God does indeed contain nature, or matter, or corporeal things in Himself, according to Malebranche. But he contains them only as immaterial entities, as Ideas, divorced from all materiality. . . . Thus the perception of the material world as material, the perception of matter as such is inconceivable. Therefore . . . material existence has no ground but in the power and the will of God, i.e. it has no ground at all in itself, and is not necessary, but merely contingent or arbitrary being. [Malebranche writes: (Reply to M. Regis)] "The creation of matter is arbitrary, and depends on the Will of the Creator. If our ideas are representative, it is only because it has pleased God to create beings which conform to them. Even if God had not created any bodies, spirits would be able to have ideas of them." (III, 290–1)

In effect, Feuerbach's critique of Malebranche is that Malebranche is not Spinoza; that on theological (Augustinean) grounds, he drags Descartes' unresolved mind-body (or better, spirit-matter) dualism along with him, though he prepares the formal ground for a resolution. Again, there is the odd Feuerbachian insistence: Hobbes is not enough of an empiricist; now Malebranche is not enough of a materialist–and all this, from the standpoint of a distinctly Hegelian critique, a critique based on the concepts of organic unity in opposition of Hegelianism. Classical or "metaphysical" idealism seems to be very much more clearly the object of Feuerbach's critique than does empiricism or materialism; at any rate, the *complement* of what is lacking in the one is found lacking in the other. Where one lacks systematic coherence, or a "substantive principle," the "substantive principle" of the other lacks empirical, "qualitative" concreteness.

The schematism of the development from Descartes to Spinoza is ultimately simple in Feuerbach's version. The elements of Spinozism are already in Descartes. Malebranche develops them in a more "determinate" way–that is (to translate the Hegelian sense of "*bestimmung*"), the concepts are explicated, articulated, carried to their sharpest, most "determinate" form, and thus to their fullest consequences. Thus, in Descartes, the center of the stage of "actuality" is taken by spirit and matter. The principle of their interconnection (not yet of their unity) still remains in the wings: God operates offstage, so to speak. The concept of God itself still requires actualization. As Feuerbach puts it, "God must descend into the spheres which spirit and matter now occupy for themselves . . . they must make place for God, so that He actively intervenes at the midpoint of actuality, and takes possession of it" (III, 292). Malebranche has moved God into Spirit's place "onstage." Still, matter remains "unmoved," so to speak. "All that is needed is that matter . . . be recognized as a modification of God's essence; that what is still held formally separate in Malebranche, be united,–and lo! we have Spinoza" (III, 293).[11]

Still, the transition is not smooth. Descartes holds that we have clear and distinct ideas of two independent substances, each of which may be *conceived* in its essential attribute without the other; and further, that in addition to these, we have an idea of a third, infinite substance, upon which the conceptions of the other two are *not* dependent. Thus, the *concept* of matter requires no more than extension as its essence; that of thought, no more than thinking activity. Neither depends, for its concept, on God, as they do in Malebranche. Malebranche therefore seems to represent a more "consequent" unity of Being than does Descartes; but matter is, so to speak, driven offstage. The resolution of this dualism, not yet achieved in Malebranche, takes place in Spinoza.

SPINOZA

Feuerbach points out that for Spinoza matter and thought are independently conceivable, just as they are in Descartes; neither requires anything more than its own essence (i.e., extension or thinking activity) for its concept. This, it would seem, is a dualistic regression from Malebranche's view of both as dependent, "created" being. Yet, according to Spinoza, the very independence of both extended and thinking being is that both are identical with substance, that what they "express" is substance. Their essence lies not in the one being matter or the other thought, but in their *both* being substance. Neither matter as matter nor spirit as spirit is real in itself; only substance is real. The independence of essence, which was expressed in Descartes, now is transformed into an independence of existence—*not* of matter as matter, or of spirit as spirit, but of substance as substance, as infinite being.

Thus, the "Gordian knot" is cut; or, to change the metaphor, we can have our infinite cake and eat it too. "Actual existence is but infinite, unlimited existence, according to Spinoza. Indeed, in Spinoza's sense, the concept of existence and the concept of infinity are one and the same" (III, 345).

Thus, Feuerbach sees in Spinoza a dialectical resolution of the partiality and inadequacy of Cartesian, and even of Malebranchian, dualism; and he extols Spinoza for this "pure philosophical" advance beyond the limits of theology—that is, beyond the limits of a mind-body dualism bound to theological dualism of the spirit and the flesh. Spinoza "purifies" the question by taking it beyond the theological context.

However, in 1847, Feuerbach appends a footnote qualifying his earlier evaluation.

Despite what is said here [in the first edition], it only cuts the Gordian knot of Spinozist philosophy, it doesn't unravel it. Just as thinking and extension remain in contradiction to each other in Cartesian dualism, despite the unity of substance, so too do the finite and the infinite in Spinoza. From the infinite comes only the infinite, and from the finite, only the finite. . . . Thus, he never arrives at an organic derivation of the finite, the determinate, i.e. the actual. This, as well as all the other contradictory and incomprehensible elements in

85

Spinoza's philosophy find their explanation and resolution in the definition: "Spinoza is the negation of theology on the grounds of theology itself." or: his is that negation of theology which is itself theological. (III, 340n.)

In this formulation, Spinoza stands to "theological metaphysics" in the same relation as Greek philosophy stands to "paganism": Each is the "negation" of the other, but a negation still within the framework of what it negates; the terminology, the framework of meanings, the conceptual structure is common. What the "negation" establishes with clarity is the contradiction inherent in the negated view. What does Feuerbach see as Spinoza's chief accomplishment in this "negation of theology on the grounds of theology itself"? It was to deanthropomorphize God and to naturalize man, to make the divine natural and the natural divine, and to see man as a product of this divine nature; thus, to remove the characteristic theological concerns with man's welfare and salvation from the precincts of philosophy proper. Feuerbach writes, in 1847,

> In his own time, Spinoza's adversaries charged him with confounding God and nature. They were right. But Spinoza was right too, when he charged his adversaries, the Christian philosophers and theologians, with confounding God and man. . . . The historical significance of Spinoza lies in the fact that, in opposition to Christian religion and philosophy, he divinized nature, made nature into God, and into the origin of man, whereas the others made human essence into God, and thus into the origin of nature. (III, 373–4)

From Feuerbach's point of view in 1847, Spinoza's separation of the *object* of theology from the *object* of philosophy is crucial: For God as an object of theology *is* human essence; God as object of philosophy is nonhuman essence. Nature is defined by Spinoza, in effect, as whatever is nonhuman, in the special sense of *nonmoral*. So that religion and theology have as their subject matter only the *moral* attributes of God, whereas philosophy's distinctive subject matter is the "physical" attributes of God. Only in the latter case is there the possibility of theoretical significance, or truth or validity. "Belief, religion, theology have no theoretical significance, or truth or validity. Their value and function is a practical one, uniquely; it is to lead those who are not determined by reason to dutifulness, virtue and happiness," says Feuerbach, paraphrasing Spinoza's *Tractatus*. The theoretical object, the object of reason or of science is only nature itself, the "philosophical God without human attributes, without Justice and Mercy, without eyes or ears, this God whose activity is unconcerned with man, but acts only according to laws, who acts not with any concern for human weal . . . but only according to the necessity of his own essence" (III, 376).

The fault with this, in Feuerbach's later view, is that this *nature* is *only* an object of reason, and reality becomes for Spinoza "a nonsensible, abstract, metaphysical essence, so that the essence of nature means, for him, nothing but the essence of the understanding–and indeed, of that understanding which is conceived of as in contradiction with or in opposition to feeling, sense, intuition" (III, 376). But this is later Feuerbach, the Feuerbach who wants to rescue the "theoretical significance" of religion and theology by revealing it as the mythical, hypostatized, or esoteric form of the science of sense and feeling. The earlier criticism of 1833 *defends* Spinoza against the charges of atheism ("in the usual, tasteless sense") and amorality, by pointing to Spinoza's own notions of religiosity and goodness; and, further, characterizes Spinoza's account of the freedom of the will as consisting in that higher freedom of rationally determined action. This is a standard appreciation, on Spinozist grounds. The criticism of Spinoza's concept of substance, however, is that its unity remains abstract and metaphysical, because the distinctions and opposition between thinking and extension are not seen as *real* distinctions, *real* oppositions in substance; they remain only *apparent* oppositions, which vanish in their shared substantiality, in their common ground. Feuerbach's objection is Hegel's: Substance has no principle of self-differentiation in itself, is not itself constituted by this very opposition itself, in which alone the essence of the unity of substance can become actualized, "real" existence. But this objection itself remains a formal objection in terms of the system-defined abstract terms such as "opposition," "unity," "self-differentiation," as well as the more traditionally metaphysical terms, "substance," "essence," "existence"–in short, it remains an objection in "pure philosophy." It is only in the added remarks of 1847 that Feuerbach states the sharper criticism of Spinoza. Here, Spinoza's "theological" ground, the context from which he could not free himself, is seen in the very abstractness of his "matter" and of his "nature" itself. Spinoza fails on the same grounds that even the empiricist Hobbes failed: He is not, in effect, adequately empirical!

> The secret, true sense of Spinozist philosophy is Nature. But nature is not Nature for Spinoza–instead, the empirical, anti-theological essence of nature is, for Spinoza, only an abstract, metaphysical theological essence–it is an object, as God. Spinoza subsumes God in nature, but he also does just the reverse: he subsumes nature in God . . . [but] why do you, as a naturalist, want also to remain a theist? Or as a theist, to remain a naturalist? Down with the contradiction! Not "God as well as nature" but "either God or Nature" is the password of Truth. Where God and nature are identified or confounded, there is neither God nor nature, but a mystical, amphibolic hybrid. This is the chief defect in Spinoza. (III, 383)

In 1847, Feuerbach says that the theologians' charge of atheism against Spinoza was justified, for by 1847 atheism had already been defined by

Feuerbach as the denial not of God, as subject, but of those predicates usually associated with divinity: sympathy, goodness, justice, and so on. But insofar as Spinoza denies these godly predicates in the nature that *is* God, God becomes redundant. "Inasmuch as God is not a separate, personal Being, distinct from nature and man, he is a superfluous being; for only in its distinctiveness is there the ground and necessity for any Being." But, adds Feuerbach, "Spinoza didn't mean to be an atheist, nor could he be one, from his point of view and in his time. He therefore makes the denial of God into the affirmation of God, he makes the essence of nature into Godly essence" (III, 383).

CHAPTER IV

Leibniz: The History of Philosophy as Immanent Critique

Feuerbach followed his *History of Modern Philosophy* with a full-length study of Leibniz. This volume was to prove a crucial turning point for Feuerbach. He writes, years later, that in this study, his interest in naturalism begins; that his attention was called to the role of the natural sciences; and that a tendency in the direction of "individualism" (i.e., to the existential primacy of individuals), begins here.[1] Whether in fact this is so or whether it only seemed so to Feuerbach in retrospect, there is no doubt that the *Leibniz* presents Feuerbach as a more mature and critical philosopher, one more consciously aware of the task of historical analysis of philosophy, than the Feuerbach of the *History*. He is still the young Hegelian, but with a difference. He is still writing interpretive history of philosophy, history "from a standpoint." He is still concerned with the history of philosophy as the ever more adequate attainment of a concept of "Spirit," with the dialectical resolution of the partiality, the one-sidedness, of a previous stage, in the succeeding stage.

But the *Leibniz* study is noteworthy in three special respects, apart from its general competence as an extended and richly wrought exposition and analysis of Leibniz's philosophy: First, it contains a full discussion of the *philosophic* importance of historical studies in philosophy and an exposition of the "genetic-analytic" method. Second, Feuerbach uses his discussion of Leibniz's critique of Locke to develop his own views on empiricism. In effect, he continues his quest for a more adequate empiricism, still in the guise of an external critique, as he did in the *History*. Thus, the *Leibniz*, although ostensibly the work of a Hegelian idealist, is the dialectical proving ground for an empiricism still suppressed, but working its way to fuller and open expression–

Feuerbach contra Feuerbach, in retrospect. Third, the concluding portions of the *Leibniz* are the opening portions of the succeeding work on Pierre Bayle. The substantive importance of this transition is again retrospective: The *Leibniz* begins that critique of *belief* (distinguished from the critique of *reason*) that forms the basis for Feuerbach's distinctive materialism and so-called anthropologism. It is from this that Feuerbach's analysis of religious belief, and further, of all the modes of belief, begins, and it is thus the source of Feuerbach's most distinctive philosophical contribution. In these three respects–the exposition and evaluation of the "genetic-analytic" method, the search for an adequate empiricism, and the critique of belief–the *Leibniz* is a crucial transitional work in the development of Feuerbach's philosophy, quite apart from its continuing value as a study of Leibniz.

THE GENETIC-ANALYTIC METHOD AND THE PHILOSOPHIC IMPORTANCE OF HISTORY OF PHILOSOPHY

The very title of the work on Leibniz establishes its style and intent. It is, called in a classical German tradition, *Darstellung, Entwicklung und Kritik der Leibnizschen Philosophie.*

Feuerbach conceives the *Leibniz* to be "the second part of *The History of Modern Philosophy*" (IV, 1), the continuation of a multivolume history. But he explains the exclusive treatment of Leibniz alone on the grounds that "the essential object of this study is not that of a purely formal exposition, but instead, the sort of positive philosophical presentation which the study of the immanent development of a philosophy makes not merely possible, but necessary" (IV, 1). "Positive" is a term with a complex of connotations for Feuerbach. It means, in one sense, "appreciative," but even this is imbedded in the Hegelian context of "appreciation"–its explication demands a system. Feuerbach writes, "The study of the development of philosophy is the deciphering of its true sense, revealing what is positive in it, and presenting its Idea in terms of the temporally conditioned, finite determinations of this Idea. The possibility of development is this Idea itself" (IV, 1). Again, what appears here as rhetoric, or at best as a formal heuristic, is, in context, a technical description. "Idea," "development," or "immanent development," "true sense" are not ordinary terms here, and to take them thus baldly would be to vulgarize. But Feuerbach does qualify and define; in language more nearly explicative, he continues,

Therefore, criticism is easy, developmental study is difficult. Mistakes and deficiences demand only alertness and attention; what is valuable and good demands immersion in it, in order to be recognized. The former can be un-covered by even the most superficial inquiry, the latter only by dedicated ex-amination. The error gives itself away, it leaps to one's view; the true, the valuable in a philosophy stays to itself, in the innards of the philosophy, pro-viding its own reward, and manifesting itself only in a transformed way. (IV, 2)

Philosophical criticism, then, is never simply the exposure of error, of "mistakes," of inconsistencies or contradictions. Rather, it demands the comprehension of the *Idea* of a philosophy–its "positive" content– *and* this by means of the development of this *Idea*, dialectically. The revelation of error, then, is part of this understanding: the elimination of what is partial, false, incomplete, to get at the "rational kernel," at the "truth" contained in the husk, and therefore at what constitutes the "positive," abiding element to be preserved through the dialectical unfolding of the Idea. Feuerbach is an *echt-Hegelianer* in his method-ology here. "The true critique of a philosophy lies in its development itself, for it is made possible only by the separation of the essential from the accidental, of the unconditional from the conditional, of the ob-jective from the subjective" (IV, 2). "Development" means two things here, or connotes two aspects of one thing (if one is to remain true to the spirit of Hegelian "identity" theory). On the one hand, the "de-velopment of a philosophy" is, objectively, the dialectic of that philos-ophy itself–how *its* "consequences" "unfold" from its "ground," its "determinations" from its "Idea." Thus, to be "a philosophy" is to be a system, in which all the parts are related. But the second sense of "development of a philosophy" is the critical reconstruction of this ob-jective dialectic, "from the inside," so to speak (by "immersion in it"). This is the subjective side of "development." It means, in Hegelian terms, transforming the *object in itself*, the philosophical system as pre-sented, into an *object for me*, the philosophical system as understood; and this not so much by tracing its inner structure with one's finger, but by adopting this inner structure itself as one's own mode of philos-ophizing about what it is the system deals with. So *Entwicklung*, in the title, and in Feuerbach's procedure itself, is at the same time a ref-erence to an object (the philosophical system itself) and a procedure (the mode of apprehending the system), on the grounds that objects *are* in fact procedures, and that one learns *what* an object is by emu-lating the procedures of its development (which it also *is*). Clearly, then, exposition precedes development. But then one would remain at a flat identity with the object; Feuerbach would *be* Leibniz, and his work on Leibniz would, in effect, be identical with the work *of* Leibniz. This, in fact, is what misinterpreters of Hegel take him to intend, both in his *History of Philosophy* and in his wider theory. And this, in effect, would seem to be what Feuerbach means when he says that "the true critique of a philosophy lies in its development itself." But *Kritik* is entailed by *Entwicklung* as something distinct, namely, the *point of view* of the critique, which is inescapable, and inescapably different from that of the original development. Thus, *Kritik* is immanent in its identification with the point of view of the object of critique and transcendent by virtue of its being something more than this: a reflective inquiry into the grounds, limitations, and direction of a philosophical system. This difference is the "transformed way" in which alone the "truth of a philosophy manifests itself."

Feuerbach continues,

The method of developmental study is as much an analytic as a synthetic enterprise: analytic not only in the sense of abstracting, or deriving the general, determining concept from particular determinate ideas, but also in the sense of eliciting, from that which is explicitly stated, that which is left unsaid, but which is yet contained in an undeveloped, implicit form. Thus the hidden content is not an object of empirical perception, but rather an object of meditation. Such an analysis is synthetic also insofar as it ascertains the essential Idea of philosophy by coordinating the manifold elements into a whole, by interconnecting all the different, isolated thoughts, which on first view don't appear to have any relation to each other, or at least appear to have no express relation to each other, though they are in essence coherent. (IV, 2)

"Analysis" in the two senses that Feuerbach presents is a matter of inductive abstraction, and a matter of explication. How exactly the derivation of the general concept from particulars is to proceed and how indeed this is distinct from the synthetic activity of "coordinating the manifold elements into a whole" is not clear. Presumably, the derivation of a general "determining" concept from particular ideas is closely related to explication, in the sense that apparently isolated ideas are seen to have a common, relating property upon explication of their "hidden content."

The related term "genetic" in this method of *genetic analysis* is used *not* in a strictly historical sense, but in a logical sense. Developmental study is genetic in that it seeks to establish the *logical* derivation of "what appears as an unmediated thesis," or "an isolated idea," from its *ground*. It is, in effect, what Peirce called *abductive* logic or hypothetical inference: Given a proposition p, we hypothetically reconstruct the proposition (or set of propositions) from which p could be derived. Feuerbach demands a *systemic* hypothesis, however—a *ground*, from which a whole set of apparently unmediated, isolated propositions (or "ideas") could be derived and whose systemic relation *to each other* would be revealed in this joint derivation. *This* then reveals the "developmental" aspect of any particular idea.

But in what sense is such a *logical* "genesis" *historical?* Is it that such a genesis takes place *in* history, specifically, *in* the history of philosophy? This would indeed seem to be the most apparent answer: History reveals the development, or is grasped "in its concept" thus. But this is not what Feuerbach means. He is still too much of a Hegelian to admit some quasi-independent process of developmental history that reveals the genesis. Rather, history *is,* or is *constituted by,* this genesis itself. "Genetic" means "historical" because history is the process that this genesis unfolds. It is not a question of conflating historical and logical *genesis.* Rather, history as history *is* the generation of the consequences (the "determinations") from some *ground* or *Idea.* Apart from this, it would be nothing but the recitation of disconnected events, for even mere *chronicle* entails the (abstract) Idea of succession of events in time. Hence, it is not discovered *that* history "unfolds" in terms of a logical schema of Ground-Consequent; rather, this is the very condition of history itself, if it is to be history proper. To discover *how* a particular, concrete history unfolds is a matter of historical study. It follows that the method of this study must be "genetic-analytic," and its limitations are ever the "point of view" that is itself historically conditioned and that is itself therefore a transformation of the original "development." Feuerbach writes,

> The developmental study is therefore a genetic study, in that it derives what first appears as an unmediated thesis from its ground, and in this way *explains* what would otherwise not be grasped in its concept, as long as it remains something given only in its immediate, merely apparent form. But this genetic analysis is a historically conditioned and bounded activity. It must depend on particular data, from which it would follow, directly or indirectly, that this particular development, this genesis, and not another, is the appropriate, unmistakable one. . . . (IV, 2)

In a metaphor, Feuerbach likens such a developmental study to "organic activity":

> The development should be a reproduction, a metamorphosis. The developmental expositor has to accept what is strange and alien to him as his own, so that he can reconstruct it as if it were his own, and represent it as mediated and assimilated by his own activity. His model is not that bee which gathers pollen and brings it to the hive, but the bee which assimilates this pollen and exudes it as wax. (IV, 3)

The task of the historian of philosophy is such a "reproduction" in terms of an "internal treatment" and "transformation" that still retains the spirit of the original by emulating its own mode of philosophical dialectic. Thus, says Feuerbach, the intellect doesn't place itself in a foreign element, in its self-alienation; the thought alienates itself only in order to be *rethought*, not merely to become something seen, or believed as an external object. It remains therefore in its own homeland, in its place of origin. The force which begot the thought in the first place must be the same force which will re-beget it. (IV, 3)

In this account of a method of *empathetic reconstruction*, both the genetic and analytic components of the method are seen to be derived from some more fundamental commitment: that the historian of philosophy *participates in* the very thought process of the philosopher whose work he is reconstructing.

THE CRITIQUE OF MECHANISM: LEIBNIZ

Feuerbach attempts first to "derive" Leibniz from the prior development of modern philosophy; that is, he attempts a schematic construction of the development of modern philosophy from its Italian "birth," in the break with scholastic-Aristotelian philosophy, through its French, English, and German transformations.

The "babe" born in Italy is traced through its metaphorically conceived wanderings, from its birthplace to its "place of residence," which turns out, of course, to be Germany. Feuerbach's emphasis on the "national" character of philosophy was typical of his time. In German philosophy, this emphasis had its roots in Kant, Fichte, and Herder and found its systematic use in Hegel's *History of Philosophy* as well as in his *Philosophy of History* and his *Philosophy of Art*. This tradition was carried over into a German self-critique by Feuerbach, and then by Marx and the left Hegelians (e.g., in *The Holy Family* and *The German Ideology*). Thus, Feuerbach offers such characterizations as these: The Italians were capable of giving birth to philosophy, but not of raising the child. "The fate of the Italian philosophers was the fate of philosophy itself: Bruno fled to France, England, and Germany; Campanella, after a long-term imprisonment, found asylum in France" (IV, 4). The English genius, or "productive spirit," was empiricism and materialism. In France, it was "spiritualism," capable of rising to the heights, but not of sustaining them, which required the Germans.

This is the familiar "ethnic" mythology of philosophy, common to German nineteenth-century thought. Feuerbach's point here is apparently to set the stage for the hiatus in the wanderings that was provided by a non-Hollander in Holland–the Jew Spinoza. It is at this point that the *Leibniz* study is braided into the loose ends of the *History*, which had ended with a chapter on Spinoza. And it is with the contrast of Spinoza and Leibniz that the study really begins.

Feuerbach's further characterization of Spinoza in this volume, following the long study in the *History*, is itself a recapitulation of the theme of philosophy's emancipation from theology. Spinoza, "separated from Judaism but not yet become Christian, was the personified independence and freedom of thought" (IV, 6). In an extended metaphorical passage, Feuerbach describes the "arrival" of philosophy in Amsterdam thus:

Here, philosophy rested from the tumultuous extremes of Idealism and Materialism, between which it fluctuated in France; here it cleansed itself of all foreign constituents, of all the ornamentations of fantasy, all the accoutrements of anthropomorphism and anthropopathism. Here, philosophy ground lenses for its glasses, so that it could see more clearly and distinctly. Here, it achieved a pure and true image of itself. But the stuff in which it reflected itself was hard and inappropriate. Thus, what resulted was only a lithograph in black and white, lacking the colors of life. . . . (IV, 6)

We are ready, then, for the German adventure: Whereas the Spinozist lenses gave us clarity of vision, but lacked the "colors of life," German philosophy swam in color, but lacked distinctness. It was mystical and not scientific. Because of the historical circumstances of the German reformation, philosophy as scientific philosophy remained an alien, kept at the threshold by the rule of religion.

Therefore, in accordance with the religious character of the nation, religious emancipation preceded philosophical emancipation in Germany. On the one hand, in France, England and Italy, an independent philosophy begins outside of the prevailing religion, in separation from it–but in a separation which leaves religion unchallenged, in a dualism which establishes the world of belief in which reason has nothing to do, and a world of reason segregated from belief. On the other hand, philosophy in Germany begins with a conscious, reflective mediation of philosophy and religion; and even prior to *this* mediation, with an unmediated unity of philosophy and religion, as religious philosophy–as philosophy within the confines of religious feeling and belief, arisen out of religious needs. (IV, 9)

But, Feuerbach continues, such philosophy is trapped in the confines of religious, sensuous imagery, and does not attain to any really metaphysical Idea as such. It is "not philosophy, but mysticism." Religion, in "the usual, narrow sense" regards all study of the nature of things as merely worldly and vain. This, says Feuerbach, is the fundamental sense of Jakob Böhme's mysticism, insofar as he deals at all with natural philosophy, and Feuerbach accords to Böhme a preeminent place as the archetype of "German" philosophy, in this "national" sense.

What, however, is "science" or "scientific philosophy," in Feuerbach's sense? If it is not Spinoza's *Reason*, which remains too abstract and "colorless," and it is not the religious philosophy, which displaces the actual, the determinate, the natural or this-worldly with the sensuous imagery and mysticism of a reality constructed by belief, what, then, is it? It is, according to Feuerbach, the classically conceived study of the "nature of things" (i.e., natural philosophy), but not yet "science" in the modern sense, distinct from philosophy, although Feuerbach is ready to call it *naturwissenschaft*. It is, or appears to be, in Feuerbach's account of it, *the rational study of the finite*.

> Science requires an independent interest in its subject matter . . . a free, concentrated, unconditional devotion to it. But it is precisely the freedom of such an interest, such a dedication that man is robbed of by religion in the above [narrow] sense. For such an interest, such an enthusiasm, without which nothing can be accomplished in science, is regarded by religion as a divinization of the finite. The study of natural science bears only such fruit as is banned by theology—by that theology which Bacon, in his physics, called a barren virgin consecrated to God. The study of natural science awakens a free and pure interest in nature. The arts and sciences accomplish what is great and immortal only when they are free to follow their own will. But in this untrammeled and free tendency, the artistic and scientific spirit is nothing less than an irreligious spirit. To put it the other way round: only he who pursues and loves science in terms of its own demands, pursues it religiously. (IV, 9)

The essential interest of the modern period is to formulate a philosophical framework, independent of religion and adequate to the tasks of natural science. This is the *general* condition that Feuerbach sets for a scientific philosophy. But he sees this too as a historically conditioned development, related to the history of science itself. In the context of the history of science, Cartesian mechanism is the most adequate philosophical principle for its time. The concept of matter as extended substance, of *Quantity* as the "principle of material existence," of mathematical description as the paradigm of science derives, according to Feuerbach, from the fact that "the first great revolutionary discoveries of natural science were principally in the realm of astronomy and mathematical physics." This historically evoked principle of Quantity was in this sense more clearly justified than the opposing views of such "qualitative" mechanists as Digby, such "mystical metaphysicizing theologians" as Henry More, such opponents of mathematization as Pierre Poiret, such Neoplatonists as Cudworth, and such hylozoists as Glisson, all of whose anti-Cartesian views Feuerbach examines. He holds that these alternative positions are only of historical interest, but not of philosophical interest.

> From the point of view of philosophy in its world-historical development, these are only unjustified positions. The privileged knowledge-principle, from the point of view of the world spirit, so to speak, was at that time mechanism alone. As a definitive method of the knowledge of nature, no other principle of

explanation but mechanism was then available. The hylarchic principle of More, the constructive principle of Cudworth were indefinite and unenlightening principles, which did not meet the needs of the essential interests of the modern period, i.e. the material knowledge of the material. In fact, these other views contradicted these needs. (IV, 39)

Feuerbach's notion of "privileged principles" is clearly a historical relativism related to Hegel's. The *principle* is judged or justified in terms of its relevance to a historical "need"–in this case, the needs of physical science *at that time*. What would determine the "privilege" of a principle would be the facts of the history of science; that is, the nature of the dominant scientific developments of a period. It is interesting that in this instance, the *philosophical* dialectic no longer seems to be viewed as autonomous, but only as ancillary to some "deeper" historical development. This would seem to override the general framework of the unfolding of the Idea in philosophy that dominates Feuerbach as it dominates Hegel. And on these grounds, it would be unclear what "justification" Feuerbach finds for Leibnizian monadism as an *advance* over Cartesian mechanism, unless it could be shown that the development of natural science required this advance. Feuerbach finds his answer in Leibniz's own dissatisfaction with mechanism. He cites Leibniz's account of his own development. Leibniz writes,

> If I am to be counted among those who have ever been taken up with mathematics, I did not on that account neglect to devote myself to the study of philosophy, from my early youth on. I had already made great progress in the study of Scholastic philosophy when mathematics and the new writers drew me away from such studies when I was still very young. I was enchanted by the beauty of the mathematical method and its mechanical explanation of nature, and I rightfully scorned the manner of explanation of the school philosophers, which made use only of incomprehensible forms and properties. But as I inquired into the ultimate foundations of mechanics and the Laws of Motion, how surprised I was to discover that it was impossible to find them in mathematics, and that I therefore had to turn back to metaphysics. (cited by F., IV, 39)

In effect, Feuerbach's estimate of Leibniz's "advance" is that Leibniz discovered the *philosophical* inadequacy of mechanism, and not that Leibniz found it *scientifically* inadequate, nor that new developments in science "demanded" a new principle. The *description* of motion required no more, methodologically, than mathematical quantification as its "principle." But the "ultimate foundations" (*letzte Gründen*) of mechanics and the laws of motion could not be adequately comprehended mathematically (i.e., in terms of Quantity). Leibniz's rejection of a purely kinematic (Cartesian) mechanics, and his interpretation of mechanics in terms of a fundamentally dynamic principle (Force), is a chapter in the history and philosophy of physics.[2] But Feuerbach does not deal with it in this context. Rather, he is content to deal with the issue in its traditional metaphysical sense, that is, Leibniz's claim that only Force is *Being*.

What is at issue here? If a mathematical account is adequate for a description of motion, then what is missing? Plainly, for Leibniz, what is missing is the "ultimate ground" for motion itself, that is, *force*, without which the phenomenon of motion remains a ghostly appearance, or a geometric relation: no more than time rate of change of position within the Cartesian framework of extended substance. But, Feuerbach argues, the very ground for the *possibility* of such a mathematical account (e.g., in terms of differential equations) lies outside of mathematics. Mathematics gives us the descriptive schema, but what it describes is not accounted for in the geometrical concept of extended substance. What is required is the ground for the possibility of *real* motion: that is, self-motion, or an original principle on the basis of which the translated motion of mechanics could be explained, but that would overcome the inadequacy of mechanism itself as a principle of explanation.

Feuerbach states the dialectical issue in Leibniz sharply. Leibniz's dissatisfaction with the Cartesian concept of extended substance was mainly that there was no principle of motion in it, that it was, in effect, a concept of inert, "dead" matter, and therefore necessitated the unacceptable dualism of matter and spirit, and thus had to posit a *separate* agency that was active but whose activity could not be clearly related to matter. Leibniz's task then was to find a way of overcoming this dualism in Cartesian *metaphysics*, without jeopardizing the adequacy of mechanist-mathematical description in Cartesian *physics*. According to Feuerbach, it is in this attempt that the genius of Leibniz founders. What Leibniz attempted was the mediation of Cartesian dualist mechanism with Spinozist holism. He finds his solution in the concept of *force*, which is, in effect, self-activity; and he finds a home for this self-activity in his "ensouled atoms," the monads. Thus, Leibniz's "soul philosophy" or *pneumatology* is the metaphysical foundation of his critique of Cartesian mechanism, on its *philosophical* side.

Feuerbach traces the differences between Descartes' extended substance and Leibniz's alternative in order to advance the critique of and search for empiricism. The contrast, logically, is between the properties of extended substance and their negation, in Leibniz's "spiritual atoms." Where the former is extended, compound, and therefore divisible, material, and passive, the latter is unextended, simple, and therefore indivisible, immaterial, and active. But then, what more has

Leibniz done than to replace Descartes' extended substance with Descartes' thinking substance? Are not these properties of the monads all the properties of Descartes' own *res cogitans?*

For one thing, these *simple* immaterial substances are plural, atomistic. Further, what accounts for their plurality is their individuality, and their individuality is in turn accounted for by their qualitative uniqueness, that is, the difference of each monad from each and every other monad. This, their *quality,* depends on their mode of activity, or their "modifications." That is, though the monads are *simple,* their simplicity or unicity does not preclude "modification." But "modification" is not effected from without, for the monads do not have external relations. Rather, the monad *is* its mode of activity, and this activity, in Leibniz's term, is its *perception,* which is the unique way in which each monad is (internally) related to every other monad. But this perception, or mode of activity, is the monad's unique expression of *force.* Thus, the very *being* of the monad is *force* or the unique and individual mode of its self-activity, which, says Leibniz, is *spontaneous* (i.e., not causally effected from without). Here is the real breach with mechanism then: in positing the *being* of the monads in their spontaneous self-activity; in making them *causa sui,* as Spinoza's substance is, yet maintaining their plurality and *real* individuality in terms of their differentiating activity.

Yet this is not enough to account for the plurality, where plurality entails real distinction. Whereas *force* is the positive expression for the qualitative differentiation of the monads, *matter* is the negative expression for this *same* difference. Here, indeed, the Spinozist double-aspect theory comes into play, and the Cartesian dualism is set aside. Matter is not a separate and independent principle, but the "other-being" of spirit, the expression of the same reality *(force,* here, and not *substance,* in the Spinozist sense) in its inverse or negative form. Force is self-activity but what distinguishes the unique force of each monad's mode of being is the "veil" of matter, that is, the unique determination of such and such a force, such and such a mode of activity. The principle of individuation, then, is matter, as much as it is force, but matter not as positive being; rather, as the negative expression for the finitude of each monad (except one, of course: the infinite monad, God). Thus, the monads are immaterial, but their very immateriality is qualified by this view. There are grades of materiality (or immateriality) in Leibniz's sense of grades of *perception.* Feuerbach characterizes Leibniz's view thus:

> Leibnizian philosophy is Idealism. Its fundamental idea is that the soul is *not* a particular and finite substance, counterposed to which there exists another

material substance. Rather, the soul is the only substance. It is all truth, essence, actuality, for only active being is actual, true being. But all activity is soul activity; the concept of activity is nothing but the concept of soul and vice-versa. Matter is nothing but a restriction, a limitation of this activity. The monads are delimited activities, because they are bound up with matter. Matter is only the expression of the plurality of souls; it says no more than that there are uncountably many souls, and not one soul, one single substance. For matter is the difference between the finite and the infinite monad, and as such it is the source of plurality. . . . Only against the dark background of matter do the monads shine forth as myriad stars. Take matter away, and the monads vanish, and there remains only the one light of unlimited substance. (IV, 160–1)

The "immaterial" monads are thus "bound up" with matter, as the very condition of their interrelation to each other, albeit this matter has no "separate existence." The condition of *real* being is, then, *individuality*. Feuerbach is to take this emphasis seriously, in his own philosophical development. But here it poses a problem for him, for he sees in Leibniz's attempt to overcome the dualism of matter and spirit, a fatal weakness. Feuerbach sees the Leibnizian Pneumatology itself as a modified form of atomistic mechanism (in this sense, not Cartesian) that still retains the philosophical inadequacies of mechanism. He sees this as Leibniz's historical limitation.

It was the age of the dualism of spirit and matter, and the age of mechanism and materialism. The category of mechanism was the only one under which things were comprehended. Leibnizian philosophy is Idealism, but Idealism under the form of mechanism. It conceives of the life of the soul in itself under the form of a mechanical process. He conceives the *inner* under its external form. The soul is an automaton, as is the body, with only this difference: the soul is a *spiritual* automation. (IV, 181)

For all the spirituality of the monads, for all their incorporeality and the lack of the properties of the "material atoms" (e.g., hardness, extension, etc.), they are still atoms.

The soul, which is the principle of unity in itself, is transformed into a principle of division, of discontinuity. However much the monad, as an ensouled atom capable of representation, stands to others in internal relations–(for otherwise the monad would lack any content, since it is essentially a mirror of all the others)–still the ghost of the atom stands between the monads, and prevents their real connection. They remain at a remove from each other, avoiding all immediate contact, in that one doesn't encroach upon or disturb the other in any way. Therefore, the monads don't know each other as they are in themselves, immediately. One doesn't perceive the other with the heart's eye, but only as phenomenon. The monads already have the Kantian distinction between *ansichsein* and *fureinandersein* in mind. The veil of matter obscures the monads from each other. (IV, 185)

Leibniz

The separation of the monads from each other is, in Feuerbach's view, mechanistic, in that their existence, for all their internal relatedness, is *merely* individual. The *appearance* of their relations to each other is inevitably phenomenal, therefore. It exists only as appearance to, or in, the monad, as one of its *perceptions*. The "preestablished harmony" does not save the situation, for Feuerbach sees it as a hypostatization of that which *ought* to have been established as *real* relations among the monads. According to Leibniz, says Feuerbach,

> God connects the monads with each other, not because he feels like it, not in consequence of some blind and empty act of will, but because it is in the very nature of the monads to be so connected, because it is an inner possibility of the monads themselves. . . . God is the pure activity (*actus purus*) which actualizes this inner ideal possibility. He is the universal essence of the monads, the unifying power which embodies the self-sufficiency and independence which the monads establish among themselves. But Leibniz sets this universal essence itself in the sphere of differentiation and division. He hypostatizes it as a *separate* Being, or Subject, so that it becomes (or at least appears as) an alien, external power, instead of an inner, essential one. . . . [Leibniz] confuses philosophical thought with the anthropomorphic representations of theology. (IV, 136)

Leibniz should have been a pantheist, says Feuerbach, in effect. He should somehow have *retained* the plurality of individual monads, but he should have given this plurality a deeper unity than the one that is provided by the preestablished harmony. Spinoza's substance was too abstract, too "hard," and lacked real "living" differentiation. On the other hand, mechanist atomism lacked "real" unity, and mechanism in general lacked an original source or principle of motion, which Leibniz's *vis viva* was to provide. Still, Leibniz remains a phenomenalist in physics, and an atomist in metaphysics. He substitutes for the inadequacies of "external relation" in Cartesian and in atomistic mechanism an equally mechanistically conceived "internal relation"; the fault here is to lose the *real* relations among the parts of matter in the phenomenal relations as they are represented in the monad's perception. Thus, Leibniz is caught in the paradoxical position of positing as *real beings* centers of force that *exist for each other only phenomenally*. Feuerbach's critique, in effect, is that Leibniz was not *enough* of an Idealist. Were the monads really spiritual or ideal entities, then their capacity for direct knowledge of each other would be ideally unlimited; that is, every monad would have the possibility of such immediate knowledge. But, then, were the monads really spiritual, they would not be *ultimately* many, but one, as Thought is ultimately one with its own object. Their *plurality* would not be their *essence*, as it is in Leibniz.

101

Feuerbach, at the end of the book, has a striking passage, in which he gives an "anthropological" translation of his basic critique of Leibniz's "individualism":

Nature doesn't only divide and distinguish; she also relates, connects. She doesn't only individuate. The individual is only existence; the type, the species is essence, however. And the significance of the atomistic discontinuity of individuals, of individual differences, and thus the very significance of the unique individual itself vanishes in the face of the significance of the type, of essence. Nature produces individuals *en masse*, in unlimited profusion, and the lower the type or species, the more individuals does nature produce. But a being loses its specific worth, its significance, its why and wherefore, in consequence of this profusion. It becomes an indifferent and mere existent. This indifference is in fact the anguish of the life of the individual, the source of its misery, its neediness; but therein also lies the inner impulse to activity. The goal of our life is to overcome the indifference of our individual existence. It is the force behind our behavior, the source of our virtues, as well as of our vices and inadequacies. Man strives to become something distinct; he strives to attain a qualitative worth, an essential significance; and this lies only in his being different, in his uniqueness with respect to his species, or his "Idea." But as a mere individual he loses himself as only one among the indistinguishable drops of water in the tedious stream of an indifferent multiplicity. Once a man loses the interests which his individual existence specifies, he becomes aware of the indifference of his mere individuality, and he loses the sense of difference between being and non-being. His present existence becomes loathsome. He ends with suicide, i.e. he negates his non-being. (IV, 186–7)

The monadic "individuals" have been anthropomorphized explicitly in this passage; the little souls have become humanized, in this "existential" account of human individuality. But the intent of this closing passage of the book is unclear. Unique individuality is, after all, the hallmark of the monad; it is never "mere" individuality, which loses its distinctness in the type, or species, for this would be *no* individuality at all. Strictly speaking, there is no "indifferent individual" in Leibniz's scheme, for insofar as it is indifferent (indiscernible as a *unique* individual) it is, in effect, *not* individual. Still, Feuerbach sees it as a *philosophical* necessity, that the "identity" or "'unity" of individuals be "deepened," that "Idealism be purged of the atomistic and sensory constituents with which it was still confused in Leibnizian philosophy" and that "the bright and vital polytheism of the Leibnizian monadology become transformed into the rigorous . . . monotheism of transcendental Idealism."

What keeps the monadology from this "deeper" unity is its own admission of the "confused perceptions" of the monads–really, its *empiricism*, its "confusion" of thought with perception and sensation; the form of the monadology is Idealist, in that Spirit is the only reality.

But Spirit is compromised, in that it is contaminated with atomism and empiricism, with an *ultimate* residual materialism—in the definition of matter as the veil that makes the perception of the monads unclear, that makes them less than infinite. These two are systematically connected, because the extent to which the monads fall short of perfect perception is the extent of their monadicity itself. Thus, "mere" individuality and a compromising materialism are linked as the two shortcomings of Leibniz's idealism.

What is interesting here is the retrospective realization that Feuerbach chooses precisely these two elements that he criticizes in Leibniz, as the cornerstones of his own later empirical materialism. The ambivalence of the passage on individuals is perhaps best understood as the conflict within Feuerbach himself, between the commitment to the tradition of transcendental idealism and its all-encompassing *Identity*, and the attraction of an individualism, which when translated into "human" terms, seemed to require the ultimacy of *uniqueness* as a condition for humanity.[3]

CRITIQUE OF EMPIRICISM: LEIBNIZ AND LOCKE

If Feuerbach's analysis and critique of Leibniz's monadology gives us the context for his later development of *individualism*, then his critique of empiricism in this same work gives us an even clearer insight into his own later empiricism. The occasion for this critique is Feuerbach's discussion of Leibniz's critique of Locke—specifically, of Locke's rejection of Descartes' *innate ideas*.

Feuerbach begins his critique of empiricism by marking a distinction between Leibniz's concept of soul, as it pertains to natural philosophy, and his concept of soul, as it pertains to thought, reason, spirit, self-consciousness.

> Whereas Leibniz parts company with Descartes in further developing the concept of soul, by incorporating in it what Descartes had placed outside of it, as matter—namely, that which is to be distinguished from will and consciousness; still, in the philosophy of the soul as spirit, Leibniz joins Descartes once more, so that in this respect he is nothing but a more thoroughgoing, more fully developed Descartes. (IV, 138)

What Leibniz has in common with Descartes is the distinction between that which the soul knows "in itself" and that which it comes to know through the senses; between the clarity, immediacy, and certainty of the first and the mediated, "veiled" character of empirical knowledge; in short, between *vérités de raison* and the *vérités de fait*. It is on the issue of *innate ideas* that Leibniz sides with Descartes against Locke's criticism.[4] Feuerbach points out that Locke admits the reflection of the mind on its own operations as a source of ideas, but that Locke gives this only a secondary significance, in that memory and abstraction, which are such operations of the mind, are ultimately dependent on the simplest ideas (i.e., those of perception). Within Locke's own framework, says Feuerbach, the doctrine of innate ideas is plainly invalid. But, he adds, this framework itself is Locke's limitation, the boundary of his philosophical vision.

[Locke] conceived of these Ideas, as he did all philosophical matters, only as an empiricist; he understood them only in their literal, "fleshly" sense. He was bound by the raw, sensory terms in which he finds the doctrine expressed. He was a critic, but only an external critic, not a self-critic, not critical with respect to his own method of inquiry and criticism. He didn't ask himself what the significance of the concept of innate ideas is, or what it could possibly mean. Nothing is simpler than to refute (or appear to refute), a philosophical idea or system, when one approaches it merely factually, and not genetically; when one deals only with what is explicitly stated, and not with what is left unstated and is implicit, as a subject for thoughtful analysis; when one fails to separate the idea from the expression of the idea. (IV, 139)

Thus, says Feuerbach, it is easy to refute the theory of innate ideas, if one takes them as Locke does. But the theory has a deeper significance in Leibniz. When I assent to another's claim to truth, the identity of my reason and his is affirmed. But to recognize such an identity is to recognize an a priori ground in reason itself for this concurrence, even when experience mediates this concurrence. The mediation by experience is only a *condition*, not the *genesis* or *source* of the concurrence. Feuerbach sums up with an example: "Without air, water, light and heat, the plant will not produce a flower. But just as it would be crudely false to claim that the flower could be derived merely from these, its physical conditions, it would be equally crude and false to consider the senses as the sources of ideas . . ." (IV, 140).

In the first volume of the *History*, Feuerbach had taken empiricism to task for "lacking a substantial concept as its principle," and claimed against it that it could not be a system, that where it was externally consistent, it was internally incoherent and untenable. He echoed Hegel here. Yet as early as 1835 and 1837 in his letters, Feuerbach had already expressed the view that what was needed was a broadened empiricism.[5] Here the shift begins to take place. The critique of empiricism is that *in its narrow form*, it is inadequate. But now the critique begins to take the form of a tentative reconstruction: What would be required of a viable empiricism? What characterization of sense perception and feeling would provide for an acceptance of the emphasis on the empirical sources of knowledge? How is thought, the "free activity of the spirit," to be related to experience?

These questions, which are to become central in Feuerbach's break with Hegelianism and Idealism, are taken up for the first time in the work on Leibniz. It is in Leibniz's own treatment of "perception" in the monadology that Feuerbach finds the dialectical issue of the relation of thought to experience, of perception to matter. Yet here the theoretical formulation is inverted: Leibniz is seen to be an inadequate rationalist-idealist in that his concept of the empirical, or the material, world is merely a negative one: Matter is the finitude, or the delimitation, of pure "perceptual" or thinking activity. The question here, therefore, is, "How can a rationalist idealism formulate an adequate, 'positive' concept of matter?" rather than the question Feuerbach is to raise later, "How can an empirical materialism formulate an adequate concept of thought or perception?"

Feuerbach's criticism of Leibniz is that the role of perception in the monads is seen to intrude on a consistent Idealist account of the metaphysical grounds of natural philosophy. What is at issue in natural philosophy is *not* simply the question of *empirical* knowledge of matters of fact, but rather the purely *rational* concepts of motion, force, matter. In other words, Feuerbach seems to hold that natural philosophy, or natural science (which he characterizes as "the material knowledge of the material"), is first and foremost a matter of the adequacy of *concepts* about the finite, but not a matter of empirical or factual knowledge itself. Therefore, natural philosophy is a rational (philosophical) and not an empirical study. In this sense, Leibniz's monads fall short of the rationalist ideal, in that matter and motion are merely limitations, phenomenal appearances of the individuated self-activity of the monads. Matter, motion, force are not properly raised to their ideational "reality," as pure concepts of reason, and therefore as proper objects of natural philosophy. However, in the philosophy of spirit, of the soul as knowing activity–a subject distinct from natural philosophy–Feuerbach finds himself constrained to introduce the empirical in a backhanded way, to insist on its inclusion there, but not in the "raw" form in which empiricism has done it.

The "inversion," in summary, is as follows. Leibniz reintroduces the material negatively, as the "limitation" of the spiritual, in the "confused perceptions" of the monads. He does this in order to overcome the dualism of Descartes' two substances. Feuerbach first applauds him and then takes him to task for not going far enough in completely subsuming matter under the form of Spirit, in a full-fledged transcendental Idealism. But where Leibniz becomes a Cartesian once again, in holding that the soul has innate ideas, knows itself "in itself" immediately, Feuerbach again applauds him, criticizes Locke, but then proceeds to insist on a reconstructed empiricism that relates sense perception itself to the "innate ideas."

Feuerbach's own commitment to empiricism and the direction of his critique of classical British empiricism are revealed in his discussion of Locke. In a very important passage, the outlines of a rationalist empiricism (or an empiricist rationalism) are sketched in a way that foreshadows Feuerbach's later development (in the *Critique of Hegelian Philosophy* and in the *Foundations of the Philosophy of the Future*).

> In the sense in which Locke understands, and rejects innate ideas, nothing is innate in us, neither our hands and feet, nor our senses, nor our body. Whatever I cannot utilize for the purpose it serves, simply is what it is in itself. What is beyond my power, is not mine. Only by means of exercise and use, by means of activity, does our body become our own. The child in swaddling clothes doesn't yet possess his hands, his bones, as his own. In Locke's sense, man is not born out of himself. He brings nothing into the world but hunger and thirst, i.e. an emptiness, *but an emptiness accompanied by the feeling of emptiness* [my stress, M. W.], with feelings of lack and discomfort and of the empty stomach; in short, an emptiness not devoid of a drive for fulfillment; for this drive, under normal conditions, . . . has the force and capacity in itself for that which it does not yet formally possess as its own.[6] (IV, 140–1)

Thus far, Feuerbach transforms "innate," whose original reference is to *ideas*, into a generalized concept of anything we have the *capacity* to possess as our own, by means of our use, or exercise of, this capacity. The generalized extension of the term "innate" could then conceivably be used to talk about the "innateness" of real property (land, for example), because we could be said to be born with a capacity to possess this, by our use or by our activity. In this broad sense, Feuerbach would be in disagreement neither with Locke nor with the young Hegel, in terms of a social theory of property, of the *appropriation* of what is mine, by the exercise of my "capacities" or "powers" (e.g., labor).[7] But Feuerbach means it here in a specifically restricted sense. He is talking, ostensibly, about sense perception and feeling, and attributing to *them* the intentionality, the conativity, the directiveness ordinarily reserved for thought or will. In other words, sense perception itself is active, not passive; and active in the classic Greek sense of having a *nature*, a *proper virtue*, a priori. Thus Feuerbach continues,

> Hunger and thirst are, all empiricists to the contrary, two *a priori* philosophers. They anticipate and deduce the existence of their objects *a priori*. They do not derive from the sense-experience of their desired objects, but rather precede this experience, and miss its presence, without having previously had

it and lost it. Thus the sensible itself is a process, a flux, and not a last instant, nor a static resting point, nor an unmediated beginning, nor that sufficient principle of explanation which the empiricist takes it to be–a dogma which constitutes the very essence of empiricism. The empiricist thinks he has explained the origin of ideas when he derives them from the senses. He cuts everything off at the sensible, he refuses to recognize any neediness in sensibility, any dependency, or need for further explanation. For the empiricist, the sensible is unmediated, self-evident, clear, distinct and real, in itself. Thus, he mistakes the conditions for the cause, the material for the formal, the passive for the active, and mistakes the active–i.e., the soul, the spirit–for the passive. . . . The perception of an object as external to me . . . is already a purely spiritual act, already constitutes consciousness, thought, albeit thought still delimited by sensory apprehension . . . in order to look and see, one must think. The eyes and ears of the animal have their essential function only with respect to self-preservation; they are the means of his defense, and the deliverers of his life-needs. But in man they have a higher function, distinct from and independent of the satisfaction of life-needs. They acquire a theoretical significance. The senses in man are fundamentally emanations of his theoretical capacities. Man is born to theory. The senses are the means of his knowledge; but they are means and are effective as means only on the presupposition of the existence of their inner purpose–the capacity for theoretical activity, thought. The senses illuminate the world for us; but their light is not their own. It comes from the central sun of the spirit. Wonder is the beginning of knowledge, but wonder doesn't derive from the senses; rather, it derives from the spirit mediated by the senses. (IV, 141–2)

Feuerbach thus states his critical appreciation of empiricism:

Woe to the philosopher who hasn't appropriated empiricism as an instrument, who bypasses the realm of mediate powers and causes; who comes with so-called philosophical deductions, which are presented as if they had divine necessity, to the place where a rational empiricism alone will suffice; who wants to demonstrate as a truth of reason that which rests on particular, temporal, finite grounds. But empiricism fails to recognize its limits when it presents itself as self-sufficient, and claims validity as a philosophy. Then, empiricism transforms condition into cause, and the mediate into the immediate, and the fundamental. Empiricism remains at the apparent, at the individual. The concept of unity, totality, essence, substance escapes it. Thus empiricism makes the conditional origin of concepts into their essential origin; it makes the ways in which particular concepts are formed–the modes of observation, reflection, abstraction, which are often arbitrary–into general, universal and necessary modes. But observation, abstraction and reflection already presuppose thought as their principle, and thought is not possible without immanent determinations, even if these are not yet presently and effectively conscious, explicit, formal concepts, even if thought itself begins not in the activity of thinking, but in the activity of apprehending. Concepts would never arise from sensory apprehension, if this latter were not already, in its nature, a spiritual, thinking sort of apprehension. Otherwise, we would have to derive concepts from nothing. Man begins in the unity of apprehension and thinking. His object is never the particular sensible object as particular and separate.

The discrimination of particularity, distinctness, generality is a later development. Man begins with the undifferentiated totality, with unconditional universality. . . . (IV, 143-4)

Feuerbach's conditional appreciation of empiricism as a *means*, of sense perception as a condition but not the cause of our knowledge, ends with a restatement of an explicit rationalist formulation of the "essential" nature of knowing activity. If Spirit is *essentially* Spirit, then it is of its essence that it is thinking activity. If thinking is essential to Spirit, then there are concepts or ideas that are *essential*; that is, they are identical with the Being of Spirit and cannot have their origin in the senses, no more than Spirit can, *if* it is essential. That it *is* essential, says Feuerbach, is the principle of Idealism: Spirit is independent being; in its essential activity it has *itself* as its own object, it is self-consciousness. It could not then derive its essential content from the senses, from observation and abstraction, but only from reflection on its own activity.

This idealist critique of empiricism rests on the notion that the "narrow" or "phenomenalist" form of empiricism–its inadequate form –cannot account for the knowledge based on sense perception. Such an empiricism is therefore blind, and in it, the relation of sensation to thought cannot be effected. In a striking anticipation of his own later empiricism, Feuerbach already provides, in the *Leibniz*, that formulation he is to develop in his 1842 work *Preliminary Theses Towards the Reform of Philosophy* and the 1843 sequel, *Principles of the Philosophy of the Future* (discussed fully in Chapter VII). "The senses in man acquire a theoretical significance; they are fundamentally emanations of his theoretical capacity. Man is born to theory. The senses are the means of his knowledge; they are means and are effective as means only on the presupposition of their inner purpose–the capacity for theoretical activity, thought" (IV, 142). So Feuerbach writes, in 1836, in his critique of empiricism. But this already contains the sense of his own later empiricism, which requires only that this "inner purpose," this "capacity for thought" be ascribed to the very nature of sensibility itself, or that the capacity for thought is a capacity of sensibility itself. The dependence of sensibility *on* thought, as it is expressed in this earlier work, is transformed later into a ramified, "adequate" empiricism in which thought is seen to be derived from, and to be immanent in, sensibility itself. In short, later, Feuerbach will come to pose the very condition of thought as its cause, thus compounding condition and cause.

In his discussion of Leibniz and Locke, Feuerbach thus approaches the limits of those "inadequate" concepts of individuality and sensibility that he is to surpass, in his break with idealism.

In the *Leibniz*, Feuerbach had carried his critique of scientific philosophy, of the conditions of natural knowledge to its limits. In the subsequent work that completes the trilogy on the history of philosophy, the book on *Bayle*, Feuerbach addresses himself to the critique of belief and to the distinction between knowledge and belief. In this work, he begins to formulate those ideas that eventuate in his major critique of religion, *The Essence of Christianity*, which appeared three years later, in 1841.

CHAPTER V

Critique of Belief: Leibniz and Bayle

If there is one central motif in Feuerbach's whole philosophical development it is the critique of belief. The most viable systematic reconstruction of Feuerbach's philosophic position is that which relates his analysis of idealism and empiricism, of science, of ethics and religion, and of
the developmental course of the history of philosophy itself to the central
concern with the nature of human belief. Feuerbach's first published
work (after the *Dissertation*, of course), and the one that, incidentally,
shut him off ultimately from the possibility of an academic career, was
a critique of the belief in personal immortality.[1] In the third of his historical studies, Feuerbach devotes the entire work to Pierre Bayle, a figure
who would certainly not deserve such attention in any orthodox historical account of philosophy. The centrality of Pierre Bayle, in Feuerbach's
ongoing study, is symptomatic of his own growing concern with the
distinction between rational thought and belief, for this in effect is the
theme of the study of Bayle.

This work was already foreshadowed in the *Leibniz*, in which the
issue of the nature of human belief is already discussed. The immediate
context of this initial discussion of the nature of belief in the *Leibniz*
is a discussion of the dualism of body and soul in Descartes, and its
sources in the conflict between skeptical reason and Christian dogma.
Feuerbach insists that though Descartes was a good Catholic in matters
of faith, there is no trace of this belief in the essential spirit of his
philosophy.

His moral theory is stoicism, his philosophy of spirit rests on a complete independence of the spirit from everything external, his philosophy of nature
is pure materialism. He bans teleology from physics, by means of a pretty thin
subterfuge, to be sure, as Leibniz has already pointed out. . . . His Catholicism

had no objective significance; it lacked the significance of his essential being, his spirit. It had only the significance of a personal matter of a private accommodation, of an accident, of a historical situation ... [in short] a significance which was not of interest to the spirit, or to science. (III, 173–4)

"Objective significance," for Feuerbach, is defined as that which is essential to one's being, and this, in turn, in Leibnizian terms, is identified with one's activity.

Activity is the being of substance, in general: a distinctive activity is the being of a distinctive substance. Your action is your truth, your being, your spirit and essence. Your real being is only your being for others, is only your good, which insofar as it is yours, is thereby a common good. Whoever divorces his activity from his essence is a spiritual criminal. Descartes' activity, however, was scientific knowledge. True, he cloaked himself in a holy appearance, in that he excluded the subject of belief from the realm of thought, taking Pascal's maxim as his own: "Everything which is an object of faith cannot be an object of reason, and can much less be submitted to reason." But this very exception shows that the spirit feels itself to be unclear here, and that its thinking stands in contradiction to its belief. Bacon says, "Render unto belief what belongs to it," in a paraphrase of "Render unto Caesar the things that are Caesar's." But what belongs to Caesar? Only that which is not of fundamental concern to your salvation, to your soul; but render unto God what is God's, i.e. your treasures, that which is dear to you, your soul. What do Bacon or Descartes render unto belief, however? However much they might give they do not give it, at any rate, their soul, their essence, their substantial interest; they do not render unto belief that which makes them historically significant persons, that which makes them what they are. (IV, 174–5)

Feuerbach takes this as a division of the spirit within itself. For what unity of the spirit demands is not an *accommodation* of faith and reason, but something more: an identity of faith and reason, of belief and thought. Anything short of this leaves the spirit in unease over the division. Thus, belief is no less a subject of philosophical understanding than is nature; moreover, a philosophy of the human spirit that accounts only for thought and not for belief is itself incomplete, and its view of man is therefore incomplete. Feuerbach appends a long note on Descartes, with respect to this issue, which explicates further the sense of split personality that is to play such a predominant role in Feuerbach's later critique of religion. He writes,

As a philosopher, Descartes was not a Catholic and as a Catholic he wasn't a philosopher. . . . Descartes was a thinker: the substantial concern of his life was knowledge. . . . But he excluded the belief of his church from this concern. . . . If one says, "Descartes was a good Catholic," then the question arises *which Descartes?* . . . Descartes is significant only as a philosopher. Only as such did he have effect in the world, and participate objectively in it; only as such does he still exist as a living person for us. . . . The history of philosophy doesn't know of a Descartes who was a Catholic. His Catholicism belongs only to his biography. . . . Descartes himself excluded belief from the domain of thought; he accepted his belief in an unconditional way, without thought or criticism or inquiry, as it was handed down to him. In this respect, he wasn't that Descartes who is of interest to us in the history of philosophy, and whom we always have in mind when we speak of him. In this respect, he was no more than any other *indoctus* and non-philosopher. . . . Thus, his Catholicism has no more significance, or value or weight than that of any other common, thinking person. It doesn't depend on philosophical conviction. In one word, his Catholicism . . . was no more than a birthmark. (IV, 287–90, n39)

What remains unclear in this characterization of the bifurcation of thought and belief is how this is related to *philosophical* dualism. If, indeed, Descartes the philosopher did *not* mix his religious beliefs with his philosophizing, then it would appear that the dualism of mind and body has no affinity whatever with the dualism of thought and belief, but arises only as a dualism *within* thought itself. Here a distinction between two kinds of belief, or two senses of "belief," is necessary, because Feuerbach uses the term in both senses; and yet only one of these is compatible with reason, on Feuerbach's view. The dualism of thought and belief, which is an *essentially* incompatible dualism, is that between thought as essentially critical-rational, and therefore essentially anti-dogmatic, and belief as received dogma, as justified by authority. In Feuerbach's earlier characterizations of belief, in his discussion of Böhme and Luther, for example, he had linked belief to the activity of feeling, desiring, and needing and to the concrete, sensate, and affective life in which beliefs are the human responses to the witness of our present experience. In short, this latter sense of "belief" may be characterized as *witness*, rather than as *authority*, and as such it has neither the rigidity nor the articulated rational *form* of authoritative belief. Here, in the context of this criticism of Descartes' "belief," he is dealing with "belief" not as *witness*, then, but as *authority*. This is attested to by Feuerbach's substitution, in this discussion, of "dogma" for "belief," in several places. Such "dogmatic" belief cannot, in principle, be brought into unity with reason, and so the only *critique* one can bring to bear on such dogmatic or authoritative belief is the negative criticism that skepticism and rational analysis affords–that is, debunking criticism. Feuerbach does recognize that this is only the beginning of a full philosophical critique of belief, but that this is not yet the "positive," philosophical critique of the essential function of belief in human life, nor yet an examination of its *grounds*, in psychological-anthropological terms. He writes,

> Belief is recognized by the modern philosophers, but receives only that recognition which a man grants his wife, once they have been separated in their inner life–i.e. the recognition accorded her as a person entitled to certain rights. It

is not a recognition of love, or unity, but a recognition of mere toleration and accommodation. . . . It was therefore a necessary development that this internal alienation and separation of belief and reason come to open expression as a direct contradiction, as it did in the work of the acute and learned Pierre Bayle. Bayle recognized as a weakness of human understanding, that it was capable only of negating, contradicting and perplexing, therefore thrust himself vigorously against belief, holding that it was the very essence of dogma to contradict reason.[2]

So bifurcated is man that he affirms–or at least imagines he can affirm–in belief what he directly denies in reason!–a split in man, a contradiction which will remain . . . as long as there is a necessity to base religion on an external, miraculous revelation, alien to man; so long as religion is not recognized as man's own true essence, as identical with his reason. (IV, 175)

What exactly this identity of religion and reason is remains for Feuerbach's later writings to explain. In 1841, the *Essence of Christianity* was first published, and by then the outlines of Feuerbach's "resolution" were already clear. But the *Leibniz* already contains, in an as yet unclear and epigrammatic form, the kernel of this program. The more immediate context suggests only that dogmatic belief acts as a constraint on the unity of thought with itself and prevents the achievement of an all-coherent rational system, in the philosophies of both Descartes and Leibniz. But Feuerbach never clearly shows how it does so in Descartes, except to suggest that the dualism of spirit and matter, soul and body is concomitant with the dualism of thought and belief. He says only that "the expression of the Idea is in every instance the expression of the time in which it comes to be expressed, and therefore it is always encumbered by the predominating categories of that particular time" (IV, 172). This seems a fairly innocuous truism, of a Hegelian sort. But the specific content Feuerbach gives it is to point to mechanism and dualism as the predominating categories of the period under consideration, and to see the two as inseparable, because the only relation between body and soul that is conceivable under these categories is that of mechanical connection. In respect to body-mind dualism, then, its specific form is seen to be related to the predominant mechanistic model. But nowhere does he show a parallel "mechanistic" interpretation of the dualism of thought and belief. He places the two dualisms side by side, without any clear indication of *how* they are related–only *that* they are related:

This dualism reveals itself on the one hand in the unmediated opposition between spirit and matter, which was expressed in Cartesian philosophy, from which it spread and became characteristic of the general learned culture of the time; on the other hand, and most eminently, this dualism revealed itself in the inner opposition of spirit with itself, in the opposition of belief and reason–a conflict which had already made its temporary appearance in the Middle Ages, but which comes to the full light of day only at the beginning of the modern period, with the reawakening of the sciences. (IV, 172)

Feuerbach is disappointing here, because what we are led to expect is an analysis that would show the pervasiveness of the mechanistic model in both dualisms. However, only the *formal* similarity remains, between the dualism of spirit with that which is not-spirit (mind and body) and the dualism "within spirit itself" (thought and belief). Both are *dualisms*, but one may argue that both are two aspects of the *same* dualism only by showing the common ground of both. Feuerbach intimates that there is such a ground but does not carry the analysis through.

In his context, then, belief (as dogmatic belief) merely delimits the range of the free inquiry of reason; it marks off a domain beyond which reason's competence is not permitted. Thus, reason and belief constitute a dualism of mutually antagonistic elements with spirit. Under such conditions, says Feuerbach, and so long as belief was a "dominant power," reason could pursue only "a *formal*, not a *fundamental* mode of inquiry, as in the period of scholasticism and of Protestant orthodoxy" (IV, 176).

This is Feuerbach's historical explanation of why reason's fullest development was in "the quiet realm of mathematics and physics, where it avoided direct confrontation with the subject matter of belief" (IV, 176). This is an odd view with respect to physics, and especially odd because Feuerbach had earlier noted that the development of the sciences themselves was the most direct challenge to orthodox belief and that the emphasis on a quantitative, mechanist world view stemmed directly from the discoveries in physics and astronomy. Feuerbach's view has some cogency here, in that the prerequisite that mechanism imposed was the separation of physics from teleology and theology and the demarcation between belief and rational thought that was the very condition for the relatively free development of mathematical physics. In this sense, the "quiet realm" was kept quiet by that very "accommodation" that Feuerbach sees as a tentative solution at best, putting off, on grounds of expediency, a "direct confrontation." Descartes, keeping Galileo's and Bruno's fate in mind, was a master at skirting the issue, and Feuerbach recognizes this.

The effect of the "split" between belief and rational thought on Leibniz was unfortunate, according to Feuerbach:

Leibniz's great genius was not fortunate enough to belong to a period in which spirit was at one with itself. He belongs to the age in which spirit was sundered in the dualism of belief and reason. Bayle is his contemporary.[3] The character which the thinking spirit bears, under the dominion of Christian orthodoxy is therefore impressed on him. His philosophy has the general fault of remaining an inhomogeneous whole, of failing to attain its full realization in a resolute, independent and self-sufficient integrity. Theology always thwarts him, spoils his best thought, and keeps him from pursuing the deepest problems to their fullest resolution. Where he should continue his philosophical quest, he breaks off instead. Where he requires metaphysical elucidation, so that his thought can attain to its metaphysical expression, he disseminates theological ideas; and conversely, where theological ideas are at the basis of his thought, he elaborates, delimits and emends them only with additional metaphysical considerations. (IV, 176–7)

Feuerbach finds this inhomogeneity in the *Monadology* itself, in particular in the relation between the individual monads and the infinite monad–that is, God. "The image of an absolute, extramundane Will, outside and beyond the nature of things still lurks behind Leibniz's back, despite the efforts he makes to get rid of it," says Feuerbach. And it is this image of an unlimited Will that wreaks havoc with any attempt at a rational system, for under such a will, all things are possible, and where all things are possible, the distinction between rationality and absurdity is lost, and the principle of reason itself is jeopardized. Reason remains in control, holds the initiative, only as long as the limits of rationality are not transcended by some limitless, all-powerful Will. Feuerbach sees the concept of an absolute Will as the creation of human imagination, and as an incursion upon the principle of reason. In this respect, says Feuerbach, Spinoza is the true founder of modern philosophy, in that he explicitly rejected such a notion and systematically explained its origin in human feeling and in the imagination as an anthropomorphic projection of human will and desire. Leibniz succeeds only in "restricting the demon of arbitrary will; he doesn't rid himself entirely of it" (III, 181). This accounts for the gaps, the "interstices" in his philosophy. Still, says Feuerbach, Leibniz is to be honored for having gone as far and as deeply as he did, considering the time in which he worked and its predominating dualistic categories.

The work on Pierre Bayle,[4] which followed the *Leibniz* by one year, is a strange one. It is a transitional work, both philosophically and stylistically. It is the third volume, ostensibly, of a multivolume *History of Philosophy*. Yet whereas the first volume, *The History of Modern Philosophy from Bacon to Spinoza*, was a work whose very structure and title proclaimed its systematic orientation, the third abandoned the attempt at systematic exposition, and followed, both in form and content, the *anti*systematic proclivities of the book's subject, Bayle himself. Bayle was Leibniz's contemporary, not merely historically but also *dialectically*. Yet Bayle was not a critic, nor a commentator on Leibniz's work. Bayle's major work, the *Dictionnaire Historique et Critique* (1697), which was the bible of preenlightenment skepticism, preceded by many years Leibniz's most important systematic work. The dialectical contemporaneity of Leibniz and Bayle lies, then, in some deeper relation than that of mutual philosophical criticism. Feuerbach sees this relation in the "spirit of the age," that division between reason and dogmatic belief that bedeviled philosophy and kept it from the ideal unity of spirit that is the appropriate condition of reason.

What drove Feuerbach to devote an entire monograph to the "acute and learned skeptic" was the occasion itself: Feuerbach was ready to try out, in tentative fashion, the ideas that later came to full fruition in the *Essence of Christianity*. More and more clearly, as the discussion of belief in the *Leibniz* already shows, Feuerbach saw his *philosophical* task as the critique of philosophy itself, and the open wound of the reason-belief dichotomy was the place to begin. Feuerbach, still not ready for the attack on philosophy itself and upon Hegelian philosophy in particular, turns to that weakness in philosophy that he had begun to criticize in Leibniz: its inconsistency with regard to the realm of belief, its lack of *philosophical* analysis of this forbidden topic. Bayle serves Feuerbach well, in this context. For just as Bayle is not prepared to level a systematic critique, neither is Feuerbach. Just as Bayle focuses primarily on the negative critique of dogmatic, theological belief, so too does Feuerbach. Feuerbach characterizes Bayle's philosophy as a *Gelegenheits-philosophie* (philosophy for the occasion), and there is no more apt characterization of Feuerbach's monograph itself. It is a work written for the occasion, a *Gelegenheits-Buch* – the occasion being Feuerbach's own transition from *Geschichtlich-systematische Darstellung* in the classic tradition of Hegel, to free-swinging and original philosophical criticism. It is an experimental book, for all its exposition of Bayle's own writings – more experimental, less self-conscious and didactic than the *Leibniz* and the *History*. Feuerbach also says of Bayle that "he had, so to speak, no metaphysical patience" (more colloquially than the translation permits: "*Er hat, so zu sagen, kein metaphysisches sitzfleisch*" [V,335]), and, indeed, neither does Feuerbach. He progressively becomes disenchanted with idealist metaphysics and thinks he has discovered its secret. The work on Bayle has been characterized by Rawidowicz as Feuerbach's "Confessional of 1838." Rawidowicz's comment is that, "The name 'Bayle' is here to a certain extent a pseudonym for Feuerbach himself, a disguise for his gradually ripening naturalism" (Rawidowicz, L.F., p. 63). The disguise is not much of a disguise, for Feuerbach makes no attempt to have Bayle speak for him. Rather, it is clear that he is using Bayle's views as the occasion to state his own more fully and explicitly. The work is loosely constructed, and Feuerbach permits much more discursive leeway than he did in the first two volumes of the *History*.

The significance of the *Bayle* is that it gives Feuerbach the opportunity to formulate, in a fuller way, the question of the dichotomy between reason and belief. What this amounts to is (1) a close examination of Christian belief, in its specifics, and the beginning of that analysis of theology that was to be the cornerstone of *The Essence of Christianity*; (2) an examination of the strife between thought and belief in the specific terms of the strife between theology and the natural sciences; and (3) an examination of the relationship between an ethics based on religion and an autonomous ethics.

It may be useful to show the several senses in which Feuerbach had already used the term "belief" and also to indicate the broader sense in which he uses it thereafter. In sequence, there is first that "primitive" form of belief that is not *Glauben* but *Alberglauben, superstition*. Its general form is animism and anthropomorphism of the naturalistic sort, which reads human meanings into natural events. The development of this into supernaturalistic animism then divorces such meaningful events from nature and ascribes them to supernatural beings. This, roughly, is the condition of belief of the so-called pagan world view, of mythology as Feuerbach discusses it at the outset of the *History*. Christianity literally brings this *mythos* back to earth in the body of Christ, but in its spiritualized, denaturalized form, as it develops theologically the concept of the absolute divorce between the spirit and the flesh, the union of which then becomes a mystery. If belief is then primarily dealt with in terms of *religious* belief, and this religion itself is defined in terms of this or that institutionalized religion, then it is institutional dogmas, the assertions of the theologians, that ultimately become the principal objects of belief. Such *authoritative* or *dogmatic* religious belief is the one that Feuerbach discusses in the *Bayle*. Still, he had already indicated that belief, in its fundamental and genetic sense, was an intrinsic human phenomenon, not to be constrained within its historically limited modes of expression. Therefore, what Christian belief has suppressed, in its dogmatic form, is that belief that is in unity, not in contradiction, with reason, that is, a fully rational belief, stripped of its irrational form. This apparent paradox remains unresolved as long as Feuerbach does not yet provide a theoretical account of the nature and genesis of belief in man, and the *Bayle* shows this tension. But in the *Bayle*, also, the first tentative proposals for such a theory are present. What does not emerge clearly until later is the view that idealist metaphysics is itself a rarefied, abstract form of theology, that it is also the old devil, religious belief, now masquerading in rational form, but with an ultimately irrational content. The view that belief stands over and opposed to reason, that it is *au fond* irrational, is, at this point in Feuerbach's rational-idealist view, a completely pejorative characterization. Later, Feuerbach is to invert this evaluation, in the course of discovering the foundations of belief in man's own drive to self-knowledge, and in his empirical-affective experience, rather than in his "pure" thinking activity. In the sense that these contrary strains are present in the vivid and polemical discussion in the *Bayle*, the work can be viewed as an internal dialogue: Feuerbach contra Feuerbach. Rawidowicz considers it still the work of a Hegelian, though he says that it cannot be considered a philosophical work, in the sense that it does not come to grips with metaphysical or epistemological issues (Rawidowicz, L.F., pp. 64–5). Superficially, Rawidowicz is right. But in terms of any genetic analysis (in Feuerbach's own terms), the work has more than a superficial philosophical interest, and more than the interest of the personal reflection of himself, which Feuerbach sees in Bayle. The context in which he comes to deal with the metaphysical and epistemological issues in his later work is prepared here.

THE ESSENCE OF CHRISTIAN BELIEF: THE OPPOSITION OF THE SPIRIT AND THE FLESH

Feuerbach's opening sentence in the *Bayle* continues the critique of dualism begun in the *Leibniz*, but it does so in the context not of philosophic, but rather of religious dualism. "Unity was the essence of classical paganism; dualism, bifurcation is the essence of classical Christianity" (V, 113). The whole passage is instructive for many reasons, not the least of which is Feuerbach's distinction between belief as *human* phenomenon and Christian belief.

Certainly, there are many oppositions to be discovered in the pagan world view–where indeed would one *not* find oppositions?–and in consequence, plenty of struggle, suffering and evil. But these oppositions were necessary, these struggles were organically grounded, these sufferings and evils natural and unavoidable ones. But Christianity added superfluous evils to the unavoidable evils, added soul-tearing transcendental struggles to the necessary, immanent struggles, added the sufferings of the soul to bodily suffering, and to the natural oppositions added *unnatural* ones–the bifurcation of God and world, of heaven and earth, of Grace and Nature, of Spirit and Flesh, of Belief and Thought. The struggle between Church and State was only the external, political expression of an immanent opposition in mankind itself. Where man is one with himself, his world cannot fall apart into two worlds. The characteristic inner strife of the Christian world in the Catholic age was

118

specifically the opposition of Nature and Grace, sensibility and super- or anti-sensibility, humanity and holiness–in short, in the Church's own language, the opposition of flesh and spirit. (V, 113–14)

The highest virtue, according to Catholic Christianity, continues Feuerbach, is the rejection of all worldly goods and desires, the repression of all natural drives.

The specific virtue of Catholicism, the anti-natural and supernatural virtue was–and in truth still is–not love, however much this is rhetorically praised –for nature hasn't implanted hate in man, but only an inclination to love,–not belief, for man has a strong natural tendency to belief–none of these! Only chastity, or, more strictly speaking, virginity, spinsterhood, for which there is no natural inclination; on the contrary, against which Nature provides us with an opposite, and most powerful drive. Belief is easy, love is easier still, but chastity is hard. Neither belief nor love is superhuman, but chastity is. The concept of sacrifice is the highest concept of Catholicism. But what sacrifice is greater, for the natural human being, than the sacrifice to chastity, to virginity? Heaven is the final and only goal of Catholicism. But what virtue makes man heavenly and makes him the equal of the angels, and angel-pure even here on earth? Chastity. (V, 114)

The spirit, the tone of Feuerbach's writing is completely changed here. It is as if he were freed from the constraints of an academic language, from the demands of expositional scholarship, from the crabbedness of metaphysical analysis. Indeed, it is as if Feuerbach had found his *métier*–he was "home" again, in the precincts of theology and dogmatics, but not as a chastened prodigal son. Feuerbach gives full rein to his negativism and utilizes his theological training and his broad readings as a weapon in the argument. He marshals the evidence from the writings of the Church Fathers, from Augustine, from Hieronymus, from Albertus Magnus, from Peter Lombard, from Saint Anthony, from Dante, from Pope Leo X, from St. Ignatius Loyola, from St. Benedict. The thesis is then established: Catholicism, as the primary form of Christian belief, is founded on the negation, the repression of the flesh. Is it, then, by contrast, the affirmation of the spirit? Here, too, Feuerbach sees it as a compromised spiritualism. Catholic learning was encouraged, in the monasteries and cloisters. But insofar as it embodied a real drive to scientific knowledge, it was really anti-Catholic. Learning "was nurtured by Catholics, but not by them as Catholics, but as human beings thirsting to know, in contradiction to the true essence of Catholicism. Whoever would deny this would also have to deny that the combination of Aristotelianism with Catholicism is a contradiction–whereas in fact it is the clearest, most glaring of contradictions" (V. 121).

True science begins, says Feuerbach, only where the scientific spirit emerges from the cloisters, and is taken up by free men "who weren't constrained to hide the light of science under the bushel of belief" (V, 122).

Once the attack has been launched and its strategic goals made clear, Feuerbach goes on to characterize Protestant belief in the same broad terms.

The contradiction between Catholicism and the essence of man was the internal cause of the Reformation. Protestantism resolved the false opposition between flesh and spirit. With singing and joyous music, it led man from the church-graveyard of Catholicism back to his civic and human life. And first of all, it rejected celibacy as a Godless, despotic dogma which contradicted one of the natural rights of man. But Protestantism freed and rescued man only on the practical, and not on the theoretical or intellectual side. The higher claim, the right of the drive to knowledge, the claim of reason was not recognized or satisfied by Protestantism. Reason remained imprisoned in the old barbarism, in this regard, and Protestantism set up articles of faith in contradiction to reason, and insisted on their truth. (V, 123)

The essential conflict between *any* form of religious dogma and theology, on the one hand, and reason, science, philosophy, on the other, is that the first is of necessity bound to the particular and has no fundamentally theoretical, but only a practical interest, whereas the second is by its nature universal, and theoretical—that is, has no other interest, or constraint, but that of "truth as such." The critique that "universal" Christianity was seen to have leveled at the ethnically and locally limited pagan world view, in Feuerbach's account in the first volume of the *History*, is now turned against Christianity itself. However "universal" Christianity claims to be, it is nonetheless "Christian," that is, dogmatic, theological, and thus *essentially* in conflict with the spirit of science.

For theology, science is only a means to the end of belief. It urges upon science an impure, servile sense, contradictory to the spirit of science. The scientific spirit is the universal spirit, the nameless spirit—not Christian, but also not pagan. There is no such thing as Christian and Pagan mathematics, no Christian and Pagan logic, psychology, metaphysics, no Christian and Pagan philosophy. A philosophy which takes itself to be Christian and is Christian, is on this very count a deficient, limited philosophy which is in contradiction to the concept of philosophy. Philosophy is not cosmogony or theogony—it is neither Hesiodic nor Homeric, nor mythical, nor Aristotelian nor Platonic. It is instead the science of the calm spirit, of logico-metaphysical principles, of the laws which rule both nature and man. But these laws are eternal and change-less. They rule the Christian world today no less than they did the pagan world. Theology, however, is essentially *Christian* theology; its principle is not *truth as such*, but *Christian* truth—i.e., what is Christian is true. Thus its essence is not universality but particularity. (V, 135–6)

Feuerbach further characterizes the conflict of theology and the "calm spirit" of philosophy by the qualities of the *character* of the two opposed views: "Love, truth, humanity, the spirit of universality were always found on the side of the scientific man. Hate, lies, intrigue, heresy-hunting, and the spirit of particularity, on the theological side" (V, 137). This black-and-white characterization tends to polemical journalism. It is as if Feuerbach were permitting himself, finally, that "negativity" that he ascribes to Bayle. The important philosophical point is often blurred by the wide-swinging polemic, but it is ultimately clear: Religion itself, and therefore theology too, is bound by the subjectivity, the particularity, and the historical concreteness of human needs; it follows the dictates of man's practical concerns. Religion cannot be objective, because its essence is subjectivity; it cannot be universal, because the interests it serves are ever partial, particular, conditioned by this or that concrete historical circumstance; it cannot be science because it is ideology. In all of these senses, religion cannot be *philosophical*, nor can it abide a truly philosophical point of view, because "philosophy is the science which represents, in its clearest form, the spirit of science as such" (V. 138); and this is why, according to Feuerbach, theology congenitally *hates* philosophy, as the generalized and most accessible means of expressing its hatred for science.

It is only out of fear or lack of acquaintance with the spirit of the other [separate] sciences that the theologian who brings his hatred to bear against philosophy doesn't extend it to the other sciences as well. If he followed the letter of the law, and if he were militant, he would have to extend his hatred thus, for the Bible says, "Who is not with me, is against me." But then, Physics, Astronomy, Botany, Physiology, Anatomy, Jurisprudence–all, in the sense of the true believer, not being *for* Christ, are therefore *against* Christ. . . . Indeed, where does free-thinking find its source, if not in these sciences? They are not Christian sciences–therefore they are anti-Christian sciences. (V, 138)

Feuerbach qualifies this charge by ascribing such a view to "the most orthodox theologians," or "the really theological theologians." The force of this is to claim that any theologian who did not take this orthodox essentialist view was less than theological in proportion to his "backsliding" on this issue. What is interesting about this sort of exclusive essentialism is that Feuerbach adopts the *either/or* of "orthodox theology" as his own truth. If the theologian, insofar as he is *essentially* a theologian, finds the objective universality of science incompatible with the *essential* concrete subjectivity of religion, then Feuerbach as an equally essentialist spokesman for the objectivity of science finds theology incompatible with science.

This is a vague and rhetorical argument as it stands. Still, it is a framework, and it is within this framework that the more detailed and concrete arguments are brought forth. If the charge *against* theology is its very concreteness and "subjectivity," it is a charge merely against the theological claim to theoretical (i.e., universal) truth, not against concreteness or against subjectivity. Feuerbach's argument is the paraphrase of Bayle's: Science needs to be free from dogmatic authority if it is to be science at all. Scientific reason stands in utter contradiction not so much to the claims of theology, in matters of fact, but to the foundation of theology itself. This foundation Feuerbach takes to be *essentially* the belief in *miracles*. For it is the *miracle* that is the focus of that concept of God's will as arbitrary and absolutely efficacious, and of God as essentially willful. To the question of *why* the spirit of theology is opposed to the spirit of science and of philosophy, Feuerbach answers that the primary principle of this opposition is that theology is founded on the miracle, whereas philosophy is founded on "the nature of things": "The foundation of philosophy is reason, the mother of lawfulness and necessity, the principle of science; whereas the foundation of theology is the will, that asylum of ignorance–in short, the principle opposed to science: that of arbitrariness" (V, 150). Against the argument that God can be conceived as *other* than willful, and particular, or local, Feuerbach holds that

> The God of theology is a special, particular God–whoever denies this denies theology, denies its characteristic essence. He is not a God of the universe, a universal God. This latter God, who is not personal, who is not of the male, but of the neuter gender,[5] who has no proper name but only a class-name –such a God is the God of the philosophers–that hated, chimerical, merely intellectual, pantheistic God, who exists only in thought–just as the universe exists for us only in thought, and not as an object of the heart's feelings. . . . (V, 230)

But how can there be a God of the philosophers? If He is not an object of the human imagination (i.e., an anthropomorphic God), then He fails to be an object of belief. Belief requires a representation of its object in terms of the concrete and particular imagery of human experience. The "God" of the philosophers is, in effect, an empty shell, a name without reference, nothing. "Belief cannot make do with this 'nothing,' because belief requires an image, or it becomes a belief in nothing" (V, 231).

Thus, in Feuerbach's view, God either is an object of feeling or is nothing. Only that which can be represented in the concrete imagery of the human imagination, only the particular (i.e., the personal, anthropomorphic God) can be such an object. Insofar as the "philosopher's God" is an object of *rational* knowledge, He is *nothing*–an empty name. Two conclusions follow: First, because science is, paradigmatically, rational knowledge–knowledge of universal concepts–there can be no *science* of the particular; insofar as theology claims to be a science, it has no object; insofar as it claims to have an object (as a "science"), it cannot be that which is the object of belief. Second, insofar as *philosophy* deals with the predicates of its "philosopher's God" (e.g., justice, goodness, rationality, etc.), these are predicates without a subject, or predicates whose subject is merely a name, exhausted in its significance by these predicates. The philosopher's "God," as an object of philosophy, is nothing *but* these predicates, which, strictly speaking, ought then to be taken autonomously. The study of such "predicates" is then to be taken as an autonomous study, *not* as a part of theology. There can, of course, be a science of *belief*, but not of the *objects* of belief. Such a science would explain the grounds for belief and analyze the forms of belief, the genesis and the significance of these forms, the relation between belief and reason, and so on. *Such a science is anthropology.* In the *Bayle*, Feuerbach had already tentatively proposed the broad thesis of his later critique of religion: the study of religious belief and of its theological formulation as a study not of the divine nature, but of human nature. Fichte's dictum "Give me the man's God, and I will tell you what kind of a man he is" is taken by Feuerbach in a sense more literally, and more profoundly perhaps, than Fichte intended.

This theme, to be the leitmotif of the later *Essence of Christianity*, finds variations in the *Bayle* that Feuerbach did *not* pursue later, but that are of signal interest. What effect, asks Feuerbach, does the *theological* conception of God have on the natural scientist? What is the interplay of a theological conceptual framework and concrete scientific practice? Though the study of the history of science was not yet developed, Feuerbach grasps the importance of this question in an original, though fragmentary way. He considers it in terms of the question of the natural piety of the scientist, and how this is articulated in terms of current theology. He considers the question first by means of an analogy to the relation between religious and aesthetic attitudes:

An art lover, who also happens to be a pious man, will prefer paintings of religious subjects to those of secular subjects. But if our good man were to say that he owns, and views such paintings only out of religious interest, he would be lying. Certainly, he has a religious interest; but he also has an aesthetic interest, which has its own independent grounds, and is an interest which can be shared by a free-thinker or a pagan as well. That our man owns these particular paintings is due to his religious sense; but that he owns paintings at all, and beautiful paintings at that, is due to his aesthetic sense. The love of beauty in general is his strongest motivation; the religious sense only determines the sort of artistic subjects he will prefer. . . . Render unto religion the things that are religion's, but render unto Art the things that belong to it! (V, 143)

The analogy is to the relation between the scientific and religious interests of the natural scientists (or more accurately, the "natural philosophers") of the seventeenth and eighteenth centuries. The scientific interest, insofar as it constitutes an attitude, and embodies the feelings of the scientist toward his subject matter, is a natural interest—that is, a natural piety or sense of wonder concerning the object of his inquiry *in itself*. Yet the quality of this wonder will affect the *kind* of things in nature that the scientist is interested in. Here, then, Feuerbach wants to show how a particular religious conception, a particular theological framework, limits and distorts the deep-seated sense of wonder, and thus limits the range and quality of the scientist's interest. Feuerbach writes,

Basically . . . the sense of wonder about supernatural power and goodness exhibited in nature is nothing but the sense of wonder about the object in and for itself, which is tied up with the religious conception only externally, subjectively, in the feelings of the observer. This sense can also be experienced independently of the religious conception, however. And precisely because there is no necessary connection between the object of wonder and the divine properties, the representation of the object in terms of such properties merely marks the diversion from nature, the subordination of the object under the general form of a Creature, under which form it then loses that interest which alone makes it an object of scientific inquiry. As exceptional as were the natural scientists of the 17th and 18th centuries, in their way; as untiring as they were in their zeal, as rich in discovery of techniques and experiments to cast light upon nature; yet the spirit of their study of nature, as a whole, was a limited one: namely, observation of the particular. Theology, with its belief in miracles, with its ideas of a supernatural, otherworldly, personal God, governing nature according to his pleasure, ruling it as if it were a machine—this theology alienated mankind from nature, and robbed it of the capacity to feel and to think in sympathy with nature. Instead of feeling a homeward pull, a kindred sense of the essence of nature, the majority of these scientists had a feeling of surprise, of bewilderment concerning this puzzling being. Instead of a deep-rooted sense of wonder, it was a sort of astonishment, a mere inquisitiveness which drove them to the investigation of nature. And therefore, their attention was especially attracted by *curiosities*, and exceptional phenomena. *As nature appeared to their God, so it appeared to them: a mere machine* [my stress, M. W.]. Robert Boyle and Christian Sturm even wanted to ban the word *Nature* as a pagan fiction. Whoever believes in a God external to nature will never be on intimate terms with nature. . . . So it was with the early natural scientists. The idea of God, as theology represented it, was the limit, the boundary of their spirit; therefore, the representation of a spiritless, external fitness of nature. (V, 144–6)

The scientific spirit, the "calm spirit" whose touchstone is universality, is not something that arises suddenly, as a revelation. Feuerbach's view is not that of a simpleminded positivism. Rather, scientific rationalism is an achievement, and its development is marked by a struggle to free it, in its conceptual foundations, from the limiting and distorting frameworks in which it is historically embedded. In its still fundamentally theological framework, the science of the seventeenth and eighteenth centuries was, to some extent, still caught in the toils of a Christian attitude toward nature. Even the appearances of rationality (i.e., of system and of necessity in the workings of the world machine) are deceptive veils for an ultimately theological (i.e., an anthropomorphic) perspective. One prime instance of this is teleology.

Teleology appears to have the virtue of calling attention to the rational element in nature. But this is only an appearance, which one shouldn't permit to deceive him. God's wisdom and understanding were conceived only in their subjective significance, only by analogy to practical human understanding, which exhibits purpose and goal-orientation in its use of things, which are in themselves in fact entirely indifferent. (V, 149)

Feuerbach's conditions for freeing the concept of nature from such anthropomorphism are (1) a rejection of teleology in nature and (2) an autonomous, objective formulation of the concept of necessity, as the foundation for a truly scientific rationalism. Thus, the limited rationalism which still conceives necessity under its anthropomorphic form of the realization of purpose needs to be supplanted. If nature, as object of inquiry, is to be taken in its autonomous form, then whatever necessity is exhibited in nature must be conceived as its own, "indifferent" necessity, as the function of its own "inner life." This concept of an autonomous natural necessity was already formulated, says Feuerbach, in the philosophy of Bruno and of Spinoza, "the only ones who had any conception of the inner life of nature (and who preserved this idea in its purity)" (V, 149). Thus, Feuerbach estimates the importance of Spinoza's rejection of teleology, his characterization of God's will as the asylum of ignorance, as one of the critical foundations of modern science. However, the explicit formulation of the concept of natural necessity he credits to Descartes. The passages in the *Bayle*, in appreciation of Cartesian mechanism, are in striking contrast to his earlier critique of Descartes' dualism. In the *History*, Feuerbach had extolled Baconian "qualitative empiricism" as the beginning of a scientific philosophy; he now harks back to an older theme, presented now in a new variation. Empiricism is not at issue here; rationalism is. More specifically, the historic task is to free rationalism from its theological husk, and to formulate the idea of necessity in an autonomous way. Strangely enough, it is not mathematical necessity which Feuerbach takes as the paradigm of natural necessity in Descartes, but rather Descartes' theory of automatism of animals. Feuerbach rejects this theory. But he sees its historic role as the achievement of nonanthropomorphic objectivity—in the literal sense of seeing the object as an "other," and not under the projected form of the self. Feuerbach's argument runs thus:

The real accomplishment of Descartes' philosophy, in a material sense, was to turn back the study of nature to the concept of mechanism, i.e. to clear and distinct concepts, to the examination of natural, determinate causes in general. Though the extension of this principle to everything turned out to be one-sided and unproductive in its later development, yet in its initial statement the skeleton, the foundation of natural science was established. No matter how much the concept of animals as machines contradicted man's oldest convictions, no matter how much unlettered or superficially (or at least one-sidedly) cultured people still laugh at this idea of Descartes', even today, . . . still, this mechanistic conception of the nature of animals, so apparently contradictory, was the first step towards the proper recognition of their nature. It was an advance which, at one blow, undermined all superstitions in natural science, and set it on entirely new foundations, rejecting the previously accepted view which conceived of animals as willful and purposive, in the image of the rules of intelligent human activity. Previously, man took himself as the model of nature, conceived of everything in his own image, and was incapable of conceiving of anything unrelated to this self-image. Now, thanks primarily to the accomplishment of Descartes' philosophy, man was able to conceive of the other *as* an other, to attain to an objective notion of things. In fact, it was by separating the concepts of spirit and nature, that it became possible to separate from the concept of nature everything which didn't belong to it, and which had been imposed on it.

So, the most apparently unnatural view of nature [mechanism] turned out to be the first *natural* view of it. It was Descartes, therefore, and not Bacon, who was the first to express the principle of natural science clearly. The concept of which is the foundation of Descartes' assertion that animals are machines . . . is nothing else but the concept of necessity. (V, 258–9)

In terms of the formulation of Feuerbach's distinctive critique, first of theology and later of metaphysics itself, this passage is very important. Here, more clearly than before, Feuerbach outlines the program of his fundamental critique, albeit in what appears as a marginal instance. The outline is this: That the crucial step, in the progress of scientific rationalism, is the realization that what had appeared as an object, or an *other*, under the form of an anthropomorphic projection, was in fact truly *other*, and that its anthropomorphic form was in fact a projection and objectification of the human under the *guise* of otherness. The object of natural science is deanthropomorphized, is realized as nonhuman; but the object of religious belief, in its theological form, is realized as *only* human.

Thus, Descartes' automatism becomes a step in this discovery of the object in its independent objectivity. For Feuerbach, this means the discovery of the objective and autonomous necessity of nature, as nonwillful, nonteleological, nonpurposive. The limited first approximation to this conception in terms viable in the natural sciences is mechanism, the philosophical extension of the analogy to a machine, whose parts and whose activity are determined by specifiable external relations.

Mechanism isn't the idea of necessity itself, but a specific interpretation of it; i.e. a temporal, finite interpretation, but one true and necessary for its time, precisely in that sense. At a later time, when a deeper conception of nature arose, and the difference between internal and external necessity and purposiveness came to be recognized, this particular interpretation of necessity fell. But the Idea remained—for the source of this idea is the essence of nature itself. The actions of the lower animals, particularly those which cause us the greatest wonder because they appear to exhibit purposiveness, are in reality *necessary* actions. And it is this which is the true sense of the Cartesian assertion that animals are machines. (V, 259–60)

True, Feuerbach then repeats his earlier characterization of the contradiction between Reason and Belief, in Descartes. But the very *separation* of natural necessity from the realm of Belief (i.e., the realm in which necessity is ruled by will, by God's freedom to act, by miracle) becomes in Feuerbach's view, a great historical virtue.

Thus far, it is only nature that has achieved autonomous status. The predicates originally attributed to an intelligent, purposive designer and creator now lose their theological subject (i.e., God) and become the predicates of natural existence itself—of matter, or extended substance. Science is set on its proper road. But science (i.e., *natural* philosophy) does not exhaust the domain of *philosophical* objectivity. The realm of *moral* philosophy also has to attain to autonomy, that is, to freedom from the limitations and distortions imposed on it by theology. If ethics is to become philosophically objective (i.e., *universal* in its ground), if it is to become a rational science, then the ethical predicates cannot be dependent upon or inhere in a subject that is *not* universal. They, like the natural predicates, must be autonomous. In the same sense that there cannot be a theological science (e.g., a Christian astronomy), neither can there be a Christian or a theological ethics. The theologian's God, as the subject of ethical predicates, is and must be a *Christian* God, and as such, limited in conception by the imagination (i.e., empirically and historically limited), a concrete object of *belief.*

Insofar as religion is made to bear an ethical content, God as *independent* subject vanishes into identity with the ethical predicates; God is then only a name, an empty shell apart from these. Insofar as theology *retains* one or another conception of God, it remains *this* or *that* God, in the context of *this* or *that* church and *this* or *that* ritual. Feuerbach distinguishes between religion in this sense, as "positive" religion, and that "true religiosity" that is not thus bounded.

The passages in the *Bayle* that treat of "the essence of religion" fore-shadow Feuerbach's later position quite clearly. But they also contain the germs of his later confusions. They establish the framework for his ethics, because it is the divorce from "positive" or "false" religion that signals the birth of a philosophical, autonomous ethics. It is therefore worth following the development of these ideas in the *Bayle* in some detail.

For the theologian, says Feuerbach, morality derives from God. God alone is the ground of virtue, the source of goodness. The moral laws are God's commands. For the philosopher, they derive from the law which reason gives itself. According to the theologian,

> The will of God is the source of the good and the right; and God's will be done. When the philosopher argues against this principle of will as the highest principle, the theologian makes this objection [*Einwand*]: "What God or the Lord wills is good, and holy, because God can will only that which is good and holy, for he is goodness and holiness itself. Thus, my obedience is not blind." But this is a mere sophism, which in fact grants the rightness of the opponent's view. For then, the will as will is no longer the ground of the good; rather, only that divine will which is identical with the idea of the good is such a ground. . . . The theologian means that the will as will, the will, in short, completely apart from any considerations of the nature of what is willed, or of the particular nature of the object of will, the will as (in the theologian's sense) free will, or willfulness, the lordly will as lawless and irrational will–this is the source of the good. (V, 150–1)

This version of the theologian's argument for the "freedom" and "omnipotence" of God's will, in its Augustinean version, serves Feuer-bach as the springboard for a wider argument; thus he argues that the founding of the moral laws on God's will is only a special case of a more general theological "tendency," to derive *everything* or to make every-thing dependent on God's will. But the general metaphysical form of this principle is the *creatio ex nihilo*. And this "nothing" "is nothing but the ontological or metaphysical expression of the groundless or sheer will of God."

> Augustine asks, "Why does God create heaven and earth?" and he answers "be-cause He wills it." God's will is the cause of heaven and earth. But philosophy has to derive things from their natural causes, i.e. from such causes as are ma-terial for thought: from their essences, or, in the language and spirit of the new philosophy, from their Idea. (V, 152)

Feuerbach is not primarily concerned here either with the foundations of morality or with the origin of things. Rather, he is concerned with religion itself, as a "thing in the world." What is its origin? How does it arise? Does it too have a "natural cause" or is it a "creation from noth-ing." Feuerbach succeeds remarkably well in this turn of the argument.

Critique of Belief: Leibniz and Bayle

The thrust comes finally in turning the analysis of the will of God as sheer willfulness back upon its original subject—that is, morality—but in a new way. The question is no longer "Is God the source of goodness?" but "How is it that *religion* comes to be the source of goodness? How does religion acquire its typical ethical authority?" The original question of the *ground of morality* now becomes the question of the *ground of Christianity*.

The theologian's answer to the question concerning the *origin* of Christianity is that God saw fit to establish Christianity for the salvation of humanity. Thus, Christianity is founded on God's will. The philosopher, on the other hand, seeks for the "natural" causes of religion, and he finds them in the natural development of the human spirit, in universal laws of psychological development. Religion is a necessary and essential form of the human spirit—as a *stage* in development in time. It is the form of the *Volksgeist*—the popular or folk mind. As such, it is a universal form, however it expresses itself in this or that specific religion. Thus, all religions, despite their ostensible disparity, have a common ground, and common laws of development. Thus, too, the origin of Christianity, in this sense, is "identical" with the origin of any religion whatever, and is so "necessarily." Feuerbach writes, "As different as the oriental and occidental religions are, the metaphysical as well as the logical laws, the conceptual forms, the general ideas are everywhere the same. . . . The Christian religion therefore has a necessary origin, an origin grounded in the nature of religion itself" (V, 153). Beyond this, however, it is historical circumstance that shapes the particular content of a religion. So it is, says Feuerbach, that the moral content of a religion, its *ethical* character, so to speak, is the product of time and circumstance. What marked Christianity off from pagan religions is the purity and rigor of its morality. But Feuerbach traces this to the concrete historical circumstances of the founding of Christianity. Whereas classical pre-Christian philosophy conceived of the ethical Idea as *dependent* and formulated it in terms of national or political purposes, the very conditions of the founding of Christianity made its ethical Idea independent of such interests. Classical ethics was the ethics of the *Polis*, conceived in the context of a classical world (or, as Feuerbach says, "in the fresh and living memory thereof") in which political and ethical good were identified. Christianity, on the other hand, developed in the context of a complete alienation from political life.

Christianity owes its purity, its austerity, its rigor to the political and moral corruption of its time. The spirit divorced itself from all politics; with the rejection of the-worldly evil, the world as such was rejected. . . . Man was sated with life; in his pleasures he was weary of pleasure. The search for pleasure, the lust for sensual satisfaction was a desperate one, a self-destructive and self-hating search for a pleasure which turned out to be no more than a splendid wretchedness. Only in such a futile time and world could the idea of morality—the only really valid idea in Christianity—be conceived in its purity. (V, 155)

Once Christianity became identified with national or political purposes, it lost its only unique content; that is, the autonomy of the ethical Idea. Beyond this, Christianity follows the common course of all religions, such as the belief in miracles. "The belief in miracles," says Feuerbach, "is a psychological law," common to religion as such. If the argument is given that Christian miracles differ from those of the pagans, in that the former are true miracles and the latter false, this is not at all to the point. If *both* express the same "natural need," then they have the same essential source, apart from their "truth or falsity." Feuerbach sums up his view in a phrase whose aphoristic construction is to become typical of his later critique: "The belief in miracles is the essence of the miraculous" (V, 157).

Thus, Feuerbach seeks to "naturalize" religion—to make it a "fact in the world," whose essence is the nature of belief, itself a "natural" or "human" fact. In this way, the questions of the *origin* of religion and of the *character* of its universal and its specific content become an object of rational inquiry, subject to lawfulness, and hence to objective, rational understanding. The theologian *explains* religion by founding it in God's will, in miracle, in the creation from nothing. In this way, he precludes the possibility of rational understanding. The philosopher explains religion by *deriving* its origin and its characteristic content from objective, "natural" sources. These turn out to be in the universal grounds of the "natural development" of the spirit (what Feuerbach here calls *psychology*) and the particular workings of historical circumstances on this development.

Whatever Feuerbach takes from Hegel here becomes interpreted in a peculiarly *Humean* way, and this is a striking fact, to say the least, about a disciple of Hegel—particularly in light of the fact that nowhere in the three volumes of the *History* is Hume dealt with. The similarity appears in three ways: first, in the notion of a universal (human) form or disposition, whose specific manifestations are the work of historical circumstance (cf. Hume's "custom"); second, in the particular application of this notion to the "natural" or "psychological" grounds of religion; and third, in the characterization of belief as a natural activity transcending our empirical knowledge (cf. Hume's "habit of the mind"). This latter similarity appears especially clear in a passage on the miraculous transformation of water to wine:

When, for example, water is transformed into wine, this must occur before my very eyes, so that I can substantiate this miracle as an empirical fact. But what in fact do my eyes see? All I see is the mere presence of wine in place of water—one natural object replaces another, without my comprehending—i.e. without having seen—how this came about. Thus, *I believe* in the miracle, but I don't *see* it. All I see is that the wine has replaced the water in some way unseen by me. But of the miracle itself, I have no objective, sensory certainty. The senses tell me only that the wine was wine, the water was water, and that where the water was, wine appeared in the blink of an eye. They *don't* tell me that water was transformed into wine. This "fact," this unnatural and supernatural act, is no fact at all, but only a thing of belief. Just as the spatial void is not an object of the senses, or of experience, neither is the qualitative void, the infinite gap which lies between the water and the wine. Only belief can leap over this gap. (V, 158)

Here is as classical an instance of the fast-transcending nature of belief as Hume's example of the belief in causality. The form is the same: The "connection," the qualitative continuity, is not given in experience. It is supplied by belief, which, as both Hume and Feuerbach saw it, was a "natural" activity of the human mind. The ground for the similarity is not hard to find. It is Bayle, whose influence on eighteenth-century English deist thought was considerable and whom Hume could count (together with the Pyrrhonists) as the spiritual godfather of his own skepticism.

Thus far the argument for the necessary autonomy of ethics is as follows: If religion itself is a stage in the development of the human spirit, then the form that ethical ideas take in this stage is the form that theology gives them. The origin and source of morality is the "miracle" of God's will, and hence ethics cannot be rationally comprehended on its *own* grounds independently. If only obedience to God's command upholds morality, then such a morality is dependent, precisely to the extent that "God's command" is always the command of this or that conception of God. Every "positive religion"—that is, every institutionalized religion, or theologized religion—must have a particular and determinate God. Its commandments must depend upon an ultimately irrational and incomprehensible will, and obedience to them cannot therefore be rational. Therefore, such obedience cannot be *free*. Man subjects himself to the Good, but the Good has become something alien to him, something apart from his own nature. This "absolute alienation of the Idea of the Good" is in the doctrine of original sin, which, says Feuerbach, attacks the very roots of ethics. "Only when man realizes the good as his own inner essence, as his true nature, and realizes that the belief that he is ultimately sinful is itself the greatest of sins, can the good penetrate to man's own being" (V, 192).

131

The only autonomous basis for ethics is therefore man's own nature. Because theology places the ethical ground beyond man's nature, the development of an autonomous ethics requires the sharpest divorce from theology as its condition. If theology claims that God's will, as good will, is the basis for ethics, then in fact God's will as will loses its character and is an empty name for the Good. Such a theology is at the point of abandoning theology and assuming the standpoint of philosophy (V, 210). This transition becomes a transition from the religious to the philosophical stage of the human spirit. Feuerbach describes it thus in a passage that makes full use of religious metaphor:

To realize ethics as autonomous was a holy task for mankind. All the alternative theological versions of ethics deform, debase and obscure it. Only with Kant and Fichte, in whose work philosophy,–for its own salvation and for the salvation of mankind,–established itself as self-sufficient and independent of theology–only then, could the ethical Idea come into its own in its purity and full clarity. Atheism . . . was only the necessary therapeutic, transitional stage from the empirical concept of God as an external object–(of the sort to which the vulgar question "Does God exist?" is relevant)–. . . to the concept of the Godly, in and for itself; to the independent, clear comprehension both of the essence of nature, and the essence of the moral Idea. The Categorical Imperative (i.e. the unconditional moral law) was the manifesto in which ethics proclaimed its freedom and independence to the world. It was a life-giving thunderbolt out of the clear sky of previous theories of the Good. The validity of the ethical Idea could not have been established in any other way but in the naked purity of the straight-forward necessity of Duty, stripped of all of its anthropathic trappings. (V, 210–11)

Kant, says Feuerbach, was the first to write a "grammar of ethics." Fichte went even further (in the *Sittenlehre* and elsewhere). The limitation that is overcome, in this "pure ethics," is religion's need for compromise, indeed, for "capitulation."

Religion must tie its moral ideas to common workaday interests, in order to make these ideas more assimilable to humanity in general, and the particular populace to whom it appeals. . . . Ethics is not a Pedagogy whose task it is to teach and apply empirical techniques of virtue. Ethics cannot capitulate, it cannot smile benignly at man, and accommodate itself to his weaknesses. Instead, it must alarm man, shock him, shatter him. Its commands must be expressed unconditionally and without reservation, and it must bring the character of infinity, of the Ideal to the empirically oriented person, so that he cannot imagine that he already *is* what he *ought to be* and can *become*. (V, 211)

But theology, as Feuerbach has defined it, places God, instead of the *Good in itself*, as the highest ideal. Because God is necessarily "anthropopathic" and ever delimited in conception, in accordance with particular human needs, a God-grounded morality is always conditional. Such a religious morality is therefore "only a spiritualized self-seeking"

(V, 213). Again Feuerbach says that in religion, "the Good is thought under the category of Personality, and so it is not independently conceived" (V, 214). Because religious morality is condemned to express particular needs and interests, it lends itself to abuse in the name of such interests. "The impurest sense can hide behind religion. The filthiest, most repulsive convictions, the lowest personalities, the worst world conditions accommodate themselves well with religion, but never with the moral Idea" (V, 214).

Feuerbach's indictment is complete, and apparently antireligious in essence. But it is *this* religion–namely, the "positive" religion of the churches, of the all-too-worldly theologians–that is condemned by his attack. The religious impulse–the "true religion"–has been betrayed by the church, by its very nature. He reserves a place for the essential "spirit of religion," for the "true religion" (i.e., ethics), in its transcendental and categorical form. Ethics "is the spirit of religion, openly expressed, self-aware; not concealed behind deceptive fantasy images, behind obscure symbols and confused representations, but the clean, simple, straightforward word of truth, far removed from all oriental ostentation" (V, 214–5).

Thus, Feuerbach's *Bayle* reveals, in his own typical phrase, "the secret of Feuerbach" and the deepest motivations that underlay his later "anthropological ethics." The mark of the reformer is clear here; the indictment of the protester, the would-be leader of the "Second Reformation," echoes not only the language, but the content of the first Reformation. The ostentation of Rome now becomes "oriental" (i.e., in the Hegelian sense), bound to sensory imagery, to emotive expression, to concreteness and specificity of symbol. And what, indeed, did Feuerbach jokingly call himself? Why, "Luther II," of course! It may be that the similarity is formal only, that the choice of language and spirit is a historically "necessary" choice: It is the critique of a Protestant, schooled in the theology, and accultured in the values of the Reformation. But if this is so, it is only more explicit in Feuerbach than it is in Hegel, or in Kant. And the contradiction is more explicit too; for the ultimate outcome of this demand for the transcendence, in ethics, of the "empirical" in religion, of the "human, all-too human," turns out to be a return to the empirical, to concrete human feeling, to neediness as the ultimate basis for the "true religion" (i.e., ethics). Feuerbach's debt to the rationalist ethic, to the speculative tradition, to the rigorous Idealism of Kant, Fichte, and Hegel had to be paid before the reconstruction of an essentially "Protestant" ethics, on humanistic and empirical grounds, could be undertaken.

The sense of the *Bayle*, throughout, is an internal dialogue, Feuerbach contra Feuerbach, a confrontation of deep commitments. The result is the aphoristic and polemical character of Feuerbach's discussion, the apparent inconsistency in usage (in which "religion" figures both as the hero and the villain of the piece). Here, too, is the significance of Feuerbach's transparent identification with Bayle, throughout the book, and of the self-revealing characterization of Bayle's own ambivalences. What, after all, does Feuerbach hold to be Bayle's main significance in the history of philosophy? It is his *negative* critique of theology, his dissolution of its claims.

CHAPTER VI

The Critique of Hegelian Philosophy: Part I

✦

The central idea of Feuerbach's early critical and historical works is distinctly Hegelian, or more broadly, distinctly rationalist: The history of the development of concepts is the history of the development of an ever more encompassing and ever more fundamental rational consistency. According to this view, the critical task of any analysis of the history of philosophy is to point out, in systematic fashion, how far short any given philosophical system falls in attaining to the universal, absolute Idea – that is, to truth itself; and truth, in its rational expression, is self-consistent, systematic, and complete.

Philosophy is preeminently the inquiry into truth itself. The history of philosophy, therefore, presents the living process of this inquiry, and doing philosophy consists in the twofold activity of criticism and speculative construction. Criticism is the principle of motion by which the dialectic advances. Speculative construction is the formation of more adequate and more fundamental theories to overcome the partiality that criticism lays bare in previous philosophical systems. Thus, Feuerbach's reconstruction of the history of philosophy is a running critique of the inconsistencies of reason. Whenever reason finds itself complete and self-consistent in any one province, philosophic criticism uncovers the essential boundedness, the merely local character of this alleged completeness. Criticism lays bare the essential *in*completeness of reason (i.e., its inconsistency) in this or that historical-philosophical epoch. Still, in the progress from classical philosophy, through Christian philosophy, to true scientific philosophy (i.e., to metaphysics proper) the domain of reason expands, becomes ever more universal, until, in modern philosophy, with the advent of Descartes, Spinoza, Leibniz, philosophy becomes self-conscious of its universality, and self-consciously pursues it. Reason, as Feuerbach had written in the full flush of his Hegel discipleship, is one, universal, and infinite. Yet, as Hegel had shown, all philosophy throughout history has turned out to be either manifestly or latently dualistic, historically limited and finite (i.e., rationally incomplete)–all philosophy, that is, until Hegel's. Hegel, in revealing the process of philosophical development itself, had shown the end of philosophy, its τέλος. He provided it with that absolute ground that subsumed all partiality and that expressed the Idea for the first time in its full self-consciousness. The *process* was not complete, for the dialectic by its very nature shunned completion. But its reason, its meaning, its metaphilosophical characterization had now been given. The Last Judgment was no nearer, but the Messiah had come. The earthly problems of philosophy still remained, but serenity had been established in the philosophical heaven. There the absolute identity of subject and object waited serenely to be attained; there the Idea in its full self-consciousness *was* complete. True, this heaven was not *actual*, yet it could be conceived. In the Hegelian sense, its form could be thought. One could conceive what conditions would have to be met for this heaven to be actual. If the question were "What is the end of man?" the answer would be "Man's essence is his thinking activity; he is *man* insofar as he *thinks*." And if his thinking *is* his being, then the very conception, in thought, of this end–that is, thinking itself–is the fulfillment of human essence. And further, if thought itself is the coming into self-awareness of the Idea, then the Idea fulfills itself in man thinking.

So far, so good, says Feuerbach; but thinking what? Feuerbach asks. Thinking anything whatever? Apparently not, for this trivializes the matter. Thinking *something*, then; that is, thinking determinately. But every determination is a negation, a differentiation of *this* from *not-this*, and therefore, incomplete essentially. But, then, thinking the Absolute abstractly (i.e., without all of its determinations) is, in effect, thinking *nothing in particular*. This, in effect, is thinking *nothing*, which is identical, on Feuerbach's view, with *not*-thinking. How cruel is reason, which gives us an unreflective glimpse of paradise only at the moment when we lose it.

Feuerbach's *volte-face*, his apparently radical rejection of the Hegelian idealism that led to this nonthinking impasse, first became a public matter in 1839, with the publication of his *Critique of Hegelian Philosophy*. But it cannot be said that it was either a sudden break or a sharp one. It was not sudden, in that his very Hegelianism itself had prepared him for it and further, his refusal to become an "orthodox" Hegelian, already shaped the character of his break with speculative idealism. It was not sharp, in at least one important sense—the mode of philosophizing, the adoption of the *Reflexions-Manier* (that peculiar stylistic quirk of inverting and contrasting phrases in the same sentence, to which German lends itself especially well[1])—this general stamp of German speculative philosophy remained with Feuerbach long past his break with Hegelian philosophy itself. It remained with all the left Hegelians, whether their various itineraries led them to negative theologizing (Feuerbach), to political journalizing (Ruge), to solipsist anarchism (Stirner), to proto-Zionism (Hess), or to historical materialism (Marx and Engels). The Hegelian mode of thought, at least in its more superficial aspects, was ineradicable. Like the trace of one's native dialect, it could be easily noted by any trained observer with a halfway decent ear for the language.

In the *Critique*, Feuerbach examined the claims of Absolute Idealism, and found this last of the grand philosophical systems wanting. In true Hegelian fashion, he uncovered the sense in which this system, like all others, was fatally limited, and he showed where its own self-contradiction lay. But Feuerbach's critique is not a rejection of Hegelian historicism, nor a rejection of the dialectic. Rather, it is a renewed application of the very mode of analysis one would expect of a Hegelian. Its object is to show the contradiction in which Hegel's *Logic* is caught, and by extension, to show that an analogous flaw lies at the heart of Hegel's *Phenomenology*. Thus, the critique is not a refutation of this or that particular aspect of Hegel's encyclopedic work, but rather an attack on the conceptual foundations of the Hegelian *system* itself, that is, on its presuppositions. Moreover, it is, in Feuerbach's view, an attempt to rescue the dialectic from being merely empty form, by showing that the primary contradiction upon which Hegel constructs the logic of the dialectic—that between Being and Nothing—is *not* a "true" (i.e., "metaphysical" or "real") contradiction at all, but only the form, only the appearance of a contradiction. Thus, the *Critique* is neither an abandonment of Hegel's dialectical method nor a rejection of the concrete content of Hegel's applied analysis. It is principally a refutation of the absolutizing of the Hegelian categories, and of the general claim to an "Absolute" philosophy. Its main thematic content is a detailed criticism of this absolutism in the concept of the identity of subject and object. In this latter critique, Feuerbach clearly breaks with objective idealism, both in its Schellingean and Hegelian forms. This break, more than the revisions and criticisms of the *Logic*, is fundamental in the *Critique*. For the attack on idealism, and on speculative philosophy in general, is Feuerbach's first decisive move toward a reconstruction of empiricism and of an empirical materialism. The excesses of the *Logic*, of the claims to Absolute philosophy now fall into place, in Feuerbach's long-developing systematic critique, as the last, most abstract expression of mysticism, and as the latest stage of theology, appearing now in its completely metaphysical form–but metaphysical in *form* only. If, indeed, Hegel's idealism is esoteric theology, then in whatever form it masks itself, it cannot ultimately be scientific (i.e., "true") metaphysics. It must be the old, "oriental" *imaginatio luxurians*, stripped of its sensuous imagery, but nevertheless, mystical: not reason's actuality, but rather its fantastic dream. Thus, Feuerbach characterizes it as "mystical rationalism."

Finally, the *content* of the *Critique of Hegelian Philosophy* is Feuerbach's rejection of the very criterion that he had previously accepted from Hegel, for the analysis and evaluation of the adequacy of any philosophical system. According to this criterion, every philosophical system took its place in the unfolding of the Idea. Every philosophical system was a rational advance, in critically undermining its predecessors by showing their partiality and fatal limitations, and in extending the domain over which self-consistent reason held sway. True universality (i.e., total rational coherence) was the limit that the history of philosophical systems approached. And Hegel had expressed the formal concept of this very limit itself: Absolute Idea, Absolute Identity, absolute transcendence of all subject-object differentiation. The measure of the historical (i.e., conditioned) rationality of a philosophical system, hence of its truth being only relative for its time, was its progress toward this limit, with respect to other, previous systems. Thus, Hegel had projected the self-completion of reason as the very essence of philosophy, and herein, he represented the crowning point of rationalism, and its fullest *formal* expression. That is to say, the formal requirements for an achieved rationalism are set out by Hegel, but only in this abstract-formal way. Its concrete actuality could only be achieved in the attainment of reason's own "kingdom of ends," that is, in the "concrete universalization" of the Idea in human history–or (problematically) at the "end" of human history.

But what if this *rational* self-completeness was no *more* than rational –that is, the essence of *thinking* activity? And further, what if one counterposed to the *self-completeness of reason* the *incompleteness of rationalism*–that is, of total rational coherence–itself? That is, what if "thinking activity" is less than the universal essence of man, but instead, is no more than an aspect of human essence? Furthermore, what if the very conception of this "thinking activity" is the limited conception of "professional" thought? Insofar as the philosopher takes his professional thinking activity as the paradigm of human reason, he describes this activity as the essence of man. But the philosopher, as a man, is more than a philosopher. He is a living being, who exists, desires, acts—in short, whose thinking activity does not exhaust his being. But, then, the definition of man's essence as his thinking activity is inadequate, and false. However self-complete *reason* may be conceived to be, however all-encompassing rationalist *philosophy* pretends to be, it stops short of encompassing human *existence* adequately, and is therefore fatally incomplete.

Thus, Feuerbach attempts a redefinition of human essence. His approach has three interrelated aspects: He concnetrates on three criticisms—first, the epistemological critique of rationalism, as misconceiving and underestimating the role of sense perception in the attainment of knowledge; second, a major attempt at a critique of religion (i.e., of religious belief and of theology), the aim of which is to show that theology is esoteric psychology and that what religion expresses in its concept of divinity is, in fact, man's knowledge of his own, human essence; third (and on the basis of the first two), a rejection of all metaphysics, at least in its classical form. In conclusion, Feuerbach claims that classical philosophy is at an end.

Feuerbach has often been identified with one or another of these major motifs in his philosophy, or with all three, but only in patchwork fashion. My own view is that they are fully integrated in his critique and that his philosophical contribution can best be understood if one recognizes how systematic Feuerbach was in all this. His Hegelianism had trained him too well; he could not be a piecemeal philosopher. Although Feuerbach, by temperament and by style of work, preferred the fluid contours of an *approach,* rather than the rigors of a *system* in the grand manner, system there is, in the coherence and internal relatedness of the various aspects of his critical and constructive writings. Analyses are clearly related to a fuller program, and to a deeper idea of which these are the applied and detailed aspects. It is always easy to make a philosopher appear more coherent, retrospectively, than he was in fact. Here, however, the fault in much Feuerbach criticism lies in the other direction. However, Feuerbach himself rejects sheer systematicity, or coherence, as a test of truth, in his retrospective writings. He characterizes his own approach as that of a scientist, with respect to the "facts," and sees the test as an "empirical" test of the truth or falsity of the purported facts. In a "positivistic"-sounding passage, he writes,

> My essential mode of thought is not "system" but rather "mode of explanation." My relation to my subject matter—at least to that which I chose to make the main themes of my work—is the same as that of the scientist to his subject

matter. I seek to explain a fact; but not in the sense that it is somehow already "contained" in thought, not as a "fact of consciousness" to be explained by explication of its content. Rather, I seek to explain it as an empirical fact, by empirical means . . . I therefore distinguish myself utterly from earlier speculative philosophers. I don't ask, as Kant did: "How are *a priori* judgments possible?" or "How is religion possible?" but rather, "What is religion?" "What is God?" And I ask these questions on the grounds of the facts as given. The only argument that counts against me is that my facts are false, or are falsely understood, or that my explanation of them is false. (X, 344)

To move to such a position, to reject "speculative philosophy" fundamentally, Feuerbach had to go beyond his critique of the history of philosophy. He had to take on Hegel directly. He had to confront "the philosophy of the present," and to reject it.

THE BREAK WITH HEGEL

CHARACTERIZATION OF THE "BREAK" AND ITS RELATION TO THE "HISTORY"

When did Feuerbach break with his early Hegelianism? This has been a favorite question among students of Feuerbach's work, and would be trivially historical and only a matter of biographical dating if it did not involve central questions of understanding the philosophy itself. Feuerbach himself wrote a separate note on his relation to Hegel, which has been taken, sometimes as an accurate self-evaluation and sometimes as a retrospective distortion, made to fit a later view. Friedrich Jodl, an ardent Feuerbachian and the editor of the second edition of Feuerbach's *Collected Works*, takes Feuerbach's self-characterization to be essentially correct, and goes so far as to say that Feuerbach questioned Hegel from the very start[2] and that the first clear break with Hegel came in *Philosophy and Christianity*[3] in 1839 (a work ostensibly dedicated to a defense of Hegel against a critic, Heinrich Leo). Rawidowicz, on the other hand, takes issue with this view and argues at length not only that Feuerbach's early Hegelianism is unambiguous, but that as late as 1841, in the first edition of *The Essence of Christianity*, he is still Hegelian in his view of *Reason*, and that the position he took in the 1828 *Dissertation* is here but "little changed." Rawidowicz's case is based on an examination of the early writings, but also on a comparison of the first (1841) and the revised (1846) edition of *The Essence of Christianity*, from which he concludes that, "In general, it can be noted that the greatest revision is in the Introduction and in those sections of the book which deal with the basic principles of the Feuerbachian philosophy of religion. . . . The other revisions are purely formal."[4] Rawidowicz also cites the reaction of Feuerbach's own left-Hegelian colleagues, especially Arnold Ruge, who regarded *The Essence of Christianity* not as a break with Hegel, but rather as a final fulfillment of Hegelianism.[5] On the other hand, the right-Hegelian K. Rosenkranz wrote in 1842, "Who would have thought that the Hegelian philosophy, which Feuerbach defended, together with me, against Bachmann in his polemic against the *Anti-Hegel*, would have fallen so low in his view."[6]

Obviously, then, one's judgment on Feuerbach's Hegelianism depends in part on one's own understanding of what constitutes "Hegelianism." The break comes earlier or later, depending on how one interprets not only Feuerbach, but Hegel as well. Several commentators (notably S. Rawidowicz, K. Löwith, and H. Arvon) have pointed out, with cogency, the strong similarities of the "anti-Hegelian" Feuerbach and the young Hegel. Is the break, then, with some "essential" Hegel or with certain *aspects* of Hegelianism? If the latter, then Hegelianism itself cannot be the monolithically coherent system that some Hegelians make it out to be, for if it were, then one could not accept *this* and reject *that* without doing violence to Hegel.

It seems clear to me that Feuerbach does not break with Hegel or with Hegelianism as such, *except* in specific ways. It is meaningless to talk of a break with Hegel in any simple sense, because one *can* find non-Hegelian elements in Feuerbach's earliest work and Hegelian elements in his latest work. In an important sense, Feuerbach remained a Hegelian all his life. The unifying theme of his work is the progress of human consciousness, the unfolding of self-awareness. And it is Feuerbach himself who recognizes that Hegelian philosophy establishes the *form* of this development, and suggests the mode of its progress (in the dialectic of consciousness with its "other," in the *Phenomenology of Mind*), albeit in "inverted" or "fantastic" form. The break with Hegel, then, is a break with Hegelian presuppositions, with Idealism, and with the "fixed" form of the Hegelian *Logic*.

Feuerbach had already discussed the type of relation that any critical philosopher bears to the object of his criticism.[7] It is the relation that the genetic-analytic method requires–that of empathetic reconstruction *and* of critical transformation (in other terms, a relation to the object that is both immanent and transcendent). If it was Hegel who first grasped this method of analysis clearly, in his *History of Philosophy*, then Feuerbach is his heir and continuator in the best sense. But this says more: It says that Feuerbach was the critic, or the "negation" of Hegel on the grounds of Hegelianism itself. One may say that

Feuerbach prepared a place for himself in the very construction of his *History of Philosophy*, and then chose to occupy it. Having defined the role of the philosophical historian through three volumes of the *History*, and having done it with respect to the philosophy of the *past*, from the standpoint of the philosophy of the *present*, what is left to do, by the rational imperative of the approach itself, is to turn the same instruments of criticism on the philosophy of the present (i.e., Hegelianism). But in the Hegelian view, every present is transformed into a past by criticism—and by its own inexorable transiency. Feuerbach had, in effect, to criticize his *own* standpoint, insofar as it was Hegelian and to transcend it and make *it* an object of criticism. Thus, the general consensus of Feuerbach commentators who separate the "historical" phase of Feuerbach's work from his anti-Hegelianism critique, though they correctly mark a change in the quality and character of Feuerbach's philosophy, miss an important point: namely, that the critique of Hegel is nothing but a continuation of Feuerbach's *History of Philosophy*, which now includes Hegelian philosophy as itself a *historical* stage (i.e., as a philosophy of the *past*). To miss this is to miss a good part of the reason for the excitement that Feuerbach's critique engendered. After all, the critics of the present still suffered the name "left Hegelians," which bound them to the present at least in philosophical nomenclature. It was time to throw off even these ties, to adopt what was revolutionary in Hegel as a means of overthrowing Hegel himself. Then, too, the previous studies in *The History of Modern Philosophy*, the *Leibniz* and the *Bayle* become clearly more than expanded lecture notes from Feuerbach's days as docent at Erlangen. They are the necessary preparatory work for *The Critique of Hegelian Philosophy*. Even Henri Arvon, who estimates Feuerbach's *History* as a degradation of Hegel's dialectical *History of Philosophy* into a "simple procedure," is forced to conclude, "one doesn't continue Hegel except in opposing him. This conclusion is finally brought home to Feuerbach."[8]

FEUERBACH'S RELATION TO HEGEL
BEFORE THE 1839 CRITIQUE

The relation of the erstwhile disciple to his master becomes a philosophically interesting question when it bears on general features of conceptual development and the growth of knowledge. Otherwise, it may be trivially biographical and idiosyncratic. Feuerbach's relation to Hegel, before the 1839 *Critique*, is of philosophic interest precisely in that it exhibits the struggle to overcome and free himself from the dominance of the master, and shows thereby a classic dialectical pattern: from imitation, to critical emulation; to a more critical selection of the viable and enduring elements in Hegel's thought (and a critique of the "dogmatic" and "absolutizing" Hegelians who follow uncritically and blindly); to a rejection of the master's fundamental presuppositions, and the revelation of their inadequacy; and finally, to the proposition of a dialectical counterthesis.

In the 1839 *Critique*, there remains a good deal of ambivalence with regard to Hegel on Feuerbach's part. Up to the very year in which the *Critique* was published, Feuerbach had engaged in vigorous polemics against the anti-Hegelians, as we shall see. He had agonized over his "break," yet made it. But he remained wary about throwing out the baby with the bath water. Understandably, any philosopher who sees his own critical task in a historical framework is inevitably self-conscious with respect to posterity, that is, with respect to the place that his *own* philosophy and his *own* criticism will be given by future philosophers. Feuerbach recurrently exhibits this self-consciousness, in his letters, in the *Aphorisms*, and nowhere more clearly than in a note of philosophical autobiography, written in 1840 (with later additions), on his relation to Hegel. He extols Hegel in glowing terms.

When I came to Berlin, I didn't know what I wanted, so distracted and full of conflict was I. But after less than half a year of attending Hegel's lectures, my head and my heart were set right. I knew what I should do, and would do: not theology, but philosophy! Not babbling, and fanciful visions, but learning! Not believing, but thinking! . . . It was through Hegel that I came to self-awareness and to awareness of the world. It was he whom I then called my second father, as I then called Berlin my second birthplace. He was the only man who got me to feel, to experience what it means to be a teacher. . . . My teacher was Hegel, and I was his student. I don't repudiate it, but on the contrary acknowledge it even today with gratitude and joy. And, to be sure, that which we once were, doesn't vanish from our very being, any more than it does from our awareness of it. (IV, 417)

So much for the student's debt to his teacher. Now for a qualification, by way of a general point and a parable. As to the qualification: Feuerbach wants to establish himself as a "proper" anti-Hegelian and to separate himself from what he considers crass, unphilosophical, and half-baked anti-Hegelianism. He is against the orthodox, absolutizing Hegelians and against the "half-philosophers" who criticized Hegel improperly. First, then, Feuerbach tries to characterize what *kind* of a Hegelian he was, in his early period. And this seems to be aimed at those colleagues, like Ruge, who criticized his patience with the "old rubbish" and implied that he was still too much of an Hegelian. Retrospectively, Feuerbach considers that he studied Hegelian philosophy as a historian, "first as one who identifies himself with his subject matter, . . . because he doesn't know better, and doesn't know enough else; then as one who distinguishes and separates himself from his subject-matter, gives it its historical due, and in this way endeavors to assess it properly" (IV, 419). This process, says Feuerbach, is one that one comes to separate the mere form from the essence of Hegelian philosophy.

> I was an essential, ideal Hegelian, but not a formal, or literal Hegelian . . . I distinguished between the letter and the spirit of Hegel, between the *Logic*, on paper, and the idea of the logic, between what Hegel said, and what he intended. I was determined by Hegel in general, but not in particular. I was determined by him not as by a philosophical Jehovah, or Allah, but as by the Zeus of modern philosophy, who left me enough freedom to be impressed by other philosophers as well—namely, Spinoza, Descartes, Malebranche, Fichte, as well as Kant, and even Bacon. (IV, 419)

This rather idealized relation of student to master is clearly retrospective, though it certainly exemplifies the ideal of the genetic-analytic method as Feuerbach had earlier dealt with it in the foreword to the *Leibniz* (in 1837). But Feuerbach could argue that the true evaluation of this relationship was not as he saw it, or was aware of it *then*, but rather as he reflectively reconstructed it later. He does claim that he was no longer a "school Hegelian" when he wrote his "Humorous-Philosophical Aphorisms" (in 1834), and that this early work was rather the outcome of tendencies and insights of which Hegelian philosophy itself was an expression, rather than the source.

The parable concerns the matter of intellectual growth, and sees it as an analogous to social and personal growth, in the attainment of autonomous maturity.

> When I left home for the university, my favorite dish—roasted potatoes—was prepared for me, in honor of my departure. And as a child, when I watched my father eat a whole herring, I had no greater desire than to be able to eat a whole herring someday. How idiotic it would be, if a Gastrologist, who classified all people according to the food they ate, were to define a grown man as a potatophile, or a herringophile, according to the favorite dish of one's childhood, or youth. (IV, 418)

The point, of course, is that Hegelophilia was a youthful preoccupation—moreover, that it was the favorite dish of university days. "But," adds Feuerbach, "a man is a member of mankind before he is a member of a university," and he asks, "doesn't intellectual taste change with years, just as physical taste does?"

This takes care of the qualified, "essential" Hegelianism of the early years (1828–34). But how does Feuerbach account for the ardent *defense* of Hegel against the critics as late as 1839, the very year in which *The Critique of Hegelian Philosophy* appeared? This too is characterized by Feuerbach as a *qualified* defense:

> It is superficial to conclude that because one is opposed to the opponents of some idea, one must therefore be unconditionally in favor of this idea. . . . So I was *for* Hegel (in this qualified way), but only on transitional, and not on ever-binding, eternal grounds, only because I couldn't be *for* that which was raised against him. For I saw in his opponents only opponents of philosophy in general, only half-philosophers. (IV, 420)

Feuerbach goes further, and claims that even in his attack on the anti-Hegelians (specifically on Bachmann's *Anti-Hegel*, see below), he nurtured his own anti-Hegelianism in silence. "The *Anti-Hegel* was already a part of me, but because he was only a half-man, I bid him be silent. My point of view was, however, no longer a purely logical or metaphysical one, but rather a more psychological one" (IV, 420).

FEUERBACH'S DEFENSE OF HEGEL AGAINST THE CRITICS: BACHMANN, DORGUTH, LEO

While the anti-Hegelian "half-man" was condemned to enforced silence, Feuerbach undertook a defense of Hegelian idealism. Still, even in its earliest form, it was a defense that the "orthodox" Hegelians were not prone to accept. Feuerbach had caught the eye of the Hegelians with his *History*, and was asked in 1834 to become a contributor to the *Jahrbücher für wissenschaftliche Kritik* (a journal founded in 1827 by Henning, as the organ of the Hegelian school–usually referred to as the *Berliner Jahrbücher*). He contributed a number of reviews, primarily of works in the history of philosophy. In 1835, the major part of his review of C. F. Bachmann's 1833 work on Hegel was rejected, and Feuerbach published the complete review separately.[9] His first open attack on the anti-Hegelians was thus not fully acceptable to the school Hegelians themselves. Greater latitude was provided for Feuerbach with the founding of the *Hallesche Jahrbücher fur deutsche Wissenschaft und Kunst* in 1838. Here, under the editorship of Arnold Ruge, Feuerbach's distinctively left-Hegelian views were encouraged, and here were published his review of Dorguth's *Critique of Idealism* and, later, his own *Critique of Hegelian Philosophy*.

The three works to be considered here in Feuerbach's defense of Hegelian idealism cover the period of "transitional" advocacy, from 1835 to 1839. They are the *Critique of the Anti-Hegel* (the 1835 review of C. F. Bachmann), the *Critique of Empiricism* (1837–a review of F.

Dorguth's *Critique of Idealism*), and *Philosophy and Christianity* (1839–a defense of Hegel against the charge by Heinrich Leo that Hegelian philosophy is un-Christian). Thus, these works cover the same period in which the three volumes of historical studies were published (the *History of Modern Philosophy* in 1833, the *Leibniz* in 1837, and the *Bayle* in 1838). The end of this period is marked by the *Critique of Hegelian Philosophy* in 1839, and the seal is put on it in a review of J. F. Rieff's *The Beginnings of Philosophy*, in 1841; and in the same year, by the epochal *Essence of Christianity*.

This is also the period in which Feuerbach attempted, unsuccessfully, to get a university post, and his growing disdain and criticism of academic, "professorial" philosophy is in proportion to his lack of success in getting an appointment. But it is too easy to interpret this as merely "sour grapes." The growing political and clerical reaction in Germany, the split between the orthodox and right Hegelians and the young and left Hegelians, and Feuerbach's own long-term concern over the split between the "thinker" and the "Man," between the professorial condition and the human condition—all enter into the matter. Thus, Arvon's charge that the *Critique of the Anti-Hegel* was an "opportunist" work, an attempt to curry favor with the official philosophers in order to wangle an appointment, is, at best, grossly oversimplified.[10]

The importance of the critiques of Bachmann and of Dorguth, in Feuerbach's defense of Hegel, is that both of these erstwhile antagonists were to provide Feuerbach with some of the very arguments he himself was later to use against the master. In Feuerbach's reviews of historical works in the *Hallesche Jahrbücher*, he fulfilled, as he was expected to do, the role of a young historian of philosophy who had already made his mark. In the articles contra Bachmann and Dorguth, the choice of subject matter was dictated in great part by Feuerbach's own concern and his own inner struggle with the foundations of speculative idealism–that philosophic position he had adopted as his own. Thus, the dialectic between the realist-empiricist arguments of Bachmann and Dorguth and Feuerbach's still idealist position served to sharpen his own critical perception and to reinforce his earlier attempts to encompass a rational empiricism with a critical, systematic framework. The emphasis in both Bachmann's and Dorguth's works is on an anti-idealist realism, the arguments are (especially in Dorguth's work) largely materialist and "physiological" (in a way that links them to the French *ideologues*, especially to Cabanis),[11] and the question they center on is, in Feuerbach's own terms, the "central question in philosophy," the relation of mind to body, of thinking to matter. More especially, this question, as it arises in Bachmann and Dorguth, is addressed in terms of the relation of *thinking* to *sensing* in the acquisition of knowledge,[12] and thus this forces Feuerbach to take account of the distinctive epistemological issue that was to form the basis of his own later empirical materialism.

Feuerbach's Critique of Bachmann

Feuerbach criticizes Bachmann's *Anti-Hegel* on four major counts: first, Bachmann's misconception of Hegel's Logic of Identity; second, Bachmann's narrow "empiricist" interpretation of Being; third, Bachmann's views on the physical basis of mind; and fourth, Bachmann's interpretation of Hegel's philosophy of religion (as having made God finite).

First, Feuerbach attacks Bachmann's argument that Hegelian identity eliminates essential distinctions, reducing philosophy to religion, and Nature to the Idea, in asserting the identity of the terms in each of these pairs. Bachmann fails to understand, says Feuerbach, that Hegel's concept of identity does not exclude the idea of difference: "Identity doesn't extinguish the light of the understanding, the comprehension of difference; rather, identity is only an identity among *differentia*" (II, 21). Thus, the "identity," in dialectical terms, of religion and philosophy is not a reduction of philosophy to religion or vice versa. So, too, where God is "identified," as universal ground, with the existence of things, this does not thereby entail the absurdities that, for example, God "eats himself," "digests himself," and so on (as critics of Spinoza's *Identity* had charged against him). Insofar as Hegel claims that logic *is* metaphysics, says Feuerbach, he means that the categories of thought are the essential and universal form of things, for otherwise there would be an absolute hiatus between thinking and being, there would be no possibility of real knowledge, and metaphysics would be inconceivable, or at best, a fantastic dream. In short, Feuerbach accuses Bachmann of having confused the determinate, finite, and particular *ways* in which we come to know, with the *Idea* in and for itself. Such a confused concept of identity can be made to seem ridiculous, says Feuerbach, but properly understood, the Hegelian concept of identity entails only that Being is identical with the Idea in itself, and *not with* its finite representation in human thought, or in the particular, limited, and finite Idea of any philosopher. The extent of Feuerbach's objective idealism is seen clearly in this passage:

If the universal modes of thought are at the same time actually real modes, aren't they universal in and for themselves? And as such, mustn't they be grounded in something beyond us, or in the things around us? Must they not, in this case, have a divine ground and essence? Then, isn't it a foolish misunderstanding to think that when these logical-metaphysical modes, in their totality and absoluteness,–in short, as they really are–are conceived as modes of God's Being, that they are also to be conceived as the philosopher proposes them, as they appear on paper, in their finitude, particularity and separateness? These latter are the necessary ways in which a scientific exposition of these modes becomes available to human experience; but are we to attribute them to God in this form? When we make man's moral modes, in their totality and absoluteness, into God's predicates, and when we make God, in the mode of absolute Goodness, the principle of morality, wouldn't it be ridiculous to conclude from this that we thereby take God's predicates to be the list of virtues which constitute the compendium of this morality? Would we then attribute the virtues of chastity, temperance, honesty, frugality, patriotism, love of parents, etc., to God? Has our dear Bachmann charged Hegel with holding that God is constituted by the three volumes of his *Logic*? And, since the first volume has 334 pages, the second, 282 pages, and the third, 400 pages, that God's content amounts to 1016 pages *net*, and that consequently God first saw the light of day in Nurenberg, at Schrag's publishing house? These would indeed be the consequences he would have to accept, in the light of the lack of rhyme or reason in his method of inquiry. (II, 24–5)

The *Idea*, in and for itself, is not the same as the *awareness of the Idea*, which the philosopher achieves. In a passage replete with the dialectic of the Idea coming to know itself in another's knowledge of it, Feuerbach marks off philosophical awareness of the Idea from the Idea's self-awareness. The classic philosophical theology, characteristic of the Hegelian analysis, is strikingly clear here:

Philosophy is not the Idea itself, personified in a lofty mind, but is rather the awareness of the self-awareness of absolute Idea–herein lies the difference between philosophy and the Idea, and here also lies their identity. God knows himself in man, in that man knows God. But this self-knowledge of God through man is only a re-knowing, a re-cognition, a duplication of God's original, and man-independent self-knowledge. Our representations of God, insofar as he is an object for us, are only representations of the representations which God has of Himself, and in which He is an object to Himself. (II, 27)

Analogously, Feuerbach criticizes Bachmann's interpretation of the identity of Nature and Idea in Hegel. Bachmann criticized the identity of Nature and Idea as no more than the subjective assertion of the identity of the *Idea* of Nature with Nature itself. On these grounds, he asserted that the existence of Nature was independent of the Idea of Nature and that the latter did not therefore represent a true identity of subject and object, but only a subjective representation of it. But, argues Feuerbach, in good Hegelian fashion, Nature is not independent Being, for Hegel, but rather the *other-being*, or *otherness* of Idea itself. Thus, it follows that the *Idea of Nature* is not the Idea in itself, but rather the Idea's awareness of itself as *other*–or the subjective, determinate, and particular awareness of nature as the other-being of idea.

Bachmann, in confusedly identifying Hegel's concept of Idea with that of the Idea of nature (i.e., the *duplication* of Idea's awareness of itself as other) misses the point here again, says Feuerbach. The role of contradiction, in Hegel's *Logic* is not to counterpose *mere* opposites (e.g., Idea and Nature in their "rude-sophistical" sense), but rather to explain this opposition as self-opposition *in* the Idea itself (i.e., between Idea in and for itself and Idea in its other-being, or its being merely for itself). Without this concept of self-contradiction, the concept of Identity (of Identity in difference, in its dialectical form) becomes no more than the flat and superficial Identity of pre-Hegelian philosophy–the Schellingean night in which as Hegel had said, all cows are black.

Further, when Bachmann pursues his folly, confuses the identity of the Idea and its appearances, and reduces Idea to the sum of its appearances, then, "Idea is exhausted in actual, finite matter, in merely empirical existence" (II, 40). But empiricism does not exhaust the Being of Idea in and for itself. Rather, the furthest reach of empiricism is the determination of its *own* limits (i.e., the phenomenal world, the world of appearances only). This much Kant already accomplished, says Feuerbach:

> Kant is to be distinguished from Locke and from the skeptic, David Hume, by the breadth and depth of his inquiry, specifically, in that he established as the *a priori* condition of the possibility of knowledge that which they derived from experience. But the well-known consequences which Kant drew are the consequences of empiricism itself, namely, that real knowledge is limited to the realm of objects of experience (albeit Kant distinguished himself from empiricists proper in that he took the objects of experience as mere appearances). Kant therefore represents nothing but empiricism come to rational realization, and therefore to knowledge of its own limits. (II, 44–5)

Feuerbach accuses Bachmann, then, of not having gone beyond Kant's phenomenalism and bases his criticism of Bachmann's "realism" in epistemology on this point. This is important, in that Feuerbach could not make the transition to his own empiricist-realist viewpoint until he had reformulated and resolved the question concerning phenomenalism and realism, which are raised in this 1835 essay. In this respect, his discussion of Bachmann's epistemological realism is the central section of this review.

Bachmann's position was that spirit, mind, thought depended on matter and on its organization–a clearly materialist thesis. Thus, he had argued from the examples of hydrocephalic and cretinous persons that it was indeed the bodily deformation, the distortion of material organization that explained mental deficiency in such cases. Feuerbach, in a bitterly polemical way, accuses Bachmann of a "thoughtless empirical" view on the relation of mind to body and upholds a classic dualism between the materiality of body and the immateriality of mind.

> Only that which is of a material nature can be dependent on matter, but not that which is entirely different from it, i.e. that which is self-determined, self-dependent. . . . When a man suffers intense hunger and thirst, he cannot think. But does this mean that philosophy, or thought depend on eating and drinking, and consequently, on matter? Quite the opposite: insofar as I eat and drink, I satisfy the demands which nature makes upon me as an individual, and thus allay them, rid myself of them. Only then, when I am free of material demands do I participate in Spirit. Cretinism, hydrocephalism, bodily injuries which result in loss of memory or consciousness, etc., show only that man is a materially living being, and that spiritual activity, which is a distinct and separate immaterial activity, becomes man's activity only mediately, under the conditions of bodily fulfillment. For only that matter which is not lacking, which is self-completed, fulfilled, . . . is capable of overcoming or negating its materiality, and only as such can it serve as an organ of the spirit. So too, man can rise to the aether of thought only when he is self-complete, free from the sufferings of feeling, affect, worry. But it is ridiculous to make man's dependence on the disposition of his body, his needs and his circumstances into the dependence and needs of the Spirit,—as ridiculous as it would be to take the fog which lies in this valley and hides the sun from me as if it were the sun itself darkening. (II, 53–4)

Thus, Spirit, as objective Being, is distinct and independent of any individual mind, which is merely a particular and conditional "participation" in eternal Spirit. The classical distinction between subject and object, between knower and known, between man and the world should not be given up in this case: The *organ* of the spirit may suffer, but not the spirit itself.

Feuerbach continues, in a passage that reminds us of the strong Platonic and Plotinean strain in Hegelianism:

> We contain an objective and subjective world in ourselves. And we are nothing but the organs of this objective world, which we represent and actualize each according to his own constitution, as rational or insane, adequate or false, clear or obscure, fulfilled or deprived. Spirit itself, however, is that objective world in us which is independent and unaffected by us. Only one who rests content with appearances, like Mr. Anti-Hegel, confuses the individual with Spirit itself. (II, 54–5)

In a Cartesian vein, Feuerbach attacks Bachmann's argument against the identity of Being and Thinking (from the examples of the interruptedness of consciousness in deep sleep, for instance). Bachmann (following Locke contra Descartes) argued, commonsensically, that we do not cease to *be*, when, in such instances, we cease to think, or cease to be conscious. Feuerbach argues that lacking consciousness, we *have* no Being, so that in such circumstances, there is no question of whether

The Critique of Hegelian Philosophy: Part I

Being and Thought are identical. Because, as Descartes rightly holds, our Being *is* our thinking, we simply *have* no Being in deep sleep, says Feuerbach (*without* his tongue in cheek). "Where our consciousness ceases, our Being ceases." And further, "we are only insofar as we act, and indeed, only insofar as we act in that way ... which is in accord with our innermost essence" (II, 55). For the raw, uncultured man, whose only "essence" is his *sensory* satisfaction, this still holds true, for only *consciousness of a satisfaction* makes it a *satisfaction*. Thus,

Being conscious is itself man's Being. The Being of a stone or a plant is its being an object for another. But man's Being is that he is an object to himself. When he ceases to be an object to himself, as in deep, unconscious sleep ... he loses his Being. The hours of sleep are not reckoned in the diary of our life, as hours we have lived through, no more than the wormlike contractions of our stomach and the supporting motions of the ventral muscles and the diaphragm during digestion are reckoned as motions which we ourselves make. (II, 55–6)

Having defined "being human" as "being conscious," Feuerbach avoids the consequences of a monadic plurality of consciousnesses by the argument that the *Being* of consciousness does not *depend* on individuals, but is only *participated in* by them. The development of a particular consciousness in man is not, therefore, the development of Consciousness itself or of Spirit itself, but only of this or that individual consciousness, by a process of appropriation or assimilation of Consciousness itself; otherwise, there would be as many Consciousnesses, as many *Reasons*, or *Spirits* as there are individual men, which, Feuerbach concludes, is absurd.[13]

If all of this seems flatly idealist and no more than a learned echo of Hegel, still it pinpoints the precise locus of Feuerbach's trouble. If man's being is to be entirely contained within his consciousness, and if, further, this individual consciousness is nothing in itself, but only a "participation" in the Being of Consciousness as such, then human individuality, concrete human existence, individual biography, need, feeling, sensation are "nothing but" the determinate "otherness" of Universal Consciousness, and have, hence, no independent existence. Arvon, for example, attributes the vehemence of Feuerbach's polemic against Bachmann to the internal struggle that Feuerbach was waging with himself on this issue. It is clear, retrospectively, that the very issues of the relation of eating and drinking to consciousness, of matter to thought, and of sensing, feeling, worrying–the finite conditional modes of *bodily* existence–to thinking, are the issues around which Feuerbach is to build his own philosophy. In particular, it is the relation between sensing, perceiving, and thinking that concerns Feuerbach, hereafter.

In the *Critique of the Anti-Hegel*, Feuerbach begins his consideration of this issue. Bachmann had held that the subject, man, can be thought of as not-thinking, as when he is only sensing or perceiving, and that the essentialism that identified man's being with his thinking was shown to be false in this instance also. Feuerbach argues, against this, that sensing is itself a form of knowing and involves thought. He writes,

The scholiast to Plato's *Phaedrus* says correctly, if I am not mistaken, that sensations themselves are instances of knowing. Sensation is nothing but that Reason which is identical with our unmediated, individual senses, i.e. personal, sensate reason. Sensation is knowledge, but not yet knowledge in the form of universality. But thinking as such is present and active in all the activities of our senses: indeed, it isn't the kind of thinking which is speculative, scientific, reflective, profound, which is directed to the essence of things, but rather that which is directed to the existence of things, and through which alone external things are given to us—in short, it is thinking as *awareness*. Sensations are perceptions of objects. But the perception of objects as differentiated from ourselves is the work of that thinking which inheres in sensation. "Intuition [i.e. sensations] without thought is blind," Kant had already said. The eye of the eyes is conscious awareness. We see only because seeing itself is also thinking. All of our sense activities are, in this sense, activities of thought. Even in eating and drinking, we are actively spiritual and conscious. . . . Even the fact that we can hold a knife and fork at the table depends on the force of our consciousness; were we to lose consciousness, they would fall from our hands. All of our force, our activity is, in the last analysis nothing but the force, the activity of thinking. (II, 61-2)

Feuerbach insists here, as he was to insist in the review of Dorguth's *Critique of Idealism* three years later, and as he was to insist at the very height of his "physiological" materialism, that sensing already involves thinking. It was this insistence that enabled him to overcome his earlier rejection of empiricism, with the aid of his Kantian distinction between a "blind" and a "rational" empiricism.

The *Critique of the Anti-Hegel* gives us Feuerbach at the peak of his objective idealism, with an explicitness greater than that of the *History* or the *Leibniz*, because less diffuse. Yet it gives us the Hegelian Feuerbach who on Hegelian grounds already had chosen the crucial issues in Hegel on which to do battle—the question of the relation of logic to Being, of religion to philosophy, and of philosophy (and thought in general) to sensate existence, and to the material structure of human existence itself. The last ground on which to stand in this battle is the objectivity of the Idea, its transcendent reality beyond any human instance or idea of it. To this resource Feuerbach turns, in order to answer Bachmann on the criticism of Hegel's fundamental concepts: the theory of the Idea and the concept of Identity. This is the foundation stone that Feuerbach himself will remove, when he passes from defense of Hegel to critique.

His final criticism of Bachmann's views on Hegel's philosophy of religion is the least interesting part of the essay and amounts to no more than a school exercise recapitulation of Hegelian views. Only the form (almost the bare grammatical form) is of any interest here, for it is by inversion of this standard Hegelian pattern, which Feuerbach repeats here, that he formulates his later philosophy of religion. So, for example, "Human love of God is God's own self-love" (II, 79) needs only the transposition of "God" and "human" to become the later Feuerbachian formula "God's love of man, is man's own self-love" (VI, 70–1).

Feuerbach's Critique of Dorguth

Feuerbach's critique of Dorguth is of major interest and deserves to be better known as a classical defense of idealism against "physiological" materialism, on epistemological grounds. The tone is much less polemical than that of the attack on Bachmann. It is also a more mature work, philosophically, and has an elegance and aptness of phrase, a clarity of expression that characterizes Feuerbach's best work. It was written for the more sympathetic pages of the *Hallesche Jahrbücher*.[14] Dorguth's *Critique of Idealism*, the object of Feuerbach's criticism, was published in 1837 and subtitled "Materials for the Founding of an Apodictic Realist-Rationalism," and was the work of a philosopher with no professional training (*"Ohne strenge Fachbildung,"* as Jodl puts it). The pamphlet apparently influenced Feuerbach greatly, despite his open criticism, and Jodl counts it as the forerunner of Feuerbach's *Foundations of the Philosophy of the Future*. In his review of Dorguth, Feuerbach returns to a theme of his *History*, the critique of empiricism. But whereas in the *History*, he took a more or less systematic view of the inadequacy of the empiricist philosophical framework (as lacking a "substantive idea"–i.e., a metaphysical ground), here his criticism is directed toward a contemporary, physiologically oriented materialism, explicit in its assertion that thought is no more (and no less) than an activity of the brain. Feuerbach's criticism not only served, then, as one of the last of his defenses of idealism, but was his way of becoming aware of specific materialist arguments. Thus, it served as an initial testing ground for revisions and reformulations of this very materialism itself.

"What is thought? How is it to be considered in itself, how is it to be related to its object, how is it related to the Being of Nature and of Man, and to Organism?" These, says Feuerbach, at the beginning of his critique of Dorguth, are the most important and most difficult and profound questions of philosophy. Dorguth's *Critique of Idealism* addresses itself to this question in the most forthright way, answering it with a physiologically oriented empiricism. Feuerbach credits Dorguth with being more rigorously empiricist, in this respect, than the ordinary "lax" empiricism, which leaves the issue of the relation of mind to body vague and unsettled. The merely "negative" formulation of "lax" empiricism asserts only that mind is *dependent* on body, but avoids drawing the necessary consequences from this premise, namely,

If mind itself–not man, not the individual who so to speak participates in mind–but mind as such *depends on* the organism, then it follows that mental activity, thinking itself, is a purely organic activity, and consequently, when no essential distinctions are drawn between organism and matter, then mental activity is a material process. For what doesn't belong to matter cannot be dependent on it, cannot be determined by it. That which is not material is thereby also excluded from the reach, the influence of matter, for this extends no further than does materiality. . . . Therefore, the relation of dependence necessarily entails an absolute materialism. Absolute materialism only expresses openly, candidly, without reservation, what is intended by those who propose the relation of dependence of mind on body, but which they don't trust themselves to state openly and which they conceal in euphemisms. (II, 132)

Praising Dorguth for his forthrightness, Feuerbach addresses himself to the view that thinking is an activity of the brain. This, says Feuerbach, is the fundamental proposition of Dorguth's work. But it nowhere carries the sense that thought is *also* an activity of the brain; rather, it asserts that thinking is *only* a brain activity. But, Feuerbach objects,

If this proposition isn't altogether brainless, then it certainly appears to be meaningless and incomprehensible: and on the simple grounds that as long as we don't take the brain as the understanding itself, then a brain-act as such is an act without understanding. Consequently, the act of understanding, or thought, is defined as an act without understanding when it is taken to be a brain-act. (II, 133)

This *reductio ad absurdum* is preface to Feuerbach's more serious critique:

Calling thinking an activity of the brain doesn't tell us anything about what thinking is. . . . An activity comes to be known only by what it does, by its product, its object. It is what it does: its deed gives it its name. The work praises the master. By their fruits shall ye know them. The doer achieves his name in life from the objects or product of his doing: so it is with the painter, the poet, the tailor. But the product of thinking is thought. Only an examination of thought can tell us anything about thinking; and only thought can give us this. (II, 134)

The contradiction that Feuerbach sees in the reductionist view is that if thinking has its reality as brain activity, then the brain activity that accounts for the alleged chimera of Idealism (as itself a brain act) must also be taken as "real." "Idealism is so unavoidably valid, that you [empiricists] yourselves become Idealists, affirm Idealism in the very act of denying it" (II, 135). Here Feuerbach is silly, expressing a confusion: Namely, that if idealist "thoughts" exist, as brain acts (as must be admitted even by Dorguth), then they must be "true" (i.e., they are affirmed in their content as they must be affirmed in their existence). Feuerbach could, of course, have turned this into an argument against the "physiological" reduction by showing that such a reduction gives us no theoretical hold on truth and falsity, because brain acts as such are neither true nor false, but merely exist. Then the full strength of his argument that Dorguth's view tells us nothing about what thought is, in this sense (of its truth or falsity), would rest on firmer ground. But the identification of Being and Truth, in this instance, at least, is silly. It leads Feuerbach, naturally, to the following conclusion: "The knowledge of Thought [as an activity] depends on the knowledge of thoughts, of that which is thought. But what is thought? The thought is the thing as it is, while the sensible representation is the thing as it appears. The senses give us only images. Only thought gives us the thing" (II, 135).

Sense imagery, without thought, is the realm of dream, of fantasy and the imagination. If you want to know what sense imagery without thought is, says Feuerbach, then you have to ask primitive man, man in his cultural infancy. "But don't ask civilized man, who has already been tainted through and through by thought. So long as the Greeks didn't attain to rational thought, so long did they conceive of the stars as animate, divine beings. It was philosophy that transformed these images into things."

There follows a passage worth quoting in its entirety, for it gives the clearest picture of Feuerbach's critique of empiricism on rationalist grounds, and thus gives us a key to the reformed empiricism that Feuerbach later formulated. It is also relevant to Feuerbach's view of scientific thought.

When mankind rises from mere sensibility to thought, it is as if it were awaking from a dream. The distinction between the world of thought and the world of sense is then taken to be more than merely a distinction—it is seen as an absolute dichotomy, and the two are taken to be contradictory. Then, like Parmenides, mankind condemns the senses as betrayers, or like Xenophanes, sinks to a condition of skeptical doubt of any truth whatever, because thought has not yet become aware of its own character. Thought is then nothing but the activity of distinguishing between reality and appearance, between the thing and its image–an activity which the representation of things by the senses leaves unsatisfied. If the senses had satisfied man's inquiry, he would have no need of thought. In this case, he would have taken the sun to be as it appeared, and he wouldn't have come to mistrust his senses. He wouldn't have come to ask whether the sun were in fact larger, or only as large as it appeared to him. For he wouldn't have known enough to distinguish reality from appearance–much less to conceive of the Copernican system. *The Copernican system is the most glorious victory that Idealism has achieved over empiricism, that reason has achieved over the senses.* The Copernican system is not a truth of the senses, but a truth of reason. It is a system which contradicts the senses, absolutely transcends them, goes beyond them, and is inconceivable to the senses alone. Only thinking spirit–not the senses, nor the sensory imagination –could have given rise to the loftiness of this system. It was an idealistic *chimaera* for its time. It shocked not only religious belief, but the belief of the senses, and its certainty rested not on empirical, but on rational grounds. What was the argument for its certainty? That it was simpler, more natural, more reasonable than the Ptolemaic system. What logical argument does this reduce to? That it is contradictory to assert that the whole revolves about the part itself, as about a center. What gave Copernicus the strength to affirm his system? Only the belief in its rationality–reason's own self-assurance. . . . Galileo regrets that Copernicus was not fated to live in Galileo's own time, and then cries: Oh Nicholas Copernicus, how happy you would have been to live to see this part of your system (i.e. the phenomena of the orbits of Venus, Mars, and the moon, which were still inexplicable and contradictory in Copernicus' own time) fully confirmed by our own observations and research. That's how Galileo could talk in *his* own time! But now, we ought to say "Oh, Nicholas Copernicus, be glad that you don't live in *our* time, the age of the slavery of the spirit, of Historicism, of Empiricism, of Positivism. Were you to breach so audacious, so heroic an *a priorism* nowadays, you'd have to atone for such a shockingly anachronistic idealist *chimaera* in a lunatic asylum, at the very least!" (II, 135–7)

It would appear that Feuerbach leaves *no* role for the senses, in establishing scientific truth. But he does not go so far. He denies only that the senses *alone* can give rise to theoretical truths. "Experience can confirm, develop, perfect what has been discovered, but the act of discovery is an *a prioristic* act, an act of genius. And genius is nothing but the anticipation of experience, the capacity for synthetic judgments *a priori*" (II, 137). Thus does thought transcend sense, and thus is it to be reckoned as an *independent* activity. The mark of its independence is its self-differentiation–its capacity to distinguish itself consciously from its object. Oddly enough, Feuerbach takes the act of suicide as the paradigm of this self-alienation of thought and of its *independent* power. If thought is taken to be an unmediatedly organic activity, or an unmediated manifestation of the brain's power to act, Feuerbach asks the reductionist to explain how this thought can so isolate and abstract itself from its organ that it can lead to the very negation, the very destruction of its own organic basis, by suicide. He asks, "How can the manifestation of a power destroy that power itself? ... Explain to me this insurgency of the brain against itself, this being-against-itself in one and the same power to act" (II, 139). Feuerbach asserts that no *thing* can negate itself, but can only affirm itself, in existence—it *is*. No *thing*, as such, has the capacity of self-separation, self-differentiation. The very fact that man can *conceive* of thought, or of spirit cannot be explained on the basis of brain acts as merely material activity. Further, argues Feuerbach, the *concept* of body or of matter cannot arise from body or matter itself. "Where there is only matter, there is no concept of matter.... Only for a being which can differentiate itself from matter—or more correctly, only for a self-differentiating being can matter exist, just as darkness can exist only for a person with sight but not for a blind one" (II, 140). Feuerbach affirms the necessity of matter for thought itself but not in the materialist dependence relation. Rather, matter becomes (in true dialectical fashion) the condition of thought's own *self*-knowledge. Thought can know, or come to know, itself only through matter. "The goal of our life is knowledge of the spirit," says Feuerbach, "and we are endowed with body in order to differentiate ourselves from body, and thereby to become spirit by this very process of differentiation" (II, 141). "*Ohne Leib, Kein Geist,*" says Feuerbach. "Minds without bodies are mindless objects of fantasy." That activity in which spirit actualizes itself by differentiating itself from matter or from body is *thinking*. But thinking requires images, and thus sense perception and imagination are prerequisite for the development of thought. In the teleological context of the Hegelian *Idea*, the senses and sense imagery only serve the end of *stimulating* thought, which alone can discover the truths hidden behind the sense images. Even abstract thought requires images, or signs, says Feuerbach—not in order to think about these images or signs themselves but in order to abstract from them as its material. Thus, the function of brain activity is imaging activity; and further, the culmination of brain activity is therefore fantasy. Brain activity goes no further than this, and this alone is the sense in which brain activity is a necessary condition for the stimulation of thought. But fantasy is not reason. Rather, it takes the images to be things; it hypostatizes appearances; it takes imagination for reality.

Where spirit is dependent on its organ, there sensory imagery reigns, there imagination is the involuntary manifestation of brain activity. But there reigns only falsehood and deceit, fancy, illusion. Brain-activity is, therefore, only the condition, and only the negative condition of thought. (II, 142)

Feuerbach's conclusion, now buttressed by this Hegelian-idealist argument, is that "thought is not the subject of physiology, but only of philosophy" (II, 143). Only the thinker *as thinker* can know thought. And this defines philosophy—it is that thinking which takes thought itself as its object. This is what the thinker *as* thinker deals with. To take the physiological act as an act of thought is to make the same mistake as to take the act of *reading* as an *eye* activity:

When I study Plato, and think what he thought, I have to read, and in order to read, I have to see. . . . So the act of studying is *also* a sensory act for me. But seeing the letters is not yet reading, and reading is not yet understanding. One who takes the words for things, who can't abstract the thought from the sign is very far from understanding, even though what he reads is imprinted in his brain. (II, 143)

Feuerbach thus affirms the necessity of sense activity as the organic condition for thought; there is no thought without sensation or, at least, without sense imagery as its vehicle. This, in classical terms, is the role of the Imagination; but it is not the genesis of thought—only its material and its stimulus. Thus, says Feuerbach:

To take the senses as the sources of knowledge, as empiricism does, is as much as to derive the understanding (e.g., of an author) from the act of reading. For the objects of the senses, as such, were one to take away thought, are nothing but meaningless images and signs. We read the book of nature through the senses, but we don't understand it through the senses. The understanding is an act of its own, an absolutely independent act. (II, 144)

The sense of this "absolute independence" of the understanding, its a priori nature, is to bother Feuerbach seriously. At best, his argument comes to this: *Because* the understanding cannot be derived from the senses, it must, therefore, be independent. This is a negative argument. Its positive correlate is the all-out assertion of metaphysical idealism, namely, that its independence derives from the independence of thinking substance itself. But if this idealism is taken away, that is, if one does not originate the understanding in Idea or in thinking substance itself, the negative argument remains open to modification. What if one conceived of sense activity and of perception in such a way as to establish it as the *genesis* of thought, though not thereby *identical* with thinking? At the end of the critique of Dorguth, Feuerbach writes:

To try to determine anything about the objects of experience without experience is nonsense. Were a philosopher to attempt to acquire or purport to give us *a priori* knowledge in *this* sense, he would be a fool. But . . . the concept of sensory phenomena, the *understanding* of them, is *a priori*, is plainly *the a priori*, and the only *a priori* there is. (II, 144)

Knowledge of this sort goes beyond the limits of physiology and is independent of any "anthropological" or "pathological" or other "positive" knowledge, says Feuerbach. It is this that ultimately establishes the truth of idealism, and the nullity of that empiricism "which wants to murder the spirit with the anatomist's scalpel."

In this critique of Dorguth's views, Feuerbach expresses, in its latest form, his desire to account for the role and nature of sense experience within an idealist framework. He considers a reductionist, physiological materialism as the necessary consequence of empiricism, and thus identifies empiricism and materialism in this sense. And his concept of matter is still that of a classic idealism: It is inert, "dead" matter. It has no self-activity, no principle of its own self-differentiation; it merely *is* what it is, in itself. As such, it cannot account for *thought*, whose hallmark is self-differentiation, the capacity to reflect on itself, to take itself as its own object, which therefore requires the self-activity, at least, of self-separation, or self-alienation. The role of matter (and on teleological idealist grounds, its *raison d'être*), is to provide the vehicle for thought's self-differentiation, or more rigorously, to *be* nothing but the *otherness*, the self-separated aspect of thought itself, and thus, to have no independent existence. Still, there is the suggestion of an activity, in brain acts. These Feuerbach takes to be essentially acts of imaging, of forming impressions, in the traditional empiricist sense. But in his discussion of Leibniz, he had already applauded Leibniz's view that even such instances of passivity, and of receptivity, are "acts" (i.e., a *kind* of activity). Receptivity is already selectivity (i.e., it has a species nature); it is a specific capacity. Capacity itself is thus already active. Further, sensation, the brain's capacity to receive impressions, "acts" as a stimulus (*Reiz*) to thought; it is the goad to thinking activity, in the negative sense that it supplies the material of a contradiction, namely the conflict between appearance (sensory imagery) and reality (the object of thought), and thus is the condition for that dialectic that generates knowledge as a synthesis. Feuerbach requires more than this, for the *material* of the contradiction cannot as yet give rise to *real* contradiction unless there is a reflection of this contradiction *in thought*; that is, contradiction as such has its *Being*, so to speak, only in consciousness. The mere appearance, in sensation, of the elements of contradiction is not yet contradiction realized. Thus, at this stage, Feuerbach still presupposes the Hegelian dialectic as the foundation of his Critique.[15]

PHILOSOPHY AND CHRISTIANITY: REPLY TO HEINRICH LEO

The distinction between sense and reason, which runs through the critique of Dorguth's empiricism, is reconstrued systematically in relation to the distinction between religion and philosophy in Feuerbach's last defense of Hegel, his *Philosophy and Christianity*. In this work he continues the discussion, initiated in the *Bayle*, on the nature of belief, and the critique of "learned belief" (i.e., theology). *Philosophy and Christianity* was published in 1839, after the *Bayle* and the *Critique* of *Dorguth* (both of which appeared in 1838). The critiques by Bachmann and Dorguth attacked Hegel from the "left"; that is, from the point of view of empiricism and materialism. The critic whom Feuerbach deals with in *Philosophy and Christianity* attacked Hegel from the "right"; that is, from the position of Christian orthodoxy. Heinrich Leo, a professor of history at Halle, had attacked Hegelian philosophy as un-Christian, in an 1838 article in the *Augsburger Allgemeine Zeitung* entitled "Die Hegelingen" ("The Hegelings"). His charge of Hegelian "atheism" was leveled at the so-called young Hegelians, in the context of the political-clerical struggle between Catholic Bavaria and Protestant Prussia.[16] Arnold Ruge, editor of the *Hallesche Jahrbücher* and ostensible leader of the young Hegelians, had committed his publication to its first explicitly political stand on this issue, and Heinrich Leo's attack on Hegelianism signified the official disfavor into which the *Hallesche Jahrbücher* was falling. Feuerbach's defense of Hegel was in effect as much a political defense of the young-Hegelian position as it was a defense of philosophy against clerical orthodoxy. Its main lines had already been sketched in the *Bayle*: "positive" (i.e., churchly) theological religion was essentially incompatible with a free, unfettered Reason, the hallmark of philosophy. The grounds of this incompatibility, as Feuerbach already suggested in the *Bayle*, were the particularity, concreteness, locally limited and "practical" reference of religious belief, on the one hand, and the universality, the "theoretical," nonanthropomorphic, and "objective" character of philosophy or science, on the other (cf. pp. 120). The role of concrete (and therefore sensory) imagery in religious belief had also been suggested in the *Bayle*. In *Philosophy and Christianity*, the dichotomy between religious belief and philosophical reason is likewise systematically related to the distinction between sense and feelings, on the one hand, and thought, on the other. Again, the classic rationalist pattern emerges: The senses "know" (or we should say "are acquainted with") only particulars; reason alone "knows" universals. Thus, despite all attempts at reconciliation, philosophy and religion are unalterably opposed, because they represent opposed modes of knowing. "The basis of philosophy is thought; the basis of religion is feeling and fantasy" (VII, 47), writes Feuerbach. To feeling, science appears as a limited view, because the determinateness of scientific thought appears only as limitation. Science is therefore the sphere of the finite.

> For feeling, reason is a finite activity, and only fantasy is an infinite activity. Not only the determinations of intellect, but the laws of nature, which reason knows as rational laws, are limitations. But fantasy is precisely that activity which is not bound by the laws of nature, but rather rules over nature with limitless arbitrariness, and metamorphoses even the most heterogeneous things into one another. Therefore, religion is, essentially, nature dramatized. (VII, 48)

But religion as fantasy, as dramatization of nature according to the arbitrariness of feeling, does not come into conflict with science, or with theory in *this* form. This is no more than a theater for man's affective life. Religion, however, is more than the mere activity of fantasying. It also expresses itself in words, in concepts, in ideas—in short, in the currency that properly belongs to the realm of rational thought. Feuerbach proposes an analogy here: the proper mode of religious expression is symbolized by the *musical tone*, that of philosophy, by the *word*. "The word doesn't address the feelings as immediately as does the musical tone, precisely because the word determines and restricts, and thereby destroys the magical charm that lies in the indeterminate tone" (VII, 47). But philosophy clashes with religion once the latter presents itself in verbal, and therefore in conceptual, form, and appeals to the laws of the intellect in its representation. Philosophy comes into conflict with religion, then, "only insofar as religion has a literary representation—in theology" (VII, 48). Thus, says Feuerbach, philosophy has as little to do with combating the actual beliefs of believers as it has with the popular education and instruction of the people. Philosophy's task is not to criticize the belief of the believer; it knows its own limits, as any good therapist should, and takes as its proper subject matter concepts, ideas, theories. Therefore, it is not *actual* beliefs that concern the philosopher as critic, but *theories* of belief.

> For example, [Philosophy] doesn't deal with the religious belief in miracles as such, but only with the concepts and ideas by means of which the religious belief in miracles is justified as a rational belief. . . . Thus, philosophy doesn't fight belief as such. . . . This lies outside its domain—but rather, it combats *theories* of belief, belief once it has passed through the hands of the learned gentlemen, . . . once it has been divested of the immediacy of folk-belief, and has been raised to an abstract, i.e. scientific—or at least formally scientific subject. But that which has been committed to writing has lost the right to claim indisputable holiness for itself, and must permit itself to become an object of criticism and polemic. If one wants to decree that matters of faith

are not to be critically written about, then one must also decree that one may not write about such matters at all–that there be absolute silence on matters of religion. For if it is to be allowed to theologians to justify miracles and the like on bad grounds, by means of sophisms, then thinking people must also be allowed to refute such arguments on good grounds, by means of evident truths. But this refutation doesn't relate directly to the belief of believers; rather, it relates to Doctoral belief, the belief of the learned, who have betrayed the privacy of their belief. . . . (VII, 49–50)

In this way, Feuerbach attempts to answer Leo's charge of unchristianity and atheism in Hegelian philosophy. The "belief of believers," for better or worse, remains secure, if it remains in the proper domain of belief–that of sensibility, feeling, the heart. Its proper form is fantasy, but not *that* fantasy that impinges on the domain of reason, of rational law. Once this fantasy image, created by feeling, or by the needs of feeling, is taken for an object of reason (i.e., once it is taken to be a truth claim), then it has arrogated to itself the proper domain of science, or of rational thought: then its *virtual* contradictions become *real* contradictions, to be resolved (or dissolved) by rational critique.

In a sense, this proposed *Concordat* between reason and belief is an uneasy one, even on Feuerbachian grounds, for the mere description of the belief of believers as, in effect, whatever they choose to believe, evades the issue of the justification of belief. And belief without justification is irrational belief, just as the justification of belief is also irrational in substance (because it is ultimately a matter of feeling or sensibility), though rational in form. Still, Feuerbach was to hold on to his tolerance of "immediate" belief, through the whole extended critique of the foundations of such belief, in his later work. In *Philosophy and Christianity*, he gives full expression to the theme begun in the *Bayle*: The critical task of philosophy is to expose and attack *theology*, as an illegitimate intruder into the domain of thought.

Here also the fundamental themes of his critique of religion are formulated in an initial way. The central concept of Feuerbach's later critique is that of "human essence," or essential human nature. In straightforward idealist terms, such an "essence" would transcend any finite instances of it, and would be independent of, though actualized or concretized *in*, individuals. This concept had already been developed in the *Dissertation*, with respect to Reason. But even there transcendent reason was not an inhuman, or nonhuman reason. Consciousness was taken to be *human* consciousness, but not the individual consciousness of a particular human being; rather, it was that *species concept* in which individuals participated, and through which they achieved their essential humanity. Thus, the notion of "species concept" (*Gattungs-*

begriff), midway between the classical notion of abstract universal and the biological, classificatory notion of *species*,[17] is an early feature of Feuerbach's thought. That it is a variant on Hegel's Concrete Universal is clear; also, *species* is, in effect, the notion of *class*, in its conceptualist interpretation, as *class concept*: Existence is not attributed to the *class* as such, but to the *class concept*, to that *consciousness* of class inclusion that in fact constitutes the *fact* of class inclusion. Thus, the *class of men*, or the *species*, exists insofar as man is conscious of himself as a member of the class. It is not, therefore, a class of individuals per se, but only of such individuals as are *human* (i.e., members of the class, insofar as they participate in the essential property of that class), and this essential property is class consciousness, or *species* consciousness. But consciousness is not knowledge of particulars, only of universals. The very condition of class membership, then, is the conscious awareness of class nature or of species nature, which is itself a universal. Thus does Descartes' dictum that man's *being*, as *man*, in his *thinking*, become transformed into Feuerbach's notion of human essence.

The earliest discussion of this concept, in the form in which it becomes central for Feuerbach occurs, then, in *Philosophy and Christianity*. The context is Feuerbach's answer to Leo's charge that Hegel's philosophy of religion deals only with the universal and abstract, and not with the concrete and individual personality of God; that Hegel, in effect, makes God nothing but a species concept, or class concept; and further, that this species concept is that of humanity, rather than of God. One might almost say that Feuerbach borrowed his notion of species concept from Leo's pejorative formulation, and changed it only in making it laudatory and in developing it further. But it is more likely that Leo caught on to what Feuerbach (and with him, Strauss, Bauer, and Ruge) had intended, and made this the basis of his charge against the "Hegelings." In any case, Feuerbach points out that, *unfortunately*, this notion of a *human* species concept was never expressed by Hegel, and that it goes back more directly to Kant (in his *Idea for a Universal History from a Cosmopolitical Standpoint* and in his favorable review of Herder's ideas on philosophy of history)[18] and that Hegel did not carry it far enough. This is an interesting note, for it indicates, correctly, an important feature of Feuerbach's conceptual development: As Feuerbach's ideas develop, he pushes further back to concepts akin to those of the young Hegel (although Feuerbach himself did not know the early works, which were published only posthumously), and more important, to elements of Kantian, and especially Fichtean thought. This requires more detailed attention than can be given to it here, however.[19] One could say that while he adopts the central features of the Hegelian epistemology, he more and more discards the Hegelian ontology and approaches the humanist elements of Kantian and Fichtean philosophical anthropology. In this early discussion of the notion of *species concept*, he already formulates this humanist interpretation, which he had anticipated in his discussion of ethics, in the *Bayle* (see pp. 131ff.), and which anticipates the later formulation, in *The Essence of Christianity*, in a way that makes it appear, in retrospect, as a preliminary sketch of the later work.

Can the human individual conceive of anything, in thought or feeling, which does not derive from his own species-existence, from the essence of humanity? Can man shed his species-character like a skin? Isn't everything he thinks and feels determined absolutely by his species? Aren't even the most elevated ideas he can conceive ultimately derived from his human species-character? Can the fantasy, which is so unlimited in every other respect, conjure up a more exalted configuration than that of man? What is the angelic body but an "excerpt" of the human body freed from all the inconveniences that man wishes himself rid of. But if man can't even rise beyond his own sensory configuration, in his conception, how can he transcend his own essence? The positive difference between man and the animals is only this: that man's species is an object for him. Through it he has an inner life, which the animal lacks. What else are all the predicates which speculation and which religion itself can attribute to God but ideas which man derives from his knowledge of himself as species? And what is a subject without its predicates; what else is the subject at all but the sum of its predicates? Will, Understanding, Wisdom, Being, Reality, Personality, Love, Power, Omnipotence–what else are these but species-concepts of man? What is the concept of creative activity but the species-concept of activity freed from the limits of particular acts, which are bound to particular objects? What is omnipresence but human presence freed from the limitations of presence at a particular place, to which the individual is bound. Being at a place, or being in space in general is not yet negated by the concept of omnipresence, but only being at a particular place to the exclusion of other places. When St. Augustine, Dionysius the Areopagite, Thomas Aquinas, or Albertus Magnus say that God is not good, nor beautiful, nor just, nor true, but *is* Goodness, Beauty, Truth itself, and that the Good and Truth are his essence, what else does this mean–not for them of course, but for us–but that God is the real species-concept? According to these thinkers, essence and existence are not differentiated in the *Essentia Divina*, and Goodness, Truth, Justice are the *Essentia Divina* itself. What else is this but the personified species-concept of Goodness, Truth and Justice? Or are these something other than species-concepts? Who can deny this but a blind fanatic or a raving ideologist or a God-inebriated theosophist? [Feuerbach adds this footnote:] All positive species-concepts, or ideas have their origin in the fact that his species is an object for man. Only on the basis of the consciousness of species, of humankind, do I have an awareness of Justice, Love, Truth. (VII, 69–71)

There remains only one step to be taken beyond this to the humanist materialism of *The Essence of Christianity*. That step is the explicit break with Hegelian idealism, and with "speculative philosophy" in general. But it is not taken here. It is not "material" human *existence* that defines the species concept, but human *thought*—the consciousness of one's humanity as consciousness of its essential predicates; and of these as *ideal* predicates. Philosophy as such is still conceived as the mode *par excellence* of such consciousness.

Belief still remains problematic here. Feuerbach's position seems to be: Render unto belief that which belongs to it. But very little belongs to it, except the fantasy life of man, which Feuerbach appears to ascribe only to the condition of childlike innocence, prior to the age of reason.[20] Nevertheless, it is this innocence that he wants to defend against the "hypocrisy" of the theologians.

Every attempt to mediate between Dogmatics and Philosophy is a forced union, against which one should protest as much in the name of Religion as in the name of Philosophy. All religious speculation is vanity and falsehood—a lie against reason and a lie against belief, a play of pure arbitrariness in which both reason and belief defraud each other. (VII, 72)

But what belief is being defended here? What "true religion" is being upheld against the theologians? The mere *fact* of belief in itself is empty, without an object of belief. Feuerbach lamely agrees that it is in general true that one must believe in order to know, in the sense that every thinker "believes" in truth, in reason, in mankind. But if the function of belief is itself ascribed to the affective life, and to sensibility, and if these are in *essence* contradictory to reason and are the objects of rational criticism, then belief serves only as the whipping boy for reason, and has, at best, a negative significance. It offers only the "material" (i.e., the "raw material," the necessary but not sufficient condition) of contradiction, which emerges as *real* contradiction only for a reflective (i.e., a rational) consciousness. Thus, it subserves reason in the same way as sense imagery or imagination subserves thinking in general—as its "goad" or stimulus.

Feuerbach's attempt to seal off the "belief of believers" and to distinguish it absolutely from "learned" or "Doctoral" belief becomes very nearly a cry for either/or: Believe literally and truly, without interpretation, or justification, or else disbelieve. The theologians, says Feuerbach, are disbelievers hiding under the mantle of belief—"unbelieving believers," as he calls them again and again—who caricature belief. But aside from *religious* belief, Feuerbach has as yet no clear conception of empirical belief or of rationally grounded empirical belief. And as to rational belief as such (i.e., intellectual belief), the terms themselves are mutually exclusive in Feuerbach's view of the distinction between sense and reason. The word *Glaube* has no intellectual correlate, in this scheme. In one odd instance, Feuerbach seems to talk about *natural*, as opposed to *religious*, belief, but it is little more than a linguistic trick: He addresses himself to Spinoza's argument (in the *Tractatus Theologico-Politicus*, Chapter VI) that miracles are only unusual natural phenomena that we do not yet comprehend because of our ignorance. Feuerbach comments that one who explains miracles in such a way "still believes in the miracle, but believes it in the sense of disbelief which explains the miracle naturalistically" (VII, 82). We have, then, in addition to the "unbelieving believers" (a term that is at least rhetorically meaningful), the "believing disbelievers" (a term that so confuses the original Feuerbachian sense of "belief" that it must be written off as a stylistic excess). The lack of a theoretical foundation for "natural" or "scientific" belief cannot be remedied until Feuerbach makes the more radical move to an empirical grounding of knowledge. This still requires the final rejection of Hegelian idealism.

In order to take this step, Feuerbach had to reformulate radically his characterization of philosophy–and of speculative idealism in particular. In the *Bayle*, in *Philosophy and Christianity*, as also in his 1838 *Critique of Christian or "Positive" Philosophy*,[21] Feuerbach had sharply separated religious belief and rational thought, theology and philosophy, as essentially contradictory. His critique of theology, whether in its orthodox form or in its philosophically apologetic form (as "Christian philosophy"), had as one of its major arguments the separation of the dependent, particular, and practical character of religious dogma from the independent, universal, and absolutely free character of philosophy. The demand that philosophy conform to some external standard–to the teachings of the Church or of the Bible–is therefore a "vulgar and vicious demand," which in effect asks philosophy to give up being philosophy. In the *Critique of Christian or "Positive" Philosophy*, Feuerbach had attacked the formulations of a "positive," "personalistic" philosophy, in "Christian" terms, as a travesty on both philosophy and religion. He argued that both religion and philosophy were either self-sufficient, each on its own grounds, or were nothing at all. "Insofar as Positive philosophy wants to be both religion and philosophy–i.e., "religious philosophy," as it calls itself–it is neither religion nor philosophy" (VII, 133). Now, Feuerbach was to go further. He was to identify speculative philosophy, the systematic idealism of Hegel, as *itself* a form of this same "religious philosophy," but an exceptional form, one in which the contradiction inherent in theology is masked in an absolutely abstract, rationalist form. In short, the very antithesis that Feuerbach found between fantasy (as the expression and symbolization of feeling) and reason, he now finds in the

Hegelian concept of Reason itself, and in the systematic structure of Hegel's *Logic* itself, insofar as the *Logic* is the purported structure of the Idea, that which Reason concretizes. In 1839, in the same year that *Philosophy and Christianity* appeared, Feuerbach published his *Critique of Hegelian Philosophy*. The readers of the *Hallesche Jahrbücher* were presented with Feuerbach's last defense of Hegel (and of his proper heirs, the "young Hegelians") on page 481, and later in the same year, with his full-scale rejection of Hegelian idealism, on page 1657.[22]

CHAPTER VII

The Critique of Hegelian Philosophy: Part II

The stages of Feuerbach's break with Hegelian idealism may now be reconstructed. They reveal a clear dialectic, most remarkable in its sequence of criticisms and rejections. Feuerbach's work the *Critique of Hegelian Philosophy* as the capstone of this development, appears, then, not as a sudden inspiration, but as the product of a long and agonizing series of appraisals, moving through the apprentice's defense of his master to his full attack on the foundations of the master's theory.

First, there is the critique of "dogmatic belief," beginning in the final sections of the *Leibniz* and running throughout the *Bayle*, as its major theme. Next, there is the critique of the limits of empiricism and materialism, as theories inadequate to account for rationality and scientific knowledge; thus, in these two stages, there is a Hegelian "negative" dialectical critique of the joint inadequacies of blind belief and of blind empiricism; but here also, an attack upon "learned" or "justified" belief, as a perversion of the essence of belief–that is, feeling. This perversion is theology. What follows, then, is a defense of Hegel against the "orthodox" critics, whose standpoint is itself inadequate to a comprehension of the master's thought. From this, Feuerbach moves on to an outright attack on the orthodox (i.e., "Christian") philosophers, on the grounds of their fatal limitations, as "personalists," as anthropomorphizing "positive" philosophers, bound to the finitude of their sense imagery and unable to go beyond the faculty of imagination to that of Reason. (Here is a utilization of the previous theory of the limits of both "belief" and "empiricism," insofar as they can express only the affections and the abstract–i.e., nonrational–sensations.) Finally, in an unexpected move, there is an attack on Hegelian idealism itself, as "nothing but" the most rigorous, most abstract, and most rational form of this very "Christian" or "theological" philosophy itself – its "sober" rather than its "inebriated form," but nevertheless "theological." And with this move, there is a rejection of "speculative philosophy" itself as the embodiment of this deception.

Just as a consideration of Feuerbach's defense of Hegel against the empiricist and orthodox critics is necessary to understand the genesis and the content of the *Critique of Hegelian Philosophy*, so too it is necessary to consider the transitional stage in which he actively attacks the "orthodox" or "Christian" philosophers (who had attacked Hegel). The intensity of Feuerbach's philosophical activity is attested to by the shortness of the period in which the transition took place. Also, this intense period is marked by the relative coincidence of various phases of Feuerbach's thought in the two years 1838 and 1839. In 1838, before the publication of *Philosophy and Christianity*, Feuerbach had already suggested that Hegelian philosophy needed to be bypassed. And it was then too that he prepared the ground for the attack on Hegel by an apparently *different* attack on the non-Hegelian and anti-Hegelian "Christian" or "positive" philosophers, Gunther and von Baader.

This attack appeared in a review of a book by J. Sengler.[1] The main content of the review is an attack on the attempt to formulate a "religious philosophy," which (as remarked earlier) Feuerbach took to be neither religious nor philosophical. But the significance of the review goes beyond this attack. Here Feuerbach is not attacking theology as such, but "speculative philosophy," the explicit attempt to include a personal God in a systematic philosophical framework. It is here, then, that Feuerbach makes his first clear attack on the concept of "personality" and here that he formulates a view of personality, as well as of our mode of access to personality, that is incidentally strikingly like that of Kierkegaard. The personal is the singular, and as such is not an object of reason, but of belief. This aspect of the review shall be discussed later. Its relevance here is that Feuerbach takes this "positive" view of personality, in theistic terms, as the paradigm of "speculative philosophy," and sees such a philosophy as no more than a projection and objectification of the subjective individual, *as* individual. But because *individual* life is the life of individual *feeling*, of individual *wish fulfillment*, and of individual *imagination* (as the instrument of feeling and wishing, in the activity of fantasying), then a philosophy built on this basis is a fantastic, hence irrational philosophy. It is a "philosophy of absolute arbitrariness, which in disregard of all the laws of thought, thoughtlessly brings together the most contradictory things" (VII, 137).

Only the Imagination [can do this], but not Reason. What is impossible for Reason is easy for the Imagination. One can think only that which is rational, but one can represent or imagine everything possible. Thinking is an activity determined and limited by Reason; but Imagination is limitless; it is the sense-organ for that which is senseless.[2] No law and no truth exist for it. Positive philosophy has the Imagination, not thought, for its basis: it substitutes mere images for thoughts, the picture for the thing, the phantasm for the concept. It is, in short, absolutely fantastic philosophy. (VII, 138)

The paradigm of this fantasy is the absolutization of self-consciousness, in which "the speculative philosopher fosters the illusion that the object of his speculation is not his own self, but an other, divine self" (VII, 140), and then proceeds to take this other as the Absolute Person. In the double reflection of this subjectivism, the speculative philosopher then construes his own self as no more than the appearance of this other, objective self: My self-knowledge is really God's knowledge of me, and my awareness of God's knowledge of me. Feuerbach quotes von Baader on this (VII, 143): "The human spirit is known to God, and knows its own being-known; nature is known to God but doesn't know itself." Feuerbach writes this off as "mystification of the self," but explains its appeal in this way:

Philosophy is disillusion—therefore, astringent, bitter, austere, repelling, unpopular. Speculation is self-illusion—therefore easy-going, agreeable, popular, as is every illusion. The philosopher philosophizes on the essence of man, but with the awareness that this is also his own essence. The speculator speculates on this without this awareness, because, unlike the philosopher, he fails to distinguish between his own individual essence, and the general essence of mankind. He takes his own essence to be that of an other, and he deludes himself. The speculator is a Tautologue. He thinks he is expressing something more than himself, but he only says the same thing twice—he goes round and round in a circle about himself. (VII, 142)

After a few more pithy characterizations (e.g., "Speculation is philosophy in the condition of sleep-walking" [VII, 141], "Speculation is drunken philosophy" [VII, 153]), Feuerbach ends with a surprising note. Until now, he had attacked "Christianizing" philosophy on the grounds of its confusion of objective essence, as that which is truly universal, and therefore an object of rational thought, with subjective, individual esssence, as that which is merely personal. He had charged speculative "positive" philosophy with crude anthropomorphism. He had said all the things one would expect of a rationalist Hegelian against the subjective aspects of Fichtean and Schellingean philosophy. He had belittled the claims of "objective" identity of self and God in "positive" terms as no more than the projection of a fantasying self, unrestricted by the laws of reason. But at the very end of the essay (after an admonition to heed the Socratic dictum "Know thyself," offered gratis to the "positive" philosophers,) Feuerbach says, quite unexpectedly,

The Critique of Hegelian Philosophy: Part II

Philosophy must, in any case, surpass and go beyond Hegelianism. It is speculative superstition to believe in the actual incarnation of philosophy in a particular historical phenomenon. How can you want to be philosophers, and at the same time confine the eternally creative life of the spirit in narrow time-space limits? There was a time when Aristotle was philosophically and rationally valid. Haven't this time and its beliefs vanished? Won't it be the same with you and with your beliefs? (VII, 153)

There is certainly nothing earthshaking in the proposal that any philosophical system will have its day, and then become a thing of the past. The historical relativity of various philosophies was a well-embedded feature of the Hegelian view. Still, the Absolute hung over the succession of philosophies as a sign in the heavens: "Your philosophy is relative with respect to *this.*" This much messianic Hegelianism had achieved: It had given the true believers a glimpse of heaven. But Feuerbach is here insisting that this heavenly apparition is itself merely another in the parade of philosophic "eternal verities," and that this too shall pass; that the alleged "Absolute" is no absolute at all, but is another fantasy objectified, and as fantasy, no more than an absolutization of the limited, historical person of the philosopher himself. Up to this point, Feuerbach had set up the rigorous rationalism of Hegel's *Ideenlehre* as the measure of the inadequacy of *other* philosophies. "Speculation" stood for the most rigorous and critical self-consistency of thought on the assurance that the Being of thought was the Being of reality itself–that the rules and laws of thought were the rules or laws of Being and that philosophy was nothing less than the process of revelation, in consciousness, of this Being. Speculation was, therefore, not merely the methodological self-examination *of* thinking *by* thought, but the ontological discovery par excellence of Being itself. In its subjective aspect, this speculation is "the awareness of the self-awareness of the Absolute Idea." But this subjectivity is given its objective metaphysical status by the concept of Absolute Idea as Truth, Reality, Being itself. But now, Feuerbach is ready to overthrow all the Absolutes, to reject not only Christian theistic metaphysics, but Hegelian metaphysics as well. When Feuerbach includes, in his critique of speculation, the proposal that Hegelian philosophy be surpassed, its sense is not yet that Hegelian philosophy is the *same* as "positive" speculative philosophy, but rather that *even* Hegelian philosophy needs to be transcended. What Feuerbach demands, at the end of the Sengler review, is a simplification–not merely a rejection of the metaphysical absolutes, but a rejection of speculative systems in toto, a rejection of this whole mode of philosophizing. It is not a demand for a *more* inclusive system than Hegel's, but a demand for an end to system building. He links the system-building propensities of

German idealism to the luxuriant excesses of the Imagination itself, and sets against this the austerity of a "simpler" and "more natural" approach.

Only the simplest intuitions and foundations are the true ones. The most important historical, natural and psychological phenomena lend themselves to explanation and to comprehension in a much simpler and natural way (and for that reason in a less contradictory way) than that which speculative philosophy has thus far provided. Speculative philosophy in Germany should rid itself of the prefix "speculative," and in the future it should become (and call itself) straightforward "philosophy"–philosophy without prefix. Speculation is drunken philosophy. Philosophy will become sober once again. Then it will be, for the spirit, what pure well-water is for the body. (VII, 153)

The direct sequel to this passage in the *Critique of Christian or "Positive" Philosophy* is the opening passage in the *Critique of Hegelian Philosophy*, published a year later.

THE REJECTION OF IDEALISM

It is not clear that Feuerbach rejected idealism as such, in his 1838 critique of "positive" philosophy and of speculation. Nor is it clear that Feuerbach merely lumped Hegelianism and "positive" speculative philosophy together, in the review of Sengler.[3] But the criticism that Feuerbach leveled at "positive philosophy" was a forerunner of his Hegel critique, nonetheless. His rejection of the absolutization of individual self-consciousness, in positive philosophy, established the pattern of his rejection of the Hegelian *Idea*, and formed the basis for his critique of Hegel's *Logic*. Much of the groundwork of the Hegel critique was laid, therefore, in the 1838 review. But in 1839 we have a sharper, a more independent Feuerbach. Although the sense of respect for Hegel is still there, the critique is an open and clear rejection of the metaphysical and logical foundations of Hegelianism–a rejection, therefore, of Hegelian idealism itself, and not merely an attempt to reconstruct or improve Hegelianism. The 1838 call for a philosophy that goes beyond Hegel is answered by a foundational critique of Hegel, in 1839.

The *Critique of Hegelian Philosophy* centers on several interrelated but distinguishable issues: (1) There is an initial critique of the Hegelian claim to an Absolute philosophy and of the claim that such a philosophy is absolute *because* it is presuppositionless. (2) This is developed as a characterization of the essentially dialogical or communal character of philosophic thought. That is to say, the understanding, and its instruments, demonstration and proof, are of the nature of species knowledge, and the necessary condition for such knowledge is a community of thinkers and therefore of a means of communication, that is, language.

(3) This "material" condition of communication also becomes the condition of philosophy, and therefore philosophic ideas are not themselves the end of philosophy (i.e., the inquiry into truth) but only the instrument of this inquiry. (4) Given this instrumental character of any philosophic theory, it is then seen that the identification of any particular philosophic theory with Absolute truth is a basic confusion, a hypostatization of the means as itself the object of philosophy. Hegel's *Logic* and the *Phenomenology of Mind* are both seen to exemplify this confusion, the logic in its allegedly absolute, presuppositionless "beginning" with Being itself, and in the confused Hegelian notion of Nothing; the *Phenomenology* in its confusion between actual sense awareness (or sensory consciousness)[4] itself and its representation in thought. Hegel is charged here with a fundamental error with respect to sense perception in the *Phenomenology*. (5) Feuerbach then goes on to expose Schellingean *Natur-Philosophie* as itself an inverted idealism, merely a restatement, in "objective" language, of the hypostatization of self-consciousness that is the hallmark of subjective or egoistic idealism. (6) Hegelian philosophy is then seen as the last, most abstract form of this "speculative" tradition, but one still grounded in the same fundamental error that all idealism makes. (7) The critique ends with a proposal for a philosophy based on human species knowledge, on a dialogue of speculation with itself. Human experience is seen as sensuous experience, and not merely theoretical. Any attempt to transcend this experience results in a blind anthropomorphism, a hypostatization of *human* categories as if they were objective or transhuman categories. The Hegelian form of this hypostatization is characterized as rational mysticism.

It can be seen from this rough sketch that Feuerbach moves decisively away from the rationalist idealism that characterized the *History*, the *Leibniz*, the critiques of Bachmann and Dorguth. What is more, he goes beyond the "left" Hegelianism of Strauss and Bauer, and beyond the attempts to interpret Hegel in a viable way that still retains the centrality of critical (or self-critical) consciousness as itself the sole foundation of philosophy. Although the sense of the term "empirical" as Feuerbach uses it here is still not clear, the move to accommodate an "empirical" standpoint, to found philosophical reflection on empirical *existence* or on concrete "human" existence is clear. An examination of this important transitional work will help to make clear Feuerbach's starting point for the "reform of philosophy" that he undertakes thereafter.

The *Critique* begins with an attack on "Absolute" philosophy, and with a satirical characterization of Hegelianism (reminiscent of Marx and Engels' style in the later *German Ideology*).

German speculative philosophy stands in direct opposition to ancient Solomonic wisdom. Whereas the latter saw nothing new under the sun, the former sees nothing but the new under the sun. Whereas the Oriental lost sight of the difference for the sake of unity, the occidental forgets unity for the sake of difference. Whereas the oriental, in its indifference, with respect to eternal Oneness, arrives at an apathy bordering on idiocy, the occidental intensifies its sensibility to difference and variety to the fever heat of an *Imaginatio Luxurians*. When I say "German speculative philosophy," I mean especially the presently dominant Hegelian philosophy. For the Schellingean philosophy was really an exotic growth – the old Oriental Identity in German soil. (II, 158–9)

The hallmark of Hegelian philosophy, says Feuerbach, by contrast to the Identity philosophy of Schelling, is the principle of *difference*. Where Schelling's philosophy swallows up all differences in a sheer Identity, Hegel's philosophy accentuates difference to an extreme. This "differentiating spirit" reveals itself in Hegel's presentation and treatment of history.

Hegel fixes on and treats only the most glaring differences among various religions, philosophies, ages and cultures, and then only in a process of ascending stages; what is common, similar, identical is pushed entirely into the background. The form of his presentation and his method itself is only that of exclusive Time, and not also that of the more tolerant framework of Space. In his system, there is only subordination and succession, and nothing of coordination and coexistence. To be sure, the most recent stage of development is always that totality which subsumes all the prior stages in itself. But since this latest stage is itself a temporally-determinate existence and therefore has the character of its own particularity, it can only subsume the previous stages by sucking dry the marrow of their independent significance, which they possess only in their own full freedom. Hegelian method prides itself on following nature's own course. To be sure, it models itself on nature; but the copy lacks the life of the original. (II, 159–60)

The point of this criticism of the "exclusive" mode of temporality is that Hegelianism admits "reality" only to that last, most contemporary stage of development that all "lower" stages only subserve teleologically. This, says Feuerbach, is the "monarchical" tendency of a temporalistic philosophy, which loses sight of the necessary and contemporary coexistence of *all* the stages. The leaf may be the precondition for the flower, in Hegel's dialectical sense, but this cannot mean that flowers appear only on defoliated plants. The animal kingdom may subserve human ends, but this does not mean that animals do not also have an independent existence. The coexistence of individuals in "tolerant" space belies the overweening repression of individuality in the hierarchical "end reality" of Hegel's historicism.

The development stages in nature don't merely have historical significance. They are indeed "Moments," but Moments of the simultaneous totality of nature, and not of some distinct, individual, totality which is itself, once more, only a Moment of the universe, i.e. of the totality of nature. It is otherwise in Hegelian philosophy, which has only Time, and not also Space as its Form of Intuition: Totality, Absoluteness is asserted to be a predicate of a particular historical phenomenon, so that the stages of development have no independent significance as existents, but only as historical ghosts, as shadowy "moments," as homoöpathic droplets continuously existing in the absolute stuff. (II, 161)

Although this is not yet an explicit rejection of the Hegelian dialectic in toto, it is one of the earliest criticisms of it as a construction forced not only on nature, but on history itself. To be sure, it "copies nature," but the copy is "lifeless." The more usual, and usually more superficial, charge against Hegel's dialectic, made by later critics, is that it vitalizes nature, and sees a "living process" where there is none. Feuerbach's criticism is not that "nature" is *not* dynamic, that "process" is *not* historical, but that "nature" and "process" are constituted by *independently* existing individuals, which are more than mere "moments" in the overarching process. Feuerbach's initial charge is that Hegel "differentiates" out of all proportion, that he articulates difference and deemphasizes the common. Now, however, he charges that Hegel swallows up the *differentia* in the temporal "Now," in which they only exist as historical "moments," that is, as the historical *explicata* of the present reality, as its "negated and subsumed" constituents, synthesized to the point of extinction.

Skepticism, Feuerbach had said, is the starting point of modern philosophy. Now this skepticism is leveled by Feuerbach against the Absolutization of Hegelian philosophy. But Feuerbach, in this case, is turning the characteristic Hegelian critique of preceding philosophies against Hegelianism itself. Hegelianism had, like preceding systems, exempted itself from the very critique it leveled at other philosophies. In *Philosophy and Christianity*, Feuerbach had written,

Every religion claims Truth for its own, claims real miracles for itself alone, claims for itself alone an unconditionally divine origin—precisely because it doesn't take itself, or at least its own origin, as a subject for critical reflection. . . . Every religion is rationalistic against other religions, as e.g. Minucius Felix, Cyprian, Tertullian and Augustine were rationalistic against the gods of the pagans. The rational monotheism of the Church Fathers lies only in its opposition to the polytheism of the pagans—but with respect to itself, it is blind; it makes itself the exception to the general rule, and doesn't consider valid for itself what it takes for granted as being valid with respect to other religions. (VII, 64)

The *form* that the critique of Hegel takes gives us an interesting clue to Feuerbach's critical development. It turns out that it is not only historical religions that fail to examine their own foundations with the same rational acuity they level at their predecessors, but historical *philosophies* as well. The critique of Hegelian philosophy proceeds isomorphically with Feuerbach's prior critique of religion, and indeed, this latter becomes the model for his critique of classical idealist philosophy in general. But to Feuerbach this suggests more than a formal similarity. If the history of philosophy is a process of critical "negation" and transcendence of earlier views, which uncovers their partiality, then the dialectic of the Idea, the "odyssey of the spirit" proceeds from victory to victory in the sureness of the identity of its method with its substance. But if the very foundation of this progress, the Idea which thus unfolds itself (literally: "*develops*"), is itself nothing but the historically limited, conditional concept of a particular philosophy, then it too–or at least the claims for it as the "Absolute" essence of philosophy–must also become subject to criticism. Feuerbach's move is to note the *formal* similarity of the foundations of theology and the foundations of "Absolute" philosophy, namely, the irrational, uncritical, and uncriticized notion of an absolute, or unmediated *beginning*. Once the connection is made, then Feuerbach can draw on the whole arsenal of his critique of theology–especially in the *Bayle*, in *Philosophy and Christianity* and in the Sengler review–and turn it, by an easy transformation, into the basis for a critique of philosophy itself. Feuerbach's critique goes further, too. It is not merely accidental that theology and speculative philosophy are formally similar. The formal similarity has a profounder sense: Speculative philosophy is nothing but a form, albeit a disguised, rationally appearing form of theology, itself; or as Feuerbach puts it, "the last refuge, the last rational support of theology." The speculative idealist positing of Absolute Idea as the essence of Being is, therefore, nothing but the rationalist form of religion, not in the language of the heart, but in the abstract, and hypostatized language of the intellect, in philosophical language. This latest of theologies, like those preceding it, claims for itself Absolute truth, eternal validity, finality, against all the previous theologies. The critic's task is to expose this. Feuerbach writes,

Thus, e.g., the Christian religion, especially in its historical dogmatic development, is proclaimed as the absolute religion, and in support of this view, emphasizes only that which distinguishes it from other religions, and ignores what is common in all religions, the nature of religion itself, the only absolute which lies at the very basis of all the various religions. So it is with philosophy also. According to the Hegelians, Hegelian philosophy is proclaimed as the absolute philosophy, i.e. nothing less than Philosophy itself–if not by the master, then at least by his pupils, or at least by his orthodox pupils–and in a way which is entirely consistent with the teachings of the master. Not long ago, a

The Critique of Hegelian Philosophy: Part II

Hegelian–in every other respect, a man of astute thought–attempted to establish formally, and to his own mind, unshakeably, that Hegelian philosophy is "the absolute actuality of the Idea in Philosophy." (II, 161)

The fundamental error of such a view, says Feuerbach, is that it does not critically raise the question of how the species can be actualized in an individual. But this is the main question. "What good are all the proofs that the Messiah has come, if I don't believe, in the first place, that a Messiah will, or must, or can appear?" (II, 162). In effect, says Feuerbach, such a view is no more than the belief in Incarnation in philosophical guise; and this latter is a belief founded on faith, not on reason, and cannot therefore be accommodated in philosophy. It is a fundamentally irrational belief. The analogy to the belief in Incarnation is not merely a rhetorical analogy, for Feuerbach. He begins to realize it as a systematically significant analogy, which reveals the profound delusion of speculative idealism in general, and of Hegelian idealism in particular. In a perspicuous passage, Feuerbach gives a preview of the sort of analysis he is to pursue in *The Essence of Christianity*:

Goethe says, "only collectively does man live humanly." Profound, and what's more, true! Only love, admiration, honor–in short, only affect, only feeling, raises the individual to the level of species, as when we are exalted by the beauty of a person worthy of our love, we exclaim: She is Beauty, Love, Goodness itself! But reason . . . knows nothing of the actual, absolute Incarnation of the species in a particular individual. . . . Whatever enters into time and space must obey the laws of time and space. The God of limitation stands as guardian of the gate. Self-restriction is the condition of entry. Whatever becomes actual, becomes so only by virtue of its determinateness, its delimitation. The incarnation of a species, in all its aspects, in the form of a single individual would be an absolute miracle, a prodigious transcendence of all the laws and principles of actual existence–it would, in fact, be the end of the world.

Clearly, the belief of the Apostles and of the early Christians in the imminent end of the world is intimately connected to their belief in the Incarnation. With the appearance of the Godhead at a particular time and in a particular form, time and space are already transcended, and nothing else can be expected but the end of the world. History is no longer thinkable: it is without sense and purpose. Incarnation and history are absolutely incompatible: where the Godhead enters into history, there history ends. But if history pursues its course as before, then the theory of Incarnation is factually refuted by history itself. . . .

But it is the same with theories of Incarnation in art and in science. Were Hegelian philosophy in fact the absolute actuality of the Idea of philosophy, then the end of reason would have, as its consequence, according to Hegelian philosophy itself, the end of time. But if time pursues its sad course, now as before, then the predicate of absoluteness must be denied to Hegelian philosophy. (II, 162–4)

There is an appeal to common sense here, and on this ground an attempt in this passage at a *reductio ad absurdum* of the eschatological consequences of the incarnation theory. "Time," as Feuerbach appeals to it, is ordinary day-to-day time, and "history" is no more here than the flux of ordinary events. These clearly pursue their sad, ordinary course, regardless of what metaphysics or theology has to say about them. It seems odd, perhaps, in a present-day context, that Feuerbach should have to strain so hard to establish the conditionality of Hegelian philosophy, or of any philosophy whatever. But apparently more is at stake, for Feuerbach, than merely bursting the bubble of Absolutist pretensions among the orthodox Hegelians. If it were only this, then the commonsense appeal would, in itself, be crass and antiphilosophical at best. What is at issue in this general denial of "Incarnation" in philosophy is the specific denial of the Hegelian claim to a presuppositionless beginning; thus, it is a critique of the Hegelian concept of *Being*.

Feuerbach is careful to qualify his attack: Hegel himself never made such explicit, preposterous claims. Only his orthodox followers did. But they follow, nonetheless, from Hegel's own system, and especially from his *Logic*. The preposterous consequences, the absurdity of an "incarnation" of the Idea of Philosophy itself may be overdrawn for rhetorical effect. Nonetheless, this is what the more enthusiastic "absolutizers" of Hegelianism openly proclaimed. But Feuerbach's reaction, in 1839, is no longer the left-Hegelian attempt to correct the "misinterpretation," but rather an attempt to find its source at the root of the Hegelian *Logic*. If the consequences are absurd and contradict the facts of ordinary experience, then the source of the contradiction must be tracked down to the premises themselves, to the axioms of the system. The fact that Feuerbach, almost surreptitiously, appeals to such empirical grounds as the test of the *actual* contradiction to which Hegelian philosophy leads is perhaps not even realized by him at this point. "Actual existence" means only something qualitatively vague, somehow related to time and space as the conditions of "finite" existence. But does the phenomenal now sit in judgment on the noumenal, for Feuerbach? Is Feuerbach, after long years of Hegelizing, backsliding to a quasi-Kantian view, as some commentators have suggested? The answer, if we take Feuerbach's brand of empiricism seriously, is clearly *no*, and his later discussion of Hegel's *Phenomenology* will show why.

The basis for the critique of Hegel's *Phenomenology* is the critique of Hegel's *Logic*, and, in particular, of the concept of *Being* in the *Logic*. The initial attempt to show that Hegelian philosophy is a conditional, temporally determined philosophy is merely the preparation for the attempt to show that the concept of Being in Hegel's philosophy is also no more than a conditional and limited concept, and not that "absolute presuppositionless beginning" from which philosophy *as such* must now forever take its departure.

> Every philosophy appears, therefore, as a specific phenomenon of its time, with presuppositions. It appears to itself as presuppositionless, as indeed it is, relative to earlier systems. But a later time recognizes that this philosophy also has its presuppositions. (II, 165)

The presupposition of which Hegelian philosophy itself is critical is the unconditional absolute of Fichtean and Schellingean philosophy (the "Absolute I" of Fichte, the "Absolute Identity" of Schelling). But Hegelian philosophy, as a particular stage of the progress of thought, is bound by the limits of that tradition it takes as its object of criticism. "The only presuppositionless philosophy," writes Feuerbach, "is that which has the freedom and energy to doubt itself, which learns from what stands in opposition to it" (II, 180). But, says Feuerbach, recent German philosophy has not had this character; rather, it *starts* by presupposing its own truth. The mediation of such presuppositions takes the form of explication, as in Fichte's case, or further development, as in Hegel's.

> Kant was critical with respect to the old metaphysics, but not with respect to himself. Fichte presupposes the truth of Kantian philosophy. He seeks only to raise it to the level of a science, which derives from a common principle that in Kant remains separated and disunited. Schelling, similarly, stipulates the truth of Fichtean philosophy on the one hand, and on the other revives Spinoza as the counterposition to Fichte. Hegel is the Fichte mediated by Schelling. Hegel argues against Schelling's Absolute . . . but at the same time posits the truth of the Absolute, . . . and charges Schelling only with mistaking its form. (II, 180–1)

So, through this whole tradition, a common underlying presupposition is made, and its mediation is not a fundamental one, of questioning this basic presupposition, but rather only a process of sharper, more consistent formulation, explication, improvement upon the form this presupposition takes. Feuerbach proposes, then, to question this presupposition in its most refined, most rigorously scientific form, in Hegelian philosophy. In an imaginary dialogue with a Hegelian, Feuerbach asks,

> Doesn't Hegelian philosophy begin with a presupposition also? "No," answers the Hegelian, "it begins with nothing but that which is entirely unconditioned, with the beginning itself." Really? But isn't it already a presupposition that philosophy must make a beginning in the first place? "Well, it is self-evident that everything must begin, and so must philosophy." Granted. But such a beginning is accidental, indifferent. The kind of beginning that philosophy is supposed to make is quite different from this; it is supposed to be that which begins of itself, which is First, in the metaphysical sense.[5] Is the concept of *beginning* no longer an object of criticism? Is it unconditionally true

and universally valid? Why can't I give up the concept of beginning at the very outset? Why can't I start unconditionally with the actual? Hegel begins with being, i.e. with the concept of Being, or with abstract Being. Why shouldn't I begin with Being itself, i.e. with actual, concrete Being? Or why shouldn't I begin with Reason? . . . What's the harm, as long as I can later show that my presupposition is only a formal, apparent one, but is in fact nothing more than this. (II, 165–6)

Thus, Feuerbach does not criticize the making of presuppositions, but rather the tendency in philosophy to absolutize these presuppositions, to take any presupposition as ultimate, unconditional, and immediate— therefore, as necessary. All philosophies are based on presuppositions. But the philosopher's task is not merely to criticize and show what presuppositions *other* philosophies are based on, but to examine the presuppositions of one's own position as well. One might ask, on what basis (or on what presuppositions) is even *such* an inquiry based? And is this not, in effect, an infinite regress? Feuerbach would agree, and this is in fact the point of his statement that all presuppositions are only apparent, or *formal*, that is, for the sake of this or that inquiry. Not all presuppositions are equally valid, and the progress of philosophy is precisely in unmasking the invalidity, the sources of self-contradiction in any presupposition scheme. Instead of being an attack on the dialectic, Feuerbach's position seems to be a more rigorous application of this all-dissolving critical method, at the expense of its *ontological* interpretation in Hegel's concept of the Idea. In short, the absoluteness of the Idea stands in contradiction to the essential anti-absolutism of the dialectic. Hegel had shown the flaw in Schelling's concept of the Absolute. He had shown that Absolute Identity is not unconditioned, but entails a process of self-differentiation. But at the "beginning" and "end" of this process, we merely come full circle: The process is bounded at its beginning and end by this same Absolute. This is the tension, the contradiction in Hegel's system. What is more, it shows the limits of system building itself. Any system ("in the strong sense," adds Feuerbach) is a closed circle, which at the end comes back upon its beginning. This is its character as a *formal* system; but then it must remain *formal*. Its presuppositions must remain formal, and cannot be taken for anything more.[6]

Feuerbach makes an interesting point here, with respect to his previous discussion of language as the instrument of thought, of the "word" as the object of reason. Where Hegel holds the Logic to be the actual form of thought itself, the formal character of the "awareness of the self-awareness of the Idea," as Feuerbach had pointed out earlier,[7] Feuerbach now suggests that the Logic can *at best* be only the form in which thought is presented, for purposes of communication, *in language*, and not the form (or the forms) of thought in itself. With this, the ontological claims of the *Logic* are cut down to claims only about the forms of human communication. The claim to have exposed the structure of truth about Being then turns out to be no more than the more modest claim to have exposed the structure, or the conditions of human knowledge of truth, insofar as truth is *demonstrable*–that is, insofar as it is communicable to an other. But if the identity of Being and Idea is the foundation of the claim that the unfolding of the Idea is in fact the unfolding of the objective truth about Being itself, then Feuerbach's delimitation has one of two consequences: Either this truth turns out to be no more than the "truth" conditions of the use of language, rather than of *Being* as such, or such a truth, in the expository form of linguistic "demonstration," is a truth about the species character, the "essence" of man. And language, communication between two or more, *is* in fact what constitutes humanity as a species. The first consequence is the more skeptical and negative of the two. The second *uses* the linguistic characterization to propound the more radical view that not Being as such, but *human* Being is the subject of philosophy; that what is revealed in consciousness is true not by virtue of the identity of Being and Idea, abstractly, but rather by virtue of the identity of human Being and human consciousness. This tendency toward what appears as a Kantian anthropologism is qualified by Feuerbach's later emphasis on empirical consciousness as noumental, and not merely phenomenal, but this remains to be dealt with later.

Feuerbach develops this line of thought by first distinguishing between *systematic* thought and thinking as such.

Systematic thought is not thought in itself, or thought as it is, in essence, but only thought as it is presented to itself. Insofar as I present, or exposit my thoughts to myself, I place them into time. What is concurrent in my thought, what is grasped by an insight which transcends succession, becomes, in its exposition, sequential. (II, 167)[8]

This much, says Feuerbach, Hegel grasped in a more rigorous way than did, for example, Fichte. Thus, what I begin with, in thought, is indeterminate, and becomes determinate only insofar as it is revealed in the successive moments of its exposition, in its presentation to thought as an object of thought. What is revealed at the "end" of this process is what was already contained in the indeterminate form, but now it is made an object *for* thought and is not merely *in* thought. But however well elaborated this view is, in Hegel, it remains *thought* that presents itself *to* itself; that is, the whole dialectic is ultimately an inner process of thought itself.

To be sure, says Feuerbach, thinking *is* an inner process. It is unmediated activity, insofar as it is self-activity. No one can do my thinking for me. I have myself to become convinced of the truth of my thoughts. Philosophy hasn't the power to *grant* this understanding or this conviction. It is only a means for achieving it. "Philosophy," says Feuerbach, "is not a creation from nothing, but a development ... of that spiritual matter which I already possess. The philosopher only brings me to awareness of what I can know" (II, 169). But he does this by means of language, by means of demonstration.

> Philosophy doesn't speak for speaking's sake–therefore, its antipathy to mere rhetoric; it speaks for the sake of thinking. Philosophy doesn't demonstrate for demonstration's sake–therefore it despises sophistical syllogistic; it demonstrates in order to show that what is demonstrated is so by virtue of the principles of demonstration; that its conclusions are legitimate, according to the rules; i.e. they are such as to express a rule of the understanding valid for every thinker. Demonstration is nothing else but the way of showing that what I say is true; nothing but the return of the externalized form of thought to its origins in thought. The significance of demonstration can't be assessed, therefore, unless one relates it to the significance of language. Language is nothing but the realization of species, the mediation of the I and the Thou, the achievement of the unity of a class or species, in virtue of the transcendence of the individual separateness of its members. The word's element is air, the most spiritual and universal medium of life. Thus demonstration has its ground only in the activity of mediating one's thought so that it can be communicated to others. When I want to prove something, I prove it for others. When I prove, teach, write, I don't do it for myself, presumably. (II, 169–70)

Thus, "truth," for Feuerbach, is not simply a "truth of language" in the formal or the "use" sense (the first alternative presented earlier, see p. 181). Rather, it is linguistic truth by virtue of its being "species" truth, that is, human truth, bound to the conditions of human communication, in the I-Thou sense. Truth, therefore, has its ground in human *Being* and is "ontological" only in this sense.

There is an odd twist hidden here. Whereas Feuerbach had argued, as a young Hegelian, that Reason, Thought, Consciousness alone are universal, one, infinite, the consequences of the present view are radically different. Reason, taken here as consciousness, or thinking activity, appears to be *private*. It is that self-activity that marks off my *individuality*, and not my species existence, my commonality. What, by contrast, enables me to recognize the rationality of others (or to *recognize* my own as well, strictly speaking) is no immediate intuition of "their" or "my" reason, but rather language–the capacity to communicate what I *mean* by means of what I *say*. "Thus," says Feuerbach,

demonstration is not the relation of the thinker, as self-contained thinker, to himself, but rather the relation of the thinker to others. The forms of demonstration and proof are not forms of reason in itself, or of the inner acts of thinking and knowing. Rather, they are only forms of sharing in thought, forms of expression, of exposition and representation, phenomena of thinking. (II, 172)

Feuerbach seems to reject the view that Logic represents the "laws of thought," because the condition of lawfulness is *not* the condition of *thinking* as such, but rather of *demonstration*, of *communication* of thought. In a footnote, Feuerbach writes,

The so-called forms of logical judgment and proof are therefore not active forms of thinking, nor causal relations *in* reason itself. . . . The so-called logical forms are only the abstract, elementary forms of language. But speaking isn't thinking–otherwise the greatest babbler would be the greatest thinker. What we ordinarily take as thinking is only the translation of a more or less unfamiliar, strange and difficult author, who, though he strikes us as congenial, is never known in the original, but only in translation into a familiar language. *And the so-called forms are valid and have application only to the language of the translation, not to the original.* [My stress, M. W.] These forms belong, therefore, not to the Optics, but to the Dioptrics of the spirit–an as yet unknown region. (II, 172n.)

In the same footnote, however, Feuerbach talks of these "derived" logical forms as standing in relation to necessary principles of thought, in the same sense that language does. These "derived" logical forms *presuppose* such "metaphysical" concepts as "Universality," "part-whole," "necessity," "ground," so that "only metaphysical relations are logical relations, only metaphysics, as the science of categories, is the true, esoteric logic–This is Hegel's profound thought." But this would presumably require that we *do* understand the "original" language of the "author," (i.e., *thought*), at least well enough to know its categories despite what Feuerbach says. The alternative is a "transcendental deduction" in Kantian terms, a reconstruction of what presuppositions *would* be necessary for the derivation of the "forms of logical judgment and proof." It is not at all clear how Feuerbach resolves this. But he keeps sharp the distinction between the "appearance," that is, thought as it is presented to us as an object, in language, and the "underlying reality" of this presentation, thought activity itself, as "original," as "a priori," as that understanding that is presupposed by philosophy.

The outward forms of *shared* thought are therefore not the reality of thought, or of thinking activity itself, but only its means, its instrument. Every presentation of a philosophical system is not itself the truth, but merely a means of *my* coming closer to the truth, by means of my own thinking activity, in short, a *heuristic* for thought. The *genius* of thought far outstrips and breaks through these forms, grasps intuitively what requires demonstrative exposition in the outward, linguistic form. It stands to outward demonstration and proof as the lyric does to the dramatic.[9] Feuerbach's analogy takes the dramatic to be the mirror in which I recognize my own thought. No one can literally "share" my thought.

The sharing of thoughts is not a material, actual sharing. The impact, the actual concussion on my ears of a sound, the impinging of light–this is a real sharing. I passively receive that which is material: I suffer it; but that which is spiritual, I possess by my own self-activity. Therefore, what the demonstrater shares with me is not the thing itself, [i.e., thought] but only its means. . . . Otherwise the philosopher would actually be able to produce philosophers– something no one has yet accomplished. He shows me my own understanding only in a mirror. He is only an actor. He only presents to me, in perceivable form, that in which I should imitate him. Expository, systematic philosophy is dramatic theatrical philosophy, in contrast to the lyrical, self-directed, material thought. (II, 173)

This discussion has for Feuerbach a specific object: the criticism of Hegel's *Logic* as *ontology*, as a logic of Being itself. All of this has been for the purpose of delimiting the role of the *Logic* to that of an instrument–a mirror for the recognition of my own thought activity. Thus, the system cannot *be* reason itself, but only its limited, outward *form*. To mistake this *formal* representation for the *material* fact of reason (i.e., thinking activity itself) is a fundamental error, and an error of hypostatization. Hegel's accomplishment, therefore, is not what his "absolutizers" have taken it to be. He does not "incarnate" reason; he merely gives a rigorous model, an externalized presentation of the abstract *form* of reason, but not its *essence*. Hegel's accomplishment, as a *systematic* philosopher, is in recognizing that the appropriate condition for demonstration *is* systematicity.

The exposition of philosophy must itself be philosophical. The exposition of thought, insofar as it is a philosophical exposition, is systematic. Through this systematicity, the exposition achieves a value in and of itself. The systematizer is therefore an artist. The history of philosophical systems is the picture gallery, the *Pinakothek* of reason. (II, 174)

In this sense, says Feuerbach, Hegel is a great artist. But he makes the fundamental error of taking the picture for the thing itself, mistaking the form for the essence. He mistakes the form in which thought appears *for others* (in its representation in a system) for the way thought is *in itself*. Feuerbach charges Hegel with mistaking relative for final goals. In this context, it is clear what Feuerbach means when he says that "the Hegelian system is the absolute self-alienation of reason" (II, 175). He means literally that the projection or the externalization of reason in linguistic or logical form – the *expressed* idea – is already the idea in its *otherness*, and, therefore, the *mediated* idea. But, then, no *system* as such can have an "absolute beginning," by virtue of the very fact that it is a system, that is, *already* the alienated or objectified and external *form* of reason, and not reason in itself.[10] Thus, the "Being" that the Logic begins with is not, and cannot be, "Being" in itself, but only the formal concept of Being, Being as it is presented for thought in its recognizable (i.e., linguistic) or conceptual form.

Here Feuerbach's criticism of Hegel becomes linked with his criticism of "speculative philosophy" in the Sengler review. There he said that speculative philosophy hypostatizes the individual self-consciousness, and takes it for objective, universal *Reason*. It takes as species existence, or essence, what is in effect the individual expression of this species existence in the philosopher's own self-consciousness. Here he modifies this argument in a significant way and says that in Hegelian philosophy, it is the objectification as universal that has the character of being merely formal, and it is the original activity as *individual* that has the character of being essential. It is not Reason as *system* that has, in itself, the character of real Being. This is only outward show, the shared form that acts as stimulus and model for my own thinking activity; that is, it is Being for an-other. The linguistic and logical form that this manifested thinking activity takes is that form under which thought grasps its objects, that is, the form of universality. But this is only the *form* of *understanding* the thought of another, the form under which intellectual community becomes possible. It is the instrument of *learning*, but not the act of *knowing*. Language, as the material condition of communication, dictates this form; and the "unity of form and content" in this context is the unity of logical form and that to which this form is relevant and from which it derives, that is, language. The unity is not that alleged between the *Logic* and Being itself.

This direction of Feuerbach's argument continues the nascent emphasis on *individuality* as the essential form of Being, which had begun to show itself in the *Leibniz*. Feuerbach's sharpest break with Hegelianism hinges on this, in his later development of an empiricism based on an ontology of individuals. Its first statement is in the *Critique of Hegelian Philosophy*, and it appears first in the criticism of the concept of Being in Hegel's *Logic*. The further development of this criticism demands a more explicit reformulation of the concept of thought, however. For if thinking activity still remains that which is ultimately real, albeit in this new version as individual, private, "mine," then we seem to be thrown back on a nominalist idealism that merges with subjective idealism and solipsism. If man's essence is his thinking activity, and, further, if this is his own, original, *individual* activity, then we seem, indeed, to be back to the Fichtean Ego, with its own activity, as the origin of all Being. This radically subjectivist line of thought, which one branch of left Hegelianism took in the work of Max Stirner, is *not* the one Feuerbach pursues, however. His road is thornier.

Feuerbach's theory of thought-as-it-is-in-itself now devolves upon the characterization of Being, as-it-is-in-itself. Feuerbach's strategy is to consider Being-in-itself first, and then to characterize the "Being" of thought in these terms. The consequence of this approach is that thought is characterized *not* as Being itself, but as a determinate *kind* of being, with which there coexist (in the tolerant framework of space) other kinds of determinate being. The seeds of Feuerbach's naturalism are in this relegation of thought, of consciousness, finally of the Idea itself, to determinate and conditioned *kinds* of being. The absolute identity of thinking with Being as such, which Hegel and the younger Feuerbach had posited, no longer obtains here.

Feuerbach's main attack on Hegel's concept of Being derives from his attack on the concept of an absolute or immediate beginning. If we begin, as Hegel does, with "pure, empty Being," then in fact we begin with nothing at all. And Hegel does in fact assert the dialectical unity of this kind of *Being* with *Nothing*. But Feuerbach accuses him of saying nothing at all, to begin with, and of positing therefore a fake contradiction between Being and Nothing.

The *Logic* says: "I abstract from determinate Being. I don't predicate the unity of *Being* and *Nothing* of determinate Being." Since this unity appears paradoxical and ridiculous to the understanding, it shoves determinate Being in place of pure Being, and then indeed, there is a contradiction in asserting that Being as *something* should also be nothing. The understanding answers that only determinate Being is Being. The concept of Being contains the concept of absolute determinateness. I derive the concept of Being from Being itself; but all Being is determinate Being. Thereby, in passing, I also posit *that* Nothing as opposite to Being, which is *not-something*, because I always relate Being inseparably to *something*. If you omit determinateness from Being, then you omit Being as well, with nothing left over. And it is nothing remarkable then for you to show that this sort of Being is Nothing. That's self-evident. If you were to omit, from man, everything which makes him man, then you could prove without difficulty that he is no man. But just as the concept of man, minus all the specific differentia is no longer a concept of man, but of some self-created being, like the Platonic Man of Diogenes, so too the concept of Being, minus its content, is no longer a concept of Being at all. As different as things are, so is Being different. Being is one with that which is, with specific things. (II, 179)

186

Just as Feuerbach attacks Hegel's concept of "Pure Being," he also attacks the "concept" of Nothing as no concept at all, as the absence of any concept. To posit it, then, as the dialectical antithesis to Being reflects on the philosophical emptiness of both of these "concepts." As Hegel himself points out, thinking is determining. Nothing, as lacking all determinations, cannot therefore be thought. Only Being can be thought, and thought cannot transcend determinate Being, because it cannot transcend itself, for the very essence of thinking activity is to think determinately. Thus, Nothing represents the very abdication of reason, as in the concept of creation from Nothing. This expresses absolute arbitrariness, willfulness without reason, as in Augustinean thought. "*Nothing* is an absolute self-illusion, the Πρωτον Ψευδοѕ, the absolute lie," says Feuerbach (II, 197). "Whoever thinks Nothing is no longer thinking. *Nothing* is the negation of thought. It can only be thought if it is made into a *something*" (II, 197). The very concepts by which Nothing is characterized are themselves determinate concepts, or concepts derived from determinate ones.

"Nothing is complete emptiness, lack of all determinations, of all content, undifferentiatedness in itself" [Hegel]. *Nothing* is in itself without differentiation? Am I not endowing this nothing somehow, just as in the Creation from nothing, this nothing is made into a quasi-stuff, so that a world can be created *from* it? . . . Nothing is complete emptiness? What is emptiness? It is empty where nothing is, but where something *should* be, or *can* be: thus "emptiness" expresses a capacity. . . . The lack of all determinations and of all content cannot be thought without respect to "content" and "determination." I have no concept of lack of determination except through the concept of determination. "Lack" expresses something missing, a fault. First I think of content, of determination, because it is positive. I think of nothing only in terms of that which is *not* nothing. . . . So affirmative, so decidedly determinate an activity is thinking, that the indeterminate, insofar as it is thought, is thought as determinate. . . . (II, 197–8)

Hegel's concept of Nothing as the antithesis to Being is "a product of Oriental Imagination which takes that which has no Being as itself a kind of Being" (II, 199), as if it were something positive. Feuerbach continues his characterization in this way:

Nothing is akin, here, to the Zoroastrian night. But it is only the limit of human powers of representation. It doesn't originate in thought, but in non-thought. *Nothing* remains nothing–therefore, nothing for thought, as well. More than this cannot be said about it. Only the fantasy makes this *Nothing* into a substantive, but only by transforming this *Nothing* into ghostly, Being-less Being. Hegel didn't inquire into the genesis of this *Nothing*, but took it at face value. The opposition which Hegel posits between *Being* and *Nothing* as such, is therefore ... not at all a universal, metaphysical opposition ... [but one which] exists only in the imagination, whereas Being exists in actuality, or rather, *is* the actual. .... (II, 201–2)

Feuerbach's argument can be seen as the other side of his rejection of Hegel's concept of pure, indeterminate *Being*–that is, as the rejection of the ontological validity of any of the abstract concepts. Abstractions like Being and Nothing are constructions of the fantasy, of the imagination, and express the limits of reason, beyond which reason cannot function (because it contradicts itself), rather than the heights to which reason can rise. The mistake is not in the fact that the imagination can fantasize pure Being or pure Nothing (at the expense of thinking), but rather that a presumably rational philosophy objectifies or hypostatizes these fantasies and makes them the absolute concepts from which all others derive.

Feuerbach says that Hegel's "contradiction" between Being and Nothing is therefore an empty, merely formal contradiction. The real contradiction to the abstract concept of Being–that is, Being as it is conceived in the Logic–"is not Nothing, but rather sensory, concrete Being. It is sensory Being which disavows logical Being" (II, 180). Feuerbach does not, therefore, reject the notion of dialectical opposition, but attempts to reinstate it in nonformal terms. "The dialectic is not a monologue of speculation with itself, but a dialogue of speculation and the empirical" (II, 180). The dialectic, therefore, requires the "real" opposition of sensory, empirical consciousness with speculative rationalism. But in order for such a dialectic to ensue, the empirical must be constituted not merely as the otherness of reason, or of the Idea itself, but on its own foundations. Otherwise, says Feuerbach, all knowledge becomes merely a matter of "subjective assurances," within the rational monologue. In contemporary terms, the monologue of "speculation" with itself, the reflexology of the Idea, amounts to no more than analytic truth, that is, merely formal truth. But the very condition of coming to know belies this. Coming to know requires the process of demonstration and is essentially a dialogue. It requires two, not one, and the very conditions of communication that underlie coming to know, in this sense, require ingression into the empirical world, require a material or empirical medium as the minimum condition for intersubjectivity.

Demonstration consists in nothing but this: convincing an (actual or possible) other of that of which I am convinced. Truth lies only in the unification of *I* and *Thou*. But the opposite of pure thought is, in general, the empirical understanding. In philosophy, demonstration consists in overcoming the contradiction between empirical understanding and pure thought, so that the thought is not only true for itself, but also for an other. (II, 183)[11]

Otherwise, it remains "subjective, one-sided, doubtful." The attempt to found certainty on pure thought, on the agreement with itself, or on rational intuition is the mark of modern philosophy from Descartes to Spinoza, and also marks the whole speculative idealist tradition in German philosophy. It is based on an absolute dichotomy between intellectual intuition and "actual" or "empirical" intuition.[12]

Because Hegel dealt at length with the whole matter of empirical understanding and the "certainty of the senses" in the *Phenomenology of Mind*, Feuerbach develops his own concept of sense knowledge in his criticism of this work. He charges Hegel with having fundamentally misconstrued his categories of sense knowledge, on the same grounds that he misconstrued the concept of Being. In the section of the *Phenomenology* that deals with "the certainty of the senses," Hegel had attempted to show that empirical knowledge of sensible particulars is dependent on the categories "Here" and "Now," which are not finite, particular concepts, but universal concepts. The tree "here," the house "here," all "vanish" as particulars, but "Here" as universal relation remains. Language expresses this truth, because we can denote particulars only by virtue of universal terms such as "Here" and "Now," and thus what is "meant" or intended by us, in our sensible certainty of impressions of particulars is not expressible in language.

Feuerbach's criticism of this view follows the line of his previous criticism. Hegel's "Here" and "Now" are *empty* universals, whose "reality" is no reality at all. The concepts "Here" and "Now" ultimately derive from particular, finite, temporal "heres" and "nows," and it is these, particular relations among actual, concrete existences that constitute the content of the universal concepts.

My brother's name is John or Adolph. But besides him, there are countless Johns and Adolphs. Does it follow, therefore, that my brother John isn't real? That only Johnhood is real? For sensory consciousness, all words are proper names, *Nomina propria*: they are no more than signs which serve sense-awareness as a means of reaching its goal in the shortest way. Language has nothing to do with this as yet. The reality of sensible, individual Being is a truth sealed with our blood. In the realm of sensibility, this means: an eye for an eye, a tooth for a tooth. In this context, this is to say: never mind this word or that word. Show me what you're talking about. For sensory consciousness, it is always language which is unreal and inconsequential. Why should this sensory consciousness find itself refuted, or be refuted merely because individual being cannot be expressed in language? Sensory consciousness finds, in this, a refutation of language, but not of sensory consciousness. And it is justified. Otherwise, we would find our life's nourishment in words instead of things. The content of the whole first chapter of the *Phenomenology* is nothing but a warmed-over hash, an inverted version of Stilpo the Megarian. . . . (II, 185–6)

The universal concepts are nothing but the abstracted, formal expressions representing the whole set of their concrete, particular instances. It is the individuals that exist, and it is the universals that are derived by "abstraction." Thus, Feuerbach rejects the Hegelian sense of "abstraction" (as a part taken out of the whole, which is its ground). In this Hegelian sense, because particulars as such are "abstract," they do not exist as such. They are, in effect, "unreal." In place of this Platonistic view, Feuerbach adopts the Baconian inductivist sense of universals as generalizations from particular instances, by "abstraction" of their common properties. Here, by contrast, universals are abstract, and existent particulars alone are taken as real. But he leaves this only in the form of an alternative assertion, and does not get into the problem of similarity, or resemblance, or analogy as the basis for abstraction of class properties.

Feuerbach admits the cogency of Hegel's analysis of the *logic* of phenomenological discourse, of the limits of *talk* about the sense awareness of particulars, but charges him with confusing the limits of talking about this sense awareness with the limits of this sense awareness itself. Therefore, he says, the *Phenomenology* is not a phenomenology of consciousness (as sensory consciousness) *itself*, but is a phenomenological *logic*, or, in effect, a metaphenomenology.

The same unmediated contradiction and bifurcation that we met at the beginning of the *Logic* appears again at the beginning of the *Phenomenology* – the bifurcation between Being as it appears in the *Phenomenology*, and as it appears as an object of sensory-consciousness. [Hegel's] phenomenological *Here* is in no way different from any other (phenomenological) *Here* that I fix upon. It appears in both cases as a universal, because it has, in effect, already been conceived as a universal. But the real *Here* is always distinct from other *Heres* in quite real ways – it is an exclusive Here. "This 'here' is, e.g. the tree. I turn around and this truth vanishes," [says Hegel]. Well, this is true enough in the *Phenomenology* where "turning around" only takes a word or two. But in reality, when I have to turn my bulky body around, the "Here" behind my back still appears as a very real existence. The tree limits my back; it excludes me from the place which it occupies. Hegel doesn't deny the "Here" as an object of sensory-consciousness, and as it is distinct from pure thought, but only denies that the logical "Here" and the logical "Now" are such objects. He denies the *thought* of "thisness," of *Haecceitas*. He shows the untruth of the uniquely particular, insofar as it is represented in the imagination as a (theoretical) reality. The *Phenomenology* is therefore nothing but phenomenological logic. Only from this point of view is the chapter on *The Certainty of the Senses* excusable. But precisely because Hegel doesn't get to deal with, or cope with sensory consciousness – (he deals with it only as an object of self-consciousness, of thought, because he takes it only as the self-alienation of thought, in terms of the latter's own self-certainty) – so the *Phenomenology* (or the *Logic*, since it all comes to the same thing) begins with an unmediated posit – or rather with an unmediated contradiction, an unmediated breach with sensory consciousness. For it begins, not with the other-being of thought, but rather with the *thought* of the other-being of thought. The victory of thought over its opposite–i.e. sensory consciousness–is therefore a foregone conclusion. (II, 186–7)

If the object of sensory consciousness as a unique particular "here-now" cannot be referred to, because of the very nature of language, then it would appear to be ineffable, in Feuerbach's terms. His acceptance of Hegel's *Phenomenology* as a phenomenological *logic* would seem to leave him no recourse but to remain silent about immediate experience. Feuerbach's solution here is not to ignore this difficulty, but to make it a central question in his later work. The form under which we come to rational awareness of objects of sense experience is *not* in immediate awareness, but in the representation in the imagination of this awareness, which makes it, in this reflected form, an object of reason. It is symbolized, so to speak, either in its affective or intellectual form (i.e., as object of feeling or of intellect). Only in a projected form, the form the language of the heart or the language of the head imposes on it, does it become an object of *critical* knowledge.

The link between Feuerbach's critique of Hegel's *Phenomenology* and *The Essence of Christianity* is a strong one, and the role of the *Critique* in Feuerbach's *Gedankengang* is crucial, a point commentators have not stressed. The structure of the phenomenological dialectic, the model of self-reflection in an *other*, which Hegel works out in the *Phenomenology* and elsewhere (in the *Philosophy of Right*, and, earlier, in the *Jenenser Realphilosophie*, for example) and formalization of this model in the *Logic*, provide the basis for Feuerbach's own view. But it was Feuerbach who first saw the possibility of a radical *inversion* of the analysis, to "stand Hegel back on his feet."

Feuerbach's critique of Schelling's *Naturphilosophie* is relevant here. Feuerbach notes that Schelling's *Philosophy of Nature* appears to offer an "objectivist" alternative to the "subjectivist" orientation of Kantian-Fichtean critical philosophy. But Feuerbach sees Schelling's philosophy of Nature as an "inverted idealism" (II, 188), which takes away with one hand what it gives with the other, in its "objectification" of Nature.

The idealist says to Nature: "You are my *alter ego*, my other *I*," but he stresses the *I*, so the sense of his statement is: "You are the *effluvium*, the reflection of my *Self*, and have no independent existence." The Philosopher of Nature says the same thing, but he stresses the *alter*. Nature is still the *I*, still your *self*, but your *other* self, and thereby real in itself, and to be distinguished from the [subjective] *I*. (II, 188)

The difference between subjective idealism and the "objectivity" of Schelling's philosophy is that the latter wants to demonstrate a posteriori what the former asserts a priori. But the Absolute Identity of subject-object, in Schelling's system, leads back to the idealist dualism of Nature and Spirit. Since there cannot be *two* Absolutes, Schelling is driven to assert the Identity itself as the Absolute. The Absolute turns out to be nothing but the *and* that conjoins the two alternative forms, or aspects, spirit and nature, in Spinoza's terms. But then the Absolute becomes itself vague, indeterminate, a *nihil negativum*. For all this, Feuerbach credits Schelling with a positive emphasis on Nature–but no more than this, for beneath this Nature lurks the Fichtean *Ego*. The *Nature* that Schelling so fully affirms in its objectivity is not objective nature at all, but only the soft-focus representation of nature in the Imagination. The unity of thinking and being turns out to be only a unity of thinking and imagining, where in place of nature itself, we have a mystical and fantastic version of it. "Philosophy then becomes beautiful, poetic, cosy, romantic, but therefore also transcendental, superstitious and absolutely uncritical" (II, 193).

The "fantastic" and "mystical" element in Absolute philosophy is the explanation of the Identity of subject and object as some ultimate truth of Being, whereas this Identity concept can be explained on natural grounds as expressing a psychological need, a conditional process of human thought. Whereas Schelling placed this Identity at the very forefront of philosophy, Hegel placed it, says Feuerbach, correctly, at the end, as the limit toward which knowledge tends, as the result of the process.

But Hegel fails as well, according to Feuerbach, because he takes this "limit" itself, this identity of subject and object, as the expression of an ultimate truth about consciousness and about Being. In this he fails to be critical, in the "genetic-critical" sense, says Feuerbach. He falls prey to a representation of the Imagination–this "achieved" Identity–and takes it to be the object of philosophy itself, a truth about Being itself, whereas it is, on critical examination, only a formal truth.

> This unity of subject and object is a principle which is as unfruitful as it is pernicious for philosophy, especially because it overrides the distinction between the subjective and the objective, and frustrates any attempt to deal with genetic-critical, conditional thought, or with the problem of truth. Hegel was led to take representations which expressed merely subjective needs, as objective truths, because he failed to go back to the origins, to the needs which give rise to these representations in the imagination, and took them, instead at face value. (II, 195)

Thus, Hegel passes from the extreme of a hypercritical subjectivism to the other extreme of an uncritical objectivism. Genetic-critical method, on the other hand, takes the *origins* of this theory of identity to be its proper subject matter, says Feuerbach. If these origins are psychological, that is, if one can explain the origin of such theories in terms of "secondary causes," then this is philosophy's proper task. "The principal subject matter of genetic-critical philosophy is what are usually called secondary causes" (II, 194).

What these "secondary causes" are is not entirely clear in Feuerbach, but he gives a general characterization of them as the traditionally conceived *physical* causes of natural events and the *psychological* causes of our ideas and concepts. Previous modes of physical and psychological explanation were superficial, says Feuerbach, because in psychology the logical foundations were not recognized, in physics the metaphysical import was ignored, and in nature the rational structure was not seen. Feuerbach here intends to explain why the idealist critique of empiricist science, from a rationalist-metaphysical viewpoint, was a telling critique. What empiricism left without philosophical foundation, idealism supplied, but in fantastic, inverted form. Feuerbach says that the reunion of these two traditions requires an empirically and naturalistically oriented rationalism (or a rationally oriented empiricism), in which the superficial ad hoc eclecticism of the one and the luxuriant imaginative unity of the other are both overcome, in which the particular evidence of the senses serves to discipline the speculative insights of the human mind. He sets this forth, therefore, as his program.

At the very end of the *Critique of Hegelian Philosophy*, Feuerbach gives us an almost unprepared-for paean to nature and to man, which marks not so much the conclusion of the *Critique* as critique, as the introduction to an alternative philosophy. The abstract *Idea* is left behind, or rather reappears under its new *human* form. What was *Absolute* in Hegel becomes *human* in Feuerbach. What was a logic of Being becomes a psychology of human concept formation. The dialectic of consciousness, as the "awareness of the self-awareness of the Idea," becomes a dialectic of human consciousness, whose Idea, that is, whose essence, is no longer Being as such, but rather human essence, human being. "Hegelian philosophy is rational mysticism" (II, 195), Feuerbach had written in the *Critique*. The revelation of this mystery lies in man's self-revelation, the dialectical process of realizing as human, and therefore natural, what had been projected in the imagination as superhuman and supernatural. The means of this revelation is the restoration of human experience, in its sensory and affective modes, as the origin, the "secondary cause" in terms of which philosophy and religion can be explained. In the passionate last passage of the *Critique*, Feuerbach writes a preamble to the new philosophy:

The highest object of art is the human figure–(figure not only in the narrowest [visual] sense, but also in the sense that poetry deals with man)–The highest object of philosophy is human essence. The human figure is no longer a limited, finite one. . . . Human essence is no longer a particular, subjective essence, but a universal one, for man has the universe as the object of his drive for knowledge. But only a cosmopolitical being can take the cosmos as his object. The stars are not merely the objects of unmediated sensual intuition. We know this much: they follow the same laws as we do. Therefore, all speculation is vain, which seeks to go beyond nature and man–as vain as that art which wants to give us instead only grotesque caricatures. Just as vain is that speculation which has recently arisen against Hegel–the speculation of the "Positivists," which instead of going beyond Hegel, fell far behind him, in that it failed to understand the meaningful hint that Hegel, and before him, Kant and Fichte gave, each in his own way. Philosophy is the science of the actual, in its totality. But actuality is encompassed by nature (in the most universal sense of the word). The most profound secrets lie in the simplest natural things, which the fantastic speculative philosopher, yearning for heaven, merely kicks aside. The return to nature is the only source of salvation. It is false to place nature in contradiction to ethical freedom. Nature possesses not only the mean workshop of the stomach; she also has built the temple of the brain. She gave us not only a tongue . . . but also ears, which alone can be thrilled by the harmony of tones, and eyes, which alone can be entranced by the heavenly, selfless essence of light. Nature opposes only the freedom of fantasy, but not rational freedom. (II, 203-4)

This romantic blend of the "return to nature" and "rational freedom" sounds like nothing so much as that Renaissance humanism that Feuerbach had noted in the *History* as liberation from the introverted speculative fantasies of repressive scholasticism. But it is transplanted here into Reformation soil, and it will bear, even in its excesses, the characteristics of the Hegelian seed out of which it developed.

The *Critique of Hegelian Philosophy* is a fundamental critique in that it rejects Hegelian idealism not so much in its details, or in its structure, as in its underlying assumptions. It is a critique of the foundations of Idealism. Feuerbach does not take Hegel to task for "logicizing" nature, nor even for imposing the dialectic of the Idea on phenomenology, that is, on the science of consciousness. He takes him to task rather for mistaking the sense of what he was doing. He wants to make that Hegel who represents the *consciousness* of the course of philosophical speculation and system building into a *self*-conscious Hegel, one who recognizes his own system as itself a hypostatization of the *Principle* of self-consciousness. One could say that where Hegel represents the consciousness of self-consciousness, the awareness of thought as an object of thinking, Feuerbach represents a further awareness, namely, that this very process of coming to awareness of thought is not a transcendental, "spiritual" process, in itself, but is a process of distinctively human existence. As such, its ultimate foundations are in the necessities of human life itself, in the sense of man's natural existence as a creature of needs, of sensing and feeling, as well as thinking. These needs are individual needs, in existential terms. They are *my* hunger, *my* thirst, *my* pleasure and pain. Thought does not represent these needs *as such*, for these lie beyond or below the threshold of *reflective* awareness. Rather, thought constitutes the "Dioptrics of the Spirit," that is, the unique way in which these needs become known as *human* needs, or indeed, the way in which these needs become humanized. This is a "Dioptric" because it is only by reflection, or to follow the metaphor more closely, by *refraction*, of these needs, and their projection on the screen of "humanity," that man comes to *know* them, as distinct from merely *having* them. This "screen" is the human image, man as he knows *himself* through knowing *others* as human. The condition of this knowledge is intellectual intercourse with other men. And the foundation for this intercourse is not the *conatus* of thought itself, but the *Eros* of the human need for other human beings, as a condition of their very existence. The polarity of the Spirit, and its dialectic as a self-differentiating process, is thus seen by Feuerbach as the reflection of this more fundamental dialectic. Relations within Spirit, between "self" and "other" as abstract terms of a logical relation, are nothing but reflections of the concrete relations between "self" and "other" in human terms, that is, between oneself and other human beings. The fantastic projection of these relations in Hegel's *Logic* (and, in effect, in the *Phenomenology* as well, as representing the *logic* of these relations as they are reflected in one's awareness) is, therefore, nothing but the representation of the varieties of man's dependency upon, and his necessary relations with, other men. "Anthropology," as Feuerbach is to repeat again and again, "is the secret of theology," and therefore also of speculative philosophy and metaphysics.

This is Feuerbach's program. He conceives it as a demystification and a demythologization of theology, and of the most abstract form of theology, that is, idealist speculative philosophy. Its purpose, henceforth, is to rehumanize the Gods, by exposing the process of their deification. The first step is to make philosophy self-conscious, in these terms, to introduce a "reform." The next is to use this reformed standpoint as the instrument for an inquiry into the foundations of theology and religious belief, those phenomena that provide the clearest subject matter for a "Dioptric" analysis. The outcome, it is hoped, is a repossession of the whole realm of human knowledge that purports to be knowledge of something more as in fact nothing but man's self-knowledge, the esoteric form of his consciousness of *himself*, as human.

CHAPTER VIII

The Philosophical Context
of Feuerbach's Critique of Religion

The philosophy of the future has the task of leading philosophy out of the realm of departed spirits back to the realm of embodied, living spirits; out of the godly felicity of a world of thought without neediness, back to the realities of human misery. For this purpose, the philosophy of the future requires no more than a human understanding, and human language. But the ability to think and speak and act in authentically human terms belongs only to the human species of the future. The present task is not yet to represent this new humanity, but to draw mankind out of the morass in which it is sunk. . . . The task . . . is to establish the critique of human philosophy on the basis of the critique of divine philosophy. (II, 245n.)

With these words, Feuerbach introduced his 1843 work, *Foundations of the Philosophy of the Future*. In that same year, there appeared the second (revised) edition of a work that had first been published two years earlier, in 1841: *The Essence of Christianity*. It was in this latter work that the substantive "critique of divine philosophy" was undertaken, and it was this work that made the anonymity-seeking Feuerbach a major public figure in German thought. The history of the writing and the publication of *The Essence of Christianity* is instructive, but need not be gone into here.[1] The impact of the work was great. It represented a major break with the whole dominant speculative tradition of German idealist philosophy. It promised to be the key to a complete reinterpretation of both theology and metaphysics. It introduced an empiricist and materialist-oriented humanism into a philosophical tradition in which this emphasis had been alien. Feuerbach's critique of religion built on, but overshadowed the "higher criticism" and historical critique of Christian dogma and Christian theology which Strauss, Bauer, Lützelberger, Daumer, and others had instituted. It made "ardent Feuerbachians" of the young Marx and Engels. It is the one work for which Feuerbach is popularly known to this day and has appeared in numerous editions and translations over the last century.

And yet it is a work whose substance and whose leading idea is simple and even ancient: that man created the Gods and that the Gods embody man's own conception of his own humanity, his own wishes, fears, needs, and ideals. Xenophanes, Euhemeris, Lucretius, among others, had already grasped this idea clearly, in their own contexts, in ancient times. Every "true" religion itself had, in the clearest way, leveled its critique of idolatry at precisely such anthropomorphism in *other*, that is, "false" religions. The whole tradition of demythologization had a long philosophical heritage, and the critique of personification in religious conceptions had gone far beyond theology, in the conceptions of God in rationalist philosophy, from Descartes, Spinoza, and Leibniz to Hegel. The French *Eclaircissement* had, in vigorously anticlerical terms, adopted Bayle's skepticism and turned it into a weapon against orthodox belief. A comfortable deism, compatible with the new spirit of mechanism in science, had banished God to the interstices between worlds, where Lucretius would have placed Him, and required His services only to provide the hypothetical first push for the world machine. How backward could German philosophy have been to be shocked, indignant, or joyful over such a stale revelation?

Though the leading idea is essentially simple, Feuerbach's development of it, and his application, is complex, inventive, and striking. What Feuerbach sought to do was not to *state* the idea, but to trace its present significance. The trouble with a *bald* reading of *The Essence of Christianity* is not that it does not hold one's attention or that its revelations seem old hat. It is, on the face of it, an exciting book (though repetitive) and an original one. What it says about religion has rarely been said as well, or as passionately. What it condemns, in theology, has rarely been condemned so sharply and so systematically. Still, with this alone, the book remains, though effective, largely superficial: a competent "popular" work, full of quotable aphorisms, and marvelously acid polemical asides, but hardly a *philosophical* landmark. What gives the work its depth is its context in the development of Feuerbach's thought. Feuerbach himself said that the work, though written in a style suited to the educated layman, was primarily a work addressed to scholars and to philosophers, who would recognize what he was up to, and whom, in fact, he was criticizing. There are, therefore, two levels at which the work may be read. First, there is the manifest thesis that man creates the Gods in his own image. But, second, there is the latent and deeper thesis concerning the nature of concept formation not only in religion and theology, but in philosophy itself. In this deeper thesis, Feuerbach's critique of "divine philosophy" becomes the basis for a critique of metaphysics, and of the whole history of modern philosophy as "abstract" theology. The effect of this critique is the anthropological reduction not simply of religion, but of philosophy proper. In this "reduction," the foundations of philosophical speculation on human needs, wants, and fears are to be laid bare. Philosophy itself is to be demystified and recognized as the refracted, abstract image of concrete human existence and the esoteric expression of human consciousness and self-consciousness. Thus, *The Essence of Christianity* combines an expositional and critical clarity about its main subject matter, religion, with a deep-going philosophical critique of *philosophy*. But the latter has to be dug out of the work. It is not yet explicit.

The Essence of Christianity is the direct outcome and the culmination of the *Critique of Hegelian Philosophy*. Without this context, much of its significance is lost. Certainly, it derives from the initial critique of religious belief in the *Bayle*, and many of its epistemological and metaphysical points relate to earlier work, in the *Leibniz* and the *History*. But its main thrust is in the application of Feuerbach's "genetic-analytical" method to a specific subject matter, ostensibly religion, but really *religious consciousness*, as the paradigm of *human* consciousness in general, and hence, of universal significance. What Feuerbach sets out to examine is the process of concept formation in religion. But insofar as the "true" subject of religion itself is man, what Feuerbach really intends to do is to examine the process of concept formation in man's knowledge of himself as man. In short, he purports to reveal the psychological and epistemological process of man's self-conception.

Feuerbach takes this process to be a historical one: It is cumulative, it develops, it matures. The domain in which this human self-revelation takes place is the religious consciousness. But this is not an undifferentiated consciousness. It is as varied, as concretely differentiated as are the varieties of religion. Still, it has its fundamental patterns, and it has a universal ground in those aspects of human nature that are universal in essence, though they are of necessity particular in their concrete or existential expression. This universal ground, this essential humanity, which man as much creates in himself, as he discovers it, is the "mystery" of religion, its true object, or that which it hides under the external form (i.e., under the imagery) of its imaginative constructions. Because there is a real subject matter—that is, human nature or human existence—at the basis of religious consciousness and because this reality has *universal* human features, the inquiry into the structure and the content of religious consciousness is a scientific inquiry into a "real" or "natural" subject matter, namely, human consciousness. The methodology of such an inquiry is translation or reduction into "natural" terms of the imagery or *super*natural form of expression of religious consciousness.

Insofar as religious consciousness expresses a natural truth in esoteric or Aesopian language, the reasons for this inversion need to be explained. This, again, requires a study of the *psychology* of religious concept formation. Insofar as the content or subject of this truth is man himself, reflection on this content, in its natural form, is *anthropology*. In its fantastic, Aesopian form, this reflection is theology. Thus, "Theology is nothing but esoteric Anthropology."

This reflection upon religious consciousness is not the original religious consciousness but theology. The original and immediate content of religious consciousness is not a matter of theoretical reflection, but of human action: human feeling, human need, human will, human belief. This content cannot be "negated" by theory, because its mode of existence is not theoretical. It is, rather, the empirical content of religious experience. The mode of knowing it is *in* experience. And because the only experience *I* can have (in the direct sense of experiencing, living through) is my *own*, religion is ultimately a matter of *personal* experience. This direct, personal experience is not *religious*, however, until I recognize it as *human*. This I can only do by recognizing it as my experience of an other, of something *not*-me, who is however, essentially *like*-me. The privacy of the direct experience of feeling, need, love, awe, fear, respect is mediated by the *otherness* of its object. It is out of this dialectic of feeling, of sensibility, that my own self-consciousness, as *human* self-consciousness, arises. I know my own humanity only in the process of acting humanly with respect to an other. I am not an *I* except with respect to a *Thou*.

Thus begins the Feuerbachian dialectic, whose starting point, in distinction from the Hegelian, is the existing individual, the concrete and particular organism whose existence is dependent upon the fulfilment of its needs, and the fulfilment of whose needs is dependent on a relation to what is beyond it—other beings and other things, man and nature. The source of human consciousness, as of human self-consciousness, is in the natural conditions of human existence themselves. These natural conditions include bodily needs such as hunger and thirst, certainly. But just as naturally, they include love—not yet as the *conatus* of thought, but as the *Eros* of living, needy existence.

There are, for Feuerbach, really two subject matters here: first, *what* is revealed, in religious consciousness, about its immediate subject matter, man; second, *how* it is revealed, in the specific forms of religious thought, and in the "false" reflection on this thought (i.e., theology).

Feuerbach's "critique of divine philosophy" is thus both a positive assessment of the "true" content of religion and a negative polemic against theology. Religion is the *alienated form of man's recognition of his own nature.* Theology, on the other hand, is *the theoretical alienation of man's nature, as not yet his own.* Feuerbach's self-appointed task is to translate the alienated form of man's recognition of his own nature into unalienated, human terms. But this requires also that he repudiate, on theoretical grounds, theology's alienation of man's nature as *not* his own, that is, by a critique of the "contradictions" in theology. This gives us Feuerbach's twofold division of the work into a "positive" and a "negative" part. The first deals with the "positive essence of Religion," or religious belief; the second with the "negative or false essence of religion," or theology.

The apparent theme of the work is religion, in particular the Christian religion, as the mode of consciousness in which man comes to know himself as man. This same theme becomes almost obsessional with Feuerbach, and it forms the heart of the major part of his work thereafter. It is easy, therefore, to characterize Feuerbach as essentially a philosopher of religion. But this is true only in a specifically qualified way. Feuerbach is a philosopher of religion only in the sense that Hegel could be characterized as a philosopher of history, or Kant a moral philosopher. But this is to characterize philosophy and philosophers in crude textbook fashion, in terms of stilted departmental divisions. It would be more apt to characterize Feuerbach as a theoretician and critic whose empirical or applied domain is the phenomenon of religious consciousness. He writes in the preface to the second edition of *The Essence of Christianity*:

I am nothing but a natural scientist of the spirit; but the natural scientist can do nothing without instruments, without material means. In this capacity–as a natural scientist–I have written this work, which consequently contains nothing but the principle of a new philosophy, one essentially different from previous philosophy, and one which is confirmed practically, i.e., *in concreto*, in application to a particular, concrete subject matter, but one which has universal significance: namely, to religion, with respect to which this principle is presented, developed, and carried through to its consequences.[2] (VII, 282; S: I, 16)

The "new philosophy" thus has the critique of religion as its point of departure. But it has the critique of philosophy itself as its aim. This critique therefore proposes the "end of philosophy" in its present form, and its replacement by a "new philosophy." Feuerbach aims at nothing less than a philosophical revolution.

There are personal contexts–biographical, temperamental, stylistic

–that help to explain the specific character of Feuerbach's program for a revolution in philosophy. These are closely interwoven with the explicit philosophical motives. No small part in Feuerbach's move toward a "new philosophy" was played by his exclusion from the professional ranks, and his relative isolation from "professional" philosophy. His reaction was bitter in its tone, substantive in its import. His rejection of "professional" philosophy as "professorial" philosophy leads him to say of Hegel as "professional philosopher":

> In Hegel, this role reaches its culmination. He is the ideal realized, the model of a German professor of philosophy, a philosophical Scholiarch. The Absolute Spirit is none other than the Absolute Professor, the professor who practices philosophy as a profession, who finds his highest bliss and his destiny in his professorship, who takes the standpoint of the professorial lectern to be the all-determining, cosmological and world-historical standpoint.[3]

Thus, when Feuerbach declares "my philosophy is no philosophy," he is specifically rejecting the professional, professorial philosophy of his time, that is, the speculative philosophy of both the Hegelian and the Schellingean stripe. He is also rejecting *systematic* philosophy in general. He finds the whole temper of intellectual *construction*, of formal-logical systematicity, repugnant to the spirit of his own philosophizing. "Empiricism," as the antithesis to "mere" speculation, presents itself to Feuerbach in romantic terms, as direct, qualitatively immediate, "flesh and blood" philosophy–as having to do with existence itself, and not with its fantastic reflection in the imagination. However much Feuerbach is to insist on a "thinking," or philosophically reflective, empiricism, later, his growing temperamental affinity for the individual, concrete, and existential has the effect of muting and diffusing the more technical analysis that a reflective, logically and epistemologically sophisticated empiricism demands. The empirical tendencies are, in Feuerbach's own mind, associated with religious consciousness, in its original, untheological form, on the one hand, and with what Feuerbach regarded as natural science, on the other. These two, religion and science, are man's most direct confrontation with the dual, human-natural fact of existence–on the one hand, in terms of the feelings, on the other, in terms of sense perception.[4] The "feel" of things, just as the "feel" of one's own existence, lends itself poorly to expression in the tough logic of analysis or in the abstractness of speculative construction. Feuerbach is enough of an artist to surrender to the temptations of evocative aphorism, of striking phrase, of metaphor. Also, he recognizes a certain impatience in himself and a certain lack of systematic rigor. Feuerbach wrote to his friend, Christian Kapp, in 1840 (the year that *The Essence of Christianity* was composed):

I am meant to be a researcher and a thinker, but not a teacher, at least not a professional teacher. I lack a certain talent: the formal-philosophical, the systematic, the encyclopedic-methodological talent—at any rate, I haven't cultivated it, nor have I, in the present condition of philosophy and science, put much value on it.[5]

Feuerbach, in this same letter, refers to a certain cryptic characteristic in his work, a tendency to repress systematic conclusions:

My works deserve only limited recommendation. . . . I suppressed what was best, kept it to myself, limited myself extremely, set myself only limited goals, dealt with the whole from only a certain point of view. My works therefore have a crabbed, sharply delimited but striking character. They all end with a great dash–. What youth addresses itself to, namely general ideas and overviews, decisions as to the plan, method, form and essence of philosophy, i.e. its history,–I dealt with not in general, but only indirectly and in concreto, so that no one should see it. I remember distinctly how I conceived of the work From Bacon to Spinoza–History of Modern Philosophy as an introduction to a treatise on the history of philosophy, and meant to use it as the point of departure for my larger idea—had it completed already in my mind—but I kept it choked within me.

From this, and from other evidence,[6] it becomes clear that even in *The Essence of Christianity*, the deeper thesis is veiled from clear view, and does not attain to explicit *philosophical* statement—though, here, ostensibly he was finally speaking his mind. The assessment of the work is therefore a more complex task than has hitherto been recognized. In a work that deals specifically with the ways in which human consciousness becomes aware of its own nature only in veiled, esoteric, and symbolic forms, Feuerbach himself offers us the parable, but does not point the *moral* of his thesis.

For this, two reasons may be suggested: (1) Feuerbach's ambivalence between his philosophical and political radicalism, on the one hand, and his desire for anonymity, on the other; (2) his antisystematic bent, and his failure to go beyond the exemplification of his deeper thesis to an explicit philosophical statement of it, *beyond* the context of his study of religious consciousness.

There is an ongoing tension in Feuerbach himself between the characteristic desire for anonymity and his desire to be the innovater, the reformer, the Second Luther, the overthrower of the false representative of God on earth, the philosophical Pope, Hegel. That this is a temperamental and deeply personal ambivalence is readily suggested by the traumatic character of Feuerbach's break with Hegel, whom he called his second father, as he had called Berlin his second birthplace. There is the temptation to speculate on the personal psychological character of Feuerbach's ambivalence and it may indeed be a suggestive and useful analysis. But there are other grounds for the anonymity seeking that are closer to the surface, and whatever the psychological constituent may be, the sociopolitical and professional reasons are clear. Despite Feuerbach's repeated disclaimers, university posts were sought for him, unsuccessfully, over a period of several years.[7] The political and clerical reaction to the radical views of the young Hegelians, as well as to the allegedly anti-Christian, or at any rate, antiorthodox views of Hegel himself, were intimately connected with Feuerbach's apprehensiveness over his own and his family's security. Feuerbach struggled with the issue of safety and risk in these terms, and the record of his correspondence substantiates, in explicit terms, the apprehensions that are only implicitly revealed in the cautions, the indirections, and the suppression of more open conclusions in his philosophical works.

Feuerbach's politics, his personal temperament, his understanding of the political situation in Germany in the decade before the revolution of 1848, and, thereafter, his relation to the professional or professorial community all enter into this.[8] But the actual, complex connections between all of this and his philosophical views and mode of expression require more than an account of his explicit *political* attitudes. Such an approach would merely beg the question, or substitute another in its place. There is no attempt here to do more than to indicate the nature of the problem. To do more requires a separate and different study. But the larger context, which is relevant here, is clear: Feuerbach's *thèse manquée* is in part explained by his apprehensions concerning the political consequences of a public reputation as a radical. That he overcame these apprehensions to the extent that he did is, as Schuffenhauer rightly remarks, a sign of his courage.[9] But that the clarity of his thesis, in this work, suffered from these ambivalences is the sign, or the scar, of this personal struggle in its philosophical context.

These, then, are two aspects of the *first* reason for Feuerbach's failure to achieve a clear philosophical statement of his deeper thesis: the personal desire for anonymity, on temperamental grounds generally and on the grounds of the ambivalence of Feuerbach's rejection of Hegel, on the one hand; his desire for political anonymity in the context of the political and clerical reaction to his work, and the dangers it presented, on the other.

There is, however, another and almost obvious reason, which the genetic analysis of Feuerbach's own work suggests, namely, that although he grasped the deeper thesis in a way profound enough to enable him to exemplify it brilliantly and suggestively, he did not yet grasp it in a conceptually clear enough way to enable him to articulate it in the clearest philosophical terms. He was aware of this too. His statement that "the ability to think and speak and act in authentically human terms belongs only to the humanity of the future" is an acknowledgment of this. So too are his reiterated statements of dissatisfaction with *The Essence of Christianity*, with its incompleteness, his own lack of clarity, the critics' misunderstanding of it, and his lifelong attempt to explain, clarify, and enlarge on the thesis of the work. In one sense, he is still enmeshed in the Hegelian scheme, as the structure of the work and its principal model of self-alienation show. In another sense, his radical phenomenological and ontological inversion of this very Hegelianism bespeaks something entirely new, and Feuerbach's language is not yet adequate to its clear expression.

My task, in presenting the substance of *The Essence of Christianity*, is not merely a task of exposition, however critical. It is rather a task of reconstruction, an attempt to dig out latent from manifest content. Such a reconstruction cannot simply restate what Feuerbach appears to be saying, nor simply assert whatever the interpreter wishes he had said. To the extent that a philosophical reconstruction is not merely a subjective exercise of reading one's own views into the work, retrospectively—or recreating it in one's own image—it is constrained by the context of Feuerbach's own development, both prior to and subsequent to the work. This is to grasp the work as a work in process, as the work of a philosopher who is grappling with an idea, difficult and elusive, and who is not yet fully aware of its implications.

To this end, in the present chapter, the work will be considered first in its relation to the works that preceded it. Then, its formal structure will be considered, as it reflects the Hegelian scheme of thesis and antithesis in the dialectic. Its manifest content, Feuerbach's analysis of religious consciousness as inverted human self-awareness, will be examined, in particular, for its relevance to classical philosophical questions in their religious and theological form. Then, the latent thesis will emerge, it is hoped, as a thesis in epistemology and in phenomenological psychology, and as a radical reinterpretation of what philosophy itself is. In short, the latent thesis is a metaphilosophical thesis —not about man as such, but about man as a philosophizing being. Although the manifest content plainly deserves the title *The Essence of Christianity*, the underlying thesis might well be titled *The Essence of Philosophy*.[10]

Feuerbach's Critique of Religion

The Philosophical Context of "The Essence of Christianity" in Feuerbach's Earlier Works

When *The Essence of Christianity* appeared in 1841, its effect was overwhelming. The orthodox theologians and the "positive" philosophers of religion were quick and sharp in their criticism and in their condemnation of the work. The left Hegelians were enthusiastic in proclaiming the work a radical and successful attack on the very foundations of the "sterile" speculative and "Christian" philosophy that was then current. They hailed Feuerbach as their philosophical leader, became, as Friedrich Engels later described it, "ardent Feuerbachians."[11] It was a shocking work. This is due in part to the style, to the choice of the particular subject matter of Christian belief and dogma, and to the explicitness of Feuerbach's condemnation of theology. The basic effect of the work, however, is due to its radical formulation of the human foundations of religious belief, its total inversion of a philosophical-theological framework that had dominated Christian thought for well over one thousand years, as well as its striking naturalist "reduction" and reinterpretation of the central symbols and rituals of Christianity. Still, if what has been said in the preceding section is correct (concerning the deeper philosophical thesis latent in the work), the philosophical implications of the work were largely missed.

In retrospect, one can find the themes in *The Essence of Christianity* scattered throughout everything Feuerbach had hitherto written. The major elements are these: (1) the Hegelian account of the dialectic of self-differentiation, of self-"estrangement," of self-projection, and Feuerbach's defense and critique of it (in the critique of Bachmann's *Anti-Hegel*, in his defense of Hegel against Heinrich Leo in *Philosophy and Christianity*, and in his own *Critique of Hegelian Philosophy*); (2) the distinction between philosophy and religion, or more accurately, between philosophy and theology (in the *Bayle*, in *Philosophy and Christianity*, and in the Sengler review); (3) Feuerbach's treatment of *Feeling, Imagination, Wish,* and *Fantasy* in the cited works; (4) his adoption and reinterpretation of Hegel's phenomenological analysis and his definition of the "species concept" in relation to religious thought; (5) the critical account of "Incarnation," of the universal in the particular, in its philosophical form in "positive" and "speculative" philosophy, (in the Sengler review and in *The Critique of Hegelian Philosophy*); (6) the account of the communal or shared character of thought, and the role of language, and of material sign, (both in its earliest version in the *Dissertation* and in the *Critique of Hegelian Philosophy*); (7) the account of the metaphysical problem of the relation of mind to body, and the correlative epistemological problem of the relation of sensing and feeling to conceptual thought. All of these themes are to be noted in the historical works (especially the *Leibniz*), in the Critique of Dorguth's materialism, and in the section of the *Critique of Hegelian Philosophy* that deals with the *Phenomenology*.

THE HEGELIAN MODEL OF SELF-ALIENATION AS THE CONTEXT OF FEUERBACH'S PHENOMENOLOGY

Central to Feuerbach's analysis is the *model* of self-differentiation, self-"estrangement," self-projection, which lies at the heart of the Hegelian dialectic. Hegel's use of the model in a variety of interpretations is based on the fundamental ontological or metaphysical claim of the Hegelian system, namely, that in all of these contexts—whether phenomenological, historical, aesthetic, natural—there is *one* underlying process, that of the Absolute Idea unfolding itself. The dialectic of self-differentiation is therefore the universal form of this process, revealing itself throughout all the aspects of Being and Becoming. Feuerbach makes no such systematic or explicit ontological claim, both because he eschews the very idea of such a philosophical system (as the self-delusion of speculative philosophy) and because he rejects the objective Idealism on which this unity of process is based. Instead, Feuerbach takes this dialectic as the formal structure or model of *learning*, of coming to know, of concept formation, in particular. Therefore, he constrains it within the context of a phenomenological logic, a logic of the process of consciousness as it comes to know itself, as self-consciousness. In Feuerbach's interpretation of Hegel's phenomenology, the subject of this dialectic is not the *Idea*, but rather man as a species being. Thus, the "culmination" or τελος of this dialectical phenomenology is man's self-knowledge as a species being.

The essential features of this dialectical model are as follows: the basic formal relation within the model is the relation of subject to object. This is the necessary relation, the presupposition of the whole schema. This requirement is presented by the very fact of consciousness itself (which is the subject matter or "interpretation" of the formal dialectical model). Consciousness—or awareness, in the most general sense—requires an object. To be conscious is to be conscious *of* something. In short, there is no sheer consciousness as such, without an object. Such sheer subjectivity is utterly empty. The subject, in consciousness, must therefore present itself (or be presented with) an object, as *other* than itself. Whatever the object may be *in itself* (outside of consciousness, and here it is characterized in the Hegelian dialectic as a sheer abstraction, not yet realized or "concretized" in relation to a subject), it becomes an object *in* consciousness only insofar as it is "for another," that is, insofar as it is an object for some subject. Thus, the very condition of consciousness is a separation or differentiation *within* consciousness. Using the term "self" now, not in its personal or subjective reference, but only as an index of reflexivity, this is to say that consciousness is necessarily *self*-differentiated or *self*-separated. This does not happen *to* consciousness; it is not an event. It is a definitional condition of consciousness itself. Just as the "object in itself" is an abstraction (i.e., empty of content), so too the "subject in itself" is an abstraction. The *process* of consciousness, therefore, is one that takes place as an appropriation by the subject of its "other," of the object. In this process, the abstract "object in itself" becomes an "object for me" or for the subject. The crucial move, however, is that the "other" that the subject grasps *is consciousness itself* in its aspect as *other*, so that *self*-consciousness is a relation in which consciousness as subject is aware of *itself* as object. This is the sense of the phrase "the other-being of consciousness" (*Das Anderssein des Bewusstsein*) in Hegel's *Phenomenology*. In this stage of the process, consciousness is objectified, or projected into its form as an *other*. Self-differentiation is therefore a self-objectification (*selbst-vergegenständindigung*) of consciousness. In other terms, consciousness as subject takes itself as its own object, but as if it were an other, *external* to itself. Thus, the process is described also as a *self-externalization* (*selbst-entaüsserung*).

Feuerbach requires as the condition for consciousness not merely the other-sidedness, or the other-being of consciousness, or self (as merely the outward reflection of the subject). He requires "real" or "existential" duality: The other must be *really* other and not merely the otherness of the *I*. It must be an ontologically or existentially independent *Thou*. This existential duality is the real, not the merely apparent or confused, condition of consciousness. And because it is sense perception that "gives" us the knowledge of existent "others," it is not merely the conditional, but the essential prerequisite and basis for consciousness itself, and therefore also the basis for the development of self-consciousness. The achievement of self-consciousness is the achievement of knowledge of the other as *like* myself, *in terms of the qualities of consciousness itself*. This constitutes *species* knowledge, knowledge of myself insofar as I am *species*-identical with this other. But it does *not* require *existential* identity with the other; that is, he is not the same person or individual I am; for if "he" were the same as I, this "otherness" would be only a sham, a specious appearance. It would be "otherness" only as it is thought, in conception, but not "otherness" as it is in objective fact. Feuerbach's claim is that objectivity, or the independent reality of the other as *other*, is given to us by the senses, with respect to objects of sense, (i.e., *natural* objects). And the objectivity or independent reality of the other *as* other is given to us through *feelings*, particularly those of *need* or *love*, about certain objects, characteristically, *human* objects or persons. Clearly, on these grounds anything that is an object of need, of love, of fear, of any of the "feelings," in this broad sense, is *taken* to be human or personal. But clearly not all such objects are, in fact, other human beings. One may be mistaken about the objects one takes to be human. And, apparently, if such objects are apprehended by us as objects of feeling, then Feuerbach's view would seem to lead to a blatant anthropomorphism. But Feuerbach's point, apparently simple, is nevertheless an epistemologically subtle one. We may be mistaken about what the *objects* are to which we attribute humanity. But we are *not* mistaken in our attribution of this predicate to these objects. In other words, it is not the predicates that are mistaken, but the subject to which we attribute these predicates. We may, anthropomorphically, take a stone or a tree (i.e., sensible, "natural" objects) or a ghost or a dream figure (i.e., imaginary, "fantasy" objects) as human. But these objects are not themselves human beings. Rather, they serve as surrogates for the proper objects of this attribution, as *objectifications* of these *human* feelings, but as mistaken objectifications. We have transferred the feelings, which require objects, (feeling verbs are also accusative, as sensing verbs are), to non-human or to imaginary human objects. We have, in short, made a category or a species mistake. We have included in our half-formed and vague species concept things that do not belong in it. The predicates that prompt us to this misinclusion are the predicates of the species *properly conceived*, but *misapplied*. The discovery of the proper subject of these predicates, according to Feuerbach, is the growing self-awareness of man as himself the subject of these predicates. Thus, love of God is love of man in its esoteric, symbolic but not yet self-conscious form. Fear of the gods or of anthropomorphically conceived forces in nature is the form that fear of other men takes. Reverence for God's design in nature is reverence for man's own rational understanding of nature. The monuments raised to God are monuments in honor of man's own architectural ability to *build* such monuments (literal instances of the proverb "the work praises the master"). All the external objects of feeling become, upon enlightenment, self-directed feelings. They are the objective aspects under which man adores his own nature. The idolatrous form of this self-realization is boundless individual egoism–the individual man as God. And this is, of course, the way in which Feuerbach was immediately misread by the critics. But Feuerbach's sharpest attack is upon such idolatry. The fundamental distinction in his work is that between the existing individual man as the finite and incomplete instance of the species, and human nature as such, which is the infinite character of the species, its essence, or that unlimited potentiality or capacity humanity has for being "truly" human. The individual adores not himself, as a human individual or person, but rather his species nature, his infinite capacity for humanity. The expression of this infinite capacity is given in man's highest ideals, his highest expression of love, of respect for reason, of morality. The form of this expression has historically been religious. The subject of man's attribution of these human or essentially human predicates has been God. The realization of the *humanity* of these predicates has been the humanization of God by the truly religious. In Christianity, says Feuerbach, this reaches its highest point in the concept of God as man, in Christ. But the impetus to the hypostatization of these human predicates as divine, in the first place–the systolic movement of religious consciousness–is precisely the realization that individual men are not, nor can they become, identical with the object of their striving. Kant's "kingdom of ends" is that in which "ought" is fully realized in "is." Feuerbach's "kingdom of ends" is that in which an "authentic humanity" is fully realized in every individual. For both, it is a limit, and for Feuerbach, *not* a limit *in history*, but outside it; therefore, not in the world, but beyond it. But Feuerbach's "beyond" is treated not as a *jenseits* in the heavenly sense. Rather, it has the character of an extrapolation from the *diesseits* in terms of a glimpse of the capacities that this-worldly man, as *species*, has, but that he realizes, at any historical point, as not fulfilled. The static or hypostatized embodiment of the fulfillment of these capacities is God. But the very history of belief shows that every concept of God is itself conditional, limited, the best that is *then* conceivable. The metaconcept of God's *infinity* shows recognition of this, but still under the aspect of God's infinity, that is, the infinity of His attributes (which is to say, our incapacity to know them all, or to know them in their full perfection). What Feuerbach regards positively as the healthy (one might almost say soul-saving) instinct of religious consciousness is its insistence on a humanized God, a God-man.

Once the mystery of hypostatization is revealed, the divine predicates –God's humanity and His infinity–are seen to be human predicates. The *real* object of man's religious consciousness is seen to be the divinity of mankind and the infinity of man's capacities. Man, in effect, worships his own humanity, as a *feeling* being, and his own infinite capacity to comprehend himself, and nature, as a *rational* being. He celebrates his own species capacities for human feeling and for rationality, under the guise of his worship of the divine predicates.

This humanist credo is given its systematic support in terms of an analysis and a reduction of the *content* of religion to what concerns the human, by means of the epistemological and psychological model of self-differentiation, self-separation, self-objectification discussed earlier. And this model remains the thoroughly Hegelian, thoroughly dialectical feature of *The Essence of Christianity*. Thus, the critics who point to Feuerbach's rejection of the Hegelian dialectic take an exceptionally superficial view of it. It is human consciousness and the process of concept formation involved in self-knowledge that constitute the essential subject matter of the work. Feuerbach's *model* for this consciousness, and for this process, is throughout Hegelian and dialectical, though his *interpretation* of the model is distinctly anti-Hegelian in that it is anti-idealist.

THE DISTINCTION BETWEEN PHILOSOPHY AND THEOLOGY

The distinction between philosophy and religion is already made by Hegel in terms that are akin to Feuerbach's. In the *Phenomenology of Mind*, Hegel had written,

> In the previously considered formulation, in which *consciousness, self-consciousness, reason* and *spirit* were distinguished, *religion* was also considered as the consciousness of absolute Being in general – but only from the *standpoint of consciousness*, which is conscious of absolute Being. But absolute Being in-and-for-itself, the self-consciousness of spirit, was not treated in these formulations.[12]

Hegel's view here is that Religion presents man to himself as species, as collective, historical, or universal Man. But in religion he presents his species nature to himself as an objective universal, as an object "out-there," as *other* than himself. This objectification of Absolute Spirit is the content of theology. But it is a *consciousness* of the object, and not yet a *self-consciousness* of the object as the other-sidedness of the subject, that is, of Absolute Spirit itself. The actuality (*wirklichkeit*), in Hegel's terms, of Absolute Spirit is its self-identity, the moment of return upon itself, its consciousness of itself as its own object. Theology, however, only *represents* this object, so that it is not unmediated reality as such that is the object of theology, but only reality as it is *thought about,* or as it is dressed in the garment of a representation. But, says Hegel, "actuality doesn't enjoy its full rights in this representation—namely, not to be merely the outer garment but to be independent, free existence."[13]

In Hegel's terms, consciousness represents the relation between the *I* and the *not-I*; the object of consciousness is not realized as identical with the subject. But this is as far as religion goes. It represents Absolute Being, Absolute Spirit in its mediated form as other. Further, the conditions of its *representation* always give the *form* of this absolute content in a mediated or determinate way. Only in the philosophy of the Absolute, specifically, only in the *Phenomenology* itself, does this limitation become apparent. Kojève takes this to mean that only in the Absolute Identity of the spirit with itself, only in the condition of the identity of the particular and the universal, or in concrete terms, of the individual with the state, is the "otherness" of the theological representation overcome, and then,

Man will see that the absolute-essential reality is also his own reality. At one blow, it will cease to be *divine*. He will come to know it not in a theology, but in an Anthropology. And this Anthropology will also reveal to him his *own* essential reality: it will replace not only theology, but philosophy as well.[14]

Kojève goes on to say that only such an "atheistic interpretation" of the passage is compatible with the rest of the *Phenomenology*.

Whether or not we accept the "humanist" or "atheist" implications of Hegel's discussion of religion in the *Phenomenology*, it is clear that Hegel's characterization of theology's *content*, and of the *object* of religion as Absolute Being, known only in the outward form of *consciousness of an object*, is structurally close to Feuerbach's. It is *not* clear that one may take Hegel as an incipient Feuerbachian, though one would have to read him as grossly more "transcendental" than he is, in fact, not to feel the force of Kojève's "humanist" interpretation of "Absolute Spirit," or of "Absolute Reality." Kojève's suggestion of an *Anthropology* that supersedes the one-sidedness of both theology and (pre-Hegelian) philosophy seems to be directly inspired by Feuerbach. But one could say that Feuerbach intended to fulfill this very suggestion in Hegel's *Phenomenology of the Spirit*, to write his own *Phenomenology* in which the reidentification of man's essence and his existence is set up as the purpose of the work.

In his earlier works, Feuerbach's own distinction between philosophy and religion took the object of religion to be the *concrete*, the *particular*, the historically limited and finite; that of Philosophy to be the *universal*, the *unconditioned*, the *infinite*. Theology was there condemned for its crassness, its this-worldliness, its concern with the here and now, hypocritically concealed by its fig leaf of concern with the divine and the eternal. By their very nature, Feuerbach had argued, philosophy and science could not be "Christian" or "Jewish" or "Mohammedan." In the *Bayle*, Feuerbach opposed *thought* and *reason*, the domain of philosophy, to *feeling* and *fantasy*, the domain of religion, as mutually irreconcilable (cf. VII, 47, cited on p. 161). In *Philosophy and Christianity*, he had made the point that *contradictions* do not arise in religious belief itself, because the realm of contradiction is in thought, whereas in the realm of imagination, wish, fantasy, all things are possible. Thus, there are no *real* contradictions in feeling, only in reflective thought (see p. 162). Only where religious content is transformed into reflective thought, in *theology*, do contradictions arise. The two-part structure of *The Essence of Christianity* follows this formulation: Part I deals with the "true or anthropological essence of religion," but Part II, which deals with the "false or theological essence of religion," has in all but two of its chapter headings the phrase "the contradiction of. . . ."

Thus, the form of Feuerbach's characterization is the same as Hegel's: Religion is the consciousness of Absolute Being (Hegel) or of human essence or nature (Feuerbach) as an *other*, "set over against it." Theology incorporates the original religious projection as a systematic, explicit dogma, as a *metaphysical* article of faith. It makes the psychological process of religious concept formation into an ontological and metaphysical "truth"; it works up the material for contradiction into a *real* contradiction, by giving it systematic, rational form. In *The Essence of Christianity*, Feuerbach describes it thus:

Religion is the relation of man to his own nature—therein lies its truth and its power of moral amelioration—but not to his nature as his own, but rather as an other nature, separate and indeed counterposed to his own. Therein lies the untruth of religion, its limits, its contradiction to reason and morality; therein lies the evil-begetting source of religious fanaticism, therein the chief metaphysical principle of bloody human sacrifice: in short, therein the ultimate source of all the atrocities, all the horrifying scenes in the tragedy of religious history. (VI, 238; S: II, 307–8)

But what theology "fixes" is already contained in the character of religion, for Feuerbach writes,

The character of religion is the immediate, involuntary, unconscious contemplation of human nature as an other nature. But when this objectification of human nature is made an object of reflection, of theology, it becomes an inexhaustible mine of lies, illusions, deceptions, contradictions and sophisms. (VI, 257; S: II, 330)

Theology is therefore the systematization of illusion.

This much is already contained in the earlier writings, and *The Essence of Christianity* is an elaboration and explication of this theme. But philosophy as such, with which so much of the earlier writings are concerned, does not enter explicitly into the considerations in *The Essence of Christianity*. To all appearances, the aim of the work is to supplant theology with anthropology, once the divine is revealed as human. The connection with philosophy is oblique. Theology is the philosophically rationalized *form* of religious consciousness. That is to say, it is a reflective, systematic enterprise; it hews to the norms of philosophy, and its apparent subject matter, insofar as theology deals logically and metaphysically with the questions of Divine Being, is the same as that of philosophy. In Feuerbach's early view, theology is incomplete or false philosophy, because *its* Absolute is *not* the "free, independent, universal and infinite" Absolute that is the object of self-conscious, thinking Spirit (i.e., of philosophy). But this latter absolute is the *Idea* of Hegel's *Logic*, the *Spirit* of his *Phenomenology*; it is Being itself, in its self-conscious self-identity, in the philosophical spirit. "Christian" or "positive" philosophy took this Idea or Absolute Spirit to be God, and Feuerbach had already criticized this view in his review of Sengler's work. Speculative philosophy, the object of his criticism there, had been characterized much in the same way as theology. It was, in effect, theology parading now not in the theologian's garb, but in that of the philosophy professor. But the error is essentially the same: the subjective (i.e., concrete, particular, individual) faculties of the individual philosopher himself are mistaken for the objective, universal, "metaphysical" essence of man, and as such are hypostatized as a transcendent, absolute essence. Hegel, as the *non*positive, allegedly un-Christian philosopher, is at first spared from this criticism, and in fact defended against the orthodox version of it, in *Philosophy and Christianity*. But then Feuerbach goes further and includes Hegel's *Absolute* as itself the latest and "sober" version of this "drunken speculation," which posits the Absolute as it is conceived in the thought of a philosopher as the "incarnation" of Being, or of the Idea itself (cf VII, 142, 153, cited on pp. 170–71). If speculative philosophy, the tradition from Kant and Fichte through Hegel, is to be identified *as a whole*, with the error of hypostatization ascribed initially to theology, then neither philosophy, in this sense, nor theology are to be spared, in the anthropological reduction. This implication, present in the works of 1838–9, must certainly underlie the explicit attack on theology itself that is made in *The Essence of Christianity*. Hegel's philosophy overcomes the weaknesses, the contradictions in the speculative tradition that preceded it. That much is conceded by Feuerbach. But it carries these contradictions along with it, and repeats them in the most abstract, "scientific," and rigorous form. The major contradiction remains a *real* contradiction in Hegel. His resolution of it is only a resolution of its *formal* expression, in *thought*, but not a resolution of its *material* expression, in *fact*. It is the "contradiction" between thinking and being, the "formal" solution of which is the subsumption of being *in* thinking, in the self-identity of self-conscious consciousness. This formal or abstract resolution is idealism, and in rejecting this, Feuerbach rejects, in effect, philosophy itself, insofar as it is idealist.

To sum up this developmental story, what begins as the sharpest distinction between theology and philosophy, on Hegelian grounds, ends as an identification of theology and philosophy (idealist, speculative philosophy), based on the rejection of Hegelian idealism. Once this identity is established, the critique of theology can be taken as an implicit critique of idealist philosophy itself. That this was Feuerbach's intention is made explicit by his remarks in the preface to the second (1843) edition of the work. After noting that he has written this work in as nontechnical a style as possible, so that it may be understood "by every educated and thinking person," he writes,

Nevertheless, my work can be appreciated and fully understood only by the scholar . . .; for though it is a completely independent production, it is at the same time a necessary consequence of history. I very frequently refer to this or that historical phenomenon, without expressly naming it, thinking this to be superfluous; and these references can be understood only by the scholar. So, for example, in the very first chapter where I develop the necessary consequences of the standpoint of feeling, I refer to the philosophers Jacobi and Schleiermacher; in the second chapter, I allude chiefly to Kantianism, Skepticism, Deism, Materialism, Pantheism; in the chapter on "The Standpoint of Religion," where I discuss the contradiction between the religious or theological, and the physicalist or natural-philosophical view of nature, I have in mind the philosophy in the age of orthodoxy, especially Cartesian and Leibnizian philosophy, in which this contradiction presents itself in a particularly characteristic way. Therefore, the reader who is unacquainted with the historical presuppositions and intermediate stages of my work, will miss that upon which my arguments and ideas hinge. (VII, 292–3)

"History" and "historical presuppositions" refer here to the history of philosophy, specifically. This gives us another clue, therefore, to the work not only as a philosophical critique of religion, and of theology, but of philosophy as well–a critique Feuerbach was to make explicit in subsequent works.

This is stated even more explicitly in Feuerbach's remark that "we criticize speculative philosophy only by means of the critique of religion. . . . The critique of speculative philosophy merely follows as a consequence" (VII, 298).

FEELING AND IMAGINATION

The most important *epistemological* analysis in *The Essence of Christianity* is that concerned with the role of feeling and imagination in the process of religious concept formation. It is this analysis that gives us the specific content with which Feuerbach invests the Hegelian model of self-alienation. It is also the other of the two sides of Feuerbach's empirical orientation: The first deals with the senses, the second, with feeling. Between them they form the basis for man's knowledge of the natural world, and of man. In that feeling is the distinctive capacity for *human* self-recognition, it is the empirical basis for Feuerbach's humanism. The context for Feuerbach's treatment of feeling, and its instrument of expression, the imagination, is his earlier discussions, in the *Bayle*, in *Philosophy and Christianity*, in the Sengler review, and in a number of other essays. The character of Feuerbach's analysis is rationalist, but in a distinctively qualified way. The romantic counterposition of sentiment and reason, which runs through much of the literature and philosophy of the eighteenth and nineteenth centuries, had various emphases. In Hume, and in Kant, the domain of the feelings, of sentiment, of the "practical will" was clearly distinguished from reason and then, with great difficulty, related to it once again. The classical rationalist distrust of the senses and of feeling (e.g. in Descartes, in Spinoza) resulted in a sublimation of these "faculties" in the Cartesian mathematical and rational "institution," in Spinoza's "intellectual love of God." The German idealist tradition had, with varying emphases, developed Kant's distinction between Pure and Practical Reason; but Kant's *Third Critique* (*The Critique of Judgment*), in which the dialectical unity of freedom and necessity, of spontaneous feeling and rational *moral* freedom (under a concept) was attempted, remained his most problematic work. The question "How can immediate feelings be moral?" remained, within the rationalist context, a difficult one. Fichte's emphasis on the practical, active Ego, on doing, on activity, and on the role therein of the stimulus of feeling found its continuation in the feeling-centered philosophies of Jacobi and Schleiermacher, especially in the context of religious feeling. Hegel assigned this complex of feeling faculties to the lowest order of organic response. He wrote, "to remain at the level of feeling, and to be able to participate only at this level constitutes the anti-human, the animal element of our nature."[15] "Sensibility," in the organic sense, is dealt with together with "irritability" and "reproduction," as a function of the nervous system.[16] The more complex feeling of desire (Begierde) represents, in Hegel's Phenomenology, the negative character of self-consciousness that takes itself as an outward object in itself, but not for itself.[17] It is this same unknowing self-consciousness that Feuerbach takes as his subject in religious consciousness. Desire must have an object. Its object in both Hegel and Feuerbach is self-consciousness— the universal or species consciousness. But desire is unconscious of the nature of its object, and takes it for another, not-itself. The satisfaction of desire is the incorporation of the object in the subject. But this satisfaction is the negation or transformation of desire into its "opposite." This aneignung or appropriation (i.e., making one's own) is the passage from consciousness to self-consciousness, but only its initial stage, in Hegel.[18] The awareness of desire is a feeling of self as incomplete, or unhappy. This "unhappy consciousness" is, in effect, the feeling of one's own feeling, or feeling as the object of feeling. This condition of neediness, as felt need, which Hegel identifies with life as against self-consciousness,[19] is taken over by Feuerbach as the very condition of human existence and as the ultimate source of religious feelings, insofar as the fulfillment of these feelings, in fantasy, is the actual theogony, the birth of the Gods. Thus, it is not human misery in itself that creates the Gods, but the satisfaction this misery finds in the imagination, as the instrument of wish fulfillment, which creates and appropriates the objects of these wishes and desires; which, in effect, objectifies them, so that they can be appropriated. But this illusory satisfaction of the "unhappy consciousness" is, at best, replaced by a more abstract illusion, in Hegel: the abstract identity of self-consciousness with itself. This transcendental solution, the "highest good" as self-contemplation, which Aristotle had already formulated and which Hegel had placed at the pinnacle of his system, is rejected by Feuerbach as the latest, most abstract form of religious fantasy, in the garb of systematic, speculative philosophy. Religion as waking dream, as the "opium of the people," in Feuerbach's (and later in Marx's) critique, also has its "philosophical" form, not only as philosophically formulated religion (i.e., theology) but as "religious" (i.e., fantastic) philosophy.

However sharply Feuerbach rejects the Hegelian resolution of the contradiction within self-consciousness, he nevertheless adopts the form of this contradiction as Hegel presents it. The "unhappy consciousness" (Das unglückliche Bewusstsein, in Hegel's phrase) is the self-alienated consciousness, which has its own essence as its object, but only as outward or projected object. This "split-consciousness" or "double-consciousness" (*in sich entzweite Bewusstsein*), as Hegel calls it,[20] is in fact the subject of *The Essence of Christianity*. The mechanism of this *entzweiung* or split involves the role of *image* in thought. And the faculty of image production, insofar as *self*-consciousness is concerned, is the feeling-directed *imagination*. In Feuerbach's earlier writings, the difference between *belief* and *thought* is that the ultimate object of belief is always the *image*, whereas the object of thought is the *thing itself*, or the *fact* (see p. 122). Belief is therefore, for Feuerbach, always caught in a self-delusion once it is taken to be literal or "scientific" in its import—that is, once the objects of belief are accorded a real or a metaphysical status. The *image* is always a finite and conditional *representation* of an object. Insofar as belief claims to be absolute, its object is claimed to be absolute as well—that is, unconditioned, infinite, universal. This absolute claim of belief therefore takes the subjectively finite representation, the representation of the concrete and particular objects of feeling, as the objectively infinite reality; or conversely takes these finite representations as the *incarnation* of the Absolute. The belief of the believers, the spontaneous and original religious consciousness, tends to the very opposite of this. It tends to take the alienated form of self-consciousness in its personal, concretely human sense; it brings God down to earth; it conceives the imaginary object in its literal, even sensible form: God as man, as present in nature, as present, literally, not only in history, but in individual form. Theology, on the other hand, *fixes* the alienated *image* of self-consciousness as a wholly other, absolute, supernatural and superhuman essence.

The essence of religion is the projection of human essence as other. The essence of theology is the "absolutization," the metaphysical hypostatization of this other, as real, or as the only essentially real Being. Imagination plays the role of providing the object of this hypostatization, or of this entification. But imagination, in Feuerbach's view, is not "imaginary." It is the real reflex of real existence—of *that* existence which constitutes the distinctly human. It is the expression of human needs, human desires, human feelings. What makes this distinctively human is that it is the consciousness of an object of feeling. But this "unhappy" consciousness is the veiled, unconscious or unknowing form of the consciousness of one's *own* feeling, that is, it is *selbstfühlende Gefühl*. To the extent that one is aware of one's own feelings, in the sense of having feeling itself as an object of feeling, one is a *conscious* being in the human sense, for this self-conscious feeling has as its object not merely this or that *particular* feeling, as a form of sensibility or

217

irritability in the organic sense – an itch or a feeling of hunger, whose objects *are* in fact outward, physiologically particular objects. Rather, this self-conscious feeling has the nature of feeling itself as its object, that is, the *species* nature of feeling. Such a feeling is given only to human beings who are at the same time the subjects and the objects of the feeling. It is a feeling toward that which is *human* in another, and thus entails, unknowingly, the species concept of humanity itself. It is feeling toward another who is like oneself, and thus it transcends the particularity of mere sensibility; it has a universal as its object – that is, an *essence*.

It can only be suggested here that this view has much in common with Kant's view in the *Critique of Judgment*, but its "dialectic" is peculiarly Hegelian.

The characterization of fantasy in Feuerbach's earlier works emphasizes its lack of self-limitation, its penchant for "infinitizing" its particular representation. Insofar as fantasy imposes no self-limitations, it is essentially lawless, arbitrary. But insofar as fantasy *remains* merely fantasy (i.e., the work of the imagination), it is not self-contradictory, for it can be self-contradictory only with respect to a logic, a system, a concept – all of which it eschews. In the critique of Dorguth's materialism, Feuerbach had taken this fantasy activity, this image production, literally, in Dorguth's own terms, as a brain act. In this context, it has a common form with sensation, which is taken, in its "activity," as the production of "impressions" of sense, in the brain. The difference between "images" of sense and of feeling is that the former are attributable to the action of outward stimuli on the brain, the latter to the internal stimulus of the "heart," that is, of inner feeling activity. But in both cases, these are "brain acts," not acts of *thought*. They are, says Feuerbach, the sine qua non of thinking, its stimulus, or *Reiz*, so that there is no thinking without images. But they are only the matter, not the *essence* of thinking activity. They merely are what they *are*, that is, are neither true nor false. In the Dorguth critique, Feuerbach appears to be a full-fledged mind-body dualist, when he speaks in these terms. But he modifies this in Hegelian idealist fashion, by subsuming the "otherness," the "materiality" of brain acts as no *more* than the other-sidedness of thinking activity itself. Matter has no independent being, it is only "matter" insofar as it stands to thought in the relation of object to subject. Its inertness or passivity – in effect, its nonbeing – is mediated only to the extent that it has the capacity to be taken up in thought activity as an object. The "image" in this sense is unreal, or has only the qualified reality of being a thought object. It is thought's *other*, the *condition* but not the *cause* or ground of thinking.

But once Feuerbach gives to feeling activity the status of the concretely existential mode of human being, this "unreality" of the image is transformed into the unreality of the image *as it is reflectively conceived or thought about.* The reality that the image as such represents is the essential reality of human essence itself, and not anything less. The image is therefore the signature or emblem, the material sign, of the distinctively human reality of feeling. Though feeling still has no law, because it does not operate under the determinations of a concept, it is nevertheless now become lawful in another sense. The "lawfulness" or "purposefulness" of feeling is not conceptual, but existential; it fulfills itself not in thought, but in life, that is, in the life of the species. Its fulfillment is humanity itself, and the process of its fulfillment is the humanizing of the species, its attainment of the full capacities of the species.

The condition of this process is the condition of all phenomenology: the dialectic whereby the subject comes to know himself as capable of and therefore responsible for the species attainment–that is, comes to know himself as human. This condition is the subject-object relation of consciousness, through which alone self-consciousness is attainable. And this requires the objectification, or the projection in outward form, of this species character, as object of consciousness. The instrument of this objectification is the imagination. Its content–that which is objectified–is *feeling* itself. The positive relation between the subject and the object, in its broadest terms, is *love*–not egoism, but the love of another as oneself. The condition for this love of another as oneself is self-knowledge. The itinerary of the progress of self-knowledge requires the image-forming activity of the mind. This fantasy, or dream work of the imagination, becomes *systematically* illusory only in theology. When the scales of theology fall from the eyes of man, the illusion is shattered, anthropology replaces theology, man knows himself for what he is. The millennium of self-conscious rationality has arrived.

The bulk of *The Essence of Christianity* is taken up with the examination of this process of imaginative projection, and its humanist or naturalist "reduction." But the process itself, examined here in an array of concrete instances, in good empirical fashion, is never explicitly or theoretically treated in the work. It remains part of the deeper thesis of the work and is indicated by Feuerbach's discussion in earlier, as well as in later, works.

The rationalist character of Feuerbach's treatment of the *image* (e.g., in the *Critique of Positive or "Christian" Philosophy*, in the Sengler review) is made clear in his charge that speculative philosophy substitutes images for thoughts. But what exactly distinguishes image from thought, rather than one sort of image from another, is not made clear. Feuerbach echoes the traditional rationalist view that images, as copies or representations of things, are obscure, and that the clear light of truth is best apprehended directly by thought or by the intellect. But the distinction remains epistemologically obscure. Historically, it has served as a framework for epistemological discussion, rather than as a material contribution to the clarification of epistemological questions. The root of image in feeling–especially in desire–is, on the other hand, a boldly suggestive idea, with clear psychological and empirical implications. The role of fantasy, dream, illusion in relation to wish and feeling is a basic theme in contemporary psychology, and Feuerbach's suggestion is a basic source of this emphasis, just as his works, especially *The Essence of Christianity* and the later *Theogony*, are deep-going *empirical* studies of this theme.[21]

THE "SPECIES CONCEPT" (GATTUNGSBEGRIFF) IN THE EARLIER WORKS

What pertains to the notion of "species concept," so central in *The Essence of Christianity*, cannot be encompassed in a brief note, nor need it be fully treated here. It is in fact the basis for Feuerbach's theory of *Universals*, in both ontological and epistemological terms. The references to this question in the Hegelian literature and in philosophical literature generally, are too vast for cogent comment here.

It is germane, however, to examine how this species concept figures in the post-Hegelian polemic, and how indeed Feuerbach modifies it to meet his needs. Here, oddly enough, it is Hegel's orthodox critic, Heinrich Leo, in his attack on the "Hegelings" (especially Michelet and Strauss), who provides the distinctive interpretation. Leo had charged that Hegel's philosophy was "un-Christian" and that the young Hegelians had reduced God to a mere species concept. That is, they had reduced the concept of God as a Person, in His concrete individuality, to that of God as abstract Universal. He writes, "This party [the young Hegelians] denies every God who is at the same time a Person. . . . This party openly teaches atheism."[22] The "species concept" that Leo attacks is the concept of God as Myth, as expression of the myth-forming capacities of the folk soul, as Friedrich Strauss had characterized it. The charge is not, therefore, that the concept of God is *im*personal, in the sense that the mythical representation has no personality, but that as mythical "personality," God is denied actual "personality," concrete existence. Conceptual "existence," mythical or fictive "existence," falls short of the actual existence of the divinity as person. If one goes beyond the Straussian "demythologization" to the "positive" concept of God, as philosophically conceived Being, then the "personal" content, even of the myth, evaporates into the abstract categories of Being, or Essence. Leo wants to hold on to the evangelical God who was crucified, was buried, and was resurrected; he wants to retain the *personality* and historical existence of Christ as witness to the existence of God. If not only the mythical "personality" is a human conception, but even the abstract, philosophical Being, or Essence, is a human conception, a projection of human self-consciousness in its abstractly reflective outward form, then this is complete "atheism." It first relegates the personal God to the status of an object of folk imagination; then relegates the "philosopher's God" Himself to the status of object of the philosopher's imagination. This is what Feuerbach's critique of speculative philosophy amounts to. But in this move, Feuerbach has not fully resolved the question of the status of the species concept. He has not, in short, decided what status universals have, or what the ontological or epistemological status of "species being" is. He has only interpreted it as a human concept, whose reference is not a transcendentally existing God, but a this-worldly humanity. But what the denotation of "humanity" is is not yet resolved. Leo had charged that "this party openly teaches a religion of exclusive this-worldliness."[23] But "this-worldliness" is not simply the collection of all the individual *concreta*, the existing particulars as such. Rather "this-worldliness" (*diesseitigkeit*) is the conceptual reflection in consciousness of this world, of the totality of both actual and possible existents. Therefore, this *diesseitigkeit* is other than the world it reflects. It is (in Hegel's terms in the *Phenomenology*) the *entzweiung*, or the duplication in consciousness of the "simple unity" of Being, mediated by its *actual* plurality, its actual form taking (*Gestaltung*), its actual determinateness. It is the grasping, in conception, of the essential unity of a collection of particulars, akin to Kant's *transcendental unity of apperception*. Hegel resolved this problem of the many-in-the-one by deriving the manifold from the dialectical unfolding of the simple unity. This process of "unfolding," grasped in the form only of the separate particularity of each "member," takes each particular as in-itself, and is in Hegel's terms the *abstract* concept of *life*. The process grasped *as process*, however—that is, in the internal relatedness of each of these "members" to the whole—is the *organic* concept of *life*, or (in Hegel's barbarism) *lebendiges leben* ("living life"). The manifold, taken in its "simple generality," Hegel calls "species," or "simple species" (*Gattung*). Still, the simplicity, or unicity, of the object of a species concept cannot be merely the collection itself, but its principle of unity, that which makes it a *collection* at all and not merely a *given-one-by-one*. The consciousness of species already involves universals as objects of consciousness. But it involves them first only as *other* than consciousness. In Feuerbach's terms, as in Hegel's, the consciousness of a universal as merely *other*, as mere *object*, leads to the conception of such a universal as *in itself*— in short, to a Platonic hypostatization of universals as *entities*. It gives the status of independent existence to such universals, in the same way that the senses give the status of independent existence to sense objects, as particulars. The "certainty of the senses" is paralleled by the "certainty of consciousness" with respect to its objects. This species certainty is dialectically mediated, in the movement to *self*-consciousness, when the universal as object is taken to be consciousness itself. It is then taken as the *I* that is at the same time subject and object; and insofar as the *I* is the particular, that is, "myself," consciousness takes *itself* as object under the form of particularity. Just as the hypostatized universal, as "other," is abstract, so too the universal now reduced to particular self-consciousness, to an individual ego, is abstract. Feuerbach's critique of egoism as the hypostatization of individual self-consciousness (in the Sengler review), and his attack on the "mystification of self-consciousness" in "Christian philosophy," is essentially an elaboration of this aspect of the *Phenomenology*. The "Incarnation theory," in which a concrete particular is invested with the attributes of the universal (or the "species"), breaks down at this point, according to Feuerbach.

What, then, is the "proper" object of species consciousness? What is the ultimately revealed reference of the species concept? What is its domain, so to speak? In Hegel's terms, *self*-consciousness is the object of species consciousness in this way: The *ostensible* object of species consciousness is the manifold grasped in its simple unity. But the actual manifold, in its organic flux and in the form taking of this flux, is life itself. The reflection of the organic unity of life in consciousness is *other* than life itself; that is, the *species* appears only to the consciousness of life, exhibiting this simple unity only upon its reflection in consciousness. Thus, Hegel says, "in this result, life refers to something other than itself, namely, to consciousness, for which it appears as this unity, or species."[24]

The appropriation of this unified manifold as object, in species consciousness, is still the "negative" aspect of this dialectic. This unity is still "unorganic, general Nature," in Hegel's terms. Its principle of self-activity is not yet given. It is taken as *independent* Nature, "species as such" or *self-consciousness as an object of consciousness*, still under the aspect of an *other*, unrealized as self-consciousness. The fulfillment of the dialectic, that is, the identity of self-consciousness with itself, is achieved only when self-consciousness is its own object or is the object of another self-consciousness. In Hegel's terms, life is the objectified form of the self-activity of self-consciousness. Thus, the dialectical identity of self-consciousness with itself is the hidden content of the consciousness of the organic unity of life. This incomplete, not yet fully self-conscious identity is what Hegel characterizes as desire. The satisfaction of this desire is achieved when self-consciousness has self-consciousness itself (or an other self-consciousness) as its object. ("*Das Selbstbewusstsein erreicht seine Befriedegung nur in einen andern Selbstbewusstsein.*"[25]) The "other" self-consciousness is, however, as much an *I* as it is the object of I. "Insofar as self-consciousness is the object, it is as much *I* as it is object—with this, the concept of Spirit is already present . . . : The *I* that is *We*, and the *We* that is *I*."[26] Thus, Hegel arrives at the self-conscious species concept, *Spirit*, which connotes the recognition of the subject in the object, or the symmetry of the subject-object relation, now taken in its manifest form to be a reflective relation, as the self-consciousness of *Spirit*. What is, on the one hand, a subject with respect to an object, is, on the other, the object of that same object now taken as subject. The self achieves its fullest self-knowledge, its "satisfaction," in being known to another self that is identical in essence with it; or it knows itself in knowing this *other* self as identical in essence with it. This instance of "being a self-consciousness for a self-consciousness" involves the self-alienation and then the self-identification, or self-return, that characterizes the systole and diastole of this dialectic.[27] It constitutes the essential phenomenological meaning of "*coming to know*," for Hegel, and it is this "coming to know" in its paradigmatic case as "coming to know oneself" in *essence*, that is, as *Spirit*, not as abstract individual.

The preceding journey through the looking glass (or the reflecting mirrors) of the phenomenological dialectic is worth the patience of the traveler. For it becomes clear on close inspection that the concept of species in Feuerbach derives from this dialectic. Feuerbach's humanistic-naturalistic interpretation of species concept is structurally identical with Hegel's. Yet this interpretation remains open to confusion. The confusion to which the term *Gattung* gives rise comes from two sources: First, it stems from an attempt to *simplify* its meaning, and to take it in the logical or biological sense of *genera* or *species* as classificatory index: that is, to take it merely as denoting the criterial attributes that members of a species have in common. The second source of the confusion, paradoxically, is *not* to take it in this latter sense *at all*, but to seek some transcendental notion of species as ideal form or principle, apart from its rude classificatory use. For Hegel, as for Feuerbach, "species" is a concretely referent term. Species are actual, in life, that is, in "living nature." The species *concept* is not this living nature *in itself*, but only as it is reflected upon as an object for consciousness. Hegel wants to find the ontological ground for the very possibility of such a species consciousness in the nature of consciousness itself. Thus, living nature is, for him, nothing but the external form, the projection, and, thus, the objectification of the nature of consciousness itself. Feuerbach's move has a Kantian flavor: He finds his ontological ground for the possibility of species consciousness in limiting the "living nature" that embodies this species to *human* nature. Moreover, the dialectical relation between consciousness and its object, in Feuerbach, rejects the notion of an a priori essence either in the object, mankind as living nature, or in the subject, the consciousness of man. The "essence" of man is infinite, in the sense that it is the *process* of this dialectic itself, rather than any stage in it or any transcendental final cause that underlies it. Man *creates* his essence infinitely in the process of developing a self-consciousness with respect to his existence. But without existence there is no consciousness; without this "real" consciousness of his existence, no self-consciousness. On the other hand, without self-consciousness, no man. In the dialectic as an evolutionary process, man creates himself as man, in the very process of coming to self-consciousness. And this self-consciousness entails the consciousness of himself as species, that is, the consciousness of himself as identical in essence with other selves, *insofar as they are self-conscious selves*. Self-consciousness, in this *species* sense, is the essence of humanity, the mark of man's separation from the brutes.

In the *Bayle*, Feuerbach had already argued that the limits of species *conception* are the conditions of species existence, and he there identifies *species existence* with human *essence*; that is, the essence of man is his existence *as species*. He had written, "Can the human individual conceive of anything, in thought or feeling, which does not derive from his own species-existence, from the essence of humanity?" VII, 69).[28] But in this passage, Feuerbach conceived of "derivation" as a universalization of particular human traits, freed by the fantasy from "this-worldly" limits, and carried to infinity, or to perfection, so to speak, but derivable nonetheless from their this-worldly, human origins. For the species concept itself to be *really* unlimited, however, it must take as its reference something that is itself unlimited, infinite, according to Feuerbach. He finds this "real" infinity in man as species; and he finds the source of the infinite species *concept* in man's capacity to take his species *existence* as an object of consciousness.

Feuerbach's Critique of Religion

The gist of Marx's criticism, in the *Theses on Feuerbach*, is that "species existence" is in itself an abstract term, and that Feuerbach fails to grasp the essence of man in the concrete historical terms of man's "sensuous practice." In the sense that Feuerbach did not grasp this historical practice in the political-economic terms of Marx's conception of praxis, Marx is surely right. Nonetheless, it is clear that Feuerbach did think of "species existence" in terms of a historical process, at the level of the historical phenomenology of human consciousness. That is to say, he dealt in detail with the modes of reflection *in consciousness* of characteristic human experiences. It may be said that where Marx and Engels were concrete (i.e., in historical political-economic terms), Feuerbach was abstract; but that where Feuerbach was concrete (i.e., in the psychology and phenomenology of conscious experience), Marx and Engels remained abstract. An adequate notion of species existence would have to be "concrete" in both of these respects, and would have to show how they bear on each other.

To return to Feuerbach's notion of the species concept: The requirement for the Feuerbachian dialectic is the same as that for Hegel's: this species nature in order to become an object of consciousness needs to be objectified. The process of this objectification begins with man taking himself as an object, but conceiving of this object as *other* than himself. This *necessary* stage of the dialectic is the unconscious anthropomorphism that characterizes religious consciousness. This latter includes, for Feuerbach, everything from outright primitive animism, to myth, to the classic forms of Judaeo-Christian belief, to the "positive" philosophical concepts of God, in the ostensibly *de*anthropomorphized and *de*mythologized forms of metaphysical speculation. In short, the species concept goes through a history of transformations before it comes to be *consciously* realized as man's *own* self-conception, the form of his own self-knowledge. Where man sees the Gods, he sees nothing but his own nature in the form of the Gods. Therefore, a self-conscious, enlightened study of the concepts of God, in religion, as well as of the detailed relations between man and his God, prescribed in the sacraments, especially in baptism, and in Holy Communion, reveals the true or anthropological content of religion, its reference to man's own nature. This examination is, in effect, the program of the "positive" first part of *The Essence of Christianity*. But its philosophical or epistemological framework is the phenomenology of human consciousness *in general*. The work is, therefore, in a fundamental way, Feuerbach's *Phenomenology of the Spirit*, structurally similar to but radically different in ontological interpretation from Hegel's *Phenomenology*. To approach the work in any narrower framework than this is to lose its philosophical significance. Further, to miss the structural kinship to Hegel's *Phenomenology* is to fail to comprehend that *The Essence of Christianity* is a thoroughly dialectical work, in its fine structure, as well as in its two-part organization, as thesis and antithesis. It is not incidentally, but essentially a study of religion; but only of religion taken in this broad, epistemological context.

INCARNATION THEORY

The concept of *species* is one aspect of Feuerbach's approach to the relation of the universal to the particular. A cognate aspect of this same problematic relation is his treatment of *Incarnation*. The problem is the classic metaphysical and logical one of the relation of the one to the many, of essence to existence, of the forms to their exemplification—the central dialectical problem in ancient Greek philosophy and an archetypal problem through the whole history of human reflection. Feuerbach's treatment of it in terms of Incarnation is an example of his genius in playing variations on what one might call a root metaphor. The concept of Incarnation has at least three distinctive senses in Feuerbach's work. First, it denotes, in straightforward fashion, the Christian mystery of incarnation, of Christ as God incarnate, of the God-man. But beyond this particular "Christian" sense, Feuerbach takes incarnation as an essentially *religious* concept, in general, a characteristic element in *any* religious consciousness whatever. Therefore, in a second "anthropological" sense, incarnation is the characteristic of the universal religious impulse to regain, in the form of concrete, individual human existence, what was given up in the projection of human nature as *other* or divine nature. The God who is absolute moral judge, who transcends all particularity in His infinite being, is also the God who is my own private and personal solace, who descends from the otherworldly heaven to walk among men in visible form, to feed them, to heal them, and to suffer the pains of mortal flesh. This second sense is the reflective or critical interpretation of the first "literal" sense. These two senses are standard enough—the metaphor *is* a metaphor only if it has an interpretation that is not metaphorical. The third sense is a crucial one, however, for here Feuerbach extends the "Christian" metaphor by relating it explicitly to its expression in non-Christian, "philosophical" terms. This usage has an *ironic sense* in Feuerbach's criticism of "Absolute" or speculative philosophy. The "incarnation" is no longer explicitly religious, for it is not God who has become man; nor is it anthropological, for it is not human essence that has been objectified in a sensible image, in an imaginative symbol. In speculative philosophy, the philosopher takes his own philosophy as the "incarnation" of absolute and universal truth itself, as the final attainment of the self-consciousness of Being itself. But Feuerbach is not merely exploiting a metaphor for the sake of irony. His references to Hegel as the "Messiah," as the personal embodiment of Absolute Spirit, as the "Absolute Dalai-Lama," and so on, are ironic enough (see pp. 176–77); and even more bitter is his attack on so-called Positive or Christian philosophy, for its Incarnation theory (see p. 171). But the irony has a systematic intent. The analogy between the Incarnation concepts of the "true believer" and the speculative philosopher rests on an essential relation between the thought processes in both cases. In Feuerbach's view, the incarnation of universal and infinite attributes in an individual involves a logical contradiction. The real "incarnation" of the universal can be fulfilled only in an actuality that is *itself* infinite, whose essence, as infinite, is identical with its existence. This essence, however, is not God, to whom this identity is classically attributed, but that which the term or the concept "God" represents, that is, mankind, the species as such. But individual existence is not species existence. The species transcends any finite individual in its existence, though it is comprised of nothing but the totality of individuals, insofar as they are human, that is, are aware of themselves as members of the species. Thus, the attribution of universality and infinity to any individual cannot be the work of reason, which is constrained by the principle of noncontradiction, and hence cannot rationally formulate such an identity of the infinite universal and the finite individual. Rather, such an identity is the work of imagination, which is unfettered in this regard. What imagination expresses in outward or objective form is the unlimited wish, the dream, the satisfaction of the desires of man's feelings, the ultimate and infinite fulfillment of *subjective* needs. In imagination there is no real contradiction, because its rule is not the rational principle of noncontradiction (see p. 218). Yet the philosophical claim to have embodied Absolute truth is itself nothing but this wish fulfillment in abstruse form; it is the imaginative incarnation of the subjective faculties of desire, feeling, and so on, in the guise of rational thought. This "philosophical" deception has its double movement just as does its religious analogue. First, the "Absolute" philosopher projects his own, individual self-consciousness, as if it were a divine, infinite (i.e., "Absolute") and "other" truth. Then he recovers it, and discovers his own philosophical system to be the *incarnation* of this universal truth. Thus, Feuerbach's comment that the speculative philosopher is a *tautologue*, that he thinks he is saying two things but is only saying the same thing twice (see p. 170), sums up his criticism of this philosophical version of Incarnation theory.

This much of the third sense of "Incarnation" is already contained in the earlier reviews and critiques, as we have seen. The concept is systematically tied to Feuerbach's analysis of the relation between philosophy and theology, and reflects the sense in which Feuerbach takes speculative philosophy to be nothing but a form of theology. But whereas theology has an explicit Incarnation theory, speculative philosophy replaces the divine subject of incarnation with abstract philosophical terms. The very concept of incarnation is a nonphilosophical or antiphilosophical one (i.e., a nonrational concept). Its source is in imagination. It is here that we see the cutting edge of Feuerbach's criticism. Speculative metaphysics becomes nothing more than a rigorously conceived, but nevertheless nonrational expression of the imagination. If its claims are taken at face value, then speculative metaphysics is fraught with contradiction and is a false representation of what it claims to represent, that is, truths about Being itself. However, once the intimate relation between the process of metaphysical or speculative construction and that of religious construction is laid bare, then the translation or reduction of metaphysics to its "natural" or human content follows the same procedure as does the reduction of religious metaphor. In this qualified "anthropological" sense, speculative metaphysics is as rich an expression of the self-consciousness of the human species as is religious thought. It shares the character of theology, as esoteric anthropology. The metaphysical questions of existence, of creation, of causality, of freedom and determinism, of the relation of body to mind, or of matter to spirit all turn out to be interpretable as "natural" or "human" questions in Feuerbach's reduced sense. Thus, the history of philosophy, just as the history of religious thought, provides us with the empirical material for the study of the primary features and processes of reflective consciousness; it is the source book for the systematic study of concept formation, as it has in fact taken place. One of the principal keys to the solution of the cryptogram this history presents is the explication of the concept of Incarnation. This background, then, permits an interpretation of Feuerbach's discussion of Incarnation theory in *The Essence of Christianity* in terms of its connotations as a critique of philosophy itself, and not alone of religion and theology.

IMAGINATION, LANGUAGE, AND THOUGHT

Feuerbach's analysis of the concept of Imagination underlies his critique of Incarnation theory and is a fundamental theme in *The Essence of Christianity*. In effect, the analysis of Imagination recapitulates the dialectic of alienation of Hegel's *Phenomenology*. Hegel's account of objectification in sense perception and in "organic" desire, or sensibility, is adapted by Feuerbach as the framework for his account of objectification in the process of image formation.

The most general description of this framework is something like the following: Thought, consciousness, awareness must have an object, must be "of," "about," or "directed toward" something other than itself. Empirical thought has its object as external. Its "outness" (in Locke's phrase) or its "externality" is given. That is to say, the object is taken unmediatedly or intuitively as "other." This direct or naive realism is mediated by reflection. The "otherness" of the object is not merely given "in itself." It is *given to* a subject, so that its "in-itselfness" is mediated by this relation. Kant's move was to embody this relation as the necessary condition of any experience whatever. The subjective interpretation of this Kantian position (e.g., in Fichte) is now founded upon the *ontological* status of the object itself in its being given to a subject. This is taken to mean that the object is a mediated mode of the subject's *own* self-activity, or its projection of itself, its self-duplication as outward object. The condition of objectivity (i.e., being an object for a subject) is now transformed into the *essence* or the *definition* of objectivity, as this relation itself *in* the mediated subject, or in Fichtean terms, as grounded in the Ego. This Ego activity is creative, therefore, in that the presumably "given" object of consciousness is, in this version, a *created* object. Its "givenness" is only the naive apprehension of its otherness, but not the reflective awareness of this "other" as self-alienated Ego. This creation of objects of consciousness is the "free activity" of the Ego. It is the freedom of creative act, in the sense of its being self-activity and not an activity caused by something other than the self. This "free activity" is not lawless, or arbitrary, but is rational, that is, lawful, activity insofar as it exhibits the autonomy of the self— its self-imposed lawfulness, its activity in accordance with its own rule, which constitutes its rational nature. However, to the extent that the Ego is not actually rational, to the extent that it falls short of rationality, its creative activity is contaminated by the heteronomous influences of nonrational desires, feelings, passions—those modes of apprehension that are directed toward objects that are nonrational in precisely the measure that they are not fully under the rule of the Ego's rationality. Therefore, this activity is not fully autonomous, but heteronomous, and to that extent it is not free. This "human bondage to the passions" is the common feature of the rationalism that finds its culmination in Spinoza's *Ethics*, in Kant's *Metaphysics of Morals*, in Fichte's *System of Moral Theory*. Hegel's development of this thesis in the *Phenomenology*, as in other works, gives it in its most rigorous, systematic, and abstract version. In this sense, Hippolyte justly says that Hegel's notion of the "unhappy consciousness" in which this theme of self-alienation is worked out is the central motif in the *Phenomenology*.[29]

This serves as the framework for Feuerbach's analysis of Imagination. Because all consciousness must have an object, the object that is created by an *unfree* consciousness, or Ego activity, is not an object that is constructed according to autonomous reason, but one that bears the imprint of the "lower" faculties of sense, desire, feeling, and so on. The mark of this nonautonomous representation is the "limited" character of the object thus created. This sense of "limitation" here goes back to Plato's account of the forms and their copies. What limits the *ideal* forms is the condition of their exemplification in material or sensible form. The *copy* or exemplification of the form, as sensible image, is thereby removed from the perfection of true form; it is a distorted shadow. This "imperfection," by degree of removal from the perfect original, becomes, as we know, a central theme both in theology and in metaphysics. It finds its clear expression, in Feuerbach's view, in the Incarnation theory and in the theory of the Trinity. Here, however, it is given a paradoxical form. The incarnation, though it is a corporeal embodiment of the ideal form (and therefore a copy or exemplification or manifestation), nevertheless is identical in perfection and in essence with the original: The Christ *is* God. But this violates the conditions of the "copy" model, that is, that the copy is less perfect than the original. In this sense, the identity of ideal form and copy, of God and Christ, remains a "mystery." The limited object of the unfree or passionate or "unhappy" consciousness in its "nonmysterious" form is less perfect than the object of free or "happy" consciousness. By contrast, the object of a fully free, autonomous consciousness (i.e., of reason) is not thus limited. Its freedom is its autonomy; it acts only in accordance with its *own* necessity, as rational nature. Its freedom, in Hegel's phrase, is the recognition of its own necessity, that is, the recognition of no *other* necessity but that of its own rational nature. Hence, its object is nothing but the objectification of this inner nature, and is, in this sense, unlimited, infinite, universal, absolute. The capacity to produce objects limited by the passions, sense, feeling–objects of sense or of desire or feeling–stems not from reason but the imagination. The objects of consciousness that imagination produces are sensible objects. They differ from objects of actual sense perception only in that they are *felt* to be freely produced, whereas the latter are not and exhibit an intransigence to our will or desire. But they are like the objects of sense in that they are *images* or sensible *impressions*, they have the form of sensible objects, they are clothed in the garments of sensibility, they are "pictures," in the broad sense. Here the illusiveness of imagination presents itself: On the one hand, the appearance of these images is *like* that of sense impressions. On the other hand, the images are *felt* to be free creations, in the fact of their being conformable to our wish and desire and in their being nonconforming to the laws under which we apprehend the objects of sense perception. Thus, these images give the *appearance* of free creative activity, and thus we are led by this feeling to attribute to them also the properties of the *proper* objects of free, rational activity, namely, *infinity, universality, absoluteness*. The *images* as objects of feeling are given the status of *thoughts* as objects of reason. This self-deception is the characteristic error of that power of imagination that mistakes itself for reason proper.

Here, then, is the framework of Feuerbach's charge that theology, the reflective theory in which imagination arrogates the place of reason, is *systematized* self-deception; and here is the source of Feuerbach's charge that in this, theology embodies a fundamental contradiction. Rational reflection effects the realization that objects of imagination are in fact objects of imagination, images produced by feeling, desire, wish, no longer mistaken to be objects of reason, or of thought. The tendency to take imaginary objects as *sensibly* real, as concrete, perceptual objects is, according to Feuerbach, characteristic of religious consciousness. God is given sensible form, He appears in the flesh, as an individual human being. He appears in history as a person. By contrast to this religious consciousness, theology takes these imaginary objects as objects of rational thought, as rationally real, or "transcendental" objects. Further, speculative philosophy abstracts this same imaginary content and makes metaphysical "substance" of it. The believer's God and the philosopher's God are polar opposites in this sense. The one is a concrete individual person; the other is an abstract essence. Feuerbach's conclusion that theology, and speculative philosophy, especially in its "Christian" or positive form, is the very negation of religion derives from this polar distinction.

The psychological content of Feuerbach's discussion of Imagination is in his characterization of the feeling of limitlessness in imaginative activity. He ascribes this to the fundamental character of feeling, as tending to its own fullest satisfaction, following no law and allowing no limitation but that of feeling itself. The image is the objectification of this full satisfaction. In terms of the process itself, image formation objectifies this "infinite" striving to satisfaction. The term "infinity" is used by Feuerbach in the sense it had acquired in Hegelian philosophy: The "infinite" or unlimited satisfaction of feeling is not a matter of either quantity or degree of satisfaction, but of its lack of limitation by any other nature than that of feeling itself. The felt freedom of this feeling activity, in image formation, is its lack of either empirical or rational constraints. Because neither the limits of empirical nature nor the rule of reason are imposed on imagination, it is infinite in its own mode, in accordance with its own nature. It is self-fulfilling activity. The objects of feeling are therefore nothing but objectifications of this "infinity" or unlimitedness of the nature of feeling itself; or in Feuerbach's reflexive formulation, "The object of feeling is feeling itself" (VI, 11; S: I, 46). Therefore, also, *in* feeling itself, there can be no contradictions. These arise only in the reflection upon feeling, which regards it from the point of view not of feeling, but of a nature alien to feeling, that is, that of thought. But this contradiction itself is only "formal," that is, in accordance with the laws of rational *expression*, which is, in Feuerbach's terms, only the reflection of the "real" contradiction in consciousness. This "real" contradiction is that between the satisfaction of feeling in the imagination and the satisfaction of feeling in "real life," in the empirical or natural world.

Thus, for all the inner reality of the world of imagination, the "real" or this-worldly constraint on imagination lies in empirical nature. Imagination is therefore the flight, the reflex *away* from the intransigeance of empirical reality. But it is an unconscious flight. It cannot *know* itself as such. The rational realization of the illusiveness of imagination requires the reflection in consciousness of a "real" contradiction, that between imagination and empirical fact. And the necessity of this contradiction must therefore lie in the fact that man *exists* as a natural, empirical being, in the natural world, and not only as a self-sufficient feeling being. The lack of existential constraints would in fact lead to unbridled hallucination, to a total affirmation of the imaginary world as real. But because man's existence as natural being is the prerequisite for his existence as feeling being, such an affirmation would eventuate in his self-destruction as natural being. The immediate objects of feeling, desire, and so on, as organic sensibilities, are this-worldly. I love this person. I desire that object. But the nature of feeling is such that faced with limitations upon the satisfaction of these natural wants in the world of man, feeling fulfills them internally, in imagination.

The work of imagination is thus the satisfaction of unrequited natural feelings, such as desires and needs. This inner satisfaction is possible only to a being who can know what he wants well enough to be able to form an image of it as an object of consciousness. But the real satisfaction of unrequited wants is possible only to a being who can distinguish the illusory satisfaction within the imagination from real satisfaction in such a way as to redirect activity from one to the other, to turn from the image of the object, now objectified and held before him, so to speak, to the object of which it is the image. This *rational* realization of the relation of image to real object, the reading of the metaphor as nothing more than metaphor, is at the same time the realization of the function of imagination: *It is the process of coming to know the object of feeling, and not just the immediate fulfillment of feeling in itself.* Imagination, then, provides the stimulus to the process of rational knowledge. The image is "the material of thought," in Feuerbach's phrase. Fully self-conscious rationality is attained only when the image is known to be no more than an image. The contrast with fact is given by empirical knowledge. Rational activity is therefore the mediation of imagination and empirical knowledge. Its ultimate subject matters are sense and feeling. Reason is nothing but the mediated, reflective level of sense and feeling, or, in good Hegelian terminology, reason is nothing but fully self-conscious sense and feeling.

This is the direction Feuerbach's "dialectic of sensibility" is to take. This is the form of that marriage of rationalism and empiricism he wished to achieve. But the necessary bond of that marriage is the faculty of image formation, which is neither rational nor empirical in its essence. Feuerbach nowhere explicitly recognizes how closely his proposed solution of this problem of the status of the imagination with regard to reason and sense perception approaches Kant's, in the *Third Critique,* nor does he ever attain to the philosophical explicitness of Kant in this regard.

This theory of Imagination links up in an interesting way with Feuerbach's treatment of language. In his *Critique of Hegelian Philosophy*, Feuerbach had distinguished thought from language as original from copy. He had given the original or native character of thought as private, internal activity, and, as such, unshareable with others (see pp. 181–4). This is already a radical revision of his early Hegelianism in the *Dissertation* and in the *History*, in which thought itself *is* the community of thinkers, is their universal bond, the unity of *I* and *Thou*.

The critique of Hegelianism entailed a rejection of this view, as expressing only the reflected *idea* of community in thought, but not the community itself, and thus exhibiting the fundamental error in Hegelian idealism of hypostatizing the *thought* object as a real or as the ultimately real object. The sharing of the content of thought requires the objectification of this content in sensible (i.e., public) form, which is no more than to say that communication requires language. But language as such is the *translation* of thought. The original is not given, only its copy is. And such a copy, as public object, is the condition of community, of *shared* thought. Therefore, the actual species, mankind, can become aware of its species nature, or can become self-conscious, only by the instrumentality of language, of the word as image of the thought. So far, then, language shares the formal character of Imagination. It is the projection, in outward form, of the *image* of a human faculty, and is in this way the means whereby human consciousness becomes aware of its own faculties or its capacities, that is, of that which constitutes its nature. But whereas the private or inner imagery of feeling is not available to other minds than my own, and is "free" in the sense of being limited only by my own feeling nature, the public imagery of language is not free in this way. Once feeling or thought is expressed in language, then the forms of language are its limits. It is required to follow the "rules" of language, and is no longer a "free" image. Now, the "rules" of language are, for Feuerbach, nothing but the natural conditions of the material structure of language—its grammar. In this sense, any public objectification of feeling or thought is limited by the structure of its material or sensible medium. Feuerbach had suggested that different media are more or less appropriate to such objectification. For example, the musical sound is the most appropriate medium for the expression of feeling, the word for the expression of thought. The influences of Hegel's aesthetic are clear here. Both musical sounds and words constitute a "language," that is, an instrument for the sharing of feeling or thought, of feeling no less than of thought. Thus, for Feuerbach, all the forms of art, no less than the forms of religion and philosophy, are public objectifications of human capacities under the limitations of their medium of objectification, their "language" or means of communication.

The formal structure of language or its laws, in Feuerbach's view, are not the intrinsic conditions of thought in itself. Rather, they are the conditions of *demonstration*, that is, of the outward, public or shared form of thought. Thus, as Feuerbach argued in the *Critique of Hegelian Philosophy*, the laws of logic are not laws of thought in itself, but laws of language. Only in such a context does the logical law of noncontradiction arise. Therefore, only in the linguistic *image* of feeling or thought can formal contradiction arise.[30] Further, only insofar as the work of the Imagination, as instrument of feeling, is represented not only in a sensible, but in a linguistic form (i.e., insofar as the image of feeling is retranslated, or reflected upon, as an image of thought) can there arise contradictions. But these do not arise in the Imagination itself. The consequences of such a view are that, though Imagination and language share the property of "imagery," that is, sensible representation in a medium, the conditions of the linguistic image are different from those of the image of feeling, or the image of Imagination proper, as instrument of feeling. The difference is that once the image becomes expressed in the public medium of the word, or verbal language, it is limited by the laws of language. And insofar as the function of language, in Feuerbach's view, is demonstration, it is limited by the laws of logic. Contradiction arises only in the dialectic (literally, in the verbal dialogue) that constitutes the actual community of thought. In Feuerbach's terms, this dialogue is not mere "talking," but rather discourse or reasoning. The history of this discourse, in its essential form, is the history of philosophy. Philosophy is therefore the rigorous pursuit of verbal dialogue, according to the laws of language, and thus philosophy imposes the law of contradiction on the material of free imagination, once this material is recast in linguistic, that is, rational, demonstrative, or "philosophical" form.

How do Imagination and language contribute to the constitution of the actual human community, that is, the species existence of man? Feuerbach's claim is that this community is constituted fundamentally by feeling–by shared feeling. The outward form of this shared feeling is the system of projected images of feeling, as objects of public consciousness. This construct of the Imagination is religion. As construct, it is hypostatized as an independent object–as a person–and is taken to be both other than human *and* human at the same time. For the imagination, there is no conflict here. For reason, however, there is an outright contradiction. The systematic embodiment of this contradiction is theology, and in its most abstract form, it is speculative philosophy. This contradiction is resolved by recognizing the derivation of the image from its original, by recognizing the real reference of this image as human nature. Thus, the religious image is the imaginary construct, or representation of man's real species existence, in its most direct embodiment as an object of consciousness, albeit an unmediated, naively realist consciousness, which takes the image as an independent entity.

Religion is, in this way, the most direct expression of the actual community. The relation between this religious image and thought is once removed from this direct representation. Insofar as the image is the material of and the goad to thought, thought is the reflection upon this representation of the Imagination. In its outward expression in language (i.e., in philosophy), there is only the *representation of the representation of* the community. The community of thought achieved in linguistic communication is not the actual community, but its reflection, or the *idea* of the community. Language as such does not constitute the human community, but is the means of its self-consciousness as community. Man, says Feuerbach at the outset of *The Essence of Christianity*, is the only species to which its own species nautre is an object. That is, only man is a self-conscious species. Only by means of language does he achieve this self-consciousness. But language is secondary, in this dialectic, to the representation of the Imagination. Only the imagination presents the object, that is, species nature, as an object of consciousness. It is unknowing self-consciousness. Only by the distinctions of reason, the dialectic of language, does this unknowing self-consciousness become knowing self-consciousness. The Hegelian frosting on the phenomenological cake is that because man's species nature *is* his consciousness of himself as species, that is, his self-consciousness, we arrive, by reason, at the *self-consciousness of self-consciousness* (i.e., of the species, as object).

The "positive essence of religion," its representation of human essence in the Imagination, passes over to the "negative essence of religion," the uncritical reflected form of this imaginary construct, in theology. From this antithesis, the dialectic moves to the synthesis by way of the negative critique of theology. This synthesis is the *critical* reflection of the positive essence of religion, that is, anthropology. The original subject matter of religious consciousness is rescued from its heavenly alienation and brought back to earth, no longer in the form of imagination, as Messiah, but in the form of "positive science," as Man. Moreover, language is now known *as* language, as the reflection of the *idea* of the human community, or species nature, and not the direct reflection of its *existence*. There is but a short step from this to Feuerbach's "materialistic" formulation: Thought is the reflection of sensory and feeling existence. Existence–in Feuerbach's terms, the natural existence of the human being as a sensing and feeling creature –is ontologically prior to thought, as sensing and feeling are prior to language, or as sensibility in general is prior to consciousness.

There are difficulties in this formulation, particularly because Feuerbach had earlier insisted that *even* sensing and perceiving (being selective) require thinking. But his general direction is clear. Religion, in its native "positive" form, is closer to man's *existence*, as sensible being, than the reflection upon religion, in "negative" theology. The critique of theology, and of speculation in general, is intended as a self-conscious return to the empirical, to the concretely sensible existence of man. The desired achievement is the critical empiricism or empirically directed rationalism that Feuerbach set as the goal of the "new philosophy."

There is an interesting footnote on the status of language in Feuerbach's reply to R. Haym's criticism of his philosophy.[31] R. Haym had objected that religion, as such, cannot be "derived" from external nature, that physical nature cannot be used as the grounds for an explanation of religion. Feuerbach, although agreeing with Haym's objection, points out, however, that the "nature" at stake is not physical nature as such, but rather that physical nature which provides the conditions for human existence, that nature in which the human species could originate. In the course of this discussion (further considered on p. 389), Feuerbach raises the question of what language would be appropriate to consideration of this "natural bond between man and nature." His answer is that the expression of this bond is human existence itself, that the original "language" of man's dependence on nature is the fact of his existence itself, and that human language is only the copy of this "language of nature," that is, the reflection of human existence. "Isn't existence that which is prior?" asks Feuerbach:

Isn't human speech struck dumb in the face of the language of nature, in the rumbling of thunder, in the roaring of the storm-wind, in the crashing of waves, in the noise of a volcano? But isn't it this language of nature which is the decisive language of life and death, being and non-being? Aren't there peoples who have no other word for God than they have for thunder, whose loftiest expression and conception is therefore nothing other than an expression for the shattering effect that the sound of thunder has on their feelings? Isn't it obvious here that the word is only a copy; but that the original, the ultimate ground is the sensible impression? Doesn't the word come forth only when the first overwhelming impression of natural violence has subsided, and man returns from his feeling of dependency and awe of nature to self-awareness, to self-feeling? (VII, 511–12)

Feuerbach further agrees with Haym's suggestion—he finds it "brilliant and original"—that "the critique of reason must become a critique of language." "Splendid!" notes Feuerbach, "but however much I agree with the author's view of the 'transcendental' significance of language, I find it difficult to discover that transcendental significance . . . which the author attributes to it" (VII, 511, n.). Language has "transcendental significance," for Feuerbach, in that it transcends the private individuality of thought and is the expression of species consciousness. But language does not have the "transcendental significance" of species *existence* itself. Language is not to be confused ontologically with the *being* of the species. Species existence is primarily sensate existence, which is the direct "expression" of the bond between man and nature. Language is only the copy, the dependent reflection of this existence. This is, of course, a later Feuerbachian view, more explicitly sensationalistic (in 1848) than its earlier, still indecisive expression in the *Critique of Hegelian Philosophy* or in *The Essence of Christianity*.

In the realm of nature, the "universals," as real classes, are ontologically derivative from the primary existence of individuals; that is, they are constituted and not primitive "entities" in the ontology. This is also the case in that natural realm constituted by the "bond" of nature and man, which Feuerbach conceives of as *human nature*. In this "nature" too, the individual is existentially prior to the species. The species concept, or species knowledge, is therefore predicated on the priority of knowledge of the individual. The genesis of species knowledge begins necessarily with knowledge of the individual, or, strictly speaking, with the representation of the individual as an object of consciousness. On these grounds, the precondition for species knowledge, that is, for the genesis of the concept of the universal, is the representation of the individual, which only sensation and feeling afford. The ontological priority of the individual is therefore reflected in the epistemological priority of the individual. These are the systematic grounds for Feuerbach's empiricism in the domain of natural knowledge and for his "anthropologism" in the domain of human knowledge. For in this latter area, the imagination serves as the appropriate instrument for the representation of the individual. The imagination presents us with a *Thou*: but at the same time with this *Thou* as infinite and universal. And it is this *potential* contradiction, actualized only upon rational and empirical reflection, that embodies the process of the development of species knowledge. That is to say, the represented *Thou* as individual is the *beginning* of this process (though not the "real" beginning ontologically, which is individual existence itself, but rather the epistemological beginning, that is, the representation in consciousness of the existing individual). The *Thou* as species concept, as "universal" Thou —that is, mankind as such—is the *end* of this process. This classically "inductive" progress, from particulars to universals, from individual concept to species concept, generates the unresolved dialectical "contradiction" that the imagination presents to reflective thought and to empirical knowledge. The representation of this universal concept in its most abstract logical form is the Hegelian concept of *Being*, as an embodiment of the contradiction between an abstract and "empty" concept of the universal, and its concrete realization in the domain of individuals. As such, Hegel takes it as the "absolute beginning" of the dialectic, not merely in logical terms, but in ontological terms as well. *Being* is the first term of the dialectic. Feuerbach's critique of Hegel, as we have seen, rests on the rejection of this "first term" as anything more than the *logical* first term in the rational reconstruction of the dialectic in reflective consciousness. Thus, he takes the Hegelian logic as a reconstruction after the fact, in *inverted* form, of the actual process in human thought or in existence. Once this inverted form is hypostatized, the phenomenology and ontology are viewed in this inversion. The result is that the rational or logical reconstruction after the fact is mistaken for the primary ground, the necessary a priori conditions, of the fact itself, of which it is a reconstruction. Thus, for Hegel, the individual existent becomes an expression or a mode of the ontologically prior species concept – that is, a moment in the unfolding of the Idea. Feuerbach proposes, instead, that the species being is ontologically derivative from the individual existent, but from an individual "I" that arrives at a consciousness of itself as a species being.

THE MIND-BODY PROBLEM: STAGES IN FEUERBACH'S FORMULATION IN THE EARLIER WORKS

Feuerbach's formulation of the mind-body problem may be traced in three stages. (1) In his initial consideration, he considers the traditional dualism of body and mind in the modern form, which takes Descartes' *Cogito* and his theory of two substances as its point of departure. Here, Feuerbach is a fairly orthodox idealist, in the speculative tradition. Very soon, however, his "genetic" method leads him to shift the framework of the problem. (2) In the second stage, Feuerbach considers the mind-body problem not only in terms of the dialectical difficulties of its philosophical formulations, but in terms of the origins of these very formulations themselves, in religious thought. The "resolution" of the mind-body problem is no longer taken to be a dialectical or "philosophical" resolution. Rather, Feuerbach seeks an explanation of how it came to be a problem in the first place. Feuerbach, in effect, proposes an elimination of the traditional "problem" by a shift in framework. But if this is to be more than a gross commission of the "genetic fallacy," the new framework has to have its own theoretical basis. (3) In the third stage, Feuerbach finds this basis in his concept of human nature. That is to say, the analysis of the typical modes of human feeling, belief, thought, the phenomenology of human consciousness, shows us how the mind-body problem is *generated*. Feuerbach claims to resolve the problem by demystifying it. This demystification entails removing the mind-body problem from the realm of metaphysics, explaining it in terms of its "natural" causes (i.e., human nature), and thus reducing it to its anthropological significance, and restating it in these terms. These stages follow, in broad outline, the course of Feuerbach's whole philosophical development up to the publication of *The Essence of Christianity*.

The Idealist Formulation in the Early Works

Feuerbach's earliest consideration of the mind-body problem comes in the *Dissertation*, and it is a restatement, in more or less orthodox Hegelian terms, of the classic idealist position, which takes mind or consciousness as its fundamental category and derives body or matter as the "other-sidedness" of consciousness, or reduces it to the mental. The point of departure for Feuerbach's treatment is Descartes' formulation of the problem, in which two contexts may be clearly distinguished. (1) Descartes' first concern is the question of man's nature, in the form of the question of what constitutes man's *Being*. Descartes answers this in striking fashion in the *Cogito* argument. Man's *Being* or his *Essence* is his thinking activity. Man *is* insofar as he thinks. His thinking is his being. (2) The second context is Descartes' concern with nonthinking substance, that is, with matter, characterized by extension. In this second context, thinking and extension, mind and body, are conceived as two independent substances, as *res cogitans* and *res extensa*. Now the first context may be interpreted in a purely phenomenological way, in that what is at issue is the characterization of consciousness qua consciousness, as an activity of reflection of consciousness upon itself, in introspection, or in terms of its intentionality, or its directedness toward its objects. In this context, the objects of consciousness are taken in a phenomenological sense, and not yet in an ontological sense. The only "ontology" concerns the *Being* of consciousness or of mind itself, and this is characterized functionally in terms of an activity. The second context, however, introduces the ontological problem with regard to the difference between mind and body. Feuerbach sees the sources of Cartesian dualism in this shift from the phenomenological to the ontological mode (or in Feuerbach's term, the "ontotheological" mode). Here the problem is not man's nature, as thinking being, but rather the classical problem of *substance*. The functional notion of *thinking activity* is translated into *substance* terminology, as *res cogitans*, to which there stands opposed, in the Cartesian two-substance dualism, *res extensa*, the corporeal matter that is the object of empirical or sense knowledge. Feuerbach's estimate, in the *History*, is that Descartes' *Cogito* is the real point of departure for modern philosophy, because it states the essential thesis of the idealist view, that man's essence is his thinking activity. Whatever the ontological extensions of the *Cogito* in terms of substance dualism, in its initial form it accords well with Feuerbach's view of what philosophy is ultimately about: man and his nature. In the *History*, Feuerbach interprets the *Cogito* in a most rigorous phenomenological fashion. In this context, insofar as man does not think, he has no being, and thus he does not exist as man at all (see p. 151). So, too, in the *Dissertation*, human consciousness is taken as identical with man's species existence. The identity of *I* and *Thou*, in consciousness, constitutes man's being, and it is also this that constitutes Reason as One, Universal, and Infinite.

Further, in these early works, Feuerbach adopts the German idealist resolution of the mind-body dualism, which comprehends body, or matter, or nature as nothing but mind, or spirit in its other-sidedness, in its objective, self-alienated form. The argument here is the one developed in the tradition that stems from Leibniz and goes through Kant and Fichte to Hegel. This argument provided a resolution to the problems engendered by the mechanistic framework of two externally related substances, by proposing a shift in the framework, from interactionist or parallelist mechanism to a functional or dialectical view of the relation between mind and body. This involved a switch from the Cartesian concept of Being, as either *res cogitans* or *res extensa*, to the Leibnizian proposal for a radically relational concept, not in terms of substantive *thing*, but as *activity*–in short, a move from *substance* concepts to *function* concepts of Being. Still, the Cartesian influence persists even in this alternative formulation. On the functional or dialectical view, "body" as such has no essence because it is "inert"; that is, it has no inherent principle of motion or self-activity. Whatever "essence" body has is that which is derived from that which does have a principle of self-activity, that is, from mind. Because, in the Cartesian formulation itself, only mind, or thinking substance, is self-active, the functional view draws the radical conclusion that body or external substance, *in itself*, is *nothing*. It is something only insofar as it is the "other being" of mind or thinking activity. In his discussion of Leibniz, Feuerbach finds the full dialectical difficulties of this position realized in Leibniz's concept of matter, as the "negative expression" for the qualitative plurality of the monads (see p. 100). Matter is nothing more than the mutually limiting character of the monads, insofar as each one is uniquely what it is, as individual, and therefore not identical with any other. This "limitation," the "veil of matter," is therefore in itself nothing. It does not express the individual quality, the spontaneous self-activity, of the monads, or their "perception," in its "positive" form as *force*; neither does it express any substantive property of the monads as material, because they are immaterial. Feuerbach had estimated Leibniz's view as a resolution of the substance dualism of Descartes by way of rejection of the framework of mechanism. In effect, Leibniz had dissolved the mind-body problem by making body itself a function or an expression of the relations among self-active essences. This relational desubstantivization of body[32] provided for idealism a concept of body as nothing in itself, but only a delimitation of spirit, through its actualization in determinate, particular form. The Leibnizian emphasis on *relations* as constituting the essence of any determinate being carries over into the speculative tradition and into Hegelianism in particular. In Feuerbach, it becomes the characterization of human essence as that set of relations which *constitutes* the species—specifically, the relations, in consciousness, between an *I* and a *Thou*.

Only in Hegel does Feuerbach find the full working out of the idealist thesis in a consistently monistic way. The issue between body and mind, matter and spirit, is reduced to that of the self-separation or self-differentiation of spirit. The *vis viva*, the inherent principle of activity, is no longer the reductive notion of self-*motion*, with all the mechanist connotations of motion as change of place. Nor is it the postulated *force* that is the mode of activity of the monads. Rather, it is the "movement" of thought itself. This "movement" is separated into its "moments," and the process as a whole is laid bare, in its logical structure, as *dialectic*. In the dialectic of self-differentiation, thought is taken *only* as activity. Mind is no longer a substance but an activity, and the *Being* of this activity, no longer substantival, is the totality of this process itself. The traditional polarity of mind and body is then seen as a polarity generated by the very self-activity of mind or thought, by the very nature of this self-activity as self-differentiation. Here there is no substance "mind" that has the attribute "thought" in the traditional subject-predicate formulation. Rather, "mind" is nothing but thinking activity itself, in the formulation of the identity theory. Body is therefore not substantivally distinguished from mind, but is only the aspect of mind as self-differentiated other—the aspect under which mind appears to itself as an object under the form of sense awareness. Body is only the *qualified* other-sidedness of mind, or only one level of "objectivity" insofar as whatever appears to thinking activity as "other" is its "object." The fullest extension of this view, ontologically, is the panpsychist "objective idealism" that suffuses the cosmos with mind and makes the existence of any object whatever dependent on its being an object of thought. The theological analogue is not missed, either by Hegel or by Feuerbach. The dependence of all Being on God is the pervasive theme of this idealism in its theological form, from its Neoplatonic form in Plotinus, Augustine, Erigena, through its variants in Renaissance and Cambridge Platonism and in Berkeley, among others. In a sense, Descartes' *"Cogito ergo sum"* and Berkeley's *"Esse est percipi"* express this same basic idealist thesis, in the active and in the passive moods, respectively. In the former, *thinking* is *being*; in the latter, *being thought is being*. But clearly the first, as active, is generative or independent being, the second, generated or dependent being.

Again, the two contexts in which the mind-body problem appears become distinct. On the one hand, the full-blown ontology of Spirit may be taken in its "cosmic" sense, as dealing with Being as such. On the other, we may translate from this framework of panpsychistic, "objective" idealism into the more modest language of human conscious-ness, and take the whole problem of "being" as relevant only to man's "being," and the "being" of things as relevant only insofar as they relate to or are involved in human existence and human consciousness. But what grounds are there for making a choice between the two alternative emphases? Should the mind-body problem be conceived in its modest "human" form? Or is this modest form only the local instance of a cosmic-metaphysical problem of the relation between matter and spirit? Or is it an ontotheological problem of the relation of Logos and Nature, God and World? On systematic grounds alone, the choice would be a matter of philosophic taste, or temperament, or a function of previous condition of (philosophic) servitude. As a systematic Hegelian idealist, Feuerbach is caught on the hook of classical "metaphysical" formulations. But as critical historian of philosophy, Feuerbach gets off the hook by a "genetic" twist. He shifts the whole framework in which the problem is conceived.

The Genetic-Critical Analysis of the Origins
of the Mind-Body Problem in Religious Thought

The second stage of Feuerbach's formulation is an answer to a different question than is posed in the first. The first step toward such a critique is a genetic analysis of the origins of the dualist distinction. The question that traditional philosophy asked is "How does one account for the duality of body and mind, nature and spirit? And how does one relate the terms of this dualism to each other in a systematic way?" The question that a genetic-critical inquiry asks is "'How does one account for the *concepts* of mind-body dualism in philosophy? What are their origins, and what explains the centrality of this dualism in philosophical thought?" The point of this is not merely historical, but critical. It is an attempt to discover what the concept expresses or is intended to express, beyond what its formulators or users *take* it to express.

The mode of inquiry that Feuerbach calls "genetic-analytic" or "genetic-critical" undertakes to trace the sources as well as to analyze the systematic development of the idealist view of the mind-body problem. In the *History*, Feuerbach traces the early, "inadequate" expressions of this dualism, in religious and philosophical thought. He follows them through their "pagan" and "Christian" forms to their open "philosophical" forms in the Renaissance and in seventeenth-century rationalism. What Feuerbach seeks is the origin (or the original sin) that generates traditional dualism. He finds it in religious anthropomorphism. The attribution of "spiritual" properties to nature is seen to derive from this anthropomorphism, from the original attribution of *human* properties to nature. This expresses a naive unity of man and nature, which is broken by the reflective realization of man's distinctiveness, of his separation from nature. The separation of the spiritual from the corporeal, the view that culminates in the world-denying asceticism of early Christianity, is seen as the dialectical negation of this naive or "natural" anthropomorphism. On the one hand, nature is stripped bare of personality, including its central "spiritual" or "animated" properties. Personality, on the other hand, in its abstraction as "divine personality" or "eternal spirit," is stripped bare of all "material" or "natural" properties. The material and the immaterial are thus consciously counterposed. The "spiritual" properties, life, mind, consciousness, are then taken to be immaterial. Residual nature, bare of these properties, is taken as "inert," "dead," in a word, "material."

These two "moments" in Christianity, the *anthropomorphic* and the *ascetic*, are seen by Feuerbach as the dialectical opposites that constitute the contradiction in "inadequate" idealism, which the subsequent history of philosophy seeks to resolve. In the first, man sees nothing but himself in nature, takes nature in the form of *human* nature. In the second, he sees nothing of himself in nature, takes it as totally alien. The philosophical expression of this world denial is in the concept of Being as self-activity, as *causa sui*, as substance. To the extent that being is conceived of as self-activity, and man takes his own essence—that is, his consciousness, life, self-activity, freedom—as this Being, nature is conceived of as negative, or non-Being, as inert, dead matter. To this concept of nature as "dead matter" is attached the concept of corporeality, in the mechanistic sense of "extended body."

Man's *natural* being is, therefore, nothing in itself; and therefore his body, as the form of his natural being, is also nothing. His life, as his Being, is not his bodily "life" (for the body as such has no life). His real life is only his nonbodily, immaterial or spiritual life. So, too, nature, in which his body exists, is nothing.

The analogies to the metaphysical formulations of the dualism and its resolution in idealist terms are trivially clear. Hegel recognized them no less than did Feuerbach. In the *History*, however, Feuerbach did not go much further than this recognition and elucidation of the genesis of the dualism. The bulk of the *History*, much of the *Leibniz*, in its discussion of the relation of Leibniz to Descartes, and much of the *Bayle*, are concerned with the ways in which this dualism appears in its systematic philosophical expression. But only in the *Bayle* and in the earlier *Thoughts on Death* (1830) does Feuerbach suggest *why* the dualism arose, on any other grounds than those of the dialectic movement of thought itself. In the *Bayle*, Feuerbach had attributed the world-denying asceticism of early Christianity to its recognition and rejection of the political and moral corruption of the time. What the early Christians expressed *theoretically*, in this asceticism, they practiced, in their denial of this-worldly lusts. The theory, therefore, derived from the practice, according to Feuerbach. In the *Thoughts on Death*, Feuerbach saw the projection of a life beyond death as the fulfilment in the imagination of an *incomplete* life. He saw these as the psychological grounds for the belief in the immortality of the soul. The separation of the two worlds, the *Diesseits* and *Jenseits*, provides the ground for the mind-body dualism that systematizes this immortality wish (cf. I, 55–6).

In the *History*, Feuerbach comments on the "one-sidedness of spirituality," or "negative religiosity" only in terms of the ideal of an all-encompassing, monistic truth that comprehends the flesh and nature as much as it does spirit. Even in the *Bayle*, he described the "outer" struggles between church and state as nothing but "the external, political expression of an immanent opposition in mankind itself. Where man is at one with himself, his world cannot fall apart into two worlds" (see p. 118). Thus, the *cause* of the dualism is in man's spirit, in its immanent contradictions. But what exactly this spirit is, and what gives rise to contradictions in it, is left here in its idealist form, as the expression of the dialectic of the spirit in man's consciousness. Feuerbach prepares the ground for his naturalist reduction by exposing the sources of this breach, in religion. In the *Bayle*, he characterizes the opposition of flesh and spirit as "the essence of Christian belief." It is not until he gives the full characterization of the natural human grounds for this belief itself that a theoretical explanation of the sources of the dualism is forthcoming in any but Hegelian idealist terms. This explanation is to come only in *The Essence of Christianity*.

The "Natural" or "Anthropological" Formulation of the Mind-Body Problem

Merely to trace the philosophical formulations of mind-body dualism to their sources in religious thought is not yet a theoretical contribution. At best it is intellectual history, only the *material* for theory. To trace the original religious bifurcation of spirit and flesh, body and soul to *its* sources means to go beneath the level of articulate conceptual expression, to find what it is that gives rise to this articulation itself. Here Hegel had supplied a theory. The *Idea* was postulated as the substantive reality of which this whole development was the manifest or actual expression. The theoretical entity, *Idea*, had to be charged with all those properties (as *necessary* properties, and therefore as constituting the essence of the *Idea* itself) that were required to account for the actual expression. Because the actual expression, in the history of religious and philosophical thought, proceeded by critical opposition of concepts, the source of this opposition was to be attributed to the *Idea* itself, in its process as dialectic—that is, as self-negating, self-differentiating activity of thought. In this sense, Hegel was the first to attempt to offer a *theory* of concept formation in philosophy, and to state it in sustained, systematic form. It was the whole tenor of the left Hegelians to interpret the history of religious beliefs and of dogma as a symbolic history, whose meaning lay in the myth-forming propensities of the folkspirit. Thus, the outer, legendary history was the creature of an inner need, which bespoke some underlying universal *human* activity of imagination and belief. So Hegel's theory of concept formation was first modified in its application to religious concept formation. However, Feuerbach did not modify Hegel's theory. He supplanted it. It is clear how much he owed to Hegel, how closely the structure of his theory derived from Hegel. It is even clear that on one "humanist" interpretation of Hegel's Phenomenology (*Kojève's*) one may take Hegel to be saying in implicit fashion what Feuerbach was to say explicitly. But it needs also to be clear that Feuerbach's theoretical basis for interpreting the genetic account as he did is different from Hegel's in fundamental ways.

The third stage of Feuerbach's formulation asks the question "What are the sources in the nature of human consciousness itself that lead man to bifurcate mind and body, flesh and spirit?" Again, "What is it in the nature of human existence that gives rise to the reflection of this dualism in conscious thought?" In other terms, Feuerbach asks here, what are the *natural*—that is, "anthropological"—*facts* of which mind-body dualism is the *conceptual* expression? What is the *real* dualism that this conceptualized dualism represents? The real dualism, according to Feuerbach, has an "anthropological" source. It derives from man's incomplete knowledge of his own species nature, and of the "natural bond" between his nature and physical nature. In short, dualism, in its conceptual form, is the expression of the degree of man's ignorance. In his ignorance, the relation between his organic existence, in the world, and his sensing, feeling, and thinking is not understood clearly. Therefore, the representation of this relation takes on the outward form of a relation among discrete entities: In the first place, as personified entities, as "other" superhuman or divine persons; in the second, as abstract entities, substances, faculties, powers. Mind-body dualism thus has a natural ground, not in nature as such, but rather, in the nature of the consciousness of nature. Relations among these entities are expressed in esoteric or symbolic form in religion, which gives the dualism its mythical representation and resolves it mythically as well—that is, in the imagination. The abstract representation of this dualism is in philosophical ontology, in the various abstract theories of mind-body relation. The attack on the problem on "natural" or "anthropological" grounds comes only with the concrete analysis of the relations between sensing, perceiving, feeling, thinking as *human* activities, and no *more* than human activities. Thus, the dualism is not *ontological*, but *phenomenological*; or in Feuerbach's terms, *psychological*. The natural-scientific approach to the mind-body problem, as distinct from the metaphysical, or theological or religious-affective approaches, thus has two aspects, in Feuerbach's view: first, the conceptual ground-clearing (getting rid of prejudices and delusions, for example), necessary to place the problem in its natural, anthropological context; second, the study of man's nature, to discover what the actual relations between thinking and being are. Feuerbach takes the first task as his principal one. The second involves the analysis of sensing, feeling, thinking, imagining, as objects of empirical-scientific study, that is, of psychology. In the works prior to *The Essence of Christianity*, he is little concerned with this latter task. Only his discussion of Dorguth's *Critique of Idealism*, on the relation of brain acts to thought, deals with this explicitly, and in a still predominantly idealist way. But his attempt to comprehend and develop an empirical point of view leads in this direction. In the later works, in which his sensation-oriented empiricism comes to full expression, he attempts to deal with the mind-body problem in this new empirical way.

The key aspect of Feuerbach's critique of Dorguth that is of concern here is his refusal to accept a reductive materialist monism as a solution to the mind-body problem. On the contrary, Feuerbach's argument is the idealist one: Not only is matter incapable of thought, but matter itself arises only as an object *for* thought. In this sense, brain acts are the indispensable conditions for thinking, not in the materialist sense of being the basis or the ultimate ground for thinking being, but in the dialectical sense of providing the object necessary for thinking activity. When Feuerbach writes, in the critique, "without body, no mind" (see p. 157), he does not mean that thinking activity is an activity of body, of corporeal matter, but that thinking activity requires, as its *other*, body. He accuses Dorguth and the "absolute materialists" of failing to answer the problems of mind-body dualism, by failing to account for thought. Matter as such cannot "think itself," because as matter–that is, as determinately *this or that thing*–it has no principle of self-activity, or of self-separation. Thus, it merely *is* what it is, and cannot be an object for itself. On methodological grounds, too, Feuerbach attacks "absolute materialism" as being incapable of dealing with thought, with ideas, without being caught in self-contradiction. Ideas are then neither true nor false. They just *are*, as brain acts are, and there is nothing to distinguish Fichte's idealism, as brain act, from Dorguth's materialism as a different brain act. Idealism cannot then be "false," nor materialism "true," on the reductive materialist's own grounds. Both are merely existing brain acts. Feuerbach upholds a real distinction between thought and matter, in this argument, which is as sharp an assertion of mind-body dualism as Descartes'. But Feuerbach has available the alternative view of dialectical idealism, with its self-differentiating spirit, to fall back upon. The dualism seems then to remain, in this critique, a matter of methodology: The proper method of philosophy is to consider thought only in terms of thought, not in terms of physiology, or physics (see p. 155). Thus, philosophy addresses itself only to concepts; it is conceptual analysis. Thinking activity alone is the object of philosophical thought. The difficulty arises because there are sciences, concepts, and thoughts that deal with *non*-thought. If there *is* physiology, then are we to study this "physiologically," that is, *without* thought? Or is thought implicated in the study of any object whatever, ideal, material, mental, physical? If it is, as Feuerbach so often insists throughout the early works, then philosophy differs from other sciences not in its method, but only in its subject matter. Empirical knowledge, unlike philosophy, requires the senses, and instruments, like the anatomist's scalpel. However, the *meaning* of this empirical activity is illuminated only by thought. We may *see*, but we cannot *read*, without thought, says Feuerbach. The difference between philosophy and the empirical sciences is not a matter, then, of thought-ful vs. thought-less activity, because the *method* of thought-ful analysis permeates, or should permeate, both philosophy and science. Rather, it is a difference in the subject matter, and in the mode of thought appropriate to it. But even here Feuerbach is not a dualist, or pluralist, concerning *modes* of thought; he is a dialectical monist. That is, the varying modes of thought, each "appropriate" to its subject matter, are more or less enlightened to the extent that their differentiated subject matter is systematically related to the substantive concepts that philosophy alone deals with. Thus, every mode of thought is more or less philosophical–that is, "speculative"–in the Hegelian idealist sense, and they all strive for the condition of philosophy, that is, knowledge of the *idea* of the subject matter, not merely of its appearance; of its *principles*, not merely of their representations. The implications of the critique of Dorguth and of Absolute Materialism, are not the surface appearances of a dualism of brain acts, on the one hand, and thoughts, on the other, and some mode of necessary interdependence of the two. Rather, on systematic grounds, the implications are nothing less than the full-blown monism of Hegelian idealism, and its system of the sciences. Though Feuerbach never develops this aspect of Hegelian thought, as Hegel did in the *Jenenser Realphilosophie* and in the *Encyclopedia*, and never developed a systematic *Naturphilosophie* in this sense, this monism remains the ground for his early critique of reductive materialism. Mind and body are therefore neither independent nor even merely interdependent substances or realities, nor are they merely different subject matters requiring alternative methods of inquiry. On the all-embracing presupposition that Being is One, that Truth is One, the relative abstractions, mind and body, and the relative modalities of thought are ultimately aspects of *one and the same* Being-and-Truth. But because "where there is matter alone, there is no concept of matter" (see p. 157), the foundation for a science of matter must rest on thought, for which alone the *concept* of matter can arise.

It is not until Feuerbach begins to emphasize the central and original role of sense experience in thought that he modifies this early idealist view and approaches the resolution of the mind-body dualism from a different point of view. Only then does he begin to approach a *systematic* alternative, which relates the genetic account of the *origins* of dualism to the analytic-empirical account that proposes a materialist solution to this dualism. In this later formulation of the mind-body problem, the origins of the dualism in the psychological process that enter into religious concept formation, in the opposition of the spirit and the flesh, are related to the dichotomy between theory and practice, between thought and existence that characterizes the concrete life of man itself. The epistemological grounds for this dichotomy, in the separation of concrete, sensory activity from the activity of imaginative and abstract thought, and Feuerbach's proposal for a reunification *in theory* of these two poles, is the concern of a later chapter in this book. The bare outline of the later formulation is this: Sensation and feeling are the conditions for thought. And organic, physical existence is the condition for sensation and feeling. Only an existing being can think. Therefore, the mind-body problem dissolves, when the false dichotomy between organic, physical existence and thinking activity is overcome. But it can be satisfactorily overcome only if one can show that matter is capable of consciousness, that is, that matter can become conscious, and self-conscious. Feuerbach could not show this. But he later enthusiastically endorsed that physiological materialism that attempted to show how man's organic activities are related to his thinking activities, how bodily conditions affect thought.

CONCLUSION

The Essence of Christianity is both a culmination and a beginning. Because it represents the passionate expression of a newly won position, it has the vigor, the brilliance, and the spontaneity of a first statement, never matched, in this respect, in Feuerbach's later work. The foregoing discussion sought to establish the manifold contexts out of which this work grew. The purpose is to see the work as more than it appears to be, and to establish the basis for interpretation of what is called here (somewhat awkwardly) the "deeper thesis." Without this context of Feuerbach's earlier development, the work tends to remain a tour de force of the popular sort, establishing another of the easily remembered "popular" landmarks in philosophy, notorious for their degeneration, in the sad course of the history of philosophy, into catchphrases for the semicultured. The work is a culmination *not* of Feuerbach's philosophy, but of his transition *to* a philosophical position developed only in later works, and by other philosophers. In this sense, Rawidowicz's estimate is only qualifiedly correct, when he says that "this shift in Feuerbach's philosophizing developed first with respect to philosophy of religion, for in fact he hadn't yet penetrated to his new point of view in metaphysical and epistemological terms."[33] The philosophy of religion was Feuerbach's first and abiding love; that much is true. But its centrality to precisely those metaphysical and epistemological issues that constitute the essential content of Feuerbach's philosophical work is what transformed a temperamental and intellectual predilection for the subject matter of religion into a more profound instrument of analysis. Rawidowicz is more accurate in his estimate of Feuerbach's critique of religion as a *transitional* step. Feuerbach had remarked that the critique of speculative philosophy could be undertaken only through the critique of religion. Rawidowicz comments correctly that

From many considerations, one may conclude that Feuerbach understood the empirical, historico-philosophical analysis of Christianity pretty much because he wanted to carry forth his main attack on speculative philosophy in this way . . . as if his major work in the philosophy of religion were no more than a means, a preliminary to his unwritten philosophical-metaphysical *magnum opus.*[34]

It is in the sense of the critique of religion as a *philosophical* critique, on the one hand, and a critique *of* philosophy, on the other, that *The Essence of Christianity* fulfills its role as the springboard for Feuerbach's mature philosophical position.

Religion as the Self-alienation of Human Consciousness: The Phenomenology of Religious and Theological Concept Formation

The Aim and Method of The Essence of Christianity

In the foreword to the first edition of *The Essence of Christianity*, Feuerbach writes that "the object of this work is to show that the supernatural mysteries of religion are based on quite simple, natural truths" (S: I, 4). The tradition of debunking, of exploding the "myths" of religious belief, is as old as philosophy itself, and had its birth in Ionia. The traditional mode of demythologization is to show that the objects of religious belief are natural and not supernatural, earthly and not divine objects; that the objects of belief are not literally what they are taken to be, but symbols, whose referents are readily accessible to an enlightened "natural" view. The obverse method of theological exegesis even lends a hand here. Where the holy text is literally descriptive, the description itself becomes esoterically the symbol for a deeper meaning, in the dramatic unfolding of God's purpose. So the very distinction of exoteric and esoteric interpretation develops into a two-edged sword, available for the purpose of reading not only the supernatural in the natural, but the natural in the supernatural as well.

The two elements necessary to such an "exegetical" enterprise, whether from the theological or the natural points of view, are the two aspects of a given subject matter: what it appears as, or is taken to be, and what it really is. Further, these two have to be related; for the interpretation to make sense, it has to follow some rule of interpretation, or a *Hermeneutic*. The relation in which these two stand to each other, in Feuerbach's analysis, is the classical one of image (or copy or representation) to original. The content of religious consciousness is the image. The demythologization consists in revealing that the image is nothing *but* an image, and not what theology or speculative philosophy takes it to be. Feuerbach works on two levels here: On the one hand, *The Essence of Christianity* takes the religious image as its *real* subject matter, by way of a critique of theology's hypostatization of the image as a nonimaginary *object*; on the other, Feuerbach is concerned with the psychological process that generates the image and that therefore explains what it is an image of. He writes,

> In this work, the images of religion are not taken to be thoughts–at least not in the sense of speculative philosophy of religion–nor are they taken to be things. They are taken to be images, that is to say theology is not treated as a mystical pragmatology as in Christian mythology, nor as ontology, as in speculative philosophy of religion, but rather as psychic pathology. (S: I, 4–5)

Feuerbach's "reduction" of the content of religious thought is therefore not in the simple classical reductive tradition, of reducing divine to natural objects (e.g., the Gods to powers or phenomena of nature as such). Rather, it is a phenomenological reduction (not in the Husserlian sense of this phrase, of course) to the sources, in human consciousness, of religious imagery. In this sense, religion is seen not to have any natural "objects" per se. It is not rocks, trees, or mounds of earth that are worshipped in animistic religions, no more than it is the Gods who are worshipped in anthropomorphic religions. These, the ostensible objects of worship, are only representations or images–the "rocks" no less than the "Gods." The objects of religious consciousness are not objects in nature at large, or nature in itself. They are, rather, the transformations of such "natural" objects by the imagination into objects for man. As such, they express the *human* relation to these natural objects. This relation, then, is the real object of religion. The religious image is therefore inevitably "anthropomorphic" in this sense; the object of religious consciousness is always a *humanized* object, an object seen under the aspect of its being an object for man. Such objects do not exist independently, in an external nature. They have no "nature" of their own, apart from the human nature with which they are invested. In this religious consciousness, it is not the case that "man is the measure of all things"[1] in the simple sense that nonhuman objects are mistaken as human. The objects of this consciousness *are* human, in fact, though they *appear* as nonhuman or superhuman. It would be more proper to say that "all 'things' are the measure of man," in the sense that the objects of religious consciousness are the images of human nature, projected in an objective form. It is through these images that man comes to know his nature, but in religion, he does not recognize that it *is* his nature, and thus mistakes the image to be something other than an image. What religious consciousness does achieve is the sense of this image as a *Thou*: Its imagery is human, personal. The relation to the object of religion as an object for man is a relation to an other taken in the *form* of the self. This is the truth of religion that Feuerbach wants to rescue from theology's perversion of it.

What the religious consciousness, in its naive, unreflective form, is unaware of is that the objects of belief, which appear to belief as real objects, are real only in the phenomenological sense: What consciousness is aware of, in this case, is human consciousness itself; or more precisely, the representation of human consciousness as an object for consciousness (i.e., in the form of an image). It is the character of belief that its objects are concrete, particular objects. Feuerbach had developed this view in the *Bayle* and in *Philosophy and Christianity*, in distinguishing reason from belief. He repeats it in the foreword of the first edition of *The Essence of Christianity*.

The image underlies the essential difference between religion and philosophy. Religion is essentially dramatic. God himself is a dramatic, i.e., personal being. Take away the image from religion, and you take away its thing, and you are left with nothing but the *Caput Mortuum* in hand. The image, as image, is the thing of religion. (S: I, 4)

The "thing" here is generically taken to mean the entities that are taken to be real, in the framework of religion, that to which the believer is ontologically committed. The entities that populate the religious universe are images. This is the sense of Feuerbach's statement. But it is only the critical philosopher–not the speculative "Christian" philosopher, the theologian, or the true believer–who knows these entities to be images, who is aware of their character. This establishes the purport of Feuerbach's inquiry. Knowing the content of religious consciousness to be the image and knowing that this consciousness takes the image to be a thing, the genetic-critical philosopher asks, "How does this image formation take place? And what explains the hypostatization, the entification of the image?" The "simple, natural truths" to which the "supernatural mysteries of religion" are reduced are, therefore, truths about human nature–specifically, truths about the psychological processes that literally *create* the "supernatural mysteries." They are truths about religious concept formation, and because of their universal scope, truths about concept formation in general.

The analysis, says Feuerbach, is also an analysis of theological-philosophical (i.e., "speculative") concept formation, because the ghost of the supernaturalism of early Christianity still haunts the secularized theology and philosophy of the present. "Ghosts," writes Feuerbach, "are shadows of the past. They necessarily lead us back to the question: what was the ghost when it was still a creature of flesh and blood?" (S: I, 6).

The present work, he continues, though it deals with the past, deals also with the present ghosts, so that though the content of the work is "pathological, or physiological," in the sense that it is an empirical-phenomenological account of the genesis of the religious illusion, its purpose is also "therapeutic or practical" (S: I, 7). That is, it aims to cure us of the illusion by revealing its etiology and providing us with the key to its demystification. The "therapy" for this "psychic pathology" is the revelation of the real meaning of the illusive imagery, the explication of the symbolism.[2] The psychic "health" to be achieved is man's clear self-knowledge, stripped of its fantastic trappings. The moral consequence is the freedom that this self-knowledge affords: Man is no longer to be ruled by a blind alter ego, by his alienated self as an unconscious "other," but by his humanity as his consciously realized species nature. Moral freedom, the autonomy whose condition is rational self-knowledge, is thus the product of this therapy. The relation between virtue and self-knowledge, the profound truth of Socratic philosophy, is clear in this as in Feuerbach's later writings. γνῶθι σαυτόν – the Greek dictum "Know thyself" – was, in fact, one of the titles that Feuerbach considered before deciding on *The Essence of Christianity*.[3] The means to this self-knowledge is the study of concept formation, not as an abstract science, but in its deeper philosophical sense: To understand concept formation is to understand what is essentially *human* about man – his consciousness. The science of concept formation, which involves both the analysis of concepts and the study of their genesis – the "genetic-analytic" method that Feuerbach propounds – is what philosophy is concerned with. But not as with any other science, for *this* science is the actual study of human nature itself: It is the paradigm of self-knowledge, insofar as self-knowledge is species knowledge, and the very essence of the human species is its capacity to know itself as species. It is in this sense that the work is phenomenological, and can be seen in its derivation from Hegel's *Phenomenology*.

Feuerbach explicitly claims a "scientific" character for his work, likening his method to that of "analytical chemistry": "The method that the author follows here is thoroughly objective. It is the method of analytical chemistry. Therefore, whenever necessary and wherever possible . . . documentation is offered to legitimize the conclusions achieved by the analyses – i.e., to show that they are objectively based" (S: I, 5).

He thus takes his analysis to be an empirical analysis, whose facts are the phenomena of religious consciousness themselves. The "documentation" here is empirical evidence of this subject matter; its *images* as they are set forth in the Bible, in the writings of commentators and theologians, and in the folk expressions of believers. These "human facts," the expression of human consciousness in the images, the material signs of religion (and in their reflected-upon, theological form as well) therefore constitute the empirical subject matter of *The Essence of Christianity*. Feuerbach saw *The Essence of Christianity* as an exercise in the application of his new method, that synthesis of rational and empirical methods of analysis that he called "speculative-empirical, speculative-rational or genetic-critical."[4] He considers his method to be in "absolute contradiction" to the a priorism of speculative philosophy and of Hegel's logicism. It is only in answer to the "clamour excited by the present work" that Feuerbach, in his preface to the revised second edition, develops this theme explicitly.

Hopefully, now that I have, often step by step, supported my analysis with historical evidence, if the reader is not totally blind, he will be convinced and will admit, even if reluctantly, that my work is a faithful and correct translation of the Christian religion out of the Oriental picture-language of fantasy into plain, comprehensible or ordinary language. My work has no pretension to be anything more than a faithful translation – to speak plainly: an empirical or historico-philosophical analysis, a solution of the enigma of the Christian religion. The general propositions, which I set forth in the Introduction are no *a priori*, self-invented products of speculation. They have arisen out of the analysis of religion; they are only, as indeed are all the fundamental ideas of the work, factual expressions of man's nature – and especially of his religious nature and consciousness, – converted into thought, i.e., set forth in general terms, and thereby made available to the understanding. The ideas in my work are only conclusions, consequences entailed by premises which themselves are not merely ideas, but objective facts, either living or historical facts. . . . (VII, 280–1)

The notion that one can draw general conclusions from empirical "facts," without a priori, "speculative" premises is a central and difficult notion of empirical science. It involves the so-called problem of induction and what Karl Popper has dealt with at length as the "demarcation problem," the question of what separates science from metaphysics. Feuerbach, in this place, is not concerned with these questions, though he deals with them at length elsewhere. He is content to make clear how sharply he has broken with speculative philosophy, in one of his most striking and oft-quoted passages:

I unconditionally repudiate *absolute*, immaterial, self-sufficing speculation – that speculation which creates its material out of itself. I am worlds apart from those philosophers who pluck out their eyes the better to think. I require the senses for my thinking, above all, I require my eyes; I found my ideas on those materials which can be appropriated only by means of sense-activity. I do not generate the object from thought, but on the contrary, thought from the object. But only that is an object which exists outside my head. . . . The maxim of previous speculative philosophy: "All that is mine, I carry with me" – the

256

old _omnia mea mecum porto_–I cannot, alas! appropriate. I have many things outside myself, which I cannot carry around in my pocket or in my head, but which I nevertheless look upon as belonging to me, not only to me as a man– this is not now in question–but to me as a philosopher. I am nothing but a natural scientist of the spirit; but the natural scientist can do nothing without instruments, without material means. In this capacity–as a natural scientist– I have written this work, which consequently contains nothing but the principle of a new philosophy, and one which is confirmed practically, i.e., _in concreto_, in application to a particular, concrete subject matter, but one which has universal significance: namely, to religion, with respect to which this principle is presented, developed and carried through to its consequences. My work is therefore not to be counted as a production to be placed in the category of speculation–although in another sense it is the flesh and blood result of pre- vious philosophy; on the contrary, it is the direct opposite of speculation, the dissolution of speculation. Speculation has religion say only what speculation itself has thought, and expressed far better than religion. It determines what religion is without letting itself be determined by religion. Speculation never gets out of itself. I, however, let religion speak for itself. I am only its listener and interpreter, not its prompter. Not to invent, but to discover, "to unveil existence" has been my sole purpose; to see correctly, my only endeavor. (VII, 280–3; S: I, 14–18)

This somewhat rhetorical rejection of idealist "a priorism" in favor of what Feuerbach conceives to be an "empirical" method, akin to that of the natural sciences, has been interpreted as "the result and high point of Feuerbach's break with the Hegelian system, as well as with Christian 'positive' philosophy."[5] The qualified sense in which this is a break with the "system" has been set forth in the discussion of _The Critique of Hegelian Idealism_ (see pp. 179ff.). It is a rejection of idealist panlogism, a rejection of Hegel's "presuppositionless beginning" with _Being_. It is therefore a rejection, on phenomenological grounds, of the _ontological_ premises of Hegelian idealism. But it is not a break with the dialectical _method_. And if "system" means reflective reconstruction of systematic relations between thinking and being, then _The Essence of Christianity_ falls within the methodology and the structure of the Hegelian "system," especially with respect to the crucial work here, the _Phenomenology of Mind_. In fact, Feuerbach's claim is that he reveals the true import of the Hegelian system as against the import that an objective idealist ontology claims for it. The subject-object dialectic of the _Phenomenology_ is, after all, the structural framework of Feuerbach's analysis in _The Essence of Christianity_. It is Feuerbach's _interpretation_ of this formal structure and its dialectical mode that makes him dis- tinctively Hegelian. This _interpreted_ system is empirical, in Feuerbach's terms, because he explicitly takes the elements in the system to be hu- man, existential realities, and not ideal or transcendental entities. But these "realities" are ontological only in the sense that they are the real, or existential, *creations* of human consciousness; they are *phenomenologically* "real"; that is, they are the "concrete" images of thought. Feuerbach is quite clear that he is *not* doing classical metaphysics: He eschews "Reality," "Being" as such. Nor is he doing anthropomorphic philosophy of nature. (This is precisely what he accuses Schelling of doing.) He is doing *phenomenology*, and his empiricism here consists in taking the phenomenological "objects" as his facts; his "natural science" consists in his taking these "objects" to be no less "natural" than the objects of other natural sciences. Phenomenology is therefore the natural science of the spirit (i.e., of human consciousness). It has no transcendental, nonnatural, or metaphysical subject matter. Finally, Feuerbach considers his method "scientific" in that it is philosophically analytical *and* systematic. "Scientific," in the then current sense of *wissenschaftlich*, meant rational reconstruction of the results of empirical or other analysis in theoretical (i.e., *universal*) form, in the form of laws or principles.

This may be taken (and was taken, by the early critics of *The Essence of Christianity*) as an implicit ontology, one that takes the phenomenological realm as that which is ultimately "real" for man. Physical nature, man's existence in the world, so-called material reality, then seems to be swallowed up in consciousness, or in experience, and thereby, a new kind of subjective idealism is introduced. Feuerbach does not take this course, though he recognizes the temptations to such an interpretation. He avoids it by an all-important distinction: Man's consciousness is not his existence, but only the reflection of his existence. It is the means whereby his existence becomes known to him. Phenomenological "existence," the "facts" with which the work deals, is not yet existence per se. It is the form of man's knowledge of his existence. It is not the ultimate fact, but its most immediate representation, the material for thought. The subject of this phenomenological "existence" is concrete, individual man, a being who eats and drinks, who is part of nature in this necessary bond, as well as one who thinks. The *whole* man, the union of body and soul, becomes an object of knowledge only in his self-representation, only in the objectified *image* of his existence. He cannot *think* eating and drinking except under the form of an image. It is the separation of the image from the fact, the copy from the original that Feuerbach sees as the self-alienating *systole* of religious consciousness. The object of Feuerbach's analysis is the re-relation of the image to its source, in human existence *as a whole*, in the organic life of sensation and feeling. Therefore, the method of the analysis is to trace the meaning, the sense of the image, the projection of the various aspects of man's real existence, as natural, sensory, feeling, and thinking being, to its sources in this existence; to show, in effect, that it *is* an image of man, and to recognize what kind of being man is, *from* the image. Feuerbach says that his philosophy

does not identify the *idea* of the fact with the fact itself, so as to channel actual existence through the point of a pen, and reduce it to existence on paper; rather, it separates the two, and precisely by this separation attains to the fact itself; it recognizes the fact, the true thing, not as it appears as an object of abstract reason, but as it is an object of the real, complete man, thus, as it is itself a complete real thing. (VII, 282; S: I, 17)

There remains a dialectical difficulty, as to what precisely this "real thing" is. It is "real man," in Feuerbach's view. But man knows his existence directly only through the senses, and through feeling. His existence as individual, or as particular man, is all the existence there is, in this sense. Yet Feuerbach talks of species existence, of human essence as the real object of a human consciousness. This problem of the relation of species to individual, of essence to existence, presents one of the chief difficulties that Feuerbach's *empiricism* has to resolve. Apart from what has been said about it in the previous chapters, it will be seen to be a central theme in *The Essence of Christianity* and in later works. Feuerbach's attempt at a resolution of this difficulty of the relation of species to individual may shed light on one of the major current philosophical problems of scientific empiricism.

THE FORMAL STRUCTURE OF "THE ESSENCE OF CHRISTIANITY"

Apart from the dialectical structure of the phenomenological analysis in the work, *The Essence of Christianity*, in its formal structure, follows the classical dialectical pattern of thesis and antithesis. The work is divided into two parts, the first of which represents the (unmediated) thesis, as the second represents the antithesis. The expected dialectical synthesis, which would fill out the Hegelian triad, is not structurally represented in a third section, but is in the discussion in the first and second parts; that is, it is implicit throughout the work. In broad terms, Feuerbach characterizes the subject matter of the first part as *Religion*, that of the second part as *Theology*. The synthesis is the restatement of the first part, but in its true, mediated sense: The object of religion is man; thus, the true essence of religion is anthropology, the study of human nature. The spontaneous, immediate, or naive religious consciousness recognizes this truth, but only in symbolic, alienated form. Theology systematizes this alienation, objectifies the human essence of religion in its wholly other form, as God. Where religion believes in the God-man, theology makes the implicit contradiction explicit. Thus, in classic dialectic fashion, theology is the negation of religion, actualizes the contradiction at the heart of religious consciousness, and hypostatizes the internal division in human nature (between individual and species) as a metaphysical division between man and God. The *content* of theology is, however, the same as that of religion: It is still man but in his most alienated form. The secret of theology, its translation, is anthropology. The translation into ordinary terms of the reflective abstractions of theology is the negation of theology, and the reinstatement of its original religious content in the new self-conscious form of man's knowledge of his own nature, *as* his own nature. The three stages may then be called (1) the religious, (2) the theological, (3) the anthropological. The third, as synthesis, is contained in the first two, and Feuerbach's purpose is to show that in both the thesis and the antithesis, his conclusion—namely, that theology is anthropology—is already contained. He offers an example of the relation between the parts of the work:

In the first part, I show that in religion, the son of God is an actual son, is the son of God in the same sense in which man is the son of man, and I find therein the truth, the essence, of religion in that it affirms and realizes a profoundly human relation as a divine relation. In the second part, by contrast, I show that the son of God—not indeed in the unmediated sense of religion itself, but in the reflection thereon—is not a son in the natural human sense, but in an entirely different sense, which contradicts nature and reason, and is consequently a son only in an absurd and incomprehensible way. In this negation of human sense and understanding I find the untruth, the negation of religion. Thus, the first part is the *direct*, the second the *indirect* proof that theology is anthropology. Therefore, the second part necessarily refers back to the first; it has no independent significance, and its only aim is to show that the sense in which religion is interpreted in the first part must be the correct one, because the counterposed sense is nonsense. (VII, 285; S: I, 20)

It would appear that Feuerbach is identifying *religion* with *anthropology*. But this is not his thesis. Religion is not reflective, its object is the object not of reason, but of feeling—its object is always the concrete particular, the *existential* under the form of its sensuous image. Reflection-thought-philosophy requires universals for its objects—that is, *essences*. Only theology presents the content of religion in this form. But form and content are in contradiction here. The concrete particular is hypostatized as if *it* were the universal (as in Incarnation theory; see the discussion on pp. 226ff.). It is this particularity of content that anthropology overcomes: It takes the essence of man as its object, but in rational form, not in the form of the sensuous, pictorial imagination. It raises the content—the *real* content of religion, man's *essence*—out of its particularity not only in form, as theology does, but in content as well. Thus, anthropology transcends the fantastic image of this essence, in religious belief, as well as in theology, and makes the esseence itself an object of thought. Existence is *lived*, not *thought*. It is the proper object of those faculties of consciousness that "know" the particular, in the sense of direct acquaintance with it. These are the senses and feeling; and the instrument appropriate to the representation of this particular content is the imagination (see p. 233). Rational knowledge—that is, self-conscious thought activity—takes universals, essences, as its objects. It is only in the analysis of the relation between sensing and feeling, on the one hand, and thinking, on the other, that this dichotomy of existence and essence is resolved by Feuerbach. Thus, the very outward structure of *The Essence of Christianity* already presents, in its form, the essential epistemological problem of Feuerbach's "speculative" or "rational" empiricism, and with it, the central metaphysical problem of an *essence* that is at the same time a concrete existence—that is, that heritage from Hegel, the concrete universal.

Finally, Feuerbach does not interpret the dialectical three stages historically, but systematically. He does not, as he did in the *History*, attempt to show a temporal development of this sequence, and eschews historical interpretation, considering alike the "living" and the "historical" evidence. The "theological" sources include, together with the Pentateuch, the Prophets, the Gospels, and "proper" theologians (e.g., Augustine, Luther, Bonaventure, Bernard of Clairvaux, Böhme) and the "speculative" philosophers (e.g., Giordano Bruno, Leibniz, Kant, Hegel). "Theology" is explicitly taken to include "speculative philosophy." The various sources stand cheek by jowl, without any historical order, arranged only in accordance with relevance to the topical structure of the work. Feuerbach concerns himself, as he says, only with "speculative theology or philosophy" and not with "vulgar theology, a kind of trash from which I would rather keep as clear as possible" (VII, 286; S: I, 21).[6]

THE THEMATIC STRUCTURE OF
The Essence of Christianity:
FEELING, WILLING, THINKING

Because the general purport of the work is to show that the real content and the true object of religion is man's own nature, the argument consists in two main propositions: (1) that man has a specifiable nature or essence; (2) that the language of religious consciousness and of theology can be shown to deal with nothing but this essence; or that the language (including here the imagery and symbolism) of religion can be translated into the language of anthropology, whose sole object is man. In the two introductory chapters, Feuerbach attempts to state these two general premises, under the headings "The Essence of Man in General" and "The Essence of Religion in General."

The structure of the argument may be seen to derive from the general model of human nature that Feuerbach adopts. It is not a new model, but, on the contrary, the most classical model of all: the "tripartite soul" of Greek thought, which has dominated philosophy for more than two millennia. In Feuerbach's interpretation, man's essence consists in *feeling*, *willing*, and *thinking*, and it is on this triadic framework and on the interrelations among these constituent faculties or properties that *The Essence of Christianity* is constructed. It is in terms of these properties that Feuerbach pursues his reductive analysis of the content of religious consciousness. It is important to note at the outset (especially in terms of the main criticisms that were leveled at the work) that Feuerbach considers this human *essence* to be man's *consciousness*; that thinking, feeling, and willing are activities of man's essence as *conscious* being. And it is this alone that he chooses to deal with here. Man's existence, as a natural or material being, his *actual* relation to physical nature, to the world outside his conscious nature is dealt with only under its phenomenological aspect–that is, as it appears to man in *terms* of his own nature, as it mirrors his nature for him. Feuerbach's restriction here, which he never makes fully clear in the work, but only in later polemic and discussion, has understandably led to much confusion and misunderstanding of *The Essence of Christianity* and will be seen in later discussion (see p. 274) to be the source of the two main charges of *subjectivism* and *abstractness* that were leveled at the work (the first, from the "right"–that is, from the orthodox theologians [e.g., Julius Müller]–the second, from the "left," principally by Marx and Engels). Feuerbach's justification for this restriction of human essence to consciousness is that his subject matter, in this work, is religious consciousness, and that the very content of *this* consciousness is limited to and properly concerns itself *only* with man. Therefore, whatever religion or speculative theology or philosophy say about nature is only a symbolic or esoteric statement about man. Anthropomorphism is therefore the essence of religion.

Feeling, willing, and *thinking*[7] constitute man's consciousness, as his essential nature. The process in which man becomes aware of this nature is therefore the process in which man becomes conscious of his consciousness, or makes his consciousness itelf the *object* of consciousness. In order to make an object of this consciousness, or species nature, its constituents, as well as the complex relations among them, have to be represented in objective form, as the material of consciousness. This representation, or image of the constituents of consciousness and of their relations is, in its unmediated, spontaneous form, the content of religion. Feuerbach's analysis of this content can be reconstructed, therefore, in terms of these three constituent properties of man's essence (knowing, feeling, and willing) and in terms of the dialectical process of emerging self-consciousness in which these properties come to be known as human, and come, therefore, to be known in their essential relations to each other. Thus, although the chapters of the work only loosely reflect this structure, all the aspects of the Christian religion with which Feuerbach deals are seen to be the symbolic forms of man's self-knowledge, as knowledge of his *feeling, willing,* and *thinking* capacities. The further step in the dialectic of this *Phenomenology* is the consciousness of the unity of these capacities in man, and thus the organic *self-consciousness* that this represents.

Under the aspect of *feeling,* or *love,* Feuerbach analyzes the central symbol of Christianity, Christ, in terms of the "mysteries of the suffering God." He analyzes the Incarnation, as well as miracles and prayer, resurrection and immortality. Thought-intellect-reason is seen in its alienated form in religious consciousness, under the aspect of the Creation, or "the cosmogonical or world-creating principle in God," and in terms of the divine attributes of infinity, and necessary existence. The metaphysical concepts of God as the necessary ground of all existence, of identity of essence and existence in God, as well as the concepts of Providence, Predestination, Design—in short, the classical ontological and teleological formulations are seen to derive from this context of man's projection of his own intellect as an object of thought. *Will,* in its religious expression, is seen to be embodied in the concepts of divine morality and justice, of God's perfect goodness, and of the tension between divine law and divine mercy. The unity of man's consciousness, the expression of his recognition of this unity, in his *self-consciousness* is the "phenomenological reduction" of the concept of the Trinity, as the mediated unity of rational law and sensibility or love. What then follows is the analysis of the sacraments—Baptism and Holy Communion. Here Feuerbach copes with the question of how man's natural functions, his physical existence, his "necessary bond with nature" are taken up into the religious consciousness. The water, the bread, and the wine become "religious" symbols, not of nature as such, but of man's dependence upon nature for his existence.

This bare sketch of the thematic structure is wholly inadequate to convey the fluidity and interrelatedness of Feuerbach's discussion, and gives this structure only in its mechanical, abstract form, as a guide to the systematic nature of the work. The alternative treatment of these same themes in Parts One and Two under the "opposite" aspects of religion and theology makes for the complex underlying architecture of the work. In fact, one may say that Feuerbach presents his thought in terms of two simultaneous and overlapping dialectical structures: (1) the dialectic of the self-alienation of consciousness, in its "immediate" form, in religious consciousness; and (2) the dialectic of this "immediate" form with its reflected form in theology. Feuerbach was not the master of dialectical construction that Hegel was. But both the formal and thematic structure of *The Essence of Christianity* attest to his ability to exhibit his meaning in a dialectical framework.

CONSCIOUSNESS AS THE ESSENCE OF MAN: THE REAL SUBJECT OF RELIGION

This section is an attempt to explore Feuerbach's concept of "human essence," especially to understand the term "essence," and to see (1) if Feuerbach's use conforms to the philosophic position that he claims as an empiricist and naturalist critic of idealism and (2) what philosophical problem remains on such an empiricist-naturalist view.

What, precisely, does Feuerbach mean by the "essence of man," and how is this the "object" of religion? This is the central question, and the answer to it hinges on the analysis set forth in *The Essence of Christianity*.[8] The question is the classical one concerning universals, and the relation of the universal to the particular. In the *Dissertation*, Feuerbach had adopted the idealist view that the *form* of consciousness (as distinct from its differentiation in determinate modes of knowing) is one, infinite, and absolute. This *form*, which is *Reason*, is universal, in that every act of knowing is necessarily *of* this form, or "participates" in it, in good old Platonic fashion. Each individual act of knowing cannot be an essence in itself, or there would be as many essences of thought as there were individuals thinking. Such "thought" would lack the community or universality that the concept of thought requires (i.e., without which it is not a concept of *thought* at all). Feuerbach had written that "insofar as essence is actually essence, it must be simple, homogeneous, undifferentiated in itself, unified, not manifold and self-differentiated as individuals are" (IV, 342; see p. 43). He had concluded that Reason alone, the *form* of thought, or its essential mode of activity, was such an essence; that man's essence was that which transcended all individuality, all individual men, and that, therefore, "Reason is neither finite nor merely human," with the clear implication that insofar as man "participated" in reason, he transcended his individuality and attained to universality (i.e., to absolute identity with all other [rational] men–to identify with the *species* itself). All other modes of relation among men (as examples he offers "love" and "friendship") are limited and finite in nature. But "insofar as I think, I am all men" (IV, 306). Thus, the condition of unity, which essence requires, is fulfilled only in thought, and "thought is therefore the absolute essence of man as species" (IV, 341). This "essence" turns out to be the *Spirit* of Hegel's *Phenomenology*. In the previous discussion of the species concept and the relation of essence to existence (see Chapter VIII, pp. 220–6), the development of the concept is traced in Feuerbach's earlier works. But the central theme, first stated in its idealist version in the *Dissertation*, remains: man's "essence" is his consciousness. "Essence" remains, in its classical sense, the universal in virtue of which the particular individuals transcend their individuality, and are "one" or "unified." But now, Feuerbach gives this essence an entirely phenomenological status. It is no longer the ground of Being, in its ontological sense in idealism; rather, it is the ground of being *human*. Moreover, it is not "transcendental." Its "existence" *is* the human community constituted by the activity of consciousness. It is only in the characterization of this community that Feuerbach justifies his claim to have abandoned idealism. For the essence that this community constitutes is no longer Reason, in the intellectualist sense of the essential form, or activity of thought, but rather the unity of sensing, feeling, willing, and thinking that makes the whole consciousness of man. Further, the community of reason, which the idealist Feuerbach took as primary, is now seen to derive from the community of sensing and feeling, the immediate relation of man to nature and to other men, as the sources and the contexts of his existence. In the by now much abused and hackneyed (by contemporary existentialism) formulation, then, man's essence is seen to proceed from his existence, and from his existence as a creature of sense and feeling. In another sense, man *creates* his essence, by the activity of his consciousness. He does not "participate" in it, except as an individual who is born into the society of men. All that this essence transcends is man's finite individual existence, but not his species existence. As such, as species existence, his essence is his humanity; it is not more than human, but *only* human. His essence is identical with his existence as species. The sense in which this essence is phenomenological is that its *Being* consists not alone in *consciousness* as such, in the substantive, idealist sense, but in the *consciousness of this* "*consciousness*," as itself the universal or species existence of man.

The phrase "the object of religion is the essence of man" then translates as follows: Religion itself is a form of human consciousness, more particularly, that form of human consciousness whose object is not anything external to man, but is his own essence. His essence is his consciousness. Therefore, in religion, man takes his own consciousness as an object of consciousness; he comes to *self*-consciousness by means of representing his essence (i.e., his consciousness) to himself as an object of knowledge.

The logical problem that this reflexive relation within consciousness presents was already solved by Hegel in the dialectic of self-alienation, especially in the *Phenomenology*. Identity, as *self*-identity, is taken to be the limit toward which this dialectic moves and, concurrently, it is the characteristic that informs this motion itself. As such, it is not a transcendental identity, beyond the process itself, but the principle, or the rule according to which the process unfolds. Thus, consciousness as *subject* is related to consciousness as *object*, not as in a logical identity relation, in which the terms may be substituted. Rather, the two must be determinably different, and their difference lies in the mode of their relation to each other. The subject is a subject only with respect to some object; the object is an object only for some subject. Their "identity," or dialectical unity, in this sense, is in the interdetermination, or interdependence. Under this condition of interdetermination in the dialectic, the object is always in the relation of being *other*, with respect to the subject. Under any other condition, namely, that in which the subject has no "other" as object, there can be no object, nor can there be a subject; and in this unmediated or undifferentiated self-identity of such a "subject" with itself, no possibility of consciousness, but only of flat, unmediated existence—mere "Being in itself." This condition of "otherness" requires, therefore, differentiation, duality, as its ground. Only where there are two can consciousness arise. (The notion of Absolute Identity seems therefore to be beyond the dialectic itself. Such an absolutely self-identical consciousness would be *no* consciousness at all. This is the sense of Hegel's critique of Schelling's notion of Absolute Identity—"the night in which all cows are black.")

Where the "other" is *nature*, as it is in that relation of consciousness that is sensibility, or sense perception, this "other" is itself a nonconscious object, and so, in this respect, its essence is different from that of consciousness itself. However, where the "other" is an object to which consciousness is attributed, it has this essence in common with the subject, and insofar as it does, it may be called a self-relation, in terms of this common essence. Thus, the relation of consciousness to itself requires that as *object*, this consciousness be differentiated from the subject consciousness, that it be presented under another form, that is, *objectified* only by virtue of its differentiation.

Religion as Self-alienated Human Consciousness

Any *representation* requires the imagination. In the imagination, the object of consciousness is presented not merely in its otherness, as an independently existing object of sense perception (i.e., as a natural object in itself), but in the sensible form, or image of an object as it is created by consciousness itself–that is, by its power of imagining or representing "sensible" objects that are not "present" as objects of sense perception but that are nonetheless "present" to the imagination. The "freedom" of the imagination is this power to create objects without the limitation of natural laws, but within the limits of the forms of sensible representation, that is, within the limits of sense imagery. These limits constrain the imagination to the representation of objects as particulars, as concrete, individual images. In this form, the objects are not essences, but may be the material *signs* of essences. The object can be an *essence* only when it is a universal, not a particular, and therefore, *not* an image. But what, then, is the phenomenological representation of a universal? At best, given this interpretation of the condition of "otherness"–that is, that the other requires a representation under the forms of the imagination–for consciousness, the universal cannot be *presented* as such, but only represented, by a symbol.

The problem arises, how is one to distinguish the image (which itself is always a particular and can be represented only under the forms of concrete, i.e., sensible particularity), in the case when it is an image *of* a particular, from the case when it is the sign vehicle for a universal (i.e., when it symbolizes an essence)? How is Christ, for example, as image of an individual man, in religious consciousness, to be distinguished from Christ as the symbol of man's "infinity of feeling" (or in Feuerbach's still more striking phrase, as the "self-confession of human sensibility")? Man comes to know his essence, his universal nature, only under the form of an image. This seems clear enough as far as it goes. But how does man come to know that this image represents an essence? What distinguishing character does *such* an image have? Feuerbach offers no theoretical clarification here. Instead, he offers an analysis based on the premise that the image symbol *may* be thus interpreted. He offers an interpretation, but not yet the justification or the theoretical argument for such an interpretation. It comes to that sorest of problems in metaphilosophy, the choice of frameworks. That one *may* choose the framework of "naturalistic reduction" is a plain matter of fact, once such a framework is clearly constructed. This much Feuerbach accomplishes: He constructs the framework, in *The Essence of Christianity*. But that there is a well-constructed framework that one may choose to adopt is a matter of fact, and does not yet approach the question of why and whether one ought to choose *this* framework rather than an alternative one. Feuerbach's argument for the choice of this framework may be derived from a reading of the work's dialectic: theology as the negation of religion; anthropology as the negation of the negation, in which the content of the thesis (religion) is *aufgehoben* in the synthesis (anthropology). Religion and theology are *shown* to be "nothing but" anthropology, by virtue of the possibility of such an interpretation. But to show that such an interpretation is possible is not the same as to show that such an interpretation is true. Feuerbach argues cogently that the image has an interpretation as the symbol of a universal. But it is not made clear what the argument *for* this interpretation is, nor what the *rule* of interpretation (or the "hermeneutic") is, in *The Essence of Christianity*. The problem of universals or essences, in its phenomenological form, remains, therefore, one of the central theoretical problems in Feuerbach's philosophy, as it is one of the central philosophical premises of his work.

Despite the persistence of this problem in Feuerbach's formulation, the empirical direction of his view of essence is shown in his now revised concept of the nature of consciousness, which is this essence. The intellectualist emphasis on rational *thought* as the essential character of this consciousness is revised by Feuerbach. In another place, he is to substitute *"Sentio ergo sum"* for *"Cogito ergo sum,"* to emphasize this change. Just as the physical organism is the necessary condition for thought activity, so too the activities of such an organism in sensing and feeling are the prerequisites for thinking. The *whole* man, as object of phenomenology, is a unity of these activities, and only with respect to such a unity can "consciousness" be adequately dealt with. The "species consciousness," for which essences or universals alone are objects–what Feuerbach calls "consciousness in the strict sense"–is involved with feeling and will, because only under these forms does it become itself an object for consciousness. The account of *how* feeling and will become species representations, what the psychological process of this representation is, in its specific form in religion, is the most strikingly original content of *The Essence of Christianity*. The thesis of the work is that in the realization of this symbolic representation *as* symbolic, in this analysis of the image *as image*, we are at the end of an illusion,[9] we arrive at the "self-disabusement, the self-consciousness of religion" (VII, 290; S: I, 25).

At the outset of *The Essence of Christianity*, Feuerbach writes,

Religion rests on the essential difference between men and animals–animals have no religion. . . .[10] But what is this difference? The simplest and most general, as well as the most popular answer to this question is–consciousness: but consciousness in the strict sense. For it can't be denied that animals are conscious in the sense of having feelings of self, and of being able to make sensory discriminations, to perceive and even to judge of external things by means of particular sensible signs. Consciousness in the strictest sense, is present only to a being to whom his species, his essential nature, is an object. The animal is certainly an object to itself, as an individual–therefore it has self-awareness–but it isn't aware of its species-nature. Therefore it lacks consciousness in the strict sense–(a word whose root is *scientia*; in the German: *Bewusstsein*, whose root is *Wissen*). Where there is consciousness, there is a capacity for rational knowledge.[11] Rational knowledge is the consciousness of species, of universals. In life, we deal with individuals. In science, with universals, species. But only a species to whom his own nature is an object can understand other things or beings in their essential nature. (VI, 1–2; S: 35)

This capacity for species knowledge establishes man in two "worlds"; Whereas for the animal, the "inner" and "outer" life are one and the same, simple and unitary, man leads a double life. In his relation to himself as species, man has an "inner life," a life of dialogue:

Man thinks, i.e., he converses, he speaks with himself. The animal cannot transact any species-functions without some individual external to it. Man, on the other hand, can transact the species-functions of thinking and speaking –for these are true species-functions–without the need of any other. Man is at once *I* and *Thou*. He can put himself in place of another, precisely because his species, and not only his individuality, is an object for him. (VI, 2; S: I, 36)

Here Feuerbach reinterprets his own and Hegel's earlier views on the relation of the individual to the species, in terms of a dialectical model of finitude and infinity. Finitude is the condition of being limited or determinate with respect to some *other*. Finitude is therefore the condition of all existences, because to exist means to be determinate, to be in relation to some other. Infinity, on the other hand, is self-relation, or being undetermined by any "other" but the self.

In Hegel's dialectic, the *ansichsein*, the *being in itself* of any determinate object or thing, is a contradiction, because to be determinate is to be *for an other*, to be limited by a relation of *füreinandersein*, of *being for an other*. It is in this sense that any determinate existence has its *essence* in an other, or, strictly speaking, in the whole set of its relations to every other that determines it. It *is* nothing but the set of its relations as object for others. The *essence* of any determinate thing, or being, therefore, is realized only in this totality, and so in Hegelian terms, the *essence* is in the *whole*, in this totality, which is to say that only this *whole* is infinite, because to talk of anything "beyond" it would be to talk of something less than the *whole*, and therefore would be a contradiction in terms. If there is nothing beyond the whole to which this whole itself can be an object, it stands in relation to nothing "else" and is therefore unlimited, or infinite. This lack of any relational determinations by "others" is the condition of empty *Being*, the first term of the dialectic, which in this sense is equivalent to its "negation," *non-Being*, in the sense of *nothing determinate*. The relevance of this concept of infinity, in phenomenological terms, is that consciousness is infinite only if it is determined by nothing beyond consciousness, or is an object to nothing beyond it; if it were, this "other" would determine it, in this relation, and consciousness would be the finite object of something else. Again, the subject consciousness would be limited by its relation to any object that was other than consciousness. But consciousness without an object is no consciousness at all: The very nature of consciousness is awareness *of* an object. Ergo: The only object that does not determine consciousness, or delimit it as finite, is an object that is *not* other than consciousness and that *is* therefore consciousness itself. The "absolute essence" of consciousness is therefore the consciousness *of* consciousness, unmediated by any "other." The mediated consciousness of consciousness, in Hegelian idealist terms, is the appearance of consciousness to itself under the form of an "other." This apparent otherness has to be both recognized and overcome. This, therefore, is the dialectical process of the *Phenomenology* in which consciousness comes to self-awareness, or realizes its essence.

In the idealist version of this phenomenological dialectic, self-realization culminates in full self-consciousness, that is, in the full realization *by* consciousness that its real object, underlying all the appearances, is consciousness itself. In this unfolding of the consciousness *of* all the relations of consciousness to "others" as modes of self-relation, consciousness realizes its own infinity, that is, its own lack of any but self-relations, its lack of any "other" determination.

Feuerbach had explored and developed this phase of the Hegelian idea of infinity in his *Dissertation*. There he had considered the determinateness of all the modes of knowing that have objects other than "thought" itself, as only the partial modes of this ultimate self-relation, and therefore infinite in only a *relative* sense (see pp. 40–1). Their limitation is in the nature of their objects, and their objects are the "contents" of consciousness, but not its "form." These modes of knowing (i.e., modes of the self-relation of consciousness in this mediated form) include sense and feeling ("sensibility," broadly speaking) whose content is appropriate to these "limited" forms. But here the argument takes a peculiar turn. Each of these limited or finite modes of consciousness is limited only with respect to its objects as "other." But the objects of sensibility are themselves not limits on the *form* of sensibility, because these objects *are* sensibles and therefore share the "essence" of the mode of consciousness for which they are objects. For example, seeing takes objects of sight only; hearing takes objects of hearing; feeling, objects of feeling. The universe, for a being whose only mode of consciousness is sight, would be constituted exclusively of visual objects. This does not mean the visual appearances of "things," for the "things" of such a universe would be nothing but such "appearances," and they would be distinguishable as "appearances" only by a being not limited to sight alone. Such a universe would be *infinite in its kind* (i.e., within the framework of this particular sense).[12] Thus, the mode of consciousness—for example, sight—would be *infinite in its kind*, because there would be nothing in it that was "other" in essence from the mode or form of sensibility itself. This permits one to talk, in this qualified way, of the "infinity" of sensibility *with regard to its appropriate objects*. The "content" (e.g., sense objects) is identical in "essence" with the "form." Within the framework of sensibility alone, there are no "external" constraints, and therefore there is a sort of "infinity," or lack of limitation. Only *thought* delimits this (relative) infinity, because in its appropriation of the contents of sensibility, the various sense modalities do impinge on each other, insofar as they are taken to refer to the "same" object: that is, the "thing" as it is an object for thought. But such *determinate* thought is in turn delimited insofar as its objects are the now determinate objects of sensibility. These finite modes of thought constitute the "knowing" that Feuerbach in the *Dissertation* distinguishes from "thought" that has only itself as an object (see pp. 37–8). Here again, the *form* of thought is different from its determinate *content*, which is the "data" of sensibility. Only when the *form* of thought, or its "essence," becomes an object *for* thought is there an identity of form and content, in the simple sense that the form of thought—its essential mode of activity—is the content that thought presents to itself. Insofar as thought transcends the limits of any mode of sensibility, its object is the *thing*, and not the "appearances" that this *thing* has, under the aspect of this or that mode of sensibility. But in knowing the *thing* merely as object of thought, thought is determined by the constitutive modes of sensible knowledge whose "appearances" form the actual content of the *thing* as object, that is, its set of relations as sensible object. Only when the modes of knowledge of such things are themselves objects of thought does thought transcend its sensible content and take the *form* of this knowledge as its appropriate content. As such, thought is empty of any sensible or empirical content and has only a formal content. In the Hegelian development of this "transcendental dialectic," the Kantian notion of self-determination is made explicit. Such a form-content identity is Reason, and because it is not other-determined, it is, in Kantian terms, autonomous rather than heteronomous—or in Hegelian terms, infinite rather than finite. This relation of thought to its "essence" is, therefore, the "infinity of thought."

This is the dialectic that Feuerbach pursued in the *Dissertation*, in 1828. In 1841, the formal framework of this theory of infinity remained almost intact. Its interpretation and emphasis had changed, however. The "infinity of consciousness" is no longer the identity of the form and content of *thought*, in the rationalist intellectualized sense of the abstract *Idea*, but rather the identity of form and content that includes *feeling* and *willing*—the activities of sensibility, and of action or practice—as much as it includes the more abstract activity of reason (as that thought that has its own form as its content). In effect, what Feuerbach wants to do is to *empiricize* and *voluntarize* the Hegelian *Idea*—to take the *Idea* of the *Logic* and the *Spirit* of the *Phenomenology* and interpret them as much with respect to feeling and will as with respect to reason. The rationalist dictum that proclaimed the essence of man to be his thinking activity is now modified to include his feeling and willing activity. Unless feeling and willing are included, man's essence becomes abstractly intellectual. Man represents his essence to himself as much as an object of feeling and of will, as an object for thought. Under each of these modes, because it is a representation *of* his own essence and not of some "other," man's consciousness is infinite, in the sense previously discussed.

This discussion of the "infinity of consciousness" is intended to forestall that interpretation that takes Feuerbach to be making merely a rhetorical and sentimental point about the infinity of human consciousness, in some sort of paean to the human spirit. Paean it is, but hardly a merely sentimental one. "Infinity" here means not some vague cosmic extent or power of human consciousness, but the nature of that consciousness that takes man himself as an object, and is therefore *self*-consciousness, *self*-knowledge. The term "infinity" prescribes that the object of knowledge in this instance is man's own "essence"—that is, the totality of relations in which human consciousness is the subject and human activity in every one of its modes is the object, each mode being without limit in its own sphere. Thus, the sense of Feuerbach's characterization of his thought as "anthropology" hinges on understanding what he means by "the infinity of consciousness." The claim that religion has this human activity, and this alone, as its object is tantamount to the claim that religion is anthropology (in its imaginative or fantastic form). Feuerbach writes,

The essence of man, in distinction from the animals, is not only the ground, but also the subject of religion. But religion is awareness of the infinite. Therefore, it is nothing but man's awareness of his own infinite . . . essence. An actually finite being hasn't the vaguest comprehension, and certainly hasn't any conscious awareness of an infinite being, for the limits of one's being are the limits of one's consciousness. The awareness of a caterpillar, whose whole existence is limited to a particular species of plant, doesn't go beyond this limited realm. It might distinguish this plant from other plants, but it knows no more than this. Such a limited, but therefore infallible, certain "consciousness" is not even called "consciousness," but "instinct." Consciousness in the strict and proper sense, and consciousness of the infinite are indivisible. Limited consciousness is no consciousness at all: consciousness is essentially of an all-inclusive, infinite nature. *The consciousness of the infinite is nothing but the consciousness of the infinity of consciousness. To put it differently: in the consciousness of the infinite, the conscious subject has the infinity of his own essence as his object.* [My stress, M. W.] (VI, 2–3; S: I, 36–7)

This passage, and others like it, led to a criticism of Feuerbach's "anthropologism" and a confusion concerning his aims (see pp. 274–5). What Feuerbach seems to be saying is that the *entire* scope of man's consciousness is taken up in self-knowledge. And therefore, religion, as the awareness of the infinite, encompasses all there is for consciousness to know. If the object of religion is man, then man, or his species nature, exhausts the knowable universe: The "infinity of consciousness" seems then to take up all the available space in the universe, and the idealist implications are clear: Nature, as external to man, has no being. We are caught in an anthropocentric predicament. Man's universe, insofar as it is an object of his consciousness, can only be a *human* universe, if indeed consciousness is infinite in the sense previously described. The entire function of the representation of objects *for* consciousness becomes a self-mirroring one.

What is the essence of man, of which he is conscious? What constitutes the species-nature or the proper humanity of man? *Reason, Will* and *Love.* A fully realized human being has the capacity to think, to will and to love. These are the fullest realizations, the greatest powers, the absolute essence of man as man, and are the goal or end of his existence. Man exists in order to know, to love, to will. But what is the end of Reason? Reason itself. What is the object or goal of love? Love itself. Of the will? Freedom to will. We know in order to know, love in order to love, will for the sake of willing—i.e., to be free. . . . The divine trinity in Man, over and above individual men, is the unity of Reason, Love and Will. (VI, 3; S: I, 37)

The nature, or "essence," of these human activities is to take themselves as their own objects. But this is achieved only by the representation of these capacities in objective form, as "others." Every object of consciousness therefore becomes a mirror for man, serves its function *for consciousness* only as an instrument for the achievement of *self-consciousness.*

Man becomes self-conscious in terms of his object: the consciousness of the object is the self-consciousness of man. Man is comprehended in terms of his object: his nature is revealed to you by means of it. The object is man's revealed essence, his true, objective *I*. And this holds true not only of mental[13] but of sensible objects. Even those objects furthest removed from man are revelations of human nature, because, and insofar as, they are objects for man. Even the moon, the sun and the stars call to man γνῶθι σαυτόν. That he sees them, and sees them in the way that he sees them serves as an indication of his own nature. The animal is affected by the light which is necessary to his life-needs. Man is affected by the indifferent light of the remotest stars. Only man has pure, disinterested satisfactions and feelings – man alone celebrates theoretical festivals of sight. The eye which gazes upon the starry heavens sees that useless and harmless light, which has nothing in common with the earth and its needs, manifested in it its own nature and origin. The eye is of a heavenly nature. Therefore, it is by means of the eye that men rises beyond the earth; therefore, theory begins with the contemplation of the heavens. The first philosophers were astronomers. The sky reminds man that his nature is not only to act, but to contemplate as well. (VI, 6; S: I, 40–1)

The inversion of religious and theological expression is the hallmark of Feuerbach's style. Here he says, in effect, "the heavens proclaim the glory of man," insofar as *any* object becomes a means to man's self-revelation. In the most explicit way, he says, "Whatever object we become aware of, is a means to becoming aware of our own essence. We cannot be involved with anything whatever without becoming involved with ourselves" (VI, 7; S: I, 41).

The charge of anthropocentric subjectivism was leveled at Feuerbach by one of the earliest critics of *The Essence of Christianity*, Julius Müller,[14] a professor of dogmatics at Halle. Müller's charge was that objects lost their reality and became no more than "illusory representations" on Feuerbach's requirement that they function only as means to man's self-awareness. Feuerbach's reply, published in the same year as the criticism, 1842, was a long, sharply worded attack upon the theological misrepresentations of his view by critics who did not take the trouble to read and understand what he said. He writes, "There is no more baseless accusation than this! From the fact that objects, insofar as man knows them, are mirrors of his essence, there doesn't in the least follow the unreality of the objects, or the mere subjectivity of knowledge" (VII, 213).

In the reply to Müller, Feuerbach also restates the limits of his work:

My Introduction to *The Essence of Christianity* is only to be understood and to be judged in relation to the proper theme of the work, to religion, in which man is related not to things outside him, but to his own nature. It arises only out of the analysis of religion, was written only after the work was essentially completed, and was only added to satisfy the demands of scientific formality, which sets forth the general before the particular. (VII, 214)

Religion as Self-alienated Human Consciousness

Feuerbach's point is that religion *is* anthropocentric, and as such, it is nothing but *self-consciousness*. All of its purported objects are only representations of human nature. Therefore, such a universe is in fact permeated by humanity, by human properties. Its "infinity" resides precisely in the reflexivity of all the relations in it. But this is the *relative* infinity of religious consciousness, or of self-consciousness in general. Insofar as religious consciousness comprehends external objects only in terms of their relation to man, to his needs and interests and feelings, it makes mirrors of these objects, it conceives them anthropomorphically. The contradiction in religion lies in the confusion between the external and internal, the attempt to regard *as external* (i.e., as independently objective) that which is at the same time no more than the projection of human properties. Thus, what is otherwise apparently nonsensical in Feuerbach takes on this peculiar sense: The object of reason is reason itself; of will and feeling, will and feeling themselves. For *this* consciousness is really *self*-consciousness, under the guise of consciousness of objects *other* than the self. In religion, the objects are *divine* objects. God is the object of religious consciousness, of thought, of will, of feeling. But, by the reflexive formula, insofar as God is, for example, an object of feeling, "God" is nothing but the nature of feeling itself (e.g., as "perfect" or "infinite" or "pure") taken as an object of feeling. God's "existence" beyond this has no meaning, in the realm of feeling. "To exist" in this sense means to exist as an object of feeling, or as the objectified nature or "essence" of feeling itself. The solipsistic implications seem clear. But this "solipsism" is not that of the individual, but of the race, or the species. It is solipsism only if it is a pretension to knowledge of a reality *external* to man's inner nature. If, in fact, the content of this knowledge is man's nature itself, then it is no longer solipsistic. The reality at stake is the reality of that consciousness itself (in its activity in thought, feeling, will) that is its own object. Feuerbach's aim, then, is to turn a virtual solipsism, as a pretended consciousness of objects, into a justifiable knowledge of a phenomenological "reality," that is, as self-consciousness. He aims to bring religion to self-consciousness, as he says, and, in effect, then, to arrive at *self-conscious self-consciousness*.

Religion, as *un*selfconscious self-consciousness, therefore mistakes self-consciousness for the consciousness of an object, that is, of God as an object. "In sense-perception," writes Feuerbach, "the consciousness of the object is easily distinguishable from self-consciousness. But the religious object conflates consciousness and self-consciousness. The object of sense is external to man, the object of religion is within him" (VI, 15; S: I, 50).

Perhaps the clearest summation of the manifest thesis of *The Essence of Christianity* is a development of this point:

Consciousness of God is man's self-consciousness, knowledge of God is man's self-knowledge. By his God you know the man, and conversely, by the man, you know his God. The two are one. What God is to a man, that too is his spirit, his soul; and what his spirit, his soul, his heart are to a man, that is his God. God is the revealed and explicit inner self of man; religion is the ceremonial unveiling of man's hidden treasures, the confession of his innermost thoughts, the open avowal of his love-secrets.

But to characterize in this way, to characterize the consciousness of God as man's self-consciousness does not mean that the religious man is directly aware that the consciousness of God is the self-consciousness of his own nature. For the lack of this very awareness is in fact the distinctive mark or religion. To avoid this misunderstanding, it is better to say that religion is the earliest, and really the indirect form of man's self-consciousness. Therefore religion always precedes philosophy, both in the history of mankind in general, and in the history of the individual. At first man misplaces his essential nature as if it were outside of himself, before he discovers it in himself. His own nature appears to him first as that of another being. Religion is the child-like condition of humanity: But the child sees his nature–man–outside of himself. In childhood, man is an object to himself only in the form of another man. The historical progress of religion consists therefore in this: that what an earlier religion took to be objective, is later recognized to be subjective; what formerly was taken to be God, and was worshipped as such is now recognized to be something *human*. What was earlier religion is later taken to be idolatry: man is seen to have adored his own nature. Man objectified himself, but failed to recognize himself as this object. The later religion takes this step; every advance in religion is therefore a deepening in self-knowledge. (VI, 15–16; S: I, 51–2)

What leads to the *illusory* self-separation of man from his essence is, however, a *real* separation. Feuerbach's thesis is not merely to *assert* that the divine is the objectification of human nature, but to explain *why* this objectification takes place. Man *is* in fact separated from his essence, and Feuerbach takes it as his task "to show that the opposition of the divine and the human is illusory, i.e., *that it is nothing but the opposition between human essence and the human individual* [my stress, M. W.], and that consequently the subject and content of Christian religion is entirely human" (VI, 17; S: I, 52–3). Human *individuality* is human day-to-day existence, the satisfaction of needs, the mortality of the moment. Man's awareness of his finitude depends on the awareness of that with respect to which existence is realized to be finite, namely, that which is *not*-finite. "The human individual can certainly feel and know himself to be limited–and herein lies his distinction from the animals–but he can become aware of his limits only because the completeness, the infinity of his species is an object for him" (VI, 8; S:

I, 43). In Feuerbach's version of the classical ontological argument for infinity, or perfection (e.g., Descartes') the feeling of finitude requires a complementary *feeling* of infinity, with respect to which the first feeling may be said to be finite. This dualism in man, his individual existence, on the one hand, and his species consciousness, which constitutes his essence, on the other, is the source of religion; or more precisely, it is the source of the religious dualism that separates man and God. Human self-alienation is the source of the *conceived* alienation of God as *other* than man, as standing over man, as *super*human. This is the original "moment" of religious consciousness, the *theogonic* moment. The reidentification of this alien essence with man's personal existence is the second "moment," the *incarnation* of God as man. Feuerbach appeals to the metaphor of systole and diastole to describe this dialectic:

Just as the arterial action drives the blood to the farthest extremities, and the venous action draws it back; just as life in general consists in a continuous systole and diastole, so too does religion. In the religious systole, man repels his own essence, repels or repudiates himself; in the religious diastole, he draws his repudiated existence back to the heart again. Only God is self-active being, only God acts of himself.–This is the act of religious repulsion. God is that being who acts in me, with me, through me, upon me, for me, is the principle of my salvation, of my good intentions and actions–consequently my own principle of Good, my own essence,–this is the act of religious attraction. (VI, 38; S: I, 77)

This, at best, is the schematic model of self-alienation, not yet filled in with the flesh and blood detail that is Feuerbach's concrete analysis of the content of the Christian religion. Man lives in two worlds, by virtue of his consciousness. He is aware of his individual existence, but is aware of it in a human way: that is, he is aware of it as finite existence. This finitude is realizable only from the standpoint of an *other*, from the standpoint of species existence. Only to the extent that man is simultaneously aware of his species existence is his existential individuality, his finitude, an object of consciousness. Out of this dual awareness arises the sense of separation, of difference between the finite and that with respect to which it is finite. Only this consciousness of infinity can be the ground for consciousness of finitude. Feuerbach's emphasis may be described in this formulation: Species existence presupposes individual existence. The species exists only in the individuals that constitute it. But individual consciousness presupposes species consciousness. The consciousness or awareness of individuality, of finitude is possible only with respect to a consciousness of infinity. In existence, there is no separation of individual from species. The species is nothing apart from "its" individuals. It has no ontological status as "essence." In short, with respect to existence, Feuerbach is a nominalist. In consciousness, however, the species and the individual are separated. The individual, *as an object for consciousness*, is nothing apart from his species character. Individuality can be consciously realized only with respect to the species consciousness. With respect to consciousness (i.e., with respect to the "objects" of phenomenological analysis), Feuerbach is as Platonistic as one could wish. Essences are universals, but their status is phenomenological only. They exist only in consciousness, and for consciousness. In consciousness, then, man sees himself as separated from his essence. He is aware of the distinction between essence and existence, and his awareness is the feeling of separation, variously expressed in religion, but characteristically regarded as the awareness of *sin*. In the religious expression, this feeling of sinfulness is the awareness of man's separation from God. But, Feuerbach argues, this expression makes sense only if that from which I am separated is *like* myself.

> I can have a sense of my sinfulness only if I feel it to be a contradiction within myself, i.e., between my personality and my own essential nature. The feeling of sin is inexplicable and makes no sense at all if it is taken to be a contradiction between myself and the divine, considered as if it were essentially different from me. (VI, 35; S: I, 73)

Nevertheless, the representation of that from which I feel myself to be separated must, on the grounds of the very nature of consciousness itself, be an *objective* representation. It is to this object, as represented, that I relate myself as "separated from." The alienation schematism is summed up by Feuerbach thus: "This is the mystery of religion: man objectifies his own nature, and then takes himself to be the object of this projected being, which he transforms into a subject, into a personal being. Man thinks of himself, is an object of himself, but as the object of another objectified being" (VI, 37; S: I, 75).

The analysis of this process of objectification, as well as of the sources of the inner duality in human consciousness that gives rise to this objectification constitutes Feuerbach's "phenomenology of religion," the phrase with which Ruge characterized *The Essence of Christianity*.[15] Feuerbach's tripartite division of consciousness, into feeling, will, and reason, gives us the framework for this analysis, and the "essential human activities" to which the content of religious consciousness is reduced, in Feuerbach's "naturalistic reduction." It remains to be seen how the content of classical metaphysical *philosophy* is also thus reduced. The suggestions will be clear, however, as the traditional metaphysical questions of creation, determinism and free will, existence and essence, the relation of the universal to the particular are dealt with in their religious and theological form.

FEELING AND THE IMAGE OF FEELING

If religious consciousness is the alienated form of human self-consciousness, then, says Feuerbach, it is the representation of feeling in religious consciousness that provides the most immediate and most fundamental access to man's knowledge of his own species nature. The object of religious consciousness is primarily an object of feeling–that is, of feeling in its basic religious sense, as sympathy or love. The object of feeling in the spontaneous and unperverted religious consciousness is, moreover, an individual person, one endowed with such concrete qualities of personality as personal existence, unique individuality, a name, a face, a body, a voice–in short, all the sensory and affective qualities that are exemplified in the ordinary human concept of personality. Such a person objectifies for consciousness its own awareness of the nature of consciousness, in the fullest sense–including here the awareness of the conditions of consciousness as those of personal, bodily existence, as well as those of social existence in a community of men. Religious consciousness, in this Feuerbachian sense, is openly and frankly materialistic in its insistence on the physical, social, and historical reality of the object of its feeling. Wherein, then, lies the alienation? For Feuerbach, it lies in the attribution of these characteristics of personality not to man's essence as such, but to its representation in the imagination, that is, to the fantasy image of these characteristics–and in the belief in the personal reality of the image as that of a being *other* than man. The incipient contradiction in religious consciousness is therefore the double insistence that the object of religious belief be human in all characteristics, and that it be *other* than human in the sense that the imagination frees this representation from all the constraints of empirical law and rational noncontradiction.

Feuerbach's analysis of the dialectic of feeling is an attempt to show the process whereby man becomes aware of his own nature as a feeling being. "Man becomes self-conscious in terms of his object: the consciousness of the object is the self-consciousness of man" (VI, 6; S: I, 40; see p. 274). Thus, man becomes aware of his feeling nature in terms of an object of feeling. But such an object of feeling is constituted by the act of feeling itself. In the phenomenological context, there are no objects of feeling as such, apart from the relation of feeling consciousness to

such objects. The "reality" of such objects is therefore a phenomenological reality—not that of *dinge-an-sich*, but only of *dinge-für-mich*—objects
constituted by my awareness of them; moreover, constituted by the
mode of my awareness of them. The object of feeling, then, becomes
my object only by virtue of my feeling consciousness; or, in Feuerbach's
Hegelian language, the object of feeling is feeling itself objectified. But
the objectification of feeling is not an abstract enterprise. The abstraction "feeling" is the philosopher's "object" stripped of its concreteness,
its immediacy, its qualities as feeling. It is no longer feeling as such,
insofar as it is not the object of an act of feeling. Rather, it is properly
the object of formal thought, of reason as a formal capacity, and as
such it is merely a formal, empty concept, a universal, or an essence.
The objectification of feeling as an object of feeling consciousness itself
requires the representation of feeling in terms of its own immediate
character. Such a representation is therefore an image of the concrete,
sensory objects that are, in the ordinary sense, objects of feeling. Such
objects are not themselves "feelings." Thus, when Feuerbach says,
"Feeling alone is the object of feeling," he is not to be taken as talking
in a poetically obscure or nonsensical way. Rather, there is a strict technical sense that he has in mind, which requires a brief detour for its
explication. For the sense of Feuerbach's reflexive expression depends on
the epistemological and psychological context of his treatment of consciousness in general, and of the concepts of *feeling* and *imagination*
in particular.

To recapitulate briefly (see pp. 215ff. for fuller discussion): Imagination is the instrument of consciousness that represents feelings under the
form of an image. An image is a particular representation (i.e., it is a concrete, sensory representation); it has the qualities of the sensory object,
for without these qualities, it lacks particularity. Imagination is, in short,
the representation of an individual, with the particular qualities that
characterize it as an object of the faculties of sense, of desire, of wish, of
feeling. Perceptual objects as such are not objects of feeling: To *see*
something is not necessarily to want it, or to fear it, or to love it. Still,
perceptual objects alone are the objects toward which, in fact, our
feelings are directed. Here we need to add: perceptual objects *or their
representation in the imagination*. The imagination fulfills the peculiar
demands of feeling that is incomplete in its satisfaction, that is, of
feelings that are not fulfilled in real objects of feeling. The feeling
capacity, in itself, is unlimited, or infinite in the sense that as feeling, it
"knows" nothing of the empirical or rational restrictions on its fulfillment. The imagination then fulfills the demands of feeling in being

itself unlimited by the laws of empirical representation–that is, of science, or of a rational ordering of empirical possibilities according to law–and therefore is capable of infinitely fulfilling, in its free construction of imagery, the infinite demands of feeling. Thus, it is not the perceptual image as such that is the object of feeling, but rather the perceptual image with all the qualities of sensory representation, which is so ordered, so created or constructed that it follows the lead of feeling and is not bound by the laws of empirical representation. In this sense, then, the image is an image of feeling embodied in the representation of a sensory object, with the concrete qualities such an object must possess to mark its individuality.

What are the objects of human feeling? They are principally objects of sympathy, for Feuerbach. That is to say, they are the objects that we take to be themselves *feeling* objects, objects to whose *own* feelings we respond *by* feeling. The dominant sense of the term "feeling," for Feuerbach, is that of *mitgefühl*, or sympathy–more especially, of love.

Feeling is therefore feeling with respect to an object taken as a *thou*, that is, as a *person*. The condition for feeling is therefore the recognition of one's own species nature, the recognition of the other as species identical with the self. The concrete form of this recognition is not the *rational* reflection on species nature, but rather the particular act of feeling itself. Here is the incipient contradiction of this feeling consciousness: The object of feeling is either a real object, taken as a Thou, or a represented object, in the form of an image, and therefore of an image that represents the species character. This latter image is a human image, or in the more complex case, a personified image of what *we* would rationally take to be nonpersonal, as in the case of animal or nature worship. The condition of the feeling image is not only that it represent an individual, but that it represent the species character (as *essence*) in this individual. The image of feeling is therefore more than the sign for a perceptual object, insofar as it already involves the symbolization of an essence. In this sense, Feuerbach speaks of it as an "aesthetic sensation." It is different in the case of mere sensory representation, in which the particular is represented only under the mode of its particularity. Feeling, then, takes as its object the sensory image of an individual, but of this individual taken as a person–that is, as invested with the species character of feeling. The person is an object of feeling by virtue of his being a feeling person; or in the more abstract locution, it is this capacity for feeling that is the object of feeling. The imagination, then, is the capacity to represent anything whatever in this way, to present feeling consciousness to itself as an object of feeling, to represent the species character in the guise of a concrete image, but one that transcends in its connotation the limits of merely sensory representation.

In this function, the imagination mediates between the abstract representation of essences as universals (i.e., as the proper objects of formal, rational consciousness) and the representation of existents as individuals. It presents the essence only in the mode of existential particularity–of individuality. In effect, it *incarnates* the essence in a particular image, taken to be an existent. For imagination does not distinguish between imaginary appearance as phenomenological object and real existence. For the imagination the image is real because the strictures neither of empirical confrontation in practice nor of rational law apply to this realm of "free" activity. The freedom, or the literally creative activity of the imagination, is ruled entirely by feeling, that is, by pure feeling that is infinite in its own mode (see pp. 270–73).

This is the context of Feuerbach's analysis of the representations of feeling in religious consciousness. But this raises some questions. What of the "feelings" that can be characterized as desires for *natural* objects, the objects, say, of physical need–food, water? Does consciousness come to recognize its own nature in such objects as well? It is clear enough, in Feuerbach's scheme, that we may be said to come to awareness of our humanity, as feeling beings, by the objectification of these feelings in an other, as objects of feeling. Feuerbach suggests (and we will later note) that the products of man's activity are themselves taken by religious consciousness as the images of the *human* capacity to create such objects; for example, in the sacraments, the bread and wine are human symbols, images of the species character of the bodily existence of the beloved, and of its necessary nutriment. The sexual love of the body of the beloved is here entangled in the very act of producing the means of the body's existence. This is the almost explicit suggestion that Feuerbach makes concerning the holiness of personal existence. "Eating and drinking is in fact, a religious act in and of itself–at least it ought to be" (VI, 334; S: II, 418), says Feuerbach, in the final paean to natural functions that concludes *The Essence of Christianity*. Art and architecture do not represent, for religious consciousness, simply aesthetic qualities in themselves. Our aesthetic appreciation of them is "nothing but" our appreciation of the human capacities embodied in images and objects, the adoration or worship of which is perhaps the most explicit form of man's adoration of his own species capacities: The temple is built for the gods, but it expresses the love of man for his own nature as a builder. So, too, any work of art, in effect, objectifies and celebrates the artistic capacities of the species; all appreciation becomes human self-appreciation.

Feuerbach is able to transform every act of religious feeling, every object of religious feeling into an expression or an embodiment of the feeling that man has for his own feeling nature. The clearest of the metaphors of religious consciousness is, in fact, the aesthetic one. If man projects his own species nature in the objects that his consciousness creates as his own mirrors, then religious consciousness is akin to, or even indistinguishable from, the image-creating activity of art. This is particularly so with respect to the image of feeling, for in constructing it, the religious consciousness functions as dramatic art. The necessary representation of the other–the object of feeling consciousness–as a *Thou* has to exhibit in its imaginative construction at least the principal distinguishing features that this *Thou* has in actual existence, as another person. These features are essentially those of a character in a drama: however fanciful the characterization, it is nevertheless *sensuously* and *affectively* recognizable as human. The Gods may wear masks, but they have to tread the boards in full view, and be involved in matters of concern to the audience. Feuerbach, like Hegel, held religion to be essentially dramatic, indeed tragic. Though he does not, like Nietzsche, investigate the common origins of religion and of tragedy, his analysis is strikingly like that in *The Birth of Tragedy*. In the drama, the recognition of one's own feeling takes place in the context of the empathic activity engendered by the projected *image* of feeling, its embodiment in a dramatic characterization–literally, in a personification. Feuerbach's view is not that we carry this "illusion" with us into real life, but that human consciousness is constrained to represent its real, "lived" life, only under the form of this "illusion." The "illusion" is illusive only to the extent that we fail to distinguish between life and art. Only when we are directly caught up in the feeling awareness that the drama engenders, without the reflective separation between image and reality that our rational consciousness maintains, does the illusion occur. The pathology of religious consciousness is that, in it, we take the imaginative representation, the "mirror" itself, to be real, and ourselves to be *its* image. To watch the faces of an audience mirror the passions of the performance is to see the religious consciousness in its clearest form.

The closely related example is that of dreaming. In the dream, we do not distinguish between the dream fantasy, or the dream imagery, and reality. In the context of his analysis of feeling, Feuerbach explicitly suggests the psychological explanation of dreaming as wish fulfillment. Though his analysis deals specifically with religion, and he does not generalize the suggestion in so many words, it is clear that Feuerbach anticipates the Freudian dream theory in its essential particulars. The lack of explicit generalization is made up for by the context that takes religious consciousness as the paradigm of unknowing self-awareness in general. Thus, Feuerbach writes,

> Feeling is of the nature of dreaming. . . . But what is the dream? The inversion of waking consciousness. In the dream, the active is the passive, the passive is the active. I take my own self-determinations as determinations from without, I take the flow of feelings as actual occurrences, my ideas and sensations as real entities outside of me, and I suffer passively what are in effect my own actions. . . . Feeling is dreaming with open eyes; religion is the dream of waking consciousness. The dream is the key to the mysteries of religion. (VI, 169; S: I, 226)

The future of the illusion is that its imagery will be recognized and understood; that its reference, as symbol, to human consciousness, and therefore to human species nature, will be clear; that the revelation of the meaning of the dream will constitute the fully aware *self*-consciousness of man. How, then, does Feuerbach reveal the dream mysteries of religion? By interpreting the dream. And because "the fundamental dogmas of Christianity are realized wishes of the heart–the essence of Christianity is the essence of feeling" (VI, 168; S: I, 226); it is the interpretation of these dogmas as images of human feeling that constitutes Feuerbach's applied analysis of religious consciousness.

The religious concepts that Feuerbach examines, as objectifications of feeling, are the following: God, as an object of personal feeling; God's incarnation in human form, and the related concept of the suffering God; and the concepts of prayer and of miracles. In his treatment of the concept of the Trinity, the relation between the Father and the Son is interpreted in this context. Feeling also enters into the religious objectifications of the other aspects of consciousness, will and reason, in his interpretation of the concepts of divine law, predestination, and creation. The Christian sacraments of baptism and Holy Communion (or the Lord's Supper) are also seen in terms of man's natural bonds as they are transformed and suffused with feeling. Thus, in the scope of *The Essence of Christianity*, feeling, as man's feeling of self as species, can be seen to be the leitmotif. The activities of reason and will, insofar as they are represented in the religious imagination, are conceived according to the conditions of feeling consciousness, that is, as unlimited or infinite, and thus free from the independent constraints of empirical action and of rational consistency.

Religion as Self-alienated Human Consciousness

Feuerbach's transformation and inversion of classical theological analysis becomes, in effect, his critique of those philosophies of religion[16] that see feeling as the essence of the subjective religious activity but ascribe an independent objectivity to the object of feeling. His philosophical argument rests on the view that in the relation of consciousness, there must be a generic identity between the subject and the object; that is, like is known only by like.[17] Thus, he says,

Everything . . . which in the sense of supernatural[18] speculation and religion, has only the significance of the derived, of the subjective or human, of the organ or instrument, in truth signifies the original, the divine, the essence, the object itself. For example, if feeling is the essential instrumentality or organ of religion, then God's nature is nothing but an expression of the nature of feeling. The true but latent sense of the phrase "Feeling is the organ of the divine" is, "Feeling is that which is noblest, most excellent,–i.e., divine–in man." How could you comprehend the divine by means of feeling, if feeling itself were not of divine nature? The divine can be known only by that which is divine–"God knows himself only through his own nature." The Divine essence, which is comprehended by feeling, is in fact nothing but the essence of feeling, enraptured and delighted with itself,–nothing but self-intoxicated, self-contented feeling. (VI, 11; S: I, 46)

The "God" of feeling is therefore "nothing but" feeling itself. And the "God" of feeling is that God who is constituted as an object, by the act of feeling–therefore, as a phenomenological object, and "real" or "existent" only in this sense. Further, once the view is taken that "feeling is the organ of the divine," and that nothing but feeling is at the root of religious consciousness, the distinction between religious and non-religious feelings is abolished. For, on this view, it is not the objects that determine the mode of conscious response, but rather this mode–feeling–that determines the objects.

What makes this a specifically religious feeling? The given object? Not at all; for this object is itself a religious one only when it is not an object of the cold understanding, or of memory, but of feeling. What, therefore, determines the object as religious? The nature of feeling itself, which every particular feeling, without distinction as to objects, shares in common. Feeling is thus held to be holy because it *is* feeling. What makes it religious is the nature of feeling, and lies in feeling itself. Isn't feeling itself thus declared to be the Absolute, the Divine? If feeling is good in itself, religious in itself, holy in itself, then doesn't it follow that feeling has its God in itself? (VI, 12; S: I, 47–8)

The God who is the object of feeling as such, unalloyed by the specificity of this or that particular feeling, is thus feeling nature itself, projected in the form of "pure, unlimited, free feeling." Any other representation of God, which one may suppose is a limitation on this projection of pure, unlimited feeling, is imposed from sources outside feeling itself. The implication here is that God's image, insofar as it has the feature that either sense perception or reason impose, is an adulterated image of feeling. Yet because the imagination can give only the concrete, sensory representation, it is inevitable that the image of "pure feeling" is always thus adulterated, or limited. When Feuerbach writes that "music is the monologue of feeling" (VI, 11; S: I, 46), he suggests that the musical sound is the purest image of feeling:

What is it that affects you when you are moved by musical sound? What do you take it to be? What else, but the voice of your own heart. In this way, feeling speaks only to feeling: thereby, feeling is comprehended only as feeling–i.e., in itself–because the object of feeling is nothing but feeling itself. (VI, 11; S: I, 46)

Thus, we have an image of an abstraction in that the figurative features of the species are not represented, as they are in the representation of God's personality. But for Feuerbach, the musical sound is already more than an aural sensation, for if it were nothing but that, it would not be distinguishable as *musical* from any natural sounds. What makes it musical is the transformation of the natural or heard sound by the musical sense, or feeling that the human listener brings. "If you have no sense or feeling for music, you perceive no more, in the most beautiful music, than you do when the wind whistles past your ears, or when the brook rushes past your feet." What makes a sound musical then is that it is perceived as the image of feeling, and, as a sensory image, it is transformed by feeling into music. But in this case, what, if anything, distinguishes *God* from *music* as an object of feeling? In one sense, although it is a sensory image, the musical sound is abstract–it is incapable of representing the full range of human feelings, in the sense that a dramatic performance can. At least, then, a God representation in musical terms remains abstract, and thus incomplete in this sense. But the sense that music imagery, in perhaps the most immediate way, is feeling imagery, suggests that the complementing of the visual or figural representation with the musical gives the total image of feeling its fullest scope. Feuerbach's influence on Wagner's early conception of "The Art of the Future" and of the music drama has its sources in this conception.[19]

In feeling, then, says Feuerbach, man cannot rise beyond his own nature. Whatever is an object of feeling is so by virtue of its reception as an image of man's feeling nature. The quantitative determination of the object, its scope, or the degree to which it is perfect of its kind may vary, but the qualities of the object of feeling are forever the qualities of man's own feeling nature. The ostensibly "higher" qualities of the divine being are therefore only projections in the scope or degree of perfection of the qualities (of feeling) that the human being can conceive himself to have. His conception of these qualities is ultimately limited by his own feeling experience, that is, the experience of self-feeling, whose object is one's own feeling nature. The representation of God, as object of feeling, is in every particular, or historical case, the projection of the particular scope or limits of man's conception of his feeling in that situation, or in that historical context. The transcendental conception, of a God without limits, is in this sense a recognition of the difference between the performance and the ideal to which it attains—that is, of the infinity of feeling, and its ultimate incapacity to be satisfied by any finite representation. It is this that, in Feuerbach's view, creates the ground for the conception of the objectified image as a real or wholly *other*, that stands over and above the individual and is something ultimately beyond him in perfection and being. Feuerbach's "feeling" has much the same character as Plato's *Eros*, the child of Poverty and Plenty, whose striving for fulfillment is therefore infinite and unlimited. The opposition of the finite and the infinite case—in other words, the opposition of the human and the divine—is the illusive representation of the real opposition, namely, that between human existence and human essence. The divine, for feeling, is human essence, the nature of feeling itself freed from the limits of actual existence—a freedom, moreover, that can be represented only in the imagination, and is thus constrained, at the very least, by its representation as an image, under the conditions of sensory, individual configuration. This image is free from the constraints of empirical action and rational law. That God can be conceived under the aspect of empirical action and of rational law concerns the God who is the objectification of the will, or of the understanding, but not the God of feeling. The representation of feeling in an image of feeling entails the concept of the incarnation of God in the form of image, that is, as individual, or as person. The religious ground for Incarnation is God's love of man. Feuerbach's reductive inversion of the sense of this image is that the belief in Incarnation is the deepest expression of man's love of man: "the ground of Incarnation is . . . the need of religious feeling" (VI, 61; S: I, 104). This need is to love others, to express the essential nature of feeling as species awareness in this feeling for others. This feeling for others, or sympathy, has as its condition the community, the presence of the beloved.

God as God, as simple essence is absolutely self-subsisting, solitary Being . . . for only that can be self-subsistent which is solitary. To be capable of solitude is a mark of character and of strength of thought. Solitude is the need of the thinker, but community is the need of the heart. One can think alone, but love only with another. In love, we are dependent, for love is the need for another being. Only in the solitary act of thought are we independent. Solitude is autarchy, self-sufficiency. (VI, 81–2; S: I, 126–7)

In the religious understanding, God is led by love to the alienation of his divinity, that is, to its incarnation in an other. God is led not by self-love, but by love of humanity. The "natural reduction" of the mystery of Incarnation reveals the deepest sense of every religion, not only the Christian, says Feuerbach. It is this: "that God is not indifferent to those who worship him." But such a God is *already* human. The Incarnation is, in Feuerbach's sense, the confession of religious atheism to this truth, namely, the reduction of God to Man.

God became man out of mercy–thus he was in himself already a human God, before he became an actual man; for human want, human misery already went to his heart. The incarnation was a tear of divine compassion, and thus only the outward appearance of a being with human feeling, and therefore of an already essentially human being. (VI, 61; S: I, 104)

Thus,

God become man is only the outward appearance of man become God; for the descent of God to man is necessarily preceded by the exaltation of man to God. Man was already in God, was already God himself, before God became man, i.e., showed himself as man. Otherwise, how could God become man? The old maxim "from nothing, nothing comes" holds for this case too. (VI, 62; S: I, 104)

The Incarnation of God requires the prior humanity of God's nature, as the ground for the possibility of this Incarnation. Only the denial of this human nature to God makes the Incarnation appear as a divine mystery, as the incompatibility of the infinite with the finite. Feuerbach concludes that the Incarnate God is nothing but the human *form* of a God already human in his nature; and that the second person of the Trinity, who is incarnate, is "in reality . . . the sole, true, first person in religion," that the concept of God as *man* exhausts the nature of the Godhead, insofar as God is an object of feeling.

Wherein is the source of the "mystery" of Incarnation, then? It is, says Feuerbach, in the confusion of the God who is an object of understanding, of reason (i.e., the metaphysician's God) with the God who is an object of feeling (i.e., the religious God). The first is a God of "universal, unlimited, metaphysical being," the phenomenological object constituted by the nature of *thinking* activity. As such, it is not an object constituted by the imagination (i.e., not a sensory or personal image). The imageless God cannot be imaged without a confusion of categories, without leading to an open contradiction for thought. As perverse as it is to adduce the Incarnation as a purely empirical fact, known by revelation in the context of a theological positivism – or, as Feuerbach calls it, "the stupidest religious materialism" – it is equally perverse, he says,

to attempt to deduce the Incarnation from purely speculative, i.e., metaphysical, abstract grounds, for metaphysics applies only to the first person of the God-head, who does not become incarnate, who is not a dramatic person. Such a deduction would be justifiable only on the condition that one consciously undertook to deduce from metaphysics the very negation of metaphysics. (VI, 63; S: I, 106)

Feuerbach's conclusion is striking, in that it suggests what he takes the Incarnation as phenomenological object to be, and thus characterizes what he means by "phenomenological object": "The Incarnation, the mystery of the 'God-man,' is not a mysterious compounding of opposites, no synthetic fact as it appears to speculative philosophy of religion, because the latter takes special pleasure in contradictions. It is an analytic fact – a human word with human meaning" (VI, 69; S: I, 113).

The Incarnation, then, is constituted as an object of consciousness, that is, of feeling consciousness. As a "fact," it exists only as such an object, that is, as a "meaning" for consciousness, whose existence *is* its meaning. The "analytic fact" is in this sense a linguistic or conceptual fact, a constituent element in the universe of discourse that is the community of men, where this community itself is constituted by dialogue, and by communication of meanings. The peculiarity of this linguistic "analytic" fact is that the "fact," as a "word," is the *image* itself: God exhibited in the form of a sensory representation of His individuality and His personality. God "exists," then, only insofar as the meaning or set of meanings which the image represents. He exists therefore by virtue of the human feelings that are objectified in the image, that *make* it an image, because the very essence of the image is that it is projected feeling. "From this point of view of feeling," says Feuerbach, "only the negation of feeling is the negation of God."

What constitutes God as an object of feeling is the feeling act. But the feeling act is, in any specific instance, an act of sympathy, of love, or of suffering, or rejoicing, for the sake of the beloved. These are the "natural reductions" of the Incarnation in its concrete, practical terms, and not in theoretical or speculative terms. Thus, Feuerbach writes,

Every prayer reveals the mystery of Incarnation. Every prayer is, in fact, an incarnation of God. In prayer, I draw God into human misery, I let Him participate in my sufferings and needs. God isn't deaf to my entreaties. He is compassionate to me, and thus repudiates his divine majesty, his transcendence of all that is finite and human. He becomes a man among men. . . . The theology which denies God's capacity to suffer denies therewith also the truth of religion. (VI, 66–7; S: I, 109–10)

To the theologian's objection (*Impassibilis est Deus, sed non incompassibilis, cui proprium est misereri semper et parcere* ["God cannot suffer, but is not without compassion, for it is always his nature to pity and pardon"–Bernard de Clairvaux, *Sermones in Cantica*, serm. 26]), Feuerbach answers, "*ware nicht Mitleiden Leiden?*" ("Isn't compassion also suffering?"). He further answers that suffering itself is a participative act: "without love, no suffering," and that only the "heart" can suffer. But what is "heart," in Feuerbach's view, except the *species* consciousness of feeling. Mere pain or uniquely private feeling are not yet human feeling. In human feeling, the heart speaks to the heart, already constituting that community, that dialogue of feeling whose condition is species consciousness. "The heart can turn only to the heart; only in itself, in its own essence can it find consolation" (VI, 67; S: I, 111). Personal suffering is possible, therefore, only if personality itself is already an object of consciousness. And this is possible only in species awareness. One comes to know one's personality only in knowing it under the form of another. Thus, Feuerbach interprets John I, 4:19: "Let us love him who first loved us" as meaning "God teaches me to love by loving me" (VI, 70; S: I, 114). I learn what love is only in being loved. I learn what my feeling nature is by virtue of my standing in the relation of object to this feeling itself, as subject. The passive-active inversion of the dream (see p. 284) is embodied in the religious inversion "God loves me." Thus,

Isn't the content of divine nature human nature, if the real content of God's love is man himself? Isn't God's love of man, which is the ground and center of religion, nothing but man's love of man, objectified and conceived as the highest truth, as man's highest nature: Isn't the proposition "God loves man" an orientalism–Religion is essentially oriental–which translates into our own language as "Love of man is the most exalted thing there is"? (VI, 70; S: I, 115)

Thus, the representation of God's love of man is the clearest proof that man objectifies himself, his own feeling, in religion. "What do I love in God? Love itself, and specifically, love of man" (VI, 70; S: I, 114).

In religious consciousness, what is primary, active, is taken to be secondary, passive. The truth of religion is its expression of the primary, active nature of feeling as man's love of man (or in the species sense, his self-love). The falsity of religion is its alienation of this feeling nature as the nature of another, nonhuman or superhuman being and therefore of human feeling activity as merely passive, or responsive. The truth of religion–that is, the natural reduction of the Incarnation–is the implicit recognition, in the act of religious feeling, that God is man, that the divine is the human. The image of feeling is the Incarnate God. Man is capable of becoming divine, in his existence, because his essence, his human species nature is already divine.

The fullest expression of this human truth, in its imaginary representation, is the Christian Passion, or what Feuerbach calls "the mystery of the suffering God." Here the religious inversion is played out in dramatic form, and the key to the mystery of Christ's suffering for man is in setting right side up what is presented upside down. The Passion represents the love of man for man in the form of a fable, as God's love for man. It is an account of this love as it proves itself through suffering. "But," says Feuerbach, "that which is the essential, real meaning of the fable, its main point in the true view of religion, is only the moral of the fable, and is only the collateral importance for religious consciousness" (VI, 72; S: I, 116). Thus, the fable is the hidden, unconscious form of an act of self-recognition. It is as if one were to say, with Hamlet, "The play's the thing wherein I'll catch the conscience of the king," where Hamlet represents the conscious recognition of the play as projection, but where the king hides or suppresses his own self-recognition. The active-passive inversion is the psychological mechanism of self-hiding. The *inversion* of this inversion, setting it right side up, so to speak, is the therapy of self-revelation. In his clearest passage on this process, Feuerbach writes,

In religion, whatever is predicate should be taken as subject, and whatever is subject, should be taken as predicate. . . . Thus, the oracular sayings of religion have to be turned around, understood as *contre-vérités*, to yield truth. God suffers–(suffering is predicate)–but he suffers for man, for others, not for his own sake. What does this mean, properly translated? Nothing but: Suffering for others is Godly; whoever suffers for others, who gives up his soul, acts in a divine way, and is a God to man. (VI, 74; S: I, 118)

The Passion, then, presents us with the human truth: Love proves itself through suffering. The suffering of Christ touches on the truths of human feeling with subtle perception. What sort of suffering moves us particularly? The suffering of the innocent. What proves love to us? The suffering of self-sacrifice on behalf of the beloved. The Passion is the proof of God's love for man, but a proof in completely human terms— or better, a proof that holds up the mirror to human feeling. "Religion," says Feuerbach, "is the reflection, the mirroring of human nature in itself" (VI, 77; S: I, 122). The Christian religion, in particular, is the religion of suffering. "Suffering is the highest commandment of Christianity–the history of Christianity is the history of human suffering" (VI, 75; S: I, 119). What does the mystery of suffering reduce to? Again, to the humanity of God, or in its true translation, the exaltation of human compassion, human self-sacrifice, human suffering for the sake of another, as divine.

"God suffers" actually means "God is a heart." The heart is the source, the domain of all suffering. A being who doesn't suffer is a being without a heart. The mystery of the suffering God is therefore the mystery of feeling. A suffering God is a susceptible, feelingful God. But the statement "God is a feelingful being" is only the religious expression for the statement "Feeling is of a godly nature." (VI, 77; S: I, 121)

God's compassion for the suffering of others is also His own capacity to suffer. "The Christian religion is so little a superhuman one, that it sanctifies even human weakness," writes Feuerbach. The God who appreciates human tears is a God of feeling, the model for man's compassion for others. The full force of the centrality of suffering in the Christian conception of love is seen by Feuerbach in Luther's phrase: "To suffer evil is better than to do good."[20] Thus, the religious image of the suffering God is the objectification of man's feeling capacity, in its concrete characteristics as compassionate, as self-sacrificing, as loving through suffering. Such an image is therefore essentially dramatic. It unfolds through incident, event, action. It is a drama of human self-revelation, and to this extent, it is the education of sensibility and feeling to its own capacities. The image of God, is, in Feuerbach's phrase, "the mirror of man" (VI, 78; S: I, 122).

CHAPTER X

Reason, Existence, and Creation: God as an Ontological Principle

Reason and Existence in Religious Consciousness

If Feuerbach sees the source of the common humanity of God and man in feeling, he sees the source of the dichotomy between the divine and the human in reason. As *feeling* draws God to man, makes of Him a suffering God, sees Him as essentially human, so *reason* makes God wholly other, objectifies Him in the form of nonhuman or superhuman perfection, separates Him from man utterly. But if, on Feuerbach's thesis, this God of reason, or of the understanding, is Himself an objectification of an aspect of *human* consciousness, it has to be shown that such a God represents an analogous dichotomy in consciousness itself. The God who is wholly other is nothing but the image of the utter self-estrangement of consciousness from itself; and the sources of this self-estrangement lie in a real dichotomy within man.

Religion is man's self-estrangement: man posits God over against himself as a separate being. God is not what man is,–man is not what God is. God is infinite, man is finite; God is fully realized, man is not; God is eternal, man is temporal; God is all-powerful, man powerless; God is holy, man sinful. God and man are extremes. . . . But man objectifies his own secret essence in religion. It must therefore be shown that this opposition, this dichotomy of God and man, which is the starting point of religion, is a dichotomy within man, of man with his own essence. (VI, 41; S: I, 81)

On this reduction, the question becomes one concerning the sources of man's concept of completeness, perfection, infinity, and so forth. What are the human sources of the divine attributes? What is it that restricts man's perfection, and man's infinity? Why is man not conceived as Godlike, but as something less?

The heart of the matter, in Feuerbach's view, lies in the contrast between feeling-consciousness and reason or intellect. The former expresses man's most uniquely personal, individual concerns. Its essence is its particularity, its concreteness. Against this, there is the transcendence of personal concern: the impersonality, the abstract universality of the judge, who stands above subjective concerns of individual men and whose criterion of judgment is the truth of the way things are in themselves, wholly apart from the limited perspectives in which they appear for man. The ultimate criterion for such truth is existence, such existence as is independent of all human finitude, and therefore independent of feeling, insofar as feeling is limited by the form or the image under which it represents itself. The representation of such *independent* existence is therefore imageless, that is, abstract, nonsensory. The properties of this God of the intellect are therefore the properties of the intellect, of reason itself. What religion represents as the object of reverence is human rationality itself, in all its features: universality, objectivity, impersonality, and in particular, *unity*, in the sense that what is universally rational is *one* and not many; and *infinity*, in the sense that reason is its own autonomous lawgiver and is not bounded by anything else. To the obvious complaint that it is, in fact, the Greek philosophical concepts of reason, the metaphysical ideas of *philosophers* that have been superadded to the concept of God, Feuerbach's reply would be that the representation of reason, under the form of a divine nature, is precisely that: a *metaphysical* notion of God, whose essence stands directly in contradiction to the notion of God as essence of feeling in the same relation that human reason stands in contradiction to human feeling. The dichotomy that theology formulates is a dichotomy *in* human consciousness itself. The deception of theology does not lie in mistaking the properties of reason themselves, but in attributing them to God as independently existing Being. The falsehood introduced here, according to Feuerbach, is the ultimate denial of the humanity of reason, in the absolute separation of the human from the divine that theology introduces. The contradition entailed by this very separation is perpetuated by theology in conceiving of the personal God, who suffers, participates in finitude, appears, and dies – that is, is human in a fundamental way. How can this personal God be *identical* with the God who cannot suffer, who is infinite, invisible, and eternal? The parable that this duality represents, whose real object is the mortality of man, as person, and the immortality of the species character of reason, is taken literally by theology. *Man* becomes the parable, God the object of the parable, its meaning. What is required, says Feuerbach, is the radical inversion: God is the parable whose meaning is man.

The concept of God as rational Being does serve, however, as the projected form of man's conception of his own rationality. Once the inversion is made clear, the history of religious conceptions of the *exis-*

tence of God gives us a rich and accurate account of man's developing self-consciousness with respect to his rationality. Here the deeper purpose of Feuerbach's critique reveals itself most clearly. It is in the concept of God's *existence* that the content of the consciousness of reason – that is, of reason's self-consciousness – is exhibited. The modes of God's existence are therefore nothing but the modes of reason's *own* existence, still veiled in the anthropomorphic and contradictory language of theology, which makes this also a personal existence. If one were to strip away the concrete imagery of personality, the anthropomorphic and anthropopathic trappings of the Christian God, then what would remain would be an abstract ontology whose object is reason itself. But this reason is now taken to be independent, objective reality, or more radically, as the domain of reality itself. But this is to say no more than speculative idealism says, no more than what classical idealist metaphysics says. Therefore, the difference between idealist metaphysics and theology is a difference in logical rigor, and in abstraction, but not an ultimate difference in principle. The alienation of *human* reason, its objectification as an independent essence, as a Being (or in the fullest monistic development, as *Being* itself) merely fulfills the theological program and represents its last stage. Feuerbach's critique of the theological concepts of the existence of God has as its real object the idealist concepts of reason, of the Idea of ultimate, independent reality itself.

In Feuerbach's interpretation of the symbols in which religious consciousness incorporates the concept of reason, he carries out a thinly veiled attack on idealist philosophy in general, and fulfills, with broader scope, the critique he had leveled against Hegelian idealism earlier. Here, however, it is not merely a local attack on the Hegelian *form* that idealism takes, but a full-scale critique of the *genesis* of idealism, in religious consciousness. Feuerbach seeks to uncover the psychological process whereby human awareness of *human* rationality becomes transformed into the hypostatization of reason as Being itself, as the ground of *all* existence. Although the elements of this analysis are scattered throughout *The Essence of Christianity*, it remains a fully coherent and systematic account, and perhaps the crucial account, in terms of which Feuerbach arrives at a materialist conclusion.

The concepts of reason, as they are transformed by religious consciousness, are presented as predicates of God. But these predicates are the very ones that transcend anthropomorphic representation, in the sense that they are rationally incompatible with personal existence, as individual, finite, concrete. The concept of man that is reflected in the religious objectification of feeling, or of sensing – that is, the concept that admits of representation in the imagination – is seen to be completely excluded in the concept of reason. In this sense, the "representation" of reason is necessarily an abstract representation, in terms of predicates that admit of no anthropomorphisms. The God who is the object of the understanding, of the intellect, of reason therefore defies representation. His nature is imageless, His predicates abstract universals, such as reason alone can know. His existence and His essence are identical, and therefore His existence itself has all the predicates of His nature, among which, of course, is necessity. The necessity with which reason characterizes itself–the very ground of the universality and self-consistency of reason–is thereby ontologized: The necessity of reason is represented as the necessary existence, the necessary Being of God. This is also true of the traditional predicates of the independence or autonomy of God's Being, its characterization as having its ground in itself, as *causa sui*. And it is true of its infinity and unity and of its productivity and creativity, as the source of all existence. This is true of its characterization as the absolute criterion of reality and of truth, where reality is seen as the *being* of truth itself, that is, where truth and reality are identical. It is also true of the concepts of God's completeness, or complete self-sufficiency, the absence of all lacks, or of all insufficiencies, and therefore the absence of all desires. Related to this is the concept of God's perfection, of God as perfect Being (which, in the classic ontological argument of Anselm, brings us full circle to God as necessary Being).

These predicates, so clearly identifiable as the classic ones with which metaphysics has characterized *substance* and *Idea*, and on which it has built the idealist identity of Being and Knowing, are not merely written off as metaphysical impositions on some originally naive religious conception, but are seen by Feuerbach as dialectically parallel to and continuous with the religious conception. Insofar as religious consciousness adumbrates the dichotomy between the spirit and the flesh, in representing consciousness to itself as disembodied spirit, it provides the basis for the theological articulation of this dichotomy. The source of this dichotomy, however, lies in the common experience of the difference between feeling, desire, subjectivity, on the one hand, as consciousness of oneself in one's distinctive particularity, and, on the other hand, the impartial, dispassionate objectivity of rational judgment, as consciousness of a rule or a law that transcends all particularity and self-interest. Such a quality, as transcending man's finitude, his self-interest, is seen to stand utterly opposed to man as finite creature of sense and feeling.

God as the opposite extreme of man, as nonhuman, or impersonal being, is objectified essence of the understanding, the pure, perfect, complete divine essence is the self-awareness of the understanding, of its perfect completeness. The understanding doesn't know the sorrows of the heart. It has no desires, no sorrows, no needs, and therefore no lacks, no weaknesses, as does the heart. (VI, 42; S: I, 82)

The ideally rational man, then, also stands above such finite concerns, exclaims "All is vanity," and releases himself from bondage to the human passions. This "pure, passionate light of the Intellect" is seen, at best, as the condition toward which man's reason strives. Its *existence* is God Himself. Such a lofty conception, however, already reflects the awareness by rational consciousness of its *own* unlimitedness and is a late stage in religious conception.

The way in which you think of God is the way in which you think of yourself. The measure of your God is the measure of your understanding. If you think of God as limited, so is your understanding limited. . . . If you think of God as, e.g., corporeal being, then corporeality is the limit, the reach of your understanding; you cannot think of yourself as without body. If you deny God's corporeality, then you empower and manifest thereby the freedom of your understanding from the limits of corporeality. In the unlimited Being, you embody only your own unlimited understanding. And insofar as you declare this unlimited Being to be the most essential, highest Being, you are in fact saying no more than that understanding is itself the *être suprème*, the highest being. (VI, 48; S: I, 89)

Reason is hypostatized, or objectified, therefore, as the real subject in which these predicates inhere. It is hypostatized, however, not as some abstract substance or Idea or form, but as God. Feuerbach separates *that* which is hypostatized from the process of hypostatization itself. The process is the *self-awareness* of reason, the stages whereby reason, or the understanding, comes to know itself. But in coming to know itself, it posits itself as an other, as its own object. In theology, this object is God, whereas in speculative metaphysics, it is Substance or Idea. In either case, it posits this object as ultimately real, as necessary existence. For Feuerbach, this represents the way in which man conceives his own rationality, and the way in which he estimates its scope in knowing truth. Insofar as man conceives of the necessity, the categoricity of reason, so does he regard God as necessary being. But the attribution of existence to this necessity arises out of the conflation of truth with being or necessary existence. On Feuerbach's account, the psychological process of this conflation is this:

Whatever man conceives to be true, he unmediatedly conceives as actual [as objectively real], because originally only the actual is taken to be true – true in contradistinction from that which is merely appearance, which is merely dreamed or imaged. The concept of Being, of existence is the first and original concept of truth. Or: at first, man makes truth dependent on existence, and only later does he make existence dependent on truth. God is man's being, conceived as the perfect truth. (VI, 24; S: I, 60–1)

Such a concept of truth, however, is bounded by the *conditions* of actu
ality or of existence, that is, by conditions of determinateness. And
because, in the Hegelian context, determinateness entails negation-
that is, being *this* entails the finitude or delimitation of *not* being *that*-
every concept of truth as bounded by the concept of determinate existence is a bounded or finite concept. Thus, man's concept of his *own*
existence, insofar as he conceives of it as *complete*, or *perfect* existence,
is fraught with contradiction, because the idea of completeness or perfection entails a transcendence of all finitude, of all determinations. In
this negation of the *predicates*, or determinations of a subject, the subject itself is negated as anything existent. The subject has no necessary
existence apart from the necessity of its predicates. Feuerbach writes,

> The necessity of the subject lies only in the necessity of the predicate. You
> are a being only insofar as you are a human being. The certainty and reality
> of your existence rest only on the certainty and reality of your human proper-
> ties. What the subject is depends entirely on the predicates. The predicate is
> the truth of the subject. The subject is only the personified, existing predicate.
> The distinction between subject and predicate is only the distinction between
> existence and essence. The negation of the predicate is therefore the negation
> of the subject. What remains of human essence if you take away all the human
> properties? (VI, 23; S: I, 60)

If the existence of any subject whatever rests on the existence of its
predicates, then the concept of God's existence depends on the concept
of His predicates as necessary, as existing. "The reality of the predicate
is the only guarantee of existence," writes Feuerbach. But such a God is
a determinate being just as a human being is determinate by virtue of
being human.

> There are as many varieties of God—or, what amounts to the same thing, as
> many varieties of religion—as there are various ways in which man conceives
> of his being as the highest, most perfect being. The particular, determinate
> ways in which man conceives of God constitute his conception of truth, and for
> this very reason, also constitute his concept of perfect existence; moreover, of
> existence in general. For [in this view] only perfect existence is really existence,
> and it alone deserves the name. God exists, therefore, on the same grounds that
> he is determinate: for the quality or determinateness of God is nothing but
> the essential quality of man himself. You cannot take away the Greek proper-
> ties from a Greek without taking away his existence. It is clear from this that
> however relative a particular religion is, its certainty of God's existence is an
> unconditional certainty. For however arbitrary, or however necessary it is that
> the Greek be a Greek, it is just as necessary that his Gods be Greek beings, and
> *just* as necessary that they be really existent beings. (VI, 24; S: I, 61-2)

The *genesis* of the concept of necessary existence lies therefore in the
concept of determinate existence as necessary, in terms of the necessity
of the determinate predicates that a subject takes. But this is not its

final form, for reason. The predicates Feuerbach talks of here are the determinate predicates of *human* existence, over and above which no others are recognized. Once the human predicates are taken in their finitude, once man's reason transcends, in its conception of universality, all ethnic, particular predicates, of being *this* man or *that* man, then the predicates of reason are seen as transcending this finite humanity and are seen in Feuerbach's interpretation as the expression of universal and therefore necessary species predicates. This recognition of species universality is reason's recognition of its *own* species universality, of its *infinity*, therefore, *in its kind*, where its "kind" is reason itself. The existence of this species universality is then taken, in its necessity, as the ontological reality of the species, that is, of the universal. This "highest" or "most perfect" of all beings is represented to reason as an *other*; that is, as *objective* reason, or the God of the intellect. The predicates of this being are no longer determinate in the existential human sense, of *concrete* personality, but only as *abstract* being. But, says Feuerbach, "A God of abstract predicates also has an abstract existence" (VI, 24; S: I, 62).

What distinguishes "abstract" from "concrete" or "real" existence for Feuerbach? Precisely the predicates of spatiality, temporality, and quality (determinateness). If these are taken to be *indifferent* predicates, then the existence of which they are predicates is an indifferent existence. If the essential difference of spatial, temporal, and qualitative modes of existence is swallowed up in some conception of their essential *identity* (i.e., *indifference*), the product is an abstract, "philosophical," or "metaphysical" existence. Here Feuerbach criticizes the Spinozist concept of *substance* as representing precisely this indifferent, hence undifferentiated, "existence." The essential determinations of concrete existence—space, time, and quality—are "contradictions," in the Hegelian context that derives from scholasticism, in that they are mutually exclusive. These "contradictories" or "opposites" are united in one and the same subject. But this "unity of opposites," insofar as it is an indifferent unity, or a sheer identity, in effect abolishes *all* determinations, by assigning them all without restriction to the *same* subject, that is, to *substance*, or, what comes to the same thing, to God. Thus, Feuerbach says of Spinoza:

He [Spinoza] speaks of an infinite number of attributes of the divine substance, but he specifies none except thought and extension. Why? Because it is a matter of indifference to know them; indeed, because they are in themselves indifferent, superfluous; because with all these innumerably many predicates I say no more than what I say with these two, with thought and extension. Why is thought an attribute of substance? According to Spinoza, it is because it can be conceived by itself, because it expresses something indivisible, perfect, infinite. Why then is matter an attribute of substance: Because, in relation to itself, *it* expresses the very same thing. Therefore, substance can have indefinitely many predicates, because it isn't their determinateness, their difference which makes them attributes of substance, but rather their indifference, their identity. Or, to put it still more strongly: substance has innumerably many predicates only for the reason that—(how peculiar!)—it has properly *no* predicate, i.e., no determinate, actual predicate. The indeterminate unity of thought completes itself by the indeterminate multiplicity of the imagination. Because the predicate isn't *Multum*, it is *Multa*. The positive predicates are actually thought and extension. With these two, there is infinitely more said than with the nameless innumerable predicates; for with these two, something determinate is expressed; I know something thereby. But substance is too indifferent, too passionless to be impressed or awed by a determinate *something*. In order not to be something determinate, it rather is nothing at all. (VI, 29–30; S: I, 67–8)

The substantive Being, in whom all predicates inhere without delimitation is, in effect, an *abstract* Being in that it lacks determinate quality. Yet it is such an abstract being that turns out to be ultimately real, to have necessary existence, on the account both of speculative metaphysics and theology. The kind of being this is, from the account of its predicates, is the Being of thought, of reason itself, whose existence is exhausted in the abstract predicates of necessity, unity, infinity, independence, and so on. It is metaphysical Being, par excellence, in that its only reality lies in these abstract, "philosopher's" predicates. The infinity of predicates claimed for such a Being, is only a formal (i.e., an *empty*) infinity, that is, only the *idea* of infinity, rather than its concrete content, as infinitely rich and varied in real determinations; that is, in the multiplicity of real differences, rather than in the indifferent unity or identity of only apparent differences. It is concrete differentiation that characterizes existence, and not the transcendence of all differences. What makes for concrete differentiation is the actual differences in the predicates of spatiality, temporality, and quality. The Being who embodies this undifferentiated unity is a Being in form only, that is, abstractly, and devoid of all determinate content. To attribute real existence to such a Being is, in effect, the work of fantasy, of imagination. What makes God an imaginary object, devoid of real existence, is the attribution of nontemporal, nonspatial, abstractly infinite qualities, in Spinoza's sense of indifferent qualities, or what is the same thing, no qualities at all. To say, as Feuerbach does, that "indifferent qualities" are equivalent to "no qualities at all" is to conceive of quality, in Hegel's sense, as concrete determination, or of being a *this-such*, in Aristotle's terms. Thus, for qualities to be "undifferentiated" is for them to be indeterminate, or what is the same thing, no qualities at all. An indifferent or indeterminate quality is thus a *contradictio in adjecto*. "Existence," says Feuerbach, "is as various as are the qualities which constitute existent beings" (VI, 25; S: I, 62). But quality is that concrete character of a thing that is given in the fullest determinateness, as an object of sensation, or of feeling; the sort of thing, therefore, that can be imaged as a this or a that, having configuration, temporal boundedness, sensory or affective distinctiveness. "Only in sensibility, only in time and space does there belong an actually infinite being, rich in determinate qualities" (VI, 28; S: I, 66). A man can be a first-rate musician, or a writer, or a physician. But he cannot perform musically, write, and heal all at the same time, says Feuerbach by way of illustration. To each determinate property there is a determinate time. The unity of these properties, or predicates, is not a unity that swallows them up in an indeterminate instant, but rather one that requires time as its condition of actualization. Now one performs; later one writes, or heals. In a rare, explicit criticism of dialectical "identity," Feuerbach writes, "Time, and not the Hegelian dialectic, is the medium of uniting opposites, contradictions, in one and the same being" (VI, 28–9; S: I, 66).

But all this holds for *actual* performance, *real* practice. In *thought*, one can conceive of such an identity, in the form of a logical, or conceptual identity. The objectification of this identity or unity in thought is the abstract Being in whom all these *differentia* are atemporally, nonspatially subsumed. Such a being objectifies the unity of thought, but not by a real, concrete, or actual unity in existence. The real contradiction of theology is to insist that such a *thought* unity is identical with the personality of God, that is, His historical, temporal, qualified existence. The rigorously consistent view of reason is thereby forced into the *via negationis*, in its objectification of its own nature, in its representation of the intellect as abstract and imageless. God, as spirit, as infinite being in this abstract sense of the *idea* of infinity, can be grasped only negatively—for example, as *im*material beings, as *un*limited, *in*finite being. That is to say, God is nothing I can think determinately, for in doing so, I *know* something other than thought itself, other than the pure form, the *actus purus* of thought activity itself. When I think determinately, it is not thought, or reason, which is then the exclusive object of my thinking, but rather thinking *something*, that is, thinking a determinate content, whose source lies outside the *form* of thinking activity itself.

Feuerbach had developed this distinction in the *Dissertation*. It is not clear to what extent he saw this rigorous rationalist separation of the *form* of thought from its actual or concrete content as his own recapitulation of Kant's transcendental idealism, or to what extent he realized, either in the *Dissertation* or in *The Essence of Christianity*, the

Kantian emphasis he had given to the objective idealism of Hegel. One may take his jokingly proposed title for *The Essence*–"The Critique of Pure Unreason"–more or less seriously in this regard. But it is clear that Feuerbach's account of this rationalist version of "thought thinking itself" is a fully conscious critical account of classical idealist metaphysics, from Aristotle to Spinoza and Hegel. The value of this metaphysics, and of its correlate ontological logic, is that it represents a rigorous account of the self-conception of human reason. But just as the ontology of this account confuses the essence of reason with existence *as such*, and derives the predicate of existence from an autonomous, independent, substantive *subject*, so too does ontotheology derive existence *from* God, as the ultimately real, substantive subject. Feuerbach makes the inversion thus: "God as metaphysical Being is self-satisfied Intellect; or better: conversely, self-satisfied, self-fulfilled intellect, which takes itself as the absolute essence of thinking intelligence, is God, as metaphysical Being. All the metaphysical properties of God are therefore actual properties of Intellect, or of the Understanding" (VI, 46; S: I, 86).

Reason (Intellect, Understanding) knows itself, therefore, in knowing God as spirit, as pure intellect, as infinite intelligence; but knows itself in the form of an other. "What the understanding, what Reason is: this God alone tells you . . . God is reason expressing itself, affirming itself as the highest Being. The imagination takes reason to be a (or the) revelation of God; for reason, however, God is the revelation of reason, in that the nature, the capacities of reason are objectified in God" (VI, 45; S: I, 85). The force of Feuerbach's dictum "The consciousness of infinity is nothing but the consciousness of the infinity of consciousness" becomes clearer here. He follows this reduction of metaphysics, and of ontotheology to predicates of human reason, further into the specific reduction of specific predicates: noncontradiction, self-cause, and so forth. In each case, the characterization of God is seen to be a characterization of reason itself, and therefore of reason's self-characterization. The arguments concerning God as first cause–for example, in St. Thomas' version of the cosmological argument for the existence of God–is interpreted as reason's self-conception as original, primary Being. In effect, in deriving all things from God as first cause, reason means to derive everything from *itself* as first cause. Thus, metaphysics says clearly and openly what theology says in the guise of religion. But the content is the same. So too with the concept of the necessary rationality of reality: What is irrational contradicts itself–therefore *is* nothing, has no reality. Reason and Being are identified here. But the theological version of this metaphysical identity says, in effect, "What contradicts reason contradicts God," inverting subject and predicate terms. The attenuated theology, which uses God as a *name* for noncontradictory Reason, would subject God's activity to the rule of noncontradiction, but would save the appearances by making this rationality God's own nature. God's freedom in acting is, in effect, his action in accordance with his own nature as rational. In this sense, Reason as independent, self-causing, autonomous, is identical in all but name with God's freedom to act in accordance with His nature. What Aristotle or Kant held out as the ideality of the rule of reason, in rational beings, is hypostatized in the theological God who *does* act as man *ought* to act. The logical notion of Identity is given a nominally theological form in Leibniz's version (of the Identity of Indiscernibles) in the notion that between such indiscernibles, God could not choose. (Einstein's "God"–"complicated, but not vicious"–also takes on this nominal form.) Examples abound, and Feuerbach merely suggests the broad characterization that all such examples would take. But his general point is clear: "Reason (the understanding) is therefore the *Ens Realissimum*, the ultimately real Being of classical onto-theology" (VI, 48; S: I, 88). The God of the understanding, or of reason, is nothing but reason objectified, deified, regarded as most excellent, perfect, necessary, primal being.

The psychological sources of this concept formation are ultimately in the absurdity, the inconceivability, the utter unrationality of reason's nonexistence. "Reason" here means the self-conscious reflection on consciousness, the *Cogito* as itself an object of thought. If man's being is his thinking, and if his awareness of being is therefore thinking's self-awareness, then to *conceive* of nonbeing is to *conceive* of nonthinking, of nonawareness, which is self-contradictory, irrational. Reason therefore affirms its own existence in its activity, as the necessity of its being what it is. It is the necessity in existence that it transfers to God, as the objectification of reason. In this necessity, it founds its autonomy, its nondependence on anything beyond it for its existence. And thereby it derives *all* existence from itself as ground. "The Understanding, or Reason is ultimately that Being which is necessary. Reason *is*, because only the existence of reason *is* reason. For if there were no reason, no consciousness, all would be nothing. Being and non-Being would be equivalent. It is consciousness which first established the difference between Being and non-Being" (VI, 52; S: I, 93). But reason takes this necessity of Being as an ontological principle: Without consciousness, without reason, there is no world. The world's own necessity lies therefore in the necessary existence of reason. God, as Reason, is therefore the "domain of all reality," the source of all Being, and is therefore the world-creating principle, in the theological image of reason. Reason therefore creates the necessity of a world out of the necessity, *to itself,* of its own existence. Therefore, the world creation is not out of *nothing*, but out of *need, Penia*: reason's need for its own self-existence. The necessity for the existence of a world lies therefore in the self-conscious existence of reason. Self-consciousness itself is therefore the world-creating principle. The teleology of reason, its self-fulfillment, its self-necessity as its own end, is thus taken to be the ultimate ontological ground of Being. "It is reason that is the self-consciousness of Being, or is self-conscious Being. It is only in Reason that the purpose and meaning of Being is revealed. Reason is the objective Being which is its own end – the final cause of things. What is its own object, that is the highest, ultimate Being; what rules itself, that is all-powerful" (VI, 53; S: I, 95).

Thus, Feuerbach, in what amounts to a paraphrase of idealist metaphysics and theology, attempts to show that the concept of necessary existence, propounded in terms of ontology, or of ontotheology, derives from the psychological impossibility of a self-denying or self-negating consciousness. The recognition of the value or meaning of existence is therefore nothing but the self-recognition by reason of its own value, as ultimate. In affirming the value and meaning of *existence* as such, man does no more than affirm the value and meaning of his own existence, as self-conscious, rational being, as the highest of all things. The term that mediates between existence as such and human existence, in this relation, is God. For if all reality is *in* God, and if all meaning and value lie in God as the domain of all reality, then by showing that this God is the embodiment of reason's self-conception, and further, by showing that this reason is man's species nature or his essence, it then follows that the meaning and value of "existence" are nothing but the meaning and value of man's rational nature as he represents this nature to himself. Again, the Feuerbachian formula is realized: The deification of reason is the deification of man's reason; thus, God is the deification of man's own nature.

This, then, is the analysis that Feuerbach gives of God as a Being of the understanding. The critical import of his argument is philosophically more crucial, however, in Feuerbach's development. For in this account, although it is manifestly a critique of the alienation of reason in religious consciousness, it is at the same time a critique of classical metaphysics. For in this analysis of the genesis of the concepts of God's predicates – necessity, infinity, autonomy, and so on – Feuerbach seeks to establish that the metaphysical concepts of substance, of Idea, and of the predicates of Being are nothing but a further development of a still religious consciousness; that metaphysics is, in effect, the continuation of theology by other means; and that the alienation of reason in the religious, theological conceptions of God's Being is brought to its fullest formal expression in idealist metaphysics. In short, Feuerbach's thinly veiled purpose is to show that metaphysics is the last stage of theology, and that the essential contradictions in theology are retained in metaphysics, though in abstract form, stripped of the imagery of personality that theology retains.

Feuerbach's analysis and critique seem to take on a Kantian character here. In deriving the metaphysical concepts of necessity, ground, first cause, and so forth, from the nature of reason itself, as the forms under which reason can conceive *itself*, Feuerbach seems to be making the antimetaphysical reduction to epistemology that Kant made. The forms under which reason can conceive of existence are the forms of reason itself, and in this sense, transcendental forms. To know the rule of reason, in the Kantian framework, is to know that self-regulating necessity that constitutes the autonomy, the infinity–the freedom, therefore– of reason. For Kant, as for Hume before him, *existence* itself cannot be derived from the conditions of reason, or from thought, however much our *knowledge* of existence is "objective," except in the sense that it is constrained by the necessary forms of reason. And Feuerbach's critique of the ontologizing idealists, and of Hegel in particular, superficially seems to be no more than a reformation of this Kantian view. The conditions of the existence of reason, the predicates under which reason knows *itself* become predicates of reality or of existence only by a metaphysical sleight of hand, a mystical and fantastic conflation of reason with Being. Kant's, and Hume's, conclusion is agnostic: The conditions of reason are not the conditions of existence as such. Or, in terms of God's Being, the conditions of our knowledge of God are not and cannot be known to be the conditions of God's existence. In this sense, the Humean and Kantian emphasis on the forms of our knowledge, and of our belief, seem to be paralleled by Feuerbach. But neither Hume nor Kant take the step that Feuerbach does, which goes beyond agnosticism, and beyond the pragmatism of belief that the others jointly propose: namely, the step of asserting that God is nothing but what He is constituted as by these forms; that there is no beyond, no *jenseits* that exceeds the scope of our knowledge, of our reason. In Feuerbach's terms, it is not the case that we can have only a finite and limited knowledge of God's Being, because of the constraints, the necessities of our faculties. It is not meaningful to say that one can or cannot *prove* God's existence rationally, or deduce it syllogistically, or as a necessary truth, from unconditionally true premises. Rather, for Feuerbach, the question of *proving* God's existence becomes a *meaningless* question once it is revealed that the "existence of God" is the unconscious religious metaphor for the existence of man's self-consciousness. There is no room, then, for agnosticism, nor as Feuerbach often reiterates, for philosophical atheism. Because the subject, God, is nothing without predicates, "God's" existence is entirely subsumed in the existence of these predicates. "A real atheist," writes Feuerbach, "in the ordinary sense, therefore, is one for whom the predicates of Divine Being . . . are nothing, but not one for whom only the subject of these predicates is nothing" (VI, 26; S: I, 63). The term "God" is therefore analytically identical with the predicates with which religious consciousness and, therefore, metaphysical theology have endowed it. There is therefore no room for the agnostic "something more" that lies beyond the predicates, or beyond the knowledge of these predicates. Although one may sometimes read such an interpretation into some of Kant's religious criticism (e.g., in the passages from *Vorlesungen* . . . that Feuerbach cites: "Fundamentally, we cannot conceive of God otherwise than by attributing to him every reality which we discover in ourselves, but attributing them to God without limitations." "God is, as it were, the moral law itself, but conceived in personified form"), one cannot push Kant further than an "as if" or an "as it were," to the full reduction of Godhood to man's conception of his *own* nature, his *own* predicates as divine. The agnostic principle remains a two-edged sword in Kant's philosophy of religion, as it does in Hume's. Therefore, the issue over Feuerbach's "Kantianism," and his affinities to Hume, that has arisen in Feuerbach scholarship is never sharply set forth as an issue of whether Feuerbach was or was not a Kantian *au fond*, but rather as one regarding the degree of his indebtedness to Kant. On one extreme, some commentators claim that Feuerbach's philosophy of religion is only the fully realized consequence of Kant's. On the other, Feuerbach is seen to be the direct heir of Epicurean, Baconian, and Hobbesian views in this regard, and therefore such a view decries the Kantian label. In between, there is the qualified view that sees Feuerbach's respect for Kant not only in his explicit statements (e.g., "Kant represents the revolution, Hegel the restoration"), but also in the content of his "anthropological" reduction. Whatever judgment one may make, it is clear that Feuerbach's reduction of the metaphysical Being of God to the species nature of human reason is more radical than either Kant's or Hume's, though it is unquestionably related in many ways to the humanist and antimetaphysical elements in the thought of both of these astute critics.

The issue of Feuerbach's critique is this: that God's Being is now seen as a phantasm of thought, *if* it is taken in the sense of metaphysical Being, in the sense of ontotheology. For the Being of metaphysics is a Being spun from the self-reflection of human reason, and is therefore nothing but the "being" of self-consciousness. It is the unconditional affirmation of one's own conscious awareness, in one's consciousness of *being* conscious. Without determinate content, such an awareness is totally formal, or abstract. Its "existence" is recognized, on rational reflection, as the condition for the "existence" of anything else, *in thought*. Simply stated, *being aware* is the logical precondition *for being aware of something*, X. But such "logical" existence is not the condition for the existence of X. The 100 imaginary dollars and the 100 real dollars may both be said to "exist," one in the imagination, the other in sensuous, qualitied space and time. But one cannot produce the 100 real dollars out of the imagination. No more can one produce existence out of reason, or thought. But if God, as metaphysical Being, *is* the being of thought—if this *kind* of Being is, in fact, self-conscious Being—then the archconfusion of this view is to derive the existence of the world from *this* being. Feuerbach concludes that however rational in form speculative metaphysics is, it still commits this mystification, this inversion of dependent and independent terms. The essence of ontotheology, as of idealist philosophy in general, is expressed in this confusion. Its clearest expression is in the concept of creation, in what Feuerbach calls the "world-creating principle in God." In his analysis of the concept of creation, Feuerbach probes deeper for the psychological sources of this concept in ego consciousness itself. In Chapter III of *The Essence of Christianity*, on "God as Essence of the Understanding," this psychogenesis is suggested, but not elaborated. Rather, in this chapter he fulfills the critique of classical metaphysics that he had undertaken in *The Critique of Hegelian Idealism*. Now the sources of metaphysical thought itself are to be laid bare: In examining the notion of God as Creator, or as world-creating principle, Feuerbach hopes to show the source of classical metaphysics in religious consciousness.

CREATION: AS SELF-DIFFERENTIATING REASON AND AS WISH FULFILLMENT

Feuerbach deals with the concept of creation in two contexts. The first is the concept of creation *out of* some primordial or original Being, that is, the creation of a world by the *self-differentiation* of some original Being. The second is the concept of creation *from nothing*, the miraculous creation that stands beyond explanation by a principle. The first is therefore rational in form, the second irrational. But both concepts are interpreted, in Feuerbach's naturalistic and psychological reduction, as expressing nothing but man's conception of his own nature: in the first case, that of self-consciousness, and in the second, that of supernatural fulfillment of wish, or the unlimited satisfaction of feeling needs, in the fantasy life of consciousness. Both of these concepts stand apart from the concept of the *origin* of the world, and Feuerbach introduces the distinction between *creation* and *origin* to mark the difference between religious and natural-scientific concepts. In the religious conception, Feuerbach repeats, man's nature itself is the object of consciousness. Insofar as the world enters into this conception, it serves only as the objective symbol for this human nature, and has no significance in itself. By contrast, the basis for the scientific (i.e., nonreligious) conceptions is the real otherness, the objective independence of the world, or of nature, from man's consciousness of himself. But Feuerbach recognizes that both concepts, the religious and the scientific, are complexly interwoven, and the framework of natural-scientific accounts of *origin* has to be disentangled from the framework of *creation* as a mystical account of self-consciousness.

CREATION AS SELF-DIFFERENTIATING AND DEPENDENT REASON

Just as God, insofar as He is a metaphysical Being, with metaphysical attributes, is an objectification of reason, or is the symbol in which reason projects its own nature as an object of consciousness, so too, God, as world-creating principle, embodies reason's self-conception as *productive* and *self-differentiating*. "God creates the world" means "God creates that which is *other* than, or *different* from God." This activity of creation is therefore an activity of self-differentiation, or, in classical terms, it is the proliferation of the *many* out of the *one*. Thus, this principle of creation finds its expression in the logic and metaphysics of the *One* and the *Many*. The sources of this abstract theological and cosmological problem are seen by Feuerbach in the difference between the nature of God, conceived as an object of the intellect (i.e., abstract, imageless, "invisible" Being, which is undifferentiated, and above all, *one*, simple and universal) and the nature of the world, conceived as an object of perception (i.e., concrete, "visible" Being, which is differentiated, manifold). In Feuerbach's reconstruction of the logic of creationist views, he shows that, on a rational account, the derivation of the perceptual manifold from the intellective abstract unity of God cannot be *immediate*. Such *immediacy* would in effect be miraculous, and thus irrational. The opposition, in logical terms, between God and world, needs to be mediated by an intermediate term. The opposed natures require the mediation of a nature that at the same time participates in the Godhead, as abstract, imageless perfection, and in the world, as finite, imageable existence. In the theological account, this function is represented by the second person of the Trinity: "The second Person, as God revealing, manifesting, declaring himself (*Deus se dicit*) is the world-creating principle in God" (VI, 98; S: I, 146). The Son, though a different person from the Father, yet, as *image* of the Father, is of like nature. "The second person, as begotten, as not *a se*, not existing of himself, has the fundamental condition of the finite in himself. But at the same time, he is not yet an actually finite Being, posited outside God; rather, he is still identical with God—as identical as the son is with the father" (S: II, 573). The possibility of such mediation, of a δεμιουργος who participates both in the nature of God, as infinite, and in the nature of the world, as finite, is not a possibility of reason, but of imagination:

> The opposition between the non-sensible or invisible divine nature and the sensible or visible nature of the world is nothing but the opposition between the nature of abstraction and the nature of sense-perception. But it is the imagination or fantasy which connects abstraction and sense perception. Consequently, transition from God to the world, by means of the second person is nothing but the objectified transition from abstraction to sense-perception, by means of the imagination. It is fantasy, imagination alone which mediates, transcends the opposition between God and world. All religious cosmogonies are fantasies, every mediating being between God and world, however one may conceive it, is a fantasy-being. The psychological truth and necessity which lies at the foundation of all these theogonies and cosmogonies is the truth and necessity of the imagination as a middle term between the abstract and the concrete. And the general task of philosophy, if it is a fully self-conscious philosophy, in investigating this subject matter, is to make clear the relation of imagination to reason, to explain the genesis of the image whereby an object of thought becomes an object of sense, of feeling. (S: II, 574)

The first approach to an explanation of the religious concept of creation is therefore to state in its sharpest form the contradiction between the two polarities, God and world, and to show that a rational resolution of this contradiction is impossible. With God, however, all things are possible, precisely because God fulfills the function of unlimited imagination, bound neither by empirical law nor by reason's rule of noncontradiction. The conceptual gap is crossed by this unbounded imagination. Rational self-consciousness, whose object is the abstract form of reason itself, nevertheless requires that its imageless object *be* imagined, if it is to relate the objects of reason to the objects of perception. The world, after all, is constituted of perceptual objects, whose character is that they are *not*-me, lie outside me, or outside my consciousness, as distinctive others. But they are not totally beyond me, beyond my consciousness, because as they can be *known* by me, they can be objects of my consciousness. The exoteric epistemology of the subject-object relation is represented in esoteric form in the religious concept of creation. Its secret, however, is revealed as a psychological process, the process by which the ego comes to know the world as nonego. The mystery of creation is reduced to the workings of consciousness itself, in coming to know its own otherness; in coming to realize itself as a process of self-differentiation–or, in the terms in which Feuerbach, following Fichte and Hegel, had already defined it, the process by which consciousness posits its own nature as an object. Feuerbach's aim, however, is to go further. He wants to reduce the abstract terminology of reason and perception, God and world, the Fichtean dialectic of ego and nonego, to explicitly human terms. He wants to descend from the heaven of speculative philosophy to the earth of human psychology. He wants to show, in effect, that both theology and speculative philosophy are esoteric expressions of a plain and profound truth of human concept formation. But the clear wish to accomplish this is tangled in the very language of speculative philosophy, which remains inadequate and inappropriate to the task. In a striking and important passage, he writes, "This world-creating process is therefore nothing but the mystical paraphrase of a psychological process, nothing but the objectification of the unity of consciousness and self-consciousness" (VI, 99; S: I, 146).

What is a promise of clarity in the first half of the sentence is lost in the obscurity of the second half. What is this "unity of consciousness and self-consciousness"? How are we to make "human" sense out of this terminology? Feuerbach provides the difficult series of reductive translations, and rescues his meaning. His paraphrase of Hegel is clear here, as he invokes again the dialectic of the *Phenomenology*: *Unmediated* self-consciousness is impossible, because the very condition of consciousness is that it have an object. The process of self-consciousness therefore requires an object as *other* than itself. This *other*, as *unmediated* other, cannot simply be consciousness itself as its own unmediated object. It too needs to be mediated. As it is *in itself*, it is not an object *for me*. Insofar as it is an *object for me*, its unconditional otherness is mediated by its being, in some sense, *like me*. The ancient dictum "Like is known by like" is once again invoked here. The middle or mediating term has to share in the nature of both mediated terms. It is therefore both *like me* and *not me*; not an *it*, therefore, but a *Thou*. The condition for my knowing the *other*–now revealed as *world* (i.e., of being *conscious*)– is that this knowledge is mediated by my knowledge of myself, in the form of another, as a *Thou* that mirrors me to myself–that is by my *self-consciousness*. Self-consciousness is therefore the condition of consciousness of the world. And self-consciousness can be achieved only by my self-differentiating consciousness that permits me to know another as *like myself* (or, equivalently, to know myself in the form of another).

This abstract Hegelian dialectic is thus seen to be formally equivalent to that between *God*, as first person of the Trinity (self-consciousness: God thinks himself), *world* (the *other* of consciousness, as unmediated), and the second person of the Trinity, the *Logos* (the mediation between God and world, the world-creating principle, the *Thou*). What is required for the next step in reductive translation is to give these phenomenological terms their psychological translations. Here Feuerbach formulates the relation as one between ego and world (in a way that presages the Freudian formulation uniquely); ego consciousness, in itself, is unlimited. Unconstrained by an *other*, it is, in the terms already discussed, in relation both to feeling and to reason, *infinite* (see p. 269). Limitation is introduced by consciousness of the world. This bounds "the impulse of my ego, my selfhood, to unlimitedness." I mediate this absolute opposition, between the ego drive, to unlimitedness, and the limitation enforced on it by an alien world. "I must introduce, prepare, moderate this contradiction by means of the consciousness of a being who is indeed an other, and thereby gives me the measure of my limitation; but in such a way as to simultaneously affirm my own nature, to objectify it for me" (VI, 99; S: I, 147). The shock, the trauma of constraint and delimitation by an alien world is mediated for me by the more sympathetic constraint of an other who is not entirely alien. I am prepared for world consciousness by my consciousness of other men.

The consciousness of the world is a humiliating consciousness—the act of creation is an "act of humility"—but the first stone upon which the pride of egohood is broken is the *Thou*, the other *I*. The ego first steels its glance in the eye of a *Thou*, before it can endure the perception of a being which does not reflect its own image. My fellow-man is the bond between myself and the world. I am, and feel myself to be dependent on the world because I first feel myself to be dependent on other men. If I didn't need other men, I wouldn't need the world either. I reconcile myself with the world, befriend it only through my fellow-man. Without these others, the world would be not only dead and empty for me, but also meaningless and incomprehensible. Only in his fellow-man does man become clear to himself, and self-conscious. But only when I am clear to myself is the world clear to me. A man existing completely for himself would lose himself, as an undifferentiated and selfless being in the ocean of nature. He would neither comprehend himself as man, nor nature as nature. Man's first object is man. The sense of nature, which the consciousness of the world as world first reveals to us, is a later development, which arises by the act of man separating himself from himself. The Greek nature-philosophers were preceded by the so-called seven wise men, whose wisdom had immediate reference only to human life. (VI, 99–100; S: I, 147–8)

This perceptive passage, however rich in psychological insight, appears to be only dimly related to the symbol of world creation, whose content it is supposed to reveal. How does the condition of *knowledge* of the world get transformed by religious consciousness into the act of *creation* of the world? The key is in the term "dependency." Man's need for the world, his dependency on it is a brute fact of his existence. The *human* sense of this existence is man's dependency on his fellow man for existence in the world. This *natural* and *social* dependency is transformed by religious consciousness as a *represented* dependency, in consciousness. It is the dependency of my consciousness on what lies beyond it, on what I am conscious of as the objective content of my consciousness, without which it would be an empty consciousness; that is, it would think *nothing*, and therefore *not* think at all. Its very existence *is* its thinking, so it has an existential need for a content, for an object. This need, this *Penia*, this requirement for *otherness*, therefore for self-differentiation, for self-alienation, as a very condition for existence, is expressed in the creative impulse, the productive activity of consciousness.

Thus, what is represented in two ways—first in the religious consciousness of man's alienation from the world, as his object; and second, in speculative philosophy (in Hegel's *Phenomenology*, for example) as the self-differentiation and self-alienation of consciousness, as its very condition for existence as consciousness—is really a *human* fact: *The need of consciousness for an object, or the need of God to create a world, is nothing but man's need of other men as the very condition of his human existence.* Feuerbach specifies that the *existence* he is talking about is human existence, and not existence in either a physical or metaphysical sense. Man's dependency on the world for his physical existence does not enter into conscious awareness as an unmediated fact, no more than it enters into the conscious awareness of any existing nonhuman being or any animal. This is a *fact* of existence, but not the *idea* of existence. What makes man's existence distinctively human is his awareness of dependency in mediated, that is, human terms: dependency on another *conceived of* like himself, anthropomorphically. Therefore, his very existence as a *human* being depends on this form of *self*-consciousness, albeit in alienated form. What the human fact of creation, then, comes to is man's *creation of his own human nature*, under the form of another. Its otherness, its alienated form leads the not fully self-conscious self-consciousness to posit a world as the symbol of this otherness, and to carry out the metaphor in the concept of *world* creation. But this "world" is not yet the real world, but rather man's projection of himself, of his own nature as world nature. The creation of a world is therefore the mystical, anthropomorphic reflection of the human fact of man's creation of his own nature, in his species activity as conscious being.

The second level of this reductive interpretation is clearly the creation of man. For if God creates man, in his own image, on the religious account, the interpretation clearly follows that man creates other men, in his own image. But God creates man out of need, out of love, ostensibly out of a desire to fulfill His own nature. Translation: Man "creates" other men out of need, love, desire to fulfill his own nature. His need is his dependency on other men for his own existence. His need for others is a self-need, an existential need. Thus, his "creation" of other men, is the creation of his own nature, mediated by the necessity of others, by his concourse with others like himself. In phenomenological terms, that is, in its reflection in consciousness, this social human dependency is describable as the consciousness of self-consciousness. Therefore, it is not merely the awareness of others, for this consciousness even animals have, but the awareness of others as *like* myself. This is, then, also an awareness of myself *in* others, and therefore the awareness of my self-awareness (or the consciousness of my self-consciousness), because the others are *like* me precisely in the sense that they are conscious of me as an other like themselves.

The "mystery" of creation is therefore the transformation of need, wish, desire, dependency into immediate fulfillment. To have a need is not yet to fulfill it, in real life. But in the life of imagination, to have a need is tantamount to its fulfillment. Whatever I express a desire for, is thereby magically "created" for me by imagination, as the instrument of unlimited feeling, which fulfills itself infinitely (see p. 281). "Creation" is therefore the act of imagination, which bridges the gap between the subject (need) and the object (fulfillment). In the case of creation, however, the need is not a sensuous or feeling need, as much as it is the need of reason itself for content, of form for matter, of the intellect for its object, if it is to be more than empty, formal activity. The echoes of all the classic theories of *Eros*, of the *Conatus* of the intellect, of the intellectual love of God, from Plato, through Plotinos, through the medieval mystics, through Spinoza and Hegel are heard here, refocused in Feuerbach's interpretation. Imagination therefore effects the unity of abstract form and sensuous or feeling content, in the fantasy of creation. The fantasy, like all fantasies, has its natural counterpart, its masked meaning, as it represents the requirement of human reason for an empirical and affective content. This in turn is nothing but the reflection in consciousness of man's need for other men, as a requirement of his very *rationality itself*; his dependency, therefore, as *rational* being, upon a community of reason. If, in any sense, human existence is rational existence, then human existence depends on the dialogue of reason. Its need finds its fantastic expression in the immediacy of imaginative fulfillment, that is, in the principle of world creation. But this expression is the "mystical paraphrase of a psychological process," and the "unity of consciousness and self-consciousness" is the psychological fact of my self-consciousness under the form of a consciousness of an other, like myself.

This rather strained and difficult dialectic of self and other, following the logic of Hegel's *Phenomenology*, leads us to an impasse, suggested earlier. If, on the one hand, reason is the activity of solitude, independence, self-sufficiency, but feeling or love is dependency ("One can think alone, but love only with another" [VI, 81–2; S: I, 126–7, see p. 288]), then this need of reason for its other, for self-differentiation, comes as a surprise. Either there is a contradiction in human nature, between reason as both self-sufficient *and* dependent, or there is a contradiction in the conception of reason as it is expressed in conceptions of God's nature. Because, for Feuerbach, the latter conception of reason or of God derives from man's awareness of his own, human reason, the contradiction must be in human reason itself. For otherwise, how could it conceive of itself as both self-sufficient and dependent. Feuerbach's earliest work—the *Dissertation*—attempted to resolve the contradiction by means of a Hegelian conception of Reason as, at the same time, One, Universal, and Infinite *and* as *constituted* by a community. The Hegelian identity theory, of unity in difference, provided the resolution of this One-Many problem. Yet it remains unresolved in the mutually exclusive predicates of self-sufficiency and dependence as it remains unresolved in the mutually exclusive characterizations of God as self-sufficient Being, and as a Being who creates the world out of need (the need of His self-realization in an other). Plato suggests the resolution, followed by later theology, that God creates the world not out of need, but out of fullness of Being; therefore, as an act of grace, not of necessity. Platonistic and Augustinean theology thereafter emphasizes this voluntarism, in the conception of a God whose free activity determines His nature, rather than one whose nature determines His activity. But such a God, on Feuerbach's reductive interpretation, would be precisely a creature of the imagination rather than one of reason, that is, one constrained by the determinations of reason, its laws and its limits. With Reason, all things are *not* possible. Self-contradiction is impossible. The principle of sufficient reason holds sway, and the principle of identity (of indiscernibles) is such that God cannot choose between indiscernibles. A dependent God, who creates the world out of need, is reason conceived of as dependent, as requiring an other, as self-consciousness in Feuerbach's and Hegel's sense. Never mind that the other is the self regarded as other, for if the *Thou* is nothing but the *I* in its otherness, the *I-Thou* is no longer real dependency, but the false appearance of dependency, the corruption of dependence on an other to mere self-dependence, which is no dependence at all. However theology or abstract metaphysics may have resolved this problem, by interpreting God's "dependence" on the world *as* such self-dependence (in the conception of God as *causa sui,* or as independent ground), Feuerbach cannot appeal to this resolution without abandoning the very ground of his analysis of the concept of creation, as arising out of the *real* dependence of human beings, and on nature, for their very existence.

One alternative suggests itself, but it is not yet introduced by Feuerbach at this point. That is, that reason itself, far from being the opposite of feeling, in its predicates, is *like* feeling, precisely in its condition of dependency. Reason requires the *other,* the *Thou,* no less than does feeling. But then reason becomes a *kind* of feeling, or a mode of feeling, and of sensibility. Or it becomes a kind or mode of perception, of sensory awareness. The difference in reason is simply that the infinite and unrestrained fulfillment of feeling, in the imagination, now comes under the constraints of reason. Thought activity, intellect, becomes nothing but rationalized feeling. To put this another way is to give the clue to Feuerbach's later development: Reason becomes the instrument of feeling, the adaptation of wish to reality, the constraint on merely fantastic fulfillment, in the Imagination. And thus it becomes the means whereby feeling both realizes its dependency and can act to satisfy its needs, not in fantasy, but in reality. It takes feeling out of itself, therefore, just as it takes mere sensory intuition out of itself.

To achieve this rationalization of feeling, of sensibility, Feuerbach has to go beyond the analysis in *The Essence of Christianity,* however. He has to go beyond this critical phenomenology of religious consciousness to a "positive" philosophy, in which these characterizations of reason and feeling form the basis for a "new philosophy."

In this account of creation, as a projection of man's dependence on other men, on his need for an other as a condition both of consciousness and of self-consciousness, the "other" remains exclusively *human.* What of man's dependence on the natural world, on matter, as a condition for his existence? Here, Feuerbach says, insofar as the world is conceived of as matter, in religious and metaphysical theories of creation, this matter itself is seen as God's mind, or the Idea, in its other-being, and not as independent substance. Even matter, in this transformation, becomes nothing but the condition for self-consciousness, and is, therefore, dependent being, having its being in being-thought.

Feuerbach characterizes this view as the "Christian" mediation of the "pagan" view that the world is "objectively eternal," and sees this as an example of the principle of absolute subjectivity characteristic of Christian thought:

> No matter how much the Christian philosophers and theologians talked about creation from nothing, they couldn't circumvent the old sayings, *From nothing nothing comes*, because it expresses the law of thought. . . . The difference between pagan eternity of matter and Christian creation, in this regard, is only that the pagan attributed an actual objective eternity to the world, whereas the Christian attributed to it only a non-objective eternity. Things subsisted before they existed, but as objects of Spirit, not of sense-perception. The Christians, whose principle is the principle of absolute subjectivity, mediate everything in terms of this principle. (VI, 101–2; S: I, 150)

Thus, "the world is eternal in God." But this means, says Feuerbach, that I can derive the world only from itself.

> The world has its ground in itself, as does everything in the world which deserves the name of a real being. The *differentia specifica*, the originating essence which determines that a particular being is what it is, is always, in an ordinary sense, inexplicable, underivable, *is* through itself, has its grounds in itself.
>
> The difference between the world and God as creator of the world is therefore only a formal, and not a real difference. . . . God's Being is nothing but the abstract, derived Being of the world as it is conceived in thought. The Being of the world is nothing but the actual, concrete, sensibly-given Being of God. Creation is therefore also nothing but a formal act. For, although what was an object of thought, of the understanding, before creation, becomes, by creation, an object of sense-perception; its content remains the same, even though it still remains inexplicable how an actual, material entity could be produced by a mental entity. (VI, 102–3; S: I, 151)

CREATION FROM NOTHING

In contrast to the idea of creation that sees it as the necessary self-differentiation and self-elaboration of reason, Feuerbach interprets the idea of *creation from nothing* as a pure expression of the imagination, freed from all rational constraints, and projecting the irrational wish to supersede all natural necessity. Feuerbach writes,

> The highest point of the principle of subjectivity is the creation from nothing. Just as the [idea of] the eternity of the world or of matter signifies nothing but the essentiality of matter, so the [idea of] creation from nothing signifies the nothingness of the world. . . . The being or non-being [of the world] depends only on the will. (VI, 121; S: I, 172)

The will, on this view, can call the world into existence, or can annihilate it, as it pleases. Thus, the creation from nothing is the highest expression of omnipotence. But omnipotence is nothing but subjectivity exempting itself from all objective determinations and limits, and celebrating this exemption as the highest power and reality there is – the power to subjectively transform what exists into nonexistence, to realize as possible anything that can be imagined; the power of the imagination, or what comes to the same thing, the power of the will which is identical with the imagination, the power of wish-fulfillment. (VI, 121; S: I, 172–3)

Feuerbach sees the deeper source of the idea of creation from nothing in *feeling*, in the tendency of feeling to objectify itself. It is the word become flesh, but in the sense that the word expresses the deepest desires of feeling, to realize itself immediately. The nature of subjective willfulness is to achieve its satisfaction without constraint. In this sense, Feuerbach sees the idea of the creation from nothing as identical with the idea of miracles, and of providence. In both cases, it is human need, human wish that is fulfilled. But what is at the basis of the wish? Feuerbach sees it ultimately as an expression of man's self-esteem, man's conviction that the world exists for his sake, for the fulfillment of his needs, that he stands at the center of creation as its purpose for being and as its beneficiary. "Providence," Feuerbach writes, "is a human excellence. It expresses the worth of man in distinction from all other natural beings and things. It expresses for him the interconnectedness of the universe. Providence is man's conviction of the infinite worth of his own existence" (VI, 123; S: I, 177). So, too, the miracle is testimony for providence; the miracle violates nature and natural necessity for man's sake.

The creation from nothing is one with the miracle, and with providence; for the idea of providence – fundamentally, in its true religious significance, where it is not yet constrained and limited by the unbelieving understanding – is identical with the idea of the miracle. The proof of providence is the miracle. The belief in providence is the belief in a power which can command whatever pleases it, and before which all the powers of the world are nothing. Providence suspends the laws of nature; breaks the course of necessity, the iron band that inexorably binds effect to cause; in short, it is the same unlimited, all-prevailing will which brings the world into being out of nothing. The miracle is a *creatio ex nihilo*, a creation from nothing. Whoever makes wine out of water makes wine out of nothing, for the prerequisites for wine are not in the water. Otherwise, the bringing forth of wine from water wouldn't be miraculous, but only a normal everyday matter. (VI, 122–3; S: I, 174)

If, in providence, and in miracles, God expresses His love of man, his concern for man's weal and woe, then the anthropological reduction of this conviction of religious consciousness is that, in his belief in providence and in miracles, man expresses his self-love and his self-concern.

The belief in a providential God is therefore belief in providence itself, in which my will, my wish, my desire are seen as God's will. "God's love of me is nothing but my own self-love made into a God," writes Feuerbach, "but this is nothing other than the belief in human worth, the belief in the divine significance of the human being" (VI, 126; S: I, 178). The secret of this mystification is explained by Feuerbach on the basis of the distinction between *ground* and *purpose* or *goal*.

If man . . . is the purpose of creation, he is also the true ground of creation as well, for the purpose of an activity is its principle. The difference between man as the purpose of creation, and as its ground is only that the abstract, derived essence of man is taken as ground, while the actual, individual person is taken as purpose. Man knows himself to be the purpose, but not the ground of creation because he takes another personal being, distinct from himself, as its ground. (VI, 127; S: I, 179)

Thus, man alienates his essence, as ground of creation, in God, in this case as well. Insofar as creation from nothing is a violation of nature, or of natural law, Feuerbach sees in it the separation of man from nature. For the creation from nothing is not an act expressing the truth and reality of nature, but rather the truth and reality of personality or of subjectivity. In asserting this as the highest truth, man marks his break with nature, or his transcendence of natural necessity. "Man differentiates himself from nature. This difference is his God—the differentiation of God from nature is nothing but the differentiation of man from nature" (VI, 128; S: I, 180). But, says Feuerbach, man thus marks himself off as a *super*natural being. The difference between pantheistic and personalistic views of God's nature is resolved here, claims Feuerbach, into the question of whether man is natural being or transcends nature. Whereas pantheism, in effect, identifies man with nature, personalism isolates or separates him from nature. One sees God as the essence of nature, the other, as the essence of transcendent human personality. The latter, subjectivist-personalist view expresses itself in the idea of creation from nothing. What is created from nothing, *is* nothing. By contrast to man's importance, to man's self-worth, the world is nothing. Feuerbach describes it thus:

The *nothing* from which the world is brought forth, is its own nothingness. Insofar as you say "The world is created from nothing," you think of the world as nothing, you clear away all the constraints on your fantasy, on your will; for it is the world which constrains your will and feeling. . . . Thus, you subjectively annihilate the world. You are one with God, in thought; He is yours alone, as unbounded subjectivity, as the soul enjoying itself alone, without need for the world, and without suffering the painful bonds of matter. In the innermost recesses of your soul, you want to deny the existence of the world. For where there is a world, there is matter; and where there is matter, there is oppression and force, space and time, limitation and necessity. Yet, there is a world, and matter. How do you get out of the clutches of this contradiction? . . . Only by making the world itself into a product of the will. . . . (VI, 131; S: I, 184)

Thus, Feuerbach reads into the creation from nothing a two-sided motive: man's projection of his self-esteem as the purpose of creation and man's denial of his identity with nature, his claim to freedom from the constraints of an external world. The two are related, in that the "unbounded subjectivity," the sheer wish-fulfilling desires for omnipotence in the first case, is the positive pole of which that negation of the world, the assertion of the nothingness of the world, is the negative pole (both expressing the same motive).

FEUERBACH'S ANTI-SEMITISM: A NOTE ON HIS ACCOUNT OF CREATION THEORY

In a chapter that is strikingly similar in characterization, in language and in metaphor to Karl Marx's later work, "On the Jewish Question," Feuerbach ascribes the origin of creation theories to the Jews. He calls creation theory "the fundamental theory of the Jewish religion" (VI, 133; S: I, 186). He cannot have meant that other peoples and other religions have no independent theories of creation. But in the context of his treatment of the Christian religion, he sees in Judaism the original form of the creation idea, in its "egoistic" or "practical," "utilitarian" form. All that is missing, in the language, is the addition of Marx's more explicitly anti-Semitic epithet: "in its dirty-Jewish form." It was a cultural anti-Semitic commonplace of the age, especially in Germany, to identify "egoism," "practicalism," "utilitarianism" with the Jews, or to use the term "Jewish" as a general term for these characteristics (as in the persistent anti-Semitic Anglo-American colloquialism "to Jew down," in talking generally about bargaining for a lower price). There is no question here of Feuerbach's anti-Semitism, in general. For his time, he was generally enlightened in his personal dealings. Nevertheless, he shared the anti-Semitic prejudices of his age, in this conception of "Jewish" practicality and egoism. Moreover, he furthered these prejudices by his theoretical treatment. He writes,

Utility, usefulness is the very first principle of Judaism. The belief in a special divine providence is the characteristic belief of Judaism, the belief in providence, in miracles. But it is a belief in miracles in which nature appears only as an object of willfulness, of egoism, so that nature serves only the purposes of willfulness. The waters divide, or join; dust becomes transformed into lice, the rod into a serpent, the rivers into blood, the rock into a spring; it is both light and dark in the same place, the sun stops in its course, or turns back. And all of these unnatural events occur for the use of Israel, ostensibly at Jehovah's command, who is concerned only with Israel, and is nothing but the personified selfishness of the Israelite people, to the exclusion of all other peoples, nothing but personified intolerance–the secret of monotheism. (VI, 135–6; S: I, 189)

The difference between "Jewish" egoism, in "Jewish" creation theory, and belief in providence and miracles, and Christian "subjectivity," in the like instances, is presumably the exclusiveness, the ethnicity of the special providence of the Jews and the universality of the Christian belief, which is no longer exclusively ethnic. Feuerbach writes,

Israel is the historical definition of the peculiar nature of religious consciousness, but still within the confines of separatism, of national interest. We have only to release it from these confines, and we have the Christian religion. Judaism is worldly Christianity, and Christianity is spiritual Judaism. The Christian religion is the Jewish religion cleansed of its national egoism, though certainly, at the same time, a new, different religion. . . . For the Jews, the Israelite was the mediator, the bond between God and man; his relation to Jehovah was his relation to himself as Israelite. Jehovah was nothing but the unity, the self-consciousness of Israel objectified for itself as an absolute essence, as national consciousness, lawfullness in general, the central point of politics. Once we are released from the confines of national consciousness, we have in place of the Israelite, Man as such. Just as the Israelite objectifies his nationality in Jehovah, so the Christian objectifies in his God, his own human essence–albeit his subjective human essence, freed from the limits of nationality. Just as the Jew elevates the requirements, the needs of his existence to the law of the world . . . so, the Christian elevates the needs of human feeling to the all-encompassing powers and laws of the world. (VI, 143–4; S: I, 197–8)

This theme had already appeared in Feuerbach's *History of Modern Philosophy*, in the distinction he drew between Christianity and pagan religions (the latter limited to national or ethnic boundaries) (see pp. 56–7). Yet here the Greeks, in their religion, are characterized by Feuerbach, in contrast to the Jews, as humanistic. They "contemplated nature theoretically," says Feuerbach, whereas the Jews regard nature only "gastronomically"!

The Greek pursued *Humaniora*, the liberal arts, philosophy; the Israelite never rose above a bread-and-butter theology. . . . Eating is the most consecrated act, or indeed the initiation of the Jewish religion. In eating, the Israelite celebrates and renews the act of creation. In eating, man declares nature to be unimportant to him. As the seventy elders climbed the mount with Moses, they "saw God, and as God appeared to them, they ate and drank." A glimpse of the most exalted being called forth in them only their appetites. (VI, 136–7; S: I, 190)

Feuerbach characterizes this not only as a historical feature of biblical Judaism, but, to make his point contemporary, adds, "The Jews have maintained this peculiarity to the present day" (VI, 137; S: I, 190). The more general point, in Feuerbach's treatment, is that this egoism is the principle of monotheism, "which collects and concentrates man upon himself . . . but makes him theoretically limited, because indifferent to everything which doesn't immediately serve his well-being. Science, like art, develops only out of polytheism, for polytheism is the open, *unenvious* all-inclusive appreciation for everything beautiful and good, an appreciation of the world, of the universe" (VI, 137; S: I, 190).

The other passages in *The Essence of Christianity*, on food, on eating and drinking as consecrations, occur in Feuerbach's discussion of the sacraments, specifically, of Holy Communion. There is no denigration there of the act; on the contrary, it is seen as man's enoblement of his dependence on water, wine, and bread, as the stuff of life. Later, Feuerbach's philosophy is to become almost grossly centered on the stomach, on digestion, on food and eating as the "secret of sacrifice," but also as the dissolution of speculative philosophy, *in fact*—the dissolution, for example, of the mind-body problem. Here, in his account of the "egoistic" motives of "Jewish" creation theory, he is content to focus on the delimited version of creation from nothing as not only subjectivity, but selfishness, intolerance, parochial practicality. It is no surprise that this parochial anti-semitism appears in Feuerbach, at this point; it is only sad that the demystifier himself could not be demystified of this old and dangerous myth.

CREATION AS ACTIVITY: DIVINE PRAXIS AND HUMAN PRAXIS

In the "positive" first half of *The Essence of Christianity*, which Feuerbach characterizes as the "true or anthropological essence of religion," he does not deal with one obvious "anthropological" source of creation theory: the analogy of God's creative activity to human praxis, to the making of things, to human creation. He does, however, develop this theme in the "negative" half of the work, on "the false or theological essence of religion." Here creation is no longer either the requirement of self-consciousness to present itself as its own object or the subjective expression of the needs of feeling or of will, to realize itself omnipotently. The first may be characterized as the rationalist creation theory; the second, as voluntarist. Here, however, man's freedom, or his feeling of freedom, is seen as rooted in his actions, in his making of things, in his deeds. Feuerbach begins by characterizing human labor, human activity as self-realizing activity that makes man a free individual.

The concept of activity, of making, of creation is, in and for itself, a divine concept; therefore it is unconsciously attributed to God. In activity, man feels himself to be free, unlimited, happy; in passivity, man feels himself to be limited, oppressed, unhappy. Activity is positive self-feeling. In general, that is positive which is accompanied by joy. But it is God . . . who is therefore the concept of pure, unlimited joy. . . . A joyful activity is . . . one which is in conformity with our being, and which we therefore regard not as constraining or forced upon us. The happiest, most delightful activity, however, is that of producing things . . . in effect, it is better to give than to receive. (VI, 262; S: I, 335)

The contradictions in theology arise, says Feuerbach, when this generalized joyful creation, attributed to God as a creation of *all*, comes into conflict with the generation and production of particular things. The religious conception of God's free activity is not interested in the physics and biology of the natural origin of things, says Feuerbach, but only in the "practical or subjectively human concept of creation." Thus, he says,

Religion has no physical conception of the world; it is not interested in a natural explanation, which can only be given in terms of the origin or generation of things. But origin or generation is a theoretical, natural-philosophical concept. The pagan philosophers were concerned with the origin of things. But the Christian religious consciousness rejects this as a pagan, irreligious concept, and puts in its place the practical or subjective human concept of creation. . . . (VI, 264; S: I, 337)

However, once the religious consciousness is constrained to understand God's activity, as human activity, in the sense of productive, creative activity, or in terms of the origin of things in nature, the concept of creation from nothing ceases to be comprehensible to it. Religious consciousness, in Feuerbach's view, demands the absolute derivation of all things from God, in an immediate act of creation. Once this is mediated by a physical or natural process, it is no longer God's free activity. Divine and human making are similar up to a point: Free human creative activity (e.g., creative thought) is a direct expression of my inner self, just as the world expresses God, directly, on the religious view. Such an activity, says Feuerbach, "is identical with my essence, is my own inner necessity, like intellectual production, which is an inner need. . . . But intellectual works are not 'made'–the 'making' is only the most external aspect of them; they rather are generated in us" (VI, 265; S: I, 339). But there the analogy with human creative activity, with human production of things, with human action as praxis, ends. The idea of creation from nothing has nothing in common with this praxis. It is interesting that when Feuerbach does give an example of human creation here, it is intellectual activity, as the expression of "my own inner necessity." The immediacy of the relation between this "inner necessity" and its expression is that between the thought and the word. Its outward appearance, as word–its externality–is accidental, not essential to it. This externality is concerned with the *process* of production, therefore with the mediation of thought and word–or thought and act, for the *act* is the outward expression of my immediacy, my inner necessity. At the beginning of the chapter on *Creation from Nothing*, Feuerbach writes, "Creation is God's spoken word; the creative word is the inner word which is identical with the thought" (VI, 121; S: I, 172). The essence of the creation from nothing is its immediacy. There is no process of self-differentiation, of self-production, but only a pure and instantaneous act of will. The creation from nothing, as Feuerbach says, violates time and space. It is not a process, but a pure act. But, then, this is no longer a model of "making," and cannot have its source in this analogy. This would be, in effect, an alien, even an irreligious determination of the concept of divine creation as creation from nothing. Once theology forces the original religious consciousness to cope with this alien determination, says Feuerbach, it forces a breach between man's self-conception as creative being–that is, as a being of creative praxis, or making– and his conception of God as creator from nothing. In effect, this is a breach between man's recognition of the requirements of his praxis and man's recognition of his desires for unconstrained fulfillment of his wish. Man may express his self-esteem in praising his own work, as an act of creation; but this has nothing in common with the self-esteem that is expressed in the ideas of providence and miracles. The first has a workaday context, in the recognition of necessity, of external constraints; the other has its context in fantasy, in the imagination, in wish. Thus, as Feuerbach points out, the idea of creation from nothing founders on the disanalogy or disharmony with human creation, as production. God creates from nothing. His "making" is a creation from nothing. But man cannot produce from nothing. Therefore, there is an absolute breach between man and God. For this difference is incomprehensible, and has no representation in the imagination, at least not on the model of human production. God therefore becomes posited as alien to man's nature, and thus, in Feuerbach's terms, as the "false or theological essence of religion." "This difference between divine activity and human activity is this Nothing," writes Feuerbach (VI, 265; S: II, 339). This difference becomes a *Nihil negativum* of the understanding, the naive recognition of which is to take this *Nothing* as an object of the understanding; to fall, therefore, into utter incomprehensibility.

In one way, it is strange that Feuerbach does not press the analogy to human activity, to production, to the generation of things as a "positive" or "true" essence of religion. If anything, the notion of God as creator, as artificer, as producer of things in their forms and their uses is the oldest of all cosmogonical ideas. Yet Feuerbach is uncomfortable with it here, precisely on the grounds that it intrudes the world and its natural processes upon the "purer" conception of God as man's essence. But man's interaction with the world, his praxis, is his essence, in a way Feuerbach was never to grasp. The categories *reason, feeling, will* are all expressions of some "inner" essence of man. Insofar as man is an active being, the "activities" Feuerbach understands are the *reflected-upon activities* of human life, as they appear in consciousness, albeit in the alienated form of religious consciousness. True, this is his proper subject matter, as he tells us explicitly. Yet in his discussion of creation, as in his discussion of "secondary causes," and of "the world," human praxis as such appears almost as if *it* were alien to man. It appears only at the point of breakdown between man's conception of his own essence as divine and his conception of God as a being beyond him, and completely alien to his essence.

There is an ambivalence in Feuerbach here. The true essence of religion is anthropology. Religion is the self-revelation of *human* nature. Therefore, it is a misunderstanding, in Feuerbach's view, to see in religion, or in religious consciousness, anything *more* or *different* from this. The true essence of religion is not physics, or mathematics, or any revelation, in whatever inverted form, of the *natural* world. Therefore, religion stands, if not opposed to natural science in its determinations, still absolutely separated from it in domain. Thus, in religion, man not only conceives of himself as God, or as divine being, but separates or differentiates himself from nature, as he separates God from nature. Every identification of God with nature or with the physical world is already an introduction of irreligiosity, except where "nature" itself is transformed into a human object, or is simply a personified projection of human nature itself. Feuerbach's ambivalence, however, is in his conception of human nature. If it is human, it is transcendent, it stands beyond nature as such. On the other hand, it is the *natural* human being whose anthropological essence is to be revealed here, *not* the transcendent, supernatural being who resides only in heaven, or in the imagination. The bond between man and nature is realized in religious consciousness, says Feuerbach, in his discussion of the sacraments of baptism and holy communion. Man's material nature there becomes reflected in his consciousness of his *dependence* on the material world for his existence, on water, on wine, on bread. But this dependence is a passivity;

it is not yet the activity of man, as creative being, that binds him to the natural world, but his dependency. Despite the positive characterization of man's free activity, in this section of the work, this free activity, or creative freedom, is *not* raised to the level of divinity; it is not seen as Godlike activity. To be sure, in one place earlier (see p. 282) Feuerbach seems to recognize this. In discussing the builder's craft, or that of the architect, he sees the object built or constructed as a glorification and objectification of the skill and capacity that human beings have. The temple built and consecrated to God is, in effect, a consecration of the divine skill of the architect. But Feuerbach's recognition is not sustained, for precisely at the point where productive human activity *is* discussed, it is *contrasted* with divine activity, to which it ultimately stands in contradiction, because the divine activity of creation, as a *productive* activity, is understood as a creation from nothing, which violates the human understanding of *human* making, absolutely. Still, one may say that Feuerbach here simply contrasts the *sources* of the creation-from-nothing idea with the incompatible sources of the creative production model. The two are incompatible, because one expresses sheer willfulness, the other, the discipline of actual realization of a project, in the activity of making. One is unmediated fulfillment, the other fulfills itself only on the condition of the mediation of making, of praxis. So be it. But then one would expect Feuerbach to have introduced a *third* theory of creation—that of creative praxis—*or*, and this is more significant still, to have introduced this aspect by way of a reinterpretation of the *first* model—namely, the model of creation as self-differentiation and self-objectification, and therefore as self-realization. But Feuerbach understood praxis only in its theoretical context—the praxis of consciousness, as consciousness' own dialectic. Marx was, of course, to choose this third alternative, *by way of* a reinterpretation of the first, and he was to criticize Feuerbach on precisely the ground of his failure to comprehend "sensuous, living, concrete *praxis.*" This failure reveals itself elsewhere, to be sure, but nowhere as precisely or as clearly as in this discussion of creation as activity.

Religion as Praxis and as Theory

"The essential standpoint of religion is the practical—that is to say, here, the subjective" (VI, 223; S: II, 291).

In the whole foregoing treatment of religion, Feuerbach constantly stresses and repeats the point that the object of religious consciousness is man, that the concern of religion is exclusively with man's weal and woe, that the true essence of religion is not theology, but anthropology.

Religion is practical in the sense that it is concerned with man's well-being. Its origin is in this concern, and its efficacy is that it provides a means for expressing this concern. But, says Feuerbach, man's well-being is a matter of concern only when it is threatened, when man realizes the precariousness and neediness of his existence. Religion is the voice of man's self-concern, the acknowledgment of his insufficiency, his dependency, his fear of death. At the same time, Feuerbach argues that religion is the image of man's infinity, his self-esteem, his capacity for love, friendship, self-sacrifice. All that man can desire for himself, all that he can imagine as possible for himself, all his dream wishes are embodied in his conception of divinity, which is therefore a conception of himself as divine, and of his desires, capacities, and possibilities as divine.

Feuerbach's sense of "practical," as I noted in the previous section, is removed from the context of practice in which man engages not himself, but a world external to himself, which he has to transform, abide, understand, in order to meet his needs. Feuerbach recognizes this breach between the subjective practicality of religion and this other practice, which we may characterize as technical-scientific practice. Religious praxis is confined to man's felt needs, as they are reflected and dealt with in consciousness. Religion, as Feuerbach says, deals with the image, not the reality. But this human essence, this reality, is a reality of thought, that is, the reality of man's conscious existence, the object of his self-consciousness. It is, in effect, a psychological reality. Insofar as thinking, self-reflection, imagination are praxis it is the praxis of consciousness, not yet the praxis of action. It *is* the praxis of action in its reflected form, but not action as such, or in itself. When Feuerbach says "man," he means human consciousness, human imagination. When he talks of human life, he means *conscious* life, the life of thought, feeling, desire. When he talks of "activity," he thinks of the activity of consciousness, in all these aspects. When he talks of man's practical activity, he means the *faculties* of desire, feeling, will, thought. These are the object-language terms, so to speak, the "realities" that Feuerbachian anthropology deals with, and that it reveals as hidden under the esoteric terminology of religious consciousness. The mistake of religious consciousness is to take the referents of its esoteric terms as other than human, to take them therefore as designations and descriptions of the nonhuman and superhuman divine being. God's praxis is therefore revealed as reflected upon and hypostatized human praxis. But what does God *do*? What is God's activity? He thinks, feels, and wills, as man does. But in the religious image of this activity, God is not merely an "inner" being; his activity is not psychological or mental. It is *real* praxis, in the sense

---

that it is efficacious, causal–in effect, *worldly* praxis. God creates the world, whether from Himself or from nothing. God feeds the hungry, helps the worthy, punishes the transgressor. If He is to be God, He has to be incarnate. He cannot simply *wish* to create a world, or *hope* that the hungry will be fed. Feuerbach, more clearly than any other student of religion, recognizes the crux of religious consciousness as the demand for an omnipotent God, one who effects what he wills, thinks, or desires. Moreover, this efficacy must be *immediate*. It must follow from God's nature, and not by the mediation of secondary causes. But insofar as it is immediate–that is to say, insofar as it is divine–it is impossible for man. Man's praxis, his living praxis in the world, is mediated. Only in the fantasy world of the imagination is it conceived of as unmediated, and therefore superhuman. But as it is superhuman, it is a wish for superhuman or divine power, not a practical, human realization of that power. Therefore, the religious praxis realizes itself not in deeds, except as they are God's deeds. As a human praxis, it realizes itself in the incorporation of the wish into an objective form. But this objective form, the objective form of *human religious praxis,* is belief–belief in miracles, belief in providence, belief in God's love of man.

Thus, Feuerbach constructs the *world* of religion as a world of belief, a world constituted by belief. Belief is the praxis of religion par excellence. It therefore stands opposed to theory, to the understanding, says Feuerbach. The ultimate violation of the nature of this belief is not disbelief, but the attempt to *theorize* it, to make it a belief *of* the understanding. This is, in its very nature, impossible. It is a contradiction of belief, from within belief itself, therefore. The nonbeliever simply dispenses with belief. Or better yet, he understands belief–the true belief of believers–for what it really is: the embodiment of human feeling, in alienated form. The *theorizer* of belief, however, is committed to both the belief *and* to the understanding that makes this belief impossible. The understanding realizes that creation from nothing is impossible for man, as *real* praxis; that the immaculate conception is impossible for man, as *real* praxis; that the miracle is an impossibility, in *real* praxis. Why? Because *real* praxis is understood under its natural constraints. Because the miracle, by definition, violates such constraints, it is impossible for human practice. Impossible for man, it is only possible for God. Thus, God is set above man as an impossible being for the understanding and as possible only for belief. The theorizer of religion is the theologian. Theology therefore is the contradiction of belief on the very grounds of belief itself.

In this way, Feuerbach establishes theology as "the negative essence of religion." But our concern here is with the distinction between divine praxis and human praxis. Insofar as divine, efficacious praxis is an impossibility for man, as praxis *in the world*, it becomes a possibility in God's world. But God's world *is this* world, and because only God can act divinely in the world, the world becomes the arena of man's *in*efficacy. In this world, God is everything, man is nothing. But in such a world, where God reigns, natural laws do not. Where God's will is law, the world's laws have no status. To know the way the world is, one has only to know the way God is. Thus, the only "theory" there can be is the "theory" of God's nature. But God's nature is the fulfillment of subjective human practical needs, the needs of the heart, of feeling, and so on. These obey no theory, no laws, except those of human feeling. Thus, where God is everything, man is everything, and the world is nothing. Man is everything for God, in his providence; but man is nothing to the world, and the world is nothing to him. Thus, his praxis in the world is nothing. For religious consciousness, then, man as man in the world, is nothing. Man as *God*, however, is everything. The breach between the two is man's absolute separation from nature insofar as he counts for something. His praxis as believer can only be concerned with his wished-for well-being, his salvation. But because his salvation lies outside this world, beyond nature, his religious praxis cannot be concerned with this world. Insofar as it is, it leads to disbelief, to irreligion, to materialism and atheism.

THE LIMITS OF FEUERBACH'S CONCEPT OF PRAXIS

According to Feuerbach, the essence of religious praxis is that it is supernatural—that is, that it transcends, in its mode and in its efficacy, the objective constraints of the understanding, the limits of the natural world and of "natural reason." It is a praxis of unlimited feeling and of the imagination, unfettered by rational or empirical conditions. Feuerbach's critique of theology is a critique of its attempt to *theorize* this religious praxis—to theorize feeling, love, the imagination, which are, in essence, antitheoretical. This antitheoretical, prerational (if not irrational) character of religious praxis comes from the very nature of religious belief, the essence of which is the denial or negation of the world and of its external necessity. The hopelessness, the unreality, the inefficacy of human action in the world constitute the very ground of religious belief or faith. The trust that what man cannot do, God can do for him, and will do for him, is what generates prayer, belief in miracles, in providence, in salvation (by faith, not by works). Religion realizes the wish immediately, without means. Real praxis is limited to what it can accomplish in the world, to what it is within human power to achieve.

But for Feuerbach, in *The Essence of Christianity*, this reality is conceived not as a world of real praxis, but as a world as it is *understood* by reason, by science. It is a world of *reflected-upon* praxis, but not joined to this real praxis in any clear way.

This becomes clear in Feuerbach's striking accounts of religious praxis, in *The Essence of Christianity*, specifically in his treatment of prayer, miracles, and the sacraments (baptism and holy communion).

Prayer is characterized as "the wish of the heart expressed with confidence in its fulfillment" (VI, 147; S: I, 202). Feuerbach writes,

The man who does not exclude from his mind the idea of the world, the idea that everything here must be sought intermediately, that every effect has its natural cause, that a wish is only to be attained when it is made an end and the corresponding means are put into operation–such a man does not pray: he only works; he transforms his attainable wishes into objects of this-worldly activity. Other wishes, which he recognizes as subjective, he suppresses or regards them as only subjective, pious wishes. In short, he limits or conditions his being by the world, of which he conceives himself as a member; he bounds his wishes by the idea of necessity. By contrast, in prayer, he excludes the world from his mind, and with it, he excludes all thoughts of mediation, of dependency, of sad necessity. He makes his wishes, the concern of his heart, into objects of an independent, omnipotent, absolute being, i.e., he affirms them without limitation. God is the yea-saying of human feeling. Prayer is the unconditioned confidence of human feeling in the absolute identity of the subjective and the objective, the certainty that the power of the heart is greater than the power of nature; that the need of the heart is universal necessity, the fate of the world. Prayer alters the course of nature; it determines God to bring forth an effect in contradiction with the laws of nature. Prayer is the relation of the human heart to itself, to its own essence. In prayer, man forgets that there exists a limit to his wishes, and is happy in this forgetfulness. (VI, 147–8; S: I, 202–3)

Feuerbach goes on to analyze prayer not as mere dependence on an other, but as a dependence based on confidence. Because, in prayer, the heart speaks to itself, is conscious of its own strength, its own worth, its omnipotence, the power of prayer is the measure of the power of one's feelings for oneself. The immediacy of wish fulfillment in prayer is not that one's wishes *are* fulfilled, but that one believes absolutely in the power to fulfill them. The attitudes of prayer, Feuerbach says, are attitudes of self-worth. The prayer asks, entreats in full confidence of fulfillment. But this belief, this faith in the efficacy of prayer is

faith in omnipotence, faith in the unreality of the external world, faith in the absolute reality of man's emotional nature: the essence of omnipotence is simply the essence of feeling. Omnipotence is the power before which no law, no external condition avails or subsists. . . . Omnipotence does nothing more than to fulfill, to realize the innermost will of the feelings. (VI, 150–1; S: I, 206)

Thus, too, with miracles: The miracle is the objective form of faith–faith as "confidence in the reality of the subjective in opposition to the limitations or laws of nature and of reason–that is, of natural reason" (VI, 151; S: I, 206–7). Miracle is "a supernatural wish realized–nothing more" (VI, 155; S: I, 211). But realized immediately, and without means. "Miraculous agency is distinguished from the ordinary realization of an object in that it realizes the end without means, that it effects an immediate identity of the wish and its fulfillment" (VI, 157; S: I, 213).

The locus of religion, then, is a praxis that is entirely inward, subjective, that effects what it effects only in the imagination and in feeling. The "world" of religion is thus this "other" world, which stands in utter opposition, is, in effect, the *negation* of this world. But, then, as we have seen in the prior discussion on creation as activity–as *tätigkeit* or praxis –even activity in this world is transformed into a fantastic reflection in the wish-fulfilling imagination, as an unreal (i.e., unmediated) activity, in which there is no process, but instantaneous realization of what is wished. Where it would seem that Feuerbach trembles on the brink of a concept of this-worldly praxis, it remains vague and unrealized.

But the question of Feuerbach's conception of "real activity" is a complex one. Insofar as "real activity" or this-worldly praxis is one that is undertaken to meet a need or a purpose, it is like religious praxis, which Feuerbach notes clearly: It is an activity of objectification. In religious praxis, the wish or the need is objectified, and satisfied in the *image*, in the externalized form in which religious consciousness comes to know itself in the objects it has produced. In prayer, the word, or speech is the objective and, according to Feuerbach, the necessary form of the wish. The heart speaks to itself, yet it does so in the externalized form of utterance–in Feuerbach's phrase, "the human soul giving ear to itself." He writes,

Prayer is the self-division of man into two beings–a dialogue of man with himself, with his heart. It is essential to the effectiveness of prayer that it be audibly, intelligibly, energetically expressed. Involuntarily, prayer wells forth in sound; the struggling heart bursts the barrier of the closed lips. But audible prayer is only prayer revealing its nature; prayer is virtually, if not actually, speech,–the Latin word *oratio* signifies both. . . . (VI, 148; S: I, 203)

Thus, too, the miracle is faith objectified. The miracle exists as a created object, "made" by faith. And, in general, Feuerbach's analysis of the self-alienation of religious consciousness is, as we have seen, based on the model of objectification taken from Hegel. But if, in religion,

the objectification is an image, mistaken for the reality that it objectifies—that is, human nature—what is the object created by real, this-
worldly praxis, by "making"?

The closest Feuerbach comes to the notion of actual productive
praxis in this work is in his discussion of activity as production or
making of things, in the discussion of creation, as we have seen. He
continues this discussion on the differences between divine and human
praxis in the chapter on "The Contradiction in the Nature of God in
General." Feuerbach begins with a criticism of the "central point of
Christian sophistry," namely, that God is to be regarded *both* as a
human being and as a superhuman being; as both abstract, universal
Being, the "idea of Being," and also as a personal, individual being.
Thus, the issue of the relation of species to individual is expressed in
this theological form, and forms the crux of Incarnation theory. But the
specific form of this "sophism" that interests us here is the relation
between divine and human praxis, that is, between the productive activity of God, as abstract being, and the notion of concrete, individual
human practice, or production.

In the preceding discussion (see p. 322), Feuerbach had characterized
the "concept of activity, of making, of creation" as a "divine concept"
that connoted free, unlimited, creative praxis. "Activity is positive
self-feeling," and "the happiest, most delightful activity . . . is that of
producing things" (VI, 262; S: II, 335). Insofar as this activity is positive,
joyful, free, it is identified as unlimited, as unconstrained by necessity
or need—therefore, as divine activity. "Hence," says Feuerbach, "this
attribute of the species—productive activity—is assigned to God" (VI,
262; S: II, 335). But it is assigned to God in its *abstract* form, and only
the most abstract or general feature of production is preserved in this
religious transformation:

every special determination, every *mode* of activity is abstracted, and only the
fundamental determination, which, however, is essentially human, namely,
production of what is external to self [my emphasis, M. W.], is retained. God
has not, like man, produced something in particular, this or that, but all
things; his activity is absolutely universal, unlimited. Hence it is self-evident,
it is a necessary consequence, that the mode in which God has produced the
All is incomprehensible, because this activity is no *mode* or activity, because
the question concerning the *how* is here an absurdity, a question which is excluded by the fundamental idea of unlimited activity. Every activity produces
its effects in a special manner, because there the activity itself is a determinate
mode of activity; and thence necessarily arises the question: How did it produce
this? But the answer to the question: How did God make the world? has necessarily a negative issue, because the world creating activity in itself negates
every determinate activity, such as would alone warrant the question, every
mode of activity connected with a determinate medium, i.e., with matter. This

331

question illegitimately foists in between the subject or producing activity and the object, or thing produced, an irrelevant, nay, an excluded intermediate idea, namely, the idea of particular, individual existence. (VI, 262–3; S: II, 336)

Several things are clear here: (1) Feuerbach regards "real productive activity" as determinate, particular, in a given mode, and as, in general, a process of externalization or objectification, that is, the production of an object by an active subject in a determinate process, about which it is appropriate to ask, "How was it done?"; (2) further, in divine praxis, *only* the abstract notion of objectification is retained, but the process, the determinateness of the mode is transcended and eliminated. Productive activity becomes a mystery, an act without a means. Moreover, in creation from nothing, it is not the transformation of an external world, or of matter *by* the subjective activity, but the actual origination of this world itself: of the *All*, but of the *All* both abstractly (as *Universe*) *and* determinately and concretely (as each individual thing). This creation concept, says Feuerbach, is recognized as a myth, once "physical science . . . makes determinate causes, the *how* of phenomena, the object of investigation" (VI, 264; S: II, 338).

Where we *began* by speaking of a producing subject creating real things in the world by its activity, as the source of the analogy to divine praxis, we are suddenly left by Feuerbach with the "production" *by Nature*, of natural phenomena. "Making," as human praxis, seems to have dropped out of consideration.

But shortly thereafter, Feuerbach addresses this activity of "making," of productive praxis, itself, and we seem to be back on the track of a positive account of human praxis: "God makes—he makes something external to himself, as man does. Making is a genuine human idea. Nature gives birth to, brings forth; man makes."

But then Feuerbach gives a strange turn to the argument:

Making is an act which I can omit, a designed, premeditated, external act;— an act in which my inmost being is not immediately concerned. . . . By contrast, an activity which is identical with my essence is not indifferent, is necessary to me, as, for example, intellectual production, which is an inward necessity to me. . . . Intellectual works are not made . . . they arise in us. *To make* is an indifferent, therefore a free, i.e., optional, activity. Insofar as He makes, then, God is entirely at one with man, not at all distinguished from him; but a special emphasis is laid on this, that his making is free in self-pleasing, in caprice, in groundless arbitrariness. (VI, 265–6; S: II, 339–40)

How is one to explain this strange dichotomous characterization of human making by Feuerbach? It is, on the one hand, "positive self-feeling," as joyful, free creation. On the other, it is mere caprice, arbitrariness, no "necessity of my inner nature." Feuerbach sees in this a breach within the human: "harmony is changed into discord; man hitherto at one with himself, becomes divided: God makes *out of nothing*; he creates,–to make out of nothing is to create,–this is the distinction. The positive condition–the act of making–is a human one; but inasmuch as all that is determinate in this conception is immediately denied, *reflection steps in and makes the divine activity not human*" (my emphasis, M. W.) (VI, 266; S: II, 340). That is to say, Feuerbach recognizes the breach between the human and the divine praxis as one between the *real* conditions of human making and the abstract conception of divine making. But he sees this breach as explicit only in theology, because only theology brings to full articulation the contradiction between creation as abstract, general productive capacity, beyond the limit of comprehensibility–that is, creation from nothing–and creation as determinate, concrete, this-worldly production. Yet his discussion never descends (or attains) to the level of description, or a characterization of this real praxis. Rather, it comes to be described as *Bildung*: as "culture" or "education"; as what the understanding comes to know *about* nature; and as what reason demands as noncontradiction.

Thus, though Feuerbach has a conception of human praxis, as determinate making constrained by empirical or natural conditions, he remains at the level of the understanding, that is, at the reflected-upon and comprehended *image* of actual praxis, at what *science knows*, rather than what *man does*. Now it is interesting that the dichotomy between divine praxis and human praxis is seen as a dichotomy between the demands and needs of feeling and those of the understanding. For it leaves unresolved the question of how the understanding *can* meet the needs of feeling, can satisfy real desires, can effect real purposes *except* insofar as these are the needs and demands of the understanding itself. The practical is subjective–this is the standpoint of religion, Feuerbach tells us. Reason and the understanding are objective; their object is the world as it is known, as it is understood, as a detached object apart from considerations of human weal and woe. This breach between the subjective and the objective–between man in the world of belief and man in the world of fact–is not overcome in Feuerbach's account. It remains a breach because the *practical* understanding, or rational praxis–the actual activity by which the real world is transformed in the image of human needs and desires–is not yet the subject of Feuerbach's thought. It remains a world out there: studied, contemplated, and understood, by an activity of the understanding, or by empirical observation, but not yet by practical intervention. The subject-object dichotomy is not overcome by Feuerbach, but is rather posited in its sharpest way, as one between two worlds: that constituted by belief, by the praxis of religion, and that *reflected* by the understanding. Only the first is a world *made*, and made only in the imagination, as a fantastic image *not* of the real world, but of the inner "world" of human feelings, needs, and desires. Only the objectification of feeling involves activity by the subject. Insofar as the natural world figures at all in the imagery, it does so only as a symbol of human need or wish. It has, so to speak, no objectivity. Insofar as the natural world is an object of knowledge, it is divorced from the activity of the subject. It is, rather, the passive image that the understanding forms on the basis of sense experience. The senses are cognitive, but they are not active.

Where Feuerbach comes closest to a conception of the natural world itself as an object of human desires, needs, purposes, this too is seen only in the active image of religious praxis. True, in *The Essence of Christianity*, Feuerbach says his subject matter is *not* nature, or natural knowledge, but rather human nature, or human self-knowledge. This was, as we have seen, his answer to Müller's critique of the work as anthropomorphic (see p. 274). But where Feuerbach does express the "positive" character, that is, the enlightened or translated version of the religious imagery, in its ostensibly unalienated form, he fails to see the natural world as an object of real praxis, but sees it only as an object of the understanding; an understanding acquired not by the subject's own praxis in the world, but rather by *Bildung*—by education, by culture, by science as "natural reason."

The understanding—natural reason, the enlightened and naturalistic conception of nature—goes beyond the "negative" contradiction-laden attempts of theology to make reason and belief commensurable. According to Feuerbach, the fantastic image of nature in religion is formed by the *wish* to have nature satisfy human needs, but to do so in a supernatural way. Thus, religion recognizes the dependency of man on nature, but only in an inverted form, which requires the violation of natural constraints and the laws of nature, so that the wish can be effected immediately. In his discussion of the sacraments of baptism and holy communion, in the final pages of *The Essence of Christianity*, Feuerbach attempts a naturalistic and anthropological reduction of the sacraments to their significance for the understanding. How would a rational and scientific mind interpret the sacraments so as to preserve their real content while negating their irrational form? Here perhaps the strengths *and* weaknesses of Feuerbach's account come forth most clearly. For although we are led almost to the brink of a conception of human praxis as the *practical* transformation and realization of nature for human needs, we are finally stopped short by Feuerbach's interpretation of this praxis itself as one of the understanding, that is, as a *reflective recogni-*

tion of the natural as what is needed by man, and even as what is made over by him in his productive praxis. But it is the natural world "made over" by an act of reflection, by the mind coming to understand this process of transformation. It is not yet the world "made over" by a process of real, productive transformation of the world itself.

Thus, in the "reduction" of baptism, Feuerbach writes, "We give a true significance to Baptism, only by regarding it as a symbol of the significance of water itself. Baptism should represent to us the wonderful but natural effect of water on the human being" (VI, 331; S: II, 415). This simple naturalistic reduction is contrasted by Feuerbach with the sacrament of Communion, in what, at first, promises to be a distinction based on praxis:

But the sacrament of water requires a supplement. Water, as a universal element of life, reminds us of our origin from Nature, an origin which we have in common with plants and animals. . . . But we men are distinguished from the plants and animals, which together with the inorganic Kingdom we comprehend under the common name of Nature;—we are distinguished from Nature. Hence we must celebrate our distinction, our specific difference. The symbols of this our difference are bread and wine. Bread and wine are, as to their materials, products of Nature; as to their form, *products of man* [my emphasis, M. W.]. . . . Bread and wine are supernatural products,—in the only valid and true sense, the sense which is not in contradiction with reason and Nature. If in water we adore the pure force of Nature, *in bread and wine we adore the supernatural power of mind, of consciousness, of man. Hence, this sacrament is only for man matured into consciousness; while baptism is imparted to infants. But we at the same time celebrate the true relation of mind to Nature: Nature gives the material, mind gives the form. The sacrament of Baptism inspires us with thankfulness towards Nature, the sacrament of bread and wine with thankfulness towards man.* [My emphasis, M. W.] (VI, 333–4; S: II, 418–19)

Where we might have expected that the distinction of the human from nature lies in the fact that bread and wine are human *products*—and Feuerbach himself suggests in this passage that it is the *production* of bread and wine, the human transformation of nature to human ends, that marks the distinction—we are finally disappointed by Feuerbach. It is not the praxis that marks the distinction, but the *consciousness of the praxis*, the human self-awareness, the gratefulness to the producer of the bread and the wine, the recognition of its human origin. But this "natural" form of the religious adoration of the creator, this self-adoration by man of his own creative-productive powers, of his ability to overcome or to satisfy his needs and his dependency by means of his work, is finally translated by Feuerbach *as abstractly* as he had earlier translated the religious adoration of creation from nothing as a *generalized* and *abstract* creation of the *All* without distinction as to determinate means or processes of creation. In short, this generalized adoration or celebration of human productive and creative powers is abstracted as a celebration of consciousness, of mind, of *Geist*, by Feuerbach. Human praxis is celebrated only in its reflected-upon form, and is comprehended only as the praxis *of* consciousness itself, albeit a consciousness of human self-activity, of man's transcendence of nature. Here the *means* of transcendence, the productive praxis that creates the bread and the wine, is left out, is bypassed. It does not constitute the essential human praxis for Feuerbach. Rather, consciousness, as self-conscious awareness of the human origin of the bread and wine, itself becomes the human praxis par excellence.

In a sense, Feuerbach's own view of this distinction between divine and human praxis can become the object of a Feuerbachian critique. Human activity, *tätigkeit*, praxis becomes an object for consciousness only in its hypostatized and abstracted form: It is conscious productive praxis taking itself as a praxis *of* consciousness; conscious production taking itself as a production carried out by consciousness itself. In short, consciousness takes itself as its own object, and sees itself objectified in the *images* that *it* creates, that is, the bread and the wine. The mediation of this consciousness by real praxis, the real production or activity in the process of which this consciousness comes to form the "image," or the objects, is transparent here. It vanishes from sight. Human praxis remains, for Feuerbach, the praxis of self-consciousness, unmediated by "concrete, sensuous, living praxis," or mediated by it only as the means by which this self-consciousness can represent itself to itself. Thus, the consciousness of the natural world is only a *form* of the self-consciousness of man, albeit that form in which he sees himself as transcending nature, by transforming it in consciousness as his *own* object.

This is the inversion, the anthropological reduction of religious consciousness by Feuerbach. The supernatural is "super-natural" only insofar as it is human, and human insofar as it marks the self-consciousness of the distinction between the human and the natural. The hints, the ingredients of a theory of human praxis are contained here, but in their reflected form. Here the reflection is not in the imagination, as in religious praxis, but in *thought*. It is religious consciousness secularized, demythologized, but now cast in the form of philosophy. We have descended from heaven, but not yet to earth.

The Essence of Christianity marks Feuerbach's greatest achievement: his unraveling of the process of objectification in its psychological form, as a process of human self-knowledge. The self-differentiating *Idea*, in Hegel's *Phenomenology of Mind* or in the *Logic*, creates its other out of itself as the condition for its self-reflection, as its mode or process of self-consciousness. Feuerbach takes the Hegelian *Idea* and transforms it as the species consciousness of man, coming to know itself in its objectified and alienated form in religious consciousness. The species being that is the object of this consciousness, hypostatized as God, as divine being, is therefore known only symbolically, as an imaginary *other*-being. Therefore, for Feuerbach, religious consciousness is the paradigm of this alienated form of species self-consciousness, and he reveals its "secret," he disalienates it by showing that the divine *is* the human taken as a species being, and therefore as transcending human finitude, individuality, dependency insofar as the species as such transcends these limits. But the species transcends these limits, for Feuerbach, only in the modes of consciousness itself, as feeling, will, thought. As a species it *is* itself, or it has its essence, *in* these modes. The species activity is therefore feeling, willing, thinking. These modes objectify themselves in the praxis of this consciousness, according to Feuerbach, as objects of feeling, objects of will, objects of thought. The "world" that is created by this activity is therefore a world constituted by objectified feeling, objectified will, objectified thought. But it is therefore the world *as* human species being. Just as for Hegel, Nature has no independent being in itself, is nothing but the *other-sidedness* of Spirit, so too, for Feuerbach, in *The Essence of Christianity*, Nature is the *other-sidedness* of species consciousness. It is objectified species consciousness. But with this difference: Nature provides the material; consciousness, or the human mind, provides the form in which this material becomes an object for human beings. The praxis of consciousness, insofar as it is an activity of objectification, transforms or informs the material or natural world, makes it an object. The distinction between man and nature becomes a conscious one, according to Feuerbach, in the recognition (or self-recognition) by consciousness of its form-giving activity. But insofar as man takes himself, and not nature, as his object, consciousness provides *both* the matter and the form, because the essence of man is his consciousness. His being is conscious being, and his recognition of himself as a species being resides in his recognition of consciousness as the species nature (albeit consciousness now widely understood as including sensibility, feeling, willing, thinking, and not just thought itself).

Where, then, does the break with idealism come in Feuerbach? Is the substitution of human species being for the Hegelian *Idea* anything more than a substitution of a humanist idealism for the more abstract rationalist idealism of Hegel? Where is the bond between an independent natural world and the "world" of human consciousness? For Feuerbach, as for Hegel, the bond cannot lie outside consciousness, but must be within consciousness itself. It lies in the directedness of consciousness upon an object, in the intentionality of consciousness itself. The bond to nature, to an objective world, therefore lies in the very form of consciousness as requiring an *other*, that is, in the subject-object relation that is the essential form of consciousness. But if this is then interpreted as a self-relation, in which the object of consciousness is consciousness itself, as will, feeling, desire, sensation (i.e., as ultimately self-consciousness), then the *other* has no real otherness, no independent otherness, and we are back within the charmed circle of idealism. If we are no longer caught within the egocentric predicament, then we are certainly still caught within the species-centric predicament. The *Thou* as other is only an other as an instantiation of species consciousness. It is an other only by virtue of its being, like the self, a conscious being.

Does Feuerbach transcend this anthropocentrism, then? In *The Essence of Christianity*, he appears not to, and this was the earliest criticism of this work. But there is a break in the circle, in Feuerbach's very notion of the genesis and purpose of this species activity. In religious praxis, the practicality that is the essence of belief is the concern for human well-being, for the relief of suffering, for the satisfaction of needs, whether needs of the heart, of feeling, or for sustenance. The recognition of the other, as well as the form in which the other is constituted as an object of belief or of feeling, derives from *dependency on* the other. The praxis of belief is a needy praxis. Only for God is praxis a joyful, free praxis, stripped of necessity, creative for its own sake, or arising out of the very nature of divinity as creative. The creation, the praxis that makes its objects out of need is a human praxis. What it expresses is the need for the other, the need for its objects. Man needs God because man needs man. Thus, the creation of God by the praxis of belief is an expression of the dependence of human beings on each other. According to Feuerbach, consciousness of an other as a being like myself, in the *I-Thou* relation, is the species nature. The very recognition of oneself as a species being *is* the very *act* of species being that constitutes the species itself as a species. But this is only the *form* of species being. Its *content* is the need for the other, the dependence upon the *Thou* as an existential condition. In this interpretation the essence of species being is not species consciousness as such, but the dependence of man on man, which expresses itself *as* species consciousness. The *activity* of species consciousness, its praxis, is its expression, or its objectification of this dependence.

For Feuerbach, this objectification of dependence in religious praxis takes the form of language and symbol–the prayer, the miracle, the ritual, the sacrament, the Incarnation, the concepts and forms of God.

The dependence of man on man is supplemented, however, by the dependence of the species on nature. But this too takes the form of an anthropomorphized nature–nature as that which satisfies, or can satisfy human needs. This objective other–whether other human beings or nature–appears concretely as the origin of consciousness itself in the form of the *feeling* of dependency. This feeling of dependency or of need is the immediate source of the activity of consciousness, and as a source, it has to be within consciousness, it has to be conscious feeling, desire, want, which rises to full self-consciousness only in the praxis that objectifies this feeling of dependency. In religious consciousness, this objectification takes place by way of the praxis of belief, as a world-constituting praxis. The imaginary world of belief comes to be understood as the fantastic reflection of real human needs or dependency only when the secret of this belief is revealed, that is, when we recognize that religion, and its rationalized or "negative" essence, theology, is only an esoteric anthropology.

We may characterize Feuerbach's achievement here, in Hegelian terms, as "abstract negation," namely, the negation of the alienated form of religious consciousness, without yet an achievement of the "positive" content of this consciousness as involved in and as a reflection of the practical this-worldly activity that constitutes the human species nature. But this is to require of Feuerbach that he transcend his own critique. Insofar as he opens the way for a negation of the religious *form* of human self-knowledge, he retains the "positive" content of religion in its anthropological form, as unalienated, demystified human self-knowledge.

What is crucial here is the shift in *Problematik* that follows from Feuerbach's critique of religion, namely, the transition from the concept of praxis, in its fantastic or symbolic religious form to its worldly form. Though Feuerbach conceives this worldly form of praxis still as a praxis of reflection, of knowledge, he is to take still another critical step. The rationalized, secular form of religious consciousness, stripped of its imagery, of its anthropomorphism, and abstracted from its human origins and its human content, is speculative philosophy. This too remains otherworldly, according to Feuerbach. He then proceeds from the critique of religion to the critique of philosophy itself. Here the program calls for a conclusion concerning philosophy parallel to that which Feuerbach arrived at for theology, and for religious consciousness in general, namely, that philosophy itself has to be negated, as the last, esoteric form of theology; that philosophy itself has to be transformed from a theory that reflects an inverted, fantastic psychological process to one that reflects living human praxis in the world. Finally, this negation of speculative philosophy calls for a positive theory of human praxis, and for a theorized praxis, that is, an actualization or realization of theory *in* the world, by means of this praxis.

Feuerbach's achievement here has been viewed differently by various commentators. For some, Feuerbach already contains the kernel of Marx's program–"To make philosophy worldly, and to make the world philosophical," changing it by means of a theorized political and scientific praxis. For others, Feuerbach remains on the reflective side of praxis, as Marx himself held. In this view, Feuerbach remains a *secularizer* of religion, on the grounds of religion itself, and not yet a revolutionary.

The Essence of Christianity is not Feuerbach's last work. It is the last work of his transformation from Hegelian idealism to naturalistic and secular humanism. In the works that followed, Feuerbach was to draw more explicit and more radical conclusions from his critique of religion. In particular, he was to transform the critique of religion into a critique of philosophy itself, and to develop that distinctive notion of *Sinnlichkeit*, of sensibility, which links him most clearly with the French eighteenth-century materialists, and with the development of a humanist-materialist epistemology.

As striking as these later works are, both rhetorically and philosophically, they are not as interesting, subtle, or innovative as what had gone before. They represent the resolutions, or attempted resolutions, of problems, given a new framework. But they do not constitute, as does the earlier work, the very formation of this framework itself. And this, it seems to me, is the most exciting part of any philosophical or scientific program.

The Critique of Philosophy and the Development of a Materialist Humanism Part I: Empiricism, Sensationism, and Realism in Feuerbach's Later Works

Feuerbach's critique of religion is the *Vorschule*, the preparatory school and testing ground, for his critique of philosophy itself. In *The Essence of Christianity*, Feuerbach brings to bear those instruments of philosophical and methodological critique that he had forged in the earlier writings, and in his break with Hegelian idealism. These are, principally:

1. *The anthropological "reduction"*: the method of interpreting or translating the content of religious belief and of its theorized form, theology, into its human correlate–the inversion of the divine as human. The operative reductive phrase here is "nothing but."

2. *The humanist interpretation of the Hegelian Idea*: the reconstitution of the objective *Idea* of Hegel's *Phenomenology of Mind* and of the *Logic* as human essence, or *species being*, and the derationalization of this essence as not merely a reasoning or thinking essence, but also a sensing, feeling, willing essence; moreover, the insistence on the *practical* character of this essence or nature, as it is expressed in belief, and the revelation of the contradiction between the practical and the theoretical, in theology, as a contradiction between belief and understanding; correlatively, the attempt to integrate or connect sensibility (sense perception and feeling) with thinking itself, and to comprehend this sensibility as a species-specific or human mode of activity and receptivity.

3. *The emphasis on the concrete individual as the "real existent"*: the relegation of the universal to an object of thought alone, realized only *in* consciousness; and the interpretation of consciousness itself as this universal, as the *object* of consciousness, that is, as self-consciousness. This leads to difficulties, if not outright contradictions, in Feuerbach's notion of species being as this universal itself, that is, to the objective

existence of species being *as* self-consciousness, realized not as an independently existing "real," but as constituted by the species awareness of individuals, in what may be regarded as an (Aristotelian) conceptualist position on the question of universals. The critique of Feuerbach from the "left" (e.g., by Stirner, Marx, and Engels) rests squarely on this issue, in the charge that Feuerbach's individuals are not concrete enough, that his species being is too abstract, and that his humanism, therefore, remains an abstract humanism.

4. *The "genetic-analytic" or "genetic-critical" method*: the approach which takes the essence of a philosophical or theological idea to be revealed, in showing its sources within the framework or problem setting in which it arose. In the *History*, Feuerbach had followed a Hegelian model of developmental stages, revealing a dialectic in the history of philosophy in which problems arise and are first resolved *within* a framework before the framework itself is replaced more radically. Thus, we have as typical locutions in Feuerbach: "The resolution of this contradiction [between "universality" as reason, and "particularity" as the religiomythical forms of ancient thought, bounded by ethnic and sensory representations] within paganism itself, is pagan philosophy" (III, 1); or of Leibniz, that he overcomes the dualism of spirit and matter, in an age of mechanism, only by recasting idealism under the form of mechanism (IV, 181); or of Spinoza, that he is "the negation of theology on the grounds of theology itself" (III, 340n.).

The works that followed the publication of *The Essence of Christianity* fall into two groups, roughly: first, those in which Feuerbach elaborates, defends, and sometimes revises his fundamental critique of religion (e.g., *The Essence of Faith in Luther's Sense: A Supplement to The Essence of Christianity* [1844], *The Essence of Religion* [1845], *Lectures on the Essence of Religion* [1851], and the *Theogony* [1857]); second, those in which he develops the consequences of the critique of religion as a critique of philosophy itself and in which he develops his "positive" doctrine, that is, his sensationalist realism, his anthropologism, his humanist materialism (e.g., the *Preliminary Theses Towards the Reform of Philosophy* [1842], *Principles of the Philosophy of the Future* [1843], *The Dualism of Body and Soul, Flesh and Spirit, Once Again* [1846], "The Natural Sciences and the Revolution" [1850], *The Mystery of Sacrifice or Man Is What He Eats* [1862], and *On Spiritualism and Materialism* [1863–6]).

It is somewhat surprising, not altogether so, that the corpus of Feuerbach's works, from 1842 to the 1860s, large as it is, is rather simple to comprehend and offers very little that is substantively new. Feuerbach's reputation rests on two things: (1) his striking and masterful critique of religion, his discovery of an essential critical standpoint that permitted him at once to pay serious attention to the content of religion and to criticize it in a profound philosophical-anthropological way; and (2) his critique of speculative idealism and his formulation of an alternative "philosophy for the future," a humanist materialism, based on a thoroughgoing sensationalist epistemology. Where his later works are more than elaborations of the themes in his critique of religion, they are attempts at this new philosophy. With varying emphases, it may be called anthropologism, sensationalism, materialism, humanism; and so it has been variously taken up by later followers, interpreters, and critics of Feuerbach.

What Feuerbach lost, in the later works, was a certain philosophical subtlety of thought. Whereas the earlier works, from the *Dissertation* on, are often knotty, sometimes obscure, but almost always sophisticated treatments of epistemological and metaphysical themes, the later works show a certain simplification, and in places, even a crudity of thought. The simplification is deliberate. Feuerbach had discovered his own style, and meant to be understood not only by the learned, but by the intelligent layman as well. The revisions in style and language through the three editions of the *Essence of Christianity* are clear evidence of this intention.[1]

But the stylistic shift, from the learned to the lay language, from the Latinate barbarisms of speculative philosophy to a plainer and more popular German vocabulary and syntax, was no isolated literary matter for Feuerbach. It was occasioned by a shift in philosophical viewpoint, and a shift in viewpoint about philosophy itself. Style was taken to be the outer form, the show of the writer's intentions, his sense of his audience, and of the philosophical spirit of his work. The humanization and deprofessionalization of his style was, for Feuerbach, a personal expression of his own antiprofessionalism (i.e., philosophical professionalism or "professorism") and of his sense that the writer and the man had to be in intimate union. In an early literary effort, little noted (*The Writer and the Man*, published in 1834, when Feuerbach was twenty-six), he had written, " 'Do you want to recognize and judge the man in the writer?' Yes . . . . because the writer reveals his true self, which is at one with his creative spirit, in his writings . . . . it is in these that his true being can be recognized and judged" (I, 343–4). And in his *Diary* (1834–6, published in 1846 as part of the *Fragments Towards a Characterization of My Philosophical Curriculum Vitae*) Feuerbach added, "One writes for others, not for oneself. In any case, I can't write for myself alone. What I write must be directly addressed towards another person, or to humankind in general. Therefore, I write as clearly and lucidly as possible. I don't want to torment other people with my writings" (X, 168). A more despairing view of the gap between thinking and writing appears in the *Posthumous Aphorisms* (edited by Grün, and first published in 1874):

> We always are more and think more than we write. Writing involuntarily fixes the self in a one-sided way. Our otherwise fluent ideas, which are bound up in our living intercourse with others, become static and fixed as soon as they are put on paper. From the written page, one can't read back or conclude anything more than what the person is on paper. There is an infinite difference between the paper-person and the real, living person. (X, 346)

As one reads Feuerbach, however, much is revealed by the style, the tone, the character of his writings. The early works are critical, serious, exciting. There is much of the voyage of discovery in them, the sense of one's own powers, and a certain public show of learning as well. The struggle between professional scholarship and authentic self-revelation is clear on the printed page, but it is subordinated to the sense of excitement in the discovery and formation of a critical framework. The later works, in general, are deliberately simpler, not less combative, but sometimes more petulant, impatient, even defensive, sometimes endlessly repetitive. Yet there is a certain confidence and clarity about the later works: "I have arrived at a clear revelation of the secret of religion, of theology, of philosophy. My new framework puts the philosophy of the past in perspective, reveals it in its true light. The philosophy of the future starts with this revelation." This is what Feuerbach seems to say, and there is a sense of impatience in the way in which he presents the new "positive" philosophy. It is as if he were saying, "Isn't it clear and self-evident? What could be simpler? Only look and see, open your eyes, and the truths I point to will speak for themselves!"

Both in a personal and a philosophical sense, *The Essence of Christianity* was the watershed of Feuerbach's philosophical development. He had begun by fashioning a critical method–the so-called genetic-analytic method–on the foundations of the Hegelian dialectic. The earlier works were all leading somewhere. From the *Dissertation* through the historical works, the shorter critical reviews, the defense and then the critique of Hegel, Feuerbach becomes successively more skeptical of abstract or speculative philosophy, more intrigued with a nominalist ontology of individuals, more and more concerned with the empirical, the concrete, the human. In *The Essence of Christianity*, Feuerbach arrived at the first full and systematic use of this new framework. He knew he had said something new. It was acknowledged as such by those closest to him, the left Hegelians, who received the work with great enthusiasm. And it was widely attacked by the "other camp," which was all the more evidence of its import. Here, too, Feuerbach could exercise his theological learning, he could open up his style, give reign to his feeling for imagery, for the striking phrase, for the dialectically inverted aphorism. Feuerbach was *in medias res*, and in the middle of his own thing. The rest was consequences. The voyage of discovery was over. Now the task was to consolidate, expand, elaborate; moreover, to develop the consequences of the critique of religion for the critique of philosophy. But these consequences themselves had the air of the method of reduction in mathematics, that is, the solution of a new problem by its translation into the form of a problem already solved. The critique of philosophy *was* the critique of religion–especially of religion in its theorized form in theology–*if* it could be shown that philosophy was "nothing but" theology, stripped of its irrationality, its contradiction-laden attempt to reconcile feeling and thought within religious consciousness, its encumbrance by the imagery of sense and feeling, and the imperatives of faith. If the secret of (speculative) philosophy is theology, and the secret of theology is anthropology, then the secret of philosophy is also anthropology. Q.E.D. Thus, if philosophy is "nothing but" rationalized theology, and if theology is "nothing but" rationalized religious consciousness, or belief; and further, if religious consciousness is "nothing but" human self-consciousness as yet unaware that the object and concern of belief is the human, then philosophy is "nothing but" this very same human self-consciousness, in its doubly alienated form. The naturalistic and anthropological reduction of philosophy to its human content, *and* to its human intent, is therefore the final enlightenment, the return of man to himself as his own object, as species being. The Hegelian *Idea* thus returns to itself, in self-recognition, but recognizes itself as the *Idea* of the human, the hypostatized self-consciousness of the species, but therefore, not yet as the species itself; rather, only as the species *ideated*, reflected in consciousness, and therefore in the form of a universal as an object of thought. But the species is not thought alone, nor reason alone. It is constituted by living, feeling, needy, finite individuals who *also* think. The revelation of the Hegelian *Idea as Idea*, as the *image* of species being for thought, is the dissolution of the *Idea* as a self-subsistent or objective entity. Only man, only the human, is the real object. The *Idea* is the reflection of this being in thought, or, more accurately, the reflection of this being to itself in thought. Philosophy finally comes to know itself for what it is.

Thus, for Feuerbach, the grounds and methods of the critique of theology become the grounds and methods for the critique of philosophy itself. Just as Feuerbach's "negation" of theology is not to serve to destroy religion, but rather to reveal it, to unmask or demystify it, to show it for what it really is, to bring religion to full self-consciousness, so too the "negation" of philosophy is not to destroy philosophy, but to reveal, its true essence, in the human. True, the *form* of theology is destroyed, and so too is the *form* of philosophy. But this is done in order to lay bare its real content, the rational kernel inside the irrational husk (to borrow a metaphor from Marx that he had borrowed from Feuerbach).

There is a difference between the position arrived at in *The Essence of Christianity* and what follows it, however. The difference lies in the specification of what counts as "the human," the true object of both religion and philosophy. As we have seen, in *The Essence of Christianity*, the human that is projected as the divine is the being that is *in itself* a feeling, willing, thinking being. The objects of feeling, willing, and thinking are, however, feeling, willing, and thinking itself. The *images* of religious consciousness are these very features of human conscious life. Thus, though the reference of the image, or of the religious representation–that is, the reference of the Word, the prayer, the act of belief–is taken to be God, or Christ, or Mary, or the Trinity, it is really human feeling itself, will itself, thought itself that clothes itself in these representations, and, in reality, knows itself *through* them, albeit in alienated form. The difficulty, from an epistemological point of view, is in establishing the reference of any act of consciousness to anything beyond consciousness itself. Insofar as the *Thou*, the other person, is the object of consciousness, it is only as an embodied consciousness: consciousness recognizing itself in the *Thou*. For the *Thou* is one's *own* species being recognized as an other, and one's own species being lies precisely *in* this recognition of the other as another consciousness like oneself. The problem posed by the anthropocentric predicament is, clearly, the problem of knowledge of the *other* as nonconscious being, as what is not-human, that is, as nature, or the "external world." Feuerbach is acutely aware of this problem, and in the last sections of *The Essence of Christianity*, begins to address himself to it, but, as we have seen, inadequately.

The position he arrives at in the later works is largely an attempt to cope with this question. It is the question of an epistemological realism, that is, of a view that the object of consciousness (or of knowledge, properly speaking) is independent of the act of consciousness, that it exists in an ontologically independent way, and is not only an object *for* consciousness. Feuerbach could not simply return to a Kantian position, positing the *thing in itself* in such a way as to put it forever beyond access by the knowing subject. Fichte and Hegel had already transformed the *thing in itself* into a *thing for us*, by the radical move of making the alleged *thing in itself* the Ego itself, or consciousness itself, which comes to be known, therefore, because it is not *beyond* consciousness, but *is* consciousness (or the Ego) in its own other-sidedness. This, in fact, is the position Feuerbach adopts, simply transforming the abstract or metaphysical *Ego* or *Idea* of speculative philosophy into the *human*, into species being itself. But how to break out of the circle of idealism then? What does it mean to interpret this *other* as the human, or as species being? What purchase on reference *beyond* consciousness does this afford us epistemologically?

Feuerbach's resolution of this problem lies in his "positive" theory. Beyond the critique of what the object of consciousness is *not*, of what it is mistakenly taken to be–*God*, or the *Idea*–is the question of what this object *is*. Feuerbach's anthropologism yields only a humanist answer, inadequate in that the human "object" of consciousness is simply this consciousness itself, though finally recognized *as* human and not superhuman. But this is merely a replacement of the alienated religious or theological humanism with a secular humanism. And this replacement is at best a negative achievement, an outcome of critique. It posits no new object beyond that already posited by a world-denying religion; it does not yet posit a world. It negates the *other* world, but it does not yet give us *this* world. Feuerbach's emphasis on a "this-worldly" interpretation of religion gives us this world only as the human *itself*, and not yet either a human world (i.e., a world within which the human *also* exists as this-worldly) or a natural world (i.e., a world that exists beyond the human, insofar as the human is taken *only* as consciousness, as the act of recognizing oneself as a species being). This second *desideratum*, this need for objective reference, Feuerbach answers with his *sensationism*, his theory of the senses, or of sensibility as the context of the *givenness* of this world, as an other. The positive doctrine is then an empiricist realism, or a sense realism. What is given to sensation, or to sensibility (the term *Sinnlichkeit* is difficult to render precisely in English because of the philosophically loaded connotations of any of the usual translations) is not simply sensibility itself. Sensibility is not its *own* object, as feeling, will, and thought are. Sensibility does not simply reflect the human to itself under the form of sensibility. It gives us the material world *directly*, and without mediation. It is the act of immediate certainty that an external world exists, and is, as such, veridical and incorrigible.

Two questions arise here: (1) How will Feuerbach deal with the Hegelian critique of sense certainty, the opening critique of *The Phe-*

nomenology of Mind? There Hegel had shown that the appearance of immediate certainty in sense awareness is immediately compromised by the act of consciousness; that ostension, as pure, dumb reference to a *this* or a *here* or a *now* is immediately involved with universals, and that its particularity and immediacy is a chimaera. (2) How will Feuerbach avoid the subjectivism of classical empiricism (or of later sense-datum theories) in which the external world vanishes into my own sense awareness, becomes merely a bundle of sense impressions, or is relegated to the status of a mental construction *from* such sense data? In short, how will Feuerbach develop an empirical *realism* as against an empirical *phenomenalism*, and how will he develop this as a materialist, as against an idealist epistemology?

These traditional terms are not especially enlightening, because they remain philosophically vague, though they serve to link certain traditions of solution together. Yet what Feuerbach ends up with, or *wants* to end up with, is an empirical materialism, or an empirical realism, as the positive answer to speculative idealist philosophy. He has to negate Hegel without reverting to Locke or to Berkeley. He has to resolve Kant's dualism, of *phenomena* and *noumena*, without reverting to Hegel. And one thing more: He has to link his anthropologism with his empirical realism.

If there is the promise of anything new in the "positive" doctrine of Feuerbach, it is this latter. The characterization of the senses as human opens up for Feuerbach the possibilities of a reinterpretation of empiricism itself that is as much of a reform of empiricism as his critique of speculative theology and philosophy is a reform of idealism. Just as consciousness becomes more than thinking alone, in its abstract, intellectual, or rational form, in the critique of religion, so too in the critique of philosophy sensing becomes more than the mere operation of a sensory apparatus. The senses are *human* senses. They are therefore already endowed with an intentionality, with a human content, beyond sensation itself, taken in its narrower significations. They are the senses of a dependent, feeling, loving, willing, conscious being, and therefore they are more than abstract deliverers of bare sense data. But this makes them active, or at least, interpretive and no longer immediate in the traditional sense; or so it would seem. And here Feuerbach runs into real trouble in his "positive" doctrine: for his requirement of external reference is that sensibility be *passive*, that it give what is there, that it not reflect or intrude consciousness upon the given, but that it deliver up the given *tout court*, as *really other*. Feuerbach's *sensationism* thus faces the traditional problems of empiricism. Feuerbach's *anthropologism* offers a promise of resolving these problems. His later works exist in the tension between these two views. In a larger sense, Feuerbach's later work exists in the tension between the idealist and materialist traditions, and its virtue is that it transforms both of these traditions in a promising way.

FROM THE CRITIQUE OF RELIGION
TO THE CRITIQUE OF PHILOSOPHY

In 1842 and 1843, Feuerbach published two works in which the transition is made from the critique of religion to the critique of philosophy itself. The first—*Preliminary Theses Towards the Reform of Philosophy*—appeared originally with the term "Reformation" in the title, which was changed to "Reform" in the revised second edition of the work as part of the *Collected Works* published in 1846. But the ambition to carry out a "second Reformation" remains clear in the text, belying the modesty of the change in title. The second work—*Principles of the Philosophy of the Future*—appeared only after, as Feuerbach tells us, he had "cut it like a barbarian." Of it, he writes in the Preface to the First Edition, "These principles contain the continuation and further justification of my *Theses Towards the Reform of Philosophy*, which was banned by the most arbitrary decree of the German censors."[2]

The two works are systematically connected, for in them Feuerbach launches a critique of philosophy that, as he sees it, is the consequence of the critique of religion pursued in *The Essence of Christianity*. In both works, Feuerbach begins with a recapitulation of his critique of religion and of theology. In the *Principles*, he then goes on to a more or less historical sketch of the development of modern speculative philosophy as the continuation of theology by other means. The main object of this sketch is a critique of Hegelian philosophy, not for its own sake, but as the fullest exemplification, and most thorough development of the whole historical tradition of speculative philosophy, from Descartes and Spinoza and Leibniz through Kant, Fichte, and Schelling, to Hegel. This brief sketch, often aphoristic in style, then leads to the analogous treatment of Hegelian philosophy and speculative theology: the inversion of the categories of traditional metaphysics, and of the Hegelian phenomenology and logic, as themselves "nothing but" objectifications of the characteristics of human consciousness itself. This prepares us for the "positive" doctrine—the "philosophy of the future"—which is to transcend the Hegelian standpoint, and replace it with an anthropological and empirical standpoint, as the "negation" of abstract speculative idealism.

In the *Theses,* Feuerbach posits the methodological analogy between his critique of religion and his critique of philosophy, thus:

The method of reformative critique of speculative philosophy is in principle no different from that which one would use in philosophical critique of religion. In both cases, all one has to do is to make the predicate the subject and make the subject the object or principle–in other words, just turn speculative philosophy right side up, and you have the naked, pure truth. (II, 224)[3]

In the *Theses* and the *Principles,* then, Feuerbach simply carries forward the method of invertive interpretation carried out earlier in *The Essence of Christianity.* Just as, in *The Essence,* Feuerbach had shown that the divine predicates are to be taken as the subjects, and the subject–God–is to be taken as predicate, here the philosophical predicates of *Being*–the "God" of the metaphysicians–are taken to be the subjects, and the subject itself is taken to be human, that is, human thought itself. Thus, for example, where in religious language, the assertion is "God is love," Feuerbach had interpreted this to mean that "Love is God," that is, human love, the feature of human species feeling, is itself raised to an abstract, divine status, is adored as an object. In speculative philosophy, on the other hand, the divine predicates (e.g., necessity, unity, infinity, etc.) are taken to be predicates of *Being;* and *Being* itself is identified with consciousness, as a hypostatized, objective reality. By the anthropological reduction, Feuerbach then goes on to argue that this objectified consciousness–the *Idea*–is "nothing but" human consciousness as thinking or reason, and that all the metaphysical attributes of *Being,* or of the *Idea,* are "nothing but" attributes of this human thinking itself, taking itself as its own object. Thus, the "object" of speculative philosophy is shown to be the subject (i.e., human thinking), just as the "object" of speculative theology–God–is shown to be man, as feeling, willing, thinking being.

The *one-sidedness* of speculative philosophy is that it takes its subject-object–the human–only with respect to *one* feature of this human essence, that is, thinking. The *this-worldliness* of speculative philosophy, by contrast to theology, is that it takes theology's *God* to be *thought,* as thinking consciousness, or as reason. But the remaining *otherworldliness* of speculative philosophy is that it hypostatizes this reason or thought itself as a superhuman, objective entity. Thus, though reason expresses itself in human thought, for Hegel, it is not thereby reduced to human thought. Rather, it is both transcendent and immanent, in Hegel's view. But for Feuerbach, the transcendent nature of thought lies not in an objective *Reason* or *Idea,* but rather in the species nature of man, as transcending the finitude of the individual thinker. It is not transhuman, but transindividual. Where for Hegel, the transcendent nature of the Idea is both ontologically and logically prior to its immanent nature–for example, in human consciousness or in history (these are only the *means* of its unfolding or self-development)–for Feuerbach, the immanent nature of thought–thought as the property of concrete, finite individuals, and therefore as dependent on their existence, that is, on their sensate, practical individual existence–is both ontologically and logically prior to the transcendent nature of thought. Here Feuerbach's nominalism with respect to existence, and his conceptualism with respect to essence, or to universals, begins to come to the fore. What is interesting, historically, is that Feuerbach had already raised these questions for himself earlier, and had often adumbrated or even formulated his critical views (e.g., in the *Dissertation* [1828] and in *The Critique of Hegelian Philosophy* [1839]). His nominalism had begun to emerge as early as the *Leibniz* book (1835). In the *Theses* and the *Principles*, what we observe is a culmination of this earlier development, rather than a sudden change in view. Thus, for the reader of Feuerbach's works, both the *Theses* and the *Principles* are strangely reminiscent of the earlier works, but no longer in the mode of critical self-questioning and development. Rather, the style is assertoric and polemical. Where, in the Dorguth and Sengler reviews (1838), he had argued against empiricism and materialism, these very arguments now come home to roost in his reformulations of his own empiricism and materialism.

The method of inversion in the critique of philosophy almost appears as an account of Feuerbach's own philosophical development. In the somersault in which Hegel is turned upside down and stood upon his feet, we can recognize Feuerbach in almost every *stage* of the reversal. That is, we can see the process of transformation and inversion in the development of Feuerbach's own works. The critique of philosophy, in Feuerbach, then comes to appear not only as a dialectic of philosophical positions that Feuerbach describes in *others*, but as a self-critique, in which the dialectic of Feuerbach's own development shows itself. His critique of theology and of speculative philosophy is thus not simply a liberation, *by* Feuerbach, from the illusions of others, but a self-liberation, because Feuerbach is at once theologian, speculative philosopher, and critic, in his own development. What is overcome is thus preserved in its "rational form." The intriguing suggestion is that what Feuerbach *is* as a philosopher is largely constituted by what he conceives philosophy to be. He produces himself, so to speak, out of his own conception. He *is* his own self-conscious object, generating his critique as a series of negations of what he finds in himself.

In effect, he exemplifies the dialectic in his own progress through

"God, Reason, and Man," his "first, second, and last thoughts" as he called them. But Feuerbach is not the history of philosophy embodied. Rather, he incorporates this history, in his own unique way, and then serves as critic of this very incorporation. The reader may fail to recognize Spinoza, Kant, or Hegel in Feuerbach's version. But the very historicity *of* the history of philosophy—in this case, its being a history Feuerbachianized—is what makes it the distinctive object of the Feuerbachian critique. Further, this makes the history of philosophy appear such an extraordinarily appropriate object for the critique. The passages in the *Theses* and the *Principles* in which Spinoza, or Kant, or Hegel come under the Feuerbachian critique make it appear almost as if these philosophers said what they said, and in the way in which they said it, so as to be *proper* objects for the critical method of inversion that Feuerbach uses. The alternative conclusion is, of course, that Feuerbach had discovered *the very key* to the philosophical scriptures. How could he then fail to unlock one secret after another?

Once the key to Feuerbach's critique is recognized, the whole enterprise becomes a litany of inversions in which a point-for-point analysis of the main theses of speculative philosophy yields a series of "nothing but" reductions, like those in *The Essence of Christianity*. This would be a tiresome exercise, were it not for the insights that occur along the way and that make the critique plausible in its details. One by one, the dragons of speculative philosophy are slain—or better, reduced to human size. To mix a metaphor, and to borrow one from Feuerbach, the "ghosts" that are the objects of speculative philosophy appear once again as the living human beings they were, before they became the "departed spirits" of speculative theology and philosophy. The attributes of *Substance*, or of *Being*, or of the *Ego*, or of the *Idea*—whether in Spinoza's version, or in that of Descartes or Leibniz, or Kant, or Fichte, or Schelling, or Hegel—are all seen to be attributes of human thought itself. The Absolute becomes humanized, and *infinity, necessity, unity,* and so on, are all "reduced" to abstractions from the properties of human thought itself. Feuerbach shows that the metaphysical categories and characteristics that speculative philosophy posits are "nothing but" the categories and characteristics of the God of the theologians, cleansed of imagery and contradictions. Speculative philosophy is revealed, finally, as the last and most rational form of theology itself.

Moreover, this series of negations, reductions, inversions—these *aufhebungen* of traditional metaphysical ideas—now pose sharply the need for a "positive" doctrine, which breaks out of the circle in which consciousness eternally takes itself as its own object. "Metaphysics is esoteric psychology," Feuerbach writes. But an adequate psychology must now take into account not thought alone, but also sensation and feeling as well, in the context of practical human life.

How is one to break out of the circle of consciousness, however? The critique of speculative philosophy goes no further than to reveal this circle for what it really is; to disabuse us of the apparent objectivity, whose object turns out to be consciousness, or thinking itself, in its various philosophical objectifications. Is there a source, within theology or within speculative philosophy itself, for the objectivity of what is *not*-consciousness, of what lies beyond consciousness? Is nature, matter, the external world totally swallowed up in speculative theology or philosophy as nothing but God's *own* thought, or consciousness' *own* other-sidedness? As no more, then, than the other-being of the *Idea*?

Here Feuerbach introduces a new theme, and starts on a new path. The identification of God with Nature, in pantheism, is seen to be *more* than merely the objectification of the *consciousness of* Nature, or the consciousness of man's distinction *from* Nature. Feuerbach seems to be aware of the problem posed in the last sections of *The Essence of Christianity* concerning the grounds for an awareness of what exists beyond man, as an object *other* than his own nature, that is, as the natural or material world. In the *Theses*, this is only dimly suggested, in always compromised ways, as if Feuerbach were flirting with a more open materialism, but not yet ready to assert it. In the *Principles*, this treatment of *pantheism* as the transition to *materialism* is more explicit, but still problematic and not worked out. The issue is this: "Materialism" for Feuerbach ultimately connotes the material existence of human beings, and this in turn has its reality in their neediness, their dependency, and the sensibility, which is the mode in which finitude, the limits of the human and the recalcitrance of the "other" as really other all make themselves felt. "Matter" then does not appear as an abstraction, for Feuerbach, but only as the "concrete," given in sensibility and need. It is established, or constituted, so to speak, by these needs, and by sensibility, and its "externality" is also a quality recognized in these modes of conscious existence. Feuerbach then *derives* the independence of Nature, of the material world, from neediness and sensibility itself. But then he seems to be caught once again in another version of the Hegelian circle, which he criticizes, for the externality or the self-subsistence of the material world has no ground beyond what is given in sensibility itself. As a *condition* of sensibility, this externality begins to take on the features of the Kantian a priori structures of the understanding, which are derived from the understanding itself, as the transcendental conditions for its possibility. Analogously, Feuerbach seems to posit externality, an objective material world beyond the senses, as the a priori condition for the possibility of sensation –that is, as a transcendental deduction from sensibility itself.

The preoccupation with Nature, with the materiality of human existence itself, insofar as it is *of* and *in* Nature, develops as a sustained theme in Feuerbach's later works. In 1845, he publishes *The Essence of Religion*, which attempts to fill out the missing half of *The Essence of Christianity*, that is, precisely that half of religion that derives from the human recognition of an *external* nature, as its object, rather than from the human recognition of human nature itself as its object, as in *The Essence of Christianity*. This theme is further developed in the 1846 work *The Dualism of Body and Soul, Flesh and Spirit, Once Again*, in the 1848–9 *Lectures on the Essence of Religion*, and most explicitly, by way of an almost reductive physiological materialism, in his discussions of Moleschott's work, in "The Natural Sciences and the Revolution" (1850), and in *The Mystery of Sacrifice or Man Is What He Eats* (1862). His more methodological discussion of the question of a philosophical materialism is in *On Spiritualism and Materialism*, a late and incomplete work (written in 1863–6 and published in 1866).

The three main themes of the *Theses* and the *Principles* are (1) the methodological and historical sketch of the transition from the critique of religion to the critique of philosophy, especially in pre-Hegelian philosophy; (2) the critique of Hegelian philosophy itself as "rationalized theology"; (3) the "positive" doctrine, as an initial and uneasy combination of Feuerbach's anthropologism, his sensationism, and his nascent materialism. Let us examine these somewhat more closely.

At the beginning of the *Theses*, Feuerbach writes,

The secret of *theology* is *anthropology*, and the secret of *speculative philosophy* is *theology–speculative theology*, therefore, which differs from the ordinary sort in that it brings the latter up to date, makes it definitive, realizes it, and does so by making the worldly the Divine Essence which ordinary theology, out of fear and ignorance, puts off beyond reach and makes otherworldly. (II, 222)

Similarly, in the *Principles*, he writes, "The essence of speculative philosophy is nothing but God's essence in its rationalized, realized, contemporary form. Speculative philosophy is the true, consistent, fully rational form of theology" (II, 246).

The sections in both works that constitute the negative critique of speculative philosophy simply show how this translation is to be effected. Thus, in the *Theses*, we have such passages as the following:

The essence of theology is the essence of man, but taken as transcendent, and posited as if it were external to man; the essence of Hegel's *Logic* is thought made transcendent, human thought posited as if it were external to man. (II, 226)

Metaphysics or Logic is a real, immanent science only when it is not separated from the so-called subjective Spirit. Metaphysics is esoteric psychology. . . . Hegel's Absolute Spirit is nothing but the abstract, so-called Finite Spirit alienated from itself, just as the infinite essence of theology is nothing but abstract, finite essence. (II, 226)

The "Absolute Spirit" is the "departed spirit" of theology which still lurks as a ghost in Hegelian philosophy. . . . Theology is belief in ghosts. But whereas ordinary theology casts its ghosts in the form of the sensuous imagination, speculative philosophy casts them in the form of non-sensuous abstraction. (II, 227)

So, too, in the *Principles*, Feuerbach repeats this formula in several variations, but with a fuller range of historical examples. The main point seems to be a Hegelian one: A rigorous and consistent rationality rids itself of the sensuous imagery that clings to the "ordinary" forms of representation of the *Idea*, to its figurative modes of comprehension, and makes it finally an object of pure thought. Thus, Feuerbach writes,

Just as once the abstraction from everything sensuous and material was the necessary condition of theology, so was it also the necessary condition of speculative philosophy, with this one difference: that the abstraction of theology, whose object is an abstract being, nevertheless at the same time represented it as a sensuous being, as itself a sensuous abstraction; and thus the abstraction of theology is an *ascetic* abstraction; while the abstraction of speculative philosophy is only a spiritual, thinking one, only a scientific or theoretical abstraction, with no practical significance. The beginning of Cartesian philosophy –namely, the abstraction from sensuousness, from matter,– is the beginning of speculative philosophy. (II, 256)

What it means, for Feuerbach, to say that the theologian's God has no "practical significance" for speculative philosophy is that this God is ultimately dispensable, once He delivers the goods. The "goods" are "prime mover," "ground of being," and so on–abstract principles required *by* the system of the world, but not immanent principles *of* this world, concretely. Descartes and Leibniz still conceive of God as immaterial, divine being, says Feuerbach. God is still

a principle of philosophy, but only as an object distinct from thought and therefore as a principle only in general and only in the imagination, not in actuality or in truth. God is only the first and general cause of matter, of motion, of activity; but particular motions and activities, determinate actual material things are conceived and known as independent of God. Leibniz and Descartes are idealists only with respect to the general. When it comes to the particular, they are just plain materialists. (II, 256)

But God–the philosopher's God (e.g., the perfect thinker, the pure activity of the intellect of classical speculative theology and philosophy) –is an absolute idealist. For God, all things are known

without the senses or the imagination; he is pure intellect, that is pure in the sense of being separated from all sensuousness or materiality. For Him, therefore, all material things are only pure beings of the understanding, thoughts; for Him, there exists no matter at all, for matter relates only to the dark inchoate representations of sensibility. (II, 255)

Such a God, says Feuerbach, is nothing but the philosopher's objectification of abstract intellect, or reason itself.

Absolute Idealism is nothing but the divine intellect of Leibnizian theism in its realized form, the systematically elaborated, pure understanding which strips everything bare of sensory raiment and turns it into a pure object of the understanding, into a thought object, which has nothing to do with anything alien to it, and is concerned with itself alone as the Essence of Essences. (II, 256)

The characteristic act of pure thought is abstraction–the abstraction from all differences, all concrete determinations. Feuerbach sees in speculative philosophy the hypostatization of this *real* capacity of thought as an external, objective essence. But this is just that abstraction that in *The Essence of Christianity*, was also seen in a contradictory way, as *both* all-determining *and* beyond all determinations (e.g., the abstract God of creation who creates the *All* from nothing, without determinate means). Thus, Feuerbach writes,

The Absolute or Infinite of speculative philosophy, psychologically considered, is nothing but the indeterminate, the unconditioned–the abstraction from all determinate being, which is posited as something distinct from this abstraction, but at the same time re-identified with this abstract essence. Historically considered, however, this is nothing but the same old theological-metaphysical Being, or non-Being, infinite, non-human, non-material, undetermined, uncreated–the pre-worldly Nothing posited as Act. (II, 225)

This immaterial Being, beyond all determinations, is not simply the hypostatized or objectified form of thought itself. For actual thought is determinate, differentiated, "concrete" in the Hegelian sense of a self-differentiating dialectic. But if the Absolute, or the *Idea* in itself, which speculative philosophy posits as an essence beyond actual or concrete thinking activity, is not simply the objectification of thought, what is it? Feuerbach sees in this conception the hypostatization of a particular capacity of thought, namely, the capacity for *abstraction*. The Absolute is therefore the projected or mystified form in which *abstraction* is posited as an object *for* thought. The Absolute, as infinite, unconditioned, necessary *Being* is therefore nothing but the objectification of the infinity, the unconditionedness, the necessity, the absoluteness of abstract thought, posited as thought's own object, and as an object that is beyond thought itself.

What is the source or origin of this capacity *in* thought itself, however? Here Feuerbach makes his empirical move. The source and origin of abstract thought is in "concrete" thinking, that is, in sensibility, in the finite modes of empirical thought. Further, if one pursues this genesis, then, Feuerbach argues, the origin and condition of this thought itself lie in what is *beyond* thinking, namely, in finite, determinate *being*, or "sensuous, material, individual, real being." We are concerned, says Feuerbach, not with thought as an abstract essence, as a *Being*, but rather with human thinking activity. This human thinking activity has its ground not in itself, as does the Absolute, nor is it *causa sui*, as Substance is in Spinoza. Rather, it has its ground in the finite–in nature, sensibility, the material world of "real human existence."

Thus, Feuerbach prepares us for the "new" philosophy that is just the inversion of the old idealist metaphysics, namely, for the "positive," realist empiricism, and for his strange mixture of humanism and materialism.

The classical issue between materialism and idealism is that of ontological priority, if not also that of logical priority. Feuerbach's critique of speculative idealism takes as its first task the reversal of these priorities, in particular with regard to that all-important notion of Hegelian philosophy, the infinite. For Hegel, the Absolute Idea is infinite, but not insofar as it is beyond all finite determinations. Rather, it is infinite as containing in itself all finite determinations. Moreover, it derives these finite determinations from itself, it generates them by self-differentiation, in the dialectic unfolding of the *Idea*. Its infinity is thus posited *first*, as the condition for this self-activity in which the *Idea* passes from its unconditioned, undifferentiated unity to its fully differentiated unity, as it becomes an *Idea* both in and for itself. But Feuerbach argues that this finitude, this differentiation in which the *Idea* concretizes itself, or passes from abstract to concrete being, is a false finitude, a merely reflected finitude, merely the finite as it is *thought*, or as a product of thought, and not as real finite and determinate existence.

The philosophy which derives the finite from the infinite, the determinate from the indeterminate *can never arrive at a true positing of the finite and the determinate*. The finite is derived from the infinite–that means: the infinite, the indeterminate becomes determined, *negated*; it is admitted that without determination, i.e., without finitude, the infinite is nothing but the finite posited as the *reality* of the infinite. Nevertheless, this negative un-being of the Absolute still remains at the foundation: the posited finitude is thus always negated and transcended. The *finite* is the *negation of the infinite*, and again, the *infinite* is the negation of the *finite*. The philosophy of the Absolute is a *contradiction*. (II, 229)

The task of true philosophy is not the recognition of the infinite as finite, but the recognition of the finite as nonfinite, as infinite, or, to put it differently, not to posit the finite in the infinite, but rather the infinite in the finite (II, 229–30).

Feuerbach goes on to argue that the finite is ontologically primary being:

The starting-point of philosophy is not God, not the Absolute, not Being as a *predicate* of the Absolute, or of the Idea–the starting-point of philosophy is the finite, the determinate, the actual. Without the finite, the infinite cannot be conceived. Can you think of, or define Quality without thinking of a determinate quality? Thus it is the determinate and not the indeterminate which is first, for determinate quality is nothing but real quality; the real quality precedes the conceived quality. (II, 230)

Finally: "The true speculative philosophy concerns nothing but what is *truly and universally empirical*. One of the deepest and truest thoughts of Hegel is what he says, though only by the way, in talking about Aristotle in the *History of Philosophy*: 'The empirical in its totality is the speculative'" (II, 231). Thus, the Feuerbachian inversion is complete. Speculative idealism, stood back on its feet, is empirical realism. Ontological priority goes to the finite, the determinate, the empirical, the individual–in a word, what Feuerbach calls the *real*.

The road taken so far by speculative philosophy, from the abstract to the concrete, from the ideal to the real, is an inverted one. On this road one will never arrive at true, objective reality, but only at the reification of [speculative philosophy's] own abstractions; nor will one arrive at real freedom of the spirit. For only the recognition of things and beings in their objective actuality makes a person free and clear of all prejudices. The transition from the ideal to the real takes place only in practical philosophy. (II, 232)

But what is this "practical philosophy"? What is the "new philosophy" Feuerbach speaks about? What is this "philosophy of the future," this new Reformation? Thus far, we have arrived at the negative critique of the "old philosophy," speculative idealism. The arguments and criticisms marshalled by Feuerbach against Descartes, Leibniz, Kant, Fichte, Schelling are all intended to show that speculative philosophy constructs the world, or being, from thought. The extended critique of Hegel, begun in the 1839 work, and continued through the

Theses and at length in the *Principles* (especially in the middle sections, 19–31) is intended as both a critique and appreciation of Hegel. The contradiction within speculative philosophy lies in its attempt to generate the finite and determinate, real world out of the ideal–that is, out of the abstract, Absolute *Idea*. But the Absolute Idea is nothing but the conceptual representation, the revelation of the *standpoint* of speculative philosophy itself. The standpoint of speculative philosophy is theory. But this is also the limit of speculative philosophy. It cannot get beyond theory, that is, beyond thought itself. So it swallows everything up *in* thought, makes of every being a *thought*-being. The negation of this idealism is the limit or boundary of thought itself–that is, that which is *not*-thought. Hegelian idealism, says Feuerbach, is the *double* negation of idealism: first it takes thought beyond itself to its *other* (i.e., to what is *not*-thought), but then this other is reestablished *in* thought, as thought's *own* other. The sensuous, the practical, the material become nothing but thought objects, in speculative philosophy. The "new philosophy," by contrast, says Feuerbach, will start from the sensuous, the practical, the material. What was included in Hegelian philosophy in its mystified, abstracted form, will be revealed as the true essence of philosophy.

This new content appears first in its old form in two ways: first, as *pantheism*; second, as the finite determinations of the Absolute. In pantheism, matter is accorded divinity. The world is God. In Hegel's dialectic, the finite is accorded status as the self-differentiation of the *Idea* itself. Neither attain to a "positive" and noncontradictory affirmation of sensuous, determinate "real" being. But both include this being in the identity of thinking and being, in *Substance*, or in the *Idea*. Thus Feuerbach writes

The Identity-philosophy differs from Spinozism only in that the dead, phlegmatic *Substance* of Spinoza is infused with the *Spirit* of idealism. Hegel, especially, makes self-activity, self-differentiation, self-consciousness into attributes of Substance. Hegel's paradoxical statement: "The consciousness of God is God's self-consciousness" rests on the same grounds as Spinoza's paradoxical statement: "Extension or matter is an attribute of Substance," and has no other sense but this: that self-consciousness is an attribute of Substance or of God –God is Ego. . . . But Spinoza's statement says nothing but that matter is substantial, divine Being; and in the same way, Hegel's means that consciousness is divine Being. (II, 223)

Such a pantheism as Spinoza's, then, is "theological atheism" or "theological materialism" and is nothing but "the negation of theology but on the grounds of theology itself" (II, 224, 264). But, says Feuerbach, this "deification of the real, of the materially existent–in materialism, empiricism, realism, humanism—this negation of theology is nothing but the essence of the modern era. Pantheism is therefore nothing other than the essence of the modern age raised to a divine essence, or to a philosophico-religious principle" (II, 264). Fuerbach ends this characterization of Spinoza's pantheism by asserting that Spinoza had found "at least for his time, the true philosophical expression of the materialistic tendency of the modern era; he legitimated and sanctioned it. God himself is a materialist. . . . Spinoza is the Moses of modern free-thinkers and materialists" (II, 266). True, this remains a speculative materialism, for matter remains an abstract object for *thought*, even here. But it is at the same time afforded the same divine status as thought, or is *identical* with thought, as an attribute of Substance.

Feuerbach plays fast and loose with the terms "materialist," "empiricist," "realist," "humanist" in his discussion here. He uses them apparently interchangeably to denote a certain philosophical standpoint *opposed* to speculative idealism. Their positive and differentiated content emerges only in various contexts and in specific arguments. Thus, he writes (in a footnote in the second edition of the *Principles*): "The difference between materialism, empiricism, realism, humanism are naturally [!] irrelevant in this work" (II, 264; IX, 286). Nor is there any later attempt by Feuerbach to sort out the differences, and it seems that Feuerbach sees all these positions as coherent from a certain point of view. What is clear, however, is that these terms, as interrelated within such a point of view, no longer have the historical meanings attached to them in previous philosophy, but are being used by Feuerbach to grapple with and to construct a "new philosophy" transcending and synthesizing the older senses. Because the "new philosophy" is still inchoate and traditional connotations are inevitable, the usage can often be confusing or misleading. But this is not a question of terminological nicety or specificity. Rather it is a philosophical question, concerning how to formulate the positive alternative, the "philosophy for the future," on the basis of the critique of speculative idealism. The terms may be seen as negations, as antithetical usages set up against their parallels in speculative philosophy: "immaterialism," "rationalism" (in the strong sense of rationalist idealism), "idealism," "theism." Indeed, Feuerbach's systematic point in his critique is that speculative philosophy is the inverted image in which the new philosophy is already contained, but in distorted forms. Thus, for example, Feuerbach sees in Hegelian philosophy an incorporation of the finite and the determinate. That is, the empirical, the real, the material —the "other" of thought—is *included* in the *Idea*, but only in a flawed and negative way. In Hegel, thought negates and overcames its "other-sidedness," transcends particularity and the empirical, in its synthetic activity. Feuerbach sees this, however, as the mere negation of the particular or of the empirical *in thought*, that is, its reduction to a *thought* particularity as a *thought* being. Thus, he writes,

"The *other of thought*" is Being. Thought which seeks to get beyond itself, to get to its "other" is thought which seeks to leap beyond the limits of its own nature. "Thought attains to that which is beyond thought"; this means that thought lays claim to what belongs not to it, but to *being*. But what belongs to *being* is *particularity, individuality*; what belongs to thought is generality. Thought thus lays claim to particularity – it makes the negation of generality, that is, particularity, which is the essential form of sensibility, into a moment of thought. In this way does "abstract thinking or the abstract concept, which has its *being* outside itself, become the 'concrete' concept." (II, 288)

Then, by way of making explicit this critique of Hegel, Feuerbach goes on to say:

Thought negates everything; but only in order to posit everything once again in thought. It has no longer any boundary in anything beyond itself, but thereby, it steps outside its immanent, natural boundaries. That's how reason, or the *Idea* becomes concrete, i.e., what should be given by sense-perception, is appropriated by thought; that which is the function, the concern of the senses, of sensation, of life is turned into a function and concern of thought. That is, the *concrete* becomes a *predicate of thought*, and *being* is turned into no more than a determination of thought. Thus, the statement, "The concept is concrete" is identical in meaning with the statement: "Being is a determination of thought." (II, 291)

Thus, Feuerbach rejects the notion of "concreteness" in Hegelian philosophy as a false, rationalized, or merely *ideated* concreteness. The real concrete is not determined by the dialectic of consciousness, by way of its self-differentiation or individuation. This puts the individual, the concrete, at the end of a long chain of ideational activity, as a result or product. That which "is," for Hegel, is therefore finally an abstract or reflected "is"; whereas what *is* ("in-itself," presumably) has its being not in thought, but beyond the limits of thought. Real existence is not consciousness or thought. In thought, what is "real" is the universal, the general, that is, the concept, abstracted from its sensuous particularities. But real particularity lies forever beyond thought.

Feuerbach's rejection of Hegel takes him to the brink of a nominalist materialism, to an affirmation of sensation as the ground of thought, and to an epistemological doctrine of direct realism in which the senses deliver up external reality as it is. But how does Feuerbach answer Hegel's critique of just this sort of empiricism (in the section on "sense certainty" in *The Phenomenology of Mind*)? In the *Logic*,

Hegel begins with *Being* and shows it to be an abstraction, empty of content, and thus indistinguishable from *Nothing*. He then goes on to generate the dialectic out of this contradiction, in *Becoming*. Thus, the finite and determinate is generated by this passage from empty Being, as an abstraction, to the fullness of concretely differentiated Being. In the *Phenomenology* Hegel begins with differentiation–the particularity of sense experience–and shows that this particularity is also abstract. Thus, Hegel rejects both the abstract universal and the abstract particular as one-sided, incomplete, empty *concepts*. But Feuerbach wants ultimately to distinguish *concepts* from *nonconcepts*, what is content *for* thought and what lies beyond thought. He rejects the Hegelian ontology as an ontological logic, just as in *The Critique of Hegelian Philosophy*, he had rejected the Phenomenology as a phenomenological logic. But logic–that which gives the account of the structure or nature of *Being*, or of *consciousness*, in the Hegelian *Logic* and *Phenomenology*–remains forever bound to what concerns thought, and not what lies beyond it. Feuerbach's ontological project is to break the real loose from the embrace of thought, to posit it in iself, so to speak.

Feuerbach's first move in this critique of speculative ontology is to expose the alleged identity of thinking and being.

> The identity of thinking and being that is the central point in the philosophy of identity is nothing but a necessary consequence and elaboration of the concept of God as that being whose concept or essence contains existence. . . . But a being that is not distinguished from thought, a being that is no more than a predicate or determination of reason or is only a conceived, abstract being is, in truth, no reality at all. The identity of thinking and being therefore expresses only the identity of thinking with itself. (II, 282)

The question, then, of how to characterize being apart from thought, or how to think what is *not*-thought–the classical issue of realism–emerges here. As Feuerbach puts it, "The proof that something *is* has no other meaning than that something is *not only thought of*. But this proof cannot be derived from thought itself" (II, 283). He goes on to argue for a view very much like Kant's: that the objectivity of what *is* is attested to by the fact that not only I alone, but others too agree on what is–a rather weak position, given Feuerbach's earlier critique of Kant. There he had cited Kant's argument that "the objects of the senses are mere appearances, though we admit in doing so that they are based on a thing in itself." Feuerbach objects to this characterization of the content of sense perception as "mere appearances," for he holds this to be the fatal split between the mind, as thinking activity, which can yield "truths" and sense perception, which can yield only appearances. Rather Feuerbach will insist that the senses give us *truth*, that is, the thing-in-itself, as objectively existing (cf. II, 278–9). But here, he argues for objectivity as intersubjectivity, in a Kantian way. How can these two alternative positions cohere? Feuerbach begins his argument with Kant's example:

The example of the difference between a hundred dollars in conception and a hundred dollars in reality–which was chosen by Kant in the critique of the ontological proof, to designate the difference between thinking and being, and which was mocked by Hegel–is essentially a quite correct example. The former hundred dollars I have only in my head; while the latter are in my hand. The former are for me alone, but the latter are also for others–they can be felt and seen. But only that exists which is both for me and for others, upon which I and others agree, and which isn't mine alone but is *common*. (II, 283)

This is practically the direct opposite of what Feuerbach had written in the Hegelian work of his youth, the *Dissertation*. There, it will be remembered, he had said that what exists for the senses exists for me alone–the senses are private–whereas what exists for thought, exists in a community of thinkers. *Thought* is what binds me to my fellow man; it alone is public. But here sensibility is taken as the public, objective mode, and thought as what is in my head alone. It is clear that the connotations of "thought" and "sensibility" have changed here. "In thought, I am an absolute subject. I let everything depend for its validity as an object or as a predicate upon me, the one who thinks. I am intolerant. In the activity of the senses, by contrast, I am actual self-active being. Only the senses, only perception give me something *as subject*" (II, 284). The senses, however, are not active. Rather they are that upon which the active, external, real object or quality acts. They are passive, recipient, direct in yielding this object to me as it *is*– that is, as active object or subject. And what they yield to consciousness is therefore not an appearance, not sense impressions or sense data, but the thing itself. But, characteristically, the senses do not yield essences or universals: they give us the finite, particular, concrete individuals, the "really existing" beings, beyond thought.

It is just these "particulars" of sense that Hegel had demolished as abstractions in the *Phenomenology*. Feuerbach takes on Hegel's argument there as well. In Hegel's *Phenomenology*, says Feuerbach, the contradiction between thinking and being appears as the contradiction between the ostensive "this" and the general or universal, which "this" becomes when it is used as an abstract term. "But what an enormous difference there is," writes Feuerbach, "between the 'this,' when it designates an object of abstract thought, and 'this,' when it designates an actual object."

This wife is *my* wife, for example. *This* house is *my* house, although everyone speaks as I do of his house and his wife as "this house" and "this wife." The indifference and uniformity of the logical "this" is here interrupted and transcended. Were we to accept the logical "this" in natural law, we would directly arrive at community of goods and wives, where there is no difference between this and that, and where everyone has a right to everything. (II, 287)

To the argument that sheer ostension, the direct pointing to a *this* is beyond language, because language expresses concepts, Feuerbach answers that "existence never depends on linguistic or logical bread– bread *in abstracto*–but only upon *this* bread, the *unutterable*" (II, 288).

The concrete is ineffable, but insofar as it is an object of the un- speaking senses, how do we come to *know*, then? How do we pass from sensation to thought? Here, finally, Feuerbach has to mediate sensibili- ty and thought, and he ends up with a characteristic sensationist view: Thinking is derived from and is a form of sensibility itself.

Thinking is no longer taken to be the self-sufficient ground of itself as it appears to be in speculative philosophy. It is dependent on what lies beyond it, that is, on sensation. The divinized form of this self- enclosed thought, the abstract essence of this autonomy, in its speculative-theological form is described by Feuerbach thus, in *The Principles*:

God is independent, self-sufficient being who needs no other being for his existence, and consequently exists by and through Himself alone. But this abstract metaphysical characterization only has sense and reality as a definition of the nature of reason, and therefore says no more than that God is an in- telligent, thinking being or conversely that only a thinking being is divine. Because only a sensory being needs things external to it for its existence. I need air to breathe, water to drink, light to see, plant and animal matter to eat, but I don't need these things in order to think, at least not directly. A breathing being can't think without air, nor a seeing being without light, but I can con- ceive of a thinking being isolated in itself. The breathing being is *necessarily* related to what is external to it; it has its essential object, that by means of which it is, outside itself. But a thinking being is related to itself alone, is its own object, has its essence in itself, is what it is through itself. (II, 249)

Thus, the speculative theology that conceives of God as self-sufficient independent being is clearly related to the Cartesian concept of thought, as that which can be conceived in itself alone; and further, to the on- tologized version of this conception, as abstract being, as the *Idea* that is its own object. If this is the nature of thought, it is not the nature of sensibility, nor is it the nature of the thinking activity of a sensate being, but only of a being that is thinking activity alone, a being of pure thought. But, Feuerbach argues, such an abstract being *of* thought exists only *in* thought as an abstraction–and an abstraction from thought itself–or better, an abstraction from a being that is both sensory and thinking being, and therefore a one-sided abstraction. Our sensory-thinking being, or our feeling, sensing, willing, thinking being is, of course, human. As human, it is *not* self-sufficient, but dependent being; and as dependent, dependent both in thought and existence. In thought, it is dependent upon sensation; in existence, upon external nature and upon other human beings. Only a naturally existing being thinks. Therefore, thinking is dependent upon existence. But the link, the connection between thinking and being, between what is in thought, or what thinking is, and what is beyond the limits of thought, is sensation. There is no thought without sensation; and also, no thought without food, drink, air. Further, there is no objective thought without others who can agree. And finally, there is no agreement without that which can be shared in common beyond thought, that is, in common sensing, a common world.

Thus, Feuerbach moves from the critique of speculative philosophy to his sensationism, and his anthropologism.

SENSING, THINKING, AND BEING: FEUERBACH'S EMPIRICAL REALISM

There is a methodological problem in treating Feuerbach's sensationism or his empirical realism. It concerns the distinction between *assertions* and *arguments*, and the problem arises because much of Feuerbach's empirical realism is set out in the form of assertions and not in the form of arguments. The question is how to treat Feuerbach's thought here, as *dogmatism*, or as critical *philosophical discourse?*

A philosophical discourse is often conceived of as an extended argument, a dialectic in which questions are formulated, posed, and answered, and where what counts as an answer to a question *presupposes* a common framework of sense and significance. Often, however, the questions and the framework are suppressed, tacit, or taken for granted as background knowledge. The virtues of a *critical* dialectic are in the presentation of the object of criticism as an *explicit* theory. The negative critique consists in a refutation or rejection on various grounds (inconsistency, incoherence, empirical falsity, implausibility, inadequacy, etc.) of the arguments given for this theory. Feuerbach's critical or negative discourse has this virtue. It presents speculative philosophy as a systematic theoretical construction of answers to questions, and then critically reinterprets first the object about which the theory poses and answers questions–as a human, and neither a divine nor a metaphysical object–and second, reinterprets the answers in the light of these reinterpreted questions. The motive of the critique is in part methodological, in part substantive: methodological, insofar as Feuerbach purports to show outright contradictions, inconsistencies, and incoherences in the theological and speculative account; substantive, in that Feuerbach claims to show what the *sources* of the contradictions and incoherences are, what the fundamental *mistake* is, in the very form and intent of the questions, and therefore, also, in the answers. Philosophical argument, in this case, consists in *showing* the mistake— that is, in reinterpreting the framework of the questions itself, to show how it leads to a mistake. For theology and speculative philosophy are not "mistaken" in the simply technical sense of logically inconsistent arguments, but rather in what they *accept* as arguments; mistaken fundamentally, then, in the presuppositions that underlie the questions and answers. Feuerbach's critique is therefore a critique of the framework, of these presuppositions themselves. Something *counts* as a mistake only when the framework is *re*interpreted, so that what theology *purports* to say, or what speculative philosophy *claims* to be true is shown not as *in itself* false, but as false about the purported object. The *mistake* therefore lies in what is taken to be the object of the questions and answers; and the systematic errors, confusions, and inconsistencies derive from this fundamental error. The critique is therefore an *interpretive* critique, or a critique *about interpretation*, as we have seen. The form of the argument is therefore an interpretive form: a *translation* or *reduction*. "This is *nothing but* that." "God is *nothing but* man's species being taken as an object of consciousness." "The *Idea*, or *Being*, is *nothing but* thought abstracted from its concrete activity, and its dependence on sensation, or material human existence, and made a self-sufficient being in itself."

In general, then, one may say that nothing counts as an *answer* unless it is an answer to a question. And further, that the understanding or interpretation of the question determines what will count as an answer to that question. The framework of philosophical discourse, and the presupposition of argument is this mutual dependence of questions and answers. One thing more is suggested by this: A proper question, or a meaningful question, is one for which it is conceivable that something *would* count as an answer—that is, the *sense* of what the domain of answers is, is somehow clear. Part of philosophical discourse, then, is the formulation of questions, or the critique and improvement of questions, in this regard: to show either that a question is *not* a proper question—is a *pseudo*question—or to show that a question is confused, and to reformulate and clarify it.

The point of all this is that much of Feuerbach's "positive" doctrine

–his sensationism, his materialism, and his realism–is presented *not* in the form of argument, but of assertion. It appears to be merely rhetorical, or simply a profession of faith. Whereas in his negative critique, Feuerbach was arguing *against* an explicit theoretical framework, in his positive doctrine his own theoretical framework is not yet clear–it is often ad hoc, eclectic, incomplete, and sometimes inconsistent. Moreover, it is not yet systematic, so that arguments or potential arguments appear only as assertions. But assertions are enthymemic arguments, at least here. The presupposed framework of questions and answers, the reinterpretation of theology and speculative philosophy, the *anthropologism* in particular, is the suppressed or tacit premise in terms of which the assertion functions *in* a philosophical argument. The aphoristic, assertoric, often dogmatic mode of presentation, especially of the earlier versions of Feuerbach's empirical realism, therefore has to be seen in context, or better, in *two* contexts: first, that of the critique and rejection of speculative idealism, and its replacement by an anthropological or humanist materialism; second, that of Feuerbach's *own* philosophical development–therefore, against the background of his earlier works, and in terms of the dialectic of his own thought. Otherwise, Feuerbach's sensationism appears dogmatic, flat-footed, superficial, and naive. But even so, it often *is* superficial and naive, and sometimes simply assertive and dogmatic. Further, as epistemological theory, it is too clearly reminiscent of Locke, or even more so, of Condillac and of D'Holbach (strikingly so, in the latter case, for both the empirical materialism, the utilitarianism, and the atheist argument against theology and metaphysics in the *Système de la Nature* have remarkable affinities to Feuerbach's work, especially his later, more explicit writings). Feuerbach later declares that the sources of German materialism are German and not French, explicitly denying D'Holbach and La Mettrie as sources (X, 155). But his own sensationism and realism are clearly continuations of the tradition of French eighteenth-century materialism, though he arrives at his conclusions from almost the opposite pole, philosophically, from that of the French *philosophes*.[4]

What remains original and of interest in Feuerbach's empirical realism is its link with his anthropologism. Here there develops a fruitful tension between the *merely* epistemological and metaphysical issues, as formulated in classical empiricism (as to the relations among sensation, perception and thought, as to the relations between sense perception and the external world, as to the issue between realism and phenomenalism, or rationalism and empiricism, innatism, and inductivism), on the one hand, and the broader questions of human existence, need, praxis, on the other. This can be seen explicitly in the tension between Feuerbach's earlier sensationism, in which the senses are *essentially* passive, and his later writings, in which the senses are seen instrumentally, as functions of an active organism, interacting with a world out of dependence, and in response to an *essential* drive to well-being and need-satisfaction. Finally, Feuerbach is to put his sensationism into the context of a larger conception of the human, approaching the questions of practical, social, moral activity as central. But initially, the theory of sensation contains only hints of this larger context, or posits it unsystematically. In short, the positive doctrine is interesting because it poses the question of the relation between empiricism, materialism, and humanism–between more strictly epistemologically and more broadly anthropological and sociohistorical contexts. Moreover, it attempts, for the first time, to bring these alternative contexts to bear on each other.[5] Thus, Feuerbach presents the *Problematik* of a *social* and *historical epistemology*. But he remains at the level of a more vague and abstract *humanist* epistemology, nonetheless.

What are the issues, then, in Feuerbach's sensationist and empirical realist epistemology? They concern (1) how sensation is the source of our knowledge of truth and of a real, external world; (2) what the relation is between sensation and thought; (3) how, in all this, the senses are human, rather than merely animal senses.

In the preface to the second edition of *The Essence of Christianity*, written in 1843, the same year as that in which *The Principles* was published, Feuerbach states his *credo*:

I unconditionally repudiate *absolute*, immaterial, self-sufficing speculation–that speculation which draws its material from within. I differ totally from those philosophers who pluck their eyes out that they may think better; for *my* thoughts, I require the senses, especially sight. I found my ideas on materials that can be appropriated only through the activity of the senses. I do not generate the object from thought, but the thought from the object; and I hold *that* alone to be an object which has an existence beyond one's own head. I am an idealist only in the domain of practical philosophy, i.e., I don't take the limits of the present and the past to be the limits of humankind. . . . The *Idea* is for me only a belief in the historical future, in the triumph of truth and virtue; it has only political and moral significance for me. But in the domain of theoretical philosophy proper, I stand directly opposed to the Hegelian philosophy, in which only the converse is true, and instead, I am in favor only of realism, of materialism, in the aforementioned sense. (S: I, 15–16)

Feuerbach therefore not only argues for a philosophical empiricism, or realism, or materialism, but claims to adopt such a view as his own method of inquiry. This presents an interesting question: Can one derive the truth *about* the senses *from* the senses? For if philosophical theory entails method, then a theory of sensationism relies on the senses as its own evidence. The truth of the statement "The real in its reality or as real, is the real taken as an object of the senses, is the sensuous. Truth, reality, sensousness are identical" (II, 296) must itself rest on the senses. In other words, what will count as evidence that the statement is true presupposes the truth of the statement. Are we in a methodological circle here? Or is the appeal of Feuerbach's argument rather a heuristic one? What, in short, would count as a philosophical argument for empirical realism, as against a mere assertion of such a realism? Presumably, not the mere assertion itself; nor the evidence of the senses. Rather, I would suggest, what counts philosophically here is heuristic rather than demonstrative, namely, what it is that is called to our attention *practically* by such a philosophical view.

But this is, in fact, Feuerbach's own argument, and it is an important one, though it is buried in the text, in various places. That he is uneasy with it becomes clear, for he maintains no methodologically consistent position. In one place, the warrant for empirical realism, for nominalism, for sensationism is almost purely dialectical; it is the *negation* of speculative idealism, and therefore sensationism has its validity as the next stage of the dialectic. But this is at best a formal argument, which *presupposes* that *negation, aufhebung,* is the road to truth. In another place, Feuerbach speaks as if the argument for empirical realism is self-evident; that the revelation of *its* truth, is like the revelation of truth and being that the senses themselves give—that is, an *immediate* revelation, an act of revelatory intuition. But elsewhere he emphasizes the *practical* difference such a view makes in what one pays attention to, and this becomes not only a practical *human* question, but a political and historical question. Preoccupations with different objects of praxis connote different interests, different worlds of praxis. Though Feuerbach never develops this view systematically, it is nevertheless stated by him clearly. For example, in *The Principles,* he writes,

Empiricism or realism—by which is here understood generally the so-called real sciences, in particular the natural sciences—negates theology; but *practically* rather than theoretically—in the actual deed by which the realist makes that which is the negation of God into the essential business of his life, into the essential object of his activity. However, he who concentrates with mind and heart only upon the material, the sensuous, denies the reality of the supersensible in his very practice; for that alone is real, at least for human beings, which is an object of their real, actual activity. (II, 265)[6]

Here, as in the previously quoted Preface, sensibility is seen in the context of practice, of activity. There Feuerbach uses the term *Sinnes-*

tätigkeit–the *activity of the senses*. Here he takes the "concentration upon the material, *the sensuous*" as a matter of attention, interest, where one's practical activity lies.

Where one's interest lies, one's proficiency also lies. . . . Where something doesn't lack significance, there is also no lack of senses or organs. Whatever the heart is open to, is also no mystery to the head. Thus, the reason why humanity in modern times lost the organs for the supersensible world and its mysteries, is that in losing faith in this world it also lost the sense for it; because the essential tendency of the modern world was anti-Christian and anti-theological; that is, it was an anthropological, cosmic, realistic, materialistic tendency. (II, 265–6)

Thus, Feuerbach contrasts pantheism, as the *theoretical* negation of theology, with empiricism, as the *practical* negation of theology. But he sees pantheism–that is, Spinoza's pantheism, which accords matter divine status, albeit abstractly and metaphysically–as the legitimation and sanction of the "materialistic tendency of modern times."

But if empiricism or empirical materialism is the *practical* negation of the supersensible, of the very object of speculative idealism, then the role of theory–for example, of Feuerbach's empiricism–is to turn the practical attention away from the supersensible to the sensible, that is, to legitimate or encourage a mode or direction of praxis. The import of the philosophical argument is therefore its consequences for praxis: It reformulates the questions to be asked in such a way that what will count as a proper answer *cannot be given by philosophy, as speculation*, but only by sense experience or empirical practice itself, and notably, by the natural sciences. This is the strong positivist strain, and also the pragmatist strain in Feuerbach's sensationism. It is to be distinguished from the older, direct-realist arguments that he gives as legitimations for such a *change* in attention, and in practice. And it is clearly the sense in which he regards his philosophy as practical.

Nevertheless, in more narrow and traditional epistemological terms, the sensationism is formulated in an independent way, at first. In the *Theses*, this is barely sketched, in a rough-and-ready way. Though there is an emphasis on "Being" as finite, determinate, and as an object of sense perception, there is no elaboration of sensibility as such. What is affirmed is simply that being precedes consciousness, that thought derives from being, and that being, somehow vaguely has to do with the "heart" and not the "head," and with sense perception rather than thought. What *is* clearly stated is the *passivity* of sensibility, as compared to the *activity* of thought. Feuerbach still carries over the traditional view, common to both empiricism and rationalism (in their classic seventeenth-century forms) that the senses are passive and recipient, and the mind self-active. But he identifies this passivity not with a speculative or contemplative passivity. Rather, he takes it in its connotations as *suffering, needy, dependent*; nevertheless, as merely *receptive*, as what is acted *on* by what lies beyond it. In the *Theses,* Feuerbach writes,

The genuine tools, the organs of philosophy are the head—the source of activity, of freedom, of metaphysical infinity, of idealism—and the heart, the source of suffering, of need, of sensualism. In theoretical terms: thought and perception. For thought is a need of the head, as perception, sensing, is a need of the heart. Thinking is the principle of the School, of the System; perception is the principle of life. In perception, I am determined by the object; in thought, I determine the object. In thought, I am *I*, in perception, I am *not-I.* The veridical, objective thought, the veridical, objective philosophy derives only from the negation of thought, from the determinateness of objects, from passion, from the source of all desire and need. Sense-perception gives us being, unmediated, identical with existence; thought gives us being as mediated existence, as distinguished and separated from existence. Only where essence and existence are united, where thought and perception, activity and passivity are united, where the Scholastic dullness of German metaphysics is united with the anti-Scholastic flesh and blood principle of French sensualism and materialism, only there is life and truth. (II, 235)

Further, Feuerbach says that a philosophy that has no *passive principle* in it necessarily has the empirical as its opposite, is one-sided in positing Being as sheer activity. For this leaves out the principle of *life*—that is, of feeling, suffering existence. "A being which doesn't suffer is a being without being. But a being which doesn't suffer is nothing but a being without sensibility, without materiality" (II, 234). Here, too, Feuerbach inherits the old dualism, in which *matter* is the passive, recipient principle (which he, in the traditional male-suprema-cist metaphor, identifies as the "feminine principle"), insisting only that the duality between *action* and *passion* needs to be overcome in a unity—that is, of thinking and sensing. But the ground of this unity is not clear here, except in the vague sense that thought "derives" from sensibility.

In the *Principles,* the sensationism is elaborated further, however. The dualism of thought and sensation is criticized there, just as is the identity of thought and being.

Kant's philosophy is the contradiction of subject and object, Essence and existence, thinking and being. Essence, here, belongs to the mind, existence, to the senses. *Existence without essence is mere appearance*—these are the sensuous things—*Essence without existence is mere thought*—these are the essences of the mind, the *noumena*; they come to be thought, but they lack existence—at least, existence for us, objectivity. They are the things-in-themselves, the true things, but not actual things, and consequently not things for the mind, i.e., neither determinable nor knowable by it. (II, 278–9)

But the resolution of this contradiction, in the identity of mind with its object, equally fails to give us reality, because the object is transformed into a merely *thought* object. Feuerbach's argument is not against the Kantian *distinction* between the knowing subject and its object as known, but rather against the view that the object as known is mere *phenomenon*, mere appearance. He also does not object to the immediate unity of subject and object in identity philosophy. Rather, he objects to it as an identity *in the mind*, or in thought alone. Feuerbach's alternative, then, is to interpret the Kantian view as one in which existence is known by the senses *not* as appearance, or as *phenomenon*, but as it is in itself. The senses *directly* apprehend the thing in itself. Therefore, they are not constructive, or active, or interpretive, for then we would have the mediated things-for-us of Kantian phenomenalism as the sole objects of our knowledge of the external world. The senses are therefore transparent, veridical, and immediate.

A realist epistemology replaces a phenomenalist one, but in the form of a *direct* realism, quite in the spirit of that problematic view of the French eighteenth-century materialists, in which "natural" sense experience was taken to be the source of all knowledge and truth, and the veil of thought, especially in the corrupt forms of theology and metaphysics, clouded the clear vision of this experience and introduced error and distortion. In effect, Feuerbach gives us an empiricized version of the older "natural light" or "natural reason" theories (e.g., of the Augustinian and Cartesian tradition), except that the organ that possesses this "natural light" is not thought, but sensation.

In a long passage in *The Principles*, Feuerbach attempts to show that the very notion of the truth of an idea, in thought, presupposes the *source* of this truth in sensation. If the idea is not to be *mere* idea (i.e., if it is to be more than a mere thought), its "self-realization" requires its negation (i.e., that it be *more* than just an idea, and this "more" is what lies beyond it). But this "not-idea" beyond thought is sensation. Thus, what "realizes" the idea is sensation. "The reality of the idea is sensation" (II, 295). But, argues Feuerbach, if this is so, this presupposes that "reality and sensation, independent of the idea" is truth. Thus, "Truth, reality and sensibility are identical" (II. 296). Now this is certainly confusing, because the "identity" of sensing and being simply makes sensation itself *the* reality, while at the same time, it is to be a human faculty that gives us what lies *beyond* ourselves, and presumably beyond sensation as well. Feuerbach is only dimly aware of the problem here, though he does address it in later work.

Here he indiscriminately uses *Sinnlichkeit, Sinnliches Wesen, Sinnen-objekt* interchangeably and carelessly, so that "sensibility," "sensuous being," "sense object" all run together, and the distinction between sensing and what is sensed is lost. The intention, however, is clear, despite the confusion: It is to affirm that in sensing, in the fact of sensation itself, there is necessarily and intuitively given an objective, real thing, *external* to us, and independent of us. The claim is made that this is *what* sensibility *is*, and it is not raised as a question about *what* sensibility gives us. If it *didn't* give us finite, determinate, real things, it simply would not be sensibility. Similarly, the real is that which is sensible–that is, that which *can* be sensed. The senses are defined in terms of reality, and reality in terms of the senses–as "sensuous being." *By definition*, then, the senses give us the real. But just what this "giving" is is not clear. It is, as far as one can tell, presentational immediacy. One cannot get behind it, because it is precisely that which is at the limit, at the boundary of consciousness, the transition point from the *I* of consciousness to the *not-I*, from thought to being, from self to world.

But then Feuerbach turns in a strange direction. He denies this immediacy of sensation, in two ways: First, he says that what *is* immediate for human consciousness is not pure, unalloyed sensation, but rather what is given by the imagination, or by fantasy. This is indeed a strange shift from the standard direct realist view, which is that of *naive* realism, namely, that what appears to the *uneducated*, or naive observer is what *is*–that so-called appearance and reality are one. But Feuerbach argues instead that the naive observer is naive just in that he is prone to anthropomorphize, to see things by the mediation of imagination. What *appears* as immediate, then, is in fact mediated by the imagination. The task of philosophy, then, is to strip away the distorting veil of the imagination, in order to *get at* the pristine sensation itself, which therefore *becomes* immediate only by an effort–a mediation of the mediation, or a negation of the negation–that removes the veil. Thus, Feuerbach writes,

The sensuous is not the immediate, in the sense of speculative philosophy, in the sense that it is the profane, obvious, thoughtless, the self-evident. The unmediated sensuous intuition comes a good deal later than the imagination and fantasy. The first perception people have is itself only that given by the imagination and fantasy. The task of philosophy, of science in general consists therefore not in leading *away* from the sensuous, the real, but rather in arriving at it–not to transform objects into thoughts and images, but rather in making visible, i.e., objective, that which is invisible to the ordinary, common eye.

People first see things only as they appear to them, not as they are; see in things not what they really are in themselves, but only as what they are represented as being; people put their own human nature into things, and don't distinguish the object from the representation of it. The image lies closer to the uneducated, subjective person than the true perception of the object; for in this perception, the person is torn out of himself; in the image, he remains within himself. [In perception, the object is the acting and speaking person, and I only watch and hear. In the image, by contrast, I have the floor to speak. The perception contradicts me, the image always yields me the right to speak. In the image, I am *judex in propria causa* [judge in my own case].] (II, 305–6)[7]

So sensation (or sense perception, for the sensing-perceiving distinction is not made here) is not so simple after all, for Feuerbach. It is *not* immediately given, *tout court*, but has to be achieved *as* immediate. Moreover, the suggestion therefore is that this sensibility, as achieved, is a *product* of scientific inquiry, that it makes what is ordinarily invisible, visible. It is an achievement of culture and education, and therefore of history. It is a sophisticated immediacy, a learned openness to the directly given or an unlearning of what stands in the way–that is, the religious, or theological, or metaphysical fantasy, as much as the naive anthropormorphism of the "uneducated, subjective observer." This turn opens up a different conception of sensibility, then, from that of classic empiricism, whose senses are naive, unconditioned, or, at least, undeconditioned, the bare workings of a sensory apparatus.

Feuerbach's *second* denial of the immediacy of sensation is related to this first denial. If the senses are, on the one hand, *products* of the enlightenment that a critical philosophy and science bring, they are also *human* senses and thus are not merely animal functions of a physiological apparatus, though they are *also* that. But the "animal" is human, and, therefore, has human needs, interests, drives, and a human physiology. Therefore, however immediate sensation is, it is mediated by the *kind* of organism, the sort of being, man is. In a highly original and interesting section near the end of *The Principles* Feuerbach writes,

It is by no means only through thinking that the human being distinguishes himself from animals. Rather, his *whole being* constitutes his distinction from animals. To be sure, he who doesn't think is not a human being, but not because thinking is the cause, but rather because it is a *necessary consequence and property* of being human.

We don't have to go beyond the domain of sensibility itself, therefore, in order to recognize the human being as ranking above animals. The human being is not a particular being, as is the animal, but rather a *universal* being, thereby not a limited and unfree, but an unlimited free being for whom universality, unlimitedness, freedom are indivisible. And this freedom doesn't consist in a *particular* capacity, in the Will, any more than universality consists in a particular capacity, in the capacity to think, or in Reason–this freedom, this universality extends to his whole being. Animal senses are a good deal sharper than are human ones, but only with respect to particular things, which stand in a necessary connection to the animal's needs; and they are sharper precisely because of this determination, this exclusive limitation to something specific. The human being doesn't have the sense of smell of a hunting dog, or a raven, but only because the human sense of smell is a sense which encompasses all kinds of odors, and is therefore a free sense, indifferent with respect to particular odors. But where a sense rises beyond the limits of particularity and its bondage to need, it also raises itself to *independent, theoretical* significance and dignity: *Universal* sense is *understanding*; universal sensibility is *mind [Geistigkeit]*. Even the primordial senses, smell and taste, elevate themselves, in the human being, to spiritual and scientific acts. The smell and taste of things are subject matters for natural science. Yes, even the human *stomach*, however contemptuously we look down upon it, is not an animal stomach but a *human* stomach, because it is universal, and is not limited to particular kinds of food. That is why the human being is free from the fierce voracity with which animals befall their prey. Leave a human being his head, but substitute the stomach of a lion or a horse–he will certainly cease to be human. A limited stomach conforms only to a limited, i.e. animal sense. The moral and rational relation of the human being to his stomach, therefore, consists in treating it as a human, and not as a beastly stomach. Whoever sees the human being as no more than a stomach, puts the stomach into the class of animals, and consigns the human being to bestiality in his eating. (II, 315–16)

Sensibility, then, takes on "theoretical" status, for Feuerbach. It is an expression of human activity, human needs, human character; moreover, it is a universal sensibility *because* the human is a universal being in his activity or in his capacities. *Forms of sensibility are therefore forms of life* (to borrow a phrase from Wittgenstein, and to change it somewhat). But then what is *excluded* from sensibility? As "universal sensibility," it is thought itself. The notion of a *common sensory*, going back to Aristotle's *De Anima*, of judgment or intellect as generalized sensibility, a view popular in eighteenth-century British and French thought, seems here to find its echo in a reduction of thought to sensation, which is, finally, surprising. But not entirely so. For Feuerbach's model of the generality of the senses, or of human sensibility, is not simply that of a combination, or association of the standard five sense modalities in some general sense. Nor is it Helvétius' *sentir, c'est juger*, nor even yet the "higher sense," at the center of the web, in Diderot's account in *D'Alembert's Dream*. Rather, Feuerbach sees *each* sense as a humanized one, as developed by the life activities, or life needs of the human species. Therefore, he sees sensibility in general as a ramified and differentiated universality. There is a strong physiological overtone, in this and other passages, which develops most fully in the later works, especially in *The Mystery of Sacrifice or Man Is What He Eats* (1862). But the physiology is also human–it concerns organs that have been shaped to conform to human functions and needs. Moreover, this is not a merely physiological or biological characteristic; the senses are products of and expressions of human culture. Thus, in *The Principles*, Feuerbach goes even further:

Art, Religion, Philosophy or Science are only manifestations or revelations of the true human essence. The human being, the complete, true human being is only he who has an aesthetic or artistic, a religious or moral, a philosophical or scientific sense; in general, he who excludes nothing human from himself. *"Homo sum, humani nihil a me alienum puto."* [I am human, nothing human is alien to me.] This statement, taken in its most universal and highest sense, is the motto of the new philosophy. (II, 317)

The problem is that such a ramified sensibility, which now includes an aesthetic "sense," a religious "sense," a moral and even a philosophical "sense," is no longer clearly *sensation* at all, although it may be what sensation *becomes* when it becomes socialized, historicized, acculturated. The suggestion is that there is a *dialectic of sensibility* itself, in which the primordial sensateness becomes more complex and begins to mirror the ramified world of human activity itself. But this is no more than a suggestion in *The Principles*. Or rather, it is something more than a suggestion. It is the point at which Feuerbach's sensationism and his anthropologism are tangent to each other, or even intersect. The result is less than systematic, but more than eclectic.

In this less than systematic way, Feuerbach does effect a certain reform of classical empiricism. For all the vagueness, the lack of rigorous and constructive analysis of sensation and thought, for all the poetizing rhetoric into which the argument dissolves at crucial points, there is a hard core of theory to be salvaged. Problems abound in it, but it is suggestive and provocative. In brief summary, it is this: Sensibility is the mode of direct encounter with what lies beyond the *I* of consciousness. It is the mode of consciousness that has its object in a *real* other, and not simply consciousness itself taken as its own other. But this direct encounter is attested to not in reflection upon it, in which it too becomes an *idea* or a *thought*, but rather in practice–that is, in this-worldly, bodily activity. The locus of this activity is not at some sharply demarcated border between *I* and *it*, between consciousness and being, but rather is the original locus of being itself, a spatiotemporal here and now, a concrete *being here now*, a *Dasein*.[8]

"Being-here [*Dasein*] is the primary being, the primary case of being determined" (II, 306). For Feuerbach, this "first determination of being"–being here and not there–is also, at the same time, a determination of real otherness: The other is there, where I am not. *Dasein* therefore involves *both my* being and the world, the *other*, in which my being is determined as mine, bounded, set in relation, both acted upon

and active. The force of Feuerbach's statement, then, that *"Being here [Dasein] is primary being"* is that primary being is already being in the world, already determined by its relation to an other, and is not abstractable in isolation as a "subject" that has *then* to be put in relation to an object. (Heidegger's debt to Feuerbach seems clear here.) Sensibility is therefore to be understood not on the "observer" or "perceiving subject" or "spectator" model of empiricist epistemology, but in terms of a model of a being that is already involved in the world by its very nature. The context of *sensation* is therefore this primary involvement, this *Dasein*; and as we have seen, this *Dasein* itself is a human *Dasein*. In this sense, Feuerbach at least suggests a sensibility involved in the mode of existence and the mode of activity or praxis of this being, a functional and praxical sensibility. However, this is not easily compatible with the passivity Feuerbach attributes to sensation.

The problems arising thus far in this earlier version of Feuerbach's sensationism in the *Theses* and *Principles* may be schematically formulated in the following way: (1) the *immediacy* of sensation, or the identity of the subject and object of sensation, and (2) the *identity* of sensation and thought.

IMMEDIACY

If sensibility is immediate, in that it gives us the real, or reveals truth directly, then there seems to be an absolute identity of sensation with what is sensed. In effect, this identification of sensation with the sensible seems to lead to an egocentric predicament no different from that of speculative idealism, except that here the subjective circumscription of "being" is determined by sensation instead of thought. For since it is only the individual who senses, how is *my* sensation to be accorded objectivity, or "reality," as not merely mine. We have seen that Feuerbach's initial answer here is that sensibility is intersubjective–that different individuals can *agree* on what is given in sensation. But the standard argument on "other minds" can be leveled in a specific version here: One individual's knowledge of another individual is possible only *by* sensation itself, as Feuerbach also insists. Therefore, the "agreement" that is allegedly intersubjective has its ground only *within* sensation itself, and like the merely *formal* identity of thought with itself, for which Feuerbach criticized idealist philosophy, we have a merely formal agreement of sensation with itself, or within the circle of sensibility itself. The "objectivity" of the object of sense, if it is guaranteed only by agreement among sensing subjects, is no more than the reified or externalized form of sensation itself. The object as "real" is real only insofar as it is constituted by (or in) sensation. Feuerbach's first ploy, then, to give the warrant for the objectivity of sensation in inter-subjective agreement, fails if sensation is identical with its object, or *"is"* reality and truth. Feuerbach's second ploy, however, is to simply assert that senses *give* us the real immediately. But this fails too, because it is not an argument but a dogmatic assertion. It may be true, but in this form we have no more reason to think it is true than to think that the alternative view–that *thought* gives us reality–is true. It is clear from this why Feuerbach then needs *passivity* as the essence of sensation. For the very character of passivity entails "being acted upon," or pre-supposes an external agent, therefore an *active* object. Now this is the Lockeian account in the causal theory of perception, and is the con-ceptual presupposition of the empiricist terminology of "sense impres-sions," for example, in Hume. But it is subject to Humean skepticism itself, because we cannot know that a sensation is an "impression"–that it is causally the result of an external agent, simply from the "impres-sion" itself–*except* in the sense that its *being* an "impression" already entails its being "impressed" (just as the conceptual sense of being an "appearance" entails being an appearance *of* something). But this brings us back to that immediacy that simply asserts what it sets out to prove, namely, that sensation *gives* us the external or real *otherness* of things immediately. Thus, Kant derives the *noumenon*, the indepen-dently existing thing in itself, as the *presupposition* of sensibility. But Feuerbach's critique of Kant is precisely that this "reality" beyond sensibility has to be derived, as a presupposition, in *thought,* and there-for remains only a *thought* reality, at the same time both unknowable in itself *and* posited. Feuerbach wants it given *in* sensibility itself. And because it cannot be given directly and immediately if the sharp dis-tinction is maintained between the sensing subject and the object, Feuerbach seems to dissolve this distinction between the identity of sensation and what is sensed, in his notion of immediacy.

Feuerbach is aware of this problem in later writings, and even, im-plicitly, in the *Principles*. But here the account is not coherent and con-sistent on this point, so that the issue remains problematic.

IDENTITY

If sensation is identical with thought, on the thesis developed initially in the *Principles* and expanded in later works, that is, if thinking is generalized or universalized or cultivated sensibility, then Feuerbach's whole argument for sensationism falls to the ground. For he argues that the very condition of objectivity, of knowledge of the real, is the distinction between thought and *not*-thought (i.e., what lies beyond thought). Sensation is introduced just as this negation or "interruption" of thought, and speculative idealism is criticised for subordinating sensation to thinking, deriving sensing from thinking, and thus identifying sensation and thought in a way that leaves thought enclosed within itself. But if thought is nothing but sensation, or we derive thought from sensation, then the identity is simply reaffirmed, except that here, thought is reduced to sensation, rather than sensation to thought. In any case, the condition set by Feuerbach, that knowledge of the real is of what is itself *not*-thought, or of the negation of thought, is violated if thought then is taken to be identical with sensation, which in turn is supposed to be *not*-thought. Had Feuerbach here insisted that there is a *unity* of thought and *not*-thought, that is, a dialectical unity of opposites, or that sensation *is* this unity, he might have found a resolution here, at the cost of accepting the dialectical notion. But he explicitly rejects this notion of unity of opposites as an unacceptable contradiction in the Hegelian logic, in his critique of speculative identity theories; and he does so on the ground that the idealist identity swallows up the "opposition"–of sensation and thought–*in* thought, leaving sensation only as a reflected-upon "opposite" of thought, but not as real, negative *not*-thought.

Here too, Feuerbach implies a solution to the problem, both in the *Principles* and in later works, in his views on the "unity of thinking and being" in the human being himself. But though the framework for the resolution of this identity problem is given by Feuerbach, in the context of his anthropologism, it is not explicitly connected to his sensationism. Here, too, the account remains inconsistent and eclectic though the elements for a solution are present.

One may ask whether these two problems, of the relation of sensation to the object of sensation and the relation of sensation to thought, are not the typical problems of the empiricist tradition. And it seems clear, on first consideration, that the *immediacy* and *passivity* of sensation are also typical features of the empiricist account, as are also the veridicality of sense data, and their nature as *givens* or as simply known "by acquaintance" in Russell's sense. These are features that seem to derive from the classical Lockeian and Humean contexts, and they turn up again in the twentieth-century Anglo-American development of sense-datum theory. But Feuerbach's involvement with these problems is arrived at by a different route, and therefore the very framework in which these problems arise is different from that in which they arise in empiricism. Feuerbach himself recognizes this difference, in a note published in the *Nachlass* concerning his own progress toward empiricism: "I went over from the supersensible to the sensible; from the untruth and unreality of the supersensible, I drew out the truth of the sensible. Naturally, my approach and my task is quite different from the task of those who start unconditionally with the sensible" (X, 343).

We may note one difference immediately: The problems that derive from the British empiricist tradition presuppose a model of sensation and perception that is largely mechanist in conception, in which external causal action by contact on a passive recipient is the *initial* or a priori context of the theory. Aside from what classic empiricism imputes to the mind as an associative activity or as an inductive mechanism, Locke's *tabula rasa* is the *beginning* condition of knowledge and perception. "Immediacy" and "passivity" here are therefore the mechanical immediacy of direct contact and the passivity of a recipient surface, leaving apart the question of awareness or consciousness, which is itself conceived on the model of reflection, as the forming of images or impressions on a reflective or impressionable medium. Feuerbach approaches the question from an entirely different direction, or rather works his way back to these problems. In a manner of speaking, he derives a posteriori from his critique of speculative idealism a formulation similar to that which has a priori status within the very framework of empiricism. He generates the problem for himself, therefore. But this means that the Feuerbachian concept of the immediacy and passivity of the senses is different from that of classic empiricism. The passivity and immediacy of sensation is not presupposed by him within the framework of a spectator theory or a mechanist model of perception. Rather, he arrives at these features of sensation as conclusions from his critique of speculative idealism. Thus, the concepts are mediated by this context of their development. The explication, the reasons given for the immediacy and passivity of sensation, comes out of the *negation* of the idealist theory, which, by contrast with empiricism, begins with a self-active consciousness or an Ego, and derives sensibility from thought, and not thought from sensibility.

Feuerbach, in a rather cryptic note in the *Nachlass*, suggests a historical analogy to this development. He writes, "Leibniz wanted to improve on Descartes, and come to an understanding with Locke. Only Kant finally brought this about" (X, 321). This aphorism is followed by another: "The identity of thinking and being is the identity of thinking and sensing. There is no way I can compare any being with a nonexistent being" (X, 321). If we recall Feuerbach's critique of Kant's *noumenon*, as the thing in itself that cannot be known, the sense of this last aphorism would seem to be that there is no way of linking thought to being except through sensibility, that only a sensible thing is more than nothing for thought, whereas the thing in itself is nothing for thought. But the problem with Locke's theory is that the correspondence of the ideas with their external causes cannot be known, because only the ideas can be known, and we have no access beyond them to their alleged causes. Locke's realism dissolves in Hume's phenomenalism, and therefore into his skepticism. But Feuerbach's suggestion that Kant does come to an understanding with Locke is odd, unless we take Kant's formulation as giving that identity which Feuerbach demands. Another aphorism in the *Nachlass* states: "Thought without sensibility is nothing; conversely, sensibility without thought is nothing–that's really the heart of the Kantian system" (X, 317). By contrast to his critique of Kant in the *Principles*, Feuerbach shows a deeper appreciation of Kant[9] in his later work, just on this point of the indispensability of sensation for thought. So, for example, he writes: "Kant represents the revolution, Hegel the restoration. What Kant overthrew–the rule of the supersensible–Hegel reestablished" (X, 318).

It is from this context of the development of speculative philosophy that Feuerbach derives his *Problematik*. How he thereafter resolves the questions of the immediacy and passivity of sensation owes little to the empiricist tradition, and much more to the anthropologism that Feuerbach also derived from his critique of theology and speculative philosophy.

But there is another reason why the problems do not come up in the typical empiricist way. Feuerbach already has in mind the *ramified* theory of sensibility, that is, the anthropologized, functional, activity-laden theory of sensibility, in which the senses are more than physiological or animal senses. This is directly in conflict with the *standard* views concerning immediacy and passivity, which regard these properties of sensation as deriving from or presupposed by a reductive mechanist model of perception. *Passivity* is suffering, need, dependency. The activity it connotes is not simply the action by contact of a material cause, but rather, the specific activity of an organism that overcomes this need. Dependency already connotes a sense of what will overcome it or satisfy it. The notion of *action* is therefore functional, not mechanical, as is the notion of need-satisfying *object*. *Immediacy* also is, as we have seen, mediated immediacy–an immediacy achieved by culture, reason, technical progress, in which the original fantasy, the veil of imagination, is removed. Feuerbach's epistemology therefore has resources for dealing with the problems of the identity of sensation and the sensible, and the veridicality of the given. But these resources are not systematically deployed.

When Feuerbach does speak of the immediacy of sensibility, it is a fairly unmistakable immediacy.

> Only that is true and divine which needs no proof, which is immediately certain by itself, which speaks for itself and is convincing in itself, which carries the immediate affirmation of itself, in itself—that which is simply, decisively and indubitably clear as the sun. But only the sensible is clear as the sun. It is only where sensibility begins that all doubt and disagreement end. The secret of immediate knowledge is sensibility. (II, 301)

> Modern philosophy was in search of something immediately certain. It therefore rejected the groundless and baseless thought of the Scholastics, and founded philosophy on self-consciousness. . . . But this self-consciousness of modern philosophy is itself again no more than a thought entity, mediated by abstraction, and therefore dubitable. Only the object of the senses, of perception, of sensation is indubitable and immediately certain. (II, 300)

No problems of appearance, illusion, hallucination, no relativity of perception, no subjectivism, or solipsism of the senses for Feuerbach! None of the host of typical empiricist or rationalist moves regarding the gap between perception and reality. For Feuerbach, all perceptual error is error of the imagination or of judgment clouded by representation. The locus of error is shifted from the periphery to the center, from sense to judgment, from perceiving to thinking, from the concrete to the abstract.

Yet, in later works, Feuerbach seems to be aware of some of these problems. Or at least he reformulates his sensationism so as to avoid them. In 1848–9, for example, in the *Lectures on the Essence of Religion*, he writes,

> I understand the course of development of the history of religion, as also of psychology and philosophy as corresponding to the course of development of humanity in general. Just as nature is the primary object of religion, in my view, so too the sensible is primary in psychology and in philosophy generally; but primary not only in the sense of the word in speculative philosophy, where the primary signifies the point of departure, but primary in the sense of indispensability, that which is self-confirming, or true in itself. Just as little as one can derive the sensible from the spiritual, so little can nature be derived from God. For the spiritual is nothing apart from and without the sensible. Spirit is only the essence, the spirit *of* sensibility . . . the first belief of man is the belief in the truth of the senses, and not a belief which contradicts the senses, such as theistic or Christian belief. . . . Man originally believes only in the existence of that which his own daily existence gives witness to, in terms of what affects him in a sensory and feelingful way. The first evangelists, the first, the most infallible, religiously authentic evangelists of mankind, not con-

taminated by priestly fraudulence, are the senses. Or, to put it more strongly, man's senses are his first gods. For the belief in external, sensible gods depends only upon the belief in the truth and divinity of the senses. In those gods who are sensible beings, man divinizes only his own senses. (VIII, 107–9)

Here Feuerbach takes the argument for the truth of the senses as an argument for the hidden truth of nature religions. This is no longer an epistemological argument, but a genetic argument, like that in *The Essence of Christianity*. What it *means* to worship a sensible, perceivable God is to worship the truth, the reality, of the senses. But here the circle is closed: Sensibility attests to itself, is self-confirming. What is objectified is not the *truth* of the senses, but the *belief* in the truth of the senses, which is quite another thing. The ground here is not epistemological primacy, but as Feuerbach says, indispensability. The argument for the truth of sensibility is a practical one. We need it to derive the truth of thought from what lies beyond thought. The analogy of sensibility to nature simply underwrites the status of what is sensible as like that of what is natural, namely, what human beings are dependent upon for their existence. It is the *feeling* of dependency that gives evidence of something *other*, something beyond oneself, on whom or on which to depend. The externality of nature or of the sensible is nothing but what is entailed for belief by the feeling of dependency on what lies beyond oneself. The witness of sensibility is the truth of neediness as a human condition, therefore.

Also in 1848, in his reply to a critical review of *The Essence of Christianity* by R. Haym,[10] Feuerbach writes on the difference between the natural object and our sensations or our perception of it:

The taste-bud is as much a natural entity as salt is, but it doesn't follow from that, that the taste of salt is immediately and as such an objective property of the taste-bud, or that what salt is, as an object of sensation, is the same as what salt is in itself; nor that the taste of salt on the tongue is a dispositional property of the salt, conceived of apart from sensation. So too, the human being is a natural being, just like the sun, the stars, plants, animals and rocks. But at the same time, the human being differentiates himself from nature, and consequently, that nature which is within the human head and heart is differentiated from that nature which lies outside it. (VII, 516)

More explicitly, in the later work *Spiritualism and Materialism* (1863–6), in the section on *The Critique of Idealism*, Feuerbach writes, "My sensation is subjective, but its ground is an objective one. I have a sensation of thirst because the water outside me is a necessary constituent of my existence – is itself the ground and condition of my existence and of my sensation itself" (X, 221). In effect, then, sensation is identical with being, with external reality, in the literal sense that I incorporate an external nature, a material reality in myself. I am corporeally constituted by this external stuff and it constitutes the very being, the very existence of my sensibility itself. Here Feuerbach begins to approach a thoroughly materialist theory of sensibility, *on the very model of incarnation theory itself!* The "I" who senses, lives, acts is itself an incarnation, an incorporation of the external, natural world. Sensation is a dispositional property of matter, once this matter has been organically absorbed, transformed into living stuff, and comes *literally* to constitute the sense organs themselves as material organs. The seat or origin of sensibility is then the *need* of the very organs of sense for what constitutes them—a kind of natural affinity for what goes into their constitution. Thirst, then, is my body's need for water as a condition of life, of existence. The *sensation* of thirst is nothing but this need, this dependency expressed by my body. Sensation then becomes a functional or dispositional property of an organism, and therefore, no longer passive in the mechanistic sense, as that which is *acted* on from without, but "passive" in this other sense, of needy, dependent—and, as such, the source or ground of the *activity* of the organism itself.

In this same section, Feuerbach discusses the range of human physiological needs (e.g., for air, food, water) in a critical comment on Schopenhauer [11] (whom he calls here "an idealist infected with the 'epidemic' of materialism"). Schopenhauer had written, "Sensation of every sort is limited to the inside of our skins, thus cannot contain what lies beyond this skin, i.e. what is external to us." Feuerbach argues against this:

The object is not only an object of the senses for us; it is also the foundation, the condition, the presupposition of sensation. We possess an objective world under our skins, and this alone is the basis on which we posit a world corresponding to it, outside our skins. We sense "inside our skins"–but inside a skin which is porous, and in fact, has about seven million pores on the total surface of a grown man, i.e., openings, exits to what is beyond the skin, say— seven million pores in the skin, whereby we breathe–and in addition, in the specific organ of breathing, the lung, no less than six hundred million air-filled cells! What is breathing, in fact? Nothing but a fleshly admixture of our blood and the external atmosphere, in particular with the oxygen in the air. But the lungs are not sense organs, the air which we breathe in through the skin and lungs is no affection of our nerves, no sensation or representation of ours. We take in actual air as it is; i.e. in a material, objective, chemical way. We breathe before we see, hear, taste, smell—we breathe because without air we cannot live. Without breathing, no oxygen . . . without oxygen, no combustion, no heat, without heat, no sensation, no animation. . . . Air is the first demand of sensation and of life . . . but we don't only breathe–we eat and drink. What we eat and drink, that must we also see and hear, feel, smell. But we mustn't remain at this sentimental relation. We chew and grind [what we eat] with our unaesthetic teeth, not only to taste it–taste, like other senses, is here *only a means* [my emphasis, M. W.]–but in order to incorporate it in ourselves, to transform it into flesh and blood, to make its essence our essence. . . . "I do not sense myself," says the idealist. I certainly sense myself when I sense thirst; but I sense myself thus as a water-needy, unfortunate, miserable self. . . . (X, 220–1)

This physiologized version of sensation in the later works thus establishes a different model from the earlier one. First, it clearly distinguishes the object of sensation from sensation itself. But then it *re*identifies the subject and the object, by incorporation; it makes the object of sensation into the organ of sensation, by the transformation of natural elements into living flesh and blood,[12] and then defines sensation itself as *only a means* in this process–that is, the necessary means for the awareness of the *need* for natural elements, the expression of this need, and the necessary means for the recognition of what will satisfy this need.

This is clearly an activity-oriented, practical account of sensation, in which the identity between sensing and what is sensed is the material identity effected by a bodily process. But where is *truth*, or the epistemological context of this sensation, then? It is in the actual bond or correspondence that sensation effects, in the very life activity of the organism. Here Feuerbach attains to an anthropological-biological, if not yet historical or social, account of sensation. The "reality" that sensation attests to is therefore only relatively external: It becomes real for us, in the actual practice or process of incorporation, by our actual life activity. The reality–as a sensible, material reality, not "given" to sensation, but literally *acquired* by it, in its function "as a means only" for our life activity–is therefore *both* external *and* internal to us. The human being is *imago mundi*, not as passive reflection, but as self-constituted out of a natural world by his organic activities themselves.

In this sense, Feuerbach may speak of the "truth" of sensibility as a "truth of existence"–as something true about the conditions of our existence. But this is either a metaphorical or a novel use of "truth," not yet connected to the epistemological question of the relation of sensation to thought. True, Feuerbach talks of the dependence of thought on sensation as of the dependence of a thinking being on existence. There is no disembodied thought, except as an abstraction *in* thought itself. But once Feuerbach makes the anthropological-physiological move, in this later characterization of sensation, it raises several questions concerning sensation and thought. First, if thought is identical with sensation, or is simply a cultivated, generalized mode of sensibility itself, then presumably it too is a certain "incorporation" of the natural world–it too is *imago mundi*, not as contemplative reflection, but as an activity in which the world *becomes* thought. The physiological model developed by Feuerbach in his later works considers this question in terms of the relation between thinking and the brain as the organ of thought. The brain then becomes a highly generalized *sense* organ. Second, however, if thought is ramified, generalized sensation, and if it is the individual who senses-thinks, what happens to the *sociality* of sensibility, to the argument that consciousness, sensibility, is an *I-Thou* relation? What happens to the *species* concept of the human, which is the product of Feuerbach's earlier development.

To deal with these questions, it will be useful to consider those works in which Feuerbach more fully develops his conceptions of the relation between human beings and nature, and his more explicit materialist conception of human nature itself. These, then, form the basis for an epistemological theory of the relation of thought to sensation, and of thought to reality, that goes as far as Feuerbach will go in his formulation of an anthropologized epistemology and a materialist humanism.

The Critique of Philosophy and the Development of a Materialist Humanism Part II: Anthropologism and Materialism: Nature and Human Nature in Feuerbach's Later Works

The human bond with nature, which is expressed in Feuerbach's view of sensibility, is most fully discussed in several of the later works. The first full-scale treatment of this question is in the sequel to *The Essence of Christianity*, namely, *The Essence of Religion*, published in 1846. Here the dependency of human beings on nature is seen as the correlative source of religious belief to the dependency of human beings on each other, which Feuerbach treated in *The Essence of Christianity*. These themes are developed further in many of the later works, notably the *Lectures on the Essence of Religion* (1851) and the large, late work Feuerbach considered his best, the *Theogony*,[1] a survey of these themes in other religions as well as the Christian (e.g., in ancient Greek and Roman religion and myth and in Judaism). The human dependency on nature, and the theme of the common materiality of man and nature already noted earlier in Feuerbach's physiological emphasis, is set forth in "Natural Science and the Revolution," *The Mystery of Sacrifice*, *Spiritualism and Materialism*, as well as in a number of shorter articles and reviews.

In *The Essence of Religion*, human belief in the Gods is not simply rejected, but explained. As in *The Essence of Christianity*, the real object of this belief is seen to be different from what the believer represents it as. The real intention of the believer is, however, hidden from him by the image, the imaginary object that *stands for* the real object. The reductive translation is therefore a point-for-point dedivinization, demythologization, demystification of the object of belief.

But what does the human being express in his belief? His life needs, his desires, his fears, his understanding. Belief is therefore the form of expression of life, and therefore its cognitive content reveals how the human comprehends himself, albeit in the forms of imagination (i.e., in alienated form) in the religious consciousness.

But human life is material existence, which requires the sustenance of the world of nature for its continuation. The awareness or feeling of this dependence on what is *other*, beyond one's own being, as the source and support of one's being, is the source of all religion. This, briefly, is the theme of *The Essence of Religion*.

The work as a whole is forcefully written. It is direct, striking, revelatory in tone. It is, perhaps, the best written of Feuerbach's works, and also the least technical, the most readily available to popular comprehension. The earlier polemic with speculative idealism, with its "internal" philosophical jargon, its sometimes tortuous reasoning and inversions, is largely completed in *The Principles* (though Feuerbach continues the argument throughout later works, and elaborates it in specific ways.) So, too, the major work of interpretation of religious belief, *The Essence of Christianity*, had already established the pattern and logic of Feuerbach's critique. *The Essence of Religion* is therefore simpler, clearer, more assured. Moreover, its theme is, in a sense, less surprising and shocking than was the sacrilegious theme of *The Essence of Christianity*. That human beings adore nature and personify it as divine is less threatening to the Christian, in particular, than the view that human beings have elevated themselves as their own God. For the believer, both the humanity of Christ *and* his divinity are at the heart of Christian belief. A desacralization of this mystery of incarnation strikes too close to the core of faith. Nature worship can more easily be dismissed by the Christian as paganism, and therefore Feuerbach's critique of it can be accommodated by the Christian as in accordance with his own understanding. Thus, though *The Essence of Religion* has been called the handbook of atheism, it leaves room for a humanist religion. Only insofar as Feuerbach's thoroughly anthropological reduction is carried to its limits, does his critique of religion in *The Essence of Religion* become thoroughly atheistic; and then, only qualifiedly so, because God is restored as human species being, and the content of religion is retained in this humanist form. A more radical critique would require that one go to the social, practical, and historical sources of religious belief and of the institutionalized forms of this belief; that one assess the social and political functions of religion, and of theology, beyond the more abstract human functions of belief, that is, the expression of *general* human dependence on nature and on other human beings. But that more radical critique, as we know, is post-Feuerbachian, however much it depends on Feuerbach. It is also pre-Feuerbachian, in that it already has its political expression in the militant, anticlerical skepticism and atheism of the French enlightenment (e.g., in Voltaire, D'Holbach, and Diderot). Feuerbach remains a *philosophical* rather than a political or social or historical critic of religion. He wants to rescue its human essence, to understand it, rather than to fight its outward institutional forms. Thus, insofar as his is a strongly negative critique, it is a critique of *theology*, fundamentally. As a critique of the "belief of believers," it is rather an appreciative critique, an attempt at enlightenment, the revelation of a hidden truth.

What is of interest in the larger picture of Feuerbach's philosophical development, in *The Essence of Religion*, is the articulation of his naturalism, both with respect to a more general ontological view and with respect to the unity of the human and the natural. He begins *The Essence of Religion* with a recapitulation of a view already expressed in *The Essence of Christianity*:

That being which is differentiated from and independent of either human being or God—which latter is dealt with in *The Essence of Christianity*—that being which is without human properties, human individuality is in truth nothing but *nature*. . . . For me, "nature," like "spirit," is a general term used to designate those beings, things, objects which man distinguishes from himself and his products—these he collects under the general term "nature"; but it is not a general being, abstracted and separated from the actual things, not a personified or mystified being. (X, 3–4, and fn.)

The thesis of the work is summarized succinctly by Feuerbach: "The feeling of dependency which people have is the ground of religion. The object of this feeling of dependency . . . is originally nothing but nature. Nature is the first and original object of religion, as the history of all religions and peoples fully shows" (X, 4).

It is only when this actual dependency is raised to awareness, says Feuerbach, that the human being

raises himself to the level of religion. Thus all life is dependent upon the change of seasons; but only the human being celebrates this change in dramatic representation, in festive acts. Such festivals, however, which do nothing but express and present the change of seasons, or the phases of the moon, are the oldest, first and most authentic forms of human religious consciousness. (X, 4–5)

Here Feuerbach comes close to a conception of the social differences in religious belief, but only as close as a geographical differentiation, through differences in natural environment:

A particular human being, or people, or race doesn't depend on nature in general, nor on the earth in general, but rather on this place, this country; not on water in general, but on this particular water, this river, this well. The Egyptians are not Egyptian outside of Egypt, the Indians are not Indian outside of India. . . . (X, 5)

There are no revelations here, because Feuerbach is antedated in this view at least as far back as Xenophanes, and it is a commonplace of the eighteenth-century atheist and Enlightenment literature. The thesis of the work is therefore neither original nor striking. But here again Feuerbach shows his talent for interpretation. It is in the details of the interpretation that the interest lies, and in the renewed use of the inversive and reductive method that Feuerbach adds something new. What is attributed to the Gods by religious consciousness expresses the particular comprehension of nature and the particular forms of the feeling of dependence on nature. Thus, God as *omnipotent, eternal, self-identical, all-encompassing, universal, unmeasurable, infinite* being is nothing but nature itself, which appears to man in this way; also, as *unknowable, mysterious, beyond conception,* yet *lawlike, nonwillful, independent of human will, unmoved by human needs or wants,* and so on.

All of these properties which stem only from the representation of nature later become abstract metaphysical properties, as nature itself becomes only an abstract object of reason. From this point of view, in which man forgets God's origin in nature, where God is no longer a being of sensuous form, but a being of thought, this means that the God who is distinct from what is human, who is deanthropomorphised, is nothing but the essence of reason. (X, 14)

Here again, abstract thought turns a sensuously imagined object of belief into a thought object, into a mere reflection of human reason itself.

But what is at issue here is precisely the *otherness* of nature. In contrast with *The Essence of Christianity,* in which the *other,* as God, is nothing but the human subject hypostatized, Feuerbach here wants to achieve a conception of the other as *really* other than the human, that is, objectively and distinctively *non*human. Yet insofar as nature is an object of human dependency, the expression of this dependency still remains an expression of the human. One might argue, then, that the *full* content of religion, whether it takes the human *or* nature as its object, is a human content. How does the expression of dependency upon an object attest to the *independent* reality of that object, rather than simply to the reality of the feeling of dependency *itself,* taken as an object? Is Feuerbach, even here, caught in an anthropocentrism in which the objective existence of a nature external to human being dissolves into nothing more than the existence of a *feeling of* this self-differentiation from nature?

Feuerbach appeals to no new arguments here. It is *sensibility, feeling* that implicates the *other-being* of nature, its "originality" or "independence," as the necessarily presupposed object of this feeling or sensation. It is from the nature of the *feeling of dependence* that there derives the belief that there is something external to the self to be depended on. What we are given, then, is not an epistemological argument for the truth of a naturalistic view, but rather a phenomenological argument for the grounds and character of the feeling, the consciousness that *generates the belief* in a nature external to human beings.

But Feuerbach makes an interesting point in this context. Though he does say that the sense of the objectivity of nature, as something beyond man, is grounded in the awareness of dependence on what is beyond man, he adds that "the notion of human essence as an objective essence which is differentiated from the human, or in short, the objectification of human essence has as its *presupposition* the humanization of an objective essence which is taken to be different from the human, or *the notion of nature as a human essence*" (X, 54).

What Feuerbach claims here is that the *primary* conception of objectivity is that of the objectivity of nature; and only derivatively does there develop an objectified conception of human essence. The conception of God as the objectified form of human self-consciousness has as its precondition the conception of God as the humanized form of a nature that is already taken to be objective. Earlier, Feuerbach had argued that the consciousness of an other as a *Thou* precedes or is the condition for the consciousness of oneself as a species being. This was the theme of *The Essence of Christianity* and the basis of its epistemological account of *self-consciousness*. But here we have a rather different proposal: that the recognition of an *other* begins not simply in the recognition of another person, but rather in the recognition of *nature as an other person*, in the transformation of *sheer* otherness into a *Thou*. This unification of nature with human nature thus precedes and is a precondition for the self-divinization of man.

But what does Feuerbach see as the psychological or human motive for this objectification, or this unification of the natural and the human as an objective being? Is it only the feeling of dependency itself, or something more? Feuerbach writes, "The feeling of dependency on nature is ... the ground of religion, but the *overcoming of this dependency*, the *freedom* from nature is the *aim* of religion" (X, 34).

The function of religion with respect to nature, is to make it acceptable, to soften it, to humanize it, to make human beings at home in it. But for religious consciousness, nature as God is *both* humanized, personified, made a mirror for human needs, fears, desires, *and* at the same time seen as *non*human. Feuerbach notes this apparent contradiction, and attempts to explain it.

Religion presents us with the remarkable, yet easily understandable, even necessary contradiction: that while religion, either from a theistic or anthropological
standpoint adores the human in the form of the divine, because the divine
appears as something utterly different from man, as a non-human essence, in
just the opposite way, from the naturalist standpoint, the non-human [Nature]
is adored as divine just because it appears as human. (X, 31)

In both cases, then, what is common is the notion of objectivity: in
the first case, by the *objectification of the human,* and in the second, by
the *humanization of the objective.* But, as we have seen, the second has
priority, according to Feuerbach, and is presupposed by the first. If we
take this seriously, however, then the contradiction is not easily resolved.
For in both cases, the *objectification* has the form of what is at one
and the same time *both* human and not human; that is, it is a unity
of opposites. To take this one step further, then, in its epistemological
connotations: objectivity is a *unity* of man with nature, or has as its
presupposition the intermixture of the human and the natural, or their
interaction. In talking about anthropomorphic nature religions, Feuerbach says:

The human being does not radically differentiate himself from nature, nor
nature from himself. He therefore takes the feelings which a natural object
arouses in him to be immediate properties of the object itself. The beneficent,
good sensations and feelings are caused by good and beneficent nature; the bad,
maleficent, hurtful sensations, heat, pain, cold, hunger, illness, are caused by
an evil nature, or at the very least, by a nature in the condition of evil, of
malevolence, anger. Thus, unintentionally and unconsciously, man transforms
nature into a feeling being, a subjective, i.e. human being; and insofar as this
is done unconsciously it is done necessarily, though this necessity is only a
relative, historical one. (X, 30)

The important statement here is that, in this condition, human beings
do not radically differentiate themselves from nature, nor nature from
themselves. They are, therefore, at one and the same time affirming the
natural character of the human and the human character of the natural.
They are religious naturalists, so to speak, and their religiosity consists
only in conceiving of this unity of nature and human nature in the
form of the imagination, that is, in the sensuous imagery of the belief
that, for example, the sun and stars are human beings or have human
agency and will. The converse belief would presumably be that actual
human beings *are* the sun, the stars, and so on, and of course this identification occurs, as in the deification of rulers as natural forces, Pharoah
as identical with the sun or with the Nile, or a tribal chief as identical
with the totem animal. Presumably, then, this unity of man and nature
is simply the unenlightened form of that naturalistic humanism that is
Feuerbach's own position. But the dialectical difficulty here is that in

nature religions, nature is *not* regarded as *independent being*, but as the *other-being of human nature*. By contrast, presumably, for an enlightened naturalism, or materialism, human beings would be regarded as the *other-being of nature, or as nature humanized not as a whole, but only in human beings themselves.* The boundary between nature and the human is thus maintained only if not *all* of nature is seen as human, but only the human itself is seen as that part of nature which has *become* the human. Otherwise, Feuerbach's naturalism, here, remains a secularized anthropomorphism.

This is, in effect, analogous to the problem of *real* otherness, the objectivity and independence of the real, which arises in Feuerbach's theory of sensibility. There it remains a purely epistemological question, up to the point where sensibility itself is treated as an expression of need, dependence—that is, as a function of a living organism interacting with an environment. The parallel move is made in *The Essence of Religion*, in which religious belief, in its sensuous-practical form, as an expression of need and dependency on nature, is seen as functional, as expressing the practical relation of man and nature as an interaction—one in which both dependence and mastery are expressed—and therefore as an expression not simply of *feeling*, but of praxis.

Feuerbach begins to arrive at such a view, but does not articulate it fully. In the view that the *aim* of religion is the satisfaction of needs, the overcoming of that dependency, the feeling of which is the source of religion, Feuerbach introduces once again the distinction between the praxis of the religious imagination and this-worldly, concrete human praxis, which he had discussed in *The Essence of Christianity* (see pp. 321ff.).

Religion—at least in its origins, and in relation to nature—has no other task and no other aim than to transform an alien and inhospitable nature into a familiar, hospitable one; to take a nature which is, in itself, inflexible and iron-hard, and to soften it in the warm fires of the human heart and to turn it to human benefit. Thus religion has the same aim as learning or culture, which is to make nature theoretically comprehensible and practically compliant in the service of human needs; but with this one difference: what culture and learning try to achieve with *means* (and indeed with means themselves derived from nature), religion tries to achieve *without* means, or, what comes to the same thing, through the supernatural means of prayer, belief, sacraments, magic. (X, 40)

Again, Feuerbach trembles on the brink of a notion of praxis. For to "make nature practically compliant in the service of human needs" by actual means derived from nature seems to describe the actual *work process* itself, the transformation of nature by purposive, need-satisfying labor. The terms Feuerbach uses for this capacity to meet needs remain, however, *Bildung* and *Kultur*, but never *Arbeit*. Even where the concept of human labor or production is specific, as it is in the following passage, the metaphor of "production" or of "creation" turns out to be *birth*, or *fatherhood*, just as in *The Essence of Christianity*, it turned out to be literary or intellectual creation.

> Wherever man raises himself above nature, becomes a supernaturalist by his will and understanding, where man conceives of himself as having dominion "over the fish of the sea, over the birds of the sky, over the beasts in the field and over all that creeps upon the earth," there this Lordship over nature becomes the most exalted image, the highest being. The object of his adoration, the object of his religion becomes therefore the Lord and Creator of nature. . . . Only what I can bring forth, produce, do I have completely under my dominion. Only from the fact of my authorship does my property-right derive. The child is mine because I am its father. Only in creation does Lordship become proven, actualized. (X, 48)[2]

This analogy from human *capacities* to God's powers of action is different, however, from the analogy from human *wishes* to God's powers of action. In *The Essence of Christianity*, God's creative power, his power to create *ex nihilo* and at will, without constraint, without specific determinations, without means, by *omnipotence*, that is, by magic, was explained by Feuerbach as the projection of the willed or wished-for omnipotence of human feeling. Here, however, the notion of divine mastery and power over nature is seen to be projected from human mastery and power over nature, in the fact of human skill and art. Here Feuerbach comes closest, perhaps, to a positive notion of praxis—and stops short! For example, he considers the distinction between animal "skills" or instinctive abilities and the human understanding of these skills, as in the flight of birds or the weaving of a spider's web. He then argues that the human comprehension of the flight of birds projects this as a comprehension the bird must also have, in order to fly. But, says Feuerbach, this imputes to "blind" Nature—that is, to the bird's instinctive ability to fly—a *theoretical* understanding of the laws of nature that only human beings can acquire. Therefore, says Feuerbach, if nature is discovered to operate according to laws, we mistakenly impute an intelligence to nature that is, however, nothing but our own intelligence in the understanding or discovery of such laws. Thus, man

> makes the birds' flights dependent on his [human] insight into the mechanics of flight, makes the concepts he has abstracted from nature into *laws* of nature, which he then supposes the birds to apply to their flight, the way riders apply the rules of riding, or swimmers the rules of swimming. But there is this difference: that for birds, the application of the skill of flying is an innate capacity. The flight of birds rests on no art. (X, 57)

But whence comes the human knowledge of the *art* of flying, of the mechanics of flight, or, the "theoretical" understanding of the spider's construction of a web? In Feuerbach's view, it comes from *studying* birds and spiders, and imagining what I would do if I had to fly or spin a web. Thus, such knowledge is gained by "abstraction from nature," that is, by passive, intellectual observation, but *not* from the exercise of a real human capacity, not by emulative human praxis. The closest Feuerbach comes to contexts of actual praxis, in his account of the projection of human capacities as properties of a divine nature, is in a footnote:

Since in general the premise of all arguments which transform nature into a God, is a *human* premise, it is no surprise that the conclusion is also human, or resembles the human. If the world is a machine, or a house, then naturally there must be a designer or an architect. Are natural things as indifferent to one another as are human individuals, who can be directed and united for any arbitrary purpose of state–e.g. military service, or road-construction–only by a higher power; then naturally there must be in nature also a Regent, a governor, a general-in-chief,–a "captain in the clouds," for otherwise everything would dissolve in anarchy. Thus, man, at first unconsciously, makes of nature a human work, i.e., he makes *his* essence the fundamental essence of nature; and if he later (or simultaneously) becomes aware of the difference between the works of nature and the works of human art, he takes his own essence to be that of another, but analogous and similar being. (X, 58n.)

In his anthropologism, then, Feuerbach only rarely goes beyond generalized and abstract conceptions of human activity or human sociality. In *The Essence of Religion*, for all its clarity concerning the grounds of religion in the feeling of dependency on nature, this feeling itself and the forms of dependency remain ahistorical, only vaguely social. However, there are two passages in *The Essence of Religion* that go beyond the previously cited footnote in their more specific allusion to the social and political sources of the religious imagination. In the first, Feuerbach notes the transition from nature gods to civic gods. In the second, he decries this transition.

As soon as man passes from being merely a physical being to becoming a political one, or in general, a being who distinguishes himself from nature and concentrates himself upon himself alone, so too his God passes from being merely a physical being to becoming a political one who distinguishes himself from nature. Man attains this differentiation of his being from nature, and of his God from nature only through his association with other people in a commonwealth. Here, the former objects of his consciousness and his feeling of dependency, the powers of nature, are replaced by powers which exist only in his mind or his imagination, that is, political, moral, abstract powers, the power of law, of public opinion, of honor, of virtue. His physical existence is subordinated to his human, civic or moral existence. The power of nature over life and death becomes merely property and an instrument of political and moral power. (X, 43–4)

The notion that the Gods then become instruments of political or social power is clearly suggested here, but not elaborated except by bitterly ironic examples, concerning the use of religion to dazzle, subordinate and control by fear the now hapless slave or citizen. Feuerbach's bitterness is even more direct in the second passage, which echoes his disdain for urban life and expresses his romantic pastoralism, reminiscent of passages in Rousseau's *Discourse on the Origins of Inequality Among Men*. In comparing "Eastern" and "Western" man, he draws the analogy between the country dweller and the city dweller:

The former is dependent on nature, the latter on other people; the former guides himself by the state of the barometer, the latter by the state of the stock-market; the former by the invariant constellations of the Zodiac, the latter by the ever-changing signs of honor, fashion and opinion. Only the city-dwellers make history, only human "vanity" is the principle of history. Only he who is able to sacrifice Nature's power to the power of opinion, his life for his good name, his bodily existence to his existence in the mouth and memory of posterity—only he is capable of historical deeds. (X, 46–7)[3]

Herein lies a clue to Feuerbach's anthropologism and to the limits of his naturalism and materialism. The distaste for the city, for politics, for the mercantile, industrial, and technical aspects of modern life is clear throughout Feuerbach's life. He is disillusioned with university life and its pretensions, though he tries unsuccessfully (and his friend Kapp tries on his behalf) for several years to get a professorship. He is bitter at the political and clerical reaction, which has had direct consequences not only in the censorship of his work, but in the persecution, arrest, and later suicide attempt of his brother. He lives in rural Bruckberg, studies geology, reads works on science, observes nature in an amateur and often poetizing way. He is apathetic, skeptical, and unhopeful about the Revolution of 1848, which he regards as premature and unprepared for, and is not surprised when it fails. In none of this can one read a direct relation to his philosophical work in any simple sense. Yet there is the strong suggestion of the detached observer, the contemplator, for whom practice is not technical or political or social, but intellectual. He understands science as the observation of nature and as the theoretical abstraction from experience, but not as itself active experimental intervention. The "practical" is indeed that which has to do with human needs and interests—and, abstractly, also with the *means* for satisfying those needs. But Feuerbach's examples are always limited to *general* needs for sustenance and not yet the particular concrete means of satisfying them. Where he is concrete, it has to do with the psychological, affective, and sensual needs and desires, which he clearly sees as natural or material, or as embodied in "real flesh and blood beings." The sociological, the political-economic, the scientific-technical are just over the horizon for him, almost within view. But his view is that of a transitional figure, seeing the shape of the "philosophy of the future" but not yet its details.

Thus, the unity of nature and human nature is formulated by him in terms of conceptions of both nature and the human that remain abstract, somewhat romantic, *pre*scientific, and *pre*political. Still, the *direction* of his conceptions is *pro*scientific and *pro*political. The more direct statement of his views here betrays a naïveté not found in the earlier works. For he is, in effect, stepping on new ground. His empiricism and anthropologism lead him to more and more explicit materialist views, but it is a materialism that is in one sense a throwback to French eighteenth-century materialism, with its distinctive emphasis on the organic, the physiological, and on the material origins of the organic in the inorganic.

In *The Essence of Religion*, he gives a thoroughly materialistic account of the evolutionary origins of organic life, very much in the spirit of the passage in Diderot's *Letter on the Blind* or of similar formulations in D'Holbach or La Mettrie:

The earth wasn't always in its present state. Rather, it has come to its present condition only after a series of developments and revolutions, and Geology has discovered that in these various stages of development there had also been various plants and animals which now no longer exist, nor have even existed for ages. Thus, there are no longer any trilobites, encrimites, ammonites, no pterodactyls, no Ichthyo- and Plesiosaurs, no mega- and dinotherirems, etc. But why not? Apparently because the conditions for their existence are no longer present. But if the end of a species of life coincides with the end of its conditions, so too does the beginning, the origin of a species of life coincide with the beginning of its conditions. Even at present, when plants and animals, at least of the higher orders, originate only in organic procreation, we see how, in remarkable and as yet in unexplained ways they appear in numberless multitudes as soon as their appropriate conditions of life are given. The origin of organic life is therefore not to be thought of as an *isolated* act, as an act which follows *after* the development of the life conditions; but rather the act, the moment when the temperature, the air, the water, the earth in general takes on such feature, the oxygen, hydrogen, carbon, nitrogen entered into such combinations as were necessary for organic existence, is also to be thought of as the very same moment when these elements united to form organic bodies. Therefore, when the earth, by force of its own nature so developed and cultivated itself that it took on a character compatible with, and appropriate to human beings, that is, so to speak, when it took on a human character, it could then bring forth human beings by its own powers. (X, 19–20)

397

In effect, in *The Essence of Religion,* in the midst of his *phenomenology* of the *belief* in an objective nature, as it expresses the feeling of dependency on nature, Feuerbach gives us a straightforward natural scientific argument, and not an epistemological one, concerning the natural origins and character of the human species. He identifies the very conditions for a change in quality, for the disappearance or emergence of a species, for the origins of life, with the *fact* of that emergence itself. He sees in nature, therefore, the necessary and sufficient conditions for life, and for the origins of human life. Man is not *in* the world, merely; he *is* the world in one of its manifestations. The objectivity of nature is, therefore, not simply a question for epistemology, or for phenomenology, but a theoretical scientific question. Here Feuerbach seems to switch ground quite radically. For the derivation of the bond between the human and the natural here takes the natural, objective world as its starting point, and then attempts to derive the phenomena of life, human nature, and consciousness from nature, in a straightforward naturalistic or materialistic monism. The question is no longer one of how one gets *to* an objective reality, starting from the *I,* from consciousness or the Ego, or even from human species nature or sensibility; rather, it is the question of how one gets to human species nature, consciousness, the Ego, starting from objective, material nature.

This, then, is what Feuerbach seemed to have meant when he stated earlier, "I do not generate the object from thought, but rather the thought from the object" (S: I, 15). But what is the warrant for this radical shift? Is it simply a *volte-face,* from a subjectivist to an objectivist standpoint? Or is it rather a consequence of the empirical realism itself? For the evolutionary argument for the natural origins of life and of man *depends on* the evidence of geology, chemistry, biology; and these, in Feuerbach's view, constitute just those *ramified* modes of sensibility itself–the "seeing with open eyes"–that give us real, objective existence as an object of knowledge. This becomes clear in another passage in *The Essence of Religion:*

"The origin of life is inexplicable and incomprehensible." So be it. But this incomprehensibility doesn't justify you in the superstitious consequences which theology draws, on the basis of the deficiencies in human knowledge, doesn't justify you in going beyond the domain of natural causes. All you can say is: "I can't explain life on the basis of *those* natural phenomena and causes which are known to me, or on the basis of those which are known to me thus far." But you can't say: "It is impossible in general to explain life on the basis of nature," without pretending to already have exhausted the last drop in the ocean of nature. This incomprehensibility doesn't justify you to explain the inexplicable by the postulation of imaginary beings, it doesn't justify you in deceiving and deluding others by an explanation which doesn't explain anything; it doesn't justify you in transforming your *non-knowing* of natural, material causes into the *non-existence* of such causes, or in deifying or personifying your *ignorance*, to objectify as a being, in order to transcend your ignorance, that *which does no more than to express the nature of this ignorance*, as a *lack* of positive, material grounds for explanation. For what else is this immaterial and/or incorporeal, non-natural, unworldly being by means of which you explain life, other than the precise expression of the ignorance of material, bodily, natural, cosmic causes, of the fact that such being is not an object for you? But instead of being so honest and modest, so as to say: "I don't know any basis, I can't explain it, I lack the data, the materials," you transform this lack, these negations, vacancies in your head, by means of fantasy, into positive beings, which are *immaterial* beings, i.e., are *not material or natural beings*, just because you don't know of any *material or natural causes*. While ignorance is contented with immaterial, incorporeal, non-natural beings, her inseparable partner, the wanton imagination, which always carries on its affairs only with the highest and super highest beings, elevates these poor creatures of ignorance to the rank of *super*-material, *super*-natural beings. (X, 26–7)

Feuerbach develops this argument concerning natural evolution and adaptation further, in his *Lectures on The Essence of Religion*, delivered two years after the publication of *The Essence of Religion*. Here his argument for natural causes is directed against teleological conceptions of nature, against the theological conception of nature as providential and therefore created by design, by a beneficent God.

It is not a cause for wonderment . . . that we find here on earth the requisite and appropriate conditions and means for the life of man and animals. . . . We are not children of the [planets] Saturn or Mercury, but Earth-creatures, earth-beings. . . . Where there is such a temperature that water can exist as liquid, and not only as steam or ice, that is, where water exists which can be drunk or soaked up by plants; where there is air which can be breathed, where light is of the strength and intensity which corresponds to the capacities of animal or human eyes, there are also present the first causes and origin of animal and plant life; and there it is natural, indeed necessary that there be plants which are appropriate as nutriment to animal and human organisation. If one wants to wonder at this, he should wonder in general at the existence of the earth, and limit his theological wonderment and his theological arguments to the primary, so to speak, astronomical properties of the earth. Once the earth is given, as this individual, particular planet, distinct from all other planetary bodies, we have, in this individuality of the earth, the conditions or rather, the origin as well of all organic individuals. For only individuality is the principle, the ground of life. (VIII, 161–2)

Feuerbach goes on to give an account of the earth's own individuality as the product of material principles of "attraction and repulsion," and to explain the composition of the earth as a differentiated whole made up of an already heterogeneous matter. This natural heterogeneity of the material elements in turn is seen as an ultimately nonteleological one, so that final causes are eliminated even from the ground or origin of nature itself. The view of matter as some universal, undifferentiated stuff is seen by Feuerbach as "a human abstraction, a chimaera":

Matter is fundamentally already a self-differentiated being; for only a determinate, differentiated being is a real being. As nonsensical as is the general question of *why* anything is what it is, equally nonsensical is the question why anything is the specific thing that it is, e.g., why Oxygen is odorless, tasteless, and heavier than the atmosphere, why it ignites under pressure, and why it never becomes liquified even under the greatest pressure,[4] why its combining weight is expressed by the number 8, why it combines with hydrogen only in the proportions 8:1, 16:2, 24:3. These properties define the individuality of oxygen, i.e., its determinateness, its particular character, its essence. If I were to eliminate these properties which distinguish it from other elements, it would cease to exist, it would cease to be what it is. Therefore, to ask *why* oxygen is what it is, is particular, and why it is not something else, is no more than to ask *what* oxygen is. But why is it? To this, I answer *because* it is; it belongs to the essence of nature. It is not what it is for the sake of sustaining fire, or the breathing of animals, but rather, because it is what it is, fire and life can exist. Where the conditions or the grounds for something are given, the consequences cannot be avoided. Where the stuff, the materials for life are given, there too life cannot fail to exist, just as once oxygen and a combustible body are given, the process of burning necessarily follows. . . . (VIII, 162–3)

Feuerbach adds here too that our present inability to explain is not the ground for a resort to teleology or to supernatural explanations:

I am far from claiming that this superficial account constitutes an explanation of the origin or essence of organic life. We are far from the stage of science at which this problem will be solved. But we know or are capable of knowing at least this much, that just as we are now given birth and are sustained by natural means, so too we are originated by natural means, all theological explanations to the contrary. (VIII, 164)

And if there are in fact many natural phenomena, for which the physical or natural basis has not yet been discovered, it is absurd to seek refuge in theology on the grounds that we do not yet have a physical or natural explanation. What we don't yet understand, our successors will understand. (VIII, 168)

These passages, reminiscent of Dr. Saunderson's exhortation in Diderot's *Letter on the Blind* or of Spinoza's exhortation against the will of God, or Providence as the "refuge for ignorance," are characteristic of the mode of the enlightenment argument against religious superstition and the appeal to occult causes. Their form is therefore not novel. At the same time, however, in the context of Feuerbach's critique of religion and theology, and his epistemological characterization of sensibility, or sensation, as that form of immediate knowledge of existence that requires the *removal* of the fantastic constructions of the imagination, in order to achieve its immediacy, this appeal that Feuerbach makes to "natural causes" and "natural explanation" identifies the locus of that reality to which sensibility ostensibly gives us access.

The appeal to scientific explanation is an appeal to what can be known by the observation of nature. But scientific observation is no longer merely "looking and seeing." Sensibility, therefore, cannot be naive empirical observation. But how do we go from the "direct" evidence of the senses to science, from seeing, touching, smelling, to chemistry, physics, biology? What is the nature of inference, of judgment, of speculation, of thought *in* science? What, in effect, is a *scientific* "sensibility"? That there is such a thing Feuerbach assures us. But the elaboration of this idea, beyond its programmatic proposal, remains rudimentary, and finally devolves upon a fairly characteristic older model of a "central organ" of judgment, which compares, distinguishes, and establishes connections among the data of sensation. In short, Feuerbach falls back upon an associationist empiricism, or else substitutes a bald claim that the senses give us connections and wholes, and not merely parts.

Feuerbach's explicit materialism, his theory of mind-body identity and of the physiological unity of man and nature, adumbrated in these views of natural origins of life, his views on natural science itself as practical sensibility, are developed in a number of the later works, to which we now turn.

THE MIND-BODY QUESTION: THE DEVELOPMENT OF FEUERBACH'S MATERIALIST MONISM IN THE LATER WORKS

The relations between the physical and the mental, that classic locus of the philosophical argument between materialism and idealism, and between monism and dualism may be discussed in several contexts. First, there is the so-called mind-body problem, which locates the issue *within* the human being, as one concerning the relation of consciousness or thought to bodily existence. In religious consciousness, this expresses itself as the question of the relation between the flesh and the spirit, between this-worldly, mortal, transient, and suffering existence and the existence of an immortal and immaterial soul. In physiological and psychological contexts, it becomes a question of the relation between the brain (or, more broadly speaking, the whole physiological organism) and thought. Epistemologically, the question becomes wider in context: How can the mind know an external world, *or* its own body, if the first is mental and incorporeal and the second is physical and corporeal? Once Descartes poses the issue by defining the human being as *essentially* a thinking thing, as *res cogitans*, this same question can be posed in its anthropological context: How is the human, as essentially a conscious being, related to nonconscious material existence, that is, to nature? Second, therefore, the relation of the mental to the physical is posed as a question concerning the relations between man and world. Out of this, there arises that dualism within the philosophic discipline itself, between so-called *moral philosophy* and *natural philosophy*, that canonizes the split between mind and body, as one between two distincitive subject matters of philosophical investigation, and writes it into the actual university curriculum for more than 200 years. Under the rubric "moral philosophy," then, fall all those subjects having to do with the human. Beyond "morals" itself in its narrower ethical connotations, this includes history, politics, economics, anthropology. Later these come to be characterized as the so-called *Geisteswissenschaften*, introduced in the late nineteenth-century movement of Dilthey and others that built upon Fichte's characterization of the distinctiveness of these "human sciences." Today's demarcation between the "social sciences" and the "natural sciences" continues this division, both in those modes that continue to maintain a radical distinction (e.g., the phenomenological, cognitivist, action-theoretical, intentionalist, and *"Verstehen"* approaches and methodologies in psychology, history, and the social sciences); and in those modes that seek to overcome the distinction (e.g., behaviorist and so-called positivist approaches to the social sciences that seek accommodation to the methods and outlooks of the "natural" sciences, in particular, to the model of mathematical physics).

There are therefore two related but alternative emphases here: first, on the largely metaphysical and epistemological questions concerning mind and matter, and second, on the largely methodological and anthropological questions concerning man and world.

Feuerbach's struggle with these questions takes place in the context of his own preoccupation with the mind-body question both as an epistemological and an anthropological question. In the development of his own philosophical thought, as we have seen, this interplay is constant. But if one were to ask where the priorities lie, for Feuerbach, they are clearly anthropological. And herein lies the fruitfulness and the heuristic force of his views. He recognizes, time and again, at various stages and in various formulations, that the epistemological questions cannot stand by themselves; that questions concerning the relations of sensation and perception to thought, of knowledge to reality, of belief to truth are "epistemological" in the narrower sense only as questions for an abstracted theoretical standpoint, and are therefore "theological" or "professorial" questions, whose solution demands the broader contexts of human life, human need, human action. From his own "professorial" philosophical works—the *Dissertation*, the studies in the history of philosophy, the critical review articles, the defense and critique of Hegel—he progressed to the critique of religion. But here his concern is *thoroughly* anthropological, and his critical reconstruction of the *epistemology* of religious belief and of its "negative essence" in theology establishes the human foundations of the processes of knowledge and self-knowledge. If Kant can be said to have effected a "Copernican revolution" in epistemology and in moral theory, rediscovering the transcendental grounds of knowledge, belief, and moral action *within* human perception, reason, and judgment, then Feuerbach may be said to have continued this "revolution" by reducing Kant's appeal to a transcendental rationality—which is the essence of "any rational being whatever anywhere in the universe"—to that of human species being itself, to its own intrinsic, this-worldly, practical (in his limited sense), but not yet historical essence. Where Kant sharply distinguished the transcendental from the anthropological (e.g., in his methodological remarks at the beginning of *The Metaphysical Foundations of Morals*), Feuerbach may be said to have founded the transcendental upon the anthropological.

In this light, the later works on the mind-body problem, and on the relations of nature and human nature, tend more and more clearly to a naturalist and materialist monism, to a unity of mind and matter, man and nature. The difficulties here are posed by the temptations to a reductive and vulgarized materialism, to a denial of the qualitative differences between the *mental*-physical and the *nonmental*-physical, or between nature humanized and nonhuman nature. But Feuerbach is too much an heir and appreciator of the idealist tradition, with its emphasis on the distinctiveness and irreducibility of spiritual and mental life, to fall easy prey to a reductive and eliminative materialism, which holds, for example, that consciousness is "nothing but" self-active matter. For one thing, he is an apt critic of abstract materialism, of the objectified "matter" that is a construction and an object of a merely theoretical consciousness, or of a mathematical or mechanistic conception of matter, such as Hobbes' or Descartes' where the categories of *quantity* and *extension* reign supreme. Nor is Feuerbach ready to accept the theologized "matter" of Spinoza's monism, though here the transition from the mechanistic to the organic conception of matter, as a self-active and self-differentiating totality, is already suggested. Thus, Feuerbach is faced with the necessity for a synthesis: a nonreductive materialism that retains the distinctiveness of spiritual, human life but rejects the dualism that calls upon two exclusive metaphysical categories for a resolution of the problem. The synthesis—a problematic one—lies in Feuerbach's notion of *sensibility*, whose early difficulties we have already examined. Where he asserts, rhetorically, that sensibility is the *unity* of the material and the spiritual, of "real," independently existing nature and consciousness; or where he asserts, equally rhetorically, that *Man* is the unity of body and soul, nature and thought, he sets forth the programmatic ideal of his philosophical resolution of the problem. But his abhorrence for and rejection of the Hegelian identity of opposites—his characterization of this "identity" as a mystification in which thought simply takes as identical in reality that which is identical only in thought—leads Feuerbach to seek a more difficult solution. The unity of what is the same *and* different cannot be, for him, a postulated dialectical or logical principle. It needs to be worked out concretely, so that the differences within this unity are retained in thought but are realized as distinctions in reality itself.

It may appear from this that Feuerbach stands at the threshold of a naturalistic or materialistic dialectic. But if this is so, this dialectic, this unity of same and different, devolves not upon nature or matter as such, but only upon the *human*. In other words, the *objective* dialectic Feuerbach retains from his Hegelian past leads him to reject *both* the dialectic of consciousness as such, and the dialectic of *Being* or of matter as such. He rejects both the idealist and the materialist dialectic in their "abstracted" forms, either as a dialectic of the subject, generating objects out of itself, or as a dialectic of the objective world, generating subjects out of itself. True, this latter "objective" dialectic is approximated in his evolutionary naturalism, in which human nature and human consciousness, like organic life, are constituted by the necessary and sufficient material conditions for these phenomena. But Feuerbach is neither systematic nor sustained in this view. Rather, the *real* subject-object unity is neither thought, nor being, but *human* being, regarded as living, conscious, needy being, in which nature and spirit interact in the very fact of sensibility itself. Feuerbach's ontology is therefore a *human* ontology, both material and spiritual. But it is not the double-aspect unity of Spinoza's *substance*. Feuerbach's *Substance* is *man*. His materialism, as far as it goes, is a humanist materialism, his *Being* or *Substance* is *human being* or *substance*. Nevertheless, as to the question of ontological priority, which remains the touchstone of the difference between materialist and idealist emphases in philosophy, Feuerbach says in *The Lectures on the Essence of Religion*: "The unconscious being of nature is, for me, the eternal, uncreated being, the primary being, but primary in time, not in rank; the physically primary but not morally primary being. Conscious, human being is secondary, which emerges later in time, but is primary in rank" (VIII, 26–7).

Ontological primacy, then, is a more complex question than simply that of priority in causal or temporal terms, for Feuerbach. The world precedes man; it is the precondition for his existence, the origin and sustenance of his being. But if, as Feuerbach himself says (about the *practical negation* of theology by empiricism), "that alone is real, at least for human beings, which is an object of their real, actual activity" (II, 265), then that alone is *practically* "real," for Feuerbach, which is the object of his preoccupation and activity. The ontological primacy of the human then becomes clear as that primacy in terms of which, and on the grounds of which, the temporal primacy of the natural is established. Feuerbach contra Kant can thus be transformed into Feuerbach contra Feuerbach here, with regard to his materialism. Just as Kant, according to Feuerbach, *failed* to establish the independence of the *noumenal*, because he derived it as a presupposition of sensibility, and therefore only as a conceptual reality, so too one may level a Feuerbachian critique of Feuerbach, because he derives the independnce of the natural or material world as a presupposition of *life*, of human existence, derived from the facts of human existence itself, as dependent and sensuous existence. The question remains: How can one go any further? Is the anthropocentric limit of our knowledge to be transcended? Can our ontology transcend our existence? One may say that for Feuerbach, our existence is *constantly* transcended, but only *in particular*—that is, what was once a limit of our knowledge is overcome, but only by human means. The attempt to overcome this limit by superhuman means is the fantasy of religious wish and imagination. The only transcendence, then, for Feuerbach, is the continuing self-transcendence of the individual in the history of the species. The only objectivity there is rests in this process. "History," he writes, "is the humanization of humanity" (X, 313). Materialism, for him, is no more than the human recognition that what appears to be *beyond* us, as totally other, external, unknowable, is appropriated by us, humanized by us, in our inquiry and activity. Objectivity is not "there," it is acquired; but by a being whose essence is this very acquisition itself, its life practice, its *sensibility*, therefore, in Feuerbach's terms. Just as we incorporate and humanize the world, by breathing its air and drinking its water, we incorporate, appropriate, humanize the world, as an object of our knowledge, by sensation and thought. We absorb the object through our pores, so to speak, make it identical with ourselves, and recognize this identity itself not as an immediate "internal" one, only, but as, at the same time, an identity of the "outer" with the "inner."

These are the major themes and directions of Feuerbach's later works, in his treatment of the mind-body problem and of the unity of the human and the natural.

In 1846, Feuerbach published (as his additional commentaries on the 1843 *Principles*) *The Dualism of Body and Soul, Flesh and Spirit, Once Again*. The issue confronted here is that between physiology and psychology as alternative approaches to the bodily and spiritual characteristics of human consciousness. Feuerbach had dealt with this question earlier, in his Dorguth review of 1838, arguing there against Dorguth's reduction of thinking to brain activity. There Feuerbach had said that thought could not be conceived except through itself alone, and that although thinking was *also* an activity of the brain, it was not *only* an activity of the brain, that is, was not reducible to a physiological account. Here Feuerbach presents the then current views on the distinctions between the disciplines of neurophysiology and neuroanatomy, on the one hand, and psychology, on the other. The methodological dualism is seen to be founded on a conceptual dualism: For psychology, there are no nerves, no heart, no stomach, no spatial entities, but only sensation, thought, consciousness itself as an object. True enough, say Feuerbach; but this is only a reflection of the fact that this views the matter subjectively, from the "inside" of thinking and sensing itself, so to speak.

In the desire and enjoyment of food, I know nothing of the stomach; in sensation as such, as a subject matter for psychology, I ignore the nervous system; in thinking as such, I know nothing of the brain. But to conclude from this *subjective* lack of consideration of the nerves and the brain to an *objective* nervelessness and brainlessness and to a generally incorporeal being, in and for itself, is in fact so much as to say that because I can't know and feel, from within myself, that I have parents–(everyone knows only from others that he has been procreated)–one should therefore conclude that I am self-created, that my being owes its existence to no other origin. (X, 123)

But, Feuerbach argues, the difference lies in the fact that the object of knowledge and the mode of inquiry differ between psychology and physiology.

The difference doesn't lie in the object as such but rather in the method and way in which it is known. [In Psychology], the method is one which is identical with its object, it is unmediated, *living*; in [Physiology] it is mediated, dead, historical. The frog is a living, sensing, perceiving being, a *subject*, only for itself. But for me, as an object of vivisection, it is only a material being, only an *object*, for the frog's own sensation as such cannot in any way be an object for me. Living, sensing, perceiving as such can only be immediately apprehended through themselves and are inseparable, and undifferentiable from the living, sensing, perceiving being, subject or organ. (X, 123–4)

Here Feuerbach grounds the unity of the psychic and the physical on its functions (e.g., life, sensation, etc.) and sees the sources of dualism in the alternative ways in which these functions themselves can be known. This is, in effect, a double-aspect approach like Spinoza's, or like Schopenhauer's. (Schopenhauer says, for example, that mind is knowledge a priori of the Will, and body is knowledge a posteriori of the Will, but the object–for Schopenhauer, the Objective Will as reality –is the same, known in different ways.) Thus, Feuerbach argues further that although it is not given *in thought* as such that thinking is a brain act, it does not follow that *in itself* it is *not* a brain act. "What is *for me* or *subjectively* a purely immaterial, non-sensuous act is *in itself*, or *objectively* a material and sensuous one. . . . Just as *for me*, my body belongs to the class of imponderables or has no weight, even though in itself, or for others it is a heavy body (X, 125 and fn.). Thus, though I may be able to *think* of myself as differentiated from my body, that is, in my consciousness, nevertheless, in actual being, this separation cannot take place. The distinction between the subjective and the objective is therefore a distinction in standpoint, not in reality. Feuerbach draws the analogy: "The writing Schiller is subjective spirit, the printed Schiller is objective spirit . . . a similar difference to that between the creating author and his work as an object of the appreciative reader can be found within ourselves" (X, 128). Feuerbach proceeds then to argue against the typical dualist views of the unity and simplicity of the soul, and the plurality of the body, as a composite. His argument is two-sided: First, that the soul, or mind, is as internally differentiated and as composite as its content–that is, from the very point of view of consciousness itself, "Our *I*, our consciousness is as differentiated as its content is" (X, 129) and second, that the compositeness of the body is such only abstractly, insofar as it is an object, but not as a living organism itself, in which condition it is an organic unity, an "individual."

If one reduces the organic body in terms of an abstract, material characterization, as here in terms of a composite thing made of parts, then it becomes necessary to explain the phenomena of organic life, which contradict this characterization and representation, by means of a particular fictitious being put together out of separate and opposed properties. But this body as an organic body already possesses these properties in itself. Despite the multitude of its parts, it is "one thing," an individual, organic unity. This *organic unity* is the principle of perception and sensation. To be sure, this body can be taken apart, but with this decomposition it ceases to be an organic, living thing, it is no longer what it was. Only in death does it become a composite, divisible thing. (X, 131)

It is only in this fictitious representation of the body as a composite object that there arise the notions that the body is a merely spatial being, whereas the mind is a nonspatial or temporal being. The unity of space and time, of corporeality and thought, says Feuerbach, is *sensibility* (X, 132). The physiologist therefore has to *violate* life to make it an object of his inquiry and observation. The psychologist has to *violate* life also, then, to pretend that mind is an incorporeal or immaterial phenomenon. Here Feuerbach rejects both sides of the dualism, after finding its source in the difference in approach.

Truth is neither materialism nor idealism, neither physiology nor psychology. Truth is only *anthropology*, truth is only the standpoint of sensibility, for only this standpoint gives me *totality* and *individuality*. Neither does the soul think and sense – for the soul is only the function or event of thinking, sensing and willing, personified, hypostatized and conceived of as an actual being – nor does the brain think and sense, for the brain is a *physiological abstraction*, an organ taken in isolation, torn out of the totality, separated from the skull, the face, from the body in general. The brain is an organ of thought only as long as it is united with a human head and body. The outer is a projection and expression of the inner. The essence of life is the outward expression of life. The outward expression of the brain, however, is the head. There is no strongly marked difference between the brain of a human being and that of an ape, but what a difference between the skull or the face of a human being and that of an ape! Actually, the ape isn't lacking in the inner conditions of thinking, in the brain; only the appropriate external relations necessary for thinking are missing. . . . In a palace, one thinks differently than in a hovel, whose low roof seems, as it were, to exercise a pressure on the brain. We are different people in the open air than we are in closed spaces; narrow spaces cramp us, wide open spaces widen our hearts and spirits. Where the opportunity is missing to exercise a talent, the talent is also missing. Where there is no room for action, there is also no motivation to act, at least no true motivaion. . . . But let us not overlook the means by which nature comes to the rescue. If we can't escape the narrow confines of a prison, we seek the wide open and free spaces in our fantasy. Thus does the spirit break asunder the bonds of the body. Thus do we transcend the effects of our inner life. But just in this very resort to desperate means, whereby we may achieve in the mind what is denied us in reality, do we testify to the necessity and truth of the external relations which constrain us. (X, 135–7)

In this remarkable passage, Feuerbach arrives at the clearest statement of his conception of mind-body identity: The identity is not, reductively, that of the mind with the body, *as body*; nor of the body with the mind, *as mind*; rather, the identity, or the unity, is the *totality itself*, as a functional or organic one, that is, as an *activity* of living, thinking, feeling, willing, whose organic condition is certainly a material or physical body, but only a body of a certain kind, the *acting* body, *whose externality is a relational one*, and that therefore cannot be reduced to a composite or aggregate physical thing except in death. In short, Feuerbach arrives here at the notion of a qualitatively distinct aspect of nature, whose organic unity and whose external conditions of life join in that emergent quality of *sensibility* that is the functional unity of inner and outer, world and individual. Feuerbach writes, "Sensibility is the *ultima ratio*, the *summa summarum*, the theory of the senses is the theory of what is ultimate, of that in which all secrets are revealed. The outer is the fulfillment of the inner" (X, 138). Further, "The division of the human being into body and soul, into a sensible and non-sensible being is only a theoretical division; in *praxis*, in life, we negate this division" (X, 140). And here again, as in the *Principles*, Feuerbach asserts the distinctiveness of the human as against the animal senses: "Man distinguishes himself from the animals only in that he is the living superlative of sensualism, in that he is the most universally sensible being in the world" (X, 143–4). Universal sensibility is however not merely the universality, the manifoldness of each sense modality, nor merely the aggregate combination of seeing, hearing, touching, tasting, smelling. Rather–and here Feuerbach proposes a variant on an earlier statement of his–the senses deliver a contentful and universal input, but do not yet in themselves attain to cognitive or rational thought.

"We read the book of nature by means of the senses, but we don't understand it by means of the senses." True enough! But we don't bring any sense into nature by means of the understanding. We only translate and interpret the book of nature. The words that we read therein with the senses are not empty, arbitrary signs, but rather determinate, appropriate and characteristic expressions. . . . The senses tell us everything, but in order to understand what they tell us, we have to relate them to each other. To bring the revelations of the senses into such connection is called *thinking*. (X, 150)

Here, unfortunately, Feuerbach ends the work. Thinking, he suggests, is the internal activity of judgment: combining, associating, comparing the sensible truths of nature by means of some central process. Feuerbach adds a footnote in which he talks of a "central organ," distinct from the sensory organs and nerves, whose function it is to "concentrate and collect the data of the senses, to compare them, to distinguish them, to classify them" (X, 148 n.). This function, whether described as "mind" or in anatomical-physiological terms is itself, he says, a sensible reality– neither disembodied "spirit" nor dispirited "brain." But what? According to Feuerbach, a real *something*, an actuality, a *Dasein*. Does Feuerbach progress beyond the conception of an innate judgmental faculty of an older associationist empiricism here? Are the senses, almost clearly characterized as life *functions*, as *activities* of a living being, now once again reduced to the passive messengers of the outer world? Is this "central function" *itself* also sensibility, or "generalized sensibility," or thought? For all the teasing novelty of Feuerbach's mind-body unity as "sensibility," we are left with an abstract and confused "entity" or "function," albeit one that promises to overcome the abstractions of "mind" and "body" in the dualist view. The closest we can come to the *sense* of "sensibility," then, is that it is an interaction; and as such it is the ultimately "real" thing, of which body and mind are one-sided abstractions. It is like nothing else so much as what John Dewey was later to formulate as "experience."

This explicit identification of sensibility with reality occurs again and again in the later writings. In the *Lectures on the Essence of Religion*, Feuerbach writes "Sensibility is in my view nothing else but the true, existing unity of the material and the spiritual, not the manufactured and thought up unity of the two. Therefore, for me, sensibility is as much as reality" (VIII, 15). Reality, therefore, is not matter, not nature, not corporeality as such but the unity of matter and mind in sensibility. But Feuerbach is not yet settled, even on this point. One way to read Feuerbach is to resort to his contemporary, John Stuart Mill, who, in his *Examination of Sir William Hamilton's Philosophy*, defines matter as "the permanent possibility of sensation." That is to say, the material world is that which *can be known by the senses* but is not itself "sensibility," nor is it constituted *by* the actuality of sensation, but only by that which is potentially sensible. Is this Berkeley brought up to date, as Lenin thought of similar formulations in Mach, Plekhanov, or Bogdanov, in his critique of "empirio-criticism," a form of empirical realism similar to Feuerbach's? Is *Esse* identical with *percipi*—is *being* identical with *being perceived*? Or rather with being *perceivable*? Feuerbach never quite gets off this hook. In his posthumously published *Aphorisms*, he writes, in a passage critical of Kantianism:

How is it possible for things which are not sensible to affect our senses? How can it be that *noumena*, things-in-themselves, can be pure objects of thought? How can they at the same time exist for our sensibility, insofar as they are presupposed by it, i.e., how can they determine sensible representations, how can they allow themselves to be represented as that which they are not, i.e., as sensible things? How is it possible for beings or things to be sensible objects or to be sensibly represented unless they are at least sensible *potentialiter* (to use Aristotle's term)? . . . Insofar as [the a priori forms of sensibility] are pure intuitions of our sensibility, they "show themselves" only as mere forms of our sensibility! How much better it would be to sacrifice this *a priori* knowledge and to throw ourselves into the arms of a straightforward empiricism, which shows us things as they are, in that they determine us by their presence, rather than by their absence, and which are not modeled and determined by our preconceived concepts? (X, 322–3)

Here again there echoes that plea for the self-evidence of the senses, whose epistemological warrant *cannot* be given from within sensibility itself except as revelation; but whose real argument, for Feuerbach, is the connaturality of sensation and the sensible, between the organs of sense and their objects, and ultimately, therefore, between mind and body, consciousness and matter.

The materialist argument degenerates, however, into a purely physiological one when Feuerbach discovers Moleschott. Up to that point, he was prone to the kind of naturalism we have seen in *The Essence of Religion*, in which the internal constitution of the human is an internalization of an outer nature, or nature humanized. This materialist tendency reaches its fullest expression in Feuerbach's review of Moleschott's work *Lehre der Nahrungsmittel* (*Theory of Nutrition*, 1850).[5] Here, in Moleschott, Feuerbach finds the "sensuous" unity of thinking and being, of man and nature exemplified in the act of eating itself! Nature becomes literally incorporated into man. Thinking has its basis in body chemistry! "No phosphorous–no thought," Feuerbach quotes from Moleschott. And he draws both the epistemological and the "revolutionary" consequences of Maleschott's work.

Written two years after the 1848 Revolution, Feuerbach's essay "The Natural Sciences and the Revolution" expounds a thesis that *not* politics, but the natural sciences themselves are the real bearers of the social revolution, insofar as they reveal the processes of nature as those of constant growth, change, decay, and replacement of the old with the new. Somehow these lessons of natural science are to become political lessons for mankind. How is it, Feuerbach asks, that during a period of strict censorship in Germany, the natural sciences were nevertheless permitted to continue their free, unhampered research?

Isn't this a glaring contradiction? What is the basis however, for the liberal attitude towards the Natural Sciences? Only the narrow understanding of the government, which doesn't know of the secret, subversive connections between Natural Science, and Religion, Philosophy, and Politics. At first glance, on superficial consideration, anything that has to do with the Natural Sciences seems to be the most harmless, blameless thing there can be; what is further from the rush and drive of the political world than Nature. What sort of connection can there possibly be between the laws of Nature, and the play of intrigues in our politics, between the needs of life, and the luxury articles of our

Ministers and Deputies? . . . The natural scientist sees how everything in Nature is in continual progress, how Nature never falls back to a stage it has
already passed, how a man never becomes a boy again, nor a woman a girl,
nor a fruit a blossom. . . . He sees how the old always dies in Nature, indeed,
how it acts as the fertilizer to give forth a better future. How ridiculous the
reactionary miracle-makers seem to the natural scientist, when they fancy that
they can merely eradicate and ignore the content-full years of history, and try
to force mankind back to an anomalous past, try to make children out of men.
The natural scientist sees how there is nothing that is isolated, or single, in
nature; moreover, he sees how everything hangs together in a magnificent and
necessary whole, indeed, how the natural elements are divided into separate
classes, grounded in fundamental differences, and how these separate classes
finally resolve into the unity of the whole. (X, 4–5)

The whole is internally differentiated in nature; but it is not a frag-
mented, incoherent, squabbling whole. The scientist views the whole
from a cosmopolitan viewpoint, says Feuerbach. He is above the petty
squabbles of German politics, but he is not beyond politics. His very
scientific viewpoint itself, says Feuerbach, leads the scientist to certain
political, ethical conclusions. The scientist compares Nature with Society, sees truth in Nature and sees untruth in Society, and decides to
apply the truth of Nature to Society, in a mood of scientific enlightenment. "The view of Nature ennobles man above the tighthearted limits
of suffered rights; it makes man communistic, i.e., free-thinking, and
free-giving" (X, 7).

Granted rights are ridiculous to the scientist, says Feuerbach. What
is a right cannot be granted; communal, equal, universal rights are the
dictates of nature, of the whole.

Such are the communistic concepts of State and Right to which Nature leads
us. And still, the limited understanding of the government permits such great
freedom to the natural sciences, and places only philosophy under police surveillance. Only philosophy! How ridiculous! How harmless, how poor and
defenseless philosophy in comparison with the natural sciences! How easy it is
to hinder its dangerous effects on the public! What is needed to cut a philosopher short? No more than a professor of philosophy,–and what is easier to
obtain than one of these? When a revolutionary philosopher comes forth, all
you need to do is to get a professor of philosophy to write against him, and the
poor philosopher is, in the eyes of the public at least, dead as a doornail. The
philosopher, whose only instrument is the unfaithful, many-meaninged *word*,
can be annihilated easily, by simply twisting one word, leaving out one parti-
ciple, and changing the meaning of the clearest, most uncontradictable sentence.
How can the loose, fleeting word-connections that the mind is concerned with
stand up against the definitive, internal connections of chemical elements?
What are the paper periodicals which support philosophy, against the solid
molecular structure of the natural world? . . . (X, 8)

Feuerbach had expressed a similar analogy earlier, in the *Lectures on the Essence of Religion*. In a metaphorical mood, he had written,

Just as in a republic, only those laws obtain which express the will of the people, so too in nature, there obtain only laws which correspond to its own nature. . . . In short, just as in a republic, at least in a democratic one, which is the only one intended here, only the populace rules, and not princes, so too there are no gods in nature, but only natural forces, natural elements and beings. (VIII, 173-4)

Here, however, the natural "democratic" rule of law is taken as the model of states and politics, the natural "equality" of nature, as the model of social equality, of communism. Charming as Feuerbach's argument may be, it reveals the naïveté of his political understanding, for the work was written after the 1848 Revolution (though, of course, in the dismay Feuerbach felt over petty politics). The political "dangerousness" of natural science may lie in the political and ethical lessons the scientist may draw from nature. But historically the lessons drawn from nature have been of all sorts. Aristotle concluded "from nature" that hierarchy and domination were natural, and justified slavery and the subordination of women thereby, in the *Politics*. The divine right of kings was modeled on "nature," as were the concepts of racial supremacy, male supremacy, and social Darwinism. Thus, the conception of nature, as Feuerbach correctly noted earlier in *The Essence of Religion*, becomes itself a projection of human social structure and interests. But the natural sciences *are* revolutionary insofar as they give human beings the means to overcome their ignorance and their dependency, the means to deal with human want, misery, and ignorance. Feuerbach recognizes this clearly in his appreciation of Moleschott's work, however extravagant the excesses of his conclusions. Chemistry—that great industrial and technological science of nineteenth-century Germany—had direct implications for human welfare, in particular in its applications to agriculture, in the understanding and provision of foodstuffs. The slogan of Moleschott's work, popularized in the pun *"Der Mensch ist was er isst"* –"Man is what he eats"[6]–may be interpreted to have the social implications that man is himself a product of his productive activity, that he creates himself in the labor of producing the means of his subsistence and in the social organization that assures this production and reproduction of species existence. But this is to stretch Moleschott's intentions. Marx regarded Moleschott as a "vulgar materialist" precisely because the social and political contexts of the human production of sustenance were left out of account, in the flat insistence on the physiological materialism of human existence. Schopenhauer, on the other hand, nailed

him sarcastically as a "Barber's helper."[7] Feuerbach's appreciation of
Moleschott especially focuses on the consequences of this physiological
materialism for his sensationism and for the mind-body problem, resolved at last in the stomach.

This work, though it deals only with eating and drinking, which are regarded
in the eyes of our supernaturalistic mock-culture as the lowest acts, is of the
greatest philosophic significance and importance. Yes, I go even further, and
maintain, that it alone contains the real "Fundamentals of the Philosophy of
the Future" and of the present; that we find the most difficult philosophical
problems solved here. How former philosophers have broken their heads over
the question of the bond between body and soul! Now we know, on scientific
grounds, what the masses know from long experience, that eating and drinking
hold together body and soul, that the searched-for bond is nutrition. How
philosophers used to quarrel over innate ideas, or ideas from the outside, how
scornfully they looked down upon those who derived the origin of idea from
the senses! Now, it is as impossible to speak of innate ideas as to speak of
innate food or innate heat, which plays such an important role in natural
science under the name of *calor innatus*. Now we know that respiration is the
most important source of heat, that air is an essential part of us, that we pump
it all in from the outside, that we have nothing that is our own, that we come
on the world as have-nots, as communists, in that nothing is in us which doesn't
also exist outside of us, that we are stuck together ultimately, out of acid, nitrogen, carbon and hydrogen, out of these mean, simple elements, so infinitely
capable of combination. . . . (X, 12–13)

Just as God, Substance, the Trinity are "nothing but," the projections
of human consciousness, so is man "nothing but" a combination of
chemical elements. And yet our so-Christian government, says Feuerbach, permits the natural sciences, and particularly the most revolutionary of all, chemistry, to go on researching, investigating, and attacks
philosophy, when the philosophical debates are being dissolved by the
nitric acid of chemistry.

How the concept of Substance has vexed philosophy! What is it, I or not-I?
Spirit or Nature? Or the unity of both? Yes, the unity. But what is said thereby? Only Sustenance is substance; sustenance is the identity of spirit and nature. Where there is no fat, there is no meat; but where there is no fat, there
is also no brain, no spirit. And fat comes only from sustenance. Sustenance is
the Spinozistic Ἑν καί παν, the all-encompassing, the essence of essence. Everything is dependent on eating and drinking. The differentiation of essences is only the differentiation in sustenance. . . . Being is one with eating;
Being means eating; what is, eats and is eaten. Eating is the subjective, active
form. Eaten is the objective, suffering form of being; but both are indivisible.
. . . How philosophers struggled with the question, what is the beginning of
philosophy?–I or not-I, Consciousness or Being? Oh, you fools, who stand in
open-mouthed bewilderment before the solution of its beginning, and still
don't see, that the open mouth itself is the entrance into the innards of Nature,
that the teeth have long ago cracked his problematical nut over which you are

racking your brains even today. Therefore, thinking must begin, when we begin to exist; the *Principium Essendi* is also the *Principium Cognoscendi*. The beginning of existence, however, is sustenance. Sustenance, therefore, is the beginning of consciousness. The first condition for bringing something to your head and your heart, is bringing something to your stomach. What was called *"A Jove Principium"* is now become *"a ventre principium."* The old world stood the body on the head, the new sets the head on the body; the old world derived matter from mind; the new has mind originate in matter. . . . "A full stomach studies nothing." Right, but as long as the stomach is full, the head has nothing of the contents of the stomach. Food becomes brain, once it is digested; becomes blood. The "full stomach" is an absurd objection. The fact remains: the material of Sustenance is the material of thought. . . . (X, 13–15, 22)

The ethical, political significance of this is that all culture, convictions, all social being is determined by food. "If you want to better the people, give them better food, instead of declamations against sin" (X, 22).

Moleschott carried the half-truth to its most absurd lengths: a vegetarian has a vegetarian character; meat-eaters are strong-willed, and so on; the energy of the English workers is explained by their eating roast beef, and by contrast the laziness of the Italian Lazzarone is the outcome of a vegetarian diet. Feuerbach cites such passages from Moleschott approvingly, in this review, and concludes that a German revolution will never be accomplished by eaters of cabbage and potatoes. The basis, the real basis for revolution, is a diet for the proletariat consisting of . . . beans!

In such a universe, a new subjective anthropocentrism is introduced, centered around digestion. The world is a great animal, and its systole and diastole, the dynamic of its being is eating and being eaten! What is behind this crude reductionism, this gastrointestinal vision of the world? A grain of truth, certainly; and perhaps the polemical and rhetorical overemphases Feuerbach required to assert his utter break with idealism. The anthropological unity of man and nature is not an ideated unity, nor even a felt unity. It is a "real" unity. But as a materially existing being, the reality of the human is necessarily organic. If life is the precondition of thought and food the precondition of life, then food is the precondition of thought. "When I am hungry, I think of my stomach. When my hunger is stilled, then I have time and freedom to think of my head. *Primum vivere, deinde philosophari.* First, to live, then to think or philosophize" (X, 100).

Material existence is the precondition of thought, and the material brain is the only basis of consciousness. But the dialectic that makes Feuerbach so rich in his explanation of the phenomenology of religious consciousness, and that characterizes his activist sense of life activity as the unity of thinking and being, is lost here in the caverns of the stomach. This sensationist, physiological *dialectics of digestion* remains ultimately passive, in a way similar to that in which sensation is passive for Feuerbach. The dialectic of I and Thou is one between two active beings, each the other's other. The dialectic of man and nature is ambivalent in this regard: Feuerbach wants to insist on the causal agency of the objective world as a warrant for its reality, its objectivity. Therefore, the senses give us this objectivity in their very passivity, in the fact that they are *acted on*. The object is active, the subject passive, here. In eating and digesting, as in breathing, the natural functions are indeed *active, living*, and therefore *act* as well as *being acted on*. There is an exchange of air, water, food for life. But the *activity* of acquiring food, the agent's external activity as a living being–that is, his productive, social activity –is left out. The essence of life, for human beings, is only one-sidedly given if it is the physiological act of eating and digesting. But in a fully two-sided dialectic, not only the eating of food, but the obtaining, the production, and reproduction of the means of existence would have to be taken into consideration. The dialogue between my stomach and the world, in real activity, is mediated by the dialogue between production and consumption, the social dialogue of human praxis that Marx developed in his political economy. In this dialogue, there develops communication, circulation, distribution, the forms and relations of production, the historical development of forms of social life–in short, social and historical human phenomena. Feuerbach was not able to arrive at such a view. The passivity of the Feuerbachian context is implicit in even the social expression of Feuerbach's view: "If you want to better the people, *give them better food*, instead of declamations against sin." A worthy, charitable sentiment, but still caught within the concept of what can be *given to a recipient*, rather than what can be taken or produced by a self-active, self-sustaining, and self-creating agent.[8]

The further development of Feuerbach's "Diet-materialism" in his 1862 work *The Mystery of Sacrifice, or Man Is What He Eats*, is nevertheless an interesting one, not for its insistence on the unity of mind and stomach, but for its review of the pervasiveness of the incorporation metaphor in religious and mythical contexts, in etymology, and as a key to sacrificial practices. Feuerbach had dealt with the question of eating and sacrifice earlier, of course, in his discussion of the Christian sacrament of Communion, in *The Essence of Christianity*. Also, in the *Lectures on the Essence of Religion*, he had discussed the apparent "contradiction" that men venerate what they destroy, in consumption. In discussing *hunger* as the origin of dependency feeling, he writes, hunger is nothing but the need of my stomach for food, become an object of my consciousness or feeling; nothing therefore but the feeling of dependency on the means of my sustenance. From this amphibolic, i.e. equivocal and actually two-sided nature of my dependency feeling, one can explain . . . why human beings religiously venerate the plants and animals which they destroy, consume. (And the Christians, in fact, eat their own God.) (VIII, 100)

Here, in this later work, Feuerbach notes the characterization by Homer of various figures in the *Iliad* by what they eat, for example, the "horse-eaters," the *Glactophages* (milk-eaters), and of course, the lotus-eaters. In the *Odyssey*, he notes, Polyphemus is characterized as *anthropophage*, man-eater. In the Greek historians as well, Feuerbach notes the same use for characterization of various peoples: *Ichthyophages*, *Akridophages*, *Rhizophages*, *Agriophages*, and so on. And, as Ambrosia is "immortal food," the Gods too "are what they eat." More to the point, he leafs through such eating metaphors in Greek, Judaic, and Indian literature (e.g., in the *Bhagavad-Gita*) and in local German usage, stopping especially on the alternate names of the Gods in Greek mythology, in terms of what was offered in sacrifice to them–their essence therefore being identified with what they were fed. He brings this analysis, of course, to the Christian sacraments, and points out as well that the etymological root of the word "sacrifice" in Latin–that is, *immolare*–means "to salt," from the practice of salting both the sacrificial animal and the knife used in the sacrifice. So too, he sees the common source of the salt metaphor as the concept of *cleansing* or purification with salt (as in Judiac *Kashruth*), and in the *Iliad*, in which the pollutions are cast into the sea, and in the notion that the sea washes away all the sins of man. Salt also becomes symbol of friendship, trust, *because* it is a food symbol. The circumcision sacrifice, the covenant with God of the *Brith*, is seen to be derived (by Gesenius) from the root *"barak,"* which connotes *eating*. In all this, Feuerbach exercises a fine talent for this sort of symbolic interpretation, but he drives it to excess, permitting himself to say, finally (even if only in a literary-metaphorical way) that the brain is the "stomach" of the senses: As eating is to digesting, so sensing is to thinking. The fact that we still use the metaphor, in such usages as "digesting a thought," is abused by Feuerbach in the interests of an organic materialism that finally reduces his finer epistemological insights to their grossest form.

But in part, this is because he has no more apt model of thinking that is conformal and coherent with his theory of sensibility. The unity of sensation and thought is not yet a clearly differentiated one, though it is clear that he wants to establish the *continuity* of the two, and to preclude a dualism.

The unity of nature, *beyond* the unity of man and nature, attracts
Feuerbach as a scientific thesis corresponding to his own anthropological monism. His evolutionary argument for the continuity of the inorganic and organic finds a sympathetic correlate for him in the work of
the physician and neurologist Dr. Friedrich Wilhelm Heidenreich. In
1858, Feuerbach wrote an appreciative essay shortly after the death of
Heidenreich. Heidenreich was a personal friend of Feuerbach,[9] and
both a practicing physician and an experimental researcher, the author
of several works: *Elements of a Medical Physics,* which included *Book I,
The Life of Inorganic Nature* (1843): *Physiological Induction, a Contribution to Medical and Neurological Physics* (1846), and *Elements of
Therapeutic Physics* (1854). Heidenreich's work emphasized the *physical* continuity of the organic and inorganic, and suggested structural
levels within this continuity. "The unity of man and nature, the unity
of nature with itself in all the variations of its causes and effects—the
Idea of the unity of all life" is the way Feuerbach characterizes Heidenreich's views (X, 34). He writes, further,

It has long been a problem . . . to investigate and to establish the relations of
living processes to various dynamic, chemical and mechanical processes of
organism. Moreover, worthy and ingenious works are wasted on the useless
struggle between vitalism—i.e., the theory of a separate life force—and chemism
and mechanism. If one would only attain to the point of view that all living
stuff is a unity, is only one, but at its various stages appears as chemical, sometimes as mechanical, sometimes as dynamic, a different and better state of
affairs would obtain in physiology. We would recognize that digestion is an
activity of organic chemistry, that the motion of our joints, our chewing and
biting, is mechanical; that perception by means of the sense organs is a dynamical phenomenon. (X, 35–6)

After this neat separation of the unity of all life into its various aspects, Feuerbach approvingly quotes Heidenreich's explicitly reductionist statement (*Therapeutic Physics,* p. 12) that "soon the time will come
when all of physiology will be resolved in a physics and chemistry of
organic life, and very little will remain of the previous so-called specific
or vital, and pathology and therapy will have to follow, so that the
whole business of healing will be reasonably considered in terms of therapeutic physics and chemistry" (cited in X, 36). Feuerbach is as enchanted
with this physicochemical reductionism, in which physiology as such
disappears, as he was by the physiological reductionism of Moleschott,
earlier. The only relief from an outright eliminative reductionism comes
in the view that nature has levels or stages of organization, and that "the
identity of the laws of the organic and inorganic is not in any way
an identity of the phenomena" (X, 37). For example, though Heiden-

reich reports, in his *Physiological Induction*, on phenomena at the physiological level *like* those of electromagnetic induction, he says that the physiological case is not reducible to the electromagnetic case (i.e., in which changes in a magnetic field induce an electrical current, and vice versa).

Feuerbach does not take the step of speculating on the emergence of thought processes within this differentiated unity of nature, but only considers sensation as a "dynamical" rather than chemical or mechanical phenomenon. There is no clear logic or analysis of reduction here, but that it is compatible with Feuerbach's *general* reductive methodology is clear. For what is preserved, in the reduction, is the true, specific nature of the phenomenon (whether sensibility, life, or the human content of religion) once the husk of mistaken conceptions (e.g., vitalism, idealism, theism) is removed.

Feuerbach's faith in the ability to arrive at all these truths by scientific inquiry and by an empirical philosophy of knowledge is testimony to the sustained, though nonprofessional interest he maintains in the natural sciences throughout his years in Bruckberg. But further, it testifies to his strong attraction to an outright physicalism, which remains at odds with his anthropologism, or if anything, is subordinated to it, in Heidenreich's terms, as a "physics" of life, or a physiological physics. His concern for the physical sciences remains rooted in his primary concern over the phenomenon of the human.

Throughout his later works, in this regard, there reigns a concern with questions about the nature of space and time. In the *Theses* and the *Principles,* Feuerbach had strongly criticized the Kantian notion of Space and Time as merely *forms of sensibility,* or as a priori forms of perception. In the *Theses,* there occur the most forthright statements of all:

Space and time are the forms of existence of all beings. Only existence in space and time is existence. . . . The negation of space and time in Metaphysics, with respect to the being of things, has the most harmful practical consequences. Only he who everywhere adopts the standpoint of space and time is capable of good sense and practical understanding in life. Space and time are the first criteria of *praxis.* A people which excludes time from its metaphysics, which therefore deifies eternal, i.e. abstract existence removed from time, also excludes time from its politics, deifies the anti-historical principle of stability, which is against right and reason. (II, 232–3)

Space is then seen as the condition of *Dasein. Being-here* entails the concreteness, the specificity, the individuality of actual existence, the separation of a thing or a being from what it is not and from *where* it is not. Without spatial and temporal *limitation,* says Feuerbach, there is no quality, no energy, no need. "Existence without needs is redundant existence," he writes (II, 234). In the *Principles*, he continues this objectivist view of space and time:

Space and time are not mere forms of appearance. They are conditions of being, forms of reason, Laws of being as well as of thinking. *Dasein* [being-here] is the first mode of determinate being. *Here* I am–that is the first sign of an actual, living being. The index-finger points the way from nothingness to being. *"Here"* is the first boundary, the first division. . . . (II, 306–7)

There follows a disquisition on the phenomenology of the "determinateness of location," on the "Here" and "There," which is obviously intended to kill two birds with one stone: the merely *formal* status of space and time, as forms of perception in Kant; and the merely *conceptual* or *linguistic-logical universality* of token-reflexive terms such as "Here" and "Now" in Hegel's account in the *Phenomenology of Mind*. In the *Lectures on the Essence of Religion*, some years later, he deals with the *origins* of the abstract concepts of space and time, taking them simply as mental abstractions from common properties of things in our experience, in a rather flat-footed empiricist manner. He writes, in what must be a lapse of attention, that human beings "abstract space and time from spatial and temporal things." To say things are spatial and temporal is, of course, already to have an abstract concept of the abstracted space and time. But Feuerbach means something more, and it becomes clearer: The abstracted space and time concepts become *hypostatized*, as actual, generative beings. The conditions of the existence of things come to be thought of as that from which they *derive* their being. Thus, space and time come to be identified as gods, or as God (which Feuerbach says, in effect, is what Newton has done with space) (VIII, 147). Eternity too is nothing but the "species-concept of time, abstract time, or time separated from all time differences" (VIII, 148). Against Kant, he argues here that

Things do not presuppose space and time, but rather, space and time presuppose things, for space or extension presupposes something which is extended, and time presupposes motion–for time is a concept derived from motion, and presupposes, therefore, something which moves. Everything is spatial and temporal; everything is extended and in motion. Fine. But the extension and motion are as different as the extended and moving things are. All the planets move around the sun, but each has its own motion . . . all animals move, but how infinitely different is this variety of motion! And every sort of motion corresponds to the structure and mode of life, to the individual nature of each animal. How then can I explain and derive this variety on the basis of space and time, of bare extension and motion? Extension and motion are, rather, dependent on that something, that body or being which is extended or in motion. (VIII, 148)

There is nothing here that takes us beyond either Aristotle's *Physics* or Bacon's *Novum Organum*. Feuerbach wants to restore the qualitative and objective basis for the abstractions of time and space, to deny the geometer's qualityless space and time as anything but abstractions, to get at Kant via Newton. But this amateurish account, despite its philosophical allegiance to a reputable space-time theory eschewing the absolute container space of Newtonian mechanics or the "equably flowing" time *in* which events take place, rests on an essentially unsophisticated intuition, buttressed by Feuerbach's nominalism and his sensationism.

In his late work *Spiritualism and Materialism*, in the section on the critique of Hegel, Feuerbach criticizes Hegel for making Spirit both independent of space and time and yet involved in space and time. In a play on the space-time concept, he ends a passage on the "disease-phenomena of Hegelian psychology, and of the Hegelian time and place of residence. . . . Let us grant Hegel the honor which is due him, for his time, the time of transcendental, romantic reaction; but let us not forget that even the 'Absolute Spirit' is time-and-place bound!" (X, 192). But here, of course, Feuerbach is playing with the notion of the historical relevance of Hegel, in *his* "time and space." Yet for all the metaphorical word play, Feuerbach had suggested that "space and time are the first criteria of *praxis*," and had insisted on the specificity of human action as time and space bound – all the preparatory ground for a *historical* theory of human praxis. But the suggestion remains a suggestion, and goes unfulfilled.

Feuerbach repeats his earlier formulations in various places (e.g., where he says, "Space, like time, is a form of perception; but only because it is the form of my essence and being, because I am in and of myself a spatio-temporal being, and only as such do I sense, perceive, think" (X, 215), but in one place in particular, in speaking of time, brings it into connection with a peculiarly anthropological, human dimension. In *Spiritualism and Materialism*, in a section on *Eudaimonism* subtitled "Natural Evil and Time" discussing human essence as the drive to happiness, he writes,

Time is not merely a form of perception, but an actual life-form, and condition of life. Where there is no precedence and succession, no motion, no development, there is no life and no nature. But time is inseparable from development . . . it is one with nature, one with temporal things. But are these things *things-in-themselves*? I cannot tell. But for myself, who cannot separate myself from time, these temporal things are also things in themselves; for me, time itself is real, as the Sun, planets and comets which move in space and time are real, and *is therefore something in itself* [my emphasis, M. W.], something beyond and outside my mind. . . . Both essence and appearance fall, not beyond, but to this side of time and space, in my view. . . . Nor do I complain of my own complete this-sidedness (with respect to time and space). I do not find any inexplicable and irresoluble contradiction with the human drive to happiness here, as I do in theology and metaphysics. No! There is no other cure for incurable illnesses, the evils and abominations of the world of nature and of man, than time. (X, 252–4)

This is no longer the time of natural motion, but the time of human suffering and redemption, the human time that alone gives the condition for the fulfillment of human needs, or for their cessation with death– all *this* side of time and space, in *this* spatiotemporal world and in no other world of a spaceless, timeless eternity. This is the older Feuerbach speaking. But it is the Feuerbach who also wrote three major works on the question of death and immortality, over the long range of his career, and who was preoccupied with this question, seeking a humanist and naturalist answer consistently. Though this aspect of Feuerbach's work has not been dealt with here, and is worth a separate monograph, it is perhaps the most deeply humanistic aspect of his work, and rather than betraying a sense of despair or of the futility of life, it becomes a background for his passionate demand for self-fulfillment in this life and for his confidence in the transcendence of finitude both in individual and species life.

SPECIES BEING, INDIVIDUALITY, AND CONSCIOUSNESS: FEUERBACH'S LAST THOUGHTS ON SENSIBILITY, MIND, AND TRANSCENDENCE

Feuerbach began his work with the species concept of consciousness, with the I-Thou relation in which individuals transcend their mere individuality in thought. He found this transcendence, or the wish for transcendence, expressed in its imaginary form in religion, in the concept of God, of Immortality, of Freedom–the regulative ideas of the Kantian system. Later he developed the concept of the transcendent *other* in terms of the community of the senses, that is, in the objectivity of sensibility, which joins us as individuals to each other and makes us at one with nature. Dependency and sensibility go hand in hand here. It is by means of sense and feeling that the other becomes real for us, that we testify to its reality by our life activity itself. Only individual existence is real existence, says Feuerbach. Only needy existence is real existence. But the very *fact* of individuality *as* neediness, the fact of *Dasein* as a primordial relation of being with being, implicates the other as the necessary condition of individuality itself. Individuality is not, therefore, *selbst-sein*, being oneself, but *mitsein*, being with another.

There is no boundary to be crossed between an isolated subject, an *I*, and a detached object, an *it* or a *Thou*. The distinctiveness of subjectivity, of the *I*, for Feuerbach is that its very being as a *human* individual is its recognition of itself as a species being, which involves the recognition of oneself *in the other* and of the other *in oneself*. Community therefore becomes the dialectical prerequisite for individuality itself.

What is involved here is the knotty problem of the species concept in Feuerbach's thought, which we have dealt with on several occasions earlier. In the late works, in particular, in *Spiritualism and Materialism*, Feuerbach returns to it once again, and with respect to that most difficult and least-resolved problem in his philosophy, that of *thinking*.

The most explicit earlier discussion of the difficulties of the species concept is Feuerbach's 1845 reply to Max Stirner's critique of *The Essence of Christianity*. It seems clear that Stirner had touched a nerve when he accused Feuerbach of dissolving the real, existing individual into an abstract species being, an abstract universal. For was that not precisely what Feuerbach himself had criticized in Fichte, in Hegel, in speculative idealism, and in speculative theology? It has also been suggested (Gordon, 1975) that Stirner's critique of Feuerbach struck Marx with its forcefulness to the extent that it was the real source of Marx's critique of Feuerbach, and the proximate cause of Marx's "abandonment" of the concept of species being and of his turn to a more direct nominalism. That the issue persists in various forms is witnessed by the fact that, at least in Marxist philosophical and political contexts, the issue remains alive in the form of the concept of class-consciousness, and in the old debate over a "class in itself" and a "class for itself," initiated by Lukács' work *History and Class-Consciousness* (1923). Its ethical and political genealogy goes further back, to Rousseau's discussion of the *General Will*, in the *Social Contract*, and to Kant's conception of a Universal rationality as a transcendental norm on which alone a self-legislating, autonomous, and thereby free and moral will could be based. Hegel's conception of species is problematic, because it is at once transcendent and immanent. But here too lies Feuerbach's problem, *and* his solution, which is essentially Aristotelian, that is, conceptualist. For Aristotle, the individual is ontologically prior, the species dependent on and existing only in and through individuals. So too for Feuerbach, *except* that the individual is individuated only *as* a species being. The human individual, by nature, is human *just in being a species being qua individual*–never a bare particular, a *this*, but always a *this such*; not by virtue of *participating in* or *expressing* a prior universality, as in Plato or Hegel, but as constituting the species, by this human individual's very mode of being. Where Feuerbach begins this analysis, he is Hegelian in the sense that thought itself, as "one, universal and infinite" *is* the species being. The species is generated in consciousness, in the I-Thou relation of consciousness. Where Feuerbach ends is unclear. Sensibility bears the burden of species universality in the middle works (e.g., in the *Principles*), but it is not clear what role or function is left for thought, except as synthesizer of sensibility–and that leaves sensibility short of the centrality which Feuerbach wants to afford it. Feuerbach's apparently renewed interest in Kant, in his later years, was prompted perhaps by this search for an adequate conception of the relation of sensibility to thinking. In 1858, he writes to Wilhelm Bolin that he is planning to do a separate study of Kant–an intention originally unfulfilled after the early *Leibniz* book, in 1835. In the letter, he considers whether he ought to return to Kant, to tie his work to Kant's, as its continuation. "Whether I will return to Kant–truly, a large step backwards–remains to be seen," he writes (XII–XIII, p. 226, letter 246, March 26, 1858).[10] However, this project is *not* undertaken, and Feuerbach's interest, especially in the question of Kant's views on the a priori forms of sensibility (i.e., Space and Time) are expressed only sporadically, as we have seen. What remains at issue, then, is the species concept, specifically as it relates to the universality of sensibility *or* of thought–that is, the sense in which sensibility or thought are themselves to be conceived of as the this-worldly modes, the *human* modes of transcendence, on the *basis* of individual existence, but beyond the limits of finite individuality. Feuerbach's bold and programmatic declaration, in the *Theses*: "to posit the infinite in the finite" now has to be brought to bear on the question of human transcendence, of how the finite individual is self-transcendent, as an infinite species being. The metaphysical question becomes a human question. Infinity becomes an issue not for thought, but for life. The species, then, represents for Feuerbach not a fixed "nature," but an essentially self-transcending one; and not a logical or conceptual self-transcendence, but a living, temporal transcendence, whose dimension is the future.

In the 1845 reply to Max Stirner's criticism, "On *The Essence of Christianity* in relation to *The Ego and Its Own*" (the latter, the title of Stirner's popular work), Feuerbach passionately defends himself against Stirner's charge that he had lapsed into an abstract humanism in his concept of species being. Feuerbach defends himself on two counts: First, that he had in fact made clear that only individual existence is real this-worldly existence and that the whole spirit of his defense of sensibility is to show that only sensuous, individual existence is real, as against the abstract essences of Christian-theological belief. Second, that the individual's reality is such that, at least in the case of human beings, there is no *I* without a *Thou*, that sensuousness, need, dependency, implicate the *Thou* as the necessary complement to the *I*; and that *species being* is no more abstract, therefore, than this necessary bond between *existing, mutually dependent individuals*. Feuerbach argues, polemically, (speaking of himself throughout in the third person, by initial): "This work of F.'s [*The Essence of Christianity*] differs essentially from all his earlier works, in that here for the first time he progressed to the *truth* of sensibility, here for the first time discovered Absolute being as sensible being, and sensible being as Absolute being" (VII, 298). Further he argues, "for F. the individual is the absolute, i.e., the true, real being" (VII, 299), "but though to be an individual is indeed, to be an 'Egoist,' it means equally, and indeed, *nolens volens*, to be a *Communist*" (VII, 300). That is, the *I* needs the *Thou*. The I is a communal, as well as an individual being. But what is the *species* (*Gattung*) if *not* an abstract being, as Stirner charges? The individual expresses his individuality, says Feuerbach, in *love*. But love of an other is itself the deepest recognition of individuality.

The species signifies . . . for F. not an *abstractum*, but rather only the *Thou*, the other, generally those individuals who exist beyond me, who stand opposite me as a singular, self-fixated individuals. When, for example, F. says "the individual is limited, the species unlimited," all he means is: the limits of this individual are not the same as the limits of the other individual, the limits of the contemporary human being are not the limits of the human being of the future. (VII, 302)

He then continues, in a striking way, to affirm his positive view of the *human* essence of religion:

To have no religion is *to think only of oneself*. To have religion is to think *of others*. And this is the only religion that will persist, at least as long as there isn't only one "singular" human being in the world; for as soon as there are *two* people, where there are man and wife, we already have religion. *Difference* is the origin of religion – the *Thou* is the God of the *I*, for there is no me without you. I depend on you: No *Thou* – no *I*. (VII, 303)

Finally, Feuerbach answers Stirner's charge that he "dresses his (F.'s) materialism in the garments of Idealism."

Oh! how this charge comes out of thin air! Listen, you "singular" one: F. is neither an idealist nor a materialist. For F., God, Spirit, Soul, Ego are mere abstractions; but equally so are Body and Matter mere abstractions. Truth, being, reality is only sensibility itself for him. . . . But even less so is F. an idealist in the sense of absolute Identity, which simply unites both these two abstractions in a third. Well, then, F. is neither materialist, idealist nor identity philosopher. What is he then? He is in thought, as in deed, in the spirit, as in

425

the flesh, in essence what he is in sense–a human being; or better still, F. posits the essence of humanity only in community: he is a communal being, a Communist. (VII, 309–10)

For all the polemic fervor, the sentimentalism about love as the bond between I and Thou, the insistence on this philosophical, anthropological "communism," some things begin to be clear: the *species being* does not exist in itself, but only in the relation, the interaction, of *I* and *Thou*; that is, it is constituted only among individuals. The community, the commonalty, is *not* an entity, therefore not a hypostatized, independent being, but a relation, or as Marx was to say (in the *Theses on Feuerbach*, yet!), an *ensemble of relations*. Though this sketches the ontology of species and individual, it is far from satisfactory as a resolution of the problem, because the *bond*, the existential relation itself, remains vague, abstract. It is "love," or "sensibility," or "dependence." Thus, though Feuerbach argues strongly for the *individuality* of species beings and for their sensuous concreteness, the bond that *makes* them species beings remains abstract. Stirner may have been right in his criticism, then; but about the wrong thing. If the species nature consists in the relations among individuals, then however concrete the individuals are asserted to be, they can, in the logic of the interdependence of individuals on each other for their very individuality itself ("*Kein Du– Kein Ich*") be *no more concrete than the relations in which they stand to each other*; a point Marx was to drive home.

Feuerbach addresses this theme once again in the 1848–9 *Lectures on the Essence of Religion*, reaffirming this earlier view, but reflecting on the logic by which the species concept *comes* to be abstracted from the individuals. "It is not necessary," he writes, "for the sake of recognizing the significance of general concepts, to deify them, to make of them independent essences distinct from individuals or particulars" (VIII, 151). He is talking here about the Virtues (e.g., constancy) as well as of such human capacities as will, reason, wisdom, "whose value and reality are not lost, nor given up, therefore, if I regard and know them as human properties" (VIII, 152). Feuerbach then goes on to generalize this analysis with regard to species concepts:

What holds here for human virtues, holds as well for all general or species-concepts. They don't exist apart from the things or beings [who have these properties], are not to be differentiated nor made independent of the individuals from which we derived them. The subject, i.e. the existing being is always the individual; the species only the predicate, the property. But senseless thought separates the predicate, the property, from the individual, the abstraction from the individual, and makes this abstracted property its object, and establishes it, in this abstracted form, as the essence of the individual, and determines the differences among individuals as no more than individual, i.e.

in the sense of accidental, indifferent, unessential differences, so that for think-ing, for the mind, all individuals are fused together in one individual, or better, in one concept, the kernel of which thought claims for itself alone. The husk is left to sense-perception, which gives us the individuals as individuals, i.e. reveals them to us in their plurality, difference, individuality and existence. So that, what is in actuality the subject, the real being, is made by thought into a predicate, is taken as the essence. (VIII, 153)

This is perhaps Feuerbach's most explicit passage on the species con-cept. But it sets it forth only negatively, in its corrupted or hypostatized form. The positive argument still depends *either* upon the epistemologi-cal argument, from the commonalty of sensibility; or it depends upon the anthropological argument, from the necessity of the I-Thou relation. This fully coherent account can be derived only from whatever synthesis Feuerbach is able to effect between the two.

The existential strain in Feuerbach expresses itself in his reversal on the role of thought and sensation. In the early writings, the I-Thou rela-tion establishes community, species being in thinking; in the later writ-ings, in sensibility, and in feeling. (Where earlier, the senses were private, separative; later, *thought* separates.) Thus, in the late work *Spiritualism and Materialism*, Feuerbach says, "Thought differentiates the species from the individual; but life and love make an indivisible One of what thought has separated; makes the individual 'Absolute Essence'" (X, 144). But then thought is pathological, it would seem, and stands op-posed to those Feuerbachian virtues "life and love." Over and over again, Feuerbach repeats the litany in the later works: The senses give me *other* individuals; thought, only myself. But where is that healthy, enlightened, sensuous thinking that is bound to sensibility, has its roots in sensuous existence? Has it been eternally corrupted by the Hegelian disease, so that even Feuerbach cannot set it right again, and can only see it as the source of cognitive pathology, of reification? "The philo-sophical soul is right," says Feuerbach, "when it asserts *Cogito ergo sum, scilicet philosopharum*. I think, therefore I am thinking substance, *res cogitans*, or philosopher; wrong, however, when it passes unmediatedly from thought to being . . . when it makes Logic the Physics of the soul, or rather, when it hands that job to Logic to do" (X, 165).

Feuerbach does, finally, pass over to a more or less coherent notion of the positive relation of sensation and thought, though it remains sketchy. The requirement for a coherent view is that although thought *maintains* its abstractive function, and is not reduced to sensation, it nevertheless remains in a unity with sensation, and does not pathologically separate itself as its own, "senseless" (i.e., speculative) object. The first difficulty in effecting the unity of thought and sensation arises from the dumbness, the ineffability, the sheer givenness of sensibility, which Feuerbach continues to insist on even in the late works. "The individual is untranslatable, irreproducible–except in appearance or with respect to certain characteristics [Here, a bow in the direction of the Kantian *phenomenon*, as the mere appearance of sensation, but not its essence, M. W.]. The individual is inconceivable, indefinable. It is the object of sensuous, immediate, intuitive knowledge alone" (X, 144).

How this ineffable intuitive immediacy is shared is, of course, a mystery, unless the sharedness, the intersubjectivity of sensation is also, somehow, given in immediate intuition. But so far, no help. The truth of sensibility, the common, human truth is, finally, an inexpressible truth. It does not help the theory of mind, or of reflective consciousness, to say that it is a *lived* or *sensed* or *felt* truth. For then, thinking has no role except to distort and displace this truth. Nor does Feuerbach have the option to identify thought immediately with the ineffable immediacy of sensation, for this would be the travesty of identity philosophy in reverse. Where the former absorbed sensibility into thought, denying it its reality as *not*-thought, here thought would be absorbed in sensation, denying thought its distinctiveness as *not*-sensation. Poor thought! Feuerbach closes the door on a dialectical solution with this later critique of Hegelian dialectic: "The absolute identity (or rather confusion) of opposites and objects has placed . . . the issue in mystic darkness instead of in a clear light" (X, 190).

The remaining appeal is perhaps in the older temptation to physiologize thinking activity, to see it as some distinctive brain function. Here Feuerbach says some interesting materialist-sounding things, but bypasses the question of thought and sensation. He talks here (in *Spiritualism and Materialism*) of the functional interaction of thought and brain, but he does not establish the characteristic activity of thought, except as–thinking. "Only in thinking, does the brain become the actual organ of thought; but thought itself develops, becomes fluent, capable, on the basis of the developed organ of thought. Can one speak here of an exclusive cause or an exclusive effect? What is effect becomes cause, and vice versa. 'The body is the instrument of the soul,' but conversely, 'the soul is also the instrument of the body' " (X, 197). Similarly, Feuerbach speaks of thought as "the activity of a bodily organ," and *therefore* capable of having bodily effect. (X, 206). But this, for all its apparent body-soul identity, or functionalism, is a weak and unworked out interactionism, in which, were the "function" of this bodily organism, the brain, anything different from brain activity itself, we would be back with Cartesian dualism again–just what Feuerbach wants to avoid. We were better off with Feuerbach's earlier double-aspect views, expressed in his *Dualism of Body and Soul* essay, where a neutral monism was maintained, and where "body" and "soul," "brain" and "mind," were simply methodological differentiations, or abstractions introduced by differences in modes of access.

Finally, in the *Posthumous Aphorisms*, in the collection of comments on "Problems in the Theory of Knowledge" there occurs a series of observations extending the earlier notion of thought as a more generalized, more universal mode of sensibility itself.

Feuerbach writes,

The prejudice of Idealism is based on the abstract conclusion: *whatever is in the effect is also in the cause. Thought presupposes a thinking essence.* This is entirely false. Only an empirical being, as a sensible subject thinks. Thought is a necessary property of sensible being at its highest stage, *is the property of an individual being which differentiates itself from its species* [my emphasis, M. W.]. (X, 297)

Here at last we have a clue to the functional *difference* between sensation and thought. Sensation, to be sure, gives me myself as individual. The senses do not give me species being. Thus, an individual that separates itself not simply from other individuals, but from the other as *its species*, is capable of thought–and thought then consists in this separation. Thought separates–so Feuerbach has told us. It makes distinctions. But any old distinction will not do. The possibility of the distinctive separation that thought effects lies in conceiving the other as a species being, and not simply as another, indifferent individual. But this recognition lies in sensibility itself, Feuerbach says: not in sensation qua sensation, but in sensation as a function of, expression of, awareness of dependency, need; in short, in the *intentionality* of sensibility. Here sensibility is no longer passive, but directed upon an object out of a felt need, interest, purpose. But to make sensibility teleological or intentional in this way is to see it as active, constructive, and not passive. Sensing is acting, not just receiving. This ramified, intentional sensibility, the *anthropologized* sensibility alluded to already in the *Principles*, is *on the way to thought*. But it is not yet thought.

Still, Feuerbach goes further:

Sense perception (*Anschauung*) gives me not only individuals; it gives me also identity, interconnection of individuals–not only trees, but forests. Sense perception is not without understanding–not the boundaries of an act of understanding. I apprehend the same as same, I distinguish. The understanding separates and combines but only what is sensible, from which it abstracts for purposes of generalization and simplification, by overlooking the singular. (X, 298)

But where the passage begins with an *understanding* sensibility, it ends with a sensibility that delivers its data *to* the understanding for abstraction. Still no clear or coherent continuity of sensation and thought. But Feuerbach continues to explore this avenue:

Thinking is only a developed, elaborated, further sensing, extended to what is not present, a sensing of that which is not actually sensed; the seeing of that which is not seen. We see only gross, external motion, mass-movement, but we don't see the internal, smaller components of sound vibrations. We think it, we see it, though mediated by what we do see–raw motion. We infer it. Is there then anything absolutely unseeable, in this sense? (X, 298)

Seeing the unseen is imagining, or representing what something would look like could we see it; and this we infer from what *is* visible. But then thinking is *nothing* but the secularized imagination, which in religious consciousness filled in the gaps of the invisible with the imagination, projected the invisible by analogy to the visible, created its objects as representations of species being: God or Nature. If indeed thinking is possible only for a being that differentiates itself from its species, then the precondition is the conception of species–that is, the *imagining* of a universal, the representation in the mind of what is *not* seen, the forming of a concept, albeit "inferred" from sensibility itself.

Feuerbach's objective pull expresses itself strongly, here, however. The basis for this self-differentiation, he says, is not *in* thought. Rather, thought reflects it. "I am not differentiated from external things and beings because I differentiate myself from them, but I differentiate myself from them because I am physically, corporeally, only conscious being, only being insofar as it is conscious, represented being" (X, 298).

Thus, the abstraction of thought is not merely an abstraction *from* thought, but reflects the *ab*-straction, the separation, the individuation of my being itself. This self-differentiation derives from sensibility, not from within thought itself. "Not thinking thought," writes Feuerbach, "not thought which has itself alone as its subject and object, as its own organ and function, but rather seeing-thought, hearing-and-feeling thought. Or conversely, thinking-seeing, thinking-feeling" (X, 302). Thus, thinking sensation or sensate thinking–the *postulated* but as yet unexplained unity of sensation and thought. As to objectivity, only sensate thought is capable of it. "Whoever abstracts from the sense, the only testimony of something other than the world of thought, has robbed himself of the means of transition to an objective world, and can no more demonstrate the existence of the external world than one who extinguishes the light, or blinds his eyes can demonstrate the existence of light" (X, 308).

The best we can make of this fragmentary theory of sensibility in its relation to thinking leaves us far from satisfied. There are the clues to a "rational empiricism," the hoped-for project of Feuerbach's earliest break with speculative idealism. There is the suggestive but as yet crude direct realism, first of the passive and immediate and hopelessly ineffable senses that "*give us* existence," though we cannot think it. Finally, there are the cognitively imbued senses that give us both trees and forests, but that are only mysteriously related to a sensibility that "sees what is absent" and is strangely brother to the imagination—that veil of appearance which was originally to be pierced. Most gloriously, there is the passionate humanism, uncompromisingly rooted in this world, as part and parcel of nature, and yet transcendent; nature made sensate, transformed into an object of love, of veneration, recognized as mother and father to our needs, source of our being and sustenance, and the only theater of our redemption. A materialism fraught with sensuality, spilling over into excesses of physiologism, but never removed from the heart (as close as it is to the stomach); a failed but suggestive epistemology; and beyond all, a respect for his subject—the human—in all of its modes.

Feuerbach lets himself go in a passage in the *Posthumous Aphorisms*, which, for all its rhetoric, expresses the seriousness and love the philosopher feels toward his subject:

The human being stands consciously upon an unconscious foundation: he is here involuntarily, he is a necessary being of nature. Nature works in him without his will or knowledge. He calls his body his own, and yet it is absolutely strange to him. He eats with enjoyment, and what drives him to hunger is some other thing. He eats, and still he has neither the ground nor the consequence of his eating in his control, neither in terms of his knowledge, or his capacity. He must eat. He is a stranger in his own house, he suffers all the burdens and sorrows, has all the pleasures and joys, without as yet being master of his own estate. He is placed at the peak of dizzying heights, below him extends an inconceivable abyss. He knows neither his beginning nor his end. He is sooner in possession of his being, than he can know its foundations. He is both not-self and self. His not-self is the basis, the ground of his religion, his freedom in contradiction with his necessity. He has only the results, not the principles, the premises in his power. He sees, hears, feels, thinks as necessarily as the sun shines and the flower blooms. He belongs to nature—is its necessary product, he is deeply rooted in her. He is here not by his own will, but by that of another: it is nature which called him forth, without any demonstrable or conceivable cause. Obscure is the origin of man, for his nature is itself obscure. Only in that genesis which we see primarily in non-human nature, do we have any image of our own origins: we have it within ourselves, in what we take to be the involuntary essence of nature. Man comes into being, he is not created. Only once he has come into being, can he create himself, does he become a product of human knowledge. (X, 306)

Notes

Preface

1 See my discussion of these questions in "Consciousness, Praxis and Reality: Marxism vs. Phenomenology," in P. McCormick and F. Elliston, eds., *Husserl; Expositions and Appraisals* (Notre Dame, Ind.: University of Notre Dame Press, 1976.

2 *Denis Diderot and Ludwig Feuerbach–Studies in the Development of Materialist Monism*, Ph.D. Thesis, Columbia University, 1952. (Available through University Microfilms, Ann Arbor, Michigan.)

3 "Imagination, Thought and Language in Feuerbach's Philosophy," in Hermann Lübbe and Hans-Martin Sass, eds., *Atheismus in der Diskussion: Kontroversen um Ludwig Feuerbach* (Munich: Chr. Kaiser Verlag, 1975), pp. 197–217.

Chapter I
Prefatory Reflections by Way of an Introduction

1 See Phillip Frank, *Modern Science and Its Philosophy* (New York: Collier, 1961), p. 48.

2 Similarly, in the parallel debate over the "young" and the "old" Marx, I am clearly on the side of those who see Marx as dialectical throughout, no less so in *Capital* than in the *Manuscripts*. See my discussion on "The Young and the Old Marx" in N. V. Lobkowitz, ed., *Marx and the Western World* (Notre Dame, Ind.: University of Notre Dame Press, 1967), pp. 39–44.

3 Karl Popper, "What Is Dialectic?" in *Conjectures and Refutations* (New York: Basic Books, 1962), pp. 312–35.

4 This has been attempted more frequently in the history of literature, the history of science, and art history (e.g., in the works of George Thompson, György Lukács, Vernon Parrington, Arnold Hauser, Max Raphael, Ernst Fischer, Christopher Candwell, Hessen, among others). In philosophy, Benjamin Farrington has attempted such a Marxist account of ancient Greek philosophy and science, which, though interesting and provocative, is not

yet adequate. (*Greek Science* [Hammondsworth: Penguin Books, 1949], Vols. I-II.)

5 See my essay "Diderot and the Development of Materialist Monism," in N. Torrey and O. Fellows (eds.), *Diderot Studies II* (Syracuse: Syracuse University Press, 1952), pp. 279-329.

Chapter II
Early Hegelian Epistemology: The Dissertation

1 The *Dissertation*, entitled *"De ratione, una, universali, infinita"*–*Dissertatio inauguralis philosophical Auctore Ludovico Andrea Feuerbach, phil. Doct., Erlange MDCCXXVIII*, was first published in an incomplete, free adaptation in German by W. Bolin, in the *Collected Works*, edited by W. Bolin and F. Jodl (1903-11), in Vol. IV (pp. 299-356). The full Latin text was published in the republication of the *Collected Works*, edited by Hans-Martin Sass, in an additional volume (XI) titled *Jugendschriften von Ludwig Feuerbach* (Stuttgart-Ban Cannstatt: Fromann Verlag [Günther Holzboog], 1962), pp. 11-50, with Feuerbach's footnotes, pp. 51-68. S. Rawidowicz discusses the *Dissertation* briefly and notes the way in which the Feuerbachians–for example, W. Bolin, F. Jodl, and K. Grün–tended to underplay the "Hegelianism" of the work in favor of their view of Feuerbach as non-Hegelian, or as a very early defector from "orthodox" Hegelianism. Cf. S. Rawidowicz, *Ludwig Feuerbachs Philosophie...* (Berlin: Reuther & Richard, 1931), pp. 15-19. (Reissued [Berlin: Walter De Gruyter & Co., 1964].)

2 A. Kojève, *Introduction à la Lecture de Hegel* (Paris: Gallimard, 1947). Somewhat less than half of the French text, originally collected from notes and transcriptions by Queneau, was translated into English as *Introduction to the Reading of Hegel*. James Nichols, tr., and Allan Bloom, ed. (New York: Basic Books, 1969). See also Irving Fetscher's edition of Kojève, *Hegel–Versuch einer Vergegenwärtigung seines Denkens* (Stuttgart, 1958). Kojève's "humanist" interpretation of Hegel's *Phenomenology of Mind* was enormously influential in the formation of the French school of Marxist (and anti-Marxist) phenomenology, especially Sartre and Merleau-Ponty, and through them, Frantz Fanon. It may be said to have introduced an indirect or parallel "Feuerbachian" strain, emphasizing the humanist and existentialist aspects of the Hegelian dialectic of self and other, *I* and *Thou*. This was reinforced, of course, by the discovery and influence of Marx's early writings, the so-called humanist or Feuerbachian Marx of the *Economic-Philosophic Manuscripts* of 1844-5, and the *Excerpt Notes of 1844*. See the collection *Writings of the Young Marx on Philosophy and Society*, Lloyd Easton and Kurt Guddat, eds. (Garden City, N.Y.: Doubleday, 1967), Introduction, esp. pp. 26-32.

3 Cf. Rawidowicz, op. cit., pp. 15-20; also the fine, though brief discussion by Claudio Cesa, *Il Giovane Feuerbach* (Bari: Editori Laterza, 1963), pp. 80-94; and Henri Arvon's passing remarks, in his *Ludwig Feuerbach ou la Transformation du Sacré* (Paris: P.U.F., 1957), p. 11. Also see Gustav Riedel, *Ludvik Feuerbach a Mladý Marx* (Praha: Statni Pedagogičke Nakladatelstvi, 1962), p. 15, where the typical brief remark on the *Dissertation* is made, that

Feuerbach was then an "uncritical Hegelian," an absolute idealist, holding to the identity of reason and being.

4 Cf. Hegel, *Philosophy of Nature*, M. H. Petry, tr. (London: Allen and Unwin, 1970), Vol. III, §§ 343–4, esp. pp. 48–9. "The plant is not yet objective to itself. . . . The plant's negative selfhood is not yet self-relating."

5 See note 1. Bolin, one of Feuerbach's disciples, and coeditor with F. Jodl of the *Collected Works*, argues that Feuerbach shows his independence from Hegel in the very structure of the *Dissertation*, which fails to exemplify the triadic division of Hegel's works, and of that of his followers. Cf. *L. Feuerbach, Sein Wirken und seine Zeitgenossen* (Stuttgart, 1891), p. 70. Cf. Rawidowicz's criticism of Bolin's view, op. cit., p. 15.

Chapter III
History of Philosophy: Genetic Analysis as the Critique of Concepts

1 "*Zur Rezension Hegels Werke. Vollständige Ausgabe.* XIII u. XIV Bd. *Hegels Vorlesungen über die Geschichte der Philosophie, Herausgegeben von Dr. Carl Ludwig Michelet . . . Berlin 1833.*" The review was published in September 1835 in the Proceedings of the *Jahrbüchern fur Wissenschaftliche Kritik*, Nos. 46–48. A briefer version, with minor editing, appeared under the title "*Hegels Geschichte der Philosophie,*" in the 1846 *Collected Works*, Vol. II, pp. 44–61 and in Vol. II of the Bolin-Jodl edition. In the new Schuffenhauer edition of the *Gesammelte Werke* (Berlin: Akademie Verlag, 1969), it appears in Vol. 8 (*Kleinere Schriften*, I), pp. 44–61.

2 Feuerbach's role as intellectual herald but nonparticipant in the revolution of 1848 bears a superficial resemblance to that of the French eighteenth-century *Philosophes*, but the analogy breaks down rapidly. The question of Feuerbach's relation to and attitude toward the 1848 revolution, and toward politics in general, is discussed by S. Rawidowicz, op. cit., pp. 312–17. As Rawidowicz remarks, Feuerbach's radicalism in his political expression was matched by his almost absolute passivity and withdrawal from political activity. Though he was elected as a delegate to the revolutionary Frankfurt Parliament of 1848, he sat there in almost total silence, and is described in Ludwig Bamberger's *Memoirs* as (together with Freiligrath) "the most outstandingly silent member of the Frankfurt Congress" (cf. Rawidowicz, op. cit. p. 315). In ideological terms, the Marxist characterization of Feuerbach is given succinctly by Schuffenhauer, in the *Introduction* to his critical two-volume edition of *The Essence of Christianity* (Berlin: Akademie Verlag, 1956), Vol. I, p. v: "Feuerbach is the most significant and most influential representative of pre-Marxist bourgeois materialism in Germany. In the period of ideological preparation for the revolution of 1848, his work is the consistent expression of the world-outlook of the bourgeois-democratic opposition." But Feuerbach's contempt for the Frankfurt Parliament and its "Parlamentgeschwätz" ("Parliamentary babbling"), as he called it, could hardly be characterized as the attitude of an ardent revolutionary. Lenin's frequently quoted remark that "Feuerbach did not understand the 1848 revolution" (*Philosophical Notebooks*, Vol. 38 of the

Collected Works [Moscow: Foreign Languages Publishing House, 1961], p. 63) echoes Marx's own critique of Feuerbach's "passivity" as it reflects itself also in his philosophical work – that is, that Feuerbach did not understand concrete, sensuous human praxis. This question is dealt with especially in Chapters X and XII of the present work.

3 The term "The Hegelings" ("*Die Hegelingen*") was coined derisively by the historian Heinrich Leo in his attack on Hegelian philosophy as "un-Christian." Leo's attack is the occasion of Feuerbach's work in defense of Hegel, "*über Philosophie und Christentum in Beziehung auf den der Hegelschen Philosophie gemachten Vorwurf der Unchristlichkeit*" (1839), which is discussed fully in Chapter VI. See also Chapter VI, note 16, below.

4 Feuerbach notes that the same significance is attributed to scholasticism in Tenemann's *Geschichte der Philosophie*.

5 Rawidowicz, op. cit., p. 63.

6 In his note to the 1847 edition of the *History*, Feuerbach discusses this further:

> The reduction of natural science to Descartes's rational principle is justifiable only in the respect that the first principles of our natural science, up to the present, coincide essentially with this principle of Descartes' philosophy – i.e. they are mathematical, mechanical principles. Despite this, Bacon is not only the founder of natural science in its empirical sense alone, (as the original text characterizes him), but the true father of science. For it was he who was the first to recognize the originality of nature; to recognize that nature cannot be conceived in derivation from mathematical or logical or theological presuppositions, or anticipations, but can and ought to be conceived and explained only out of itself; whereas Descartes, on the other hand, makes his mathematical Mind the original of nature. Bacon takes nature as it is, defines it positively, whereas Descartes defines it only negatively, as the counterpart to Spirit. Bacon's object is actual nature (*die wirkliche Natur*); Descartes', only an abstract, mathematical, artificial nature. (III, 22)

7 Cf. Feuerbach's characteristically Hegelian formulation in his critique of Hobbes: "Empiricism has no beginning, no middle, no end; that is, it has no principle, it has no substantive concept as its principle. As its objects, so also are its concepts themselves merely relative, conditional; it is not and cannot be a system. Even when it is externally consistent, it is internally incoherent and untenable" (III, 79). Rawidowicz, who assesses the *History* as clearly the work of a Hegelian rationalist-idealist, still correctly notes the early interest in an "enlightened" empiricism, especially in the correspondence (cf. 1835, 1837 letters to Kapp, see note 16 below). Rawidowicz writes, "Thus, in the freer expression of the letters, the tendency to the adaptation of empiricism to philosophy is shown. Despite this, it does not indicate any break with Hegel, who, moreover, should not in any case be counted as an opponent of empiricism" (Rawidowicz, op. cit., p. 52n.). Jodl (in his introduction to the *History* in the S.W. II, Vol. III, p. ix) also points to Feuerbach's early appreciation of empiricism and naturalism, in his treatment of Bacon (III, 33), Gassendi (III, 113), in his critique of Boehme's idealism, and the comparison to Bacon (III, 134). Jodl too sees the History as "essentially still under the sway of the Hegelian philosophy" (III, vii),

though not dominated by the fabulous construction, imposed by the dialectic, in the *Histories* of Hegel and Erdmann. Even the fact of *beginning* with Bacon, rather than Descartes, as the founder of modern philosophy, on the grounds of Bacon's break with the "principle of authority" is seen by Jodl as evidence of an early independence. The *History*, though the work of a Hegelian, is significant, says Jodl, in its representation of the inner struggle between two *weltanschauungen* in Feuerbach (III, xi).

8 The reference is to Hobbes, *Philosophia Prima, VIII*, 20 and *Logic*, VI, 5. See *Hobbes' Works, Latin*, William Molesworth, ed., Vol. I (contains both *Philosophia Prima* and *Computatio sive Logica*) (London, 1839).

9 It is this first sense (i.e., "abstract," "quantitative") that Marx and Engels later characterize as "metaphysical." Their critique of "metaphysics"–especially seventeenth-century metaphysics in the philosophies of Descartes, Spinoza, and Leibniz–and of Hobbes' "abstract materialism," derives directly from Feuerbach's analysis here. They write, for example, "Hobbes was the one who *systematized* Bacon's materialism. Sensuousness lost its bloom, and became the abstract sensuousness of the *geometrician. Physical* motion was sacrificed to the *mechanical* or *mathematical, geometry* was proclaimed the principal science" (K. Marx & F. Engels, *The Holy Family*, R. Dixon, tr. [Moscow: Foreign Languages Publishing House, 1956], p. 173). (See especially Chapter VI, pp. 168–73, for the sketch of the history of philosophy and the roots of materialism.)

However, this rejection of metaphysics here, as in Feuerbach's own rejection of metaphysics as "speculative philosophy," has to be understood in its context; otherwise it is too easy to identify this view with the late nineteenth-century and early twentieth-century positivist rejection of metaphysics–by Mach, Schlick, Neurath, or Carnap, for example–and also to fail to recognize the complex way in which Feuerbach's and Marx's views *are* related to this positivism.

10 Jakob Böhme, *Theosophische Sendbriefe*, Br. 20, 3; and *Von die Drei Principien*, Vol. IV, pp. 7, 8.

11 Feuerbach notes that Malebranche approaches a position close to this, in the *Entretiens sur la Métaphysique*, where he says that "extension is a reality, and all realities are to be found in the infinite. Therefore God is extended *as well as* are bodies, since God possesses all perfections. But God is not extended *as* bodies are. . . . He hasn't the limitations and the imperfections of his creatures." The original passage is in Nicholas Malebranche, *Entretiens sur la Métaphysique et sur la Religion*, Armand Cuvillier, ed. (Paris: Librairie Philosophique J. Vrin, 1948), Vol. I, viii, p. 263:

L'étendue, Ariste, est un réalité, et dans l'infini toutes les réalités s'y trouvent. *Dieu est donc étendu aussi bien que les corps* [my emphasis, M. W.] puisque Dieu possède toutes les réalités absolues, et tout les perfections. Mais Dieu n'est pas étendu comme les corps. Car, comme je viens de vous dire, il n'a pas les limitations et les imperfections de ses créatures.

What Malebranche gives with one hand, he takes away with the other, because now we no longer have an identity of God with matter or extension, but rather a divine matter and a profane matter–*two* sorts of extension!

Chapter IV
Leibniz: The History of Philosophy as Immanent Critique

1 *Nachlass*, ed. K. Grün (Leipzig and Heidelberg: C. F. Winter, 1874), Vol. I, p. 50. Rawidowicz writes this off as a later interpretation by Feuerbach and holds that it is not to be found in the work itself (op. cit., p. 60). Cf. also Windelband, *Geschichte der Neueren Philosophie*, Vol. II, 1907, p. 382.

2 The literature on Leibniz's role in the history of physics is large and growing, and so is the estimate of the relevance of his metaphysical *and* mathematical views to contemporary questions in both quantum mechanics and relativity theory. Concerning his historical importance, Max Jammer, the historian of physics, writes, "Strictly speaking, Leibniz's concept of force is what we call today kinetic energy, but conceived of as inherent in matter and representing the innermost nature of matter. Because of the great importance attached to this concept in Leibniz's metaphysical and scientific outlook he may rightly be considered as the first proponent of modern dynamism in natural science" (M. Jammer, *Concepts of Force* [Cambridge, Mass.: Harvard University Press, 1957], pp. 158–9). Regarding Leibniz's metaphysics, in relation to his physics, Professor Joseph Agassi, in his essay "Leibniz's Place in the History of Physics" (*Journal of the History of Ideas*, Vol. 30 (1969), pp. 332–3) notes perceptively: "Leibniz found unsatisfactory Descartes' view of matter as pure extension: matter, says Leibniz, is both extension and force, and by force he meant both passive momentum and active kinetic energy. And so, when Leibniz decided that extension was not essential to matter, he decided that force alone is; extension, then, is the order of relations among points endowed with force."

3 For the fuller discussion of this issue in the later works, see Chapters IX, pp. 264ff., pp. 277ff., and XII, pp. 422ff.

4 Feuerbach notes with approval Leibniz's comment that in dealing with deeper philosophical matters, "*Locke a raisonné un peu à la légère.*" (Cf. Leibniz's letter to Burnet, 8/24/1697, and to Montmort, 3/14/1714.)

5 In a letter to Christian Kapp (June 27, 1835), Feuerbach writes, "My deepest conviction is that philosophy will come on better times only when it will cease to neglect the empirical, but will instead master and lay claim to it" (XII–XIII, p. 294). What he means by "empirical" is not clear, but he goes on to say that this change must take place otherwise than by the "so-called application of philosophy to the positive sciences which has been the case until now" (ibid.). He means, it seems clear, Schilling's *Naturphilosophie* in particular, but perhaps also Hegel's. Rawidowicz thinks that he *does not* mean Hegel, nor that it indicates a "break" with Hegel this early, because "Hegel should not in any case be regarded as an opponent of the empirical" (Rawidowicz, op. cit., p. 52n.). This goes a bit far, if it is intended to reflect Feuerbach's own view, for just a few years later, Feuerbach is to make just this same charge against Hegel, and against speculative idealism in general.

In another letter to Kapp (November 1, 1837) Feuerbach remarks, "Full freedom is now necessary in order to carry out my plans. A broader empirical basis is necessary for a philosopher. To botany, natural history, anatomy, physiology I have already dedicated a full year. . ." (XII–XIII,

p. 313). Feuerbach's notion of the "empirical" remains epistemologically vague as yet, though he links it to the study of the natural sciences.

6 Though Feuerbach never deals with it explicitly, the Platonic model of *Eros* is plainly relevant here, as it is later in Feuerbach's fuller discussion of the *double* nature of dependency (e.g., see Chapter XII p. 391). In Plato's account of the myth, in the *Symposium, Eros* is born of the union of *Poros* ("plenty") and *Penia* ("want," or "lack"), and as child of both parents is therefore *both* aware of his neediness *and* of what would fulfill it.

7 Feuerbach never gets that far, however, because his concept of "capacity" or "power," in human activity always falls short of the notion of concrete praxis as labor. See Chapter X, p. 325, and Chapter VII, p. 188. Cf. Locke's discussion of "powers" in an epistemological context (*An Essay Concerning the Human Understanding*, Bk. II, Chapt. 21) and his "labor theory" of value and of original property right (*Treatise of Civil Government*, Chapt. V, and *Two Treatises of Government*, Bk. II) in *The Works of John Locke* (London: 1823 [reprinted by Scientia Verlag, Aalen, Germany, 1963, Vol. V, pp. 352 ff.]). Hegel's views on this in *The Philosophy of Right* are well known (cf. "On Property," Sect. 41–70, and "The System of Needs," Sect. 189 ff.), but his most striking passages are in the less well known sections of the early *Jenenser Realphilosophie*, on "Will" and "Desire," especially on the concepts of labor, tools, and the transformation of possession into property right (e.g., pp. 194 ff., and the section on "practical Spirit," pp. 213–17). (Cf. Hegel's *Jenenser Realphilosophie II, Die Vorlesungen von 1805–06, aus dem Manuscript herausgegeben von Johannes Hoffmeister*, in the *Sämtliche Werke*, Georg Lasson, ed. [Leipzig: Felix Meiner Verlag, 1931], Vol. XX).

Chapter V
Critique of Belief: Leibniz and Bayle

1 The *Todesgedanken*, first published in 1830 as *Gedanken über Tod und Unsterblichkeit* in Nürenberg, was of course preceded by the 1828 *Dissertation*, but it was Feuerbach's first postdoctoral publication. Though published anonymously, its author was soon found out, and the "scandalous" work in effect closed off the possibility of a university post for Feuerbach thereafter. What is of particular interest is the editing that Feuerbach did for the republication of the work in his 1846 *Collected Works*. The title was shortened, and so was the work, by more than a third. In the edited version, as Rawidowicz notes (op. cit., pp. 20–21, esp. n. 2 on p. 21), the Hegelian language and structure of the original was radically emended by Feuerbach. The procedure is reminiscent of Marx's elimination of much of the explicit "Hegelianism" of the *Grundrisse* of 1857–9 in his totally reworked magnum opus, *Capital* (for which the *Grundrisse* were the notebooks). The motives were at least in part similar: an eye on the reading audience, and an attempt to detach from the Hegelian label with its connotations, after both Feuerbach and Marx had transformed their Hegelianism in a critical way. Rawidowicz is eager to point out (loc. cit.) (against the views of Rawidowicz's particular *bêtes noires*, the Feuerbachian editors Jodl, Bolin, and Grün, who argued that Feuerbach began to give

up his Hegelianism from the very start) that the first edition of Feuerbach's work establishes his Hegelianism clearly. The facsimile reproduction of the first edition of the *Gedanken* . . . is in the added Volume XI of the *Sammtliche Werke* edited by Hans-Martin Sass, 1962. The 1846 version, *Todesgedanken*, appears in the Bolin-Jodl edition of the *S.W.*, in Vol. I, pp. 1–90, together with Feuerbach's later works on these questions: *Die Unsterblichkeitsfrage von Standpunkt der Anthropologie* (*The Question of Immortality from the Standpoint of Anthropology*), 1846, 1866.

2 Feuerbach refers here to the articles "Deuxième Eclaircissement sur les Athées" and "Manichéens," in P. Bayle, *Dictionnaire Historique et Critique*, Fifth Edition, 1760, pp. 630 and 306, respectively. The readily available English translation is P. Bayle, *Historical and Critical Dictionary-Selections*, with an Introduction and Notes by Richard H. Popkin, tr. (Indianapolis: Bobbs-Merrill, Library of Liberal Arts, 1965), esp. pp. 151ff. and 409ff.

3 Bayle's dates are 1647–1706; Leibniz's are 1644–1716. Bayle's *Dictionnaire* was published first in 1697. Leibniz's *Monadology* is one of his very late works, published in 1714.

4 *Pierre Bayle–Ein Beitrag zur Geschichte der Philosophie und Menscheit* (Ansbach: Verlag C. Brügel, 1838) (actually off the press in March, 1839). The work was reprinted unchanged, from the original plates, in 1844, by Otto Wigand in Leipzig (Feuerbach's publisher thereafter), and then appeared in a revised and corrected edition as Volume V of the Bolin-Jodl *S.W.*, and as Volume 4, of the new *Gesammelte Werke*, edited by W. Schuffenhauer (Berlin: Akademie Verlag, 1967).

5 Cf. Spinoza's letter to Hugo Boxel, October 1674: "The distinction you drew, in admitting without hesitation Spirits of the male sex, but doubting whether any female spirits exist, seems to me more like a fancy than a genuine doubt. If it were really your opinion, it would resemble the common imagination that God is masculine, not feminine" (*Chief Works of Benedict de Spinoza*, R. H. M. Elwes, tr. [New York: Dover Publications, 1955], Vol. II, p. 380, Letter LVIII [LIV]).

Chapter VI
The Critique of Hegelian Philosophy: Part I

1 A typical example of this inversion is in Feuerbach's sentence: *"Das Bewusstsein des Unendlichkeit ist nichts als das Bewusstsein des Unendlichkeit des Bewusstseins"* ("The consciousness of infinity is nothing but the consciousness of the infinity of consciousness").

2 Friedrich Jodl, *Ludwig Feuerbach*, 2nd ed. (Stuttgart: Fromman Verlag, 1921), p. 4.

3 Ibid., p. 10. On Jodl's own grounds, however, the *Critique of Christian or "Positive" Philosophy* (1838) would seem to be a more explicit break.

4 Rawidowicz, op. cit., pp. 81–2.

5 Rawidowicz cites Ruge's letters, in which he wonders that Feuerbach still has so much patience with "the old rubbish," that is, Hegelianism (op. cit., p. 84n.). The original introduction is in the first edition of 1841 and is reprinted in Schuffenhauer's critical edition of the work (Berlin, 1956). The first *Gesammtausgabe* (1846) contains the revised introduction which

is reprinted in the *Sämmtliche Werke* edited by Bolin and Jodl (1903–11).

6 Cited by Karl Löwith in his introduction to the republication of the *Sammtliche Werke*, 1960, Vol. I, p. xii. See also the discussion on Feuerbach's review of Rosenkranz's critique of Bachmann; and the comment on Feuerbach's early reservations about the Hegelian dialectic, in Claudio Cesa, *Il Giovane Feuerbach* (Bari: Editori Laterza, 1963), pp. 242ff. and 267, respectively.

7 This discussion is in Feuerbach's introduction to the book on Leibniz.

8 Henri Arvon, *Ludwig Feuerbach ou la Transformation du Sacré* (Paris, P.U.F. 1947), p. 24.

9 See F. Jodl, *Foreword* in *S.W.*, Vol. II, p. ix; also Cesa, op. cit., pp. 242ff. The review, ostensibly commissioned as a review of Karl Rosenkranz's *Sendschreiben über die hegelsche Philosophie an den Professor Bachmann* (Königsberg, 1834), centered, however, on Bachmann's work, *Über Hegel's System und die Nothwendigkeit nochmaligan Umgestaltung der Philosophie* (Leipzig, 1833). The review was published in its revised form as *Kritik des AntiHegels. Zur Ein Einleitung in das Studium der Philosophie* (Ansbach, 1835).

10 Cf. Arvon, op. cit., p. 28.

11 The tradition of what one may call a "physiological" or "medical" materialism is itself remarked on by Feuerbach, in his late work *Spiritualism and Materialism* (1863–6). He writes, "Medicine, above all pathology, is the native soil and source of materialism" (X, 165); and argues further that German materialism derives from native rather than French soil: "Nothing is more mistaken than to derive German materialism from [D'Holbach's] *Système de la Nature*, or worse still, from La Mettrie's truffle-paste" (X, 155). (The "truffle paste" is an allusion, of course, to La Mettrie's alleged death from gluttony, a myth apparently, but divine justice in the eyes of his enemies.) But he sees this German origin as "religious," that is, rooted in the German Reformation. The connection – the "genealogical connection between materialism and Protestantism" (X, 157) – is symbolized for Feuerbach in the fact that Paul Luther, Martin Luther's son, was a physician, not a theologian, and therefore, somehow, a "materialist." For all this, the French "physiological-medical" tradition of materialism is clearly influential in Feuerbach's own work, and he protests too strongly *precisely* about D'Holbach's *Système de la Nature* and La Mettrie's *L'Homme Machine*, passages from which echo in Feuerbach's later works. La Mettrie, like Cabanis, was a doctor. Cabanis' work, *Rapports du physique et du moral de l'homme* (Paris: Crapat, Caille et Ravier, 1802) is exemplary of this tradition. On Feuerbach's later enthusiasm for such views, see his 1858 article on Heidenreich (*S.W.*, X, pp. 32–40) and his works on Moleschott's materialism. See my full discussion of this in Chapter XIII.

12 On this too, in relation to French eighteenth-century materialism, see my "Diderot and the Development of Materialist Monism," in N. Torrey and O. Fellows, eds., *Diderot Studies II* (Syracuse, N.Y.: Syracuse University Press, 1953), pp. 279–327.

13 Cf. Feuerbach's similar argument on the unicity of reason, in the *Dissertation*; see Chapter II.

14 Feuerbach's critique was published in 1838. In 1841, the *Hallesche Jahr-*

bücher, under Ruge's editorship, had to relocate in Leipzig, because of the censorship, where the journal continued as the *Deutsche Jahrbücher* for two short years. In 1843, it was banned in Saxony as well.

15 This aspect of Feuerbach's continued Hegelianism, in the period to 1839, can be noted also in his review articles on the works of Kuhn, Erdmann, Hock, and Bayer. That he still held positive views concerning the dialectic, and "the reality of contradiction," in this period, is noted by Rawidowicz, op. cit., p. 65. However, the qualification that matter as such cannot be self-contradictory, in the negative sense that it has no inner principle of self-differentiation, indicates the direction of Feuerbach's later abandonment of the dialectic at least in *this* sphere.

16 On this, see W. Bolin, foreword to *S.W.*, Vol. VII, p. vi; Arvon, op. cit., pp. 31–2; W. Schuffenhauer, *Introduction* to his critical edition of *The Essence of Christianity*, 1956, Vol. I, p. xxxvii. (Schuffenhauer gives the fullest account of the political context of H. Leo's attack. See also Hans-Martin Sass, *Untersuchungen zur Religionsphilosophie in der Hegelschule, 1830–1850*, Inaugural Dissertation (Münster, 1963), pp. 194–5; and especially H. V. Sybell, *Klerikale Politik in 19 j.h.* (Bonn, 1974), pp. 78ff.

17 See the discussion by Louis Althusser, on the question of "species being" and the difficulty of translating *"Gattung,"* in his *Translator's Note*, in *Ludwig Feuerbach–Manifestes Philosophiques* (Paris: P.U.F., 1960), pp. 6–7.

18 See Immanuel Kant, *On History*, with an introduction by L. W. Beck, ed. L. W. Beck, R. E. Anchor, and E. L. Fackenheim, tr. (Indianapolis: Bobbs-Merrill, Library of Liberal Arts, 1963). The volume contains both Kant's *Idea for a Universal History from a Cosmopolitical Standpoint* and *Review of Herder's "Ideas for a Philosophy of the History of Mankind."*

19 On this question, see Rawidowicz, op. cit., pp. 235–57 and 266–73 for a full discussion of Feuerbach's relations to Kant and Fichte. Also, W. Schuffenhauer, who argues against Rawidowicz's view, op. cit., Vol. II, note 112, pp. 686–7, and note 116, pp. 688–91.

20 Cf. Feuerbach's passage "For this reason, Christ bids us to become as children...," Vol. VII, pp. 152–3.

21 This critique by Feuerbach was a review of J. Sengler's work *Über das Wesen und die Bedeutung der spekulativen Philosophie und Theologie in der gegenwärtigen Zeit, mit besonderer Rücksicht auf die Religionsphilosophie* (Heidelberg, 1837). Feuerbach's review was published in the *Hallesche Jahrbücher* in 1838 and republished in a shorter, edited version, with some additions, as *Kritik der Christlichen oder 'positiven' Philosophie* in the 1846 edition of the *Sämmtliche Werke* (Leipzig), Vol. I, pp. 128–54.

22 The full text of *Philosophy and Christianity* was published later in the year, at Mannheim. Only the first part appeared in the *Hallesche Jahrbücher*.

Chapter VII
The Critique of Hegelian Philosophy: Part II

1 See Chapter VI, note 21 for the details on Sengler's book.

2 "Das Sinn-organ für das Sinnlose," a pun that goes through in both German and English.

3 Auguste Cornu takes Feuerbach's attack on "speculation" in the Sengler

review as also an attack on Hegel. See his *Karl Marx et Friedrich Engels, Leur Vie et Leur Oeuvre* (Paris: P.U.F., 1955–70), Vol. I–IV, Vol. I, pp. 149–50. Schuffenhauer (op. cit., Vol. II, p. 667, n. 107) corrects this misidentification of "positivism" and "Hegelianism."

4 I have translated *Sinnliches Bewusstsein* as "sensory consciousness" in most instances, instead of as "sense awareness," because the latter carries the connotation of "acquaintance knowledge" in Anglo-American philosophy. The difficulties of this latter view need to be kept distinct from the difficulties of the Feuerbachian-Hegelian usage at this stage. In Chapter XI, I discuss at some length the compounding of the difficulties in the mixture of uses and models, when Feuerbach's empiricism develops in the direction of a direct realism, complete with immediate sense awareness.

5 *Wissenschaftlich Erst* is translated here as "First in the metaphysical sense," which seems clear from the context, and from the "speculative" sense of *Wissenschaft* here; and because of the difficulties in using the English term "scientific" in this context.

6 Cf. Kierkegaard's critique of Hegel's notion of immediacy, of "immediate beginning," and of "system," in his *Concluding Unscientific Postscript to the "Philosophical Fragments,"* tr. D. Swenson (Princeton, N.J.: Princeton University Press, 1941).

7 See pp. 148ff.

8 Cf. Schopenhauer's view of mathematical intuition, in *World as Will and Representation*, E.F.J. Payne, tr. (New York: Dover, 1966).

9 Cf. Schopenhauer, op. cit., pp. 248–50.

10 Cf. Kierkegaard, op. cit.

11 Cf. Feuerbach's passage, at Vol. II, p. 169.

12 Throughout this discussion, Feuerbach uses, as synonymous or correlated terms, "empirical," "sensory," "actual," "concrete." *Sinnlich*, as in *sinnliche Anschauung, sinnlicher Verstand, Sinnlichkeit*, functions in several related ways, covering "sensation," or more broadly "sensibility," and also the more complex "sense perception" (for which *Wahrnehmung* is also used) and the general sense of "empirical knowledge." But the ontological implications, and the notion of synthetic, or empirical truth are also contained here. "Concrete" and "actual" are, in this context, terms that apply to determinate Being–this is, Being as it is, materially, or in existence, and not (as Feuerbach would say) "Being" as an empty name that does not even denote a viable formal concept.

Chapter VIII
The Philosophical Context of
Feuerbach's Critique of Religion

1 See, on this, W. Bolin's discussion in his *Biographical Introduction to the Selected Correspondence*, reprinted in the added double-volume XII–XIII republication of the *Sämmtliche Werke*, H-M Sass, ed. (Stuttgart-Bad Canstatt, 1964), pp. 73ff.; also Schuffenhauer, op. cit., Vol. I, pp. xlvii–lix.

2 Marion Evans translates the first sentence here as, "I am nothing but a natural philosopher in the domain of mind" (1854 edition of *The Essence of Christianity*, p. xxxiv, reissued [New York: Harper Torchbooks, 1957]). The phrase is *ein geistiger Naturforscher*. The S.W. II omits the phrase

in concreto, which is in the original. In this third edition, in general, Feuerbach eliminates "learned" terms and translates the Latin terms and phrases of the first edition into German to make the work more accessible to the layman. See my discussion of this in "Ludwig Feuerbach: A Review of Some Recent Literature," *The Philosophical Forum*, Vol. XXII (1964–5), pp. 69–78.

3 Letter to W. Bolin, *Nachlass*, II, 20, cited by S. Rawidowicz, op. cit., p. 208.

4 Feuerbach writes, "I strove for a true, complete recognition of sensibility, on the one hand, through a renewed, deeper study of religion, on the other, through an empirical study of nature, for which my rustic existence gave me the most pleasant opportunity" (*S.W.* I, VIII, 16, cited by Rawidowicz, op. cit., p. 112).

5 *Ausgewählte Brief*, W. Bolin, ed., #102, II, 50 (November, 1840).

6 Ibid., #105, II, 57–8 (12 January, 1841). In this letter to Christian Kapp, Feuerbach's ambivalance, his concerns over his career and his public name and reputation, his disdain for professional philosophy all come through. He writes, "In the long run, I can't remain here [in Bruckberg]. I have to go on further. But by what means? I don't qualify as a professor of philosophy precisely because I am a philosopher and, indeed, a cryptophilosopher. . . . I must get out of the limited profession of philosophy that I've been stuck in until now. As wretched a thing as reputation is–it remains the Regent of the world, reputation is the writer's Capital. Capital needs to be invested as well and as quickly as possible. . . ." There is a distinctive *"anonymity vs. public reputation"* motif throughout the letter. See also W. Bolin, *Ludwig Feuerbach. Sein Wirken und Seine Zeitgenossen* (Stuttgart, 1891), pp. 19–21.

7 See W. Bolin, Biographical Introduction, *Ausgewählte Brief*, pp. 28ff. pp. 48–9, 50.

8 See on this Melvin Cherno, *Ludwig Feuerbach and the Intellectual Basis of Nineteenth Century Radicalism*, unpublished Ph.D. thesis, Stanford University, 1955.

9 Cf. Schuffenhauer, op. cit., Vol. I, p. lvii.

10 Wilhelm Dilthey, in the context of the humanistic movement of *Geisteswissenschaft*, did in fact write a work with this title, which owes much to Feuerbach. See W. Dilthey, *The Essence of Philosophy*, S. A. and W. T. Emery, tr. (Chapel Hill: University of North Carolina Press, 1954).

11 Karl Marx's enthusiasm at the time expresses itself in his *"Luther als Schiedsrichter zwischen Strauss und Feuerbach"* (published in 1843 in Ruge's *Anekdota zur neusten deutschen Philosophie und Publicistik*, Vol. II, pp. 206–8, anonymously, and signed "Kein Berliner"): "There is no other road to truth and freedom than through the fiery brook [Feuerbach]. Feuerbach is the Purgatory of the Present," *Marx-Engels Gesamtausgabe*, p. xxxix. See also Schuffenhauer, *Feuerbach und der Junge Marx* (Berlin: VEB Deutscher Verlag der Wissenschaften, 1965), which also contains the Feuerbach-Marx correspondence; and Rawidowicz, op. cit. passim, on the relations between Feuerbach, Marx, and Engels.

12 Hegel, *Phänomenologie des Geistes*, in *Sämtliche Werke* (Hamburg: Felix Meiner Verlag, 1952), Vol. V, p. 473. Kojève, in his close analysis of the *Phenomenology*, makes much of this opening passage of the chapter on religion (Chapter VII). (Alexandre Kojève, *Introduction à la Lecture de*

Hegel–Leçons sur la Phénoménologie de l'Esprit [Paris: Gallimard, 1947].)
In fact, he interprets Hegel in an almost Feuerbachian way, for he takes
absolute Being (absolutes Wesen, for which Kojève gives *Réalité-essentielle
absolue)* as connoting nothing less, for Hegel, than humanity, or the human
species itself. Kojève writes,

> What does *Absolute Being* mean to the author of the *Phenomenology of
> the Spirit?* That which is truly real isn't Nature, the natural world other
> than Man. Because, in fact, the real world involves man. Inversely, man
> outside the world is only an abstraction. *Reality* is therefore the world which
> involves Man, the Man who lives in the world. Now what is the *essential-*
> reality of this real, its "essence," its "entelechy," its "idea"? It is Man, to
> the extent that he is something *other* than the world, who at the same time
> cannot exist except *in* the world. Man is the essential real: This is an axiom
> which Hegel, like every Judeo-Christian thinker, accepts without discussion.
> *"Der Geist ist hoher als die Natur,"* says Hegel, somewhere. But the absolute
> essential reality isn't the human *individual* (the "particular"). For the iso-
> lated man doesn't any more exist in reality than does man out-of-the-world,
> or the world-without-man. The essential reality of the *Real* is humanity
> taken in its spatio-temporal completeness. This is what Hegel calls *"Ob-*
> *jektiver Geist"* (Objective Spirit), *"Weltgeist"* (World Spirit), *"Volksgeist"*
> (Folk-Spirit), but also *"Geschichte"* (History) or, in more concrete terms—
> *"Statt,"* the State as such, Society as such. (Op. cit., p. 198.)

13 Hegel, op. cit., pp. 475–6.
14 Kojève, op. cit., p. 200.
15 Hegel, op. cit., Preface, p. 56.
16 Ibid., pp. 200ff.
17 Ibid., p. 135.
18 Ibid.
19 Ibid., pp. 139–40; also on *work* as "suspended desire," p. 149.
20 Ibid., pp. 158ff.
21 It must be noted that practically none of the Feuerbach commentators take
these works in this sense, being primarily concerned with the manifest thesis
of the work, rather than with its concrete analysis of instances. Only the
theological critiques of Feuerbach take this concrete analysis seriously, but
not from the point of view of empirical psychology; rather, from the point
of view of theological dispute over the content itself.
22 Henrich Leo, *Die Hegelingen–Aktenstücke und Belege zu der sogenannten
Denunziation der ewigen Wahrheit* (Halle, 1838) cited in Sass, op. cit.,
p. 194.
23 Cited by Sass, op. cit., p. 195.
24 Hegel, op. cit., p. 138.
25 Ibid., p. 139.
26 Ibid., p. 140.
27 Ibid., pp. 141–2.
28 The whole passage is cited on p. 164. The "like is known only by like"
motif, which runs through the history of philosophy from the pre-Socratics
onward (and indeed expresses itself in animistic and mythical thought, and
in magic, as "homeopathic" or "sympathetic" causation) is given its explicit epistemological formulation by Aristotle in the *De Anima* (e.g., III,

4, 429a, 14–17). Thomas Aquinas expresses it thus: "Everything that is apprehended by any apprehending being, is apprehended according to the manner of this being's apprehension" (*Summa Theologia*, First Part, Q 75, Art. 5c), which appears to reduce the notion to a tautology. Cf. Friedrich von Hügel's discussion of this question in his *Essays and Addresses on the Philosophy of Religion*, First Series (London: Dent & Sons, 1922), p. 40.

29 Hippolyte, *Études sur la Philosophie Hegelienne.*

30 In this sense, the "grammar" of language in its demonstrative use–that is, logic. "Grammar" in the systematic sense alone can certainly encompass the *grammatical* expression of logical contradictions.

31 *Entgegnung an R. Haym*, 1848 (appeared first in the Journal *Die Epigonen*, Vol. V, 1848; reprinted in *Nachlass*, Vol. I, 1874, and in Vol. VII, 506–20).

32 "Body" is understood here as material body, or extended body. The immaterial "corpora," which have no extension are then still "substances," which makes them available as models for the monad, as a "spiritual atom," or the geometrical point, as an unextended, dimensionless mathematical entity.

33 Rawidowicz, op. cit., p. 72.

34 Ibid., p. 102.

Chapter IX
Religion as the Self-alienation of Human Consciousness: The Phenomenology of Religious and Theological Concept Formation

1 Cf. Sidney Hook, *From Hegel to Marx–Studies in the Intellectual Development of Karl Marx* (New York: Reynal and Hitchcock, 1936), p. 256, on the "Protagorean" characterization of Feuerbach.

2 The terms of the analysis are Feuerbach's, not Freud's. The connection is clear. For further discussion, see Hermann Adolf Weser's Inaugural-Dissertation, *Sigmund Freuds und Ludwig Feuerbachs Religionskritik*, Univ. Leipzig, 1936. Weser claims that Freud's definition of "illusion" is directly borrowed from Feuerbach, and accuses both Feuerbach and Freud of "hypostatizing scientific method" (pp. 70–1). Cf. also Philip Rieff, *Freud: The Mind of the Moralist* (New York, Viking Press, 1959), p. 24: "Privately [Freud] admitted to remote intellectual connections with Kant, Voltaire, Feuerbach." In a note (p. 266), Rieff says, "Both Freud's father-theory and Spencer's ghost-theory are ways of discounting religion as a form of "projection"–a type of analysis that received its classic statement in the writings of Ludwig Feuerbach, especially *The Essence of Christianity* and *The Essence of Religion*." Cf. also Rawidowicz, op. cit., pp. 348–50, for a fuller discussion of Freud's relation to Feuerbach.

3 Cf. Rawidowicz, op. cit., p. 82, n. 1; also Schuffenhauer, op. cit., Vol. I, p. iv. Incidentally, the range of alternative titles that Feuerbach considered is instructive as to his view of the purport of the work. In a letter to his publisher, Otto Wigand, January 5, 1841, he proposes: γνωτί σεαυτον or *The Truth of Religion and the Illusions of Theology*. As subtitles, he proposes: *A Contribution to the Critique of Speculative Philosophy of Religion*; and, in a wry mood, a play on the title of Kant's work: *A Contribution to the*

Critique of Pure Unreason (in *Ausgewählte Briefe*, W. Bolin, ed., Vol. II, pp. 54–6). Arnold Ruge also mentions *Organon of Unreason* as one of the proposed titles (in a letter to Professor E. Kapp, February 18, 1870, in Ruge's *Briefwechsel und Tagebuchblätter*, Vol. II, p. 346).

4 In the letter to his publisher, Otto Wigand, January 5, 1841, *Ausgewählte Briefe*, #104, Vol. II, p. 55. Cf. Rawidowicz, op. cit., pp. 100ff.

5 Cf. Schuffenhauer, op. cit., Vol. I, p. lx.

6 In the preface to the first edition, Feuerbach writes,

> The author chooses his documentary evidence from the archives of past centuries, with good reason. Christianity also had its classic period, and only this great, authentic, classic period is worth taking into account. The un-classical belongs to the forum of comedy and satire. Therefore, in order to establish Christianity as a subject worthy of thought, the author had to abstract from the cowardly, comfortable, *belles-lettristic*, coquettish, epicu-rean Christianity of the modern world, and put himself back in the times when the Bride of Christ was still a chaste, unbesmirched virgin, hadn't yet woven the rose and myrtle of the pagan Venus into the heavenly crown of thorns of her bridegroom, and didn't fall into a swoon at the sight of the suffering God; when she was indeed poor in worldly goods, but more than rich and content in the enjoyment of the mysteries of a supernatural love." (S: I, 5)

Feuerbach's supply of adjectives is never short!

7 There are some terminological ambiguities that can be set aside with a brief remark here. Feuerbach most often talks of *feeling* in terms of *love*; he uses "love" in a generic sense, to cover all the senses of *feeling for an other, as person*, that is, to encompass every relation of feeling that can be characterized as *I-Thou*. In an awkward, and sometimes confusing sense, the term "feeling" also covers feelings of awe, fear, thankfulness, and so on, for which the term "love" is not appropriate. There is a more impor-tant qualification to be made, however, with respect to the *most* generic sense of the term "feeling," which includes also "sensibility" in terms of "sense perception" and "sense imagery." The tradition for this generic use goes back to the sense of the Greek term ἀισθησις (*Aistheisis*), as connot-ing all that we would distinguish as sensory *and* emotive, that is, both sense and feeling, and the latter in at least two meanings, "sensibility" in the narrow "aesthetic" sense, and "emotion." The important point here is the relation of sense and feeling in the tradition of German aesthetics (e.g., in Baumgartner and in Kant), because Feuerbach's discussion of sense imagery in relation to feeling otherwise seems gratuitous.

Of minor concern are the terminological substitutions that Feuerbach permits himself. "Thought" is interchangeable, in most instances, with "Reason," "Intellect," or "the Understanding." The distinction between "Reason" and "Understanding," in the Kantian tradition, is not main-tained here. All the three properties are, in Feuerbach's view, *conscious*: that is, feeling and will involve thought, insofar as they are self-differen-tiable, can "appear to themselves as objects." "Thought," in its restricted sense as "intellect," means that consciousness whose object is not a sensory image (i.e., a particular), but an abstraction (i.e., a universal).

8 See Chapter II, esp. pp. 34ff., for the fuller discussion. It is significant that the *form* of Feuerbach's argument on the species nature of man changes very little, from the *Dissertation* to *The Essence of Christianity*.

9 Cf. note 2. Freud's title, *The Future of an Illusion*, is that of his most clearly "Feuerbachian" work.

10 Feuerbach takes this distinction directly from Hegel. (Cf. *Vorlesungen über d. Philosophie der Religion*, Marheinecke ed. [Berlin, 1832], Vol. I, pp. 72–5. Cf. also Rawidowicz, op. cit., p. 90.

11 In this context, I have translated *Wissenschaft* as "rational knowledge," though it is most often translated as "science." This latter translation is acceptable, and is perhaps to be preferred, but unfortunately carries the connotations of a much narrower view, in current English usage.

12 The variations and speculations on this theme are many, and it was an eighteenth-century commonplace, as, for example, Fontenelle's *Apologue des Roses*, B. Franklin's *The Ephemera, an Emblem of Human Life* (1778). It is given in contemporary form in the mathematical fantasy *Flatland–a Romance of Many Dimensions*, by Edwin A. Abbott. Diderot, in the *Lettre sur les Aveugles* puts this view in a striking way, proposing that the metaphysicians of a sightless race would locate the soul in the fingertips. Feuerbach writes,

No being can negate its essence. No being is finite to itself. Every being is infinite in and for itself, has its God, its highest essence, in itself. Every limitation of a being exists only for other beings beyond it. The life of the Mayfly is short in relation to the span of longer-lived creatures. But it is just as long, for the Mayfly, as a life of many years is to other species. The leaf on which the caterpillar lives is a universe for it, an infinite space. (VI, 6; S: I, 44)

This might suggest that animals do have their "religion," after all! But though every being may "have its God, its highest essence, in itself," only man, according to Feuerbach, has this essence as his object, that is, as an other, or for himself.

13 I have usually translated *Geistig* as "spiritual," but where the contrast is with sense perception, I use "mental." Marion Evans uses "spiritual" here.

14 In a review article in *Theologischen Studien und Kritiken* (Hamburg, 1842), Vol. I, pp. 171ff. Feuerbach's reply appeared in A. Ruge's *Deutsche Jahrbücher für Wissenschaft u. Kunst* (Dresden, 1942), pp. 65ff., and is reprinted in *S.W.*, VII, pp. 212ff.

15 In "Neue Wendung der deutschen Philosophie. Das Wesen des Christenthums von Ludwig Feuerbach," *Anekdota zur neuesten deutsche Philosophie und Publizistik* (Zürich, 1843), Vol. II, pp. 3ff. Also in Ruge, *Aktenstücke* (Mannheim, 1847), Vol. II, p. 18. Schuffenhauer cites, op. cit., Vol. I, p. xcii. (Cf. Sass, in Bibliography B, no. 28, *S.W.*, XI, 349–50.) "Infinity" from Anhang I, S: II, 424.

16 Feuerbach means the philosophies of religion of, for example, Schleiermacher and Jacobi here.

17 Cf. Chapter V, note 28.

18 *Übermenschliches* Evans translates as "transcendental," which because of its technical philosophical connotations loses the more direct sense of the

literal translation, "superhuman." See *The Essence of Christianity*, Evans, tr., p. 9.

19 On Wagner's relation to Feuerbach, see Rawidowicz's thorough discussion, op. cit., pp. 388–410.

20 Feuerbach gives "Uebles leiden weit besser ist, als gutes thun." Schuffenhauer gives this from Luther's text, as *"das Leben in Leiden viel vortrefflicher ist als alles Leben, welches in thun steht."* Luther, *Decem Praecepta Wittenbergensi, Praedicata populo,* 1518, in *Werke: Kritische Gesamtausgabe* (Weimar, 1883), p. 417.

Chapter XI

The Critique of Philosophy and the Development of a
Materialist Humanism – Part I

1 See especially Werner Schuffenhauer's masterful and thorough critical edition of *The Essence of Christianity* (Berlin: Akademie Verlag, 1956), two vols., in which all the variations of the three editions of the work are given (Lesarten, II, pp. 545–649). Especially instructive are the changes Feuerbach made in the third edition, eliminating or translating the Latin citations and changing terms from Latin to German roots, in order to make the work less "professional" and more available to the lay reader. (For example, *Cosmogonischer Princip* is changed to *Welt-Erschaffender Princip, Objekt* is changed to *Gegenstand*, and so on. See my discussion on this in "Ludwig Feuerbach: A Review of Some Recent Literature," *The Philosophical Forum*, Vol. XXII (1964–5), pp. 69–78.

2 On the publication history of the *Preliminary Theses . . .* and *The Principles of the Philosophy of the Future*, see Rawidowicz, op. cit., pp. 118–19, 129; especially the interesting exchange with Ruge on whether or not to publish the *Theses*, and on the tactics of using the scare word "atheism," *Sämmtliche Werke*, H-M. Sass, ed., letter 363 (March 2, 1942), Vol. XIII, pp. 392–4.

3 Karl Marx borrows this metaphor from Feuerbach, in characterizing his own appreciation and critique of Hegel's dialectic. In his preface to the second edition of *Capital* (written four months after Feuerbach's death), Marx writes, "The mystification which dialectic suffers in Hegel's hands, by no means prevents him from being the first to present its general form of working in a comprehensive and conscious manner. With him it is standing on its head. It must be turned right side up again, if you would discover the rational kernel in the mystical shell" (*Capital*, Vol. I, F. Engels, ed., Moore and Aveling, tr. [Chicago: Charles Kerr, 1906], p. 25).

4 On this, see my "Denis Diderot and Ludwig Feuerbach: Studies in the Development of Materialist Monism" (unpublished Ph.D dissertation, Columbia University, 1952; and University Microfilms, Ann Arbor, Michigan).

5 Alfred Schmidt recognizes this point in his view that Feuerbach's "anthropological materialism" introduces the question of a "materialist theory of subjectivity," which has until now been neglected in Marxist epistemology. See A. Schmidt, *Emanzipatorische Sinnlichkeit, Ludwig Feuerbach's anthropologischer Materialismus* (Munich: Carl Hauser Verlag, 1973), p. 119.

6 Feuerbach proceeds here to propose the union of German and French phi-

losophy, using the metaphor of the union of "head" and "heart" that Marx borrows in the well-known passage, in his *Toward a Critique of Hegel's Philosophy of Law: Introduction*, an article written at the end of 1843, in Paris, a year after the publication of Feuerbach's *Theses*. In this article, Marx for the first time introduces the notion of the proletariat as the means to "full human emancipation":

The emancipation of the German is the emancipation of mankind. The *head* of this emancipation is *philosophy*, its *heart* is the *proletariet*. Philosophy cannot be actualized without the transcendence [*Aufhebung*] of the proletariet, the proletariet cannot be transcended without the actualization of philosophy. When all the inner conditions are fulfilled, the *day of German resurrection* will be announced by the *crowing of the French cock*."

(*Writings of the Young Marx on Philosophy and Society*, L. Easton and K. Guddat, eds. [Garden City, N.Y.: Doubleday, 1967], p. 264.) Cf. L. Feuerbach (II, 236).

7 Bracketed sentences (from "In perception" to end of quotation) are missing in the 1904–11 *Sämmtliche Werke*. They are replaced in the 1970 *Gesammelte Werke*, IX, 326.

8 Feuerbach's use of the term *Dasein* here is a revision of Hegel's frequent use. Its affinities to and difference from Heidegger's use, as a technical philosophical term, probably bears crucially on the relation of Heidegger to Feuerbach, a relation noted by Rawidowicz only in passing (in commenting on Karl Löwith's "Heideggerian" interests in Feuerbach's "anthropological grounding of ethics," (Rawidowicz, op. cit., p. 507). This relation is noted also by Hook, op. cit., and is discussed in Schmidt, op. cit., pp. 123, 146n., and 229.

9 Cf. Rawidowicz, op. cit., p. 246, and Feuerbach's remark, in the *Nachgelassene Aphorismen*: "Where Kant's philosophy leaves off, at least in its concrete realizations, there mine begins" (X, 340).

10 R. Haym, "Feuerbach und die Philosophie. Ein Beitrag zur Kritik Beider," Halle, 1847.

11 On Feuerbach's relation to Schopenhauer, see Rawidowicz, op. cit., Chapter 5, pp. 284–303; and on this point, especially p. 298.

12 The passage is reminiscent of Diderot's account of the transformation of marble into living flesh, in *D'Alembert's Dream*. Cf. my "Diderot and the Development of Materialist Monism," op. cit., for a discussion of this.

Chapter XII
The Critique of Philosophy and the Development of a
Materialist Humanism – Part II

1 Cf. Feuerbach's remarks on this (X, 345).

2 Cf. Eugene Kamenka: "There are overtones in Feuerbach as in Marx, of Vico's famous *verum factum*, that man can know completely and with certainty only that which he has fashioned himself." E. Kamenka, *The Philosophy of Ludwig Feuerbach*. (London: Routledge & Kegan Paul, 1970, p. 110.).

3 But see also, on this question of the relation of models of science and politics, Feuerbach's *Lectures on the Essence of Religion* (VIII, 424–5).

4 Oxygen does, of course, become liquified under pressure, but Feuerbach may be permitted this conception limited to the chemistry of his time, and even then, to a more or less popular version of it. Still, Feuerbach's preoccupation with, and love for the natural sciences, as a serious amateur, is reflected in this passage, and in much of his correspondence (e.g., with Christian Kapp, Moleschott, and others). On the matter of Feuerbach's scientific reading and notes, there is a large folio of unedited and unpublished material in the Feuerbach archive at the *Universitätsbibliothek* in Munich. It contains Feuerbach's notes and comments on works in chemistry, biology, physics and physiology (difficult to read in Feuerbach's crabbed script), which show serious and sustained interest on his part.

5 Moleschott had been a long-time admirer of Feuerbach's work and a friend as well. In his correspondence with Feuerbach, he acknowledges his intellectual debt. In 1850, he sends Feuerbach a copy of the *Lehre der Nahrungsnuttel* (See letter 202 [XIII, 175] March 30, 1850) and in 1852, a copy of his popular work, *Kreislauf des Lebens* (see letter 219 [XIII, 195], June 24, 1952). Cf. Rawidowicz, op. cit., pp. 331–4 on Moleschott and Feuerbach.

6 Rawidowicz has a fine discussion both of the sources of this thought, and of the pun, as well as a fair-minded defense against an unthinking reduction of Feuerbach's materialism to this simpleminded physiologism. The French "gourmet-philosopher" Brillat-Savarin, in his 1825 work *Physiologie de Goût ou Méditations de Gastronomie Transcendente* (!) has as the epigraph of his work: *Dis-moi ce que tu manges, je te dirai qui tu es*. Of some interest as well is the fact that at the end of the eighteenth century, Friedrich Dicke, an educational official in Berlin, published a work in which the pun is indicated: *"Uber isst und ist: Ein Erklärung des Ursprungs des Opfer* ("Concerning isst ('eats') and ist ('is'): An explanation of the Origins of Sacrifice"). As Rawidowicz points out, this is practically the title of Feuerbach's 1862 work *Die Geheimniss des Opfers oder der Mensch ist was er isst (The Mystery of Sacrifice or Man Is What He Eats)*. All of this is cited by Rawidowicz, op. cit., p. 202.

7 Cf. Rawidowicz, op. cit., p. 332.

8 Feuerbach's appreciation of the condition of the working class is, however, deeply expressed. See especially in the late work *Zur Ethik*, in which he argues that just as there can be no happiness without moral virtue, there can be no virtue without happiness, and no happiness without the *conditions* for happiness:

Virtue, like the body, requires nourishment, clothing, light, air, space. Where people are so crowded together, as, e.g., in the English factories and workers' housing, when one may just as well call such houses pigstys, where there isn't even enough oxygen in the air to go around,–one may refer here to the incontestable facts in that most interesting and at the same time horrifying and rich work of K. Marx: *"Das Kapital"*–then there too there is no room left for morality either, and virtue is at best a monopoly of the factory owners, the capitalists. (X, 266–7)

On Feuerbach's reading of Marx's *Capital*, see his letter to Friedrich

Kapp in New York, in which he describes it as Marx's "great critique of political economy" (Letter 336 [XIII, 352], April 11, 1868).

9 Cf. Rawidowicz, op. cit., p. 236; and the correspondence with Heidenreich, in the *Ausgewählte Brief.*

10 Cited also by Rawidowicz, op. cit., p. 236.

Selected Bibliography

Althusser, L. Introduction, *L. Feuerbach, Manifestes Philosophiques*. Paris: Presses Universitaires de France, 1960.

Ardab'ev, A. I. *Ateizm L'udviga Feierbakha*. Moscow: Akademiya Nauk S.S.S.R., Institut Filosofii, 1963.

Arvon, H. *Ludwig Feuerbach ou la Transformation du Sacré*. Paris: Presses Universitaires de France, 1957.

Ascheri, C. "Feuerbach 1842: necessita di un cambiamento." *De Homine* (Rome), 1966, nos. 19–20, pp. 147–254. Also published in German as *Feuerbachs Bruch mit der Spekulation. Kritische Einleitung zu Feuerbach: Die Notwendigkeit einer Veränderung (1842)*. Frankfurt: Europaische Verlaganstalt; Vienna: Europa Verlag, 1969.

"Aspetti dell-Hegelismo del Giovane Feuerbach." *Hegel-Studien* (Bonn), Beiheft 4, 1969, pp. 205–14.

Baskin, M. P. *Filosofia L. Feierbakha*. Izdatelstvo Moskovskovo Universitete, 1957.

Bolin, W. *Ludwig Feuerbach, Sein Wirken und seine Zeitgenossen*. Stuttgart: Frommanns Verlag, 1891.

Braun, H. J. *Ludwig Feuerbach Lehre vom Menschen*. Stuttgart: Frommanns Verlag, 1971.

Die Religionsphilosophie L. Feuerbachs. Stuttgart: Frommanns Verlag, 1972.

Brazell, W. I. *The Young Hegelians*. New Haven: Yale University Press, 1970.

Bulgakov, S. N. *Religiya Chelovekobozhestva i L. Feierbakha*. Moscow, 1906.

Chamberlain, W. *Heaven Wasn't His Destination*. London: Allen and Unwin, 1941.

Cesa, C. "Aproposito dell-influenza di Feuerbach su Marx." *Rev. Crit. di Storia della filosofia*, 1967, Vol. 22, no. 2, pp. 171ff.

Il giòvane Feuerbach. Bari: Editori Laterza, 1963.

"Ludwig Feuerbach nella piu recente letteratura." *Ginornale Critica della Filosofia Italiana*, 3rd series, 1961, Vol. XV, pp. 114–27.

Cherno, M. *Ludwig Feuerbach and the Intellectual Basis of Nineteenth Century Radicalism*. Ph.D. dissertation, Stanford University, 1955.

"Feuerbach's 'Man Is What He Eats': A Rectification." *Journal of the History of Ideas*, 1963, Vol. 24, no. 3, pp. 397–406.

Selected Bibliography

Deborin, A. M. (Yoffe). *L'udvig Feierbakh-Lichnost' i Mirovozreniye*. Moscow: Kn'igoizdatelstvo "Materialist," 1923.

Dicke, G. *Der Identitätsgedanke bei Feuerbach und Marx*, Köln u. Opladen: Westdeutsche Verlag, 1960; also in *Deutsche Zeitschrift für Philosophie*, 1962, Vol. 10, pp. 380ff.

Elez, I. "Ludwig Feuerbach and Our Times." *Voprosy Filosofii*, no. 9, tr. in *Soviet Studies in Philosophy*, 1973, Vol. XII, no. 1, pp. 3–32.

Engels, F. "Ludwig Feuerbach and the End of Classical German Philosophy," in *Karl Marx and Frederick Engels, Selected Works*. New York: International Publishers, 1968.

Fetscher, I. "Hegel, Feuerbach, Marx." *Hegelstudien* (Bonn), 1963, pp. 376ff.

Frei, H. A. "Feuerbach and Theology." *Journal of the Americal Academy of Religion*, 1967, Vol. 35, no. 3, pp. 250ff.

Gabaraev, S. Sh. *Materializm Feierbakha*. Tbilisi: Izdatelstvo Akademii Nauk Gruzinskoi S.S.R., 1955.

Gagern, M. von. *Ludwig Feuerbach. Philosophie und Religionskritik*. Munich: A. Pustet Sammlung Wissenschaft u. Gegenwart, 1970.

Glasse, J. "Barth on Feuerbach." *Harvard Theological Review*, 1964, Vol. 57, no. 2, pp. 69–96.

Gollwitzer, H. "Zur Religionskritik von Feuerbach und Marx." *Verkundigung und Forschung* (Munich), 1958–59 and 1960–62, pp. 201ff.

Hager, K. "Ludwig Feuerbach–ein grosser Materialist. *Einheit* (Berlin), 1959, Heft 7, pp. 664–72.

Hook, S. *From Hegel to Marx: Studies in the Intellectual Development of Karl Marx*. New York: Reynal and Hitchcock, 1936.

Irrlitz, G. "Ludwig Feuerbachs anthropologischer Materialismus als theoretische Quelle des Marxismus." *Ludwig Feuerbach Referenten Konferenz der Zentralen Kommission Wissenschaft*. Berlin: Deutscher Kulturbund, 1972, pp. 29–53.

Jankowski, H. *Etyka Ludwik Feuerbach*. Warsaw: Ksiazka i Wiedza (Biblioteka Studiow nad Marksizmem), 1963.

Jodl, F. *Ludwig Feuerbach*, 2nd ed. Stuttgart: Frommanns Verlag, 1921.

Jung, A. "Uber Ludwig Feuerbach" (II). *Philosophisches Monatsheft* (Berlin), 1874, Vol. X, pp. 160–80.

Kosing, A. "Ludwig Feuerbachs materialistische Erkenntnisstheorie." *Deutsche Zeitschrift für Philosophie*, 1972, Vol. 20, no. 9, pp 1091–1109.

Ley, H. "Ludwig Feuerbach uber das Bündniss und Naturwissenschaft und der Dialektischer Materialismus." *Referenten Konferenz*. Berlin: D. Kulturbund, 1972, pp. 70–8.

Lombardi, F. *Ludwig Feuerbach*. Florence, 1935.

Lowith, K. *Von Hegel Zu Nietzsche*, 4th ed. Stuttgart: Kohlhammer Verlag, 1958.

"Vermittlung und Unmittelbarkeit bei Hegel, Marx und Feuerbach." *Zur Kritik der Christliche Uberlieferung. Vorträge und Abhandlungen*. Stuttgart, 1966, pp. 198ff.

Masaryk, T. G. *Die Philosophische und Sociologische Grundlagen des Marxismus, Studien zur Socialen Frage*. Vienna: Konegen Verlag, 1899.

McLellan, D. *The Young Hegelians and Karl Marx*. New York: Praeger, 1969.

Meyer, M. *Ludwig Feuerbachs Moralphilosophie*. Inaugural-Dissertation. Berlin, 1899.

Selected Bibliography

Rawidowicz, S. *Ludwig Feuerbachs Philosophie. Ursprung und Schicksal.* Berlin: Reuther und Reichard, 1931; Walter De Gruyter, 1964.

Riedl, G. *Ludvik Feuerbach A Mlady Marx.* Prague: Statni Pedagogicke Nakladatelstvi, 1962.

Sass, H-M. *Untersuchungen zur Religionsphilosophie in Der Hegelschule.* (Inaugural-Dissertation), 1830–50. Münster, 1963.

"Feuerbach statt Marx. Zur Verfasserschaft des Aufsatzes 'Luther als Schiedsrichter zwischen Strauss und Feuerbach.'" *International Review of Social History,* 1967, Vol. 12, no. 1, pp. 108ff.

"Diskussionsstrategien und Kritikmodelle in der Feuerbachkritik.' *Differenze,* 1970, Vol. 9, pp. 245–72.

Schaller, J. *Darstellung und Kritik der Philosophie Ludwig Feuerbachs.* Leipzig: Hinrichs, 1847.

Schilling, W. *Feuerbach und die Religion.* Munich: Evangelischer Pressverband für Bayern, 1957.

Schuffenhauer, W. *Feuerbach und der Junge Marx.* Berlin: VEB Deutscher Verlag der Wissenschaften, 1965.

"Materialismus und Naturbetrachtung bei Ludwig Feuerbach." *Deutsche Zeitschrift für Philosophie,* 1972, Vol. 20, no. 12, pp. 1461–73.

Schmidt, A. *Emanzipatorische Sinnlichkeit—Ludwig Feuerbachs Anthropologischer Materialismus.* Munich: Carl Hauser Verlag, 1973.

Severino, G. *Origine e Figure del Processo Theogonico in Feuerbach.* Milan: Mursia, 1972.

Testa, A. *Incontro con Marx e Feuerbach.* Urbin: Capelli Editore, 1963.

Vishinskii, P. *Ob otnoshenii Marksizma k Feierbakhizmu.* Moscow-Leningrad: Gosudarstvennoye/sotsialno-ekonomicheskoye izdatel'stvo, 1931.

Vogel, M.H. "The Barth-Feuerbach Confrontation." *Harvard Theological Review,* 1966, Vol. 59, pp. 27–52.

Wartofsky, M. W. "Ludwig Feuerbach: A Review of Some Recent Literature." *The Philosophical Forum,* 1964–65, Vol. XXII (old series), pp. 69–78.

Weser, A. H. *Sigmund Freuds und Ludwig Feuerbachs Religionskritik.* Inaugural-Dissertation. Leipzig, 1936.

Xhaufflaire, M. *Feuerbach et la Théologie de Secularisation.* Paris: Les Editions de Cerf, 1970.

Index

creation, 307ff.; from nothing, 304, 316ff., 323

creative activity, *see* praxis

Cudworth, Thomas, 96

D'Alembert's Dream (Diderot), 21, 375

Dante, 119

Dasein, 18, 376–7, 419

Daumer, A., 196

dependency, 308ff., 311–15, 324–5, 329, 338–9; on nature, 388; as source of religion, 389ff., 391–3

Descartes, Rene, 12, 50, 60–2, 74–82, 84, 97–9, 103, 110–20, 125–7, 135, 144, 150, 163, 197, 215, 239–43, 277, 352, 403, 436

Dewey, John, 1, 26

D'Holbach, 48, 367, 397, 441

Dialectic, 7–18; of being and becoming, 306; of being and nothing in the Hegelian dialectic, 188; of digestion, 416; and falsification, 19, *see also* Popper; and Feuerbach's materialism, 120–1, 404; Hegelian, 8, 15, 16–18, 22, 49, of self and other, 309, 314, of man and nature, 415–16, critique of the Idea in, 137–40; and history of philosophy, 54–65; and Marxism, 8, 21, *see also* Marx; objective, 19–22, *see also* Engels; and ontology, 15; Platonic, 15, 19, 22; Popper and Socratic dialectic, 20; of sensuality, 20–1; and social criticism, 19, *see also* Marx; Socratic, 8, 12–15, 26

dialectical analysis, 279

Diderot, Denis, 21, 25, 375, 397, 400, 433, 434, 441, 448, 450

Digby, 96

Dilthey, Wilhelm, 402, 444

Dorguth, 145, 146, 152–9, 173, 206, 218, 248, 406

dream, dreaming, 283–4

Dualism: critique of, 118; of reason and belief, 113–14, 116, 400–8

Ego, *see* consciousness

empirical method, 256–7

Empiricism, 2, 62, 106–8, 137, 152, 154; of Bacon, 67; Feuerbach's critique of, 68–72; the idealist critique of, 108; of Locke, 104, 201; and materialism, 159; as a realism, 5, 11, 365ff., 443; *see also* materialism

Engels, Friederich, 8, 13, 19, 22, 48, 54, 80, 205

Epicurus, 72

epistemology, 11, 23; empiricist, 377; and mind-body problem, 401–2; realist vs. phenomenalist, 372

Erdmann, Johann Eduard, 53, 437

Essence: definition of human essence, 139, 162, 264–6; in Dissertation, 43; and essentialism, 32; formal, 67–8; nature as human essence, 391

Essence of Christianity, The (Feuerbach), 43, 196–256, 259–62, 295, 301, 315, 321, 329, 334, 353, 383, 387–8, 393, 395, 416

Essence of Religion, Lectures on (Feuerbach), 382, 387, 388, 395, 397, 399

ethics, basis of, 132

Euhemeris, 197

Evans, Marian (George Eliot), 443, 448

evolution, natural, 397–400

Existence: abstract and concrete, 280–1, 299; God as image of, 285–92, 477; human, 237, 298, 388, 405, 422; independent, 294

Faith, *see* belief

Feeling, 263, 279–84, 287; and creation from nothing, 317; and imagination, 215–20, 231–3, 235–6; and willing and thinking, 262

Fetscher, I., 434

Fichte, J. G., 132, 144, 163, 170, 186, 215, 230, 248, 310, 347, 349, 352, 442

first cause, 302

Fischer, E., 433

Florence, 63–4

Fontenelle, 488

Foundation of the Philosophy of the Future (Feuerbach), 67–8, 153, 196

Frank, Phillip, 433

Franklin, B., 448

Freud, Sigmund, 1, 7, 284, 446, 448

Galileo, 63, 64, 114

Gassendi, 50, 72–4, 81, 436

genetic analysis, 92–4, 342

Geulincx, 76, 82

Glisson, 96

God: anthropological explanation of, 390–3; and Cartesian conception of thought, 394–5; the creator, 323–8; essence of, 43–6; feeling, object of, 122–3, 290–2, *see also* incarnation; intellect and properties of, 305–7, 313–14; love as predicate, 350; and man, 293–4; and ontology and reason, 295–6; and praxis, 331–3, 338; prediction, and divine predicates, 301–2; Reason and God, 16, 293, *see also* Dialectic, Hegelian, critique of the Idea in; Hegelianism; Substance as God in Spinoza, 83, 86–8, *see also* substance, Spinoza

Gospels, 261

Grün, K., 439
Gunther, 169

Hauser, A., 433
Haym, R., 237, 383
Hegel, G. W. F., 2, 6–8, 12–13, 15–19, 24–5, 28, 45, 47–52, 63–4, 70, 80, 116, 133, 135–95, 205, 261, 266, 300–2, 305, 310, 313–14, 316–17, 345, 347–9, 361, 420–1, 423, 444; *Jenenser Realphilosophie*, 439
Hegelianism: break with early, 136–8, 140–5; concrete universal in, 163; Feuerbach's early, 3, 10, 17, 28–47; as Idealism, 295–9; tension within in the Dissertation, 43–8
Heidegger, M., 450
Heidenrich, F. W., 418–19
Helvétius, Claude, 48
Herder, J. G. von, 163
Hess, Moses, 137
Hessen, Boris, 433
Hippolyte, Jean, 230
historical method, 2–3
history: as humanization, 405; the Idea in Hegel and, 52
History of Modern Philosophy (Feuerbach), 49–50; and Hegel's *Phenomenology*, 50–1; as historical reconstruction and projective history, 53–88; Leibniz and Bayle, 115–17, 120, 125
history of philosophy: and genetic analytic method, 90–4, 135; logic of, 49–53
Hobbes, Thomas, 68–72, 73, 76, 81, 250, 403, 436, 437
Holy Communion, 263, 324, 335–6
Hook, Sidney, 446
human essence, 139, 162, 194, 391; *see also* humanity, "I-thou"
humanity, hypostatization of, 42; *see also* reason, the Idea, God
humanization, process of, 43–5, 405
Hume, David, 2, 4, 130, 131, 149, 215, 395
hypostatization, 209, 213, 254; of reason, 297

"I-thou," 1, 10, 34–7, 188, 310–11, 314, 346, 385–6, 425; *see also* God, the Idea, self-consciousness, species being
Idea, the, 12, 31, 52; expression of, 113; in the history of philosophy, 90, 147–9, 172, 345
Idealism: Absolute, 137; defense of, 153; formulation of, 240; rejection of, 172; *see also* Dorguth
identity: concept of, 147, 152; of sensation and thought, 378ff., 380
idolatry, 209
image, as object of belief, 253–4, 267–8
imagination, 158, 169, 229–36, 280–2, 309, 313; and feeling, 215–20

immediacy of sensation, 373–4, 377–8, 380–2
incarnation, 177, 205, 226–8, 263, 277, 288–90
individuality, 35; and empiricism, 185; and human essence, 264, 276–7, 408, 422–8; ontological priority and epistemological priority of, 238–9, 344
individuals: in Dissertation, 32–48; in Leibniz, 99ff., 102–3; *see also* species being, "I-thou"
induction, problem of in Gassendi's atomism, 72–3
infinite, infinity, infinity of consciousness, 38–9, 40–2, 44–5, 232, 271–3, 357–8; *see also* Idealism, Absolute; the Idea
innate ideas, 106
intellect, *see* consciousness

Jacobi, F., 214–15
Jammer, M., 438
Jodl, Friederich, 140, 153, 436, 439, 440
John, the Apostle, 290
Judaism, 55, 212, 387; and anti-Semitism, 319–21

Kant, Immanuel, 2, 3, 133, 140, 144, 145, 152, 163, 194, 209, 214, 218, 221, 229, 230, 233, 241, 271, 302, 305, 306, 348, 352, 362, 380–1, 405, 410, 419, 420, 422, 424, 442, 447
Kapp, Christian, 438, 444, 451
Kierkegaard, Soren, 169, 443
knowing, 30–4; distinct from thinking, 37–9; as entelechy, 169
Kojève, Alexandre, 211, 444–5

Laing, R. D., 1
La Mettrie, 367, 397, 441
language, 234–8, 289; and forms of thought, 180–4; and imagination, 229–34
Leibniz, G. W., 10, 12, 62, 74, 89–103, 105–9, 113–15, 135, 159, 197, 241, 261, 352, 380, 438
Lenin, N., 435–6
Leo, Heinrich, 140, 146, 160–3, 203–20, 436
life, origin of, 397–400
Lobkowitz, N. V., 433
Locke, John, 2, 5, 103, 344, 367, 381, 386, 439
logic: of conceptual change, 49; critique of Hegelian *Logic*, 178ff., 184ff.; and dialectic, 19, *see also* Popper; and language and form of thought, 180–4
Lombard, Peter, 119
love, 263, 290–2; *see also* feeling
Lowith, K., 47, 141, 450
Lübbe, H., and H.–M. Sass, 433

458